Foreword

This Report is the seventh in this annual series assessing development issues. This year the focus is on population change and its links with development. Population growth does not provide the drama of financial crisis or political upheaval, but as this Report shows, its significance for shaping the world of our children and grandchildren is at least as great. What governments and their peoples do today to influence our demographic future will set the terms for development strategy well into the next century. Failure to act now to slow growth is likely to mean a lower quality of life for millions of people. In the poorest countries of the world, and among the poorest groups within countries, poverty contributes to high mortality and even higher fertility. It thereby creates a vicious circle: the slow pace at which development reaches the poor contributes to rapid population growth, making the elimination of poverty increasingly difficult. Slowing population growth is a difficult challenge to humanity—but a challenge that must and can be successfully addressed.

On the one hand, the situation is grave: this Report concludes that in some countries development may not be possible at all unless slower population growth can be achieved soon, before higher real incomes would bring fertility down spontaneously. On the other hand, there is reason for hope: the experience of the past decade shows that education, health, and other development measures that raise parents' hopes for their children, along with widespread access to family planning services, create a powerful combination in reducing fertility.

The discussion of population places special emphasis on the role of public policy in an area where fundamental human values are at stake. Population is a subject that touches issues central to the human condition, including personal freedom and the very definition of economic and social progress. This Report tries to do it full justice, in a sensitive and thought-provoking way, recognizing that governments and their peoples have a wide range of views on this subject.

Even with success in efforts to slow population growth, future population growth will still be heavily concentrated in what are now the poorer areas of the globe. Thus the average level of human welfare will depend largely on the degree of economic and social transformation in those areas. The poverty of those areas cannot be blamed on rapid population growth alone; the causes of poverty go well beyond population change. Nor will reducing population growth alone ensure their economic transformation. But this Report shows that slowing the pace of population growth can make a difference—and that the ingredients for doing so are also those that will increase economic growth.

The analysis of the population situation follows our annual review of global economic developments, which as in previous years occupies the first part of the *World Development Report*. It might be argued that the general public remains insufficiently aware of the growing links among nations over the past few decades, and of the extent today of international economic interdependence. In an increasingly interdependent world, low growth, fiscal and labor market problems, and resulting inflation in industrial countries have taken a heavy toll in developing countries. Exports have suffered, fear of protectionism has increased, and high real interest rates have made debt servicing a costly burden. If the industrial countries fail to regain the growth rates they managed in the 1950s and 1960s, many countries in the developing world will have great difficulty making progress in the years ahead. Indeed, the prospects for much of sub-Saharan Africa will be particularly grave.

But it is also apparent that even in a harsh international climate, the developing nations can take actions to improve their own economic performance. Developing countries share the problems of the developed, from fiscal deficits to distorted labor markets. And they have a vested interest in reducing their own trade protectionism and adopting outward-oriented policies.

Although recovery, at least in the industrial nations, is now on a firmer footing, the outlook for the years ahead is full of uncertainties. The outlook would brighten considerably if every nation took steps to improve its own domestic economic performance. But development assistance is also critical, in reviving the global economy and in addressing many of the fundamental development issues of our era, including population. Especially for the poorest countries, a substantial increase in concessional flows of funds is needed to secure development momentum. And although the direct costs of programs to reduce population growth are not large, a greater commitment by the international community is sorely needed to assist developing countries in the great challenge of slowing population growth.

As its predecessors, this year's *World Development Report* is a study by the staff of The World Bank, and the judgments in it do not necessarily reflect the view of our Board of Directors or the governments they represent.

A. W. Clausen
President
The World Bank

May 25, 1984

This Report was prepared by a team led by Nancy Birdsall and comprising Martha Ainsworth, Rodolfo Bulatao, Dennis Mahar, William McGreevey, Nicholas Prescott, and Gurushri Swamy, and assisted by Jill Armstrong. Deepak Lal and Martin Wolf contributed to Part I. The Economic Analysis and Projections Department, under the direction of Jean Baneth, prepared the statistical materials on which Part I is based, as well as supplied data for the whole Report. Peter Miovic coordinated the work of the Economic Analysis and Projections Department on Part I. Ramesh Chander supervised the preparation of the World Development Indicators, assisted by David Cieslikowski. Staff of the Population, Health, and Nutrition Department provided extensive help on Part II. The authors would like to thank these and the many other contributors and reviewers. Thanks also go to the production staff—Christine Houle, Pensri Kimpitak, Jeanne Rosen, and Gerald Martin Quinn (who also designed the cover)—and especially to the support staff headed by Rhoda Blade-Charest and including Banjonglak Duangrat, Jaunianne Fawkes, and Carlina Jones. The work was carried out under the general direction of Anne O. Krueger and Costas Michalopoulos, with Rupert Pennant-Rea as principal editor.

Contents

Text tables

Population data supplement tables

Text figures

Boxes

Maps

Definitions and data notes

The principal country groups used in this Report are defined as follows:

- *Developing countries* are divided into: *low-income economies*, with 1982 gross national product (GNP) per person of less than $410; and *middle-income economies*, with 1982 GNP per person of $410 or more. Middle-income countries are also divided into *oil exporters* and *oil importers*, identified below.
- *Middle-income oil exporters* comprise Algeria, Angola, Cameroon, Congo, Ecuador, Egypt, Gabon, Indonesia, Islamic Republic of Iran, Iraq, Malaysia, Mexico, Nigeria, Peru, Syria, Trinidad and Tobago, Tunisia, and Venezuela.
- *Middle-income oil importers* comprise all other middle-income developing countries not classified as oil exporters. A subset, *major exporters of manufactures,* comprises Argentina, Brazil, Greece, Hong Kong, Israel, Republic of Korea, Philippines, Portugal, Singapore, South Africa, Thailand, and Yugoslavia.
- *High-income oil exporters* (not included in developing countries) comprise Bahrain, Brunei Darussalam, Kuwait, Libya, Oman, Qatar, Saudi Arabia, and the United Arab Emirates.
- *Industrial market economies* are the members of the Organisation of Economic Co-operation and Development (OECD, identified in the glossary) apart from Greece, Portugal, and Turkey, which are included among the middle-income developing economies. This group is commonly referred to in the text as industrial economies or industrial countries.
- *East European nonmarket economies* include the following countries: Albania, Bulgaria, Czechoslovakia, German Democratic Republic, Hungary, Poland, Romania, and USSR. This group is sometimes referred to as *nonmarket economies.*

The World Development Indicators uses the same groups but includes only countries of 1 million or more.

In Part II of this Report, regional groupings of countries are defined as follows:

- *Sub-Saharan Africa* comprises all thirty-nine developing African countries south of the Sahara, excluding South Africa, as given in *Accelerated Development in Sub-Saharan Africa,* World Bank, 1981.
- *Middle East and North Africa* includes Afghanistan, Algeria, Egypt, Iran, Iraq, Israel, Jordan, Kuwait, Lebanon, Libya, Morocco, Oman, Saudi Arabia, Syria, Tunisia, Turkey, Yemen Arab Republic, Yemen (PDR), and the United Arab Emirates.
- *East Asia* comprises all low- and middle-income countries of East and Southeast Asia and the Pacific, east of, and including, Burma, China, and Mongolia.
- *South Asia* includes Bangladesh, Bhutan, India, Nepal, Pakistan, and Sri Lanka.
- *Latin America and Caribbean* comprises all American and Caribbean countries south of the United States.

Billion is 1,000 million.

Tons are metric tons (t), equal to 1,000 kilograms (kg) or 2,204.6 pounds.

Growth rates are in real terms unless otherwise stated.

Dollars are US dollars unless otherwise specified.

All tables and figures are based on World Bank data unless otherwise specified.

Data from secondary sources are not always available through 1983. The numbers in this *World Development Report* shown for historical data may differ from those shown in previous Reports because of continuous updating as better data become available, and because of recompilation of certain data for Part I for a ninety-country sample. The recompilation was necessary to permit greater flexibility in regrouping countries for the purpose of making projections.

Growth rates for spans of years in tables cover the period from the beginning of the base year to the end of the last year given.

Glossary

Demographic terms

Amenorrhea. Absence or suppression of menstruation.

Child death rate. The number of deaths of children aged one to four in a given year per 1,000 children in this age group.

Cohort. A group of people sharing a common temporal demographic experience who are observed through time. For example, the birth cohort of 1900 would be the people born in that year. There are also marriage cohorts, school class cohorts, and so on.

Completed fertility rate. The number of children born alive per woman in a cohort of women by the end of their childbearing years.

Contraception. The conscious effort of couples to avoid conception through rhythm, withdrawal, abstinence, male or female sterilization, or use of contraceptives: intrauterine device (IUD), oral contraceptives, injectable contraceptives, condom, spermicides, and diaphragm.

Contraceptive prevalance rate. The percentage of married women of reproductive age who are using (or whose husbands are using) any form of contraception.

Crude birth rate. The number of births per 1,000 population in a given year.

Crude death rate. The number of deaths per 1,000 population in a given year.

Dependency ratio. The ratio of the economically dependent part of the population to the productive part; arbitrarily defined as the ratio of the young (those under fifteen years of age) plus the elderly (those sixty-five years and over) to the population in the "working ages" (those fifteen to sixty-four years of age).

Family planning. Conscious effort of couples to regulate the number and timing of births.

Family planning programs. Programs that provide information about, and services for, use of contraception.

Fecundity. The physiological capacity of a woman, man, or couple to produce a live birth.

Fertility. The reproductive performance, measured by number of births, of an individual, a couple, a group, or a population.

Infant mortality rate. The number of deaths of infants under one year old in a given year per 1,000 live births in that year.

Life expectancy at birth. The average number of years a newborn would live if current age-specific mortality were maintained. Life expectancy at later ages is the average number of years a person already at a given later age will live. Life expectancy at age five and above can exceed life expectancy at birth substantially if the infant mortality rate is high.

Married women of reproductive age. Women who are currently married, or in a stable sexual union, generally between the ages of fifteen and forty-nine. Some analysts count only women between the ages of fifteen and forty-four.

Maternal mortality rate. The number of deaths of women due to complications of pregnancy and childbirth per 100,000 live births in a given year.

Mortality. Deaths as a component of population change.

Net reproduction rate. The average number of daughters that would be born to a woman (or group of women) if during her lifetime she were to conform to the age-specific fertility and mortality rates of a given year. This rate takes into account that some women will die before completing their childbearing years. A net reproduction rate of 1.00 means that each generation of mothers is having exactly enough daughters to replace itself in the population.

Parity. The number of children previously born alive to a woman.

Population growth rate. The rate at which a population is increasing (or decreasing) in a given year due to natural increase and net migration, expressed as a percentage of the base population.

Population momentum. The tendency for population growth to continue beyond the time that replacement-level fertility has been achieved because of the large and increasing size of cohorts of childbearing age and younger, resulting from higher fertility and/or falling mortality in preceding years.

Postpartum. Refers to the time immediately after childbirth.

Rate of natural increase. The rate at which a population is increasing (or decreasing) in a given year due to a surplus (or deficit) of births over deaths. The rate of natural increase equals the crude birth rate minus the crude death rate per 100 people. It also equals the population growth rate minus emigration.

Replacement-level fertility. The level of fertility at which a cohort of women on the average is having only enough daughters to "replace" itself in the population. By definition, replacement level is equal to a net reproduction rate (see above definition) of 1.00. Replacement-level fertility can also be expressed in terms of the total fertility rate. In the United States today a total fertility rate of 2.12 is considered to be replacement level; it is higher than 2 because of mortality and because of a sex ratio greater than 1 at birth. The higher mortality is, the higher is replacement-level fertility.

Total fertility rate. The average number of children that would be born alive to a woman (or group of women) during her lifetime if during her childbearing years she were to bear children at each age in accord with prevailing age-specific fertility rates.

Urbanization. Growth in the proportion of the population living in urban areas.

Acronyms and initials

CPS Contraceptive Prevalence Survey.

DAC The Development Assistance Committee of the OECD (see below) comprises Australia, Austria, Belgium, Canada, Denmark, Finland, France, Federal Republic of Germany, Italy, Japan, Netherlands, New Zealand, Norway, Sweden, Switzerland, United Kingdom, United States, and Commission of the European Communities.

EC The European Communities comprise Belgium, Denmark, France, Federal Republic of Germany, Greece, Ireland, Italy, Luxembourg, Netherlands, and United Kingdom.

FAO Food and Agriculture Organization.

GATT General Agreement on Trade and Tariffs.

IBRD International Bank for Reconstruction and Development.

IDA International Development Association.

IMF International Monetary Fund.

IPPF International Planned Parenthood Federation.

NGO Nongovernmental organization.

ODA Official Development Assistance.

OECD The Organisation for Economic Co-operation and Development members are Australia, Austria, Belgium, Canada, Denmark, Finland, France, Federal Republic of Germany, Greece, Iceland, Ireland, Italy, Japan, Luxembourg, Netherlands, New Zealand, Norway, Portugal, Spain, Sweden, Switzerland, Turkey, United Kingdom, and United States.

OPEC The Organization of Petroleum Exporting Countries comprises Algeria, Ecuador, Gabon, Indonesia, the Islamic Republic of Iran, Iraq, Kuwait, Libya, Nigeria, Qatar, Saudi Arabia, United Arab Emirates, and Venezuela.

UNCTAD United Nations Conference on Trade and Development.

UNDP United Nations Development Programme.

UNESCO United Nations Educational, Scientific, and Cultural Organization.

UNFPA United Nations Fund for Population Assistance.

WFS World Fertility Survey.

WHO World Health Organization.

1 Introduction

The past few years have produced so much turbulence in the world economy that governments and businesses have naturally been preoccupied with the short term. Now that recession is giving way to recovery, they can start to take a longer view. For developing countries in particular, the shift is welcome: development is quintessentially long term, yielding its best results when policies and programs can be designed and sustained for years at a time.

Long-term needs and sustained effort are underlying themes in this year's *World Development Report*. As with most of its predecessors, it is divided into two parts. The first looks at economic performance, past and prospective. The second part is this year devoted to population—the causes and consequences of rapid population growth, its link to development, and why it has slowed down in some developing countries. The two parts mirror each other: economic policy and performance in the next decade will matter for population growth in the developing countries for several decades beyond; population policy and change in the rest of this century will set the terms for the whole of development strategy in the next. In both cases, policy changes will not yield immediate benefits—all the more reason for starting to act immediately. Delay will reduce the room for maneuver that policymakers will have in years to come.

The economic outlook

The recession of 1980–83 was the longest in fifty years. It increased unemployment, reduced investment, and undermined social programs in almost every country in the world. It put great strain on the international trade and financial systems and caused friction between governments everywhere. But it provided many valuable lessons for economic policy because it highlighted longstanding weaknesses in every economy and in international arrangements. Unless policymakers learn from its lessons, the recovery now under way will not mature into sustained and rapid growth of the kind the world enjoyed for twenty-five years after World War II.

That much is clear from a review of the past, which is the subject of Chapter 2. It concludes that the 1980–83 recession was not an isolated event—caused, for example, by the second oil price rise of 1979–80. Its roots went back farther, to the rigidities that were steadily being built into economies from the mid-1960s onward. The rising trends in unemployment and inflation were the manifestation of increasingly inflexible arrangements for setting wages and prices and for managing public finances.

The chapter emphasizes that policy failings have characterized both the industrial and the developing countries. Because of the industrial countries' predominance in the world economy, the consequences of their economic failure have weighed heavily on the developing countries. In particular, the much publicized debt difficulties of the past two years came to a head because of the unusual combination in 1980–83 of recession and high real interest rates in the industrial countries. Industrial countries provide a market for about 65 percent of the developing world's exports. Their buoyancy—or lack of it—and the amount of trade protection they choose to employ have a critical influence on the foreign exchange earnings of developing countries. These earnings in turn will largely determine whether the "debt crisis" gradually subsides, or seriously retards the growth prospects of developing countries for many years to come.

That is one of several contrasting alternatives highlighted by the scenarios presented in Chapter 3. These scenarios look ahead as far as 1995, but they are not intended as forecasts of what will happen. They merely illustrate what might happen, depending on the policies pursued by governments and the effectiveness of governments in tackling economic problems. They show, for example, that GDP in the developing world could grow at 5.5 percent a year in 1985–95 if the industrial countries regain their momentum of the 1960s, but at only 4.7 percent a year in that period if the industrial countries do no better than in the past ten years. That would make the difference between almost every country in the world raising per capita incomes and people in many of the world's poorest countries growing steadily poorer.

Chapter 3 also explores the gains that developing countries could make by improving their own economic policies, irrespective of what happens in the industrial countries. It concludes that, if they make such improvements, some countries might be able to add close to an extra percentage point to their economic growth rates. None of these improvements can be regarded as unachievable, since they have already been achieved by some developing countries. The chapter stresses the valuable contribution that appropriate pricing policies can make to faster economic growth. In particular, it contrasts the record of countries that have adopted outward-looking trade policies with those that have concentrated on import substitution.

The predicament of sub-Saharan Africa is a recurring theme throughout this Report. Though its total GDP growth was not much slower than in other regions in the 1970s, Africa's population grew faster; for the region as a whole, GDP per capita fell during the 1970s. It could well do so again in the years up to 1995. Of the policy failings that contributed to slow growth in other developing countries, all can be found in more or less chronic form in many African countries. The scope for raising growth rates by improving policies is therefore greatest in Africa. In addition, however, many of Africa's weaknesses require extra concessional aid if they are to be tackled effectively.

Population and demographic change

While the causes of poor economic performance can be traced back twenty years, the links between demography and development can be understood only by going back even farther into the past. In the long run of history, the second half of the twentieth century stands out for its remarkable population growth. Consider that in the year 1 the world had about 300 million people. Its population then took more than 1,500 years to double. Though the general trend was rising, population growth was not steady; the balance of births over deaths was tenuous, and crises such as war or plague periodically reduced populations in parts of the world. Only in the eighteenth century did the number of people start to rise steadily. From 1750

until well into the twentieth century, the world's population grew at the then unprecedented rate of about 0.5 percent a year, faster in today's developed countries, slower elsewhere. World population size doubled again, this time in about 150 years; it had reached about 1.7 billion by 1900. In the twentieth century, growth continued to accelerate, from 0.5 to 1 percent until about 1950 and then to a remarkable 2 percent. In just over thirty years, between 1950 and today, world population nearly doubled again—growing from 2.5 billion to almost 4.8 billion (see Figure 1.1).

Since 1950 population growth has been concentrated largely in the developing countries. Though a postwar baby boom combined with falling mortality in the industrial countries, the population growth rate never exceeded 1 percent in Europe and seldom exceeded 1.5 percent in North America. At its peak, fertility in the United States meant that families had on average little more than three children; in Europe and Japan postwar families were even smaller. By the 1970s, in most developed countries fertility had fallen to a level near or even below "replacement"—about two children per couple being the level which, over the long run, holds population constant (demographic terms are defined in the glossary).

The postwar experience of developing countries was not only different but historically unprecedented. Driven by falling mortality and continued high fertility, their population growth rate rose above 2 percent a year. It peaked at 2.4 percent in the 1960s. It is now around 2.0 percent a year, because of a slightly greater decline in birth rates than in death rates (see Figure 1.1). Further decline in population growth will not come automatically. Much of the slowdown so far can be attributed to China, where fertility is already low, close to an average of two children per family. Most families in other developing countries now have at least four children, in rural areas five and more. In a few countries in which fertility fell in the 1970s, there is evidence that it has leveled off recently. For parts of South Asia and the Middle East, forecasts of a lower rate of population growth are based more on hope than on present trends. For much of Africa and Central America, population growth rates are rising and could rise still further. In Africa couples say they want more children than in fact they are having, while mortality—though high—can be expected to decline.

Furthermore, population "momentum" means that growth rates in developing countries will remain high for several decades even if couples

FIGURE 1.1

Past and projected world population, A.D. 1–2150

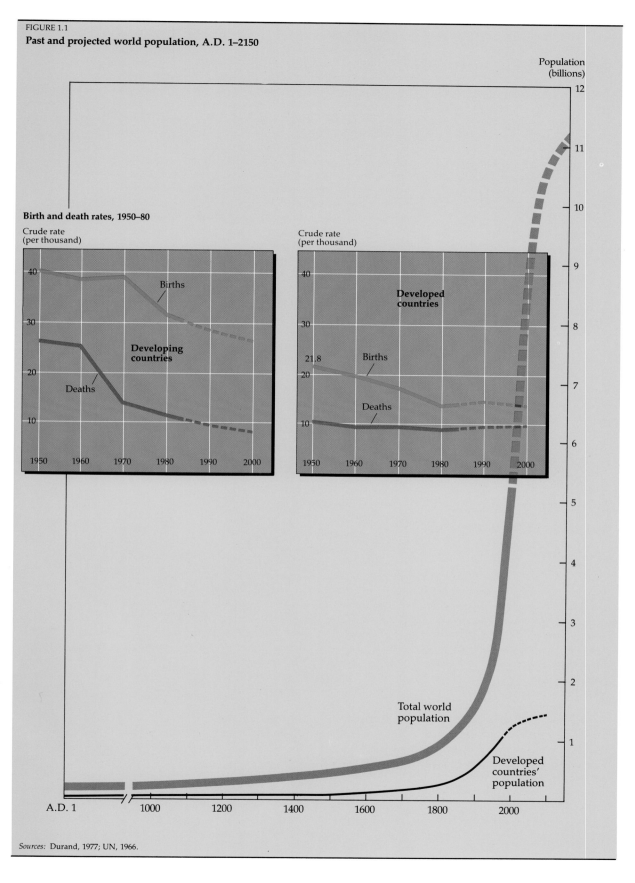

Population (billions)

Birth and death rates, 1950–80

Crude rate (per thousand)

Births

Developing countries

Deaths

Crude rate (per thousand)

Developed countries

Births

Deaths

Total world population

Developed countries' population

A.D. 1 1000 1200 1400 1600 1800 2000

Sources: Durand, 1977; UN, 1966.

Box 1.1 The arithmetic of population growth: compounding and momentum

Rates of population growth among countries tend to fall into two main groups: rapid growth countries of Africa, Asia, and Latin America, with annual growth rates for most between 2.0 and 4.5 percent; and slow growth countries, primarily the industrialized nations, with growth rates below 1 percent. In a few

Age structure in Senegal, 1980 and 2020

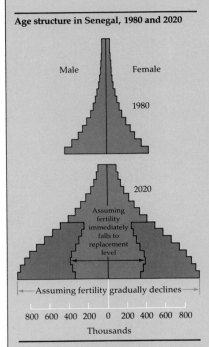

countries, including China, the growth rate falls between 1 and 2 percent (see first chart). Because of compounding, small differences in annual growth rates over long periods make a big difference in population increases. An average growth of 1 percent over a 100-year period would cause a population to multiply 2.7 times. A rate of 2 percent in the same period would bring an increase of about 7.4; 3 percent an increase of 20; and 4 percent an increase of 55. Today's population of Zambia, 6 million, would grow to more than 120 million in 100 years were growth to continue at the present rate of 3.4 percent.

Today's high growth rates in developing countries are caused not only by high fertility (between four and eight births per woman) but by the "momentum" created by the high fertility and falling mortality of the past three decades. Past high fertility and falling mortality mean women entering childbearing age now constitute a large proportion of the total population. In most developing countries, the next generation of women will outnumber the previous one. Thus, even if the number of births per woman declines rapidly, the birth rate can stay high and the total number of births can be greater than it was.

In some countries of Asia and Latin America, even with recent fertility decline (Chapter 4), birth rates remain high and average annual increases in population size are larger now than they were in 1965. Brazil's fertility rate fell from 5.8 in 1965 to about 4.0 in 1980, a decline of almost 30 percent. Yet the birth rate has fallen by only 19 percent and the total number of births has increased from about 2.9 million a year in the late 1950s to about 3.7 million in the early 1980s. The World Bank now projects that fertility in Brazil will fall to 2.1 by 2025. Yet by that year the total number of births will have increased further, to nearly 3.9 million a year.

To see how much of total population growth is due to momentum alone, imagine a population in which the fertility rate declines instantaneously to replacement level—the level at which each couple has only enough children to replace themselves (the exact number will be more than two, varying from country to country and from period to period, because of different mortality rates). The top population pyramid in the second chart shows the distribution of the actual 1980 population of Senegal by sex and by five-year age groups. The pyramid for 1980 has a wide base and a narrow top. Each five-year group is exponentially larger than the one preceding it. The bottom pyramid is actually two pyramids, which show the population distributions for the year 2020 under two different assumptions: fertility gradually declines, in keeping with the standard World Bank country projection for Senegal (the broader pyramid); and fertility instantaneously falls to replacement level (the narrower pyramid). The broader pyramid for 2020, which assumes some, though gradual, fertility decline, is shaped like the 1980 pyramid but is almost three times larger. The narrower pyramid for 2020 shows the growth that is generated by momentum alone. It has a different shape than the 1980 pyramid; its base has not expanded, yet it is 1.6 times larger.

But the smaller pyramid for 2020 does not even show the full effect of momentum, which would not have run its full course by 2020. By the time Senegal's population would become stationary (assuming instantaneous replacement fertility), the pyramid would be 2.2 times larger in area than the pyramid for 1980. In other words, the population of Sene-

Distribution of countries with 1982 populations exceeding 1 million by average 1980–85 growth rate

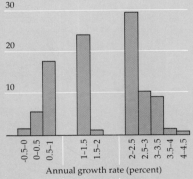

gal would increase 2.2 times from the force of momentum alone, even if fertility rates there dropped to replacement level now. The corresponding ratio of stationary to current population for the United States would be 1.3. Table 19 of the 1984 World Development Indicators provides numbers for other countries.

have fewer children (see Box 1.1); absolute annual increases will be close to or more than 80 million people a year in developing countries well into the next century. The baby "bulge" that resulted from the trends of high fertility and falling mortality that started twenty years ago is now entering child-bearing age. In China, for example, the number of women aged twenty to thirty-four almost doubled between 1950 and 1980; throughout the 1980s, as the children born in the 1960s enter their twenties, the number of women marrying and bearing children will continue to increase. To reduce population growth to 1 percent a year by the early 1990s, couples in China would need to have fewer than two children on average.

These considerations should not obscure the central fact that the world's population growth rate is falling. The latter part of the twentieth century has been a demographic watershed, the high point of several centuries of accelerating growth and the beginning of what demographers project to be a continuous decline, until world population stabilizes sometime in the twenty-second century. Though absolute numbers will continue to increase for several decades, the issue now is how quickly the rate of increase can be slowed down— and how individual countries (and the international community) are to cope with continued growth in the meantime.

The rise in living standards

Until the seventeenth or eighteenth century, life expectancy had probably changed little, and few people were literate. Since 1850, however, while world population size has more than tripled, income per person has increased perhaps six times in real terms, life expectancy has risen dramatically, and education has become widespread. Progress in education and life expectancy in developing countries has been especially notable since 1950. Even in today's poorer developing countries, primary school enrollment rates and life expectancy are above the levels achieved by richer countries eighty years ago, though income per person and adult literacy are not (see Figure 1.2).

But these averages can be misleading. Though most people are better off today, for many the gains have been small. Since 1950 it has been the countries with lower levels of income per person that have had much faster population growth. In those countries absolute increases in income have been much smaller than in the countries which began the period already richer. Consider a simple

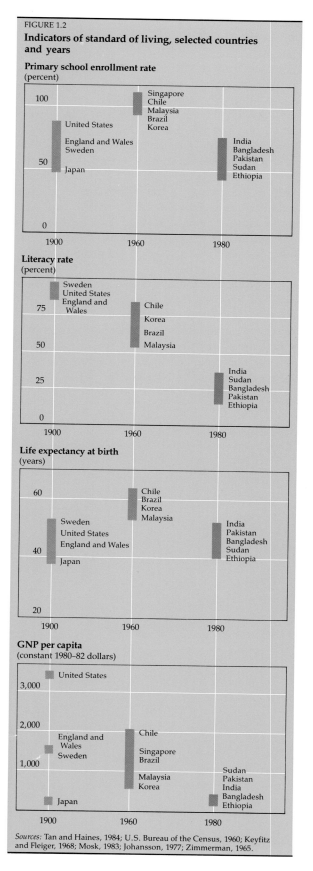

FIGURE 1.2

Indicators of standard of living, selected countries and years

Sources: Tan and Haines, 1984; U.S. Bureau of the Census, 1960; Keyfitz and Fleiger, 1968; Mosk, 1983; Johansson, 1977; Zimmerman, 1965.

example. Between 1955 and 1980 income per person in the United States grew at an average 2.0 percent a year. In 1980 dollars, average income increased from $7,030 to $11,560. Meanwhile, in India, income per person grew at about 1.7 percent a year—but only from $170 to $260 (in 1980 dollars). What had been a $6,860 income gap between Americans and Indians in 1955 had almost doubled to $11,300 in 1980; America's average income, some forty-one times India's in 1955, had become forty-four times larger by 1980. Large absolute differences in average income between developed and developing countries have persisted and have even increased since 1950 (see Figure 1.3). Among and within developing countries, differences in education and life expectancy also persist.

By 1980, 79 percent of the world's total output was produced in the developed countries, where about 25 percent of the world's people live. The remaining 21 percent was shared by the other 75 percent of people. Only 5 percent was shared among the 47 percent living in low-income countries such as Bangladesh, China, India, Pakistan, and most countries of tropical Africa.

Such comparisons raise several statistical difficulties. They exaggerate differences between poor and rich countries because not only incomes but also prices, especially for services, are lower in poor countries, and this is not reflected in official exchange rates. But even with appropriate adjustments (based on the UN International Comparison Project), the income gap between India and the United States is still estimated to have increased from almost $5,000 to almost $8,000 between 1955 and 1980. The general conclusion is inescapable: much of the world's output is produced and consumed by relatively few of its people.

The demographic future

World Bank population projections are shown in Table 19 of the World Development Indicators at the back of this Report. These, and alternative projections prepared for this Report and shown in the Population Data Supplement, are explained in Chapter 4. The projections should not be treated as predictions, but as illustrations of what can happen given reasonable assumptions. If the assump-

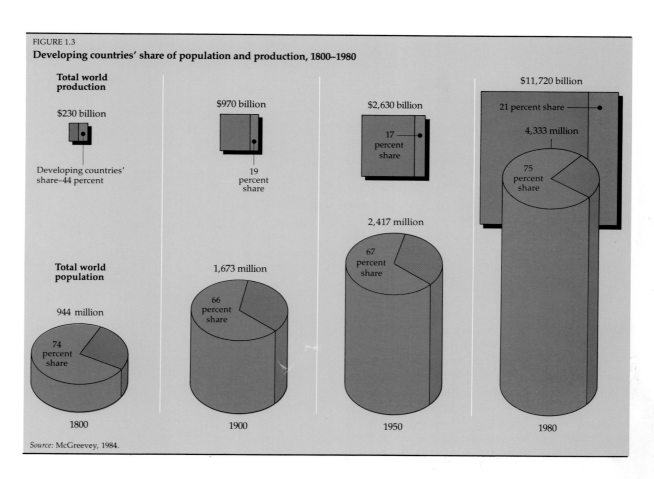

FIGURE 1.3

Developing countries' share of population and production, 1800–1980

Total world production

$230 billion

Developing countries' share–44 percent

$970 billion

19 percent share

$2,630 billion

17 percent share

$11,720 billion

21 percent share

4,333 million

75 percent share

Total world population

944 million

74 percent share

1,673 million

66 percent share

2,417 million

67 percent share

1800   1900   1950   1980

Source: McGreevey, 1984.

tions underlying the "standard" projections in Table 19 are correct, world population would stabilize around the year 2150, having risen from almost 4.8 billion to more than 11 billion (see Figure 1.1). It would reach 9.8 billion by the year 2050. The population of today's developed countries would grow from about 1.2 billion today to 1.4 billion in 2050, while that of those countries now classified as developing would grow from over 3.6 billion to 8.4 billion. By the time world population stabilized, the population of India would be 1.7 billion, making it the most populous nation on earth. Bangladesh, a country about the size of the state of Wisconsin in the United States, would have a population of 450 million. Nigeria, Ethiopia, Zaire, and Kenya, among the most populous countries in Africa, would have populations of 620 million, 230 million, 170 million, and 150 million, respectively. As a group, sub-Saharan Africa and South Asia—today's poorest countries, with the fastest population growth—would account for 50 percent of the world's people, compared with 30 percent today.

Even allowing for some error in such projections, it is clear that future population increases will be concentrated in what are now the poorer areas of the globe; the average level of human welfare will depend largely on the degree to which economic and social transformation occurs in these areas.

Are the assumptions that produce these projections realistic, and what do they imply for future human welfare? The critical assumptions are that the decline in mortality will continue until life expectancy of about eighty years is reached, and that fertility will decline to replacement level—in developing countries between the years 2005 and 2045, depending on recent mortality levels, fertility trends, and family planning efforts; and in most developed countries in the year 2010. (In the several developed countries in which fertility is now below replacement level, it is assumed to rise and then stabilize at replacement.)

In some respects these assumptions are optimistic. Consider the poorer countries of Africa and South Asia. Even with rapid income growth and advances in literacy in the next two decades, they are not likely to reach the income and literacy levels that triggered fertility declines in such countries as Brazil, Korea, and Malaysia in the 1960s (see Figure 1.2). Yet their fertility is projected to decline significantly—and even with those declines their populations will more than double in the next fifty years. A pessimist might wonder whether for

some countries it is not already too late—whether rising unemployment and increasing landlessness will overwhelm social and political institutions; whether fragile administrative systems will be unable to maintain health programs; whether, in countries that are already crowded and still heavily reliant on agriculture, mortality will rise to check further population growth.

Such speculative pessimism needs to be set against the concrete reasons for optimism. The experience of the past two decades shows that economic growth and social development are possible, even starting at low initial income levels, and that developing countries can take conscious steps to influence their demographic futures. Both mortality and fertility—the latter matters much more for population growth—can be brought down more quickly than projected. Declines need not rely, solely or even primarily, on per capita income growth. Educational change can occur rapidly; policy effort can make a difference. Moreover, the actions that would speed the demographic transition are also those which would increase economic growth.

Causes, consequences, and cures

Part II of this Report discusses three themes.
* *Rapid population growth is a development problem.* Although population growth does not provide the drama of financial crisis or political upheaval, its significance for shaping the world is at least as great. In the past three decades many developing countries managed to raise average income even as their populations grew rapidly. In that strict sense, rapid population growth has been accommodated. But the goal of development extends beyond accommodation of more people; it is to improve people's lives. The cost of rapid population growth, at least for the world as a whole, may not be a catastrophe—with luck sudden famine, war, political or environmental collapse can be avoided. But continuing rapid growth on an ever larger base is likely to mean a lower quality of life for millions of people. The main cost of such growth, borne principally by the poor in developing countries, has been and will be faltering progress against what is still high mortality, and lost opportunities for improving people's lives.

Why does rapid population growth slow development? First, it exacerbates the awkward choice between higher consumption now and the investment needed to bring higher consumption in the future. Economic growth depends on investment—all the more so if human skills are scarce and technology limited. But if consumption is low already, the resources available for investment are limited; faster population growth makes investment in "population quality" more difficult. Second, in many countries increases in population threaten what is already a precarious balance between natural resources and people. Where populations are still highly dependent on agriculture and the potential for increasing production through extending cultivation is limited, continuing large increases in population condemn many households to continuing poverty. Such increases can contribute to overuse of limited natural resources, mortgaging the welfare of future generations. Third, rapid increases in population make it hard to manage the adjustments that accompany and promote economic and social change. The growth of cities in developing countries, largely due to high rates of natural increase, poses serious management problems; so too does continued rapid growth that in some rural areas threatens permanent environmental damage.

These costs of rapid population growth differ among countries. Where education levels are already high, investment in transport and communications is in place, and political and economic systems are stable, countries are in a better position to cope with the strains of rapid growth—whether their natural resources are limited or they are already "crowded." But countries in that category—Colombia, the Republic of Korea, Malaysia, Singapore, and Thailand—also tend to be those in which population growth is already declining. In countries where the population is still largely dependent on agriculture, and the amount of new land or other resources is limited—including Bangladesh, Burundi, the Arab Republic of Egypt, India, Kenya, and Nepal—progress in the face of continuing rapid population growth will be extraordinarily difficult. Agricultural modernization and diversification into manufacturing will require large new investments in both human and physical capital, and considerable administrative and political skill to ensure efficient allocation of scarce investment resources. Even in countries with untapped natural resources—Brazil and Ivory Coast, for instance—rapid population growth makes it harder to effect the investments in complementary inputs (roads, public services, drainage, and other agricultural infrastructure) and in the human skills needed to tap such resources.

The costs of rapid population growth, moreover, are cumulative. More births now make the task of slowing population growth later more difficult, as today's children become tomorrow's new parents. Population policy has a long lead time; other development policies must adapt in the meantime. Inaction today forecloses options tomorrow, in overall development strategy and in future population policy. Worst of all, inaction today could mean that more drastic steps, less compatible with individual choice and freedom, will seem necessary tomorrow to slow population growth.

• *There are appropriate public policies to reduce fertility.* Proposals for reducing population growth raise difficult questions about the proper domain of public policy. Family and fertility are areas of life in which the most fundamental human values are at stake. This Report considers two reasons for public policy to reduce fertility. First, in the transition from a traditional to a modern economy, the private gain from having many children may exceed the social gain. This gap occurs for several reasons. For any family there are obvious rewards from many children. But poor parents especially have other reasons for high fertility. They rightly fear the risks of infant mortality because, in the absence of pensions or public support, they look to their children to support them in old age. For women who are poor and for whom other opportunities may be limited, security and status are linked to childbearing. Yet these private rewards are achieved at great social cost because part of the responsibilities for educating and employing children falls on society at large. Second, during a country's transition to a modern economy, some couples have more children than they want. This gap also occurs for several reasons. Information about family planning may be scarce or the costs of contraception high. Couples may not realize that mortality rates are falling, so that fewer births are needed to ensure that the number of children they want will survive to become adults. Couples may not be fully aware of the health risks of large families. Where young women marry early, couples do not discuss sexual matters, and parents pressure new couples to have children, there may be social as well as financial costs in controlling fertility. Thus tradition can combine with lack of information about birth control to contribute to high fertility.

Where there is a gap between private and social gains, a main reason for it is poverty. Poverty means not only low income but also lack of economic and social opportunities, an insecure future, and limited access to services such as education, health, and family planning. The gap requires public policy to provide alternative ways of securing the benefits that many children provide for their parents. Measures to improve income opportunities, broaden social insurance and pension schemes, and extend services all provide new signals to households, encouraging individuals to want smaller families. Social efforts to expand education and employment opportunities for women do the same. In short, there is a particular strategy of development in which the signals transmitted to parents encourage them to have fewer children in their own private interests.

But experience shows that all this takes time to have an effect. Population growth can be slowed more directly, and in ways that also benefit the poor. Governments can do more to encourage breastfeeding and later age of marriage, which reduce population growth by lengthening the average interval between generations. Through support for family planning programs, governments can spread information about the advantages of planning family size—making it as easy as possible for individuals to choose the number and timing of their children and helping to close the gap between the number of children parents have and the number they want. Finally, governments can use incentives and disincentives to signal their policy on family size. Through incentives, society as a whole compensates those couples willing to forgo the private benefits of an additional child, helping to close the gap between private and social gains to high fertility.

The size of the two gaps, and hence the policy actions needed, vary among countries and among different groups within each country. When couples have two or even three children, it is much less likely that the social costs of each child exceed the private costs parents are willing to bear. But if each couple has four or even six children, in a society with only limited ability to finance the education of a growing population, then it is more likely that the social optimum is being exceeded and that both social and private interests would be better served by smaller families. While there are distinctions between different types of policies to reduce fertility, in virtually every country there is some appropriate combination of development policies geared to the poor, family planning, and incentives.

The ultimate goal of public policy is to improve living standards, to increase individual choice, and to create conditions that enable people to realize their potential. Lower fertility is only an intermediate objective; a commitment to achieve lower fertility must not mean a willingness to achieve it at any cost. In fact, the successful experience of many countries already indicates it need not.

• *Experience shows that policy makes a difference.* The experience of the past two decades of population policy is encouraging. Many countries have shown that effective measures can be taken to slow population growth. Such measures are affordable: family planning programs, for example, have been successful in reducing fertility at very low cost. Such measures also respect human rights, and they complement other development efforts in enhancing welfare.

Fertility has fallen most dramatically in China, where a public policy to slow population growth includes public education, social pressure, and economic measures other governments might be reluctant to consider. But large declines have also occurred in other low-income areas: Sri Lanka and several states of India (Kerala, Karnataka, and Tamil Nadu), where education is widespread; and Java in Indonesia, where there is an active family planning program.

Within regions, countries differ. Fertility has fallen faster and to lower levels in Colombia, where family planning programs received government support starting in the late 1960s, than in Brazil, a richer country where central government involvement is minimal. It has fallen more in Egypt and Tunisia, countries with demographic objectives, than in their richer neighbor, Algeria. It has fallen more in India than in Pakistan; per capita income is low in both, but in Pakistan population policy has received less sustained support over the past two decades. The pattern of decline shows that differences in income, religion, and culture do not tell the whole story. Education, access to family planning services, the status of women, and economic and social policies that bring opportunities to the majority of people all make a difference.

The specific policy agenda for each country depends on its political culture, on the nature of the problem it faces, and on what it has already accomplished. But to illustrate what is possible, this Report provides examples of the implications for population growth of "rapid" mortality and fertility declines. These declines are for most countries more rapid than those shown in the standard World Bank projections, but comparable to what a few countries have already achieved. For most countries these declines would mean fertility rates of between two and three children per couple in the year 2000 and population growth rates of between 1 and 2 percent—moderate compared with rates today. For some countries, the declines imply eventual large differences in population size compared with the standard projection—for Kenya, about 70 million rather than 120 million in 2050 (compared with a population of 18 million today) and for Bangladesh, 230 million rather than almost 360 million (compared with 93 million today).

These alternative paths of rapid declines in mortality and fertility give only a rough guide to what is possible. For some countries, they may be too ambitious; others have already set even more ambitious fertility targets. In the longer run, some countries may wish to move to even lower or zero rates of population growth. But the alternative paths illustrate an important point: the course of future population growth and its effects on social and economic progress are well within the realm of conscious human choice.

Part I   Recovery or Relapse in the World Economy?

2   Recession in retrospect

The world has now had two major recessions in the past ten years. The recession of 1974–75 was sharp but short in industrial countries, where GDP rose by 6.1 percent in 1973, then by only 0.8 percent in 1974, before falling by 0.4 percent in 1975. In 1976, however, GDP growth in industrial countries was back up to 4.7 percent. Developing countries were less badly affected. Their GDP growth was 7.4 percent in 1973 and 5.9 percent in 1974; it fell only modestly to 4 percent in 1975 before rising to 6.3 percent in 1976.

The recent recession of 1980–83 was not so sharp but it lasted longer. In the industrial countries GDP grew by 3.3 percent in 1979, then 1.3 percent in 1980, and 1.3 percent in 1981. It fell by 0.5 percent in 1982 and is estimated to have risen to only about 2.3 percent in 1983. The developing countries were

also more severely affected. Their GDP grew by only 2.5 percent in 1980, 2.4 percent in 1981, 1.9 percent in 1982, and an estimated 1 percent in 1983 (see Table 2.1 and Figure 2.1). They had fared better in the first recession not only because it was shorter but also because, for a time, their heavy borrowing allowed them to grow. In the second recession, however, the availability of foreign capital declined abruptly after 1981. This change imposed substantial pressure on those countries which had come to rely on foreign loans as a principal way of escaping recession.

The recent recession had two proximate causes: the rise in oil prices in 1979, stemming from supply disruptions in Iran, and the disinflationary policies of governments in most major industrial countries after 1980. Both the need to reduce inflation and

TABLE 2.1
Population, GDP, and GDP per capita in 1980, and growth rates, 1960–83

Country group	1980 GDP (billions of dollars)	1980 population (millions)	1980 GDP per capita (dollars)	GDP growth rates (average annual percentage change)					
				1960–73	1973–79	1980	1981	1982	1983[a]
Developing countries[b]	2,118	3,280	650	6.3	5.2	2.5	2.4	1.9	1.0
Low-income	549	2,175	250	5.6	4.8	5.9	4.8	5.2	4.7
Asia	497	1,971	250	5.9	5.2	6.3	5.2	5.6	5.1
China	284	980	290	8.5	5.7	6.1	4.8	7.3	5.1
India	162	675	240	3.6	4.3	6.9	5.7	2.9	5.4
Africa	52	204	250	3.5	2.1	1.3	1.2	0.5	−0.1
Middle-income oil importers	915	611	1,500	6.3	5.6	4.3	0.9	0.7	0.3
East Asia and Pacific	204	183	1,110	8.2	8.6	3.6	6.7	4.2	6.4
Middle East and North Africa	28	35	800	5.2	3.0	4.2	−2.4	5.5	2.0
Sub-Saharan Africa[c]	37	60	610	5.6	3.7	5.5	3.9	1.1	0.3
Southern Europe	201	91	2,210	6.7	5.0	1.5	2.3	0.7	−0.9
Latin America and Caribbean	445	241	1,840	5.6	5.0	5.8	−2.3	−0.4	−2.2
Middle-income oil exporters[d]	654	494	1,320	6.9	4.9	−2.4	2.4	0.9	−1.7
High-income oil exporters	228	16	14,250	10.7	7.7	7.4	0.0	. .	. .
Industrial market economies	7,463	715	10,440	4.9	2.8	1.3	1.3	−0.5	2.3

. . Not available.

a. Estimated.

b. Data for 1982 and 1983 are based on a sample of ninety developing countries.

c. Does not include South Africa.

d. The estimated 1983 data exclude Angola, the Islamic Republic of Iran, and Iraq.

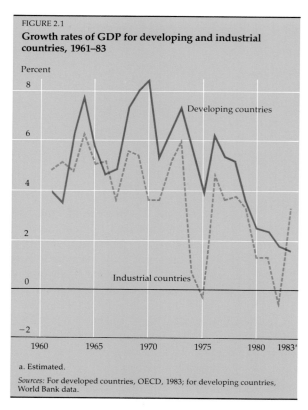

FIGURE 2.1

Growth rates of GDP for developing and industrial countries, 1961–83

Percent

Developing countries

Industrial countries

a. Estimated.

Sources: For developed countries, OECD, 1983; for developing countries, World Bank data.

the severity of the resulting recession can be understood only as a manifestation of a long-term deterioration in the economic performance of industrial countries. This deterioration may be explained in part by past policy choices as well as by underlying economic and social conditions. In an interdependent world economy, growth in developing countries is significantly affected by what happens in industrial countries (see map). To assess the prospects of developing countries, it is therefore important to consider the extent to which poor policies in the industrial world were to blame for their difficulties. To the extent that they were, improved policies in industrial countries could contribute to faster future growth in developing countries.

Industrial countries in the past two decades

Figure 2.2 illustrates the experience of seven major industrial countries since the mid-1960s. It shows that they have had marked cycles in GDP growth, unemployment, and inflation and—more seriously—adverse underlying trends. Since 1968 GDP growth has experienced three downturns, and the present recovery appears to be the third strong upswing. Inflation and unemployment have tended to follow GDP growth—in opposite

directions—with a lag in each case of about a year. The present marked downturn in the rate of inflation is the third since 1970. The rate of unemployment has not shown any significant downturns but has had three marked upturns since 1969.

The progressive deterioration from cycle to cycle is also evident. GDP growth in the industrial countries has not matched its rate of 1973 in any subsequent year. The cyclical peaks and troughs in unemployment have risen from 2.9 and 2.7 percent in the first of the cycles shown in Figure 2.2 to 8 and 5 percent in the most recent. In the case of inflation, the peaks and troughs have risen from 5.7 and 2.7 percent in the first cycle shown in Figure 2.2 to 12.2 and 7.1 percent in the most recent. Inflation has, however, fallen below its previous cyclical trough. This might be taken as a break in the tendency toward progressive deterioration, but the conclusion is not warranted. In order to lower inflation to a level still well above the average for the 1960s, unemployment rates have risen to three times the level of the 1960s.

Policy-induced problems

One explanation of why stop-go cycles have tended to be sharper in recent periods is that as

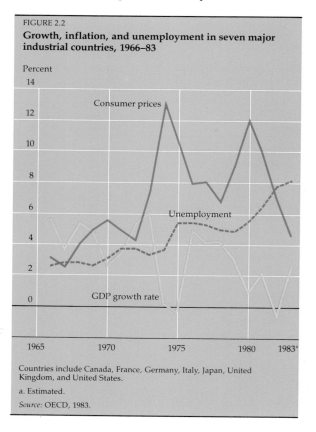

FIGURE 2.2

Growth, inflation, and unemployment in seven major industrial countries, 1966–83

Percent

Consumer prices

Unemployment

GDP growth rate

Countries include Canada, France, Germany, Italy, Japan, United Kingdom, and United States.

a. Estimated.

Source: OECD, 1983.

soon as it is widely believed that governments are embarked on an inflationary course, nominal wages rise and bond prices and exchange rates fall. The result, especially under floating exchange rates, is that inflation rises more quickly than anticipated and, in turn, the authorities are forced to choke off the expansion with monetary restraint sooner than would have been necessary with less sensitive markets.

The tendency toward slower growth can be explained in part by changes in underlying conditions. By the late 1960s the opportunities for catching up with the technology of the United States had been largely exploited by both Japan and western Europe, so one source of exceptional growth declined in significance. Another source—the shift of workers from low-productivity agriculture to high-productivity manufacturing—had also largely been exhausted. A third source—trade liberalization and reintegration of the industrial economies after World War II—though it had boosted growth for at least two decades, was no longer providing the stimulus it did earlier. Finally, the increasing share of service industries in GDP may have slowed the growth of GDP since the growth of productivity has traditionally been lower in services than in manufacturing.

Although such fundamental factors played a part in slowing down GDP growth, they cannot entirely explain the deterioration in economic performance. To begin with, some forces were working in favor of faster growth—rapid innovations in key industries such as electronics, for example. Countries might also have exploited the potential for shifting labor out of unemployment and declining "smokestack" industries to new areas, and the opportunity to expand trade with developing countries, especially by importing more labor-intensive goods in return for exports of machinery and other sophisticated products and services. Furthermore, although underlying changes in economic opportunities may explain a tendency toward lower growth, they have little to do with the stop-go pattern of cyclical disturbances combined with rising unemployment and inflation. That pattern can be explained only by the economic policies followed in industrial countries.

Two policy-induced developments deserve particular attention: first, the increasing rigidity of the labor market and the resulting strong upward pressure on real wages; and second, the growth and pattern of public spending, taxation, and fiscal deficits. The links between these are at the root of the problems of inflation, unemployment, and

slow growth. The oil price rises of 1973–74 and 1979–80 aggravated these difficulties and required adjustments which the industrial economies found difficult to make efficiently.

LABOR MARKET RIGIDITIES. In the late 1960s real wages in manufacturing in many industrial countries were rising at a rate faster than warranted by underlying productivity growth. By the early 1970s the trend was marked, except in Canada (see Table 2.2). Although there are forms of labor-using technical progress that could justify such a development, the tendency toward rising unemployment (especially in manufacturing) suggests that that is not what was happening.

If real wages are above the level at which all those who seek work can find it, there are three solutions: to let unemployment rise; to let inflation rise if wages are not indexed to prices, either formally or informally; or to try to control wages through incomes policy. Governments attempted a combination of all three. The early 1970s, in particular, witnessed efforts by several governments to achieve the required stability in the labor market through some form of incomes policy, combined with fiscal and monetary expansion. In some countries, such as Austria, Japan, and the Federal Republic of Germany, formal or (more usually) informal policies based on voluntary self-discipline among workers have had some success. In other countries, such as the United Kingdom and the United States, formal incomes policies achieved only temporary success. In general, real wage inflexibility in the industrial countries contributed to "stagflation"—continuing inflation at relatively high unemployment.

PUBLIC SPENDING AND DEFICITS. For the industrial countries as a whole, public spending rose from 29.3 percent of GDP in 1961 to 40.9 percent in 1981 (see Table 2.3). Its structure also changed significantly. Among the seven major industrial countries the share of government expenditure on defense, general administration, and economic services fell from 16.4 to 10.9 percent of GNP between 1954 and 1980. Meanwhile, the share of spending on education, health care, income maintenance, and old-age security rose from 10.5 to 23.4 percent of GNP. Most of the increase was concentrated on health care (where prices were rising rapidly) and old-age security.

The rising share of spending on health care and old-age security partly reflects increases in the proportion of old people, but increases in coverage and benefits were more important. Between 1960 and 1975 demographic change contributed about

Distribution of product among selected countries, 1982

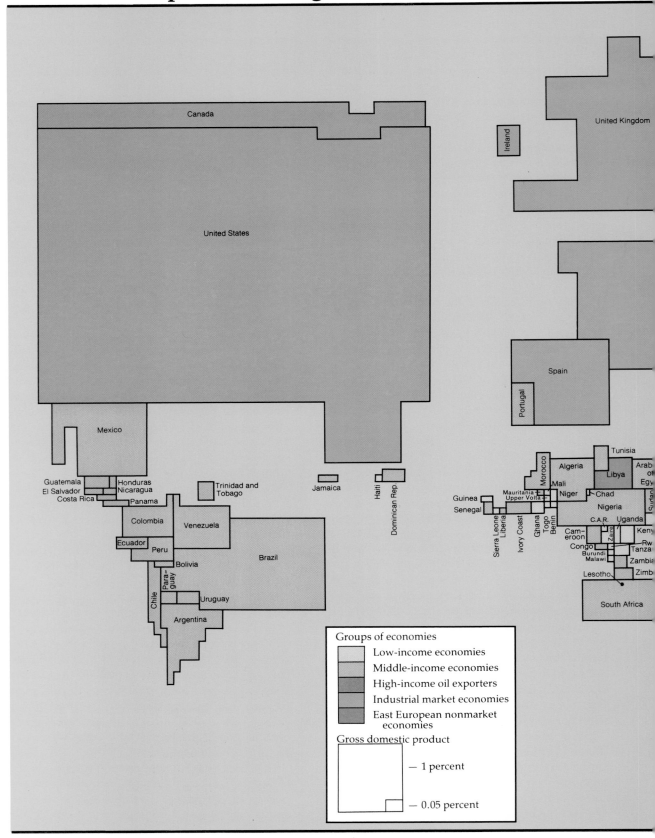

Canada

United States

Ireland

United Kingdom

Spain

Portugal

Mexico

Guatemala
El Salvador
Costa Rica

Honduras
Nicaragua

Panama

Trinidad and
Tobago

Jamaica

Haiti

Dominican Rep.

Tunisia

Morocco

Algeria

Libya

Arab
of
Egy

Guinea

Senegal

Mauritania
Upper Volta

Mali

Niger

Chad

Nigeria

Sudan

Colombia

Venezuela

Sierra Leone
Liberia

Ivory Coast

Ghana
Togo
Benin

C.A.R.

Uganda

Ecuador

Peru

Cam-
eroon

Zaire

Keny

Bolivia

Brazil

Congo

Burundi
Malawi

Rw
Tanza

Chile

Para-
guay

Zambia

Uruguay

Lesotho

Zimb

Argentina

South Africa

Groups of economies

Low-income economies

Middle-income economies

High-income oil exporters

Industrial market economies

East European nonmarket
economies

Gross domestic product

— 1 percent

— 0.05 percent

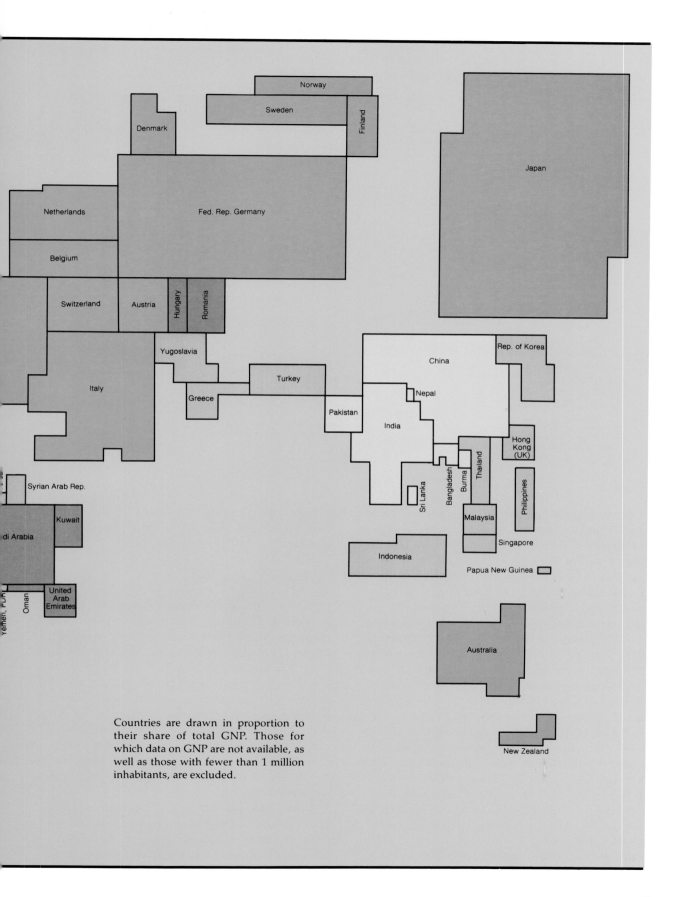

Countries are drawn in proportion to their share of total GNP. Those for which data on GNP are not available, as well as those with fewer than 1 million inhabitants, are excluded.

TABLE 2.2
Rates of growth in the real product wage and in labor productivity for the manufacturing sector and the aggregate economy, by country, 1962–78
(average annual percentage change)

Sector, measure, and period	Canada	France	Germany, Fed. Rep.	Italy	Japan	United Kingdom	United States
Manufacturing							
Real product wage							
1962–69	5.0	4.8	5.6	7.4	10.8	4.6	3.4
1969–73	3.6	7.0	7.5	9.7	12.6	5.6	3.6
1973–75	0.1	6.2	6.8	4.4	0.6	4.6	0.1
1975–78	. .	4.8	5.4	2.0	8.9	−1.4	3.0
Labor productivity							
1962–69	4.5	6.3	5.9	6.8	11.2	4.5	3.1
1969–73	4.4	5.4	4.8	6.9	8.7	4.1	3.2
1973–75	−0.4	2.8	5.2	0.4	−1.8	−1.3	−0.3
1975–78	4.5	6.1	5.0	4.1	7.3	1.2	3.0
Aggregate economy							
Real product wage							
1962–69	3.6	5.1	5.0	7.8	8.5	3.2	3.1
1969–73	2.0	5.5	6.3	7.9	12.2	3.7	2.6
1973–75	1.5	5.1	4.8	6.0	8.6	4.9	0.2
1975–78	1.8	5.2	2.7	1.2	2.7	1.5	2.3
Labor productivity							
1962–69	3.3	5.2	5.3	7.4	9.9	3.1	2.7
1969–73	3.2	5.7	5.2	6.6	9.1	3.9	2.6
1973–75	0.7	2.6	4.0	3.0	3.9	0.7	0.3
1975–78	2.0	5.0	4.5	1.3	4.1	2.0	2.1

Note: Real product wage is defined as the ratio of the nominal wage to the price of commodities produced.
. . Not available.
Source: Sachs, 1979.

20 percent of the growth of spending on social services and income maintenance, while changes in eligibility and improvements in benefits contributed 80 percent. Between 1975 and 1981 changes in eligibility had ceased to be significant. Demographic change then contributed 17 percent of the growth, and improved benefits 78 percent.

To pay for the growth of spending, taxes rose from 28.7 percent of GDP in 1961 to 37.5 percent in 1981. That increase did not cover all the rise in spending, however; public sector deficits also increased as a proportion of GDP. The significance of the general rise in public sector deficits is controversial, in part because of the difficulty of separating the effects of business cycles and inflation from those of structural trends in these deficits. It can be argued that the deficits may sometimes have acted as a valuable support for demand during a period of recession. It is undeniable, however, that, depending on the method of financing, deficits have caused difficulty in some countries at particular times. Where large countries such as the United States are concerned, deficits can have important global consequences. Insofar as they contribute

to high interest rates, they drive up the cost of borrowing, not only within the country, but worldwide.

Effects on the industrial countries

Pressures in the labor market and on public finance in industrial countries have contributed to four major problems since the late 1960s: inflation, unemployment, declining profitability, and a broadly defined protectionism.

● Inflation may be seen as the result of accommodation to labor market pressures and the result of deficit financing. One main effect of inflation is that it heightens uncertainty about the future—evidenced, for example, by the high inflation premiums demanded in long-term interest rates. This has significant implications for developing countries, which have an interest in securing medium- and long-term loans to match the long gestation period of some of their development projects. Perhaps the most important aspect of uncertainty, however, is created by the inflationary cycle itself. Experience that expansion breeds inflation

TABLE 2.3

Total public expenditure of industrial countries as share of GDP, 1961–81

(percent)

Country	1961	1966	1971	1976	1981
Canada	30.0	30.1	36.6	39.6	41.4
France	35.7	38.5	38.3	44.0	48.9
Germany, Fed. Rep.	33.8	36.9	40.2	48.1	49.3
Italy	29.4	34.3	36.6	42.2	50.8
Japan	17.4	20.3	20.9	27.8	34.0
United Kingdom	33.4	35.6	38.4	46.2	47.3
United States	29.0	29.2	32.3	34.5	35.4
Average for all industrial countries	29.3	30.6	33.3	37.9	40.9

Source: OECD, 1983.

and then policy-induced contraction is itself an important constraint on long-term investment and growth in both developed and developing countries.

• The rise in unemployment has been related to real-wage pressures, exacerbated by the productivity slowdown of the 1970s. The effect of the productivity slowdown was to lower the rate of increase of the real wage that was compatible with full employment. In the United States real wages appear to have adjusted rapidly to the new trend—they rose little after 1973 and adjusted quickly to the 1973–75 recession (see Table 2.2). In western Europe, however, the same was not true until the late 1970s. In the 1970s employment grew by about 20 million in the United States; with a similar size labor force, countries in the European Community expanded employment by only 2 million.

• The effects of real-wage pressures on employment have been exacerbated by the emergence in a number of industrial countries of both rising capital-output ratios and falling rates of profit, at least in the corporate sector (see Table 2.4). Faced with the higher costs of employing labor, firms shifted to more capital-intensive methods of production—

a natural reaction, but one that contributed to sharply rising unemployment. Among the countries where profit rates fell were Germany, Japan, the United Kingdom, and the United States.

• With real-wage rigidities, declining profitability in the corporate sector, and rising unemployment, governments were under great pressure to protect specific industries. Often protection is viewed in terms of trade measures alone—tariffs and quotas—and its costs are seen in terms of what it does to prevent other countries' exports. But protection can take many forms, including subsidies, and can be viewed more broadly as the attempt to prevent or slow change by preserving outmoded industries and firms.

Because it has taken covert and obscure forms, the evidence on the growth of protection is poor. Probably the most important protectionist policy in practice has been open-ended subsidies for specific firms in, for example, steel, chemicals, motor vehicles, and shipbuilding. In western Europe the share of public spending on subsidies was rising by the late 1960s and grew larger in the late 1970s and early 1980s. Also important have been quantitative restrictions in the form of "voluntary"

TABLE 2.4

Real rates of return on corporate capital, by country, 1962–76

(percent)

Period	Canada	France	Germany, Fed. Rep.	Italy	Japan	United Kingdom	United States
Average							
1962–64	7.9	9.7	19.3	10.4	28.2	11.9	12.0
1965–69	9.6	10.0	19.5	11.4	27.9	10.6	12.2
1970–73	9.0	11.6	15.0	10.3	21.9	8.3	8.6
1974–76	9.2	8.0	11.4	. .	13.5	3.7	7.1

. . Not available.

Source: Sachs, 1979.

export restraints and orderly marketing agreements, which violate the principles and rules of GATT. Estimates of the percentage of imports affected by nontariff barriers are shown for selected industrial countries in Table 2.5. The more effective the nontariff barrier the less the actual value of imports that enter a country. Thus estimates are only illustrative of the relative degree of protection. There has also been a growing use of "less than fair value" provisions of trade law as a form of harassment (see Box 2.1).

Quite apart from the threat to developing countries, protection damages the industrial countries themselves. First, efficiency is reduced by actions that cut the link between domestic and international prices. Second, there is an important added source of uncertainty with potentially serious effects for long-term, trade-oriented investment and thus for returns on investment.

Impact of rising oil prices

To understand the impact of the 1979–80 rise in oil prices, it is necessary first to consider the policy reactions to the jump in prices in 1973–74. That

TABLE 2.5
Percentage of industrial countries' imports covered by nontariff barriers

	Imports from	
Importer	Developed countries	Developing countries
United States	13.0	5.5
Japan	19.2	5.4
Switzerland	22.6	48.8
Sweden	1.0	7.0
Norway	8.2	10.9
Austria	15.0	8.1
EC[a]	15.1	11.8
Denmark	9.4	19.2
Ireland	15.0	9.5
France	20.1	7.1
United Kingdom	14.9	14.3
Italy	12.5	7.0
Germany, Fed. Rep.	12.6	8.5
Netherlands	16.1	19.8
Belgium and Luxembourg	19.2	29.7

Note: This table is based on detailed information on nontariff barriers available in UNCTAD. The figures measure the value of imports affected by nontariff measures in relation to total imports. Import figures are from 1980, whereas the information on nontariff barriers applies to 1983. If a country's import restrictions are rigorous, it imports little and few of its imports are affected by restrictions. Thus these figures provide little basis for comparison among countries in the total amount of restrictions.
a. Weighted average; excludes Greece.

earlier rise had amounted to an annual transfer of about 2 percent of GDP from the industrial countries, or roughly half a year's growth. But much of this could, at least initially, be borrowed back (and as the surplus available for borrowing fell between 1975 and 1979 so did the real price of oil). Although the oil price increase was damaging to industrial countries, it alone does not explain subsequent problems of slow growth, unemployment, and inflation except in the context of already existing economic rigidities.

Consider the labor market. The rise in the price of energy lowered the real wage that was compatible with full employment. It also led to an incentive to shift away from energy- and capital-intensive forms of production toward more labor-intensive methods. This substitution explains a part of the observed slowdown in labor productivity growth. Where the required reductions in real wages and real wage growth did not occur—as in some countries in western Europe—the productivity slowdown was small, but the oil price rise gave a permanent upward boost to unemployment.

In industry some capital stock had become redundant as expectations for higher growth were punctured. The changing price of energy also accelerated the obsolescence of significant parts of the capital stock, especially in such industries as steel, shipbuilding, chemicals (including petrochemicals), and motor vehicles. Governments then responded with increased attempts to prop up such industries with protection and subsidies.

Despite the failure of real wages to adjust and the declining rates of return on corporate capital, investment demand and then economic activity were partially sustained for nearly a decade by low and sometimes negative real rates of interest. The economic conditions of the late 1970s and the "debt crisis" which subsequently emerged in the 1980s can be understood only in terms of the peculiar relationship through much of the 1970s between real wages, which tended to rise faster than productivity, and real rates of interest, which stayed low.

Negative real rates of interest spurred a rapid growth of borrowing, especially by the non-oil developing countries. Although in the 1950s and 1960s the shares of different groups of countries in international lending changed only gradually, in the 1970s the non-oil developing countries' share rose sharply. The great increase in lending was largely the result of the oil producers' surplus. The industrial countries were not large net borrowers themselves; investment growth was sluggish in

Box 2.1   Administered protection and the open international trading system

An intention of the initial framers of the General Agreement on Tariffs and Trade (GATT) was that a GATT contracting party could legitimately "escape" from its commitment to keep its market open only through the use of specified exceptions such as the Article XIX safeguards provisions. Although the safeguards clause would allow a country to impose import restrictions, two important principles would be retained.

• Restrictions could not be discriminatory. They had to be applied to imports from all countries, not just a particular one.

• They had to be transparent. They could be imposed only after a finding that increased imports had significantly injured domestic production.

The recent record shows, however, a shift toward forms of "escape" that, although not inconsistent with GATT, tend to go against both these principles.

For example, in both the United States and the European Community, safeguards procedures are now used less frequently than unfair trade practice laws. The annual number of administered protection cases or investigations has been twice as high in the 1980s as it was in 1975–79, and administrative caseloads

are shifting to the less open, less transparent, forms of complaint and import restraint procedures. In 1982 and 1983 a total of 5 safeguards investigations were initiated in the United States compared with 262 cases alleging unfair trade practices. Under GATT, investigations into unfair trade practices can result in discriminatory import controls (not in conformity with the most favored nation principle) or duties on products from individual countries found to have engaged in unfair trade practices.

Furthermore, among the various sorts of cases alleging unfair trade practices, there has been a shift away from the antidumping complaint—the most transparent one—toward antisubsidy cases and other sections of US trade law. Some of these sections involve questions of fairness, such as patent infringement or policies or practices of a foreign government, that by US interpretation are inconsistent with an international agreement or are otherwise "unreasonable or discriminatory." Such cases do not involve an injury test and are not as well defined by administrative regulation and precedent as are the more traditional types of trade remedies.

In the European Community only two

safeguards cases were brought in 1983, but eighty cases alleging unfair trade practices. In addition, there were twenty-five instances of imports of a particular product from a particular country or group of countries coming under "surveillance." Surveillance involves no directly restrictive measures but is a clear warning that, if imports continue to grow, restrictions might be imposed. It discourages exporters from expanding sales by creating uncertainty about market access.

Since 1981 the Japanese government has enforced several policy measures to open its markets to imports. And in the past, Japan has not pursued safeguards or antidumping investigations and has brought only one antisubsidy case. But the Japanese government has used discretionary authority to restrict imports in order to prevent the import of new products until Japanese firms have had the opportunity to develop competitive varieties. These past policies have left a residue of uncertainty for foreign producers about market access in Japan. Once the new policies have been implemented for some time, this uncertainty, which tends to shield Japanese firms from foreign competition, should recede.

industrial countries after 1973, despite the need for expanded investment to adjust to changes in the world economy. Increased investment would have implied more rapid structural transformation, which the advanced industrial economies found hard to undertake. Indeed, uncertainty about the future course of inflation discouraged long-term investment in favor of projects having shorter pay-back periods. The latter offered greater liquidity but were less effective for restructuring the economy.

Consequences of disinflation

The disinflation of the early 1980s has its roots in the events and policies of the previous decade. It may be seen not only as a stage in the inflationary cycle but also as a determined attempt by some countries to break out of the vicious spiral of labor market rigidities, inflation, macroeconomic insta-

bility, and slow growth. There is considerable disagreement about the degree of disinflation needed to reduce inflationary pressures at any point in time. But the effects of the disinflation actually undertaken were not surprising. It is difficult to reduce inflation of the magnitude experienced in the 1970s without experiencing some loss of output and employment.

The extent of the losses, however, depends on several factors. One is the economy's flexibility in the face of reduced demand. To the extent that labor contracts take time to renegotiate and wages do not adjust quickly, reduced demand tends to produce unemployment. There is evidence that over time the rate of rise of nominal prices, especially of labor but also of some goods, has come to respond more slowly to recessions. This is not a recent phenomenon. It has merely become worse and more general over time, requiring greater losses of output and employment for each percent-

Box 2.2 Comparisons between the 1930s and the 1980s

The world depression of 1929–32 was much bigger and more widespread than any other in history. Between 1929 and 1932 the aggregate GDP of the advanced countries fell 17.1 percent and world trade by 26.8 percent. By contrast, in the 1970s the corresponding falls were only 0.4 percent and 5.0 percent in 1974–75. In 1981–82, GDP of industrial countries rose slightly and world trade fell by only 1 percent. The depression of 1929–32 was triggered by a collapse of the US money supply. In the 1980s there is no such danger of a monetary collapse in the United States, partly because of the safeguards now built into the US banking system. There are, in addition, better mechanisms for international coordination, through such institutions as the International Monetary Fund.

In nine major developing countries, accounting for 70 percent of the population of the developing world, the average peak to trough GDP decline over 1929–34 was 12.1 percent, with an average of 15.8 percent in Latin America and 4.9 percent in Asia. By contrast, except for low-income Africa in the 1974–75 recession, GDP continued to grow, though at a slightly slower rate (4 percent in 1975). In the 1981–82 recession there was a substantial slowdown in rates of growth; but even in Latin America and the Caribbean, where GDP fell in each year between 1981 and 1983, the fall since 1980 was only about 5 percent.

In the 1930s, the four main mechanisms that transmitted the depression from the industrial world to developing countries were the fall in export volume, the deterioration in the terms of trade, a perverse reverse flow of capital to the advanced countries, and the fall in the general price level.

• Exports. Data for nine developing countries show that the decline in the value of their exports in the 1930s accounted for an average fall of 5.3 percent in their GDP. Worsening terms of trade produced an additional income loss of 4.5 percent of GDP, so that change in export purchasing power amounted to 9.8 percent of GDP. Since their total income loss was 13 percent on average, a residual effect not "explained" by the direct export shocks accounted for 3.2 percent of GDP. This residual reflects the efficiency of policy in withstanding the impact of depression. It varied across countries, with positive residuals in China, India, Indonesia, and Colombia and large negative ones in Peru, Mexico, and Argentina. By comparison, the real value of exports from many developing countries, including Brazil, India, Korea, and Turkey, rose during the recent recession and for several others remained constant. Exports of manufactures in volume terms rose 6.9 percent a year from 1980 to 1983.

• Capital. In the 1920s net capital outflows from industrialized to developing countries were more than $700 million a year, primarily in the form of bonds and private investment. The flows were then reversed: in 1930–38 inflows to industrial countries averaged $540 million a year. Though much less dramatic, a similar reverse flow has begun in the early 1980s, though this time because of servicing of commercial bank debt. The countries in the 1930s (and 1980s) most affected by this reversal are mostly in Latin America, which had received the bulk of the earlier outflows of capital from industrial countries.

• Falling prices. In both industrial and developing countries the cyclical price fall from 1929 to 1932 averaged 6 percent a year. Even though nominal rates on government bonds generally went as low as 3 percent they were fixed, not variable; the fall in prices therefore created serious debt service problems for borrowers. In the 1980s high real interest rates have contributed to servicing problems; ironically, high interest rates represent in part insurance for creditors against inflation.

The combination of a drying up of capital inflows, the rising cost of servicing the existing debt, and the absence of international institutions and cooperation at the governmental level led to frequent defaults. Many countries defaulted on (but did not repudiate) their official debt obligations in the 1930s. Of the $5.3 billion of Latin American securities outstanding in 1938, $3 billion were in default. China went into default in the 1920s when civil disturbances reduced

---

age point reduction in the rate of inflation. This problem is then superimposed on the real-price rigidities, which have generated longstanding tendencies toward underemployment of resources.

A second factor is the degree to which the government's commitment to reduce inflation is credible. If people do not believe that the authorities will do what they say, they can be convinced only by experience. The more deeply rooted is their disbelief, the more protracted and painful their experience may need to be. Thus, if the extent and persistence of the monetary tightening had been fully anticipated, nominal interest rates would have declined as inflation declined. Since it was

not anticipated, the result was the worst recession since the 1930s (see Box 2.2).

Although disinflation was a major reason for the rise in real interest rates—especially short-term rates—it was probably not the only one. With growing budget deficits in the United States and in several European countries, and with the decline in the surplus of oil-exporting countries after 1980, the supply of real savings also declined. This itself would be expected to lead to a rise in real interest rates, other things being equal.

Savings rates in the industrial countries peaked in 1973 when net savings rates were 14.1 percent of GDP. Since then net savings rates have hovered in the revenues earmarked for servicing its foreign debt. Thereafter, China's creditors periodically wrote down or rolled over their loans, encouraged by occasional repayments. The penalties incurred for debt default in the 1930s were rather small. The creditor countries (mainly the United Kingdom and the United States) were already writing down their domestic farm and mortgage debt. War debts and reparations had earlier been reduced or rescheduled, which set a precedent for temporary default (as distinct from repudiation) by other borrowers.

A good deal of the defaulting in the 1930s was ultimately accepted by the creditors in wartime and postwar debt settlements. But it contributed to the collapse of the international capital market.

The world managed recovery from 1932 to 1937. The developing countries expanded their GDP by 34 percent, but trade expansion is estimated to have contributed only 6.6 percentage points of this growth. The reason for its minimal impact was the collapse of the liberal international trading system in the 1930s. Though tariffs in 1929 were somewhat higher than they had been in 1913, they were nondiscriminatory and the only barrier to trade.

The Hawley-Smoot tariff, instituted by the United States in 1930, led to a wave of protectionism. Virtually every country raised tariffs. New discriminatory trading blocs were created. Tariffs were rein-

The contracting spiral of world trade, 1929–33

Total imports of 75 countries (monthly values in terms of old U.S. gold dollars in millions).

Source: Kindleberger, 1973.

forced by quantitative restrictions and exchange controls that were also applied in a discriminatory way. World trade fell in a spiral (see chart). Developing countries, particularly in Latin America, adopted the same trade restrictions that had become the norm in the developed countries.

Though there are obvious similarities between the 1930s and 1980s—recession, a fall in world trade, the growing problem of debt, a reverse flow of capital from the developing to the developed countries—the magnitude of events in recent years bears no resemblance to what happened in the 1930s. Nor has there been any similar breakdown of the trading system that was reconstructed after the war. In addition, international cooperation both through the Bretton Woods institutions and among governments has permitted a much more effective defense against the spread of some of the worst problems of the recession.

the range of 9 to 10 percent (see Table 2.6). Household savings rates held up well in the 1970s, while corporate and government savings rates were strongly pro-cyclical. In recessions profit shares fall and governments run larger deficits. Thus a principal reason for the decline in gross and net savings rates was simply slow and unstable growth. It is as yet unclear whether there has also been a fundamental underlying trend toward lower rates of gross savings. But the high real rates of interest in the early 1980s do suggest that the credit market has become very tight and, in the event of increased demand for private investment, is likely to get still tighter.

Disinflation was successful in its immediate objective (see Figure 2.2). Among major industrial countries, the reduction in consumer price inflation was particularly sharp in the United Kingdom (from 18 percent in 1980 to 5.4 percent in 1983), the United States (from 13.5 percent in 1980 to 4.2 percent in 1983), and Japan (from 8 percent in 1980 to 0.7 percent in 1983). With few exceptions, however, even in the trough of the cycle, rates of inflation remained above the average for the 1960s. At the same time, there were serious adverse effects for world trade and the world trading system and equally—if not still more—serious effects for the international financial system.

TABLE 2.6
Net savings and savings by sector in industrial countries, 1964–81
(percentage of GDP)

Year	Net savings	Corporate	Government	Household
1964	10.8	3.4	2.0	5.4
1971	12.0	2.6	1.9	7.6
1973	14.1	2.7	2.8	8.7
1974	11.9	0.7	2.1	9.2
1975	9.0	0.8	−1.3	9.6
1976	9.6	1.4	−0.3	8.5
1977	10.4	1.9	0.4	8.2
1978	11.4	2.4	0.4	8.6
1979	10.9	2.1	0.9	8.0
1980	9.5	1.2	0.3	8.1
1981	8.8	0.6	−0.2	8.2

Note: Based on seven major OECD countries, including Canada, France, Germany, Italy, Japan, the United Kingdom, and the United States. Numbers may not add to totals because of rounding.
Source: Hakim and Wallich, 1984.

World trade grew by just 1.5 percent in 1980, stagnated in 1981, and then fell by 3.6 percent in 1982. The main reason was the sharp fall in the volume of trade in fuels. World exports of manufactures did better in terms of growth but still worse in relation to previous performance. They rose by 5.0 percent in 1980 and 3.5 percent in 1981 before falling by 2.3 percent in 1982. While the decline in the growth of world trade was largely the result of the recession itself, protection probably had some effect as well. New protectionist actions and agreements after 1980 largely concerned trade among industrial countries, especially imports into Europe and North America from Japan. There were, however, several developments that harmed developing countries, including a somewhat more restrictive renegotiation of the Multifibre Arrangement in 1981, subsequent restrictions on textiles and clothing, and further development toward comprehensive restrictions on imports of steel into the United States and the European Community.

There are two reasons the disinflation of the early 1980s created such severe problems for the international financial system. The first was the mix of fiscal and monetary policies pursued by the United States. Because of a growing budget deficit financed by borrowing in a country with a relatively low savings rate, interest rates rose. They attracted a substantial capital inflow and helped produce a large real appreciation in the dollar's exchange rate. Since the bulk of international indebtedness is denominated in dollars, the appreciation of the dollar greatly increased debt servicing costs for all, including the developing countries.

In the ten years preceding 1979, in the context of general world inflation, the US dollar depreciated about 50 percent against the German mark and about 60 percent against the Japanese yen. This tended to raise the rate of increase of dollar-denominated prices, and thus doubly helped debtors with dollar-denominated debts. The switch to global disinflation in the 1980s was accompanied by a strengthening of the dollar; between 1979 and 1982 it appreciated by 33 percent against the German mark and 14 percent against the Japanese yen. While national prices continued to rise (albeit more slowly), the average of international prices, converted into dollars, was actually falling. This greatly increased the burden carried by debtors with dollar-denominated debts; because of the tightness of international credit markets, they faced interest rates well into double figures as well as principal repayments whose real purchasing power was actually rising.

The second reason for difficulty was more deepseated. During 1960–73 the real interest rate in the Eurocurrency markets (three-month dollar rate deflated by the US GDP deflator) averaged 2.5 percent; during 1973–79 it averaged only 0.7 percent and at various times was negative. In such an environment, provided it lasts, it is almost impossible to owe too much. The tendency toward increased indebtedness was a general feature of economic life, and in no way unique to developing countries. Corporations and some governments in industrial countries tended to go increasingly into debt, as did the governments of a number of developing countries. When real interest rates jumped to almost 7 percent in 1981 and 1982, serious difficulty was bound to follow.

The difficulties were most conspicuous in the case of developing countries, particularly those which had borrowed heavily from commercial banks in the previous ten years. Although official transfers and direct foreign investment had been the major form of capital flows to developing countries in the 1950s and 1960s, they were overtaken by commercial bank lending in the 1970s. At the time, this seemed a benign vehicle for recycling the large surpluses of oil-exporting countries, and an effective way of obtaining higher investment in developing countries than could be financed through their domestic savings alone. But it also resulted in a huge buildup of commercial debt in several countries. The rise in nominal and real interest rates in the past few years and the slowdown—even halting—of new lending have made it difficult for some countries to service their commercial debt and raise the threat of a global financial crisis.

Developing countries after 1973

Thus the international environment had become less favorable to developing countries in the period after 1973 and became even less favorable after 1979–80. The slowdown in industrial-country growth hurt all developing countries, although the effect was not the same for all. Those which were exporters neither of oil nor of manufactures suffered most. The effect on oil exporters was at first more than offset by the rise in petroleum prices. Inflation in the 1970s helped to some extent all debtors. The sharp rise of real interest rates after 1979 hurt most large middle-income borrowers, most of them in Latin America. Most important, the rise in instability in the 1970s—of prices, of exchange rates, and of interest rates—complicated the tasks of decisionmakers (both public and private) everywhere.

However, interest rates and capital flows are only one determinant of growth in the developing countries. A second is their own policies; last year's *World Development Report* focused on their management of economic policies and institutions. A third influence is that of foreign trade. The maintenance of high growth and near full employment in industrial countries provides a boost to world trade. It also reduces the political pressures in industrial countries for tariffs, quotas, and other forms of protection for declining industries. More trade and less protection in turn enable developing countries to develop efficiently in line with their own comparative advantage.

The changing balance between these three factors explains the performance of developing countries, first in coping with the 1974–75 recession, then in achieving a sustained expansion until 1979, and most recently in struggling through the 1980–82 recession from which they have yet to recover. It also explains why some countries have done better than others.

Differences among developing countries

The middle-income countries of East Asia and the Pacific achieved GDP growth rates of 8.6 percent a year between 1973 and 1979, comparable to that achieved between 1960 and 1973. India also maintained its growth. Other regions did less well, especially sub-Saharan Africa. (The low growth of oil exporters shown in Table 2.1 is somewhat misleading since there were large increases in income because of improvements in the terms of trade.) Population growth rates in developing countries during the 1970s continued to be high and in some regions (notably sub-Saharan Africa) increased. In per capita terms, growth in many countries was therefore even less impressive; in sub-Saharan Africa, per capita incomes actually fell during 1973–83 (see Chapter 5).

For the purpose of assessing economic welfare, the growth of gross domestic income (GDY) is more relevant than the growth in GDP. By allowing for changes in the terms of trade, GDY takes account of changes in the rate at which national output can be converted into national consumption. All oil-importing countries experienced some worsening in the terms of trade in the 1970s. Recent improvements have not restored the terms of trade to their levels of the 1960s (see Table 2.7). The effects of the terms of trade for oil-importing countries should not be exaggerated, however. For example, between 1973 and 1979 the rate of GDP growth of middle-income oil importers of 5.6 percent a year was only a little above the GDY growth rate of 5.3 percent. Only for oil exporters have changes in the terms of trade been important; their rate of GDY growth was 9.0 percent a year compared with 4.9 percent GDP growth.

Where oil-importing countries performed well, they did so for two basic reasons. First, they maintained or increased savings and investment rates (see Table 2.8); second, they maintained or increased the growth of export volumes, especially manufactured exports (see Box 2.3). These performances in turn were made possible by the kind of domestic and trade policies that permitted an effective adjustment to external conditions. Middle-income developing countries were not uniformly successful in these areas; some may have relied too much on borrowing without adjustment. In general, though, the 1970s was a successful decade for them.

That was not true of low-income countries in Africa. Production was held back by adverse external conditions in combination with a series of domestic policies: poor incentives to farmers, costly and inefficient agricultural marketing systems for both inputs and outputs, and the maintenance of overvalued exchange rates. Between 1973 and 1982, countries such as Ethiopia, Sudan, Tan-

TABLE 2.7
Change in export prices and in terms of trade, 1965–83
(average annual percentage change)

Country group	1965–73	1973–80	1981	1982	1983[a]
		Change in export prices			
Developing countries					
Food	6.6	7.8	−16.1	−14.1	5.2
Nonfood	3.7	10.1	−14.6	−9.4	10.3
Metals and minerals	1.6	5.6	−12.0	−8.0	−2.2
Fuels	6.7	24.7	10.5	−2.6	−14.5
Industrial countries					
Manufactures	4.7	10.9	−4.2	−1.8	−3.2
		Change in terms of trade			
Low-income Asia	−0.5	−1.4	−0.1	−1.6	−0.6
Low-income Africa	−0.1	−1.5	−9.9	−0.9	4.6
Middle-income oil importers	−0.6	−2.2	−5.5	−1.9	3.0
Middle-income oil exporters	1.1	8.1	9.0	−0.4	−7.0
Developing countries	0.4	1.6	−0.5	−1.2	−0.6

Note: Calculations are based on a sample of ninety developing countries.
a. Estimated.

zania, Uganda, and Zaire experienced an appreciation of their real exchange rates, because relatively high rates of domestic inflation were not fully offset by falls in their nominal exchange rates. Even countries such as Kenya, Madagascar, Mauritius, and Somalia, which did depreciate their nominal exchange rates, ended up with a higher real effective rate or only a small devaluation.

The same phenomenon affected pricing policies, particularly in agriculture. Although nominal pro-

ducer prices have been increased in many cases, in real terms they were lower in 1982 than in 1980 in Kenya, Madagascar, Tanzania, and Togo. In some other countries—Burundi, Ivory Coast, Liberia, Malawi, Mali, Niger, Nigeria, and Upper Volta—although the prices of a few agricultural commodities have been raised, those for many others have fallen in real terms.

Governments in sub-Saharan Africa also let their public finances deteriorate. In countries such as

TABLE 2.8
Consumption, savings, and investment indicators for developing countries, 1970–81
(percentage of GDP)

Country group	1970	1973	1975	1977	1979	1981
All developing countries						
Consumption	78.9	76.5	76.7	75.3	74.4	76.8
Investment	22.7	23.8	26.3	26.1	26.9	27.0
Savings	21.1	23.5	23.3	24.7	25.6	23.2
Low-income Asia						
Consumption	77.1	75.0	75.7	75.5	74.2	76.2
Investment	23.7	25.6	25.7	25.1	27.7	25.8
Savings	22.9	25.0	24.3	24.5	25.8	23.8
Low-income Africa						
Consumption	86.6	88.6	92.5	91.0	91.5	94.1
Investment	15.5	15.1	16.4	17.9	16.9	16.6
Savings	13.4	11.4	7.5	9.0	8.5	5.9
Middle-income oil importers						
Consumption	79.5	77.5	79.1	77.1	77.9	79.2
Investment	23.6	24.4	26.7	25.4	25.7	25.3
Savings	20.5	22.5	20.9	22.9	22.1	20.8
Middle-income oil exporters						
Consumption	79.1	74.6	72.6	70.8	67.5	72.1
Investment	20.5	21.7	27.0	28.9	29.2	31.4
Savings	20.9	25.4	27.4	29.2	32.5	27.9

Box 2.3   Adjustment to external shocks, 1974-81

External shocks affect a country's balance of payments in three ways:

- The terms of trade effect on the balance of payments. When measured against a 1971-73 base as a percentage of GNP, the effect of changes in the prices of exports in relation to imports on the balance of payments over the 1974-81 period ranged from an unfavorable average of 6 to 7 percent a year for some middle-income Latin American primary producers, to a favorable 10 percent or more a year for some oil-exporting developing countries.
- The recession-induced effect. The impact on the balance of payments of developing countries because of recession in their main trading partners was uniformly unfavorable. As a percentage of GNP it ranged from an annual average of 0.05 to 2 percent or more.
- The net interest rate effect. In 1974-81 the impact on the developing countries' balance of payments of an increase in real interest rates ranged from an unfavorable 2 percent or more of GNP to a favorable 0.5 percent. The figures were generally much higher in 1979-81 than they had been in 1974-78.

As the sum of these different effects, external shocks during 1974-81 ranged from an unfavorable annual average of 7 to 9 percent of GNP to a favorable 10 percent. In a sample of thirty-three developing countries, twenty-four suffered adverse external shocks in this period.

Their responses varied considerably, measuring actual performance against what it would have been, based on their 1963-73 experience. They had four basic ways of responding: trade adjustment (export expansion and import substitution); an enhanced savings effort; that is, higher savings in relation to GNP (public and private); less investment in relation to GNP; and external borrowing.

Export expansion played a prominent role in a number of East Asian countries; adjustment through significant import substitution occurred in some Latin American and Caribbean countries and in southern Europe. Increased saving was important in a number of East Asian countries. A slowdown in investment (which lowers imports) was common in sub-Saharan Africa. And a large number of developing countries borrowed more as a way to adjust in 1974-81.

In reality, countries adopted a mixture of these methods, and can be classified on the following lines.

- Export expansion *and* an enhanced public savings effort. For this group, including Korea and Singapore, the average shock was highest at 4.8 percent of GNP a year. The effects of export expansion eventually exceeded their external shocks by one-third. Their extra savings averaged 20 percent of external shocks over the period as a whole. These countries also managed to economize on imports, which rose less per unit of GNP as time went on. While some borrowed heavily from abroad and increased investment as a proportion of their GNP, Korea sustained an investment boom with comparatively limited additional real foreign borrowing. By contrast, Singapore cut the share of investment in GNP and repaid large amounts of its real external debt.
- Export expansion *or* an enhanced public savings effort. Within this group, three patterns of adjustment may be distinguished. First, countries such as Argentina and Uruguay expanded their exports and their imports while reducing their public savings effort significantly more in 1979-81 than in 1974-78. Second, other countries, including Malawi, Thailand, and Turkey, relied on a combination of export expansion and import substitution, but a reduced public savings effort aggravated the balance of payments impact of external disturbances.

Third, a few countries (for example, Kenya) adjusted through a combination of import substitution and an enhanced public savings effort, while exports rose less rapidly than they would have, based on their 1963-73 experience. For this group as a whole, the deterioration in public savings accounted for 40 percent of external shocks. Most of these countries also increased their real foreign borrowing, which exceeded external shocks by more than 20 percent, and raised the share of investment in their GNP.

- Import substitution *and* deteriorating public savings. In this group of countries—which includes Jamaica, Portugal, and Yugoslavia—the adverse balance of payments impact of deteriorating public savings ratios was more than one-and-a-half times greater than that of external shocks. Import substitution played a dominant role in all of them, with exports rising less rapidly compared with 1963-73. All these features, present in 1974-78, became more pronounced in 1979-81. Real external financing was more important than in the first two groups, but with marked differences between countries.
- More real foreign borrowing. Morocco, Pakistan, and Spain relied overwhelmingly on external borrowing, making only a limited domestic adjustment.
- Favorably affected countries. A few countries (Colombia, Indonesia, Ivory Coast, and Nigeria) benefited from external changes because they exported petroleum or other primary commodities whose prices boomed in the mid-1970s. On average, adjustment to favorable shocks took the form of an import boom which intensified in 1979-81 compared with 1974-78, a stepping up of the share of investment in GNP, a slackening of public savings, and substantial additional real external financing toward the end of the period.

Burundi, Guinea, Mali, Malawi, and Sierra Leone, public expenditure has increased despite budgetary constraints. In many countries domestic savings collapsed in the 1970s. In Ethiopia the savings rate declined from about 12 percent to 3 percent (1973–82); Tanzania from 16 percent (1967) to 9 percent (1981); Sudan from 10 percent (1970) to about 3 percent (1978); Ghana from about 15 percent (1970) to 3 percent (1981); Kenya from about 15 percent (early 1970s) to 9 percent (1981); and Zimbabwe from about 20 percent in the early 1970s to about 10 percent in 1981. Despite foreign capital inflows, the rate of capital accumulation also fell considerably in sub-Saharan Africa.

For oil exporters, the rise in oil prices considerably increased their incomes. But the volume of their exports grew very slowly and the booming energy sector had a depressing effect on other parts of the economy. After 1982, when it became clear that the predictions of their oil revenues had been too optimistic, their relatively slow GDP growth of the 1970s was compounded by general deflation in an attempt to reduce imports (see Box 2.4).

As with the industrial countries, harsher external conditions in the 1970s exacerbated the consequences of various policy-induced distortions in many developing countries. A common response in many middle-income countries (Brazil, Korea, Philippines, Turkey, and Yugoslavia) to the 1973–74 rise in oil prices was to stimulate demand through expansionary monetary and fiscal policies and then to finance the resulting current account deficits through commercial borrowing. While much of this borrowing went to finance investment, the rates of return to both public and private investment were declining. Among the major borrowers, incremental capital-output ratios—the amount of extra investment needed to produce an extra unit of output—rose, for example, from less than 3 in Brazil in 1970–75 to nearly 4 in 1975–80, and from 3.6 to 4.5 in the Philippines. Inefficiency increased for a variety of reasons: shifts toward capital-intensive industry, low capacity utilization in various sectors, and inefficient use of resources in expanding the public sector.

Countries which saw an improvement in their terms of trade in the early 1970s also expanded their public spending. But since the improvement was transitory, the extra public expenditure increased public sector deficits and exacerbated balance of payments and debt servicing problems.

Apart from low-income Africa, the trends in savings and investment rates in most developing countries did not worsen in the 1970s (see Table 2.8). In some countries—India being a prominent example—they even improved. Nonetheless, distortions in the domestic financial system made the problems of domestic adjustment to external pressures more difficult. Thus Turkey in 1977–79 maintained fixed nominal deposit rates in the face of accelerating inflation. Brazil reduced monetary correction on financial assets in 1980.

Effects of the recent recession

In 1974–75 many developing countries were able to compensate for the deterioration of trading opportunities by exploiting the better opportunities for the migration of labor and for importing capital. Between 1979 and 1983, by contrast, most developing countries initially—and virtually all ultimately—found their external circumstances deteriorating in all significant respects.

Weak demand in the industrial countries during 1980–82 was the main cause of falling export prices for developing countries (see Table 2.7). Prices for industrial raw materials fell for the additional reason that high interest rates discouraged storage, while food prices dropped because of bumper world harvests. Overall, the prices of primary products in relation to those of manufactures reached a post-1945 low in 1982. In 1983, as economic recovery began in industrial countries, and as some supplies were limited by unfavorable weather, raw material prices started to rise again. Nevertheless, they remained lower than in 1979, and almost all developing countries faced worse terms of trade by 1983 than they had in 1980.

In volume terms, the developing countries' exports of raw materials and fuels fell absolutely during the recession. Exports of food, always relatively insensitive to income, continued to grow (see Table 2.9). Exports of manufactures, having grown at 10.6 percent a year between 1973 and 1980, rose at only 6.9 percent a year between 1980 and 1983. Given the sluggish GDP growth in industrial countries, however, developing countries did manage to increase their share of world markets for manufactures.

Among developing countries, one of the differences that weighed even more heavily in the recent recession than in the two preceding decades was between inward- and outward-looking trade policies. Previous *World Development Reports* have suggested that outward-looking policies—those in which there is rough equality between the incentives for exporting and import-competing activi-

Box 2.4 The oil syndrome: deficits in oil-exporting countries

Developing countries with only a limited range of exports—typically primary products—face potentially greater oscillations in their terms of trade than more diversified, advanced economies. The conduct of fiscal policy can be critical in determining the gains they obtain from favorable, but frequently temporary, movements in their terms of trade.

With the exception of the small group of capital-surplus oil exporters (Kuwait, Libya, Saudi Arabia), the quadrupling of oil prices in 1973–74 boosted real income, in countries such as Nigeria, Indonesia, and Venezuela by the equivalent of about 20 percent of nonoil GDP. World oil prices fell slightly in 1975–78, then redoubled in 1979–80, peaking at around $35 per barrel. As the world economy moved into recession, conservation measures in the major consuming countries began to affect the demand for energy (particularly oil). New supply sources came on stream. Prices fell by some $6 per barrel, and the sales of traditional exporters contracted sharply, in many cases to around half of their peak levels.

These swings in the availability of foreign exchange brought changes in fiscal revenues and then in public spending. There are considerable differences in the level of development and economic structure of oil-exporting countries. Nonetheless, virtually all oil exporters saw an unparalleled growth in the size and role of the public sector over this period, even in countries which had traditionally emphasized the role of the private sector. In addition to expanding their traditional functions, governments channeled their windfall gains into industry, including petrochemicals, heavy metals, and other large-scale and capital-intensive ventures, and into improvements in their transport and communications systems. Among a sample of the top nineteen developing countries with investments in projects exceeding $100 million each, all but five were oil exporters. Venezuela was responsible for twenty-seven of such projects with a total cost of $27.4 billion—equivalent to about 60 percent of its GNP in 1979 or three times its annual oil income. National oil companies in exporting countries were major sponsors of large projects.

Many countries experiencing windfall gains created or expanded programs of transfer payments and subsidies. The oil producers did not raise domestic fuel prices but chose to pass part of the windfall on to domestic consumers directly; as domestic oil consumption soared, the implicit fiscal burden of this transfer rose. In Trinidad and Tobago subsidies rose sharply to around 7 percent of GDP by 1981, not including the subsidies involved in loans to loss-making (and sometimes nationalized) firms. By 1983 it was estimated that the production costs of Caroni Sugar in Trinidad were five times those of producers elsewhere. Some 2.5 percent of the labor force was employed on public works, at wages twice as high as those available in agriculture.

A study of about 1,600 large projects (that is, those worth more than $100 million) in developing countries in the 1970s found that the larger and more complex projects had a greater tendency to overrun both in terms of cost and time. Of projects costing between $100 million and $250 million, 21 percent had significant delays or cost overruns averaging 30 percent. Of billion-dollar plus projects, 47 percent had delays or overruns averaging 109 percent. Delays of between one and two years plagued half the troubled projects; a further 25 percent had delays of three to four years.

The momentum of accelerated public investment and growing subsidies proved hard to curb when oil revenues fell. To take one example, Ecuador's public sector ran surpluses equivalent to around 2 percent of GDP in 1973–74. But these turned into deficits of some 5 percent of GDP in 1977–78, which declined with the second oil price rise, but then rose to some 8 percent of GDP in 1982.

With their improved creditworthiness, some oil exporters also borrowed heavily abroad after 1974. Algeria boosted the impact of increased oil revenues by about one-half through foreign borrowing.

The downturn in world oil markets after 1981 revealed how fragile were the development patterns of the oil exporters. The prime impact of state-led demand growth had been felt by the construction and service industries. These industries expanded their share of non-oil GDP in most cases during 1974–80, while non-oil industry and agriculture lagged. In a number of countries real exchange rates had appreciated by 20 percent or more. This reduced the incentive to develop or maintain non-oil exports and encouraged domestic producers to increase their dependence on imported intermediate and capital goods. These shifts in the pattern of resource allocation and relative prices proved hard to reverse. The massive infrastructural investments did not themselves constitute an autonomous source of demand. More seriously, the global outlook changed for many of the sectors in which investments had been concentrated. On steel, for example, in 1980 the OECD was forecasting global consumption doubling to 1,400 million tons by the year 2000. More recent forecasts project a 20 percent rise to only 900 million tons. As demand slackened, the transient boom of the late 1970s was followed by rapid deceleration in the non-oil part of economies, surplus domestic capacity, and slack labor markets. In the early 1980s, most of the oil exporters' non-oil economies were far smaller than they would have been had their growth trends in 1967–72 simply been extrapolated. In several countries contraction was accentuated by private capital outflows. Venezuela may have experienced an outflow equivalent to almost 10 percent of GDP in 1982; in 1979–82 its non-oil economy virtually stagnated despite massive investments and labor force increases.

TABLE 2.9
Exports from developing countries, 1965–83

Commodity and developing-country group	Change in export volumes (average annual percentage change)					Value of exports (billions of current dollars)	
	1965–73	1973–80	1981	1982	1983[a]	1965	1981
Commodity							
Manufactures	14.9	10.6	16.3	−1.6	6.0	7.1	134.6
Food	1.3	6.0	19.7	5.0	0.9	13.3	74.8
Nonfood	3.7	1.5	2.5	−6.1	1.7	5.4	24.5
Metals and minerals	6.3	5.9	2.6	−2.1	−1.9	4.5	26.9
Fuels	6.4	−1.3	−21.9	5.1	6.1	7.3	165.1
Developing-country group							
Low-income Asia	2.9	7.6	17.2	−3.8	4.6	5.2	36.0
Low-income Africa	4.0	−1.3	−2.6	10.6	0.2	1.9	6.6
Middle-income oil importers	8.1	7.6	12.5	−0.5	3.2	18.5	219.0
Middle-income oil exporters	5.7	−0.8	−17.0	5.2	5.7	12.0	150.5
All developing countries	6.3	3.1	0.4	1.1	4.1	37.5	412.1

Note: Data for 1982 and 1983 are based on a sample of ninety developing countries.
a. Estimated.

ties—are preferable to inward-looking policies that emphasize import substitution. To the extent possible, this equality needs to be achieved through the maintenance of appropriate exchange rates. Where some protection is imposed, export and other subsidies can offset the resultant disincentive to export producers. But export subsidies can be costly to the budget. Moreover, they introduce other potential distortions and may lead to countervailing action by industrial countries.

The benefits of outward-looking policies are felt in terms of higher growth rates in the long run and in a greater ability to adjust to external shocks. This is confirmed by a study of twenty-two oil-importing developing countries between 1979 and 1982. It found that countries with strong export growth had GDP growth of 3.8 percent a year, compared with 2.8 percent a year where export growth was average and 1.3 percent a year where it was weak. In the same sample, those countries pursuing active trade policies (including elements of both export promotion and efficient import substitution) grew faster, at 3.2 percent a year, than those which relied mainly on import restrictions.

The benefits of outward-looking policies may be gleaned from the different rates of recovery from the recession. The middle-income developing countries of Asia had a much stronger recovery during 1983 than those of Latin America, and have had a generally superior performance since 1980. They did not use borrowing to postpone adjustment to the same extent, partly because the costs of adjustment in their dynamic economies were lower. They had generally lower ratios of public

debt to GDP and almost uniformly lower ratios of debt service to exports.

For low-income developing countries, the deterioration in their terms of trade was perhaps more serious than the effects of the debt problem itself. However, low-income countries in Asia (and especially China and India) embarked in the 1970s on reforms that introduced greater flexibility in their economic structure through greater integration into the world economy, and helped raise their domestic savings rates. China has been successfully promoting its manufactured exports, while India has significantly increased its commercial borrowing since 1980–81. These policy reforms, combined with an improved institutional infrastructure, allowed them to maintain their economic growth. Sub-Saharan Africa was much less successful in adjusting, because of a legacy of poor performance and policies. In per capita terms, income is estimated to have fallen every year since 1980 in low-income African countries (see Table 2.1).

Contrary to expectations, the recession in the industrial economies did not bring down interest rates substantially. Because two-thirds of developing-country debt was denominated in dollars and much of it at variable interest, the rise in real rates meant a fundamental change in their finances. It greatly increased the costs of borrowing and of postponing domestic adjustment. Thus the impact of the recession on developing countries came in two distinct phases. The first—when adjustment was postponed by many developing countries—ended in the middle of 1982; the second—a period

Box 2.5   Paths to crisis and adjustment among Latin American debtors

Latin America's debt and growth problems drew renewed international attention in August 1982, when Mexico could not service its debt. But the problems had been brewing for some time. Since 1979 when the industrial countries entered what was to become the longest recession of the postwar period, the countries of Latin America have experienced a slowdown in economic activity and growing financial crisis. Expansionary domestic fiscal policies, the persistence of high real rates of interest on the region's variable rate debt (which accounts for over two-thirds of the region's total external debt), rapid growth of total debt, and a decline in export earnings after 1981 placed enormous pressure on the external positions of countries throughout the region.

Growth of external debt accelerated after 1973 as countries initially borrowed to compensate for higher oil prices or to finance ambitious development programs. In real terms (deflating by the dollar price of tradable goods), the debt of the major Latin American borrowers rose only slightly in the mid-1970s. But world inflation later led to a sharp rise in interest rates and a shortening of maturities on the commercial debt. Real interest rates, which had been negative during much of the 1970s, rose abruptly to a level of 15 to 20 percent for many countries. The resulting debt service rates (interest plus amortization) have increased by an amount that more than offsets the earlier inflation-induced decline of the real value of external debt. At the same time, the dollar prices of major exports fell for many countries in the late 1970s and early 1980s.

In several countries overly ambitious public investment programs, reduction of domestic savings incentives, and adoption of trade and exchange policies which had an antiexport bias exacerbated external imbalance and increased external borrowing requirements. This is illustrated by the experience of three large Latin American debtors—Mexico, Argentina, and Venezuela. Their fiscal deficits rose rapidly in the 1970s. Argentina's

increased from $1.8 billion in 1973 to $5.5 billion in 1980; Mexico's from $1.4 billion in 1972 to $5.8 billion in 1980; Venezuela's from a surplus of $3.0 billion in 1973 to a deficit of $2.7 billion in 1978. In Argentina much of the public spending was financed by direct or indirect borrowing from the central bank. In Mexico it was only with the onset of the debt crisis in 1982 that the government began to rely more heavily on central bank financing. This need not have been inflationary if the resources transferred to the government had not exceeded the normal growth in demand for reserve money. However, many Latin American countries relied heavily on fiscal drag—the process by which revenues rise automatically in line with inflation—and on the yield to the government of the "inflation tax" levied on holders of money. During 1975 and 1976, the inflation tax accounted for more than 25 percent of Argentina's GDP (and half or more of the total resources available to the government). Some countries relied less on the inflation tax because they could readily borrow abroad. As foreign loans slowed down, they resorted to the inflation tax again.

This combination of events culminated in a generalized debt crisis throughout the region unlike anything experienced since the 1930s. Since 1981, sixteen of the twenty-eight countries in Latin America have been forced to seek emergency balance of payments support from the IMF. Most of these have also had formal rescheduling agreements with their creditors.

Confronted with an external resource constraint which became acute after 1981 as a result of terms of trade deterioration and a sharp drop in capital flows, most Latin American countries cut imports and investments drastically. Domestic austerity programs aimed at restoring external balance, compounded by the decline in demand for the region's exports, resulted in the sharpest decline in output and employment that Latin America has experienced in the past fifty years. For the entire region, per capita

GDP fell by almost 6 percent in 1983. For a number of countries (Argentina, Bolivia, Brazil, Uruguay, most of Central America, and the Caribbean), and for the region as a whole, 1983 was the third consecutive year of stagnation or decline in per capita GDP. The region's per capita output has now fallen to about the 1976 level.

The challenge which now faces the Latin American countries is to shift from import- and output-cutting adjustment to growth-oriented, export expanding adjustment, since this alone is compatible with rising investment, output, and employment and is required in the face of continued rapid population growth (2.2 percent) and even faster labor force growth (3.0 percent). Strong recovery of the world economy and maintenance of an appropriate level of trade finance by commercial banks will be necessary if exports are to expand. Recovery will be accelerated to the extent that the massive outflows of private capital which occurred since 1980 are repatriated; policies to attract and hold these private savings are a necessary component of adjustment programs.

Even if more efficient adjustment policies are followed, the fiscal and trade surpluses required to service the debt will, in current financial conditions, be daunting. By historical standards even Chile's foreign debt–GDP ratio of around 85 percent would not be abnormal. But Latin American countries are paying nominal interest rates in excess of 10 percent and amortization rates in excess of 20 percent, which for the worst case implies debt service obligations as high as 25 percent of GDP.

To reestablish creditworthiness over the longer term, these countries' exports must grow more rapidly than the nominal rate of interest which they pay on their external debt. While this is a necessary condition for recovery, it is not sufficient. In the near term net capital flows will also have to increase over the low 1983 level.

of rapid and painful adjustment for some—has continued since then (see Box 2.5).

The pressures of international debt

From the beginning of the 1980–83 recession, oil-importing developing countries as a group were forced to start curbing the volume of their imports. Nevertheless, their combined current account deficits did grow—from $29 billion in 1978 to $70 billion in 1980 and $82 billion at their peak in 1981 (see Table 2.10). One reason for these increases was the rapid rise in interest payments. In 1982, for example, interest due from all developing countries, including that on short-term debt, was $66 billion—more than half of their total current

account deficit. Nevertheless, in 1982 oil-importing developing countries did manage to borrow more than they were paying their creditors in capital and interest, notwithstanding the capital flight occurring in some of them. In 1983, however, the flow was reversed, at least with respect to commercial finance.

For oil exporters the experience in the early part of the recession was markedly different from that of oil-importing developing countries, although the denouement turned out to be similar. In 1980 oil exporters ran current account surpluses and increased the volume of their imports. The higher oil prices were not sustained, however, and the volume of their oil exports fell. In 1981 they, too, slipped into deficit—of $26 billion followed by $32

TABLE 2.10
Current account balance and its financing, 1970–83
(billions of current dollars)

Country group and item	1970	1980	1981	1982	1983[a]
Developing countries					
Net exports of goods and nonfactor services	−9.8	−55.2	−80.5	−57.1	−10.9
Net factor income	−3.6	−16.4	−30.0	−43.2	−48.3
Interest payments on medium- and long-term loans	−2.7	−32.7	−41.2	−48.4	−49.0
Current account (excludes official transfers)[b]	−12.7	−69.6	−107.8	−97.6	−56.2
Financing					
Official transfers	2.4	11.6	11.7	10.8	11.1
Medium- and long-term loans					
Official	3.7	21.5	21.2	21.4	17.6
Private	4.6	35.7	49.6	33.5	39.9
Oil importers					
Net exports of goods and nonfactor services	−8.9	−69.3	−70.5	−46.9	−26.0
Net factor income	−1.5	−4.3	−14.4	−21.8	−23.0
Interest payments on medium- and long-term loans	−2.0	−21.3	−26.7	−31.7	−32.3
Current account (excludes official transfers)	−9.8	−70.3	−81.8	−65.6	−46.1
Financing					
Official transfers	1.8	9.6	9.4	9.0	8.9
Medium- and long-term loans					
Official	2.9	16.9	16.5	15.9	13.9
Private	3.7	24.6	30.8	22.0	11.1
Oil exporters					
Net exports of goods and nonfactor services	−0.9	14.2	−10.0	−10.1	15.1
Net factor income	−2.1	−12.1	−15.6	−21.4	−25.3
Interest payments on medium- and long-term loans	−0.7	−11.5	−14.5	−16.7	−16.7
Current account (excludes official transfers)	−2.9	1.7	−26.1	−32.1	−10.0
Financing					
Official transfers	0.6	2.2	2.3	1.8	2.2
Medium- and long-term loans					
Official	0.8	4.6	4.7	5.5	3.6
Private	0.9	11.1	18.8	11.6	28.9

Note: Calculations are based on a sample of ninety developing countries.
a. Estimated.
b. Current account does not equal net exports plus net factor income due to omission of private transfers. Financing does not equal current account because of omission of direct foreign investment, other capital, and changes in reserves.

TABLE 2.11
Debt indicators for developing countries, 1970–83
(percent)

Indicators	1970	1974	1975	1976	1977	1978	1979	1980	1981	1982	1983[a]
Ratio of debt to GNP	13.3	14.0	15.4	16.6	18.1	19.3	19.5	19.2	21.9	24.9	26.7
Ratio of debt to exports	99.4	63.7	76.4	79.6	84.7	92.9	83.7	76.1	90.8	108.7	121.4
Debt service ratio[b]	13.5	9.5	11.1	10.9	12.1	15.4	15.0	13.6	16.6	19.9	20.7
Ratio of interest service to GNP	0.5	0.7	0.8	0.8	0.9	1.0	1.3	1.5	1.9	2.2	2.2
Total debt outstanding and disbursed (billions of dollars)	68.4	141.0	168.6	203.8	249.8	311.7	368.8	424.8	482.6	538.0	595.8
Official	33.5	61.2	71.6	83.5	99.8	120.1	136.0	157.5	172.3	190.9	208.5
Private	34.9	79.8	96.9	120.3	150.0	191.6	232.8	267.3	310.3	347.1	387.3

Note: Calculations are based on a sample of ninety developing countries.
a. Estimated.
b. Ratio of interest payments plus amortization to exports.

billion in 1982 (see Table 2.10). In both years the oil-exporting countries drew down reserves, as did the oil importers. Their creditworthiness, too, was being questioned.

Concern about creditworthiness is related both to the likelihood that debtors, if necessary, will be willing to service their debt out of income (rather than extra borrowing) and to the economic cost of debt service. That cost depends on several factors: the ratio of debt to wealth (in the case of a country, the present value of future national income); the real rate of interest; the ease with which the necessary adjustments to spending in relation to output can be made; and the cost of making transfers in foreign exchange. In almost all these respects, creditors saw that the position of developing countries as a group was deteriorating. Between 1979 and 1982 ratios of debt to GNP had risen from 19.3 to 24.9 percent, of debt to exports from 84 to 109 percent, and of debt service to exports from 15 to 20 percent (see Table 2.11). In effect, debt accumulation was on an explosive path.

If any single event can be isolated as the turning point in the attitude of the lenders, it probably occurred in August 1982 when Mexico got into difficulties over its debt service obligations. In the context of a debt structure with short maturities and high nominal interest rates, the reduced willingness to refinance meant that these difficulties quickly spread to other borrowers. Because of the number of lenders involved, the immediate resolution of the problem also involved support by the central banks of the industrial countries and a degree of involuntary lending. Subsequently, a number of countries faced debt servicing difficulties. In 1983 there were thirty-six reschedulings involving $67 billion of debt.

It is possible to argue that the "debt crisis" was

to some extent caused by imprudent decisions by both borrowers and lenders. In some cases, this was no doubt true. But the scale of the overall strains of indebtedness was the result of an unexpected mixture of circumstances—prolonged recession in industrial countries, the strong dollar, and high rates of interest. This unexpected mixture made debt servicing more difficult, even for countries such as Korea and Indonesia, although they were able to avoid rescheduling.

For African countries, the "debt crisis" had a different meaning. Though the overall indebtedness of low-income Africa is relatively low ($22.6 billion of outstanding medium- and long-term debt in 1983), the fall in net disbursements of external finance from a peak of $3.9 billion in 1980 to $1.7 billion in 1982 has posed problems. The ability of many countries to service their debt is weak, and this is reflected in the large number of debt reschedulings in low-income Africa. Nearly half of all reschedulings between 1975 and 1983 were by African countries, with Zaire alone accounting for six, Togo for five, and Liberia for four. Most serious of all is the decline in official lending from $2.6 billion in 1980 to $1.7 billion in 1982, which will be exacerbated by the reduction in the size of the seventh replenishment of the International Development Association (IDA).

Adjustment in developing countries

To restore their balance of payments, developing countries need to make some external adjustments to raise exports in relation to imports. This has its direct counterpart in an internal adjustment that reduces real spending in relation to real output. A key question facing developing countries is the pace of the adjustment they need to make.

In many countries internal adjustments had to start with the public sector. Borrowing abroad had helped finance internal public deficits. Even when the public sector was not the only borrower, it often guaranteed foreign loans contracted by private borrowers. In a number of countries, public sector deficits had reached 10 percent of GNP by 1982; in certain cases, they were as large as 15 percent of GNP. Given the undeveloped state of domestic capital markets, such deficits could be financed (even in the short term) only by inflation or by borrowing abroad.

The extent of those liabilities can be gauged from a few figures. In 1982 the developing countries as a group had $715 billion of foreign debt. More than three-quarters was medium- and long-term. Some 60 percent of the total was owed to commercial banks; another 30 percent was due to official creditors, nearly half of which was concessional aid. More than half of total outstanding debt had been incurred by only ten countries. Their need to adjust was the most urgent of all developing countries, but others were to varying degrees facing balance of payments difficulties.

The strains increased enormously in 1982. Net disbursements of medium- and long-term private loans to developing countries fell from $50 billion in 1981 to $34 billion in 1982, with most of the drop occurring in the second half of the year. In the first quarter of 1983 net private lending was only $2.6 billion; most of this consisted of involuntary lending under the auspices of IMF rescheduling agreements. Thus the increase in medium- and long-term private lending shown in Table 2.10 is almost entirely due to the rescheduling of existing short-term debt.

Internally, the required adjustments to this sharp decline in lending have taken two forms: an overt attempt to reduce the size of the public sector deficit and a de facto increase in taxation through a rise in the inflation tax. Indeed, the acceleration in inflation that has occurred in a number of the principal debtor countries is not an accident. It is one way for existing public sector deficits to be financed in the context of the decline in foreign lending. Closing the deficits by increased taxation (whether overt or covert) has often led to a squeeze on the private sector with potentially adverse consequences for long-term investment and growth. The same adverse effects on long-term growth will occur when it is public sector investment that is cut.

Given a large enough cut in real spending, the current account of the balance of payments is bound to improve. However, experience shows that there are more and less efficient ways of achieving this result. Adjustment involves a reduction of spending in relation to output. But reductions in output itself provide no contribution to adjustment and represent pure waste. Countries therefore need to switch output into exports and efficient import substitution. If they fail to make that switch, deep cuts in spending are bound to reduce output. As a result, the attempt to reduce spending in relation to output also creates a recession.

Since 1982 developing countries have substantially improved their trade balances. For oil-importing developing countries the current account deficit (excluding official transfers) fell from $82 billion in 1981 to $66 billion in 1982 and an estimated $46 billion in 1983 (see Table 2.10). For oil-exporting developing countries the deficit fell from $32 billion in 1982 to an estimated $10 billion in 1983. Indeed, the combined deficit in 1983 was only a little larger than the interest due in that year.

In many countries these declines have resulted largely from cutting imports in relation to output and from recession-induced reductions in demand for imports. Between 1980 and 1982 the volume of imports fell by about 50 percent in Argentina and 20 percent in Brazil; it fell by 35 percent in Mexico in 1982. In Brazil imports as a proportion of GDP fell from about 10 to 6 percent between 1980 and 1983 and in Chile from 30.4 to 21.3 percent. In many cases imports have been cut to the point of consisting only of industrial raw materials and essential foodstuffs with little even for investment. Furthermore, the import restrictions employed in many indebted countries to curb imports threaten a long-term deterioration in the efficiency of trade regimes and a reduction in future growth.

Only a few countries have managed to expand exports enough to avoid serious domestic recession. Korea and Turkey, for example, had sizable foreign debts; but by following effective adjustment policies, they succeeded in expanding both their real imports and exports during the 1980s. By contrast, the real value of exports declined in Argentina and Venezuela between 1981 and 1983, was stagnant in Brazil, and rose by about 20 percent in Mexico.

Adjustment has meant a sharp decline in per capita consumption. During 1980–83 it fell by 2 to 10 percent a year in countries as diverse as Argentina, Brazil, Chile, Ivory Coast, and Yugoslavia. In all these countries, per capita consumption had grown between 1970 and 1981.

In many countries private investment suffered from weak domestic demand and high interest rates. In Brazil capacity utilization has fallen by about 13 percent since 1980. In the Ivory Coast industrial value added fell by 3 percent in 1980 and 1981, and investment (excluding petroleum) by 20 percent. As for employment, the number of manufacturing jobs in greater Sao Paulo fell by 13 percent between mid-1980 and 1982; in the Ivory Coast industrial employment has fallen by 10 percent since 1980. Distress borrowing by private firms, bankruptcies, and government takeovers have become common. In Argentina bankruptcies and judicial interventions increased from 52 in 1977 to nearly 300 in 1981. In Chile several hundred bankruptcies were reported in 1982.

Cuts in public spending have often been achieved by reducing or eliminating subsidies—not only for parastatals but also for food, education, and health. The short- and long-term consequences can be far-reaching. At one level, a reduction in food subsidies, along with devaluation, reduces real incomes. At another, a decline in spending on education and health detracts from building human capital, while less spending on infrastructure may damage a country's growth potential in the medium term. These effects may indeed outlast the resolution of the current debt problems. There is evidence that government spending on social programs has fallen by less than spending on production and infrastructure. But much of social spending undoubtedly goes to maintain staff salaries, so the materials and supplies necessary for maintaining health and educational standards may be falling much more.

The consequences of austerity are dramatic for the country concerned. But they go further than that because cuts in imports affect the entire world economy. As a group, developing countries are larger markets for the European Community, the United States, and Japan individually than any one of the three is for the other two. Developing countries are also of great importance to one another. This is a particularly serious problem in Latin America where a long history of import substitution and schemes for regional trade integration have led to significant intraregional trade, especially in manufactures. In the case of Brazil, the reductions in imports by the rest of Latin America (as well as by other developing countries) has seriously harmed its exports. Consequently, the required external adjustments are more difficult and the corresponding internal adjustments more painful.

3 Prospects for sustained growth

With economic growth reviving, attention shifts to the prospects for sustaining the recovery. Looking further ahead, governments are assessing the chances of raising long-term growth rates above their average in the 1970s. That task, as Chapter 2 made clear, depends on overcoming certain deep-seated problems that were revealed and exacerbated by two sharp rises in oil prices. The industrial countries have been slowed by the growing inflexibility of their economies, especially in labor markets, and by the upward pressures on public spending and the associated tendency toward higher taxation and periodic bouts of inflationary financing. The results have included falling returns on investment; a declining investable surplus; defensive policies of protection and subsidization; and, in consequence, slow growth and stubborn inflation. Many developing countries face difficulties which are not dissimilar to those of the industrial countries, especially policy-induced distortions in the economy and problems in controlling public spending and deficits.

This chapter begins by examining some scenarios for growth in the years up to 1995, exploring the policies and conditions that would bring them about. In particular it looks at what has to be done to restore the growth rates of the 1950s and 1960s, considering both the choices facing industrial countries and the benefits that developing countries could reap, even in unfavorable world conditions, by changing their own policies. The chapter then discusses the implications of the different scenarios for international debt, along with the related policy issues for both the industrial and the developing countries. Finally, it stresses the potential for international collaboration, especially over trade liberalization and capital flows.

A ten-year perspective

To illustrate the range of possibilities for the world economy in 1985–95, this chapter describes two basic scenarios. Designated the Low case and High case, these scenarios should not be viewed as predictions; the outcomes depend on the policies adopted in developed and developing countries. They also do not consider or allow for any exogenous shocks to the world economy that could result from, for example, a severe disruption of energy supplies.

The Low case indicates what might happen if the industrial countries were to do nothing to improve their performance of the past ten years (see Table 3.1). Their GDP growth would then average 2.5 percent a year in 1985–95, nearly the same as between 1973 and 1979. Governments of industrial countries would find it hard to control inflation, and their budgetary deficits and unemployment would remain high. Protectionist sentiment would be strong, threatening the exports of developing countries and their ability to service their debt. But protectionist actions would increase no more rapidly than in the past several years, and developing countries would still have the potential to increase penetration of markets in industrial countries.

The Low case is based on an average inflation rate in the industrial countries of 6 percent a year, in dollars at unchanged exchange rates. This is close to 7 percent in current dollars because of a presumed depreciation of the dollar after 1985 of 13 percent. This inflation rate is likely to be the average of widely divergent rates over successive cycles. With real interest rates at 3.5 percent because of the large budget deficits, the nominal interest rate would average 9.5 percent. This rate too would probably fluctuate considerably over time.

Competition for funds from the governments of industrial countries would keep real interest rates up, and so would discourage lending to many developing countries. The ratio of official development assistance to GNP in the industrial countries is presumed to remain at its historical average, so development assistance would grow at 2.5 percent

TABLE 3.1
Average performance of industrial and developing economies, 1960–95
(average annual percentage change)

Country group	1960–73	1973–79	1980–85	1985–95 High case	1985–95 Low case
Industrial economies					
GDP growth	4.9	2.8	1.9	4.3	2.5
Inflation rate[a]	6.1	9.9	2.3	4.3	6.8
Real interest rate[b,c]	2.5	0.7	5.2	2.5	3.5
Nominal lending rate[c]	5.8	8.4	11.6	6.0	9.5
Developing economies[d]					
GDP growth	6.3	5.2	2.8	5.5	4.7
Low-income					
Asia	5.9	5.2	5.8	5.3	4.6
Africa	3.5	2.1	1.7	3.2	2.8
Middle-income oil importers					
Major exporters of manufactures	6.7	5.8	1.6	6.3	5.2
Other	5.3	4.3	1.9	4.3	3.8
Middle-income oil exporters	6.9	4.9	2.4	5.4	4.7
Export growth[e]	6.3	3.1	5.5	6.4	4.7
Manufactures[e]	14.9	10.6	8.1	9.7	7.5
Primary[e]	5.0	0.9	4.0	3.4	2.1
Import growth[e]	6.4	5.9	3.2	7.2	5.1

Note: Projected growth rates are based on a sample of ninety developing countries.
a. Inflation in the United States is 3.5 percent a year in the High case and 6 percent in the Low case. But for the industrial countries as a whole, it is higher in dollars because of an assumed depreciation of the dollar of 13 percent between 1985 and 1990.
b. Average of three-month US dollar Eurocurrency rates for the periods 1960–73 and 1973–79, deflated by the rate of change in the US GDP deflator.
c. Average annual rate.
d. Does not include South Africa.
e. Historical growth rates are for the periods 1965–73 and 1973–80.

a year in real terms, with bilateral aid increasing its share if present trends in the reduction of multilateral aid, evidenced by the recent cut in the IDA replenishment (see Box 3.5 below), continue. In all their forms, capital flows to developing countries would therefore grow quite slowly.

The High case, by contrast, offers industrial economies a path of sustained and steady expansion, with GDP growing at 4.3 percent a year in 1985–95 (see Table 3.1). Unemployment would then fall steadily. Inflation would average 3.5 percent a year, in dollars at present exchange rates (and 4.3 percent in current dollars), varying only modestly from year to year. Budget deficits, particularly in the United States, would gradually be reduced—first as a percentage of GDP, then in absolute terms. With deficits being brought under control, the real interest rate is projected to fall to 2.5 percent a year, giving nominal interest rates of only 6 percent.

With lower domestic interest rates and smaller budget deficits, investment would increase. As

unemployment eases, protectionist measures subside, so developing countries would find it easier to expand their exports and to ease their debt servicing burden. Investment confidence would rapidly improve, which, along with larger aid programs, would lead to an expansion of the flows of capital to developing countries.

The Low case and developing countries

In the Low case, slow growth in the industrial countries would limit GDP growth in developing countries to an average of only 4.7 percent a year, and to only 2.7 a year in per capita terms (see Table 3.2). This supposes that developing countries, despite slower growth of their imports in relation to GDP, escape the full effects of slow growth in industrial countries.

Given considerable differences among countries, the Low case means for some little or no growth. Per capita income in low-income Africa would decline; among some middle-income oil importers,

TABLE 3.2
Growth of GDP per capita, 1960–95
(average annual percentage change)

				1985–95			
Country group	*1960–73*	*1973–79*	*1980–85*	*High case*	*Low case*	*Increased protection*	*Improved policies*
All developing countries	3.7	2.0	0.7	3.5	2.7	2.3	3.1
Low-income	3.0	2.9	3.2	3.4	2.7	2.4	3.0
Asia	3.4	3.3	3.7	3.7	3.0	2.6	3.3
Africa	1.0	−1.0	−1.6	−0.1	−0.5	−0.7	−0.3
Middle-income							
Oil importers	3.8	3.3	−0.6	3.6	2.6	1.9	3.1
Major exporters of manufactures	4.4	3.6	−0.3	4.4	3.3	2.4	3.8
Other	2.6	1.7	−0.9	1.5	1.0	0.7	1.2
Oil exporters	4.3	2.3	−0.4	2.7	2.0	1.9	2.3
Industrial countries	3.9	2.1	1.5	3.7	2.0	2.0	2.0

per capita income would grow at only 1 percent a year. China and India would grow at 4.6 percent a year, India at only 2.5 percent a year in per capita terms. Countries such as Korea and other major exporters of manufactures, affected only by the slower growth of their world markets, would get the capital they need to keep growing at 3.3 percent or more a year in per capita terms, for a total growth of 5.2 percent.

Other less creditworthy countries, such as Brazil and Mexico, would grow less, especially in the late 1980s, while their adjustment continued; in the early 1990s their growth would speed up. With their populations growing at 2.3 percent a year, per capita income of middle-income oil-importing countries as a group would grow at only 2.6 per-

cent a year over the ten years. Middle-income oil exporters would have a GDP growth of 4.7 percent a year, 2.0 percent in per capita terms. As oil prices rise, however, their GDY would grow much faster because of the continued improvement in their terms of trade.

The trade outlook would mirror growth for the different groups of developing countries. Exports by all developing countries would grow at 4.7 percent a year during 1985–95 (see Table 3.3). Manufactured exports would expand at about 7.5 percent a year compared with 9.7 percent in the High case. The reduction in growth rates of manufactured exports would be proportionately much smaller than that of industrial-country growth vis-a-vis the High case because, even with some addi-

TABLE 3.3
Change in trade in developing countries, 1965–95
(average annual percentage change)

	Merchandise exports[a]					*Exports of manufactures*				
				1985–95					1985–95	
Country group	*1965–73*	*1973–80*	*1980–85*	*High case*	*Low case*	*1965–73*	*1973–80*	*1980–85*	*High case*	*Low case*
All developing countries	6.3	3.1	5.5	6.4	4.7	14.9	10.6	8.1	9.7	7.5
Low-income	3.3	5.4	5.0	6.8	5.2	6.4	6.9	8.2	9.3	7.1
Asia	2.9	7.6	5.4	7.5	5.7	6.6	7.4	8.5	9.3	7.2
Africa	4.0	−1.3	3.5	3.3	2.2	4.5	0.5	0.9	8.9	6.6
Middle-income										
Oil importers	8.1	7.6	6.6	7.5	5.7	18.2	11.5	8.1	9.7	7.6
Major exporters of manufactures	10.5	9.6	7.2	8.2	6.3	18.6	12.1	8.4	9.8	7.6
Other	4.8	3.7	4.1	4.0	2.8	15.6	7.1	5.0	9.0	7.3
Oil exporters	5.7	−0.8	4.1	4.1	2.4	12.7	7.9	7.4	10.5	7.7

Note: Projections are based on a sample of ninety countries.
. . Not available.

tional protection in industrial countries, manufactured exports would still grow largely in line with the supply capacity of developing countries. As in the past, exports of primary commodities, however, would grow more slowly than growth in the industrial economies.

Under the Low case, net loan disbursements (private and official) plus official transfers to the developing countries would fall in real terms, from $68 billion in 1983 to $63 billion in 1995, while developing countries would pay $58 billion in interest (see Table 3.4).

The High case and developing countries

In the High case, the prospects for developing countries would greatly improve. Their GDP would grow at about 5.5 percent a year, almost as fast as it averaged in the 1960s (see Table 3.1), and at 3.5 percent in per capita terms. They would receive somewhat higher real prices for a larger volume of exports, and credit would be available at lower interest rates.

The major exporters of manufactures would do best, with GDP growth at 6.3 percent a year; some countries could manage 8 percent or more. Such rapid growth would imply that they were moving into more technology-intensive products—as is already happening in Korea with heavy engineering, for example, and in Singapore with precision engineering.

Some of the middle-income countries—such as Malaysia, Mexico, Thailand, and Turkey—could also make major structural progress in the years to

1995. The more successful would see their development proceed as Korea's did in the 1960s and early 1970s. They would begin to rely more on markets and less on government directives for the allocation of resources. And they would pursue more outward-oriented trade policies. Others would not, so there is likely to be considerable dispersion around the average of 5.7 percent growth for the middle-income group. Oil importers other than the major exporters of manufactures would grow at only 4.3 percent a year, and oil exporters at 5.4 percent a year.

Under the High case, the poorest countries would grow at 3.2 percent to 5.3 percent a year, with several Asian countries doing better. Low-income African countries would still do badly; even in the High case, per capita income would fail to rise. This is in part because the market outlook for these countries' commodity exports is not very good. The volume of such exports is projected to increase only slightly. At the same time, these countries' weak financial position means significant increases in commercial lending to them are unlikely, so they must continue to rely on concessional assistance for the bulk of their capital transfers.

World trade would grow at about 7 percent a year in real terms, given global GDP growth of about 5 percent. In a world of freer trade, trade would grow faster in relation to GDP than it did in the 1960s. Exports of manufactures from developing countries would grow at 9.7 percent a year, exports of primary products at 3.4 percent (see Table 3.3).

	Exports of primary goods				Merchandise imports[a]					
				1985–95					1985–95	
1965–73	1973–80	1980–85	High case	Low case	1965–73	1973–80	1980–85	High case	Low case	Country group
5.0	0.9	4.0	3.4	2.1	6.4	5.9	3.2	7.2	5.1	All developing countries
1.8	4.5	2.6	4.1	3.1	0.6	6.4	3.5	5.9	4.1	Low-income
0.3	7.9	2.1	4.6	3.6	−0.6	8.7	4.1	6.4	4.6	Asia
4.0	−1.4	3.8	2.8	1.9	3.5	0.1	1.1	3.6	1.6	Africa
										Middle-income
4.4	4.5	4.5	3.2	2.4	7.7	4.6	2.2	7.6	5.6	Oil importers
										Major exporters
5.2	6.0	4.8	3.8	2.9	9.7	5.3	2.8	8.4	6.3	of manufactures
3.7	3.0	3.9	2.0	1.2	4.6	3.2	−0.3	3.9	1.9	Other
3.6	−1.1	3.9	3.3	1.8	6.6	9.3	5.4	7.1	4.5	Oil exporters

a. Projections include exports and imports of nonfactor services.

TABLE 3.4

Current account balance and its financing in developing countries, 1983 and 1995

(billions of constant 1980 dollars)

	All developing countries			Low-income Asia		
Item	1983[a]	High case 1995	Low case 1995	1983[a]	High case 1995	Low case 1995
Net exports of goods and nonfactor services	−10.8	−69.5	−29.0	−8.9	−17.4	−14.0
Interest on medium- and long-term debt	−48.7	−52.1	−58.0	−1.7	−3.1	−3.1
Official	−9.7	−16.0	−17.5	−0.9	−2.4	−2.4
Private	−39.0	−36.1	−40.5	−0.8	−0.7	−0.7
Current account balance[b]	−55.8	−109.5	−78.1	−1.3	−12.1	−9.3
Net official transfers	11.0	16.6	14.3	1.7	2.4	2.1
Medium- and long-term loans[c]	57.2	74.0	49.1	4.1	8.1	6.0
Official	17.5	35.0	26.6	3.9	7.3	5.8
Private	39.7	39.0	22.6	0.2	0.8	0.2
Debt outstanding and disbursed	592.0	914.9	656.2	47.5	89.6	67.9
As percentage of GNP	26.7	21.9	17.1	8.7	8.9	7.2
As percentage of exports	121.4	80.3	71.3	99.5	85.0	78.7
Debt service as percentage of exports	20.5	12.7	13.7	9.9	7.0	7.1

Note: The table is based on a sample of ninety developing countries. The GDP deflator for industrial countries was used to deflate all items. Details may not add to totals because of rounding. Net exports plus interest does not equal the current account balance due to omission of net workers' remittances, private transfers, and investment income. The current account balance not financed by official transfers and loans is covered by direct foreign investment, other capital (including short-term credit and errors and omissions), and changes in reserves. Ratios are calculated using current price data.

The major exporters of manufactures, already accounting for 80 percent of the developing countries' exports of manufactures, would see their manufactured exports grow at about 10 percent a year. Some of them—such as the Philippines and Thailand—could do much better than others. Other middle-income oil importers would expand their manufactured exports at about 9 percent a year. Meanwhile, low-income Africa would have its manufactured exports grow at about 9 percent a year, starting from a very low base (see Table 3.3). To do this, however, it would have to reduce its reliance on western European markets and to diversify its exports, expanding into manufactured products.

Under the High case, loan disbursements plus official transfers to developing countries would rise from a peak of $83 billion in 1981 to $91 billion in 1995 (in constant 1980 dollars—see Table 3.4), a rise in real terms of only 2.5 percent a year from 1983—slower than the projected rate of growth of industrial countries.

Low-income countries would also obtain a growing inflow of capital in the High case, largely through the expansion of concessional loans from governments and international institutions. With low income levels, the sacrifice of consumption and investment needed to service loans on commercial terms is particularly painful. Yet, provided policies are reasonable, the returns to investment in poor countries can be very large indeed. Concessional assistance is needed partly to finance the development of human capital and to strengthen institutions—programs for which economic returns are high but delayed. Because the potential of the low-income countries will not be realized until these programs are in place, the role of concessional aid in promoting development is vital. Moreover, because the returns to these investments are high, aid can contribute significantly to development in the low-income countries and help to raise the global efficiency of investment.

The contrast between the Low and the High case is not merely quantitative. It amounts to a qualitative difference as well, because the apparently insurmountable obstacles of the past ten years would steadily diminish if High-case growth were achieved—or, under the Low case, would become even more entrenched. With a continuation of slow growth, millions of people in many developing countries will become progressively poorer; with faster growth, almost everybody in the world will enjoy some increase in real income. The prize that the High case offers is considerable. The question is how to win it.

	Low-income Africa			Middle-income countries								
				Major exporters of manufactures			Other oil-importing countries			Oil-exporting countries		
	1983[a]	High case 1995	Low case 1995	1983[a]	High case 1995	Low case 1995	1983[a]	High case 1995	Low case 1995	1983[a]	High case 1995	Low case 1995
	-4.3	-7.1	-5.2	-0.6	-18.8	-1.5	-12.2	-16.7	-9.9	15.0	-9.6	1.5
	-0.8	-1.3	-1.3	-22.2	-22.6	-25.5	-7.4	-7.3	-8.8	-16.6	-17.9	-19.3
	-0.4	-1.0	-1.0	-3.5	-5.1	-5.9	-2.2	-3.6	-3.9	-2.7	-3.9	-4.3
	-0.5	-0.3	-0.3	-18.7	-17.5	-19.6	-5.2	-3.7	-4.9	-13.9	-14.0	-15.0
	-4.3	-7.0	-5.8	-22.8	-40.5	-26.7	-17.5	-17.8	-14.3	-10.0	-32.1	-21.9
	1.8	2.8	2.4	3.1	5.0	4.3	2.3	3.2	2.9	2.2	3.1	2.7
	1.4	3.4	2.7	11.8	27.7	17.1	7.5	12.5	9.5	32.3	22.3	13.8
	1.6	3.2	2.6	4.3	8.6	6.1	4.0	8.0	6.1	3.6	7.9	6.0
	-0.2	0.1	0.1	7.5	19.2	11.0	3.5	4.6	3.4	28.7	14.3	7.8
	22.2	38.3	30.1	224.9	350.6	245.4	97.6	142.8	112.4	199.7	293.7	200.6
	42.2	50.2	41.4	26.3	20.5	16.0	39.8	35.0	29.2	38.9	30.4	22.3
	242.0	234.7	224.1	99.6	59.0	50.7	177.5	145.4	137.2	133.0	90.1	78.7
	24.8	19.1	20.6	20.0	10.5	11.4	28.7	20.2	22.9	21.4	16.0	17.0

a. Estimated.
b. Excludes official transfers.
c. Net disbursements.

Policy requirements of the High case

The difference between this basic Low case (variants of which are discussed below) and the High case hinges on the performance of the industrial countries. If they could regain the productivity growth and high employment they managed in the 1950s and 1960s, the High case would be achieved. There is little sign that they would be prevented from doing so by some fundamental deterioration in the rate of technological progress. On the contrary, in some fields—telecommunications, electronics, biotechnology—the pace of technical change appears to be accelerating. It therefore seems probable that faster growth depends on tackling the problems that dogged the industrial countries in the 1970s.

Deficits, savings, and interest rates

Economic recovery is likely to stimulate higher saving in industrial countries. But since the oil exporters' surplus has disappeared and the United States is running a large budget deficit, global savings rates are unlikely to regain their level of the early 1970s, at least not in the immediate future. To the extent that industrial-country recovery in the context of lower inflation leads to increased demand for money and greater investment, the prospect is that both short-term and long-term real rates of interest will remain high in comparison with those of the 1970s.

Inflationary expectations have not disappeared. In the major industrial countries, the "core" rate of inflation—measured by the rise in the GDP deflator—is running at between 1 percent a year in Japan and 9 percent a year in France; in the United States it is about 4.5 percent. While low by recent standards, these are not rates that can be ignored, especially in the light of past experience of the inflation cycle.

Given the unfavorable context, neither higher employment nor lower interest rates is likely to be brought about in any durable way merely by increasing nominal demand. Moreover, in the long run, the financing of public spending will probably become still more difficult in developed countries. In many, the political will to increase taxation is limited, but the pressures for more spending remain strong.

If they are to avoid a resurgence of inflation, most industrial countries will need to maintain tight monetary policies. Given the fiscal pressures, the real cost of borrowing is likely to remain high. For that reason alone, budget deficits will tend to grow as the real interest burden is compounded over time. The main focus of industrial countries in the years ahead should be on developing ways to reduce budget deficits.

Microeconomic flexibility

In several areas of their economies—subsidies to obsolescent firms and industries, wage and other policies affecting labor costs—industrial countries need to introduce greater flexibility in the way they accept and promote economic change. Though protectionist policies might temporarily maintain the real incomes of certain groups, they also prevent the adjustment to a country's emerging and changing comparative advantage, which alone can ensure growing real incomes of all groups in the economy. The maintenance of an open trading system is, therefore, an important means of reducing microeconomic distortions. For example, protection is costly to the country using it. The cost of "saving" jobs is higher consumer prices and inefficiencies in production (see Box 3.1), as well as loss of potential jobs in export industries, particularly if other countries increase protection as a response.

Box 3.1 Costs of protection in textiles and clothing

Motivated by a desire to "save" jobs, governments of industrial countries have introduced many restraints against developing countries' exports of manufactures. The most important of these affect textiles and clothing and have been implemented under the Multifibre Arrangements.

That such restraints are undesirable for developing countries is widely understood. Textiles and clothing constitute almost 30 percent of the manufactured exports of developing countries. They have been an essential step on the ladder of development for many countries, from the United Kingdom in the nineteenth century to Japan in the early twentieth and Korea in the 1960s and 1970s. While export restraints can benefit large suppliers who are able to raise their export prices, they are a disaster for countries such as Sri Lanka and Mauritius that are starting to enter the market, only to find the route barred.

Much less well known are the high costs borne by the industrial countries themselves. For the United States, studies of workers in the clothing industry who have benefited from the Trade Adjustment Assistance program followed their experience over several years. In the late 1970s the majority of redundant workers were able to find a new job within a year; of those who did not, many were over the age of fifty-five and opted to leave the labor force. The mean duration of unemployment for men who subsequently moved to a new job was thirty-eight weeks and for

women it was fifty weeks. They often found jobs paying as much as or more than before. The present value of the losses borne by each worker who permanently lost his (or her) original job was $10,800 before government welfare benefits, $5,600 after those benefits.

In Canada at least two-thirds (and probably close to three-quarters) of displaced workers in the clothing industry found new jobs. They were unemployed from an average of twenty-one weeks (men) and thirty-one weeks (women). The present value of the losses varied from a high of C$14,000 for the average woman in one survey, to a gain for a twenty-five year old man in the other, both before welfare benefits. The highest loss found in either of the two surveys was C$5,000 after welfare benefits for the average female worker—close to the losses found for the United States.

The cost of preserving a job to society as a whole is created by the inefficiencies in production and consumption. Based on tariffs alone, that cost for clothing and textiles was estimated to be $426 million for the United States in 1977. To preserve jobs indefinitely, protection must continue indefinitely. The present value of these costs would then be over $10 billion. At the same time, the tariffs were estimated to save 116,000 jobs. Thus the cost of permanent protection per job saved would be about $80,000, while the private benefit to the individual worker would be $5,600, a ratio of 14 to 1. In other words, a permanent policy of tariff protection would cost the United States

$1 for every 7 cents gained by workers whose jobs were preserved.

The Canadian studies estimated the costs of all the controls on the clothing trade, which were much higher than those of tariffs alone. The cost per job saved by permanent controls was estimated to be C$390,000 in the late 1970s. Because the individual worker lost only C$14,000 (before welfare benefits), the net cost to society was about C$375,000. This was needed to save each worker C$5,000, a ratio of over 70 to 1. For every one and a half cents by which the worker would be better off, one Canadian dollar would be wasted.

Developing countries also use various tariffs and quantitative restrictions (along with foreign exchange controls and broader measures such as industrial licensing and investment incentives) to protect local industries. Generally, such measures have favored production for home markets over production for export markets, and manufacturing over agriculture. Protection and other measures lead to distortions in the structure of production, consumption, and trade; these are costly to economic growth. Studies of the "costs" of such protection, such as those for the United States and Canada, have not been done in developing countries. But among developing countries, those with lower and more uniform and neutral patterns of incentives have performed better in terms of economic growth and ability to cope with external shocks.

An open trading system is also a way of capturing the potential for increased integration between developed and developing countries. And, last but not least, it is a sine qua non of a resolution of the debt problem.

For the more advanced developing economies, the next stage in their progress will carry them into industries that have hitherto been the preserve of the industrial countries. Unless the industrial countries keep their markets open, they will thwart the newcomers' progress. By seeking to retain a monopoly of such industries, the industrial countries will also be holding back their own economic growth.

The threat of increased protectionism

Slow growth in the industrial countries is the most likely trigger for a significant increase in protection directed against developing countries. It is also in this context that the adverse effects on the developing countries would be most serious, since a further decline in their exports would slow their overall growth even more. To illustrate these implications, the Low case contains a variant (Low I) which assumes that governments in industrial countries step up protection against imports from developing countries (see Table 3.5). In other respects, the industrial countries' policies and performance are assumed to be unchanged. Under these circumstances, low-income Asian countries grow at 4.2 percent a year, only 2.6 in per capita

TABLE 3.5
Growth of GDP in developing countries, Low scenario and variants, 1985–95
(average annual percentage change)

Country group	Low case	Increased industrial-country protectionism[a]	Improved developing-country policy[b]
Developing countries	4.7	4.3	5.1
Low-income			
Asia	4.6	4.2	4.9
Africa	2.8	2.6	3.0
Middle-income oil importers			
Major exporters of manufactures	5.2	4.4	5.7
Other	3.8	3.5	4.0
Middle-income oil exporters	4.7	4.6	5.0

a. Low I.
b. Low II.

terms. Low-income Africa grows at 2.6 percent a year, -0.7 in per capita terms. Even major exporters of manufactures manage GDP growth of only 4.4 percent a year, while growth of GDP in the other middle-income oil importers falls to 3.5 percent a year.

Overall, developing-country exports grow by 4.0 percent a year under Low I compared with 4.7 percent in the Low case; manufactures grow by 6.1 percent compared with 7.5 percent; and primary commodities, 2.2 percent as in the Low case. As a result, the developing countries reduce the growth in their imports, from 5.1 percent a year in the Low case to 4.3 percent in Low I. All regions are affected: exports by the major exporters of manufactures grow at only 5.2 percent a year, by other middle-income countries at 2.3 percent a year, and by low-income Africa at a disastrously low 2.1 percent a year (see Table 3.6).

The benefits of improved policies in developing countries

Just as industrial countries might make matters worse (even within the Low scenario) by resorting to protection, so developing countries can partly offset the effects of slow growth in the industrial world by improving their own policies. This is illustrated in Low II—a second variant of the Low case which assumes slow growth in the industrial world but an improved performance by the developing countries. They would achieve faster GDP growth by raising savings and investment rates, by increasing and diversifying their exports, and by using imports more efficiently as well (see Box 3.2).

As Table 3.5 shows, the improved policies of Low II would allow GDP to grow in developing countries at an average rate of 5.1 percent a year, recovering half of the difference between the Low and High cases. Low-income Asian countries would grow at 4.9 percent a year as against 5.3 percent under the High case, low-income Africa at 3.0 percent as against 3.2 percent in the High case. Major exporters of manufactures would manage 5.7 percent a year, and other middle-income oil importers 4 percent.

Developing-country exports of primary commodities would grow at 2.4 percent a year, but exports of manufactures would grow at 8.0 percent a year (Table 3.6). That would give the developing countries overall export growth of 5.1 percent a year compared with 6.4 percent in the High case, but 4.7 percent in the Low case; adding inflation, export earnings would rise at more than 13.0 per-

TABLE 3.6
Growth of trade in developing countries, Low scenario and variants, 1985–95
(average annual percentage change)

Country group	Exports of goods and nonfactor services			Exports of manufactures			Exports of primary goods			Imports of goods and nonfactor services		
	Low case	Low I[a]	Low II[b]	Low case	Low I[a]	Low II[b]	Low case	Low I[a]	Low II[b]	Low case	Low I[a]	Low II[b]
All developing countries	4.7	4.0	5.1	7.5	6.1	8.0	2.2	2.2	2.4	5.1	4.3	5.4
Low-income	5.2	4.3	5.6	7.1	5.6	7.6	3.1	3.1	3.3	4.1	3.4	4.4
Asia	5.7	4.7	6.1	7.1	5.6	7.6	3.6	3.6	3.8	4.6	3.9	5.0
Africa	2.2	2.1	2.5	6.5	5.0	7.1	1.9	1.9	2.1	1.6	1.5	1.8
Middle-income												
Oil importers	5.7	4.7	6.2	7.6	6.1	8.1	2.4	2.4	2.6	5.6	4.5	6.0
Major exporters of manufactures	6.3	5.2	6.8	7.6	6.2	8.1	2.9	2.9	3.2	6.3	5.2	6.8
Other	2.8	2.3	3.2	7.2	5.8	7.8	1.1	1.1	1.4	1.9	1.4	2.1
Oil exporters	2.4	2.2	2.7	7.6	6.1	8.1	1.9	1.9	2.1	4.5	4.2	4.7

Note: These projections are based on a sample of ninety countries.
a. Increased protection by developed countries.
b. Slow growth in developed countries but improved policies in developing countries.

cent a year. Many of the big debtors would experience growth of export earnings above that average—major exporters of manufactures would have the value of their exports grow at close to 15 percent a year—comfortably above the interest rate on their debt of above 10 percent.

What is needed to achieve these improvements? The developing countries—and the industrial world—will suffer from any action that reduces trade (see Box 3.3). They therefore need to avoid overvalued exchange rates, to provide attractive incentives for exports, and to promote efficient import substitution. Such policies would be twice blessed. Faster growth of exports and GDP would also generate a larger inflow of foreign capital. This would supplement the extra saving that improved policies would bring, all of which would then be invested more efficiently. The key to more saving and better investment lies in maintaining positive real interest rates in the developing countries.

It is also imperative that developing countries increase the flexibility of their budgets—another close parallel with the industrial countries. Many of the difficulties faced by middle-income countries in the past decade have been due to heightened public spending commitments, financed either through external borrowing or through windfall gains from higher commodity prices. When these sources of finance diminish or dry up, it is politically difficult to cut public spending, and inflation results.

Capital flows and debt

The discussion thus far has considered the effects of the performance of industrial countries and of developing-country policies on trade and the growth of GDP. Almost as important as trade in the long term, however, and far more critical in the short to medium term, are the interrelated issues of capital flows and debt. It is through borrowing from abroad that developing countries are able to supplement their own saving as well as to offset shortages of foreign exchange. Borrowing is an opportunity; but in certain circumstances it is also a snare.

Under the Low case and its variants, interest rates would be higher and the growth of exports and GDP lower than in the High case. If lenders wish to avoid debt expanding beyond the servicing capacity of the borrower's economies, net lending would then be lower while the real cost of borrowing would be higher. For the indebted sovereign borrower, the service of debt is a matter of political will, and strength of will depends on the cost of exercising it. The long-term prospect of receiving capital inflows that are not large enough to cover interest payments, combined with slow growth of export earnings (as is threatened by the Low case), implies that the service of debt is economically, and therefore politically, costly. For this reason the long-term prospects for the world economy, and hence for capital flows, depend heavily on creating

Box 3.2 Trade as an engine of growth

Foreign trade can be an engine of growth in developing countries through its effect on improved resource allocation and increased productivity. But developing countries' exports are not mechanically linked to the growth and level of prosperity in advanced countries.

In the nineteenth century in the United States changes in exports lagged behind changes in the rest of the economy. Exports remained a small and relatively constant share of GNP (6 to 7 percent). In Australia, too, growth was dominated by internal factors. Although Argentina enjoyed rates of export growth roughly similar to those of the United States and exported similar products in the last half of the nineteenth century, it grew little.

In the three or four decades preceding World War I, trade of developing countries grew almost as fast as that of developed countries (36 percent a decade compared with 40 percent). In relation to GNP, foreign trade was rising more rapidly in the developing countries than in developed ones.

The experience of developing countries since World War II further suggests that simple links between developing-country exports and income growth in the industrial countries do not adequately explain export performance. The engine of growth concept is based on the premise that developing-country exports are primary products and therefore grow in line with advanced-country income. But manufactures today account for about half the value of nonfuel exports from developing countries. A few countries account for a large proportion of these

exports (see Chapter 5), but even among countries that traditionally specialized in a single primary export, manufactures are gaining a significant share. A group of eleven such countries, including India, which account for about two-thirds of developing-country population (excluding China) has managed to raise the share of manufactures to about 50 percent of nonfuel exports (see chart). Africa is the only region in which dependence on a single primary export has not diminished.

This diversification away from primary products does not mean that foreign demand no longer matters. Developing countries depend on developed-country markets for their manufactured exports; short-run fluctuations in the demand for their exports due to fluctuations in growth in industrial countries can still be important. But the diversification of exports toward manufactures has changed the medium- and long-run competitive position of developing-country exports in developed-country markets. Their manufactured exports account for less than 5 percent of apparent consumption in developed countries, and are substitutes for goods produced within advanced countries. As long as markets for developing countries' manufactured exports remain relatively free of protective barriers, external demand constraints will not limit developing-country exports.

The experience of the 1960s and 1970s bears this out. There has been no stable statistical relation between the volume of developing-country exports and real

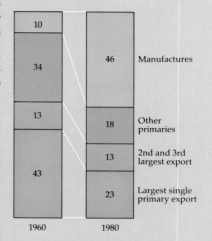

Export structure of selected developing countries (percent)

	1960	1980	
Manufactures	10	46	
	34		
Other primaries	13	18	
2nd and 3rd largest export		13	
Largest single primary export	43	23	

Excludes major exporters such as Korea, Hong Kong, and Singapore. Includes India, Mexico, Brazil, and Egypt.

Source: Riedel, 1984.

income in developed countries in the 1960s and 1970s. Developing-country exports increased twice as fast in relation to developed-country income in the 1970s; for each 1 percent change in real income in developed countries, the volume of developing-country exports increased by only 0.9 percent in the 1960s, but by 1.7 percent in the 1970s. Manufactured exports from developing countries increased at twice the rate of income of the developed countries in the 1960s, but had almost five times the rate of income of developed countries in the 1970s.

---

and maintaining cooperation on debt problems, rather than confrontation.

In the short term, the position is somewhat different. Given the effects of the recession and the growth of debt, debtors have to show that they are prepared to pay interest out of their own income. This is necessary not only to anchor the value of debt in the willingness to service it but also—in the context of high real interest rates and of low growth in indebted countries—to avoid explosive growth of capitalized interest in relation to GDP. An adverse world environment, however, makes more costly the adjustments required of many bor-

rowers. While adjustment requires action by the indebted country itself, the degree of retrenchment and its cost to the country also depend on the external environment in the next few years.

Because of the large current account deficits of many developing countries in the early 1980s, substantial adjustments have been required to cover interest obligations. The best way to have adjusted would have been to combine cuts in spending with policies to switch production into exports and into efficient import substitution. Switching usually requires a real depreciation in the exchange rate (see Box 3.4). The process is less costly if it does

43

Box 3.3 Delinking from the world economy?

Having an open trading and payments regimen encourages optimal use of available investment resources. This is a stronger argument for integrating into the world economy than that which claims that demand from industrial countries provides an ''engine of growth'' for the developing world. All countries have to trade to some extent. More inward-looking economies are not less buffeted by external shocks than are outward-looking ones. The more inward-looking an economy, the higher the proportion of capital goods in imports and the greater the costs to output of compressing imports. Similarly, the more difficulty such an economy has in expanding exports, because the smaller the proportion of output that is readily tradable. For these reasons, inward-looking countries have generally had not only lower growth but also greater difficulty in adjusting to shocks and more serious debt problems than the more outward-looking economies. The contrast between Latin American and East Asian middle-income countries in the 1980s is instructive.

Although the gains to a country from an outward-oriented strategy will obviously diminish if trade restrictions increase or external financing becomes more unstable, its position will still be better than under autarky. Some of the instability experienced by developing countries which chose fuller integration into the world economy was unavoidable, but many consequences were exacerbated by inappropriate domestic policies. Overvalued exchange rates, unsustainable public spending, and inefficient pricing policies all accentuated the short-run domestic costs of coping with a volatile world.

To achieve stability of domestic incomes by delinking from a volatile world economy can lead to lower average income than if the world economy rollercoaster is ridden efficiently. For instance, despite constraints on its development, by keeping the economy relatively insulated from international competition, India has maintained a trend in growth rate of income of about 3.5 to 4.0 percent a year over three decades. But this stability was bought at a cost: not reaping the gains from integration in the world economy during the early period when the world economy was growing. As an illustration of this loss, in 1960 the absolute size of Korea's manufacturing sector was a quarter of India's; in 1980 it was more than 60 percent of India's. Korean manufactured exports rose from virtually none in 1962 to more than $15 billion in 1980. In the same period India's manufactured exports rose from $0.6 billion to only $4.1 billion. India and Korea were different in several respects: Korea's literacy rate in 1960 was more than twice that of India; foreign capital flows to Korea were larger; and, of course, India is a much bigger country with a larger domestic market, so its exports as a percentage of total GNP would not be expected to be as high as Korea's (though they might well be in absolute terms).

Nevertheless, there were important similarities: for example, in 1960 the share of manufacturing in GDP was 14 percent in both countries, and the share of the labor force in agriculture was 66 percent in Korea and 74 percent in India. Both countries had followed an inward-looking development strategy in the 1950s. For countries with pressure of population on land and a rapidly growing labor force, labor-intensive manufacturing is a major means for providing employment. The relatively poor performance of India in increasing its manufactured exports meant that employment outside agriculture has grown much less than it could have.

---

not occur too swiftly, if a large proportion of domestic output is easily tradable—that is, if domestic and international prices are reasonably closely aligned—and if it is easy to expand exports rather than necessary to compress imports. Unfortunately, many of the principal debtor countries got into difficulties just because these conditions did not exist: their exchange rates had become seriously overvalued; their producers were heavily protected, often by import controls that reduced the incentive to sell abroad; export industries were relatively underdeveloped and, in addition, faced growing restraints in foreign markets.

Because the major debtors account for only a small fraction of world trade, the transfer of resources abroad needed to improve their current accounts should in theory be accomplished reasonably smoothly. A shift of $100 billion in develop-ing-country trade balances, the amount required to meet debt service payments, is equivalent to only 5 percent of world exports. Some of the exports of debtor countries, however, face actual or potential restrictions in foreign markets. Equally important, the domestic system of incentives is biased against exports in many of the developing countries, which makes it more difficult for them to exploit the opportunities for exports that do exist.

Partly because of the difficulty of expanding exports and partly because of this domestic policy bias against exports, imports have been cut dramatically instead, with adverse implications for growth. Moreover, there is a difference between reducing imports by reducing domestic spending—painful though that is—and reducing imports by imposing direct restrictions on imports. The latter is likely not even to produce the needed exter-

Box 3.4 Exchange rates and price adjustments: lessons from the experience of developing countries

Most governments intervene in setting exchange rates. The results are far-reaching. Severely overvalued real exchange rates (here defined as the ratio of domestic prices to foreign prices converted at the prevaling nominal exchange rate) shift resources toward less easily traded sectors and induce excess demand for imports. The resulting shortage of foreign exchange may cause higher protection against imports and additional measures to ration foreign exchange. These policies reduce efficiency by creating incentives (1) to shift resources to import substituting activities, which require more domestic resources to save a unit of foreign exchange than does exporting; and (2) to spend scarce domestic resources on "rent seeking"—the privately profitable activity of appropriating part of the rent from access to cheap, but rationed, sources of foreign exchange.

Overvalued exchange rates can arise in several ways. In Chile the nominal dollar exchange rate was preannounced and fixed in June 1979. At the same time, wages were indexed to provide full compensation for past changes in consumer prices. With falling but still high domestic inflation, the real exchange rate rose.

By 1981 imports had risen by 14.8 percent and exports had fallen by 5.2 percent. The imbalance was temporarily financed by large capital inflows that responded to capital market deregulation. But in 1982 capital flows reversed, and GNP fell by 12.9 percent. Too late, the preannounced exchange rate policy was abandoned.

Exchange overvaluation may also occur when governments follow the (quite common) policy of holding the real exchange rate constant in the presence of adverse external shocks. These imply some depreciation of the underlying equilibrium real exchange rate, although there is no simple relation between the magnitude of external shock and the degree of equilibrium exchange depreciation. During 1976–79 Yugoslavia maintained a constant real exchange rate, but the underlying equilibrium rate was falling. In 1977 the Yugoslav exchange rate was some 10 percent overvalued; by 1979 overvaluation had reached 42 percent, and exchange rates had surpassed 8 percent of GDP. In 1980 the country experienced a severe foreign exchange shortage in response to adverse external shocks, which amounted to some 3.6 percent of GDP during 1979-81. Growth

slumped from more than 8 percent to less than 2 percent, as shown in the table. It cost the Yugoslav economy almost twice as much in terms of domestic resources to earn $1 of foreign exchange through import substitution than through exports.

Turkey represents another interesting case. By 1977 a severe foreign exchange crisis and other difficulties brought economic growth to a halt. Rapid increases in the price level had far outpaced the rapid depreciation of the exchange rate after 1975 and continued to do so until early 1980. To compound matters, the country is an oil importer and the oil price increase of 1979 represented an adverse change in the terms of trade equivalent to some 2.7 percent of GDP. Starting in January 1980, reforms were instituted to correct the situation. As shown in the table, the nominal exchange rate depreciated sharply in the years 1980 and 1981, reducing the degree of overvaluation to well below its 1978 level (even taking into account the change needed because of the oil price increase). By 1981 Turkish growth resumed, and exports began growing rapidly with the exchange rate at a realistic level.

Exchange rates and GDP growth in Yugoslavia and Turkey, 1976–83

Country and item	1976	1977	1978	1979	1980	1981	1982	1983
Yugoslavia								
Exchange rate = dinars/dollars	18.2	18.3	18.6	19.0	24.7	35.0	50.3	42.8
Market clearing rate	22.3	20.4	22.6	26.9	33.5	..	..	..
Overvaluation (percent)	23.0	10.0	21.0	42.0	34.0	..	..	..
Import rents/GDP (percent)	8.3	4.3	6.4	8.2	8.6	..	..	..
Real GDP growth rate (percent)	5.3	8.4	8.5	6.3	2.3	1.4	0.8	−1.3
Turkey								
Exchange rate = Lira/dollars	16.1	18.0	24.3	31.1	76.1	111.2	162.6	225.5
Market clearing rate	..	..	38.3	72.4	103.9	112.6	..	..
Overvaluation (percent)	..	..	57.6	98.9	40.0	3.4	..	..
Market clearing rate without oil price rise	..	..	38.3	60.0	57.3	63.0	..	..
Real GDP growth rate (percent)	8.7	4.3	2.8	−0.9	−0.7	4.4	4.7	3.1

Note: Estimates of market clearing rates, percentage overvaluation, and ratio of import rents to GDP are based on modeling exercises which simulate the Yugoslav and Turkish economies during 1976–80 and 1978–81, respectively.
.. Not available.

nal surplus. The resulting rise in protection introduces a further bias against exports but does not do anything to cut spending in relation to output, as is required. Most of the major debtors have, unfortunately, adopted this second method of reducing imports.

Adjustment also needs to be accompanied by changed financial attitudes. In dealing with debtors, commercial lenders tend to push for more rapid repayment. This preference arises from their perception of risks and perhaps from their failure, acting as individual lenders, to associate a higher probability of default with fast repayment. At the other extreme, governments try to postpone adjustment as long as possible, to minimize consumption losses now even if this means larger repayment humps—and hence consumption losses—in the future.

The achievement of an adjustment ''package'' implies the recognition by both parties of an intermediate solution that does not jeopardize either the probability of repayment or the consumption of future generations. One important means of achieving this solution would be to increase the flow of equity investment to developing countries. Next year's *World Development Report* will examine capital flows to developing countries, including direct private investment.

Many developing countries have been meeting their interest obligations and are likely to go on doing so. If this process is too protracted, however, it might affect their willingness to persevere with their adjustment. They start from low levels of income and face a period of slow income and consumption growth because of their need to use current output to service past debts. That is why the longer-term prospects for the world economy will help determine whether the present ad hoc combination of rescheduling by creditors and austerity by debtors proves to be the prelude to a harmonious resolution or the prologue to a disaster.

The effect of world economic growth on developing economies is revealed in Table 3.4, which shows the balance of payments of the developing countries under the High and Low scenarios. In both cases it is assumed that lenders will wish to see debt service indicators return to their levels of 1980. The slower the growth of exports and GDP of the borrowing countries, and the higher the real interest and inflation rates in the world economy, the smaller the amount developing countries can borrow.

Under the High case the loan disbursements and official transfers to the developing countries rise by 33 percent in real terms between 1983 and 1995. Under the Low case they fall by 7 percent. In 1995 net exports of goods and nonfactor services to developing countries are $70 billion under the High scenario, a real increase of 544 percent over 1983; under the Low case they are only $29 billion, a real increase of 169 percent. Net disbursements of medium- and long-term loans less interest payments are $22 billion in 1995 under the High case. In the Low case the figure is negative: developing countries pay in interest $9 billion more than they receive in net loan disbursements. Finally, debt outstanding and disbursed rises at 3.7 percent a year in real terms in the High case and at less than 1 percent in the Low case.

In the Low case, the nominal interest rate is 9.5 percent; but because this is the rate for prime borrowers, many developing countries would face a higher rate. With a spread of 1.5 percent, for example, the interest rate for many borrowers would be 11.0 percent a year. Developing countries' exports in the Low case are expected to grow at only 4.7 percent a year in real terms, at 12.8 percent taking into account the projected increase in export prices. It is assumed that developing countries reduce their debt service ratios from the high levels of the mid-1980s to the 1980 level by the end of the forecast period. But because export revenues grow only slightly more rapidly than the interest rate, the growth of net disbursements must be restrained to meet the target debt service ratio. This restraint on net borrowing means that imports can grow only slightly more rapidly than exports (5.1 versus 4.7 percent).

Under the Low case, the developing countries would fall into three categories.

• Low-income African countries. Having little prospect of commercial borrowing, they would depend almost completely on official aid. Much of the aid would have to go directly into consumption; the private debt they now carry would have to be rolled over. Low-income Africa would receive only $2.7 billion of net disbursements of medium- and long-term loans in real terms. Their interest payments in 1995 would be $1.3 billion. Net official transfers would be $2.4 billion. Debt outstanding and disbursed would be only 36 percent higher in real terms after twelve years.

• Countries that would be hurt least by a weak world economy. Middle-income countries such as Korea, Malaysia, and Singapore would boom compared with the rest of the world and would be creditworthy as a result. China and India depend little on international borrowing, although slow growth in the industrial countries would squeeze the amount of concessional assistance they would receive.

• A group of countries that would be in and out of financial difficulties for the rest of the 1980s and possibly beyond. Some of their difficulties would be dealt with through debt renegotiations, the most problematic of which would be with the big Latin American borrowers. Having run austerity programs for years, some might effectively impose their own schedule for debt repayment. The major exporters of manufactures shown in Table 3.4, which include many of these countries, would have only 9.1 percent more debt outstanding in real terms in 1995 than in 1983. Net disbursements to them of medium- and long-term loans in 1995 would be $8.4 billion less than their interest payments. Other middle-income oil importers would be in a similar position: by 1995 their outstanding debt would rise by 15 percent in real terms, and their net medium- and long-term borrowing would be less than $1 billion more than their interest payments.

The main difference between the Low case and the variant Low I (increased industrial-country protection) is that the main debtor nations would find it more difficult than ever to service their debts. They would pay a nominal interest rate of 11.0 percent, as in the Low case, but the growth of exports would now average only 4.0 percent (Table 3.6), with nominal growth in export earnings of 12 percent. Even a developing country exporting only manufactures might find its export earnings growing at less than the nominal interest rate. Most developing countries would be starved of external capital. Debt outstanding and disbursed to developing countries in 1995 would be only slightly larger than in 1983 in real terms. Loans disbursed would be $42 billion (compared with $49 billion in the Low case.) Interest payments of $55 billion would exceed disbursements as creditworthiness falls because of the protection-induced decline in exports. Lower growth of imports would also contribute to lower overall growth. This scenario, in effect, is untenable. If the situation described began to unfold, the prospect for growth in developing countries would surely be worse than that implied by these projections.

The improved developing-country policies in Low II help, although the real growth of outstanding debt remains low for the highly indebted major exporters of manufactures and for the middle-income oil exporters. For developing countries as a whole, debt outstanding grows by only 1 percent

in real terms between 1983 and 1995.

To sum up, there are two major differences between the High and Low cases: net lending and export growth. In the High case, substantial extra borrowing is compatible with improved debt servicing for developing countries partly because the nominal interest rate is lower than in the Low case, and because export revenues grow at a higher rate. Mutual cooperation between lenders and borrowers is reasonably assured. In the Low case, export revenues grow only slightly more rapidly than the (higher) interest rate and net lending falls over the period to meet target debt service ratios. As a result, in the Low case, many developing countries end up transferring resources to the industrial world year after year. If there is, in addition, greatly increased industrial-country protection, then sustained cooperation becomes unlikely. Improved developing-country performance on its own would make the picture brighter. Nevertheless, the slow growth of industrial countries in the Low cases would balance the world economy on a knife's edge.

Poverty and low-income countries

The implications of the scenarios are best understood if their GDP growth rates are adjusted for the widely differing population growth rates of the various regions. Between the High and the Low case, per capita income growth falls from 3.5 percent a year to 2.7 percent for developing countries (see Table 3.2). Increased protection makes prospects still worse, with per capita income growth for all developing countries 34 percent below the level of the High case. In all scenarios the major exporters of manufactures grow fastest, leaving the rest of the developing world further and further behind.

It is in the low-income countries—especially those of Africa—that slow growth does most to perpetuate and accentuate poverty. In low-income Asia, however, prospects look brighter, especially as population growth continues to slow. Domestic policy improvements are essential in enhancing the prospects of low-income countries. Like the middle-income countries, they would benefit from policy changes that reduce the bias against exporting in favor of inefficient import substitution. Previous *World Development Reports* have emphasized the importance of prices in determining how well a country uses its resources. Because they are so poor, low-income countries have special reason to make the best possible use of their resources.

Because the public sector in low-income countries is large in relation to GDP, cutting imports usually means cutting public spending. Although governments may have scope for reducing spending without damaging long-term growth, budget cuts too often damage programs with the greatest capacity for raising the economy's growth potential. Some of them may be classified as current spending; but education and health budgets are better seen as investments in human capital.

Most human development programs have long gestation lags. Their output is not directly tradable and often is not even marketable. Commercial financing of such investments is therefore unrealistic. A real increase in concessional assistance is needed, and has been for several years. Yet, at times of their greatest difficulty, low-income countries have found that official aid has been falling in real terms. This trend must be reversed if low-income countries are to make any progress in the years ahead and the lot of the poorest people is not to deteriorate any further.

International action

This chapter has shown that the world economic outlook would brighten considerably if every country took steps to improve its own domestic performance. The onus on the industrial countries is greatest, because growth prospects throughout the world would be transformed if they overcame the rigidities and inflationary fears that slowed them down in the past ten years. Even without such benefits, the developing countries could do much to help themselves through policy changes that increase the flexibility of their own economies.

That said, some measures need to be taken at an international, not purely domestic, level and in a coordinated way. A trade-liberalization initiative that concentrated on the newer and proliferating forms of protectionism—various nontariff barriers, especially those affecting developing countries—would make an important contribution to restoring the momentum of the world economy. It is also essential to start liberalizing trade in agriculture. Just as the liberalization of trade in manufactures provided a once-for-all but sizable boost to productivity growth in the late 1950s and early 1960s, so the same approach to agricultural trade, combined with the reversal of the recent protectionist measures on industrial products, could boost productivity in the 1980s.

Freer trade is also vital for solving the debt crisis. For the developing countries to service their debt

without excessive cost to themselves, they will need to expand their exports rather than just reduce imports. Any worsening of global prospects in terms of increased protectionism and further rises in dollar interest rates would erode the ability and perhaps even the willingness, of borrowers to service their debt.

As in trade, so in finance there is a need for concerted international action. The success of developing countries' efforts to deal with the rigidities and distortions in their own economies depends in part on the actions of official and private suppliers of finance. For the poorer countries the main challenge for the international community is to find ways of supporting policy reform through additional flows of concessional assistance. This has been the challenge in the negotiations for the seventh IDA replenishment (see Box 3.5), the discussions for possible supplemental budgeting to IDA, and the extension of the Lome Convention.

For the middle-income countries the actions of a wide range of private and public institutions are important. Commercial banks have typically relied on borrowing countries' agreements with the International Monetary Fund (IMF) as a basis for restructuring existing claims and, in selected cases, for committing additional funds. Increases in voluntary lending by the commercial banks in the long term is an important ingredient in the restoration of growth momentum in middle-income developing countries. But the transition back to fully voluntary lending requires prudent management on the side of both borrowers and lenders. Official institutions, particularly the IMF, the World Bank, and the regional development banks can be helpful in this regard both by assisting in the design of more effective developing-country policies and by expanding their own lending in support of policy reforms (see Box 3.5). Efforts by these institutions to encourage private direct investment should also continue. Finally, it is important that official export-financing institutions adjust to the greater risks of lending to developing countries in a nondisruptive fashion. What is required need not be very dramatic for any single institution, provided they all act constructively.

Measures that would result in increased financial flows to developing countries to help them undertake structural adjustment and maintain long-term financial viability will help make trade liberalization easier by improving their short-term balance of payments outlook. In turn, liberalization would expand exports and would tend to strengthen

Box 3.5   IDA

The International Development Association (IDA) was established in 1960 as an affiliate of the International Bank for Reconstruction and Development (IBRD), to provide concessional assistance to low-income countries. Governments in the industrial world recognized that low-income countries could not afford to take on commercial loans carrying high interest rates and short maturities (even if they were forthcoming) to finance projects that had long payback periods and earned little foreign exchange. In the years since IDA's inception, the predicament of low-income countries has not eased significantly; indeed, the recent recession in industrial countries has made it worse.

IDA has met a large share of external financing of low-income countries. IDA lending, however, has not on average exceeded 2 percent of gross domestic investment in recipient countries. In 1980 in India and Pakistan, currently the first and third largest borrowers, it was less than 2 percent. Only in Bangladesh was it as much as 13 percent; it was 8 percent in Ethiopia and 3 to 4 percent in Tanzania and Sudan. Disbursements per person in 1980 in the recipient countries averaged $1.33 in IDA countries and 40 cents in countries receiving a blend of IDA and IBRD money, including India and Pakistan. In 1980 official development assistance (ODA) financed 65 percent of the current account deficit of low-income countries, and IDA contributed 16 percent of development assistance.

During 1961–82, 81 percent of total IDA commitments, which were $43 billion in constant 1982 dollars, went to countries with per capita incomes below $410 in 1980, compared with only 8 percent of IBRD lending. Because IDA countries are the poorest, nearly 40 percent of IDA funds went to agriculture and rural development, compared with 22 percent of IBRD funds. Human development, program lending, and technical assistance received about 25 percent of IDA lending, compared with 16 percent of IBRD lending.

While the terms of IDA are concessional, its projects are generally identical in scope and rigor to IBRD projects. Rates of return on IDA projects have been on average as high as on IBRD projects, but they are decidedly lower in Africa than elsewhere: the average on eighty-eight IDA projects in Africa was nevertheless about 14 percent. Since its inception, twenty-seven countries have graduated from IDA to the IBRD, and thirteen countries, including India, receive a blend of IBRD and IDA financing.

Constraints on IDA lending have recently increased. In 1961–82 commitments grew at 8 percent a year in real terms. However, because of slower-than-anticipated contributions from the sixth replenishment of IDA (IDA-6), lending in 1982 declined in current dollars to a level 30 percent below that of 1980, and in 1983 it was still 13 percent below the 1980 level. At $9 billion, the seventh replenishment of IDA (IDA-7) represents a major reduction in the concessional resources available to the world's poorest countries. It is 25 percent lower in nominal terms and 40 percent lower in real terms than the IDA-6 agreement reached in 1979. Partly because of China's membership, this reduction also represents a 70 percent cut in real per capita terms.

Some of the consequences of a decline in IDA lending are already being felt but will be intensified under IDA-7. Strict application of IDA's allocation criteria would result in allocations for India and China of more than three-quarters of IDA-7 resources. In order to prevent an imbalance in IDA's lending program, a ceiling will need to be placed on lending to these two countries (for similar reasons, a ceiling had to apply on lending to India and Pakistan in the past). Resource constraints on IDA have already induced the Association to restrict lending to India. IDA lending to India declined from a peak of $1.5 billion in 1980 to about $1 billion since then. During IDA-6, IBRD lending had to substitute partially for IDA lending as projects risked

cancellation, but at the cost of preempting further expansion in future IBRD lending. India also had to resort to borrowing from commercial markets; by 1986, borrowing on market terms may account for over half of disbursements to India. But concessional assistance would still have an essential role to play in moderating India's debt burden and in consolidating the effects of recent policy shifts toward liberalizing imports, prices, and industrial licensing.

China's allocations will increase somewhat over those of IDA-6, as earlier IDA activities were limited. But China's low incomes (about $310 per capita) and the large number of its people living below the poverty line (150 million, equal to three-fourths of the entire population of low-income sub-Saharan Africa) suggest tha a suitably broad spectrum of sectors and provinces can be covered only if a large amount of finance is available.

Sub-Saharan Afrian countries are facing some of the most adverse external circumstances in recent history. Between 1973 and 1981, low-income Africa lost as much as 23 percent in the purchasing power of its exports to buy manufactures. Per capita incomes declined. Large-scale reschedulings of official debt have taken place. Essential domestic reforms are being undertaken, but they need to be supported by concessional flows.

Africa's share in IDA has risen, from 25 percent in 1980 to 37 percent in 1983, but even increasing Africa's share by a further 5 percent over IDA-6 levels would yield less in additional resources from a $9 billion IDA than would maintaining its present share in a $12 billion IDA. With a $9 billion IDA, Africa would have a 21 percent reduction in real terms compared with commitments made in the IDA-6 period. So would thirteen countries outside Africa, including Bangladesh (where IDA lending declined by 6 percent in the past year), Burma, Sri Lanka, and Pakistan.

developing-country creditworthiness, thus increasing the developing countries' capacity to obtain and service additional capital flows. In short, trade liberalization, enlarged flows of external finance, and improved economic policies in all countries are mutually reinforcing actions in support of restoring the growth momentum of developing countries.

The links with population

Modest growth in the GDP of industrial countries means modest growth in their per capita incomes. For the developing countries there is no such easy equation. Their populations are growing by 2 percent a year, in many countries by much more. GDP growth of 2 percent or so is merely a preliminary step before they can start to improve their per capita incomes. Governments throughout the developing world cannot ignore the literal sense in which population growth affects the economic performance that really matters—the average incomes of their people. If the world is to have ten years of slow growth, many millions of poor people will by definition get poorer. Moreover, lower GDP growth makes it more difficult for countries to finance programs—in education and family planning, for example—that reduce population growth. Thus short-run difficulties have long-run consequences.

Important as these simple facts are, they do not begin to capture the links between population growth and economic development. Understanding those links requires much more than the mere counting of heads. It requires consideration of education, health, employment, incomes, culture, and personal beliefs—aspects of everyday life that explain why parents choose to have a particular number of children and what their choices add up to. Part II of this Report is about population change in developing countries. As will soon become apparent, it is also about development in its widest sense. It is affected by the macroeconomic perspective of Part I, and it gives that perspective richer meaning.

Part II   Population Change and Development
4   Demographic change and public policy

Most families in developing countries now have at least four children, in rural areas five and more, enough to ensure rates of population growth above 2 percent a year. To cut population growth means to reduce the number of children in an average family, which many governments are trying to do. India adopted a formal population policy in 1952, Korea in 1961. China, Indonesia, and Mexico have developed comprehensive policies in the past ten to fifteen years. But other governments have been more tentative. In much of Latin America political support for family planning is ambiguous; most countries in Africa have no particular demographic objectives. Should there be public concern and governmental action to reduce population growth? Along with public efforts to reduce mortality, should governments try to reduce fertility, and if so, what are appropriate policies to do so?

To answer these questions requires an understanding of, first, why fertility is high and, second, why the resulting rapid population growth slows development. Part II of this Report will show that it is the poor, with little education, low and insecure income, and poor health and family planning services, who have many children; yet it is also the poor who lose out as rapid population growth hampers development. It is this seeming paradox that provides the starting point for designing public policies to reduce fertility.

The setting for high fertility

Why do the poor have many children? Consider the issue from the point of view of parents and potential parents. All parents everywhere get pleasure from children. But children involve economic costs; parents have to spend time and money bringing them up. Children are also a form of investment—providing short-term benefits if they work during childhood, long-term benefits if they support parents in old age. There are several good reasons why, for poor parents, the economic costs

of children are low, the economic (and other) benefits of children are high, and having many children makes economic sense.

First, where wages are low, the difference between children's and mother's earnings will be small; income lost by the mother during a child's infancy may be easily recouped by the child later on. In poor rural areas, especially, children can help a lot. Nepalese village boys and girls of six to eight years work three to four hours a day caring for farm animals and helping with younger siblings. Javanese teenagers work eight to ten hours a day. Many Bangladeshi children work even longer hours; children in the Philippines and in Sri Lanka, where fertility is lower, work somewhat less. Sometimes children may also earn cash incomes. In the Philippines those in their late teens contribute as much to household cash income as do adults. And much of women's traditional work—in farming, crafts, and petty retailing—can be combined with looking after children. Other family members, including older siblings, are readily available to help.

In developed countries, by contrast, a major cost of children to parents is time lost from work—usually by the mother—or the cost, inconvenience, and uncertainty of finding child care. Nor do children contribute much to household chores and income as they grow up. One study of an American city and its suburbs found that children twelve to seventeen years old spend one hour a day doing housework, those aged six to eleven just half an hour.

A second reason that having many children can make economic sense is the lack of schooling opportunities, particularly from the age of twelve or so. For young children of primary-school age, school can often be combined with work in the house or on the farm, especially if there is a school in the village. But the choice between school and work becomes harder as children grow up. If they do not go to secondary school, they can work more themselves and, by caring for younger siblings, allow their mothers to work more. The apparent disadvantages of secondary schooling are compounded if children must live away from home or travel long distances to get to school.

As parents' income rises, as schooling opportunities improve, and as education becomes more clearly the key to future success for children, parents everywhere send their children to school and keep them there longer. In turn they often have fewer children—because schooling itself and the loss of children's help are costly, and because having two or three educated children becomes a better "investment" (for the parents and for the children too) than having many who cannot be educated.

High infant and child mortality are a third reason for having many children. Although mortality has fallen, in many parts of the developing world it is still high. One out of five children dies before reaching the age of one in some parts of Africa; one out of seven in much of Bangladesh, India, and Pakistan. Parents may feel the need to have many babies to be sure that a few survive. Where boys are more important than girls—say, for security in old age—parents may need to have five children to be sure that one son survives. Yet in poor families many births, especially if they are close together, may increase the probability of infant deaths by weakening both mother and babies.

Fourth, poor parents are worried about who will take care of them when they are old or ill. In Indonesia, Korea, the Philippines, Thailand, and Turkey 80 to 90 percent of parents surveyed said they expect to rely on their children to support them in their old age. In Egypt, especially in rural areas, poor and uneducated parents are much more likely to expect to live with (and be supported by) their children when they are old than are rich and educated parents. For many adults, the need for support in their old age outweighs the immediate costs of children.

One reason parents look to children for help in disability and old age is the lack of safe alternatives. In developed countries there are trusted institutions (banks, pensions, government bonds, insurance, and mutual aid societies) that help individuals to earn today and to save and spend tomorrow. In poor countries, capital markets are not nearly so well developed. In parts of South Asia, there is no tradition of community support; elsewhere, community support is weakening as mobility increases. For the rural poor, children are the best possible annuity, a way to transform today's production into consumption many years hence that is less risky than are bank accounts, credit instruments, and precious metals, all of which are subject to theft, inflation, and the jealousies of neighbors. Even land has to be managed to provide income and, in any case, may require children to work on it and make it a secure asset.

Fifth, in some developing countries family systems may encourage high fertility. Early marriage and childbearing are easier if the new couple can begin married life in the household of the husband's parents. For young women who have few other options, early marriage and many children may be the safest route to a satisfying adulthood and a relatively secure old age. In Africa, support from many relatives for children's education reduces the high economic burden of raising children that potential parents would otherwise bear.

A sixth factor encouraging high fertility among the poor is their limited information about, and access to, effective and safe means of contraception. The very idea of birth control may be unknown or frowned upon. Modern contraceptives may be unknown or simply not available. If available, they may be expensive, particularly in relation to the incomes of the poor—and especially if they must be bought from private doctors. For a poor family, limiting the number of children may therefore mean sexual abstinence, illegal abortion, infanticide—or, at best, ineffective and difficult traditional contraception. In some circumstances, the psychological or financial costs of avoiding pregnancy may exceed the costs of having another child.

Discussion of children as an "investment" should not imply that parents in developing countries are influenced only by economic considerations. In every society children bring parents satisfaction and pleasure. In poor settings, economic gain (where there is any) need not be the main cause of high fertility; it is more likely that economic gain (or a small economic loss) simply prevents any interest in having fewer children. The social and political functions of large families are also important, especially in poor rural areas. For better-off farmers in Bangladesh, children represent opportunities for the family's occupational diversification and hence for expansion or consolidation of its local power; a large family also has an advantage in land disputes. In Latin America, by the tradition of *compadrazgo*, or ritual coparenthood, families serve as godparents to the children of allies and friends, securing ritual bonds that are as important as blood ties in cementing alliances.

Consequences for parents

Despite the apparent advantages of many children, it is not clear that, from a strictly economic point of view, parents gain. Children may end up costing parents more than they expected. In some countries girls may require a dowry and thus be an economic burden. For households close to subsistence levels, food, clothing, and housing for children may be a burden; such costs are in fact the chief concern parents voice, even in the poorest settings, when asked about the disadvantages of having children. How much of an economic gain children provide may depend on circumstances that parents cannot easily predict—whether they gain or lose access to land, whether their children are healthy, whether they have the right balance of sons and daughters. Even old-age support is not guaranteed. Some children do not survive; daughters who marry may move to another village; sons who go far to find work may be less supportive than was hoped. Children willing and able to help may themselves face difficulties in finding well-paying work. So although parents can reasonably hope to be better off by having many children, in the end some may not be.

Consequences for children

Even when parents seem to gain from large families, children may lose. This is obviously true when births are closely spaced; the resulting harm to the health and nutrition of mothers can cause low birth weight, early weaning, and poor health of children in the critical early years. Older children may also be handicapped. Even in developed countries, studies show that children in large families and those born close together tend to be physically and intellectually inferior to other children. For middle-class families in the United Kingdom and Czechoslovakia, where food is abundant, the number of children does not affect their physical growth. But in poor families, children with many siblings tend to be smaller. In France, the United States, and the Netherlands, a large number of children in the family has a negative effect on classroom performance and test scores.

The same pattern is found in developing countries. In Nigeria, among a sample of children taking the secondary school entrance exam, children from large families scored systematically lower than those from small families. In both sets of countries, some of this effect may be due to children from large families having less educated or poorer parents on average. But in Nigeria most children contemplating secondary school would not come from very poor households, so family size probably has some independent influence on educational performance.

In developing countries, a disproportionate share of children grow up in large families that are least able to take advantage of increased educational opportunities and health services. In Brazil more than 60 percent of all children live in the poorest 40 percent of households, households which between them have just 10 percent of total income. In Malaysia and Thailand about half of all children live in households that receive just 15 percent of total income. In Colombia and Malaysia in 1974, government subsidies for education and health were approximately equal across households. But because fewer children lived in rich households, subsidies per child were twice as great for children in the richest fifth of households as for those in the poorest. Evidence from urban areas in Colombia also shows that parents themselves, at all income and education levels, spend less on each child's education once there are more than four children. Thus children from large families receive less from both public and private spending on education.

In general, children have the most to gain from family income spent on health and education. Yet family budget studies consistently show that bigger families spend proportionately more on food. Even then they may not avoid malnutrition: in one Colombian town studied, malnutrition in preschool children was directly related to the number of children in the family. Of course, high fertility may not be the direct cause of malnutrition; low income might be responsible for both high fertility and malnutrition. In either case, however, children from large, poor families are clearly disadvantaged.

So early difficulties in providing enough good food interact with later difficulties in supporting schooling. As will be shown in Chapter 6, those who receive less schooling will, as adults, tend to have more children than parents who had more schooling. From one generation to the next, an unequal distribution of income is caused by and contributes to an unequal distribution of opportunities and skills, as large family size and low investments in children reinforce each other.

If parents have many children in the hope of economic gain, the first step in reducing fertility is to relieve their poverty and uncertainty about their own future. In this sense, the persistence of high fertility in a changing world is a symptom of lack of access: to health services, which would reduce the need for many births to insure against infant and child mortality; to education, which would raise parents' hopes for their children and would broaden women's outlook and opportunities; to social security and other forms of insurance for old age; to consumer goods and social opportunities that compete with childbearing; and to family planning services, which provide the means to limit births.

The need for public policy

There are two broad justifications for government action to encourage people to have fewer children. The first is the gap between the private and social gains from having many children. Suppose that, even as each couple hopes to benefit from many children, it wishes its neighbors would have fewer, so that its children would face less competition for land and jobs. In other words, the couple's wish for society as a whole is different from its wish for itself. One reason private and social gains differ is the existence of "externalities": parents do not internalize the costs of their children to society as a whole. For example, one family's children will have little effect on the availability of land; but the children born of many families will. The same is true of the effects on forests or pasture. To narrow this gap between private and social perceptions, governments can act as custodians of society. They are meant to have longer time horizons than their individual constituents, and to weigh the interests of future generations against those of the present.

Where natural resources are abundant, so-called congestion costs caused in part by externalities may not be great, at least at the national level. But in most countries there is another source of difference between the private and social gains from many children. Health and education costs of children are heavily subsidized by the public sector, as are roads, communications, and other public services that boost jobs and income. The result, discussed in the next chapter, is that high fertility constrains the amount of resources available for investment and hence for future income growth. Even as some couples have many children because of a lack of health services and schooling opportunities, their large families make it more difficult for the public sector to extend health and schooling to all. Yet why should one couple, on its own, give up the possible private benefits of children, when its sacrifice alone would provide only minuscule ben-

efits to other families' children and grandchildren?

Even when each couple decides to have many children, and achieves its wish, it might have been happier with fewer children if it could have been sure that other couples would have done the same. Poor couples who hope their children will support them in their old age may rightly fear that, because other couples are having so many children, any one of their own children has less chance of going to school and eventually of finding a good job. Assured that each child would have a better chance of school and work in a less crowded world, each couple might be happy with fewer children.

In this setting, people will not be confident that provision of contraceptives by private suppliers will alone lead to widespread reduction in fertility. Only through the public sector can people make, in effect, a contract with each other: "If each of us has fewer children, we can rely on government support for nationwide measures (to improve access to family planning services and to create incentives for their use) to ensure that everybody makes the same decision. That way, we and our children will all enjoy a better chance in life." By developing a social contract, the government frees each individual couple from its "isolation paradox," from its need to decide alone to have more children than it would want if others were limiting their family size (see Box 4.1).

Private and social gains from children also differ in the developed countries, although usually in the opposite direction. As public social security systems develop and people have many ways to save for their old age, the private economic benefits of children diminish. At the same time their private costs rise. Thus many couples choose to have only one child or even none. In some countries governments use financial and other incentives to encourage higher fertility; this too is a population policy to achieve a common goal (see Chapter 8).

Private and social gains also differ in areas other than fertility. For the common good, legislation requires that children go to school and that everybody be vaccinated against contagious diseases. Limits, often backed by financial penalties, are placed on automobile speeds, chopping down forests, and polluting air and water. Government produces social goods and services, the benefits of which individuals cannot capture and will not produce on their own: police protection, clean water to protect health, parks for common enjoyment.

The second justification for government action to reduce fertility is that people may have more children than they want, or would want had they more information about, and better access to, easier fertility control. For example, couples may lack (or disbelieve) information about falling child mortality—or about their chance to reduce the risks to their existing children by keeping numbers down—and thus have more children than needed to reach desired family size. They may not know that by stopping breastfeeding they risk more closely spaced births. They may not be fully aware of the health risks, to mothers and children, of

as rhythm and withdrawal, which are less effective in preventing conception, or on abortion, which, if primitively performed, puts the mother's life at risk.

In this situation, the role of the government is critical. As a start, it can encourage parents in their desire to have fewer children simply by providing more information—about changing mortality and the health benefits of controlling fertility. It can encourage wider provision of modern contraceptives. This can be achieved by private suppliers,

---

Box 4.1   The isolation paradox

In a small village in Asia or Africa a father of two sons and a daughter dreams of having two or three more children. He believes that enough land might be available for each of his sons if only he could get more help in clearing, preparing, and harvesting the land he already owns. Other families, particularly those with few children, seem barely able to use the land they have; at the right price, he could buy patches of it from them. He could then amass enough land to give some to all his sons. In his old age they could work the land and support him.

Children cost that father little. They feed at the breast for two years or more. Older ones care for the toddlers and also tend animals, carry water and wood, and help in the busy times of clearing and harvesting. If the older children should become a burden, a cousin will take them in and give them work to do. Moreover, with recent improvements in health in the village more of the children born now will survive. His strategy of having a

large family to build up his wealth seems to have few risks and many possible benefits.

This is not just one man's plan. It is shared by almost every man in the village. Some may succeed; the majority will not, simply because the amount of land in the village is limited. If all families try to have five or more children, population will double in less than a generation. Most children will have less land than their fathers. If the villagers cannot coordinate their decisions, they will leave their children worse off than they were.

Economists devote considerable attention to how the hidden hand of the market makes the sum of individual decisions taken for private benefit add up to the general good. They also recognize other cases in which the pursuit of private gain can make most people worse off. One term for this phenomenon is the isolation paradox. Individuals in isolation act to the detriment of each other unless they know that their fellows will act in a manner that serves the general

well-being—and even then individuals may not act in the public interest themselves. If parents had their way, many of them would wish to limit the fertility of others; if children had their way, many of them would wish to limit their own parents' fertility.

Despite the rise in population, communities can and do adjust. People move to the cities. Technology increases land productivity. (Indonesia offers an example where population expanded slowly but steadily for more than a century after the institution of wet-rice cultivation, without notable decline in levels of living but without much improvement either.) In their greater poverty, young people may defer marriage and thus bring fewer children into subsequent generations. Parents may arrange to put children in relatives' homes away from their village. All these adjustments help to share poverty and to lessen its burden. But shared poverty is hardly the objective of development.

---

many and closely spaced births. The very idea of planning pregnancies may be unknown, especially if social norms dictate early marriage for young women and if couples do not discuss sexual matters.

Even if they know about family planning, couples may not know how to practice it. They may be reluctant to ask questions, especially if their parents pressure them to have many children. Or they may lack ready access to modern contraceptives and be forced to rely on traditional methods such

especially in towns and, for some methods (such as condoms), in rural areas as well. But private suppliers are unlikely to provide the full range of family planning services, especially in remote areas. Many modern means of contraception can be made available only with medical backup, and there is little profit in disseminating information and contraceptives where distribution systems are poor, health care is limited, and demand is unknown and possibly limited. In many countries government may need to subsidize or even organize contraceptive services. As will be shown in Chapter 7, substantial "unmet need" for family planning information and services does exist in many countries. The case is strong for support of programs to assist the poor to achieve their reproductive goals more efficiently and humanely. This would increase the welfare of parents and improve the chances of their children having greater educational opportunities, and eventually better job opportunities.

The distinction between these two justifications for a public population policy—the gap between private and social gains, and unmet need for family planning services—has not been important in practice. Support for family planning is usually how governments try to reduce fertility, a sensible first step so long as there is unmet need for information about family planning and unsatisfied demand for services. Government's role in developing and enhancing a social contract to lower fertility provides the basis for public subsidies to family planning; family planning programs have been subsidized most where a public policy to reduce fertility is strongest. In fact, family planning programs have become an important vehicle for information about the private and social costs of high fertility, and for incentives to encourage individuals to reduce family size.

Such governmental involvement has expanded in the past decade, since the Bucharest World Population Conference in 1974. There, governments adopted a Plan of Action which recognized the basic human right to choose "freely and responsibly" the number and spacing of children. There has since been substantial progress in assuring freedom of choice through family planning programs—about 95 percent of people in the developing world live in countries that support this principle.

Should governments not only ensure procreative freedom but also encourage social responsibility? The answer in this Report is a firm yes, with renewed attention to the ethical implications of incentives and other policies that go beyond family planning. A dilemma arises whenever pursuit of one set of values—improvement of material welfare through lower population growth, reduction of inequality, insurance of future security—threatens other values, such as freedom of choice and pronatalist customs and beliefs. But there is a balance between the private right of procreation and social responsibility. As discussed more fully in Chapter 8, different societies will not necessarily agree on the precise nature of that balance, but every society needs to consider it.

Lessons from history

Public concern with population growth is a recent phenomenon. The transition to low mortality and low fertility in today's developed countries occurred without any explicit public policy. But circumstances in developing countries today are different, and for several reasons that point to the need for policy action.

The agricultural age and before

For much of human history, prosperity and population growth went hand in hand. In the preindustrial age, population growth was periodically spurred by increases (often temporary) in the supply of food and declines in disease. In fact disease kept the number of people well below a level at which starvation would have become a major cause of death. Fertility in normal times was well below its biological potential, but it could rise quickly if mortality rose. Over long periods the world's population increased slowly (by far less than 1 percent a decade, compared with 25 percent a decade today).

Settled agriculture permitted a rise in population, some concentration in urban centers, and the emergence of a small nonagricultural class. In the sixteenth century population declined in the Americas because of new diseases contracted from Europe. In other parts of the world, population growth rates increased between about 1450 and 1650—to rates higher than 1 percent a decade in China, South Asia, and Europe. Even these increases were tiny by modern standards; over time and among regions, population growth continued to be irregular and vulnerable to fluctuations in mortality. Moreover, life expectancy was probably little higher in 1600 than it had been 2,000 years earlier. Everyone's health was threatened more or less constantly by disease. Only a tiny proportion of people were literate or numerate. Between 100 and 1850, the percentage of the world's population living in towns and cities of 5,000 people or more probably never exceeded 6 percent. In England between the thirteenth and eighteenth centuries, there is evidence that when mortality fell so that labor supply increased, wages fell and food prices rose (see Box 4.2).

Box 4.2 The Malthusian case: changes in labor supply, wages, and population growth in preindustrial England

Research has brought to light new information on living standards, food prices, and mortality and fertility change in England over six centuries.

- The data before 1800 fit a Malthusian model. An exogenous fall in mortality or an increase in productivity raises population growth; the increased labor supply then lowers real wage rates and raises the relative price of food and the rental returns on land. As wages fall, fertility falls and population growth slackens.

- Fertility change was more variable and more responsive to economic conditions than was previously believed. Until toward the end of the nineteenth century, in good times more people married and married younger, thus raising fertility.

- The start of the Industrial Revolution in the late eighteenth century brought a break in this Malthusian cycle. By the mid-nineteenth century fertility no longer rose along with real incomes. And the rise of living standards no longer proved self-checking in the ways Malthus feared, because productivity was advancing so rapidly.

- Both before and after the Industrial Revolution income differentials widened during periods of fast population growth.

The accompanying charts show the long-run movements of key variables from 1250 to the early twentieth century. The Black Death in the fourteenth century brought a decline in life expectancy. Total population fell and wages rose. By the middle of the sixteenth century life expectancy and total population size were recovering and wages were declining. Rents were rising in relation to wages, which redistributed income from tenants to landowners. Late in the seventeenth century, when population growth slowed again, wages rose and food prices fell.

In the eighteenth century fertility rose as nonagricultural opportunities increased and marriage rates rose. Wages failed to rise despite the gains in overall productivity associated with the beginning of the Industrial Revolution. But life expectancy did increase gradually from the early eighteenth century. Toward the end of the nineteenth century the share of income of the richest groups fell, wages rose, and fertility eventually began a sustained decline.

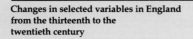

Changes in selected variables in England from the thirteenth to the twentieth century

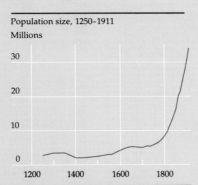

Population size, 1250–1911
Millions

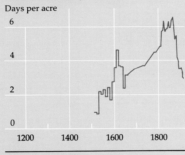

English rent-wage ratio: number of days of common labor (craftsmen) required to rent an acre of farmland, 1510–1911
Days per acre

Total fertility rate, 1540–1911
Total fertility rate

Source: Lindert, 1984.

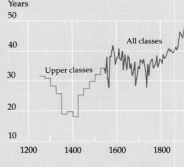

Life expectancy at birth, both sexes, 1250–1911
Years

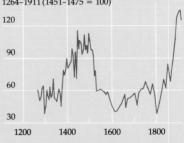

Real wage index (wage-rate of craftsmen), 1264–1911 (1451–1475 = 100)

Ratio of food prices to prices of other goods, 1400–1900

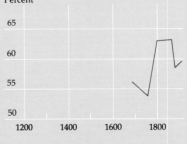

Income distribution: share of top 20 percent of households, 1600–1913
Percent

In the eighteenth and nineteenth centuries, the early phase of modern economic growth in northwest Europe, population and income increases accelerated together. Populations grew due to gradual declines in mortality and, in some areas, to increases in marriage rates as new economic opportunities opened up. Europe's rate of population growth rose from 0.5 to 1.5 percent a year.

Even that was low by modern standards, for several reasons. First, when the industrial age began in the late eighteenth century, fertility was lower than it is in developing countries today because marriage rates were low and because those who married did so in their mid-twenties to late twenties or even in their thirties. In the past two decades historical demographers have used church registers to compile new and detailed information on marriages, deaths, and births in parts of Europe. These studies indicate that as many as 15 to 20 percent of women in northwest Europe never married and that at any given time only 45 to 50 percent of women between the ages of fifteen and fifty were married. The mean age at marriage in the seventeenth and eighteenth centuries was about twenty-five in Belgium, England, France, Germany, and Scandinavia. Newly married couples had to set up their own households and thus had to postpone marriage until they were financially independent. A common arrangement was for older couples to pass land to the young in exchange for a guarantee of retirement support; such contracts occurred between different families as well as between parents and children.

The poor in particular were forced to postpone marriage; young adults often worked as servants to the better-off until they could marry. In England and Sweden the landless married later than those who owned land, except where cottage industry opened up new opportunities to earn a living. Marriage occurred particularly late in Ireland. In 1871 half the Irish women aged twenty-five to twenty-nine were still unmarried (compared with 36 percent of English women). Ireland's poverty led to late marriage and often to spinsterhood. But religious beliefs prohibited birth control, so marital fertility was high. Nevertheless, the birth rate and population growth were relatively low.

The contrast with fertility patterns today is marked. Now the key to high income is education. The rich send their children to school, so marriage is delayed and fertility is restricted. In the rural areas of many developing countries, where education beyond a few years is not available, extended family systems permit earlier marriage. The new couple often lives with the husband's parents for some time, and the family's assets are shared. What would be the financial burden of marrying young and having children is reduced in the larger household (though even today marriage does come later and fertility is lower among the truly destitute in developing countries).

No country in northwestern Europe had a crude birth rate above forty per thousand in 1800; in several (Denmark, France, Norway, and Sweden) birth rates were nearer thirty per thousand. The crude birth rate in England was thirty-four per thousand in 1850, before marital fertility began to decline, compared with forty-seven per thousand in Colombia in 1960 and more than fifty per thousand in Kenya today (see Figure 4.1). By contrast, in the Indian subcontinent in the nineteenth century, crude birth rates are estimated to have been between fifty and fifty-five per thousand.

Another reason for slow population growth in the eighteenth and nineteenth centuries was that mortality, although gradually declining, was high by today's standards. At the beginning of the nineteenth century infant mortality rates exceeded 200 per thousand live births in many communities of Europe. They were about 250 per thousand in Sweden, and were more than 300 per thousand in what is now Germany, compared with an average of 100 per thousand in low-income developing countries today. The crude death rate in France and England was about thirty per thousand at the beginning of the nineteenth century. It was twenty-three per thousand in England in 1841, twenty-eight per thousand in Germany in 1867, and more than thirty per thousand in Sweden in 1870, compared with about thirteen per thousand in India today.

As a result of low fertility and high mortality, the natural increase in population seldom exceeded 1.5 percent a year. In England it peaked at about 1.6 percent in the 1820s; in France it never exceeded 1 percent during the nineteenth century.

Finally, these natural increases were themselves partly siphoned off in emigration. About 50 million people left Europe for Australia, Canada, the United States, and New Zealand. At its peak (1881-1910) emigration was equivalent to 20 percent of the increase in Europe's population. For particular countries, it was much higher. Nearly 45 percent of the increase in the population of the British Isles during 1846–1932 emigrated, about 40

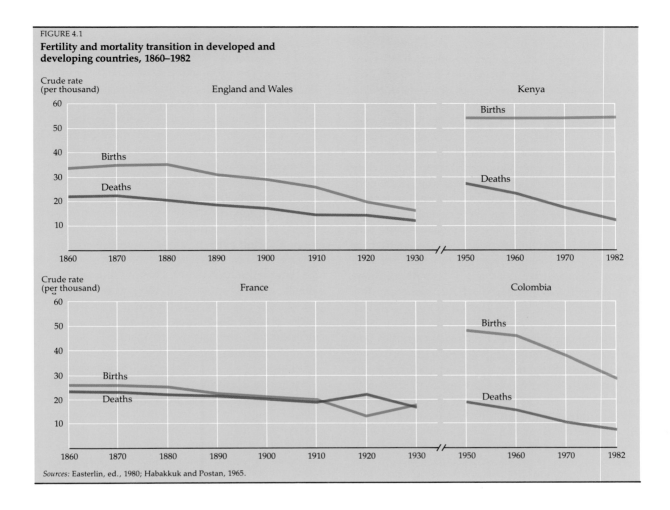

FIGURE 4.1

Fertility and mortality transition in developed and developing countries, 1860–1982

Crude rate (per thousand)

England and Wales

Kenya

Births

Deaths

Births

Deaths

Crude rate (per thousand)

France

Colombia

Births

Deaths

Births

Deaths

Sources: Easterlin, ed., 1980; Habakkuk and Postan, 1965.

percent of the mid-period population. For Ireland annual gross emigration averaged 1.9 percent of mean population in 1851–61 and 1.3 percent for the rest of the century. This was more than the natural growth of population, so Ireland's population fell between the 1840s and the end of the century. More than 7 percent of Scandinavia's population emigrated to the United States between 1880 and 1890; and between 30 and 40 percent of the increase in population of Italy, Portugal, and Spain emigrated between 1846 and 1932.

Japan in the eighteenth and nineteenth century presented a similar picture. Fertility was not high, population grew very slowly, and economic growth, although uneven, exceeded population growth so that living standards gradually rose. One explanation for low fertility was the Japanese "stem family": when they grew up, children outside the line of descent were forced to leave the household by marrying into another family or supporting themselves elsewhere. The costs of chil-

dren were shared neither within an extended family nor by the community. Nor did parents need sons to secure the line of descent; they could adopt sons from outside the family, an acceptable and frequently used option.

Detailed religious records of four villages in relatively affluent regions of Japan show that crude birth rates rarely exceeded thirty per thousand, a figure lower than would be expected in a premodern society. Death rates tended to move in line with birth rates, assuring slow but steady growth in each village. As in Europe, mean age at marriage was high, between twenty-two and twenty-five. About 40 percent of women aged fifteen to forty-four were not married. Marriage rates fluctuated with economic conditions: for people in their early twenties, from as low as 14 percent to as high as 80 percent when times were good. Couples had an average of just over three children, and mothers tended to be between thirty-two and thirty-eight when their last child was born—evidence of conscious control of family size, probably by abortion and infanticide. If it is assumed that parents did not report the births of infants killed, birth rates may have been higher than measured. Baby girls were probably the main victims, since there is evidence that more boys than girls survived.

Compared with Europe and Japan, North America, rich in natural resources and with good economic opportunities, experienced faster population growth in the nineteenth century. Fertility was relatively high, mortality was low; these conditions, together with heavy immigration from Europe, boosted the rate of population growth well above 2 percent in the early years of the century. But fertility began to decline earlier than in Europe, so the population growth rate fell well below 2 percent by the early twentieth century. About one-third of total growth in population during 1850–1910 came from immigration of working-age people.

The demographic situation of today's developed countries in the nineteenth century differed from what is happening in today's developing countries in several other respects. During the nineteenth century rural population growth in today's developed countries averaged less than 1 percent a year. By 1850 fewer than half of England's population lived in rural areas. By the 1880s Japan's agricultural labor force was already declining. In contrast, the rural population in most parts of Asia and Africa today is still growing by more than 2 percent a year, despite substantial migration to towns and cities. Technology was less advanced in the nineteenth century, so people did not need to be well educated (as they now do) to work in the modern economy. Nor did technology displace labor, as it now tends to do, especially if it is supplied by the capital-intensive developed countries. Where population growth was most rapid, in North America, land was plentiful.

All these factors—combined with low birth rates, death rates that declined slowly as a consequence of economic and not merely medical advance, and the safety valve of emigration, at least for Europe—meant that population growth never represented the burden that it now does for developing countries.

The transition to low fertility

In 1798 the English parson Thomas Malthus wrote in the *Essay on Population* his now-familiar proposition that "Population, when unchecked, increases in a geometrical ratio . . . Subsistence increases only in an arithmetical ratio." Population growth, he suggested in his first essay, could be checked only by a shortage of food and a resulting increase in deaths. The proposition rested on two assumptions: technological change could not increase food supply faster than population, and population growth (at least of the poorer classes) would not be limited by fewer births, only by more deaths. On the second assumption, Malthus later modified his views; universal education, he noted in later editions of his Essay, could give people the foresight to limit childbearing, and improved living standards could lead to "new . . . tastes and habits" before rising income induced a self-defeating rise in population. His first assumption also proved incorrect. The Industrial Revolution, beginning just before Malthus wrote, brought to Europe, and later to other economies, a new age of technological change, geometrical increases in agricultural and industrial production, and what has come to be called the "demographic transition": the transition from high to low fertility and mortality rates.

What are the lessons for developing countries in what caused fertility to decline in today's developed world, especially in what encouraged couples to choose smaller families? Three decades ago the reasons fertility declined in today's developed world might have been stated quite simply. With economic growth, living conditions improve, so mortality begins to fall. Contrary to what Malthus feared, fertility responds to falling mortality and adjusts downward, eventually producing the slower rate of population growth that prevailed before economic conditions started to improve. There is a lag between falling mortality and falling fertility, but one follows the other quickly enough so that economic gains are not eaten up by a larger population, and real incomes rise continuously.

In fact the story is not so simple. In Europe, and later in Japan, the pattern of declining mortality and fertility was not so orderly—nor is it today in developing countries. In a few places fertility decline preceded mortality decline; in others, fertility did not start falling soon after mortality did. And economic growth—if narrowly perceived as industrialization, urbanization, and the shift from family to factory production—was neither necessary nor sufficient for demographic transition.

In England fertility within marriage did not begin to fall until the 1870s, almost 100 years after the start of the Industrial Revolution and at least as long after a sustained decline in mortality had begun. Why the delay? Average real incomes rose by more than 1 percent a year in the nineteenth century. But, although unskilled workers and farm laborers (only a small fraction of the rural population owned their own land) enjoyed some increase in wages, at least after 1820, it was the upper- and middle-income groups that captured most of the income gains.

In addition, the early phase of England's industrialization permitted earlier marriage, which caused an initial rise in birth rates as rural industry provided job opportunities outside agriculture. (Such new opportunities similarly provide a rationale for early marriage and high fertility in transitional societies today.) Rural industry may not have increased the income of any one family, but it increased the number of families by giving more young people the chance to set up a household. Finally, for most of the nineteenth century the costs to parents of educating children were confined to those at the top of the income scale. Only 8 percent of school-age children were enrolled at school in 1851; despite much progress, still only 59 percent were enrolled in 1891. When fertility started to decline, it did so first among the professional middle class, which felt most keenly the need to educate its children. Only as education spread did fertility decline in all groups.

Though urbanization and industrialization came later to France than to England, fertility began to fall in France as early as the 1790s, when mortality was still high. Parish records show that families in some villages were small enough to indicate that parents were deliberately controlling fertility. Most women continued to have their first two babies within the expected interval of two to three years. Soon after the French Revolution in 1789, however, the intervals between the second birth and the third, and especially between the third and the fourth, lengthened substantially.

The decline in fertility could not have been confined to the educated. In the seventy-nine French departments for which data are available, only one in four people marrying was able to sign the parish register in 1786–90. But the French Revolution promoted what French demographers call social capillarity, the belief that one's children can rise in social status. It brought new aspirations (perhaps including the education of children), reduced allegiance to religious norms, and made individual choice (as opposed to family and communal authority) more legitimate. It also changed inheritance customs. French farming, unlike British, consisted mainly of small peasant holdings; under equal inheritance, fewer children made it easier to keep family landholdings intact.

During the nineteenth century, the idea of controlling fertility spread quickly in France. It did so also in other parts of Europe, though within linguistic and cultural boundaries and not quickly across them (see Box 4.3). By the 1830s the French birth rate had fallen below thirty per thousand. Apart from Ireland in the 1840s, during its great famine, no other European country went below that level until Belgium and Switzerland in the 1880s, followed by England and Wales in the 1890s. France never experienced a long period of falling death rates and high birth rates, which elsewhere produced a surge of population growth. Its population, once large compared with its neighbors, is now unexceptional. Perhaps as a result, a large body of French opinion has been persistently pronatalist. As discussed in Chapter 8, former French colonies in West Africa still bear that legacy.

In Sweden the demographic transition followed the classical pattern more closely. Average incomes were rising from at least the 1860s. The death rate had started falling in the 1830s; the birth rate started falling in the 1860s due to later age at marriage. Fertility within marriage decreased in the 1890s. When fertility began to decline, Sweden's economy was still largely rural, with 74 percent of the work force in the late 1880s engaged in agriculture, forestry, and fishing. Nonetheless, the economy was changing. Farm productivity had been rising rapidly from the 1860s. The percentage of farm owners in the agricultural work force rose from 42 to 57 percent between 1880 and 1930. As in France, fertility fell among landowners. Those without land of their own left for the cities or emigrated to America. Women's wage rates were rising especially fast. Education was more widespread than in England; in 1870 almost 60 percent of children were in school.

Similarly, in Hungary and Poland peasant landowners began in the nineteenth century to limit their families so that their children could inherit a workable piece of land. The fertility of landowners was consistently lower than that of landless farm workers.

Japan provides still another story. During much of the twentieth century, fertility declined gradually as marriage age rose. But fertility within marriage was as high in 1950 as it had been in 1930. Then, by about 1960, it dropped by half. There was pronatalist opinion between the 1920s and 1945 in support of Japan's expansionist policies. After 1945 the national mood changed and public policy started to favor small families. Abortion laws were

Box 4.3   The European fertility transition

Before 1880 fertility in Europe often fell where infant mortality was still high and populations were still largely rural. Fertility fell first in France (see map). This was followed, between 1830 and 1850, by declines in provinces in what are now Spain (Catalonia), Switzerland (Geneva and other French-speaking cantons), and Belgium (Wallonia)—areas that were culturally and linguistically close to the French provinces where fertility had already fallen. Some 90 percent of the provincial variation of marital fertility in Spain in 1910 was between regions (most of which were former kingdoms with different political histories and different dialects) and only 10 percent within regions. Aside from France and neighboring provinces, marital fertility had fallen before 1880 in only a few other places— some provinces in Denmark, Germany, Latvia, Servia, the Swedish island of Gotlands; and St. Petersburg in Russia.

Despite early variation, 60 percent of all European provinces began their marital fertility declines in the thirty years between 1890 and 1920, a period of unprecedented economic growth in Europe. Researchers have been unable to establish which levels or combinations of education, income, and life expectancy were critical to those fertility declines that had occurred earlier (the same is true for developing countries today). But by the beginning of the twentieth century, economic and social progress, which had spread throughout Europe, brought declines in fertility regardless of religious and cultural differences.

Starting dates of fertility transition in 700 European provinces, 1780–1969

Source: Van de Walle and Knodel, 1980.

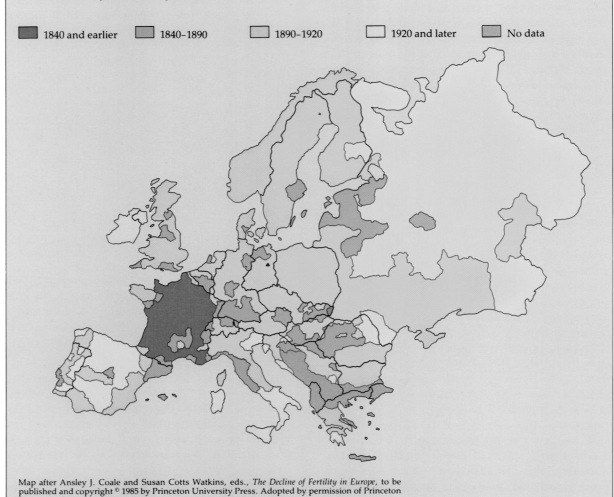

Map after Ansley J. Coale and Susan Cotts Watkins, eds., *The Decline of Fertility in Europe*, to be published and copyright © 1985 by Princeton University Press. Adopted by permission of Princeton University Press.

liberalized, and contraception, especially use of condoms, spread.

What are the lessons for developing countries?

● Fertility can decline in largely rural populations; it did so in France, Hungary, Japan, and Sweden. In France, Hungary, and Japan social aspirations and land ownership help explain why smallholders chose to limit their families. In Sweden fertility decline was associated with rapid productivity gains in agriculture and with an increase in the share of landowners among all agricultural workers.

● Economic and social opportunities for the majority of people matter. Fertility decline was delayed in England, where the real wages of farm laborers and unskilled workers rose only slowly, and where education was confined to the middle class through most of the nineteenth century. Fertility fell as education spread and became more necessary to earn a living.

● The mere idea that it is legitimate to limit births matters, but it does not spread automatically. In France and some other European countries fertility declined rapidly within cultural and linguistic boundaries, but was slow to do so farther afield. The spread of the idea that fertility control is legitimate occurs more quickly as transport and communication become easier—a potentially powerful force now in developing countries compared with Europe before the twentieth century.

● Low fertility is possible, but much more difficult, without sophisticated modern methods of birth control. In today's developed countries, late marriage and celibacy were important contributors; so, probably, were withdrawal and abstinence, abortion, and possibly infanticide. But once economic and social conditions are favorable, modern contraception speeds the decline in fertility, as the Japanese experience has proved.

Current demographic change in developing countries

Only in a few developing countries have population growth rates fallen below 2 percent a year in the past two decades. In many, population is still growing by more than 3 percent a year. In general, growth is fastest in the poorest countries. This delinking of population growth and prosperity in what is now the developing world began after World War I, when mortality began to decline. Mortality had already been falling slowly in Europe and the Americas, largely because of improved living standards—medicine had contrib-

uted little. But in the early years of the twentieth century, medical science found ways to combat infectious disease. As a result, by the 1920s and 1930s mortality decline was spreading from Europe and North America to Japan, India, and parts of Central and South America. With the introduction of antibiotics, antimalarial spraying, and the increased use of vaccination, the decline accelerated in the 1950s and spread to all developing countries. Improved communications, the consolidation of political and administrative systems, and cheaper transport all made it easier to transfer the new advances between and within countries.

Not only did this mortality decline occur rapidly; it began from higher initial levels (see Figure 4.2) and in societies where fertility levels were higher. At least initially it was not followed by fertility decline.

The current demographic condition of developing countries can be summed up in seven statements.

1. The postwar rate of population growth in developing countries is without precedent. Though in the past two decades rates of population growth in some countries have been falling because of birth rate declines, rates of growth are still unusually high, and birth rates are not declining everywhere.

In 1984 the world's population will increase by about 80 million. Most of the increase, about 73 million, will occur in developing countries, now comprising about three-quarters of world population. The combination of continued high fertility and much-reduced mortality has led to population growth of between 2 and 4 percent a year in most low- and middle-income countries, compared with 1 percent and less in most developed countries. Growth at 3 percent a year means that in seventy years population grows eightfold; at 1 percent a year it merely doubles. Current population growth in the developing economies is a phenomenon for which economic and demographic history offers no real precedent.

For developing countries as a group, population growth rates rose from 2.0 percent in 1950 to 2.4 percent in 1965, largely because of falling death rates (see Figure 4.2). Since then, death rates have continued to fall but birth rates have declined even more, so that growth has slowed somewhat. The rate of natural increase (and of population growth) in developing countries is now about 2 percent a year.

The fall in the average growth rate is due almost entirely to the birth rate decline in China, which

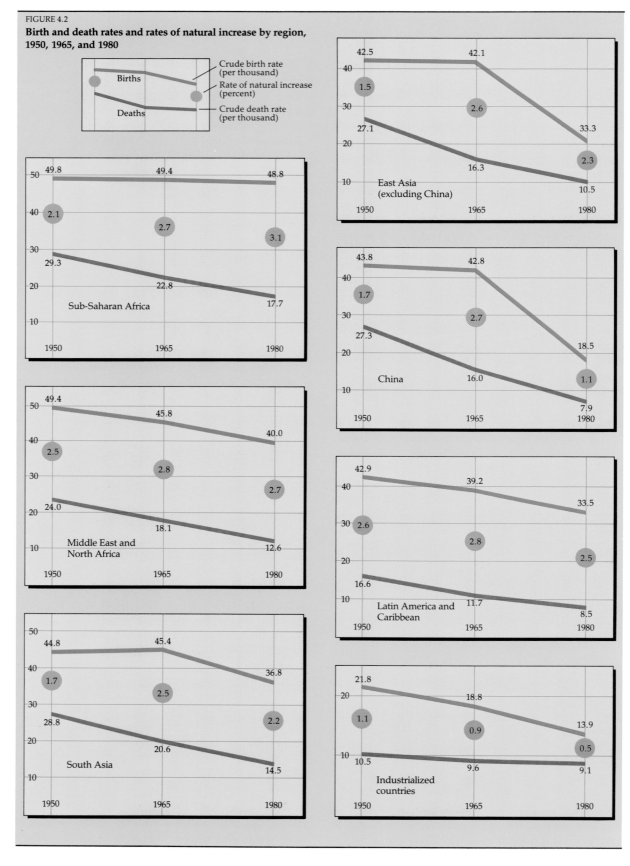

FIGURE 4.2

Birth and death rates and rates of natural increase by region, 1950, 1965, and 1980

alone accounts for a third of all the people in developing countries and where the birth rate has fallen by over 50 percent since 1965 (see Table 4.1 and Figure 4.2). Birth rates have also fallen in other countries of East Asia—in Hong Kong, Korea, Thailand, and Singapore by more than 30 percent, in Indonesia and elsewhere by 20 to 30 percent. In these generally middle-income economies, a demographic transition to low fertility is clearly under way.

In the middle-income countries of Latin America as well, birth rates have fallen more than death rates, which has slowed the rate of population growth. In Brazil and Mexico birth rate declines have been more modest than in East Asia but have still been rapid, especially in the past decade. In Colombia, Cuba, and Jamaica birth rates have also fallen. But in the poorer countries, including El Salvador, Guatemala, Honduras, and Nicaragua, birth rates are still more than thirty-five per thousand and population growth rates close to or greater than 3 percent a year. In Bolivia and Peru the growth rate is still about 2.5 percent.

In South Asia the birth rate has fallen barely enough to offset some further decline in the death rate. Sri Lanka is the only country of the region with a birth rate less than thirty per thousand. India's birth rate has fallen markedly in some states, but much less in others, and is now about thirty-four per thousand; as death rates have fallen, population growth has increased, from just above 2 percent a year in the early 1960s to 2.1 percent in 1982. In Bangladesh and Pakistan the birth rate has barely fallen and exceeds forty per thousand; population grows at about 3 percent a year. In Africa and much of the Middle East (with the exception of Egypt, Israel, Lebanon, Tunisia, Morocco, and Turkey), birth rates are above forty per thousand and have changed little or not at all; population growth rates are generally above 3 percent.

In most countries where the crude birth rate has fallen, the total fertility rate has fallen even more (see Table 4.1); the total fertility rate is the number of children a woman would have if she experienced current age-specific fertility rates of all women (see Box 4.4). The total fertility rate has fallen more because high fertility and declining mortality in the 1950s and 1960s mean that a large proportion of today's population in developing countries is now of childbearing age. Until this group has completed its childbearing years, overall birth rates will remain high, even if actual family size is small. In India, for example, because of the

TABLE 4.1

Percentage decline in crude birth rates and in total fertility rates, selected countries, 1965–82

Region and country	Crude birth rate decline 1965–82	Total fertility rate decline 1965–82
Sub-Saharan Africa		
Ethiopia	5.6	3.0
Kenya	+0.2	0.0
Nigeria	3.7	0.0
Sudan	1.4	1.5
Zaire	3.8	+3.3
Middle East and North Africa		
Algeria	6.0	5.4
Egypt	16.3	22.0
Iran	7.7	18.8
Morocco	20.0	18.3
Tunisia	26.5	28.6
Turkey	24.8	30.5
Latin America and Caribbean		
Bolivia	6.1	4.6
Brazil	18.6	30.4
Colombia	31.4	42.9
Cuba	51.5	55.6
Guatemala	17.6	21.2
Honduras	12.5	10.8
Jamaica	29.1	37.1
Mexico	23.8	31.3
Nicaragua	8.7	12.5
Peru	24.4	30.8
South Asia		
Bangladesh	9.6	14.9
India	19.9	18.7
Pakistan	15.8	22.7
Sri Lanka	20.2	30.6
East Asia and Pacific		
China	54.0	61.3
Indonesia	22.4	25.9
Korea, Rep. of	35.4	43.8
Philippines	32.0	38.2
Thailand	34.0	42.9

increase in the proportion of women of marriage and childbearing age, the birth rate would have risen by 1.1 points from 1971 to 1981, from 36.9 to 38.0, had there been no change in the marriage rate and marital fertility. (In fact, it fell by 3 points as marriage age rose and married couples had fewer children.)

2. The high fertility and falling infant mortality of the mid-1960s mean that in developing countries today about 40 percent of populations are aged fifteen or younger.

In countries such as Kenya, where fertility has declined little or not at all, more than 50 percent of the population is younger than fifteen, compared

Box 4.4 Alternative measures of fertility and mortality

Crude birth and death rates per thousand population provide an idea of the components of population growth. However, crude rates do not indicate the frequency of births and deaths at the household or individual level. Alternative measures that serve this purpose are the total fertility rate and life expectancy at birth.

The total fertility rate for the current year is the sum of the birth rates specific to each age group of women. It may be interpreted as the total number of births a woman would have if her fertility in each year of her reproductive life exactly paralleled the current fertility of women in her own and other age groups. This rate therefore does not represent the lifetime experience of any particular age group or cohort of women; it is obtained

by combining at one point in time the current fertility of women of different ages. Total fertility rates in the developing world are between three and eight.

Like the total fertility rate, life expectancy at birth is a synthetic measure. It indicates the number of years a newborn baby could be expected to live if its mortality pattern exactly paralleled that of all age groups in the current year.

The total fertility rate and the life expectancy at birth of a population are not affected by its age structure. Crude birth and death rates are. Crude birth rates will be higher if the reproductive age groups are a large proportion of the total population; crude death rates will be higher if the elderly are a large proportion.

Crude rates can therefore be mislead-

ing. For example, because the proportion of women of childbearing age has been high in most developing countries in the last two decades, crude birth rates have fallen less than total fertility rates in that period and understate the change in fertility behavior of couples. The same is true for mortality. The crude death rate in the Netherlands is higher than the crude death rate in Syria (8.4 versus 7.2 per thousand), essentially because the proportion of the population over sixty-five is four times as great in the Netherlands. Life expectancy for women however, is ten years longer in the Netherland than in Syria (seventy-six years as against sixty-six).

---

with only 20 to 25 percent in developed countries (see Table 4.2). Although the proportion of old people is smaller in developing countries, the dependency ratio—the proportion of the population under fifteen and over sixty-four to those between ages fifteen and sixty-four—is on average higher. In Japan, for example, there are roughly two people of working age to support one who is either too old or too young to work; in Kenya, the ratio is less than one-to-one. Other things being equal, if income per worker were identical in Japan and Kenya, income per person in Japan would nevertheless be at least 30 percent higher. Even within the same country there are comparable differences in age structure—and hence in dependency burdens—among families. In urban Maharashtra state (India), about half the people in the poorest 10 percent of households are younger than fifteen; in the richest 20 percent, only one in five is younger than fifteen.

The age structure in developing countries means that birth rates will remain high for some time even if each mother has fewer children. It also means the number of young people entering the labor force will continue to increase for the next two decades. For countries where fertility began to fall in the mid-1960s, the rate of growth of the labor force is now just starting to decline, though the absolute number of new workers will continue to increase until after the end of this century. In

Colombia, for example, the working-age population will increase from 15 million in 1980 to almost 25 million in 2000. In Bangladesh it will almost double, from 48 million to 84 million. The economic implications of this growth are discussed in the next chapter.

In other age groups as well, population growth in developing countries will be higher than in developed countries. The number of people older than sixty-five will almost double between now and 2000 in developing countries. In developed countries the number will increase by about a third (but by about 85 percent in Japan).

3. Neither internal nor international migration offers real solutions to population growth. High rates of natural population increase account more for the rapid growth of cities in developing countries than does rural-urban migration. Despite extensive rural-urban migration, population growth in rural areas of low-income Asia and Africa still averages 2 percent or more a year. The present scale of international migration, both permanent and temporary, constitutes a small proportion of the populations of developing countries.

Cities in developing countries are growing at almost twice the rate of overall populations (see Table 4.3). More than half the increase is due to the balance of births over deaths; the rest is due to migration from rural areas and the reclassification of rural areas to urban status. Historically, the

TABLE 4.2
Comparison of age structures in developed and developing countries, 1980

Country group	Age distribution (percent)					Total fertility rate
	0–4	5–14	15–64	Over 65	All ages	
All developed countries	7.6	15.5	65.6	11.3	100.0	1.9[a]
Japan	7.3	16.1	67.7	8.9	100.0	1.8
United States	7.9	15.0	66.3	10.7	100.0	1.9
Hungary	8.0	13.7	64.9	15.9	100.0	2.1
All developing countries	13.6	25.5	57.0	4.0	100.0	4.2[a]
Korea, Rep. of	10.6	22.7	62.7	4.0	100.0	3.0
Colombia	14.0	25.4	57.1	3.5	100.0	3.8
Bangladesh	17.9	24.9	54.6	2.6	100.0	6.3
Kenya	22.4	28.6	46.1	2.9	100.0	8.0

a. Weighted average.

urban populations of some of today's developed countries have grown even faster—for example, the urban population of the United States increased at about 6 percent a year between 1830 and 1860. But today's developing countries have started from a much larger base, so the absolute increases are much greater. From 1950 to 1980 the urban population of all developing countries (excluding China) increased by 585 million—compared with a total urban population in the developed countries in 1950 of just over 300 million.

Latin America is the most urbanized of developing-country regions. In 1980 about two-thirds of its people were urban dwellers, a level reached in today's developed countries only in 1950. Low-income Asia and Africa are still overwhelmingly rural; their current urbanization level of about 25 percent was reached in the developed countries before 1900.

The world's biggest cities are increasingly in the developing countries. Between 1950 and 1980 the proportion of urban dwellers in developing countries in cities of more than 5 million increased from 2 to 14 percent, growing at a rate of 15 percent a year. Sao Paulo, which by the year 2000 could well be the world's second largest city (behind Mexico City), was smaller in 1950 than Manchester, Detroit, and Naples. London, the world's second

TABLE 4.3
Rural and urban population growth, 1950–2000

Country group	Percentage urban population			Average annual percentage growth			
				1950–80		1980–2000	
	1950	1980	2000	Urban	Rural	Urban	Rural
All developing countries	18.9	28.7	. .	3.4	1.7	. .	. .
Excluding China	22.2	35.4	43.3	3.8	1.7	3.5	1.1
Low-income							
Asia	10.7	19.5	31.3	4.4	2.0	4.2	0.9
China	11.2	13.2[a]	. .	2.5	1.8	. .	. .
India	16.8	23.3	35.5	3.2	1.8	4.2	1.1
Africa	5.7	19.2	34.9	7.0	2.5	5.8	1.5
Middle-income							
East Asia and Pacific	19.6	31.9	41.9	4.1	1.8	3.1	0.9
Middle East and North Africa	27.7	46.8	59.9	4.4	1.6	4.3	1.6
Sub-Saharan Africa	33.7	49.4	55.2	3.1	1.0	2.9	1.7
Latin America and Caribbean	41.4	65.3	75.4	4.1	0.8	2.9	0.4
Southern Europe	24.7	47.1	62.3	3.8	0.5	2.9	.-0.2
Industrial countries[b]	61.3	77.0	83.7	1.8	.-0.7	1.0	.-1.1

. . Not available.
a. Government estimate for 1979.
b. Excludes East European nonmarket economies.

largest city in 1950, will not even rank among the twenty-five largest by the end of the century (see Figure 4.3).

Despite the rapid growth of cities, the urban share of today's developing-country populations is not increasing especially fast. This is because not only urban but also rural populations are growing rapidly, and in low-income countries from a large base, so that a considerable growth of numbers will continue in the countryside for the rest of this decade and beyond. In India, for example, though urban rates of population growth are likely to be about four times higher than rural rates in the next two decades, and the urban population could increase by 170 million, the rural population will still increase by 130 million. The rural population of all developing countries is likely to increase by another billion people by the middle of the next century. Both the rates of growth and the increase in numbers greatly exceed those of today's developed countries in the nineteenth century, the period when overall population growth in those countries was highest.

Compared with rates of intercontinental migration from Europe in the eighteenth and nineteenth centuries, present-day permanent emigration rates are small: between 1970 and 1980 emigration absorbed about 3 percent of population growth in Europe and Latin America, less than 1 percent in Asia and Africa (see Table 4.4). For India, a large low-income country, the emigration rate was only 0.2 percent. Only for a few countries are permanent emigration rates high, and these tend to be the relatively better-off, middle-income countries: Greece, Hong Kong, and Portugal.

Permanent emigration has only a limited effect on reducing the work force in developing countries. To take a simple example, even if 700,000 immigrants a year were admitted to the major host countries up to the year 2000, and all came from low-income countries, less than 2 percent of the projected growth in population in the low-income countries between 1982 and 2000 would have emigrated. By contrast, such immigration would account for 22 percent of the projected natural increase in population of the industrial market economies and 36 percent of the projected increase in the main host countries: Australia, Canada, New Zealand, and the United States.

The past three decades have seen a marked increase in temporary migration. By 1974, temporary foreign workers in Europe, numbering about 6.5 million, constituted 30 percent of the work force in Luxembourg, more than 18 percent in Switzerland, and about 8 percent in Belgium, France, and Germany. They came mostly from nearby, middle-income countries. In the major labor-importing countries of the Middle East, about 2 million foreign workers constituted more than 40 percent of the employed work force in 1975. Ghana and the Ivory Coast employed about 1 million foreign workers in 1975, mostly from Mali, Togo, and Upper Volta. Argentina and Venezuela had about 2 million workers from Bolivia, Paraguay, and Colombia.

But, as with permanent emigration, temporary emigrants constitute only a small proportion of the

FIGURE 4.3

Urban agglomerations with more than 10 million inhabitants: 1950, 1975, and 2000

Developing countries

Developed countries

1950   1975   2000

1950	(millions)		(millions)
New York, northeast New Jersey	12.2	London	10.4
1975			
New York, northeast New Jersey	19.8	London	10.4
Mexico City	11.9	Tokyo, Yokohama	17.7
Los Angeles, Long Beach	10.8	Shanghai	11.6
		Sao Paulo	10.7
2000			
Mexico City	31.0	Sao Paulo	25.8
Tokyo, Yokohama	24.2	New York, northeast New Jersey	22.8
Shanghai	22.7	Rio de Janeiro	19.0
Beijing	19.9	Calcutta	16.7
Greater Bombay	17.1	Seoul	14.2
Jakarta	16.6	Cairo, Giza, Imbaba	13.1
Los Angeles, Long Beach	14.2	Manila	12.3
Madras	12.9	Bangkok, Thonburi	11.9
Greater Buenos Aires	12.1	Delhi	11.7
Karachi	11.8	Paris	11.3
Bogota	11.7	Istanbul	11.2
Tehran	11.3	Osaka, Kobe	11.1
Baghdad	11.1		

Source: United Nations, 1980.

TABLE 4.4
Permanent emigration as a percentage of increase in populations of emigrants' countries

Period	Europe	Asia[a]	Africa[a]	Latin America[a]
1851–80	11.7	0.4	0.01	0.3
1881–1910	19.5	0.3	0.04	0.9
1911–40	14.4	0.1	0.03	1.8
1940–60	2.7[b]	0.1	0.01	1.0
1960–70	5.2	0.2	0.10	1.9
1970–80	4.0	0.5	0.30	2.5

Note: Numbers are calculated from data on gross immigration in Australia, Canada, New Zealand, and the United States.
a. The periods from 1850 to 1960 pertain to emigration only to the United States.
b. Emigration only to the United States.
Source: Swamy, 1984.

labor force in developing countries. The total number of temporary workers abroad in 1980 was between 13 and 15 million. For some countries in the Middle East, southern Europe, and Africa, temporary workers are a large proportion of the emigrant country's labor force. But for Bangladesh and India as a whole, the proportion is less than 1 percent. The same is true even of illegal migration. About 2 to 4 million immigrants were living illegally in the United States in April 1980, about half of them from Mexico. At most they would have constituted 8 percent of Mexico's total labor force in that year.

4. More often than not, current fertility and mortality rates are inversely related to income—but this rule has many significant exceptions.

The relation between average income and the total fertility rate in developing countries is shown in Figure 4.4, and between income and life expectancy in Figure 4.5. In general, the higher a country's average income, the lower its fertility and the higher its life expectancy. Some of the 100 countries used in the analysis are identified in the figures.

Sub-Saharan Africa and the Indian subcontinent (Bangladesh, India, and Pakistan) have the highest levels of fertility and mortality and the lowest incomes; fertility averages five to eight children per woman, and life expectancy is as low as fifty years. Countries of East Asia and Latin America have lower fertility (three to five children), higher life expectancy (about sixty years), and higher incomes. Some countries have moved faster than others: Brazil, Indonesia, Mexico, and Thailand are

some of the countries that achieved relatively large reductions in fertility between 1972 and 1982. At the other extreme, fertility rose slightly in a few African countries.

The association across countries also tends to hold within countries. In an individual country, those with higher income tend to have more education, better health, and—for women—more opportunities to work in modern sector jobs. As Chapter 6 emphasizes, these characteristics are all associated with lower fertility and mortality.

It is wrong to conclude, however, that countries must get richer before they can lower fertility and raise life expectancy. Average income is only one of the factors involved. As Figure 4.4 shows, some countries have significantly lower fertility than the norm for those with their income level. Examples include China, Colombia, India, Indonesia, Korea, Thailand, and Sri Lanka. By contrast, countries with relatively high fertility (given their income) include Algeria, Jordan, and Morocco, most countries of sub-Saharan Africa, Venezuela, and even with its recent decline in fertility, Mexico. China, Costa Rica, and Sri Lanka have relatively high life expectancy. These exceptions demonstrate the importance of the availability and distribution of health and educational services, the extent to which adult women enjoy a status independent of childrearing, and the access of the poor to family planning services. The reasons for the importance of these other factors, and how they interact, are discussed in Chapter 6.

5. The relation between income and life expectancy, and between income and fertility, has shifted over time.

As Figures 4.4 and 4.5 show, the same average income is associated with lower fertility and higher life expectancy in 1982 than in 1972. Since the 1920s, and especially since the end of World War II, the main reasons for rising life expectancy in developing countries have been better public health systems, educational advances, and the greater political stability that permitted these. For example, a quarter of Sri Lanka's decline in mortality after 1945 is attributable solely to the control of malaria. Rising incomes and associated improvements in nutrition and sanitation have in general played a lesser role. As a result, life expectancy is higher in developing countries than it was in today's developed countries at the turn of the century, despite income and education levels that in many countries are still lower. Life expectancy in India was fifty-five in 1982, yet India's per capita income is still below $300 a year and its literacy rate

FIGURE 4.4

Fertility in relation to income in developing countries, 1972 and 1982

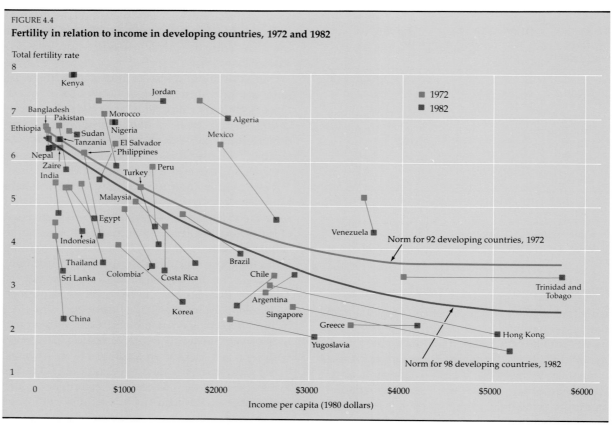

FIGURE 4.5

Life expectancy in relation to income in developing countries, 1972 and 1982

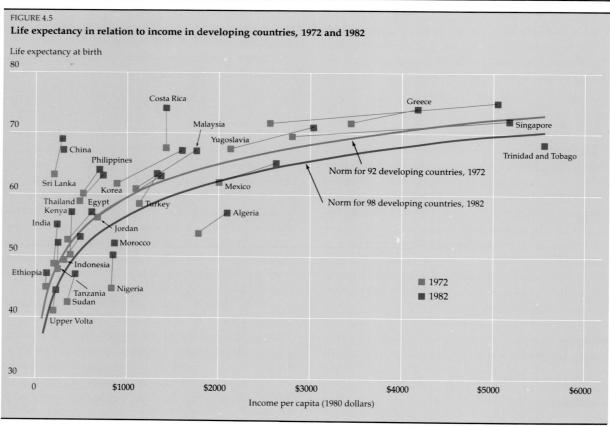

below 40 percent. Life expectancy in England, Sweden, and the United States was still below fifty in 1900, although average income (in 1982 dollars) was more than $1,000 and the literacy rate exceeded 80 percent in all three countries. One analysis indicates that life expectancy in the developing countries in 1970 would have been about eight years lower had it not been for the improvements in public health.

Fertility, too, has been declining in many developing countries faster than it did in today's developed countries. For Austria, England, and the United States it took about fifty years to go from birth rates of thirty-five to twenty per thousand, an average decline of 0.3 per year. Birth rate declines in China, Colombia, and Costa Rica have exceeded one point per year. Education and income growth have been rapid; modern communication has increased the speed with which the idea and legitimacy of fertility control can spread; and modern contraceptives have lowered the costs and increased the effectiveness of individual fertility control.

Fertility is also declining at lower levels of income. Marital fertility started falling in most European provinces between 1880 and 1930, when average income already exceeded $1,000 (in 1982 dollars), compared with half that figure when fertility decline began in Latin America and much of Asia. Between 1972 and 1982 there was a further downward shift in the income-fertility relation.

These long-term changes encourage optimism. Lower mortality and fertility can be achieved even in the poorest countries. But there is also a new cause for concern.

6. Mortality has declined everywhere, and fertility has started to decline in many countries. But there is considerable variation, and in some regions and countries the declines now seem to be stalled at relatively high levels.

Almost all countries outside Africa have experienced some fertility decline in the past two decades. But since 1975 the decline seems to have slowed and even stopped in countries such as Costa Rica, India, Korea, and Sri Lanka, where fertility levels are still relatively high (though low given income levels in these countries). In contrast, once fertility started falling in today's developed countries, it went on falling more or less continuously. Though fertility rose in Europe and the United States for two decades after World War II, total fertility rates rose only a little above 3 even during this baby boom and have declined to less than 2 since.

The reasons fertility has stalled vary from country to country. In Korea fertility is already low—a rate of 2.7 in 1982. Fertility fell as women married later, especially in the 1960s, but the marriage age for women now averages twenty-four and is unlikely to rise further. This cause of lower fertility may therefore now be exhausted. Marriage is universal, and most Korean couples want at least one son. Until that attitude changes, actual fertility will not fall to replacement level even if the ideal number of children falls to two. Some couples will have two girls and go on to another pregnancy.

In Costa Rica the total fertility rate fell dramatically from 7.0 in 1960 to 3.7 in 1978. But it has fluctuated around that level since. The use of contraception has not increased since 1976, although knowledge is widespread: 98 percent of married women know of a source of modern contraception. The fertility of uneducated women has fallen, but each still has about five children. The family planning program has flagged recently for lack of political support. More important, parents still want more than three children—an average of 3.6, say women in their early twenties, while older women favor even more.

Sri Lanka's initial decline in fertility was partly due to increases in marriage age. But since 1974 the total fertility rate has remained the same or even risen, from 3.4 to an estimated 3.7 in 1981. The country's marriage patterns are sensitive to economic conditions, especially male employment, so an economic revival in the late 1970s may have been the cause. But Sri Lankan women have one child more than they want, on average, so improved contraceptive services could reduce fertility.

In India the total fertility rate in 1982 was 4.8, down from about 6.5 in the 1950s. It has continued to fall, but very slowly. Except for the northern state of Punjab, where the Green Revolution has brought agricultural modernization, most of the decline has occurred in a few southern states in which female literacy rates are higher, infant mortality lower, and family planning services better run than in other parts of India.

In many countries fertility continues to fall without interruption. But in most, rates are still high, and the barriers to continued declines may not yet have been reached. Indonesia's total fertility rate fell from 5.5 in 1970, when the government began a vigorous family planning program, to 4.3 in 1982. It is lowest in Java, where the program has been most active. But even there it is still about 4.0; the government goal is a nationwide rate of 2.7 by 1990.

It is of course possible that the stalling may be temporary. In Korea fertility decline was checked for a while in the 1960s and then resumed. Yet stalling could also mean that initial, easily met demand for contraception has been largely saturated at a level of fertility that is lower than it was, but a level that is still relatively high. Judging from recent research on desired family size in many developing countries, this may well be the case. In the late 1970s parents still wanted about four children, even in those countries in which fertility had initially declined. The average, for example, was 4.1 in Colombia and Indonesia, 4.4 in the Philippines, and 3.7 in Thailand. Yet if each couple in a country has four children, population growth will remain rapid. Take the example of Indonesia, where the fertility rate of 4.3 is close to the desired family size. The crude birth rate is thirty-four per

thousand and the death rate thirteen per thousand, so Indonesia's population is growing at 2.1 percent a year. In countries in which desired family size is four or more, fertility will fall further only with more social and economic change, along with greater efforts to bring better family planning services to more people.

There is also some evidence that improvements in life expectancy are slowing down. In developed countries, life expectancy rose steadily until it reached about sixty; beyond that, rises are naturally slower in coming. But in some developing countries, progress has not been so steady (see Box 4.5). Much of the gain in life expectancy has come from various public health programs such as vaccination and antimalarial spraying, which generally made a bigger difference in the 1950s and 1960s than in the 1970s. This is especially true in Latin America. In Asia, and particularly in East Asia,

Box 4.5   Is the rise in life expectancy slowing too soon?

The curve in the chart represents the trend in life expectancy in developing countries. It shows that it takes about eighty years on average to raise life expectancy from forty-two years (about the level in Laos or Chad today) to seventy-five (about the current level in most industrial countries). The rise is initially slow, picks up speed, and then gradually slows again. The slowdown is particularly marked as life expectancy rises above age seventy or eighty, as in the developed countries today, because many of the diseases that kill people in affluent countries—such as heart disease and cancer—yield only slowly to expensive medical research.

During the 1950s many developing countries registered substantial gains in life expectancy. Some, such as Colombia, Mexico and Sri Lanka, outperformed the standard represented by the curve. The record for the 1960s and 1970s was much more mixed. During the 1960s Mexico gained 0.28 years in life expectancy annually, and from 1970 to 1978 Colombia gained 0.33 years annually. Even allowing for slower gains at higher levels, their progress was disappointing; if the two countries had matched the standard, they would each have gained 0.48 years annually over these periods.

The available data suggest similar slow-downs elsewhere in Latin America and the Caribbean, most pronounced in a few countries such as Argentina, Barbados, Trinidad and Tobago, and Uruguay.

Did this slowdown occur in other regions? Because the mortality data are much sketchier elsewhere, it is difficult to be sure. Some slowdown could also have taken place in sub-Saharan Africa; in Asia any slowdown was probably modest. The chart does indicate that gains fell slightly short of the standard in Sri Lanka in the 1960s, but they were greater in China and probably also in India.

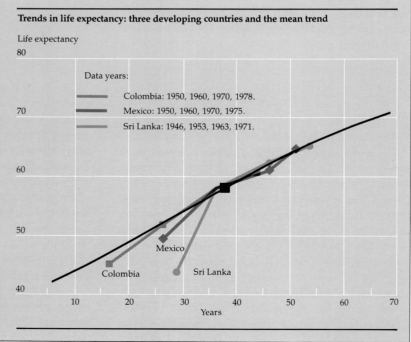

Trends in life expectancy: three developing countries and the mean trend

Data years:

Colombia: 1950, 1960, 1970, 1978.
Mexico: 1950, 1960, 1970, 1975.
Sri Lanka: 1946, 1953, 1963, 1971.

economic development has been rapid enough to offset the declining contribution of public health improvements, so life expectancy has gone on rising steadily. In India in the past decade, however, poverty and illiteracy in rural areas of the north seem to have kept infant mortality high, slowing any further rise in rural life expectancy despite economic growth. In Africa slower economic progress (in some countries, even regression) has slowed the rise in life expectancy. Rural mortality tends to exceed urban mortality, so a slightly slower pace of urbanization in the late 1970s may also have slowed progress against mortality. By contrast, the remarkable gain in life expectancy in China—from forty-one in 1960 to an estimated sixty-seven in 1982—shows what can be achieved, even by a largely rural society, through a combination of education, income gains, and a strong health care program.

For the future, increasing life expectancy seems likely to depend more than ever on improved living conditions, education for women, and better health care for the poor. Three indicators lend support to this view.

• Mortality from diarrhea in the developing world is two to three times higher than it was in today's developed countries when overall mortality levels were similar. Diarrhea is a disease of the poor, primarily of poor children. It accompanies malnutrition and is exacerbated by poor sanitation, lack of elementary health services, and lack of the basic education that might allow parents to take the necessary precautions to prevent it.

• Infant and child mortality, the major contributors to low life expectancy in developing countries, are closely linked to economic and social welfare. In Latin America infant and child mortality rates are five times greater among children whose mothers have no schooling than among those with mothers having ten or more years of schooling.

• In countries with life expectancy higher than might be expected from their average incomes—Costa Rica, Cuba, Korea, and Sri Lanka—income tends to be more equally distributed than in other developing countries. Illiteracy is also lower and health services more widespread.

7. *Further declines in mortality rates will boost population growth much less from now on than they did in the 1950s and 1960s.*

For most of the developing world, the time when declining mortality produced surges in population is passing rapidly. In part this is because mortality, though still high compared with developed countries, has already fallen considerably. But there are other reasons. Mortality declines affect population growth less when fertility is falling, as is and will be the case in most countries. Long-range population growth is less dependent on the addition of people whose lives are saved than on the number of children they subsequently bear. When fertility is high, saving a baby's life adds a great deal of reproductive potential. To save the lives of an infant girl and boy who will go on to have 6 children is to add those people plus (perhaps) their 36 grandchildren, 216 great grandchildren, and so on. But as fertility declines, so does the amount of extra reproductive capacity. The infant girl who survives, grows up, and gives birth to 3 instead of 6 children has 27 rather than 216 great grandchildren (assuming that each of her children will follow her pattern). Furthermore, as mortality declines, more and more deaths are shifted from younger to older ages. To extend the life of someone sixty years old is to keep the population just one person larger than it would otherwise be, not to boost it by that person plus descendants.

In addition, as Chapter 6 will indicate, lower mortality contributes directly to lower fertility. For the individual family, fewer deaths usually mean fewer births (though the net effect is a somewhat larger family on average). Finally, because further mortality declines depend more than before on progress in women's education and on improved living conditions and health care, programs that reduce mortality are likely to reduce fertility as well.

Demographic prospects and goals

Demographic projections should not be treated as forecasts. The purpose in making projections is to illustrate what the future could be, given certain assumptions. It is the assumptions that determine whether the projections will match reality. Some projections have been wide of the mark; for example, the size and duration of the baby boom after 1945 in the United States was unexpected. But since the 1950s, when the United Nations began producing systematic projections of world population, demographers have done well in predicting future trends. In 1963 the United Nations projected a 1980 population of 4.3 billion, only a shade off the 4.4 billion suggested by the latest estimates, and projections of world population in the year 2000 have hardly changed since 1963.

But projections for particular regions and countries have varied. The 1980 UN projection for

North America's population in 2000 is 16 percent below the 1963 projection because fertility is lower than expected; the 1980 projection for Asia as a whole is 3 percent above the 1963 projection because fertility has fallen less than expected (even though the projection for one country, China, where fertility has fallen more than expected, is below the 1963 projection).

Two critical assumptions guide the World Bank projections of each country's population.

• Mortality will continue to fall everywhere until life expectancy for females is eighty-two years. As Figure 4.6 shows, these projections essentially continue the trends that are already well established in the ten largest developing countries. They ignore the possibility of any major catastrophe, such as war or virulent disease.

• Fertility will eventually reach and stay at replacement level everywhere. When that will occur obviously varies from country to country, depending on current fertility levels, recent trends, and family planning efforts. For most developing countries, replacement level is projected to be reached between 2005 and 2025; for most countries in Africa and the Middle East, it is projected to be reached later. For most of the largest developing countries, the projections of declining fertility essentially extend declines that have been happening for several years. However, a few countries, for example Nigeria, have yet to experience fertility declines; for those countries projected declines are assumed to start in the near future (see Figure 4.7).

The consequences of these ''standard'' assumptions for the population of all developing countries are shown in Figure 4.8. As shown in the figure, the increases still to come are likely to exceed what has happened so far. This is naturally a cause for concern, but not for despair (see Box 4.6). The pace of population growth need not be taken as given—it also depends on policy. And the way societies cope with a growing population depends on economic and social policy as well as on how fast they grow.

The potential effect of policy can be illustrated by comparing population projections under the standard assumptions with two other paths: ''rapid'' fertility decline (with standard mortality decline), and ''rapid'' mortality decline added to rapid fertility decline. Country projections and the assumptions behind the standard and rapid paths are explained in detail in the Population Data Supplement. Rapid fertility decline is at a rate equivalent to that achieved in certain periods between 1950 and the present by eleven developing countries, including Colombia, Korea, Singapore, and Thailand, where at times the total fertility rate declined by almost 0.2 a year. Similarly, rapid mortality decline is based on the experience of fourteen countries, including Costa Rica, Cuba, Hong Kong, and Kenya, where life expectancy increased by at least one year every two years between 1950 and 1980 (and at a faster rate where initial life expectancy was lower).

Three points are clear from these projections.

• Even with rapid fertility (and mortality) decline, the developing world's population would more than double by the year 2050, rising to 6.9 billion. The population of Indonesia would still increase from 153 million to about 300 million, that of Bangladesh from 93 million to about 230 million, and that of India from 717 million to 1.4 billion (see Table 4.5). For countries of Africa, Central America, and the Middle East, where the proportion of young people is higher and where fertility is still high and would take longer to decline to replacement level, the increases would be much greater. Even with rapid fertility decline, Kenya would not reach replacement-level fertility until 2015, and today's population of 18 million would increase to almost 70 million by 2050. Under the standard declines, replacement-level fertility would not be attained until 2030, and Kenya's population would grow to 120 million by 2050. With rapid fertility decline, El Salvador's population would still grow from 5 million to 12 million.

• Population growth beyond the year 2000 depends critically on falling fertility in the next decade or two. As Table 4.5 shows, the difference in population size between the standard and rapid declines is not great in 2000—less than 20 percent in most countries. Under any assumption, the populations of most developing countries are likely to increase by 50 percent or more by 2000; a few, including Kenya and Nigeria, will almost double. By the year 2050, however, the differences will be huge. If fertility falls sooner rather than later in Kenya, population there in 2050 will be reduced by about 50 million compared with what it would otherwise be, against today's total population of 18 million.

• In determining the ultimate size of world population, fertility matters more than mortality. Rapid mortality decline combined with standard fertility decline would produce population in developing countries 7 percent larger in the year 2050 than that resulting from the standard mortality decline. In contrast, rapid fertility decline

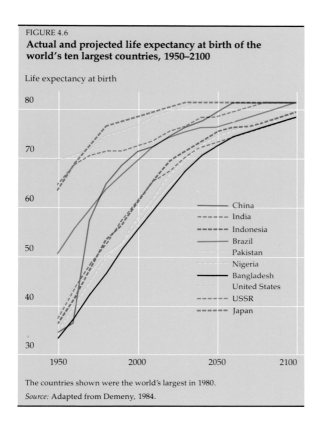

FIGURE 4.6

Actual and projected life expectancy at birth of the world's ten largest countries, 1950–2100

Life expectancy at birth

The countries shown were the world's largest in 1980.

Source: Adapted from Demeny, 1984.

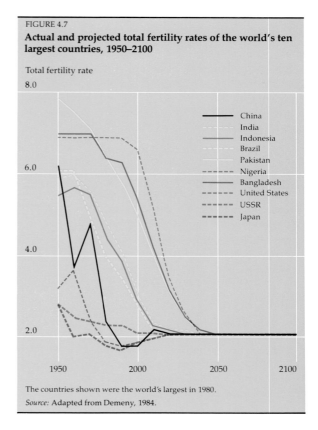

FIGURE 4.7

Actual and projected total fertility rates of the world's ten largest countries, 1950–2100

Total fertility rate

The countries shown were the world's largest in 1980.

Source: Adapted from Demeny, 1984.

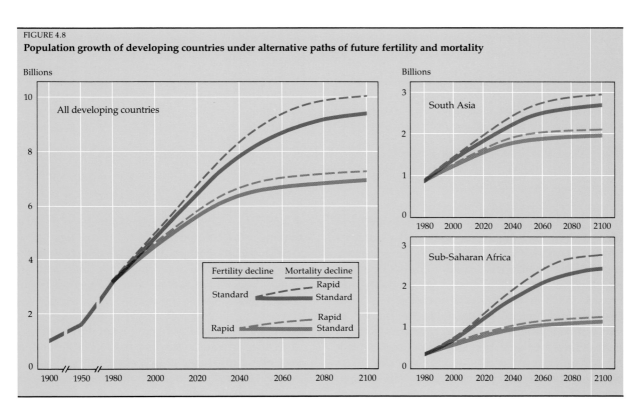

FIGURE 4.8

Population growth of developing countries under alternative paths of future fertility and mortality

75

Box 4.6   Three views of population change

The charts in this box provide three different perspectives on past and present population growth. Although each looks different, all are based on the same facts.

The top chart shows the change in the absolute size of world population from about 9000 B.C. (the beginning of the agricultural age) to the end of the present century. The middle chart shows population growth rates from A.D. 1750 to 2000. The bottom chart, like the top one, shows change in the size of the human population, but over a longer period—back to 1 million B.C.—and on a logarithmic scale.

The three charts suggest strikingly different impressions of population growth. The top one conveys the impression of an enormous population explosion beginning sometime after 1750 (the beginning of the industrial age). It points upward at the year 2000 with no apparent limit. The middle chart indicates that these recent dramatic increases have been produced by relatively small, though accelerating growth rates. Annual growth was about 0.4 percent between 1750 and 1800, crept up steadily until it reached 0.8 percent in 1900–50, and then rose sharply to 1.7 percent between 1950 and 1975. The line for growth rates points upward, but shows a recent dip, and is therefore not as dramatically threatening as that in the top chart.

The bottom chart shows that population has grown from somewhat less than 10 million on the eve of the agricultural age. In the first rise in the curve, population expanded gradually toward the limit

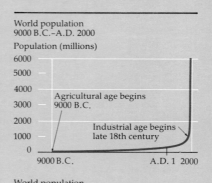

World population
9000 B.C.–A.D. 2000
Population (millions)

Agricultural age begins
9000 B.C.

Industrial age begins
late 18th century

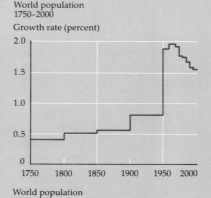

World population
1750–2000
Growth rate (percent)

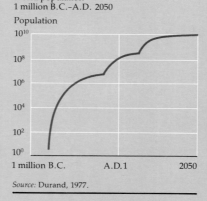

World population
1 million B.C.–A.D. 2050
Population

Source: Durand, 1977.

supportable by hunting and gathering. With the adoption of farming and animal husbandry, a second burst of population growth began. Eventually—though much more quickly than in the first case—the technological limits were again reached, and population stabilized at around 300 million in the first millenium A.D. From the late eighteenth century the industrial age triggered a third burst of population growth. It began from a much higher base and has covered a much shorter period, but on a logarithmic scale it appears no more rapid or unusual than earlier growth spurts.

Which chart best portrays the past and the prospects for the future? The top one emphasizes the special character of recent population growth, setting current experience apart from thousands of years of earlier history. It conveys a sense of crisis. The middle chart highlights the substantial acceleration in growth rates, especially in the past quarter century, that produced this expansion, and the current downward trend in those rates. It suggests that managing population growth is possible. The bottom figure underlines the likelihood of an eventual equilibrium between population and resources, achieved either by a decline in birth rates or an unwelcome rise in death rates. It calls attention to the need to achieve equilibrium by a decline in birth rates.

---

would produce a population 25 percent smaller in the year 2050 than that resulting from the standard fertility decline. Combined with rapid mortality decline, the population would still be 20 percent smaller (see Figure 4.8). Insofar as mortality and fertility declines are linked, the combined rapid path for both is more realistic; it illustrates the relatively small effect that rapid mortality decline would have on population size, especially if fertility is falling. However, the implications of a faster mortality decline are not the same for all regions. In Latin America and in East Asia, where mortality

is already low and fertility has fallen, the population in 2050 would be only 2 to 3 percent greater if rapid mortality decline were added to rapid fertility decline. But where mortality and fertility remain high—as in sub-Saharan Africa and South Asia—rapid mortality decline combined with standard fertility decline would produce a population in 2050 about 10 percent greater. But even that difference is much smaller than the difference between rapid and standard fertility decline: South Asia's population would be more than 20 percent smaller and Africa's about 50 percent

TABLE 4.5

Projections of population size in selected countries, 2000 and 2050
(millions)

Country	1982 Population	Population in 2000			Population in 2050		
		Standard fertility and mortality decline	Rapid fertility decline and standard mortality decline	Rapid fertility and mortality decline	Standard fertility and mortality decline	Rapid fertility decline and standard mortality decline	Rapid fertility and mortality decline
Bangladesh	93	157	136	139	357	212	230
Brazil	127	181	168	169	279	239	247
Egypt	44	63	58	58	102	84	88
El Salvador	5	8	8	8	15	12	13
India	717	994	927	938	1,513	1,313	1,406
Indonesia	153	212	197	198	330	285	298
Kenya	18	40	34	35	120	69	73
Korea, Rep. of	39	51	49	50	67	63	65
Mexico	73	109	101	101	182	155	160
Nigeria	91	169	143	147	471	243	265

smaller with a rapid rather than a standard decline in fertility (see Figure 4.8).

These differences between rapid and standard declines in fertility have far-reaching consequences. To take the example of Bangladesh, Table 4.6 shows what would happen to its population density and the size of its school-age and working-age population under the standard and rapid assumptions about declining fertility. Under both, population and average density will increase for the next seventy years. But the pressure on land (reflected in the projections of agricultural densities), already high, would more than double by the year 2050 under the standard assumption; under the rapid assumption, it would be higher than now in the year 2000 but would then begin to fall. The number of school-age children would almost double under the standard fertility decline by the year 2000; were fertility rates to decline rapidly, the number would still increase by 50 percent by the year 2000 but would then stop increasing. Though the number of people of working age would continue to rise under both scenarios, far fewer new jobs would need to be created if fertility declined rapidly; in the year 2050 there would be 100 million fewer people of working age. Of course, Bangladesh is just one example. And since its current fertility is high, the differences between the two projections are especially large.

The effects of a rapid fertility decline on the age structure of a country could, in principle, be a concern. It is often thought that rapid fertility decline causes a sharp rise in the ratio of old people to young, or a shrinking of the work force. In fact, this does not happen. In Brazil, if rapid rather than standard fertility decline is assumed, the number of people under twenty would be 31 percent of the population instead of 32 percent in the year 2020 (see Figure 4.9). In absolute numbers, there would be almost as many young people as there are today because of the momentum effect of today's young people becoming parents in the next two decades. As for old people, their proportion does increase rapidly, but it does so in both projections. With rapid declines in both fertility and mortality, the elderly, now about 4 percent of the population, would constitute 9.2 percent of the population in 2020, compared with 7.7 percent under the standard declines—in either case still less than the 12 percent obtaining in the United States today.

The rapid paths of mortality and fertility decline would be difficult but not impossible to attain. For India a rapid decline implies a total fertility rate of 2.2 in the year 2000 (compared with 2.9 under the standard assumption and about 4.8 today); for Brazil it implies a rate of 2.1 (compared with 2.6 under the standard assumption and about 3.9 today). These rates are below those in China (now about 2.3) and Korea (2.7) today. They require that girls who are now growing up in families of about four children have only two children themselves, whereas their grandmothers had five or six. Rapid mortality decline would mean, for Brazil, life expectancy in the year 2000 of 73, compared with 69 in the standard projection. In India life expectancy would be 65 in 2000 instead of 61.

The implied declines still produce relatively high annual rates of population growth in the year 2000: 1.6 percent in Brazil, 1.2 percent in India, and 2.6 percent in Kenya (compared with 3.9 percent in

TABLE 4.6
Population size and density in Bangladesh under two fertility assumptions, 1982–2050

		2000		2050	
Indicator	1982	Standard decline	Rapid decline	Standard decline	Rapid decline
Population density					
Persons per square kilometer	646	1,090	944	2,479	1,472
Rural population per hectare of farmland[a]	9	13	12	22	9
Population size (millions)					
Total population	93	157	136	357	212
Urban[b]	11	35	30	157	134
Rural	82	122	106	200	78
School-age (5-14 years)	23	43	33	55	30
Working-age (15-64 years)	51	84	85	246	139

Urban and rural population (from the table above)

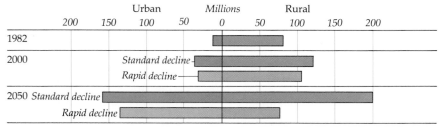

a. Farmland is defined as arable land plus land under permanent crops; the area is assumed to remain constant throughout the projection period.
b. Urban population is assumed to grow at a constant rate of 3 percent a year between 2000 and 2050.
Sources: FAO, 1981; World Bank data.

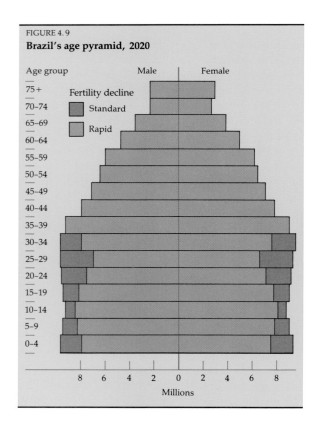

FIGURE 4.9
Brazil's age pyramid, 2020

the standard projection; because fertility is very high in Kenya and other African countries, it will probably take more than two decades for population growth rates to fall to 2 percent). In the long run many countries may wish to reduce population growth to less than 1 percent, already a goal in China. But for the next several decades most developing countries will need to make a concerted effort just to reduce population growth to a rate closer to 1 percent.

Some countries have chosen to set quantitative targets based on feasible target declines in mortality and fertility (see Chapter 8). Bangladesh has already adopted a goal of a total fertility rate of 2.0 in the year 2000, lower than the rate assumed for it under a rapid path of fertility decline. Thailand is aiming for a total fertility rate of 2.6 by 1986, and Indonesia for a rate of 2.7 by 1990. India is aiming for a crude birth rate of 21 per thousand by 1996. The rapid declines in mortality and fertility provide only one possible set of goals. They take no real account of national differences in the seriousness of the population problem, or of the social, political, and administrative possibilities in dealing with it. These are the subjects of the following chapters.

5 The consequences of rapid population growth

This chapter shows that rapid population growth—at rates above 2 percent, common in most developing countries today—acts as a brake on development. Up to a point, population growth can be accommodated: in the past three decades many countries have managed to raise average income even as their populations grew rapidly. In that strict sense, population growth has been accommodated. But the goal of development extends beyond accommodation of an ever larger population; it is to improve people's lives. Rapid population growth in developing countries has resulted in less progress than might have been—lost opportunities for raising living standards, particularly among the large numbers of the world's poor.

The conclusion that rapid population growth has slowed development is by no means straightforward or clearcut (see Box 5.1). Under certain conditions moderate population growth can be beneficial. As Chapter 4 showed, in Europe, Japan, and North America economic growth has been accompanied by moderate population growth, which may have stimulated demand, encouraged technological innovation, and reduced investment risks. Moderate labor force growth, combined with extra spending on education, can also mean continuous upgrading of the labor force with better educated workers. In sparsely populated countries, faster population growth shortens the time required to reach the population size that provides economies of scale in transport, communications, social services, and production. Some developing countries could benefit from such economies of scale, especially in rural areas. And a big population can increase a country's economic as well as political and military power; in a world of economic and political uncertainty, countries such as India and China can seem to benefit from the sheer size of their domestic markets.

But these benefits derive from a moderate increase in population. Most developing countries are experiencing growth that, by historical standards, is faster than that. Even in uncrowded countries, the long-term benefits of having more people must be weighed against the immediate costs of coping with rapid growth. In those few countries lacking the people to exploit their natural resources, immigration from neighboring countries, if politically feasible, would be less costly and more effective than a fast natural rate of population growth. And the economic success of many small countries—Denmark, Hong Kong, Singapore, and Switzerland—shows that urbanization and trade provide other means to achieve the scale economies of a large population.

There are several reasons why population growth in developing countries is today a greater economic burden than it once was in today's developed countries:

- Population growth is now much more rapid. As Chapter 4 showed, in industrializing Europe it seldom exceeded 1.5 percent a year, compared with the 2 to 4 percent that most developing countries have averaged since World War II.

- Unlike nineteenth century Europe, large-scale emigration from today's developing countries is not possible.

- Compared with Europe, Japan, and North America in their periods of fastest population growth, income in developing countries is still low, human and physical capital are less built up, and in some countries political and social institutions are less well established.

- Many developing countries whose economies are still largely dependent on agriculture can no longer draw on large tracts of unused land.

This chapter begins by emphasizing that the implications of population growth differ considerably among countries, depending on their current social, economic, and political conditions. Next it reviews how rapid population growth affects the economy as a whole through savings and investment. It then considers the experience of countries

Box 5.1 Consequences of population growth: conflicting views

The traditional Malthusian concern is that population growth will sooner or later run up against the limits of the earth's finite stock of resources. In his *First Essay on Population*, Malthus argued that the inherent capacity of population to grow exceeds the earth's capacity to yield increases in food, because of limits to the supply of cultivable land. Unrestrained population growth eventually leads to falling wages and rising food prices because, as the labor force expands, a rising ratio of labor to land leads to smaller and smaller increments in output per worker. Population growth is ultimately checked by rising mortality.

In the twentieth century this argument has been extended to the availability of energy and minerals, the effects of rising environmental pollution, and so on. In *The Limits to Growth*, Club of Rome researchers built a simulation model on the assumption that the pace of technological change would be insufficient to overcome diminishing returns arising from limited supplies of essential resources. Falling standards of living and increasing levels of pollution would lead to a population collapse within 100 years.

A related view is that some resources—land, forests, fisheries—though fixed, are renewable, but that their sustainable yields do have a maximum limit. Some harvests may exceed this maximum, but they lead to a permanent reduction in the long-run productivity of land. A population whose needs (subsistence and commercial) exceed sustainable yields will have lower per capita incomes in the long run.

The claim of diminishing returns to resources can easily be criticized for its failure to recognize that, as resources are depleted, rising prices reduce consumption and speed the search for substitutes, stimulating technological change. This criticism, extended, leads to the argument that there are no real natural

resource limits, because population growth itself brings the adjustments that continually put off doomsday. To quote from Julian Simon's book, *The Ultimate Resource*: "The ultimate resource is people—skilled, spirited, and hopeful people—who will exert their wills and imaginations for their own benefit and so, inevitably, for the benefit of us all." Simon argues that natural resources are not limited; that scarcity is revealed by prices; and that prices of resources are not rising, at least not as a proportion of the income of the United States. More people implies more ideas, more creative talent, more skills, and thus better technology; in the long run population growth is not a problem but an opportunity.

These different viewpoints each contain important truths. Some resources are finite; even if prices have not increased (and they may have done so in relation to incomes outside the United States), there have been fundamental structural changes in the balance between population and resources. Human ingenuity might be a match for these changes, but it might be able only to maintain income, not to lift millions of people out of poverty. Or it may reduce poverty very slowly: even with the assumption of technological change built into Simon's model, there are "short-run" difficulties. His short run is thirty to eighty years, and in that period he finds even moderate population growth to be detrimental to human welfare. In the short run, ideas may be lost and Einsteins go undiscovered if many children receive little schooling. Policymakers and poor people live in the short run; they do not wish to go through a period of greater deprivation to adapt eventually to rapid population growth.

At the same time, there is little doubt that the key to economic growth is people, and through people the advance of

human knowledge. Per capita measures of income should not be used to imply that the denominator, people, contributes nothing to the numerator, total income. Nor is population growth in and of itself the main cause of natural resource problems—air pollution, soil degradation, even food availability.

This Report therefore takes a position that is neither hopeless nor overly optimistic. The difficulties caused by rapid population growth are not primarily due to finite natural resources, at least not for the world as a whole. But neither does rapid population growth itself automatically trigger technological advance and adaptation. If anything, rapid growth slows the accumulation of skills that encourage technological advance, and insofar as there are diminishing returns to land and capital, is likely to exacerbate income inequalities. This is most obvious at the family level, where high fertility can contribute to a poor start in life for children. But it is also true for countries as a whole.

Moreover, the costs of rapid population growth differ greatly from country to country. Those differences are not confined to differences in natural resources. In countries heavily reliant on agriculture, a scarcity of natural resources does matter. But the underlying problem is low income and low levels of education, which are sources of rapid population growth and simultaneously make the required adjustments to it more difficult. Much of the world's population lives without the benefit of clear signals to encourage smaller families; yet these are the families and the nations in the worst position to make the adaptive responses that rapid population growth requires. That is why rapid population growth is, above all, a development problem.

in coping with rapidly growing populations—their efforts to achieve food security, the effects on their natural resources, the pressures of internal migration and urban growth, and the options that the international economy provides. Throughout this

discussion of the effects of population growth on countries, this chapter will touch on a theme introduced in Chapter 4: the implications of high fertility for poor people and for income inequality. Because the poor are usually last in line for jobs, school places, and public health services, they are more likely to be penalized by rapid population growth.

The chapter does not treat a reduction in the rate of population growth as a panacea for development; macroeconomic and sectoral policies matter at least as much. But it does show that within most countries, for any given amount of resources, a slower rate of population growth would help to promote economic and social development.

Differences among countries

The implications of population growth differ considerably among developing countries. Countries where education levels are already high, where much investment in transport and communications systems is in place, and where political and economic systems are relatively stable, are well equipped to cope with rapid population growth. This is true whether or not their natural resources are limited or their countries already "crowded," as in the fast-growing East Asian economies such as Hong Kong, Korea, Singapore, and more recently Malaysia and Thailand. But these tend also to be countries where population growth is now slowing.

Countries with untapped natural resources could in the long run support more people. But rapid population growth makes it hard for them to develop the human skills and administrative structures that are needed to exploit their resources. In Brazil, Ivory Coast, and Zaire, for example, the development of unused land will require large complementary investments in roads, public services, and drainage and other agricultural infrastructure. Natural resources are not by themselves sufficient (or even necessary) for sustained economic growth.

Where the amount of new land or other exploitable resources is limited—as in Bangladesh, Burundi, China, Egypt, India, Java in Indonesia, Kenya, Malawi, Nepal, and Rwanda—the short-run difficulties are more obvious. In some areas crop yields are still relatively low, leaving room for rapid growth in agricultural production; in others, the expansion of manufacturing industry could provide exports to pay for extra food imports. But both solutions require costly investments, development of new institutions, and numerous economic and social adjustments—all easier if population is growing only slowly.

In any society, change becomes easier if technology is advancing rapidly. From one point of view, population growth itself helps to bring about technological change: in agricultural societies it may help spur the development of new farming methods needed to maintain per capita output. In earlier centuries it may even have helped provide the minimum population required to support a small religious or artistic elite.

But throughout the modern technological era, there is no evidence that a large or rapidly growing population has itself been influential in promoting new technology. The money and research skills needed for important advances—the Green Revolution, for example—are overwhelmingly in the rich countries where population growth is slow. If anything, these advances have brought labor-saving, not labor-using, innovations. Although adjustment and technical progress can accompany population growth, slower population growth would permit them to raise average incomes all the faster.

Macroeconomic effects of rapid population growth

In a crude arithmetical sense, differences in population growth rates since the 1950s have helped to perpetuate international differences in per capita incomes. Between 1955 and 1980, GNP grew at about 4 percent a year in the low-income countries. This growth in general produced modest increases in income per person (see Table 5.1). However, in many of the poorest countries—Bangladesh and most of sub-Saharan Africa—economic activity slowed considerably in the 1970s. Coupled with rapid (and in some cases, accelerating) population growth, this economic slowdown resulted in stagnating or declining per capita incomes.

In most middle-income countries GNP growth has been much faster—between 5 and 6 percent a year—so that even with rapid population growth, per capita income grew by about 3 percent a year. Industrial countries achieved only sluggish GNP growth during the 1970s, but their low population growth—1 percent a year or less—meant that their increases in per capita income were in general almost as large as in the high-growth, middle-income countries. These increases came on top of much higher initial incomes, so that the absolute gulf between them and the rest of the world widened considerably.

The middle-income countries have shown that rapid population growth can go hand in hand with substantial gains in per capita income. But the long-run relation is more complex than that implied by a simple division of total income by numbers of people. Indeed, that simple division implies, wrongly, that people are the problem. One question is how population growth affects the distribution of income within countries, and especially growth in income of poorer groups (see Box 5.2). More generally, the question is whether a rapid pace of population growth helps or harms economic growth. There are several ways population growth can affect economic growth: through its influence on savings per person, on the amount of capital invested per person, and on the efficiency with which the economy operates.

though its effects on monetized savings are small. First, the bulk of monetized household savings in developing countries is produced by relatively few wealthy families. They tend to have few children, so their savings are little affected by the burden of their dependents. In contrast, the majority of families are poor and save little. Parents have no choice but to pay for what their children consume by reducing their own consumption or by "dissaving"—for example, by farming their land more intensively than can be sustained in the long run. If parents have more children than they want, their ability to make best use of the resources they

TABLE 5.1
Growth of population, GNP, and GNP per capita, 1955–80
(average annual percentage change)

Country group	Population		GNP		GNP per capita	
	1955–70	*1970–80*	*1955–70*	*1970–80*	*1955–70*	*1970–80*
All developing countries	2.2	2.2	5.4	5.3	3.1	3.1
Low-income	2.1	2.1	3.7	4.5	1.6	2.4
China	2.0	1.8	3.3	6.0	1.3	4.1
India	2.2	2.1	4.0	3.4	1.8	1.3
Other	2.4	2.7	4.4	2.7	2.0	0.0
Middle-income	2.4	2.4	6.0	5.6	3.5	3.1
Industrial market economies	1.1	0.8	4.7	3.2	3.6	2.4
Europe	0.7	0.2	4.8	2.6	4.1	2.4
Japan	1.0	1.1	10.3	5.4	9.2	4.2
United States	1.4	1.0	3.4	3.1	2.0	2.1
World[a]	1.9	1.9	5.1	3.8	3.1	1.9

a. Includes high-income oil exporters and industrial nonmarket economies.

Population growth and private savings

A country's savings are generated by households, businesses, and the public sector. Corporate and government savings do not seem to be related in any systematic way to variations in population growth; governments can, within limits, use fiscal and monetary measures to change a country's savings rate, irrespective of demographic conditions. Theory suggests, however, that household savings—usually the largest component of domestic savings—should be reduced by the high dependency burdens associated with rapid population growth. At any given level of output per worker, greater numbers of dependents cause consumption to rise, so savings per capita should fall.

Recent empirical studies find only minor support for this view. But many factors account for the weak link between dependency burdens and savings in developing countries; all point to the probability that high fertility is indeed a burden,

do have is harmed. Whether they are restricting investment in their farm, or in their children's education, or in security for their old age, their high fertility contributes to their poverty. But even with fewer children, poor parents might not increase their savings. Instead, they might simply consume a bit more themselves.

A second reason for the apparently weak link between savings and dependency burdens is that banking and credit systems are not well established in developing countries. Poor families (and even the not-so-poor) are unlikely to have financial savings that show up in national accounts; they are more likely to "save" by accumulating land, tools, or other assets. Even if families wanted to save in good times (say, before children are born or after children are old enough to work) and borrow in difficult times, they probably could not without paying a steep price in terms of low real interest rates for saving and high rates for borrowing. A third reason, as explained in Chapter 4, is that

Box 5.2 Prospects for poverty and population growth, 1980–2000

How would a faster decline in population growth affect the number of poor people in the year 2000? Many other economic, political, and social factors, in addition to population, will influence levels of poverty in the next fifteen years. But some simple assumptions allow illustrative estimates. In a World Bank study, the poor were defined as those with annual per capita incomes below $135 (in constant 1980 dollars). Based on the experience of many countries, projected income growth in each of forty countries (comprising 80 percent of the population of developing countries) was used to compute the change in income for the poorest groups. The findings were combined with World Bank country projections of population growth to simulate future shifts in income distribution.

The exercise showed that the predicted share of income going to the poorest 40 percent would hardly change, from 14 percent in 1980 to 15 percent in 2000. The estimated number of poor people would fall, however, because of income growth. Using the population growth rate based on a "standard" decline in fertility (described in Chapter 4), the number of poor in these forty countries would fall from 630 million in 1980 to 410 million in 2000. With a "rapid" decline in fertility, the number could be almost 100 million fewer—although at 321 million, it would still exceed the total number of people in Bangladesh, Nigeria, and Pakistan today.

Regional differences are worth empha-sizing. Economic prospects are so limited in sub-Saharan Africa that all projections point to an increase in poverty. If fertility decline occurs only as in the standard projection—and even that implies considerable decline—the number of people living in poverty at the end of the century will still increase by nearly 70 percent. With a rapid fall in fertility, the number of poor would increase by less than 20 percent—in the circumstances, a substantial achievement.

In South and East Asia, excepting China, economic prospects are better, so that a small reduction in the number of poor can be anticipated even assuming the standard fertility decline. Poverty could be reduced by almost 40 percent, however, with a rapid fall in fertility. Grouping together Latin America, the Middle East, and North Africa—where the poor are fewer than in Asia and in the rest of Africa—rapid fertility decline could help to reduce the number in poverty by 70 percent. As for China, where fertility is already low, the number of poor can be expected to decline by between 80 and 90 percent by the year 2000.

The exercise probably understates the effect of rapid fertility decline in reducing poverty. A faster reduction in fertility is likely to be associated with a narrowing of differences in educational investment by socioeconomic class, and an increase in wages in relation to rents and profits. These imply a more equal distribution of income than assumed in the projections, and a more rapid elimination of poverty.

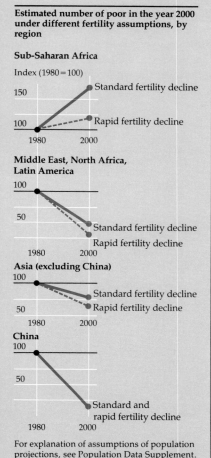

Estimated number of poor in the year 2000 under different fertility assumptions, by region

For explanation of assumptions of population projections, see Population Data Supplement.

---

poor people may see children themselves as a way of "saving" for old age.

These reasons explain why high dependency burdens reduce household savings rates in industrial countries but not in the developing world. In developing countries, though there is no direct link from fertility to household savings, they do become indirectly linked as development proceeds. For example, as more women work in the modern sector, family savings tend to rise and fertility falls; as urbanization proceeds and financial markets improve, monetized savings rise and fertility falls.

Capital widening

Although rapid population growth does not seem to influence the supply of financial savings, it clearly affects the demand for savings. To maintain income, capital per person (including "human capital," that is, a person's education, health, and skills) must be maintained. And as populations grow, "capital widening" is needed to maintain capital per person. But slower population growth releases investable resources for "capital-deepening"—that is, increasing capital per person. Of course, there may be economies of scale in the provision of schooling, health, and jobs in factories and on farms. But the evidence on education suggests that capital-widening—spreading resources over more and more people—can be counterproductive.

SCHOOLING REQUIREMENTS AND CAPITAL WIDENING. In industrial countries, school-age populations are expected to grow slowly, if at all, over the next two decades (see Figure 5.1). The same is true of those developing countries, such as China, Colombia, and Korea, where fertility has already fallen substantially. In Colombia, the number of school-age children doubled between 1950 and 1970. But it increased only slightly in the 1970s,

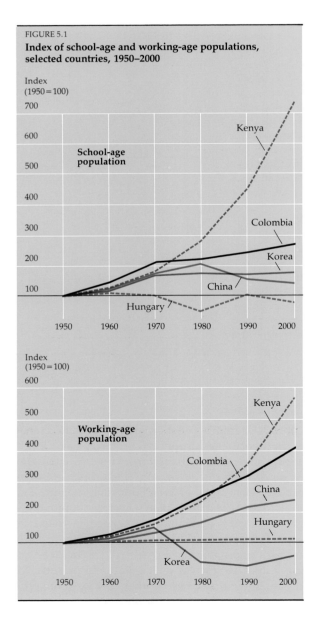

FIGURE 5.1

Index of school-age and working-age populations, selected countries, 1950–2000

because fertility had started to fall in the late 1960s. This allowed enrollment rates to rise; as the children of poor parents were least likely to have been enrolled before, the poor probably benefited most from the spread of education.

For high-fertility countries, the situation could not be more different. Countries such as Kenya face a doubling or tripling of their school-age population by the end of the century. The main implication is clear. More school-age children require more spending on education, even if the objective is just to maintain current enrollment rates and standards. As most developing countries want to improve their schools quantitatively and qualitatively, they will have to generate more national savings or curtail other investments in, for example, power and transport. If a country is unwilling or unable to make these sacrifices, spending must be spread over a larger group of school children (to the detriment of the quality of education); otherwise a growing number of children have to be excluded.

These awkward choices come after a period of considerable progress. Over the past twenty years, enrollment rates have increased at the primary, secondary, and university levels in almost all developing countries. (The enrollment rate is the number of students enrolled in schools as a percentage of the school-age population.) In some cases, progress has been remarkable. Education tends to spread as per capita income rises, but some of the lowest-income countries—Sri Lanka, Tanzania, Viet Nam—have already achieved, or are fast approaching, universal primary education.

Such achievements have substantially raised the fiscal burden of education. For the developing countries as a group, public spending on education increased from 2.3 percent of GNP in 1960 to 3.9 percent in 1974, and from 11.7 percent to 15.1 percent of government budgets. But the proportion of GNP allocated to education declined slightly over the 1970s, as did the share of education spending in government budgets, especially in South Asia, the Middle East and North Africa, and Latin America.

The budgetary downgrading of education, coupled with slower economic growth, has reduced the quality of education in many developing countries. One study showed that in Latin America public spending per primary student fell by almost 45 percent in real terms between 1970 and 1978. As a share of educational budgets, spending on non-wage items—chalk, maps, textbooks, and so on—fell in eight out of ten Latin American countries. In twenty-five of fifty-four developing countries surveyed, student-teacher ratios at primary schools have risen; of those twenty-five countries, seventeen were in Africa. Increases in class size often make sense as they raise the productivity of teachers. But in the urban areas of Malawi and Kenya, class size frequently exceeds sixty students. Combined with a lack of teaching materials, large classes make learning difficult.

Developing countries have little scope to reduce educational quality any further. The quality gap between low- and high-income countries is already enormous. Bolivia, El Salvador, Malawi, and the Ivory Coast, for instance, spend less than $2 a year on classroom materials for each child at primary school—compared with more than $300 per student in Scandinavian countries. This gap seems to be widening. In 1960, on average, an OECD country spent fourteen times more per primary school student than did any of the thirty-six countries with per capita incomes below $265 (1975 prices). By 1977 the ratio had risen to 50:1.

These differences in educational quality are clearly reflected in student achievement. Research on twenty-five countries has shown that, after approximately the same number of years in school, schoolchildren in low- and middle-income countries have learned significantly less science than those in industrial countries. Quality can also make a considerable difference within developing countries. In a study of Brazil, Colombia, India, and Thailand, the quality of schools and teachers—measured by a large number of indicators—explained more than 80 percent of the variance in student scores on standardized science tests. The poor are more likely to attend schools of lower quality (and to leave school sooner); so rapid expansion of school systems to accommodate growing populations often means that the differences in skills between rich and poor, though falling in terms of years of schooling, are persisting because of school quality differences.

As lower fertility slows the growth of the school-age population, it can ease the pressures on the education system. In Egypt, for example, if fertility does not fall, the number of children of primary school age would double by the end of the century. With the standard decline in fertility described in Chapter 4, the number would increase by 65 percent; with the rapid decline, by only 20 percent. The difference between a standard decline and a rapid one would be about 2 million fewer children a year enrolled in primary schools in the years 2000 to 2015. Fewer births in the early 1980s due to a

rapid decline in fertility would decrease the size of the age group eligible for Egypt's secondary schools and universities starting in the late 1990s.

Less rapidly growing enrollment produces considerable financial savings; these can be used to improve school quality. One projection, for Malawi up to 2015, started with the assumption that recurrent costs (essentially teachers' salaries) were held constant at their 1980 level of $12.50 per student. With unchanged fertility, the budget for primary education would double about every fifteen years, even if nothing were done to improve the coverage and quality of primary schools. Thus the education budget's share in GDP would increase from 0.7 percent in 1980 to about 1 percent in 1995 if the economy of Malawi were to grow at about 3 percent a year. The financial savings from lower fertility would accrue slowly at first, but build up considerably (see Table 5.2). Costs excluded from the projections—for instance, outlays for teachers' training and school buildings—would also fall and thus boost these savings.

With the money saved by lower fertility, the Malawi government could afford to enroll the country's total school-age population in 2005 for less than it would cost to enroll 65 percent if fertility did not fall. If the government chose to maintain a 65 percent enrollment rate, its spending per pupil could be doubled in real terms by 2015 without increasing the share of the primary school bud-

TABLE 5.2

Malawi: projected primary-school costs under alternative fertility and enrollment assumptions, 1980–2015
(millions of 1980 dollars)

Year	Standard fertility decline		Rapid fertility decline		Saving with rapid fertility decline (percent)[a]
	(1)	*(2)*	*(3)*	*(4)*	
1980	9.8	9.8	9.8	9.8	n.a.
1995	19.2	26.9	17.9	25.1	7
2000	22.5	34.6	17.6	27.1	22
2005	26.6	40.9	17.6	27.0	34
2010	31.0	47.8	17.3	26.6	44
2015	35.3	54.3	15.3	23.5	57

n.a. Not applicable.
Note: Columns 1 and 3 assume a constant enrollment rate of 65 percent. Columns 2 and 4 assume the enrollment rate increases and is 100 percent by the year 2000.
a. The percentage cost savings are the same under both assumptions regarding enrollment rates. Absolute cost savings are greater under the assumption of universal primary education by the year 2000.

get in GDP. Alternatively, all or part of the savings could be used to increase spending per pupil or to increase the enrollment rate in Malawi's secondary schools which in 1980 stood at only 4 percent. The returns to using the resources saved on account of lower population growth for improving school quality are likely to be higher than the returns to forced rapid expansion of the system if population growth does not slow. But improving quality will be difficult until a larger share of the population has access to basic education, which itself is delayed if the numbers of school-age children are constantly increasing.

The potential for cutting educational costs through lower fertility is obviously largest for those countries with the highest fertility rates. Four African countries—Burundi, Ethiopia, Malawi, Zimbabwe—could save between 50 and 60 percent of their educational spending by 2015 (see Table 5.3), whereas a rapid fertility decline would reduce educational costs by only 5 percent in Colombia, by 1 percent in Korea, and by even less in China, where there is virtually no difference between the rapid and standard fertility assumptions. But these lower-fertility countries have already gained considerably from slower population growth. For example, if Korea's fertility rate had remained at its 1960 level, the number of primary school-age children in 1980 would have been about one-third (2 million) larger than it was. Applying actual 1980 costs per student ($300) to that difference gives a saving in a single year of $600 million, about 1 percent of Korea's GDP.

GROWTH OF LABOR FORCE AND CAPITAL WIDENING. Keeping up with schooling needs is only one way whereby rapid population growth contributes to

capital widening. For most countries the same is true of jobs. In contrast to school-age populations, whose rate of growth starts to slow five or six years after a decline in fertility, the growth of working-age populations is more or less fixed for fifteen to twenty years. People born in 1980–84 will be entering the labor force in 2000 and will still be there almost halfway through the twenty-first century.

High-fertility countries face large increases in their labor forces. As an example, Nigeria's high fertility in the 1970s guarantees that its working-age population will double by the end of this century. Kenya can expect an even larger increase. Where fertility has fallen in the past two decades, the increases will be smaller (see Figure 5.1). China will experience a rise of no more than 45 percent. Korea's working-age population has already fallen substantially and will change little between now and the year 2000. In all these countries the actual labor force—people who are working or looking for jobs—will grow even faster if, for example, more women start looking for paid employment.

In countries with growing labor forces, the stock of capital (both human and physical) must continually increase just to maintain capital per worker and current productivity. Unless this happens, each worker will produce less using the reduced land and capital each has to work with. Productivity, and thus incomes, will then stagnate or even fall. Wages will fall in relation to profits and rents, and thus increase income inequalities—another example of how rapid population growth harms the poor.

For incomes to rise, investment needs to grow faster than the labor force, to ensure capital deepening. Capital deepening involves a growing demand for spending on education, health, roads, energy, farm machinery, ports, factories, and so forth. These requirements have to be traded off against extra consumption. Of course, if educational levels are rising quickly, rapid restocking of the labor force with young, better-educated people can be an advantage. But, as shown above, it is also difficult to increase educational spending per child if population growth is rapid.

Even when developing countries manage to raise investment in line with the growth in their labor force, the contrasts with developed countries are striking. The gap in educational quality has already been described. Investment in physical capital per new worker is also much larger in industrial countries because their labor-force growth is slower and their GDP per capita is so much higher. Even a middle-income country such

TABLE 5.3
Potential savings in primary-school costs under rapid fertility decline, selected countries, 2000 and 2015

Country	Total fertility rate (1981)	Cost savings (percent)[a]	
		2000	2015
Korea, Rep. of	3.0	12	1
Colombia	3.7	23	5
Egypt	4.8	27	23
Burundi	6.5	26	56
Ethiopia	6.5	25	60
Kenya	8.0	22	50
Zimbabwe	8.0	19	48

a. Compared with standard fertility assumption.

as Korea, with a high investment ratio of 31 percent in 1980, could provide only $30,000 of gross investment per new worker, compared with $189,000 in the United States, which had an investment ratio of only 18 percent. (The investment ratio is gross domestic investment as a percentage of gross domestic product.) If all investment in countries such as Bangladesh, Ethiopia, Nepal, and Rwanda had been allocated to potential new workers during 1980, each person would have had less than $1,700 invested on his or her behalf (see Table 5.4). At the other extreme, new workers in Japan would have had about $535,000 of gross investment available. Countries with the lowest absolute levels of investment per potential new worker tend to be those also facing the fastest growth in their working-age populations. Just to maintain the current small amount of investment per potential new worker, they will have to increase their investment rapidly. In contrast, developed countries can increase the capital available to each potential new worker in 2000 even if investment grows by less than 1 percent a year.

Rapid growth in the labor force has two other effects.

• It is likely to exacerbate income inequalities, particularly if many new young workers have little education. When a large proportion of workers are young and inexperienced, their productivity tends to be lower. Except for those who have more education than older workers, their starting wages will tend to be lower, and they must compete with each other. Relatively few will receive employer training to upgrade their skills. Over time, the weight of numbers of the unskilled will hold down their wages in relation to those of skilled workers. A World Bank study of what determines income growth among countries found that as overall income rises, the average contribution of individual workers without education falls—uneducated workers contribute (and probably earn) relatively less than they once did.

• It increases various forms of unemployment. Although population growth has had a relatively small effect on open unemployment in developing countries, this fact does not demonstrate any demographic stimulus to job creation. It simply indicates that unemployment is not a feasible option for most people. Open unemployment is typically found most among educated urban

TABLE 5.4
Gross domestic investment per potential new worker, selected countries, 1980

Country group	Investment ratio[a] (percent)	Gross domestic investment (billions of dollars)	Increase in working-age population[b] 1979–80 (millions)	Gross domestic investment per potential new worker (thousands of 1980 dollars)	Projected increase in working-age population 1980–2000 (percent)
Developing countries					
Bangladesh	17	1.90	1.70	1.09	74
Ethiopia	10	0.37	0.24	1.53	76
Nepal	14	0.26	0.21	1.26	78
Rwanda	16	0.18	0.11	1.66	99
Kenya	22	1.31	0.28	4.70	134
Egypt, Arab Rep.	31	7.12	0.80	8.96	68
Thailand	27	9.03	0.65	10.66	73
Colombia	21	6.21	0.62	10.10	66
Korea, Rep. of	31	18.06	0.61	29.85	45
Brazil	22	52.35	1.30	40.36	65
Industrialized countries					
Japan	32	332.80	0.62	535.04	11
Australia	24	35.53	0.16	219.35	19
France	23	149.94	0.33	461.34	13
Germany	25	204.79	0.43	481.33	1
United States	18	465.68	2.46	188.99	15

Note: Countries are listed in ascending order of their GNP per capita in 1982.
a. Gross domestic investment as percentage of gross domestic product.
b. Age cohort 15–64 years.

youths, who are presumably able to draw on family support while seeking work commensurate with their qualifications or expectations. Many others are underemployed: "invisible underemployment" (including part-time and low-productivity workers whose skills would permit higher earnings if better jobs were available) is estimated to range from 20 percent in Latin America to about 40 percent in Africa. In urban areas of most poor countries, occupations that require little or no capital—handicraft production, hawking, and personal services of all sorts—are highly visible areas of the so-called informal sector. These occupations have the advantage of using scarce financial capital efficiently, but the incomes they produce are often extremely low.

STRUCTURAL TRANSFORMATION OF THE LABOR FORCE. As shown in Chapter 4, both urban and rural populations will increase rapidly into the next century in the low-income countries of Asia and Africa. Thus, while the general concern with the provision of productive employment for urban dwellers is well founded, many countries will also face the task of absorbing considerably more workers into the rural economy. This double challenge differs from the historical experience of today's industrialized countries. Their economic growth was helped by a massive shift of labor from agriculture, where the amount of capital per worker and average productivity was relatively low, to industry and services, where they were relatively high. The two principal reasons for this structural transformation of the labor force are well known:

● As incomes rise, people spend a smaller proportion on unprocessed agricultural produce and a larger proportion on industrial products and services.

● Increases in agricultural productivity—made possible by technological innovations and accumulated investment—allow output to grow with a constant or even declining farm labor force.

As average incomes increase in today's developing countries, and as population growth rates slow, the number of workers in agriculture should eventually decline. In some upper-middle-income countries in Latin America, including Argentina, Chile, Uruguay, and Venezuela, already less than 20 percent of the labor force is employed in agriculture. But the transfer of labor out of agriculture has proceeded much more slowly in much of low-income South Asia and sub-Saharan Africa. There are two reasons: their high rates of growth of the total labor force and their low initial shares in modern sector employment.

In 1980 the share of the labor force in agriculture averaged 73 percent in low-income countries (excluding China and India); in most countries of sub-Saharan Africa it was between 80 and 90 percent. During the 1970s the total labor force in these countries grew at 2.3 percent a year. The rate of growth will increase to 3 percent a year between 1980 and 2000. The effects on the future growth of the agricultural labor force can be illustrated with some hypothetical calculations.

Figure 5.2 portrays a country in which 70 percent of the labor force is in agriculture and in which nonagricultural employment is growing at 4 percent a year. It shows, for different rates of growth of the total labor force, the time required for the size of the agricultural labor force to start to decline in absolute numbers. For example, if it is assumed that the annual growth of the total labor force is 2.5 percent (which, combined with a 4 percent growth in nonagricultural employment, is a fairly typical combination in low-income countries), the agricultural labor force would continue to grow in absolute size (though declining slowly as a share of the total) for about fifty years (point x). If the total labor force were to grow by 3 percent a year instead, the time required for the agricultural labor force to start to decline would nearly double to ninety-five years (point y). Although this example oversimplifies—for instance, it does not admit the possibility of massive urban unemployment—it does seem clear that the size of the agricultural

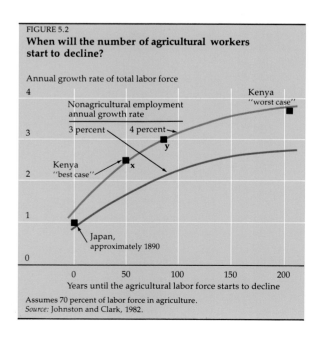

FIGURE 5.2

When will the number of agricultural workers start to decline?

Annual growth rate of total labor force

Years until the agricultural labor force starts to decline

Assumes 70 percent of labor force in agriculture.
Source: Johnston and Clark, 1982.

88

labor force in most of today's low-income countries will go on increasing well into the twenty-first century.

In western Europe and Japan, by contrast, the number of farm workers began to fall when the labor force was still largely agrarian, so there were never any significant increases in the size of the agricultural labor force. In Japan, for example, the share of agriculture in the labor force in the mid-1880s was about 75 percent—much the same as in today's low-income countries, and nonagricultural employment grew at between 2 and 3.5 percent a year in the late 1800s and early 1900s. In these two respects Japan was similar to many low-income countries today. But the total labor force was growing at less than 1 percent a year, much slower than in developing countries today (see Figure 5.2). So only modest rises in nonagricultural employment were necessary to absorb the rise in the rural work force. Between 1883–87 and 1913–17, the share of the labor force in agriculture fell by twenty percentage points and the absolute number of farm workers fell by some 1 million.

Kenya provides a dramatic contrast with the Japanese case. Only about 14 percent of the Kenyan labor force is in wage employment in the "modern" economy and about half of them are in the public sector. Between 1972 and 1980 employment in the modern sector grew at 4.3 percent a year, higher than in Japan in the late nineteenth century but somewhat slower than the growth of GDP (4.9 percent). But the rate of growth of the total labor force was very rapid—3.5 percent. There was some shift of the labor force into the modern economy, since growth in modern sector employment was faster than in the total labor force. But the shift was small. Nonwage employment—mainly in agricul-

ture—absorbed more than 80 percent of the increase in the labor force.

Agricultural output and jobs must continue to grow rapidly in Kenya: the effective demand for food is rising at about 4 percent a year, so that domestic production—or other agricultural exports to pay for food imports—must grow at least at the same pace to avoid draining foreign exchange from other sectors (if constant terms of trade are assumed). And the rest of the economy has only a limited capacity to absorb labor. The public sector accounted for about two-thirds of the growth in wage employment during 1972–80—the number of schoolteachers rose by more than the increase in manufacturing workers—but its growth is constrained by fiscal limits. Industry is relatively small and capital intensive, so its work force is unlikely to expand much.

These constraints are highlighted by the projections in Table 5.5. In the "worst" case—essentially a continuation of recent trends, with the labor force growing at 3.5 percent a year and nonagricultural employment at 4 percent—Kenya's agricultural work force would still be increasing in absolute size even 100 years from now (see also Figure 5.2). In the "best" case, which assumes the same growth in nonagricultural employment but slower growth in the labor force after 2000 (implying a decline in fertility starting in the mid-1980s), structural transformation proceeds at a faster pace. Even so, agriculture must absorb more than 70 percent of the growth in the labor force for the rest of this century. It is only after 2025 that the number of workers in agriculture starts to decline. In the meantime, how to absorb these extra farm workers productively is a critical issue in Kenya and in many other countries in sub-Saharan Africa and South Asia.

TABLE 5.5
Kenya: projections of employment by sector, under two scenarios, 1976–2050
(millions of workers)

Employment sector[a]	1976	2000	2025	2050
Nonagricultural employment[b]	1.2	3.0	8.0	21.8
Agricultural employment				
"Worst" case[c]	3.8	9.9	24.1	56.9
"Best" case[d]	3.8	9.9	12.4	4.5

a. Unemployment held constant in all years and in both cases (about 1.2 million workers).
b. Increases at 4 percent a year in both scenarios.
c. Labor force grows at a constant 3.5 percent a year.
d. Growth of labor force slows from 3.5 percent a year in 1976–2000, to 2.5 percent a year in 2001–10, to 1.5 percent a year in 2011–25, and to 1 percent a year in 2026–50.

Efficiency: allocating limited capital

Capital deepening (and associated absorption of labor into the modern sector) is not the only contributor to economic growth. Last year's *World Development Report* highlighted the importance of making better use of existing resources, as well as of innovation and entrepreneurship. Promoting efficiency often requires policy reform. For example, many developing countries have a history of subsidizing capital; subsidies have discouraged labor-intensive production and led to inefficient use of scarce capital. Even with reform, efficiency may not come easily; many technological innovations available to developing countries are labor-saving because they come from the capital-rich industrial world. But efficiency is even harder to achieve when population growth is rapid. For example, social and political pressure to employ young people has undoubtedly contributed to the large government sector in many developing countries, and in some countries to regulations designed to stop private employers from reducing their work force. Selective government concern for educated young people in urban areas has led to policies such as Egypt's that guarantee employment to all university graduates. As well as being inefficient, this policy hurts people who are not educated because scarce public spending is

TABLE 5.6
Growth rates of food output by region, 1960–80
(average annual percentage change)

Region or country group	Total		Per capita	
	1960–70	1970–80	1960–70	1970–80
Developing countries	2.9	2.8	0.4	0.4
Low-income	2.6	2.2	0.2	−0.3
Middle-income	3.2	3.3	0.7	0.9
Africa	2.6	1.6	0.1	−1.1
Middle East	2.6	2.9	0.1	0.2
Latin America	3.6	3.3	0.1	0.6
Southeast Asia[a]	2.8	3.8	0.3	1.4
South Asia	2.6	2.2	0.1	0.0
Southern Europe	3.2	3.5	1.8	1.9
Industrial market economies	2.3	2.0	1.3	1.1
Nonmarket industrial economies	3.2	1.7	2.2	0.9
World	2.7	2.3	0.8	0.5

Note: Production data are weighted by world export unit prices. Growth rates for decades are based on midpoints of five-year averages except that 1970 is the average for 1969–71.
a. Excludes China.
Sources: FAO; World Bank, 1982b.

diverted for the benefit of those who are relatively well off. Youth unemployment may also contribute to crime and instability and the resulting large amount of service employment as police and private guards in some cities of developing countries. None of these, of course, adds to national income. Crime is tied primarily to poverty and social disorder, but tends to increase wherever there are large cohorts of young people who are unemployed (including in developed countries).

Constraints on agricultural production

Food production in developing countries has increased rapidly in recent decades but has still just kept pace with population growth (see Table 5.6); in the 1970s it failed to do so in many low-income countries, including Bangladesh, Nepal, and twenty-seven of thirty-nine countries in sub-Saharan Africa. Other African countries—including Kenya, Malawi, Rwanda, and Upper Volta—managed only a slight increase in per capita food production. The output of food in China and India has also exceeded population growth since the mid-1960s, but by only a narrow margin.

In the past, increases in food production were mainly due to bringing more land under cultivation: this is still the case in sub-Saharan Africa and in parts of Latin America. About 25 percent of the world's land—some 3.4 billion hectares—is thought to be of agricultural potential. Of this, only about 1.4 billion hectares (40 percent) is being cultivated, so there is little evidence of a global land shortage (see Box 5.3).

For developing countries as a whole, however, increased acreage accounted for less than one-fifth of the growth in agricultural production over the past two decades. In part this is because land reclamation is often more costly than intensifying use of existing land; in part it is because further expansion of the land frontier is constrained in many parts of the world. In sub-Saharan Africa, for example, the development of vast areas is precluded because of such diseases as river blindness (onchocerciasis) and sleeping sickness (trypanosomiasis). The latter renders livestock production virtually impossible on some 10 million square kilometers of higher rainfall areas, 45 percent of all the land in sub-Saharan Africa. Major campaigns have been undertaken to free parts of the Sudanese savanna country from sleeping sickness, but it has not always been possible to prevent a resurgence of the disease. Moreover, insecticides used to control tsetse flies, which spread sleeping sickness, have had undesirable effects on the environment. For that and other reasons, some countries in Africa are reaching the limits of their land (see Box 8.4 in Chapter 8).

In Asia, too, further expansion of agricultural land does not appear to be an option for several countries. For example, in India between 1953–54 and 1971–72, a 66 percent increase in the number of rural households was accompanied by only a 2 percent increase in the cultivated area. As a result, the number of marginal holdings of less than one

Box 5.3 Food supplies for a growing world population

The food crisis of 1972–74 created an atmosphere of impending disaster and a renewed interest in Malthusian pessimism. More recent views point to the success of technological change in agriculture and to the conclusion that the world as a whole is capable of producing enough food for future generations well into the next century. The main issue is not the worldwide availability of food, but the capacity of nations, groups within nations, and individuals to obtain enough food for a healthy diet.

In most countries, particularly low-income ones, the staple food is cereals or coarse grains; they account for about half of total food consumption in developing countries. Over the past thirty years global grain production has doubled and, according to the FAO report *Agriculture: Toward 2000*, could double again by the year 2000. An American study, *The Global 2000 Report to the President*, agrees with this assessment. A doubling of world grain production over twenty years or so amounts to an annual growth rate of about 3.5 percent.

On the demand side, earlier projections indicated that demand for cereals and grains for both human consumption and livestock feed would rise at between 3.0 and 3.5 percent a year, depending on assumptions for population and income growth. More recent projections suggest a much slower growth of global demand. For example, the International Wheat Council's recent *Long-Term Grain Outlook* puts global cereal demand up 50 percent by 2000, equivalent to a rise of about 2.3 percent a year; a report published by the US Department of Agriculture came to similar conclusions. Both of these assessments included projections of grain that would be fed to animals. A World Bank study projects an average growth in the demand for grains of about 2.6 percent a year.

This optimism for the global situation stands in sharp contrast to the assessments for groups of countries, individual countries, and households. Various studies suggest that the gap between domestic supply and demand is projected to widen in the developing countries, particularly because of continued rapid growth in population and income. Centrally planned economies may also continue to have a shortfall. Production in the industrial world is projected to rise, albeit more slowly than in the past, while the growth in its demand is projected to level out.

On a national and household basis, the outlook is even more varied. A number of industrial countries do not produce enough grain or food to satisfy domestic demand. But their national food security is assured because the value of their nonfood exports is usually more than adequate to finance food imports. These countries also have effective methods of distributing food, though their poorest people may be vulnerable. For some of the developing countries the situation is less secure. Estimates by the FAO suggest that in the year 2000 twenty-nine developing countries may be unable to feed themselves from their own land with inputs of fertilizers, seeds, and so on at an "intermediate" level of technology (a basic package of fertilizers, improved seed, and simple conservation measures). Many of these countries are in Africa, where technology is probably below the "intermediate" level (see also Box 8.4). Outside Africa, the group includes Afghanistan, Bangladesh, El Salvador, Haiti, and Jordan.

Increasing domestic production of food is not the only solution. Many developing countries with a chronic food deficit have other options, the main one being to increase exports of nonfood goods so as to finance food imports. For those countries with transitory food deficits, a combination of more exports and better arrangements for storing food may be the answer. For some countries in Africa, to avert a food crisis will require external aid—to finance food imports in the short run and to expand investment in developing long-run potential for food and nonfood production.

Ultimately it is not countries but individuals who suffer from a shortage of food—not because of fluctuations in national production but because of higher food prices, which they cannot afford, or because of inadequate arrangements for marketing food. Their diet will improve only when their general economic state does.

Some research on the global food situation has looked well beyond the end of this century. Bernard Gilland, for example, estimates the maximum global output of food to be 7,500 million tons grain-equivalent (tge) a year. This figure was obtained by multiplying a "realistic" maximum yield of 5 tge per hectare (from the present average of 2 tge per hectare) by 1.5 billion hectares, allowing for a slight increase over the estimated 1.4 billion hectares of land currently used for food production. An additional 500 tge was added for rangeland and marine production. Presently, gross consumption of plant energy for all purposes—food, seed, and animal feed—ranges from 3,000 calories per person per day in South Asia to 15,000 calories in North America, Australia, New Zealand, and France. (Consumption of meat raises consumption of "plant energy" because the conversion of grain to meat through feeding of livestock is inefficient compared with direct consumption of grain.) Gilland selects a "completely satisfactory" average daily per capita allowance of 9,000 calories of "plant energy" (implying some meat consumption), and concludes that the earth has the capacity to support about 7.5 billion people. This population will probably be reached in the second decade of the next century. On a daily per capita allowance of 6,000 calories of plant energy—the current world average—the earth would be capable of supporting about 11.4 billion persons. That number is roughly equal to the projected world stationary population. Cultivated land could be increased more, and land-saving technological advances, especially deriving from genetic engineering, would transform the outlook, allowing for better diets even as population grows. But there are also downside risks (new crop diseases, soil erosion, and climate change).

acre increased from 15.4 million to 35.6 million and their average size fell from 0.27 to 0.14 acres. To take another example, the average land-man ratio in Bangladesh is estimated to have declined from 0.40 acres in 1960–61 to 0.29 acres in 1979–80. More people have been absorbed into agriculture, but incomes have risen little if at all. More people are probably having to earn a living as landless laborers. As their numbers have increased, their wages have tended to fall in relation to those who own (or even rent) land. The agricultural system has adapted, but in ways that have probably increased income inequalities in the countryside.

Another constraint on the use of potential agricultural land is shortage of water. In many developing countries, any large expansion of agricultural production would require some form of irrigation. Worldwide, the area under irrigation expanded by almost 6 million hectares a year during the 1960s. India has shown the most dramatic growth, with the irrigated area increasing from 28 million hectares to 55 million hectares over the past two decades, an average of more than 1 million hectares a year. In the 1970s, however, worldwide expansion of irrigation slowed to just over 5 million hectares a year. This slowdown occurred because some countries, such as Pakistan, started to run out of land that can be irrigated at an acceptable cost.

Shortage of water in many parts of India, in the Nile Basin, in Brazil, and in most of the developing countries is constraining irrigation development, and water transfer projects are being planned on an even bigger scale than those recently built in Pakistan. Countries are also putting more emphasis on groundwater development, on the combined use of ground and surface waters, on water economy, and on more advanced methods of water management. Poor water management is considered by many specialists to be the most important single constraint to irrigated crop production. Bilateral and multinational agencies are now trying to arrest the decline in management standards, and an International Irrigation Management Institute has recently been established to promote better use of water. The challenge will, however, remain formidable, especially in some countries of sub-Saharan Africa, where little or no irrigation has been used in the past. This is particularly true for the Sahelian countries, where progress has been limited mainly because of high construction costs ($10,000 to $15,000 per hectare compared with $2,000 to $5,000 in Asia), low farmer response, and poor project management.

Easing constraints

Multiple cropping—more than one crop a year from the same piece of land—is a typical way for societies to cope with rising populations. In Asia, where the proportion of potential land under cultivation was an estimated 78 percent in 1975, about 7 percent of the cultivated land is cropped more than once. For some Asian countries the proportion is much greater. In the late 1960s 52 percent of cultivated land was cropped more than once in Korea. In Bangladesh in the late 1970s, 43 percent of the land was cropped more than once.

Multiple cropping increases production and uses more labor, so that the chief resource required to feed the growing populations of developing countries is provided by the people themselves. Farm studies in Africa and Asia show that, on average, a 10 percent increase in farming intensity (defined as the percentage of time in the rotation cycle that is devoted to cropping) involves a 3 to 4 percent increase in the amount of labor per hectare. Labor input per hectare increases because, under intensive farming systems, the extra hours required for land preparation, sowing, weeding, and plant protection more than offset the reduction of hours—essentially for land clearing—associated with shorter fallow periods.

But the combined benefits of more employment and more food do not come automatically. Without modern technical packages—including purchased inputs such as fertilizers and improved seeds—and effective price incentives, the amount of labor used can increase faster than output. Less fertile land may be brought under cultivation; good land may be given less time to regain its fertility. Research into farming systems and increased use of agricultural extension services can help ensure that new farming methods are compatible with available resources, including labor. But population pressure is likely to continue. In parts of Africa, and in China, Bangladesh, and Java in Indonesia, population pressure has already forced people to work harder just to maintain income in traditional agriculture.

In most developing countries, however, labor productivity has been maintained. To forestall diminishing returns to labor, intensification of land use has usually been accompanied by better farming methods, the use of fertilizers, investments in irrigation and drainage, and mechanization. However, such measures are possible only where rainfall is favorable—or where water is available for irrigation—and where topography and soils do not impose constraints that cannot be eased at acceptable costs.

Higher population density, by permitting economies of scale in the provision of infrastructure and services, can sometimes help to induce improvements in agriculture. In the United States, for instance, rising population densities stimulated the development of the transport system during the nineteenth century. An improved transport system, in turn, greatly facilitated the growth of agriculture by lowering transport costs and by raising the farmgate prices of agricultural products. But the potential benefits to be gained from higher population densities are not always realized. In rural Bangladesh—one of the most crowded areas in the world—transport, marketing and storage facilities, as well as extension services, are all inadequate.

From one point of view, it is no small achievement to sustain an increase in population on the scale that has occurred, and continues to occur, in many developing countries. But keeping the production of food up with (or even ahead of) growth in population is no guarantee that people have a healthy diet. Where incomes are low and unequally distributed, and increases in food production are just barely ahead of increases in population size, poor people may not be able to afford the

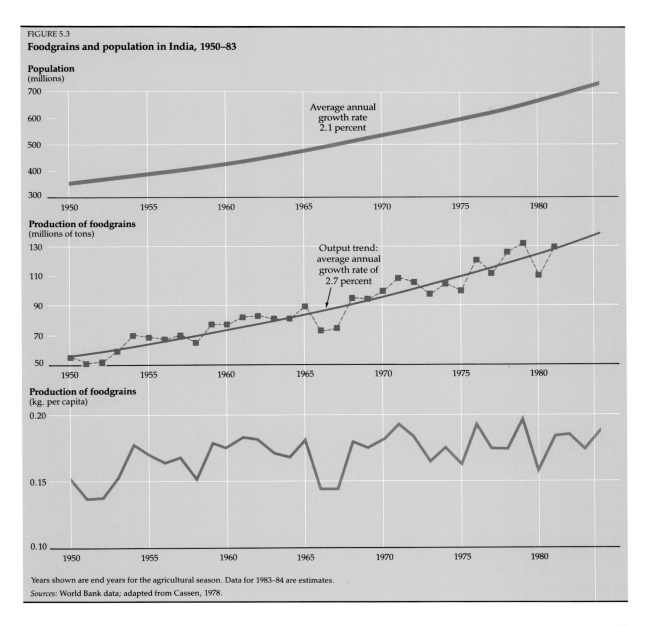

FIGURE 5.3
Foodgrains and population in India, 1950–83

Population
(millions)

Average annual
growth rate
2.1 percent

Production of foodgrains
(millions of tons)

Output trend:
average annual
growth rate of
2.7 percent

Production of foodgrains
(kg. per capita)

Years shown are end years for the agricultural season. Data for 1983–84 are estimates.
Sources: World Bank data; adapted from Cassen, 1978.

93

food they need. Although the amount of labor used in farming has risen in most developing countries, many families have had little or no increase in their income. They are particularly vulnerable when harvests are poor. As Figure 5.3 shows, India has managed to expand its food production faster than its population has grown. But output per person has varied considerably, and in bad years when food prices have risen, the landless poor probably went hungry.

Most developing countries still have potential for yield increases (see Table 5.7). But in some land-scarce countries—for instance, Egypt, China, and Korea—yields are already high. Paddy yields in Egypt in 1979–81 averaged 5.6 tons per hectare,

matching what was achieved in Japan. Because these countries also use land intensively, they need larger inputs of fertilizer to increase food production. A second group of countries are likely to go on importing food indefinitely because of constraints on land, irrigation, and so on. For a third group, although the constraints appear less severe, the process of agricultural modernization may take several decades. In the meantime, they may need to increase their food imports.

Population and the environment

Rapid population growth can contribute to environmental damage, especially when combined

TABLE 5.7
Cereal yields and fertilizer use, selected countries, 1969–81

Country group	All cereal yields (tons per hectare of harvested area)		Fertilizer use (kilograms per hectare of harvested area)	
	1969–71	1979–81	1969–71	1978–80
Industrialized countries				
United States	3.50	4.20	172.4	192.5
Denmark	3.85	4.02	331.0	331.0
Netherlands	4.02	5.69	868.0	1,121.5
Japan	5.04	5.27	426.2	532.6
Developing countries				
Africa				
Burundi	1.04	0.99	0.6	1.1
Cameroon	0.89	0.89	7.9	11.6
Egypt, Arab Rep.	3.85	4.01	115.0	188.5
Kenya	1.47	1.50	18.4	18.4
Malawi	1.00	1.18	6.6	16.1
Zimbabwe	1.08	1.36	54.3	64.2
Tanzania	0.78	0.70	3.3	6.1
Zambia	0.76	0.74	25.4	47.5
Asia				
Bangladesh	1.66	1.96	10.7	31.9
Sri Lanka	2.40	2.42	53.3	70.2
India	1.11	1.34	12.5	31.7
Korea, Rep. of	3.50	4.77	193.1	354.5
Malaysia	2.39	2.82	45.3	102.3
Pakistan	1.21	1.61	23.1	61.2
Philippines	1.30	1.59	23.5	30.7
Thailand	2.01	1.94	9.9	20.1
Latin America				
Argentina	1.71	2.20	3.3	4.4
Brazil	1.33	1.50	24.0	72.6
Colombia	1.72	2.46	43.0	69.0
Chile	1.86	2.12	106.2	84.2
Costa Rica	1.55	2.25	141.9	177.9
Ecuador	1.04	1.61	17.5	48.5
El Salvador	1.57	1.72	104.2	105.3
Guatemala	1.12	1.51	25.8	65.2
Mexico	1.52	2.11	38.7	79.8

Note: Harvested area covers all cropped areas including tree crops.
Sources: FAO, 1982; World Bank.

with certain nondemographic factors. For example, an unequal distribution of farmland, by restricting access to better soils, can help to push growing numbers of people onto ecologically sensitive areas—erosion-prone hillsides, semiarid savannas, and tropical forests. One example is the migration to the Amazon rainforests from rural areas of northeastern Brazil, where 6 percent of the landholdings account for more than 70 percent of the land area. Social changes can also bring ecological threats: in Kenya and Uganda pastoral groups, whose political power was destroyed under colonial rule, have seen their closed system of communal management converted into open access to their land. With added population growth, overgrazing and severe environmental damage have followed. Population pressure is not always the main culprit, but it almost always exacerbates the problem.

Of course, the environmental problems of the developing countries are not confined to the countryside. Industrialization and urbanization have already led to severe air, water, and noise pollution in some cities. Although such pollution is a hazard to public health, it does not pose as immediate a threat to the economic life of low-income countries as does deforestation and desertification. In dry countries, these two threats are closely linked.

Deforestation

Forests are central to the economic and ecological life of many developing countries. They help to control floods and thus protect roads in mountainous and wet areas. Floods and landslides have become serious problems in steep, deforested areas such as in Nepal (see Box 5.4). Forests also protect power production from hydroelectric schemes. When watersheds are cleared, dams often start to silt up. Less electricity can be generated (because less water can flow through the turbines); thus the economic life of the investment is reduced. For example, the useful life of the Ambuklao Dam in the Philippines has been cut from sixty to thirty-two years because of deforestation.

Satisfying the demand for firewood is a major cause of deforestation, particularly in the drier and higher regions where trees grow slowly. To meet their daily energy needs, an estimated 1.3 billion people must cut firewood faster than it can be replaced by natural growth. Unfortunately, those who are exhausting the forest seldom recognize what they are doing. The depletion becomes apparent only when obtaining adequate supplies requires more physical effort or greater expense. In the Gambia and Tanzania population growth has made wood so scarce that each household spends 250 to 300 worker-days a year gathering the wood it needs. In Addis Ababa, Ethiopia, the price of wood increased tenfold during the 1970s and now claims up to 20 percent of household income.

The scarcity of wood has profound implications for everyday life in developing countries. When there is not enough fuel to heat food and boil water, diseases spread more rapidly. In China more than 70 million rural households—about 350 million people—suffer serious fuel shortages for up to six months a year when crop residues are exhausted and wood is unavailable in deforested areas. In much of West Africa, families traditionally cooked two meals a day. Now, because wood

Box 5.4 Reclaiming the Himalayan watersheds

The Ganges river, which flows through India and Bangladesh, floods every year, causing millions of dollars of damage and incalculable human suffering. But the floods and the resulting damage are much worse than they need be. In the mountainous watersheds of northern India and Nepal, population growth has led to severe deforestation, which has caused the area's heavy rains to run off rather than soak into the soil. In the lowland areas surrounding the Ganges, population growth and competition for land

has forced many people to live too close to the river, in the path of the annual floods. As testimony to the effects of population growth, the severity of flooding has increased exponentially over the past twenty years, even though the annual rainfall has hardly changed.

To help combat the flooding, the World Bank is funding a pilot project in the Indian state of Uttar Pradesh to develop nine small watersheds covering 312,000 hectares. By planting trees over a wide area the project will attempt to reclaim

denuded hillsides. It will also encourage stall-feeding of livestock to help alleviate the damage done by roaming animals. Farmland will be terraced to slow down erosion. At the same time, the governments of Bangladesh, India, and Nepal are pursuing policies to reduce rapid population growth, a contributing factor to deforestation as well as high population density in the flood-prone areas (see Chapter 8).

is so scarce, they can do so only once a day or once every other day. A more specific example is that of soybeans in Upper Volta. They are a new crop, are exceptionally nutritious, and have grown well, but they are not popular because they have to be cooked a long time. Similar experiences have been reported in Haiti.

Managed village woodlots, fuelwood plantations, or more efficient wood stoves could do much to ease shortages. For example, a well-managed woodlot planted with fast-growing trees can yield as much as twenty cubic meters of wood per hectare annually, six times the yield of an unmanaged natural forest. However, these and other measures are not easy to introduce. They require local testing and adaptation, large numbers of trained staff, and adequate economic and institutional incentives. But the returns from forestry development can be high. In Ethiopia, where fuelwood shortages have become critical in some regions, estimated rates of return on investments in rural forestry are on the order of 23 percent.

Another major cause of deforestation is the expansion of agriculture. According to the FAO, agricultural growth involves clearing more than 11 million hectares of forest a year, primarily in response to population pressures. Unless these marginal lands are given much commercial attention—fertilizers, irrigation, and so on—they soon tend to become eroded and infertile. When this happens the settlers clear more forest, a destructive and unsustainable process. Fertilizers are often an uneconomic remedy, being expensive and ineffective in the soil and rainfall conditions of many tropical areas.

Desertification

The effects of gradually spreading desert are often confused with those of drought. But droughts, no matter how severe, are ephemeral; when the rains return, the land's inherent productivity is restored. With desertification, even normal rainfall cannot fully restore the land. In extreme cases, land may remain unproductive for many generations unless costly remedies are taken.

While drought can help to turn land into desert and make the effects more obvious to people living there, most scientists agree that changes in climate are not responsible for the vast areas of semiarid land going out of production each year. The direct causes of desertification include overcultivation, overgrazing, and deforestation. These practices strip vegetation from the topsoil and deprive it of

nutrients and organic matter, thereby exposing it to erosion from the sun and wind. These direct causes themselves spring from the pressures of rapid population growth. In trying to obtain more food for themselves and their livestock, growing numbers of people frequently overstretch the carrying capacity of semiarid areas: keeping production high during drought reduces the land's natural resilience and sets it on a course to permanent degradation.

Although some 100 countries are affected by desertification, the process is most serious in sub-Saharan Africa (particularly the Sahel), northwestern Asia, and the Middle East. Every year an additional 200,000 square kilometers—an area larger than Senegal—are reduced by desertification to the point of yielding nothing. And the process is accelerating: more than 20 percent of the earth's surface—now populated by 80 million people—is directly threatened. The human costs of desertification often include malnutrition, threat of famine, and dislocation of people who must abandon their lands to seek employment elsewhere.

Urban population growth and internal migration

Beyond a common concern, perceptions of the problem of the distribution of population vary considerably among developing countries. Some see the countryside as overpopulated in relation to its natural resources. Others complain of labor shortages in remote but resource rich areas. Most commonly, however, maldistribution is described in terms of "overurbanization" caused by "excessive" migration. In some developing countries, rapid urban growth has undoubtedly caused serious administrative difficulties. Urban life requires a complicated set of services—housing, traffic, sewerage, water, and so on—that cannot quickly be scaled up as population grows. City administrations are usually short of money, and may anyway lack the managerial skill to cope with a city that doubles its size in a decade. Where this happens, the results are familiar: unemployment, substandard housing, deteriorating public services, congestion, pollution, crime, and so forth.

An overriding concern with the negative aspects of urban growth, however, has often led policymakers to overlook some of the benefits to be gained from internal migration and urbanization. As a result, many governments have chosen to carry out costly—and often economically inefficient— programs to redistribute population. They would have done better to have concentrated on rural development in areas already settled, on improvements in urban policies and management, on elimination of price distortions (such as keeping food prices low) that encourage urban population growth, and on development of effective family planning programs to reduce rates of natural population increase.

Projections of urban growth (which were shown in Table 4.3) are not meant to predict what will actually happen—merely what would happen if historical trends continued. As such, projections are sensitive to small changes in trends. There is evidence that the rate of urban growth in developing countries slowed slightly after 1973 in response to the world economic slowdown. That decrease could produce a much smaller urban population than shown by the projections. Though this would make urban growth easier to cope with, it would (without a compensating decline in the overall population growth rate) imply faster rural growth.

The benefits and costs of urbanization

Urban growth gives rise to economies of scale. Industries benefit from concentrations of suppliers and consumers, which allow savings in communications and transport costs. Large cities also provide big, differentiated labor markets and may help to accelerate the pace of technological innovation. They also allow economies of scale for such services as water supply and electric power to be exploited. Evidence from India suggests that substantial economies of scale are found in cities of up to 150,000 inhabitants. The point at which diseconomies creep in, because cities are too big, has not been clearly demonstrated.

Against these benefits, unemployment tends to be higher in urban than rural areas. In a survey of fourteen developing countries, only one (the Islamic Republic of Iran) had a higher rural unemployment than urban unemployment rate; in six countries the urban unemployment rate was more than twice the rural rate. Surveys confirm that air pollution, congestion, social disturbances, crime, and similar problems also increase disproportionately with city size. But these problems are often aggravated by poor urban management. Typically, governments reduce the absorptive capacity of cities by intervening in labor markets (for instance, through minimum wage legislation, and licensing requirements and restrictions on small businesses), and by pursuing inappropriate pricing policies for public services. National economic policies—which provide fiscal incentives and low-interest loans to promote capital-intensive industry, for example—may also exacerbate urban problems by encouraging rural-urban migration without creating enough new urban jobs.

Whatever the cause, the drift from countryside to city is a concern to governments. A 1983 UN survey of 126 governments of developing countries found that only 3 considered the distribution of their populations "appropriate." Moreover, all three were governments of small island nations: Barbados, Malta, and Nauru. Concern was greatest in Africa, the Middle East, and low-income Asia: virtually all governments in these regions considered population distribution either "partially appropriate" or "inappropriate." As a remedy, more than three-quarters of all respondents stated that they were pursuing policies to slow down or reverse internal migration.

Between 1925 and 1950 at least 100 million people in the developing countries—about 10 percent of their rural population in 1925—migrated from the countryside to towns and cities. During the following twenty-five years, the numbers rose to an estimated 330 million, equivalent to almost a quarter of the rural population of the developing countries in 1950. Population movements within rural and urban areas, and temporary migration, have undoubtedly involved even more people, although their numbers are not reliably known.

The role of internal migration

Current high rates of urban growth in developing countries are only partly due to rural-urban migration. Natural population increase is estimated to account for 60 percent of the rise in urban populations, according to a UN sample of twenty-nine developing countries. Perhaps another 8 to 15 percent is attributable to the reclassification of rural areas to urban status. Additional evidence from India, Kenya, and several West African countries confirms this pattern.

Although fertility rates are on average lower in urban than in rural areas, differences within countries between urban and rural fertility tend to be small (see Chapter 6). Thus the effect of urbanization on aggregate fertility is limited in the short run, especially because migrants tend to be of childbearing age, raising the *number* of births in cities even when the *rate* of fertility is lower. Natural increase in urban areas is therefore substantial.

Migration then puts even greater strain on the capacity of cities to cope with rapidly growing numbers. In broad perspective, the shift of people from rural to urban areas mainly reflects the process of industrialization and the changes it brings in the demand for labor. Certain conditions in rural areas—unequal land distribution, landlessness, agricultural mechanization, natural calamities, and, in the past, forced labor migrations—have strongly influenced population movements in many countries. But, by and large, people move to towns and cities for higher incomes and better job opportunities.

For individual families, these attractions can be considerable. Once in the city, perhaps three out of four migrants make economic gains. A move from the rural Northeast of Brazil to Rio de Janeiro, for example, can roughly triple the income of an unskilled worker; the family income of a manual laborer in Sao Paulo is almost five times that of a farm laborer in the Northeast. The higher cost of urban living may narrow rural-urban wage differentials in real terms, but urban dwellers also generally have much better access to basic public services. To take one example, in rural areas of sub-Saharan Africa only about 10 percent of the population has access to a safe water supply, compared with 66 percent of the urban population.

Most studies conclude that migrants are assets to the urban economy. They are mostly between the ages of fifteen and twenty-nine and are better educated and more motivated than those who stay behind in the countryside. Evidence from Brazil, Colombia, Kenya, Korea, India, and Malaysia shows that migrants with long urban residence compare favorably with urban-born people in terms of employment and income. A World Bank study of Bogota, Colombia, found that migrants earned more than nonmigrants at all educational levels. Overall, income and employment levels are more a function of age, sex, and education than of whether a person has migrated or not.

Evidence about the impact on rural areas of emigration is mixed. Emigration seldom causes a drop in farm output. In villages of East Kalimantan, Indonesia, for instance, women have adjusted to the departure of male emigrants by working harder at rice and vegetable production. Other reactions include shifts to less labor intensive cropping patterns, increased use of wage labor, and agricultural mechanization.

Urban-rural remittances clearly benefit rural households. Village studies in India, Malawi, and Thailand, however, show that net remittances—migrants receive as well as send money—usually account for only a small proportion of rural incomes. Returning migrants can be an important

source of innovation, but only if opportunities exist to exploit their ideas. Studies in Guatemala, Papua New Guinea, Peru, and Tanzania, for example, have shown that returning migrants can introduce new crops and techniques. Other studies have found that experience gained in modern factories is largely irrelevant to the needs of small villages.

Redistribution policies

Governments have employed many different approaches to the task of slowing down rural-urban migration, ranging from direct controls on population mobility to efforts to improve economic conditions in the countryside. Few of these policies have achieved their demographic objectives, and their social and financial costs have been high. Moreover, they have often been undermined by national policies in agriculture, industry, and foreign trade.

Direct controls on mobility have been most common in centrally planned economies. China, for example, has employed controls since the early 1950s in an attempt to stabilize its urban population. These controls have taken the form of travel permits and food ration cards that can be used only in specified areas; also, restrictions have been placed on labor recruitment in rural areas by urban industrial enterprises. In some cases large numbers of city dwellers have been exhorted to move to the countryside. The "rustication" program, for instance, resettled some 10 to 15 million urban secondary school graduates in rural areas between 1969 and 1973. Administrative measures have probably helped to slow urban population growth: the proportion of the population in urban areas has changed only slightly over the past thirty years. But the costs were high to individuals, and the economy also suffered from misallocations of labor.

Less stringent controls have been used in Indonesia and in the Philippines. Starting in 1970, migrants to Jakarta had to comply with an array of bureaucratic requirements, including cash deposits and licenses for various business activities, however informal. To limit the growth of Manila, the city government in 1963 decided to charge migrants a sizable fee to enter the public school system; free education was available only to bona fide residents. In both cases, the controls proved hard to enforce, gave rise to petty corruption, and failed to slow urban growth significantly. A variant of such controls has been periodic expulsions of unemployed migrants from cities, a practice that has been attempted in parts of Africa, notably the Congo, Niger, Tanzania, and Zaire. They too have had little visible impact.

Population redistribution is commonly a major objective of land-settlement schemes. The transmigration program in Indonesia, for example, aims to ease population pressures in rural Java—with only limited success, it seems (see Box 5.5). Similarly, Brazil's TransAmazon Program did little to further the goal of reducing population growth in the semiarid Northeast. Evidence suggests that the Federal Land Development Authority (FELDA) settlement scheme in Malaysia has succeeded in slowing down intrarural and rural-urban migra-

tion. But costs have been high (about $15,000 per family in the 1970s), and "second generation" problems—increasing social differentiation in settlement areas, and renewed pressures on land as settler families increase in size—have begun to appear. Although land settlement may have important political and social objectives, a review of World Bank-assisted schemes concluded that, in economic terms, it is usually more efficient to intensify production in already settled areas than to move people elsewhere.

Governments have also tried to modify population distribution by making small and medium-size towns an attractive alternative to the major cities. Evidence from India, Peru, Thailand, and

---

Box 5.5 Indonesia's transmigration program

Indonesia's population—estimated at 153 million in 1982—is unevenly distributed over 13,600 islands, covering about 1.9 million square kilometers. A single island, Java, accounts for about two-thirds of the country's population but only 7 percent of the land area. Java has an average of 690 people per square kilometer (higher than Bangladesh); in irrigated areas the density rises to 2,000 people per square kilometer. In contrast, large areas of the other islands, including Sumatra, Kalimantan, Sulawesi, and Irian Jaya, are sparsely populated.

Java has fertile volcanic soils, which allow intensive agriculture without heavy applications of fertilizer. Some 70 percent of the island is cultivated. The other islands, however, have generally poor tropical soils. Over the years, much of the population growth in rural Java has been absorbed through "agricultural involution," a process through which land productivity is raised by adding more and more workers. But growing population pressures have contributed to ecologically harmful farming practices, such as the clearing and cultivation of steep hillsides. More than 23 million hectares have already been degraded. Labor productivity and rural incomes have declined in parts of the island, and landlessness and rural underemployment are widespread. In 1980 an estimated 47 percent of rural Javanese were below the absolute poverty line, com-

pared with 28 percent of the rural population of the other islands.

The big demographic and economic differences among the islands of Indonesia have prompted many programs for moving people from Java to the other islands. The Dutch began a resettlement program in 1905, moving 155 families from central Java to Lampung province in Sumatra. By 1932, some 27,000 people (roughly 1,000 per year) had been moved. Between 1932 and 1969 the program—which became known as "Transmigration" in 1950—slowly gathered momentum. By 1969, about 580,000 more people (about 15,000 per year) had been resettled. But since Java's population grew by some 35 million over this period, the transmigration program had only a minor impact.

With the First Five-year Plan (1969–74), the transmigration program became a national priority and was further expanded. The World Bank has supported this expansion with four loans and one credit, totaling about $350 million. Since 1969, 479,000 families (approximately 2.4 million people) have been settled outside of Java at an average cost per family varying between $4,000 and $8,000. The program has also encouraged some spontaneous migration, estimated at 1 million people since 1969. Although the transmigration program has in recent years succeeded in resettling the equivalent of a quarter of

Java's natural population increase, the island's rate of population growth actually increased slightly from 1.9 percent a year in 1961–71 to 2 percent a year in 1971–80.

Of course, the transmigration program should not be judged solely on its ability to ease population pressures in Java. Emigrants have been drawn from the poorest groups in Java and from the most ecologically vulnerable areas. Reviews of the program carried out by the World Bank found that these settlers were better off in most transmigration sites than they had been in Java. Nevertheless, average crop yields and incomes in upland areas have been low and variable. Of 592 farmers surveyed in communities dependent on rainfed agriculture, only 9 percent reported paddy yields of more than one ton per family.

The Indonesian government has set ambitious targets—to move some 13 million families from Java over a twenty-year period. For the immediate future, the government intends at least to match the target it set in the Third Five-Year Plan (1979–84) of 100,000 families a year. Costs are likely to increase as more and more remote areas are opened up, and this could constrain the program's development. Nevertheless, transmigration will continue to receive a high priority among government programs, not least because of what it can do to alleviate poverty.

other developing countries suggests that this objective is seldom achieved. One exception is Korea: through the introduction of special tax and credit incentives in the early 1970s, industrial activity and people were successfully attracted to smaller cities. One result was that population growth in Seoul slowed from 9.8 percent a year in the 1960s to 4.5 percent a year in the 1970s. But this achievement was helped considerably by a combination of circumstances possibly unique to Korea: a rapidly declining rural population, a stable government, a wide range of social services, and a booming economy.

Population growth and the international economy

Demographic change is tending to increase economic disparities between developed and developing countries. Between now and the year 2000, for example, the number of people aged twenty to forty will increase at about 2.6 percent a year in the developing countries, roughly ten times faster than in developed countries. In absolute terms, the difference is even more striking. Numbers in the twenty to forty age group will increase by 19 million in developed countries, less than one-third of the increase from 1960 to 1980. In developing countries the increase will be 600 million, one and a half times the 1960–80 increase. The size of the working-age population in China and India—which was about 60 percent larger than the total for industrial countries in 1960—will be more than 150 percent larger by 2000. Even if per capita income grows faster in developing than in industrialized countries, the absolute income gap will not decrease significantly because the initial difference in per capita income is, for many developing countries, so large. To what extent can international migration and trade reduce these disparities and alleviate the problem of rapid population growth in developing countries?

International migration

The motivation for most international migration is the same as for internal migration—higher wages. Historically, some migration may have been directly related to population pressure, but today wage differences are the main driving force. For example, in the late 1970s, an unskilled emigrant worker from Bangladesh earned up to ten times more in the Arab gulf states than he did in his own country. To the extent that population growth affects those differences, it is, of course, indirectly a cause of migration.

Despite the growing income gap between rich and poor countries and the widening gap in the size of the labor force, the scale of present-day migration is relatively small and unlikely to increase dramatically (see Chapter 4). The most important reason is the immigration policies of host countries. Their policies vary according to their economic needs, but they generally place some limits on immigration because of the effects on the wages of natives and because of social and political tensions that are often created by large-scale immigration.

CONSEQUENCES FOR THE RECEIVING COUNTRY. In general, immigration becomes controversial when new workers reduce wages—usually because the demand for urban labor is not rising fast enough to ensure that an added supply of labor will not cause wages to fall. For example, increased resistance to immigration in the United States after the 1890s was partly the result of a decline in the growth of farmland, retardation of capital accumulation, and technological change that favored capital- and skill-intensive sectors—all of which reduced the growth of demand for unskilled labor. More recently, restrictions on the use of migrant labor in western Europe increased when the 1974–75 recession began.

Host countries generally benefit from immigration; in the Middle East migrants form an indispensable part of the labor force. Host countries can also select immigrants whose skills and qualifications suit their pattern of demand (see Box 5.6). Immigration, often from developing countries, thus provides a flexible source of supply, enabling receiving countries to adapt more quickly to changes in demand than they could do without immigration. But the economic gains to host countries must be balanced against social costs. Immigration can create social tensions, often concentrated locally: whole neighborhoods exist in European countries and in the United States where adults are predominantly first-generation immigrants. Of France's 4 million foreigners, 40 percent live around Paris; in some sections of the city, more than half the primary-school children have foreign parents.

One response of host countries has been to shorten the stay of immigrants through temporary recruitment rather than permanent immigration. These efforts are not always successful: in western Europe, for example, the same workers returned, and the average length of stay increased.

As immigrants increase as a proportion of the population, they receive increasing attention and public resources. In the long run, these factors are likely to be more important than purely economic factors in maintaining limits on immigration.

CONSEQUENCES FOR THE SENDING COUNTRY. A substantial part of recent migration has involved unskilled workers. Migrant workers from the Yemen Arab Republic (constituting more than 30 percent of the national work force in 1981) were practically all unskilled. So were a large proportion of emigrants from other countries that sent labor to the booming Middle East in the 1970s—ranging from about 30 percent for Bangladesh and Jordan to about 50 percent for Egypt. About 50 percent of immigrants into Ghana and the Ivory Coast are employed in agriculture, usually as laborers. Unskilled laborers in western Europe and the United States may be more skilled than those in the Middle East, but they comprised 30 percent of migrant manual workers in Germany and more than 40 percent of temporary workers admitted to the United States in recent years. Illegal workers in the United States are largely uneducated and unskilled.

In some countries emigration has contributed to substantial increases in wages of the unskilled at home. For example, real wages of unskilled construction labor in the largest cities of Pakistan increased at an annual rate of more than 15 percent a year between 1972 and 1978 (faster than the rate of growth of wages of carpenters or masons), after remaining stagnant for several previous years. In the Yemen Arab Republic, which experienced heavy international as well as rural-urban migration, real wages of agricultural labor increased almost sixfold between 1972 and 1978. During 1975–79, they rose from 56 to 63 percent of urban wages; urban wages rose from 45 to 67 percent of those in Saudi Arabia. In Egypt the rate of increase of real wages in construction was about 6 percent a year during 1974–77, after stagnating in the previous ten years. Considering the low wages that the unskilled earn (for example, less than $2 a day in Pakistan in construction in 1977–78, less than $5 a day in Egypt in 1977), these wage increases must be considered beneficial, particularly since there is no evidence that output declined.

An additional benefit is the money that emigrants send back home. It serves not only to increase the incomes of their families but also to help finance their country's trade deficit. Workers' remittances increased from about $3 billion in 1970 to $27 billion in 1980. In 1980, remittances provided almost as much foreign exchange as exports did for Pakistan and Upper Volta; they were more than 60 percent of exports for Egypt, Turkey, and Portugal, and about 40 percent for Bangladesh and Yugoslavia.

Many countries have special schemes to attract remittances. India and Yugoslavia allow foreign currency accounts, with interest and capital withdrawable in foreign currency. Bangladesh issues import permit vouchers, which carry a special exchange rate and may be freely negotiated. China, Korea, and the Philippines have mandatory remittance requirements.

Migrant workers tend to save a lot. The average propensity to save by Turkish emigrants was 35 percent in 1971 (compared to a gross domestic savings rate of 16 percent), and as high as 70 percent for Pakistanis in 1979 (compared to a gross domestic savings rate of less than 10 percent). The average propensity to remit, which may be more relevant to the emigrant country, was lower, but still 11 percent for workers from Turkey and about 50 percent for workers from Pakistan.

With this new source of income, the living standards of many families improve significantly. A large part of remittances (about 60 percent, according to one survey in Pakistan) is spent on food, clothing, rent, and other standard household items. Many of the consumer durables are imported. Beyond using remittances to increase their current spending, families tend to repay debt and invest their extra income, mostly in urban real estate, and in agricultural land and housing. A survey conducted in 1977 in the Indian state of Kerala showed that land and buildings accounted for an average 75 percent of the value of assets owned by emigrant households. In Pakistan 63 percent of investment from remittances went into real estate, including agricultural land; in Turkey 58 percent of migrants' savings went into housing and land. Investment in equipment and financial assets has been relatively small, although in Mexico and Turkey some remittances have been invested in family-owned commercial and manufacturing businesses. How remittances are used depends on the same factors that determine other private consumption and investment decisions.

In short, emigration by the unskilled generally leads to no loss in production, and if there is a scarcity premium on savings and foreign exchange (generated from remittances), then net benefits from emigration are likely to be large. In fact, it may even be beneficial for countries to facilitate emigration by providing information to potential emigrants and organizing recruitment on an official basis. Many countries, including Bangladesh, Korea, and the Philippines are in fact doing this.

However, emigration is not totally costless. Temporary migrants and their families often suffer long periods of separation, although there is evidence that women left behind efficiently manage the household and family assets, including agricultural land. Emigration has led to a rapid rate of mechanization in Yemen Arab Republic without a significant increase in productivity, and neglect of infrastructure has led to a collapse of farm terraces. In Oman underground water channels have deteriorated. Emigrant countries may also lose when skilled and professional workers emigrate; these

form a large part of both temporary and permanent migration (see Box 5.6).

International trade: growth and limits

Trade offers more opportunities for reducing international disparities and absorbing labor in developing countries than does international migration, but the effects of increased trade on labor absorption have, until now, been limited to only a few countries.

Unlike international migration, world trade has grown rapidly in the past three decades, at 6.7 percent a year, compared with less than 4 percent a year in 1800–1913, and only 1.4 percent in 1913–50. Trade has provided developing countries with

Box 5.6   The brain drain and taxation

Between 1969 and 1979, the United States admitted nearly 500,000 professional and technical workers. Three-quarters of them were from developing countries, nearly 50 percent from Asia. During the 1970s they accounted for nearly 30 percent of the rise in the employment of physicians and related practitioners in the United States, for 12 percent of the increase in engineers, and for 8 percent of the increase in scientists.

Countries that import skilled manpower gain on two counts:

• Since professional education is subsidized (about 45 percent of revenues of institutions of higher learning in the United States, for example, come from government), receiving countries save on such public subsidies.

• Since countries can select immigrants, they can adjust more quickly to changes in demand. For example, the share of physicians (and related practitioners) in professional immigration into the United States from developing countries was 12 percent in 1969, rose to nearly 25 percent in 1973, but dropped to 11 percent in 1979 as the number of domestically trained physicians increased.

Certain developing countries have experienced heavy brain drain. Some 36 percent of temporarily recruited migrants from Sudan, for example, were professionally and technically trained.

They included as much as 44 percent of Sudan's engineers, scientists, and medical practitioners. During the 1970s professionals from the Philippines who emigrated to the United States constituted 12.3 percent of the increase in their numbers at home; for Korea the figure was 10 percent. In Bangladesh professional and technical personnel constituted 17 percent of total emigration during 1976–78, and their departure is believed to have contributed to a shortage of several types of professionals. In other countries professional emigration has been large in absolute numbers but not necessarily in relative terms. Professional and technical workers who left Egypt for the United States during 1969–79 were less than 2 percent of the increase in their numbers at home (although professional emigration to the Middle East may be larger). Indian professional emigration to the United States formed about 1 percent of the stock in 1971.

The governments of many sending countries feel that emigration is harmful because they subsidize the emigrants' education but lose the opportunity to tax their incomes. When skilled workers leave, unskilled workers may become unemployed. A country may also put a high social value on the services of professional emigrants, such as doctors and nurses, so that their emigration involves a bigger loss than can be meas-

ured solely by the loss of the money value of their services. Emigration also prevents ''internal diffusion''—skilled people moving to backward areas within a country.

These costs are hard to quantify and depend on each economy's institutional features. Some of them can be reduced or avoided by a change in the policies of the sending countries. There is, for example, little justification in subsidizing higher education when the beneficiaries are the richer elite, or when the probability of their emigrating is high. Governments may also feel that they have a right to tax the incomes of skilled emigrants, especially if emigrants remain citizens of their home country. The United States and Philippines, for example, tax their citizens when they live abroad.

There are few estimates of how much revenue would be raised by taxing emigrants. If it is assumed, however, that 90 percent of all professional immigrants admitted to the United States during 1969–79 were still there in 1979, and that within each major occupation they matched the average earnings of American workers, their total earnings in 1979 would have been about $6 billion. A 10 percent tax would thus have yielded $600 million—some 13 percent of Official Development Assistance from the United States in that year.

extra jobs, directly in the export sector and indirectly as demand for inputs and services has increased. In Korea an estimated half a million jobs in 1970 (about 60 percent of them in manufacturing) were attributed directly and indirectly to exports. For all developing countries, however, manufacturing exports have added few jobs in relation to the increases in the size of the labor force. Most of the increase in manufactured exports (and thus in total exports, since nonfuel primary exports have grown less rapidly) has been in the (now) middle-income countries. Between 1965 and 1980 manufactured exports of all developing countries increased by $128 billion, but middle-income oil-importing countries, with a population of 600 million (out of 3 billion in all developing countries), accounted for 80 percent of that increase. Five countries—Brazil, Hong Kong, Korea, Singapore, and Yugoslavia, with 200 million people—accounted for 55 percent of the increase. Manufactured exports of low-income countries, with a population of 2.2 billion in 1980, increased by only $14 billion, and those of low-income Africa by $0.5 billion (see Table 5.8). Total exports of low-income countries also grew slowly, reflecting (with a few exceptions such as India) their dependence on primary exports, which grew at only 6.8 percent a year in volume. To the extent that export revenues determine imports, primary exporters have gained little, particularly in the face of large increases in population.

EXPORTS AND EMPLOYMENT. Export success does not rely solely, or even necessarily, on a large labor force and low wages. Of greater importance are an outward-looking trade policy and a relatively skilled labor force. As discussed in Chapters 2 and 3, exports of many countries have been inhibited by inward-looking trade policies and price distortions. Ironically, employment has suffered as a result: there is now ample evidence that industries geared to import substitution create fewer jobs than do export industries. Evidence from Brazil, Indonesia, and Thailand, for example, shows that labor employed per unit of value added was twice as high in export industries as in import-substitution industries. In Korea in 1968 manufactured exports were 33 percent more labor intensive than domestic manufactures, and 50 percent more labor intensive than import-competing industries. The unskilled labor component in export industries is also generally high—50 to 100 percent higher than in import-competing ones.

The accumulation of human (and physical) capital necessary to expand export capability is, as shown above, made more difficult if population is growing rapidly. Even simple manufactures such as textiles and clothing (the commodities that developing countries typically export to start with) require skilled workers and versatile managers and entrepreneurs who can keep up with changing fashions and preferences. Modern textile plants tend to use expensive equipment: fixed capital per employee in Indian firms using nonautomatic power looms in 1963 was $1,600, more than seven times the per capita income in that year.

Table 5.8 gives some indication of the differences in human capital between low-income Africa, the least successful exporter of manufactures, and middle-income oil importers, the most successful. In both groups the labor force has grown at about 2 percent a year. But in 1960 the (now) middle-income countries had, on average, a higher adult literacy rate, a higher index of human skills (defined as the secondary-school enrollment rate plus five times the enrollment rate in higher educa-

TABLE 5.8
Export structure and human capital

Country group	Percentage of manufactures in				Value of manufactured exports (billions of dollars)		Adult literacy rate		Index of human skills [a]		Rate of growth of labor force (1960–81)
	Exports		GDP								
	1965	1980	1960	1981	1965	1980	1960	1980	1960	1979	
Low-income Africa	9.8	9.3	6.2[b]	8.7[b]	0.2	0.7	15	39	2.4[c]	19.0	2.0
Low-income Asia	37.4	41.8	13.0[d]	17.0[d]	1.9	15.4	36	53	30.0[d]	58.4[d]	1.8
Middle-income non-oil	23.0	51.6	22.0	25.0	4.3	108.9	58	72	38.0	109.0	2.2
Industrialized countries	69.6	73.5	30.0	25.0	86.9	902.3	96	99	144.0	274.0	1.3

a. Defined as the secondary school-enrollment rate plus five times the enrollment rate in higher education.
b. Based on a limited sample.
c. Secondary-school enrollment rate.
d. Excludes China.

Box 5.7 Coping with rapid fertility decline: supporting the elderly in China

Slower population growth can help developing countries raise living standards more quickly. But a rapid transition to slow growth does require adjustment—most importantly in providing security to the elderly. China's official demographic target calls for a population of 1.2 billion by the year 2000, requiring that the total fertility rate stay below 2 for the rest of this century and that many couples have only one child.

What are the economic implications of lowering fertility well below replacement level? During the remainder of this century there would be some economic advantages but they are not dramatic. If the total fertility rate is reduced to an average of 1.7 between 1985 and 2000 (which would keep population to 1.2 billion in 2000, according to World Bank projections), the school-age population would decline to about two-thirds of its 1980 level by the year 2000. The declines would be greater in those regions where many couples have already pledged to have no more than one child (see Box 8.9). Savings could be allocated to somewhat more rapid expansion of secondary education.

But, in the long run, the decline in the proportion of young people would be offset by a large increase in the proportion of the elderly. Assuming fertility rises again to replacement level after 2000, the proportion of persons in the working-age group would not fall and the overall dependency ratio would not increase in the next century. But the structure of dependency would be markedly different—with the labor force supporting the dependent old rather than the dependent young. In 1980, 60 percent of the population was of working age (fifteen to sixty-four years) and only 5 percent (about 45 million people) was aged sixty-five and over. In the year 2050—when today's fifteen-year olds are aged eighty—the proportion of the working-age group would still be 61 percent,

but the proportion older than sixty-five would be 21 percent, by then about 308 million people. This level of elderly dependency is unprecedented even in the developed countries, where the proportion aged sixty-five and over ranges from about 8 percent in Japan to 18 percent in Sweden in 1980, and is about 11 percent in the United States (see chart).

The much larger proportion of the elderly would be somewhat offset by a decline in the numbers of young people, from 36 percent in 1980 to 18 percent in 2050. Young adults would then have fewer children to support, but, for those from one-child families, no siblings to help support their parents. Consumption requirements of the elderly are about double those of children, and at present few Chinese workers (only about 15 percent of the labor force) are covered by pension schemes; very few of those covered are in rural areas.

The most severe burden will be created by the large cohorts of the late 1960s and early 1970s who are now beginning to enter the labor force. Pension funds to cover the retirement of these workers, with opportunities to earn interest and reinvest the substantial net income that such funds would receive in their early years, are urgent if present population policies continue; indeed, they may well be necessary to sustain the desired fertility decline. But they will be difficult to finance at China's still relatively low income level. In developed countries, with income per worker ten to thirty times greater than in China, each worker in 1980 supported only half as many pensioners as a worker in China would have to in the future if present demographic goals are to be met. Yet even now in developed countries, there are problems with public financing of old-age security systems.

Population pyramids, China and United States, 1980 and 2050

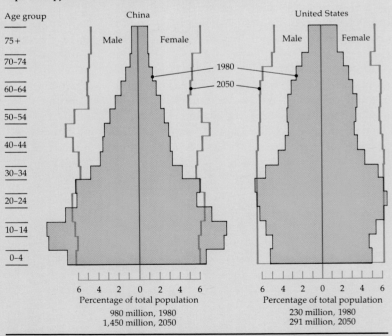

Age group — China — United States

980 million, 1980
1,450 million, 2050

230 million, 1980
291 million, 2050

tion), and a larger share of manufactures in output than low-income Africa. Low-income Asia occupies an intermediate position on most indicators; in 1960 it had a nearly comparable level of human skills and a higher share of manufactures in exports than middle-income countries. The comparatively slow increase in exports of manufactures from low-income Asia is as much attributable to inward-oriented policies in the two largest countries (China and India), at least until recently, as to any lack of export capabilities.

These simple correlations should not be carried too far. Even among the successful exporters, some countries have fared better and others worse than their skill index in 1960 might suggest. Nevertheless, these comparisons show that factors such as a literate and educated labor force, accumulation of physical capital, and economic diversity are important for growth of manufactured exports.

Conclusions

Population and development are intertwined in many ways, not all of them fully understood. Moreover, the effects of population growth may vary widely, depending on the institutional, economic, cultural, and demographic setting. Slow population growth itself requires new adjustments to support the growing burden of dependent elderly (see Box 5.7). The complexity of the subject makes it tempting to be agnostic about the consequences of rapid population growth. Nevertheless, the evidence discussed above points overwhelmingly to the conclusion that population growth at the rapid rates common in most of the developing world slows development. At the family level, as Chapter 4 showed, high fertility can reduce the amount of time and money devoted to each child's development. It makes it harder to tackle poverty, because poor people tend to have

large families, and because they benefit less from government spending on the programs they use most—health and education, for example—when public services cannot keep pace with population growth. At the societal level, as this chapter has emphasized, it weakens macroeconomic performance by making it more difficult to finance the investments in education and infrastructure that ensure sustained economic growth.

Population growth eventually slows as parents decide to have fewer children. The factors behind parents' decisions, discussed in the next chapter, then work their way through to benefit society as a whole. But it does not follow that slower population growth will be an immediate panacea for developing countries. Declines in fertility, for example, will cut the growth of the labor force only after fifteen to twenty years.

In the meantime, there are various nondemographic measures by which countries can ease those development problems made more difficult by population growth. The adoption of trade and exchange rate policies that do not penalize labor and the dismantling of institutional barriers to creating jobs would ease the employment problem. Pricing policies in agriculture and more resources allocated to rural credit, agricultural research and extension, and so forth, would increase agricultural output.

In short, policies to reduce population growth can make an important contribution to development (especially in the long run), but their beneficial effects will be greatly diminished if they are not supported by the right macroeconomic and sectoral policies. At the same time, failure to address the population problem will itself reduce the set of macroeconomic and sectoral policies that are possible, and permanently foreclose some long-run development options.

6 Slowing population growth

Experience has shown that as development progresses fertility falls. Yet, because current rates of population growth are so much greater in the developing world than they were at comparable income levels in today's developed countries, many developing countries cannot afford to wait for fertility to decline spontaneously. This message is not without hope, however, because some developing countries have already shown that fertility can be brought down significantly. This chapter examines the forces behind their success and considers the role of public policy in strengthening such forces.

It was once assumed that reducing fertility in developing countries would require a typical sequence of economic advance: urbanization, industrialization, a shift from production in the household to factory production, and incomes rising to levels enjoyed by today's developed countries. This view seemed to be confirmed by the

fertility declines of the 1960s, which were largely confined to the industrializing economies of Korea, Singapore, and Hong Kong. But fertility declines beginning in other developing countries in the late 1960s, and spreading to more in the 1970s, have been related to a different kind of development: education, health, and the alleviation of poverty. Birth rate declines have been much more closely associated with adult literacy and life expectancy than with GNP per capita. Despite high average incomes, rapid industrialization, and fast economic growth, birth rates fell less in Brazil and Venezuela between 1965 and 1975 than in Sri Lanka, Thailand, and Turkey, where income gains and social services have been more evenly distributed.

This association is not surprising. When their children have a better chance of surviving and of enjoying a wider range of opportunities, parents are willing to devote more money and time to edu-

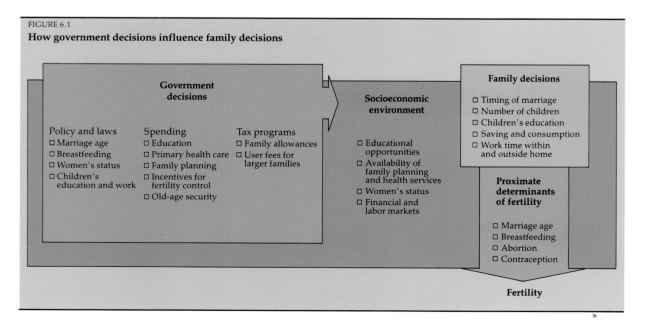

FIGURE 6.1
How government decisions influence family decisions

cating them. The gap between the private and social costs of children narrows where income gains are widely shared, credit and labor markets are working well, and people are receiving a fair return to effort and skills. Income gains often coincide with an increase in opportunities for women outside the home and for the poor, and associated changes substitute for the benefits of having many children.

But such changes come only gradually. Education, for example, cannot be transformed overnight. Nationally, literacy rates today are strongly influenced by their level in the past; in households, children are more likely to attend school if their mothers did, regardless of family income level. Expanding opportunities for women relies in part on educating women—but this occurs more slowly where parents see only limited opportunities for their daughters. In rural areas, credit and labor markets cannot be transformed overnight. All the more reason, therefore, to act now—especially because some of these changes also take time to lower fertility.

Other complementary policies can have more immediate effects. Promotion of later marriage and longer breastfeeding can reduce the birth rate at the same time it raises welfare. And the experience of many developing countries shows that public support for family planning programs, by narrowing the gap between actual family size and what couples would want if they could more easily choose, can lower fertility quickly. Where family planning services are widespread and affordable, fertility has declined more rapidly than social and economic progress alone would predict. Some examples are Colombia, Costa Rica, India, Thailand, Tunisia, and, more recently, Indonesia and Mexico.

By taxing and spending in ways that provide couples with specific incentives and disincentives to limit their fertility, government policy can also affect fertility in the short run. Government can offer "rewards" for women who defer pregnancy; it can compensate people who undergo sterilization for loss of work and travel costs; and it can provide insurance and old-age security schemes for parents who restrict the size of their families.

Each of these public policies works through signals which influence individual and family decisions—when to marry, whether to use contraception, how long to send children to school, and whether and how much family members work. The level and pattern of government expenditure

—for example, for health and education—has great potential for affecting such decisions. Education and primary health care account for between a fifth (Malawi) and a third (Tunisia) of public budgets in low-income and middle-income countries. Taxes similarly affect behavior through, for example, tax-free allowances for children and fees or subsidies on services that children use. The effects of taxes and subsidies can differ depending on the situation. Tuition and book charges might discourage parents from sending children to school and so indirectly contribute to higher fertility. But once it is clear that education is valuable, such charges are likely to encourage people to have fewer children in order to give them a better education.

Some of the ways in which government can influence family decisions are illustrated in Figure 6.1. The influence can be direct—government can make laws and issue proclamations, for example, that clarify social goals about marriage age and children's schooling. But government influence is likely to be stronger and more enduring when it is indirect; for example, through various entitlement and tax programs, government can affect the social and economic environment, which in turn affects people's decisions about marriage, children, and education. These indirect effects are so powerful because fertility itself is but one of a set of interrelated household decisions: saving, consuming, working, raising children, and sending them to school. Many of the signals sent out by government affect fertility by altering the decisions about children's education, mother's work, and the relative attractiveness of spending now or saving for one's old age. Figure 6.1 also shows that all these influences alter fertility through what demographers call the proximate determinants of fertility—breastfeeding, age at marriage, contraceptive use, and abortion.

The complexity of these relationships is both a virtue and a drawback. It is a virtue because specific government programs can have multiple effects that enhance their overall impact on family behavior. This is clearly true of family planning programs and other development programs. Such efforts work best in concert; they work only haltingly when they work alone. When various programs all work together, they make possible the steep declines in fertility achieved by countries that have simultaneously benefited from rapid economic growth, improvements in education, rising life expectancy, and expanding family planning programs. But the complexity is also a disadvantage; no one program or policy is enough to reduce fertility; nor is it easy to judge the importance of one program compared with another.

Socioeconomic factors and fertility

One possible remedy for population growth can be ruled out at the start: accepting a rise in death rates, or even a slower decline than is possible. High death rates do slow population growth. But the main reason for wanting slower growth is to improve people's well-being—to move quickly toward a balance of low death and birth rates, thus completing the demographic transition.

Reducing infant and child mortality

High infant mortality is part of the setting that promotes high fertility (Chapter 4). Parents who expect some children to die may insure themselves by giving birth to more babies than they want or expect to survive. High infant mortality can cause high fertility for biological reasons as well: breast-feeding delays the return of regular ovulation, so the interval between a birth and the next conception may be shortened if a baby dies.

In the short term, the prevention of ten infant deaths yields one to five fewer births, depending on the setting. Thus lower infant and child mortality leads to somewhat larger families and faster rates of population growth than otherwise. But effects in the long term are more important. With improved chances of survival, children receive more attention from their parents, and parents are willing to spend more on their children's health and education. Lower mortality not only helps parents to achieve their desired family size with fewer births, it leads them to want a smaller family as well.

The 1980 World Development Report reviewed policies and programs to improve health and reduce mortality. This Report focuses on measures to speed the decline in fertility for three reasons:

- Fertility will henceforth have a much stronger influence than mortality on population size; this was discussed in Chapter 4. A rapid fall in fertility is all the more urgent to ensure slower population growth without compromising efforts to reduce mortality.
- High fertility and unplanned births contribute to high infant (and child) mortality. Many children, born close together, weaken the mother and the baby and make it harder for the family to afford health care and food.
- The policies and programs that reduce fertility are more than ever those which will also reduce mortality. As shown in Chapter 4, many of the less difficult ways to reduce mortality—through antimalarial campaigns, for example—have already been exploited; further progress against mortality requires changes in people's behavior. Family planning services are an obvious example. Though primarily seen as a way to reduce fertility, family planning can be a major contributor to lower mortality—both of infants and of mothers (see Box 7.1 in the next chapter). The same is true for the education of women; women's education can lower fertility by delaying marriage, by increasing the effectiveness of contraceptive use, and by giving women ideas and opportunities beyond childbearing alone. Women's education is also a major contributor to lower mortality.

Raising income

Since children are a source of satisfaction, one might expect richer parents to have more of them. Within the same socioeconomic group, this is often so: among small farmers, for example, those with more land often have higher fertility (although their fertility is lower than the fertility of the landless—see Box 6.1). Rising incomes are also associated with decreased breastfeeding, which raises fertility unless contraceptives are used. Where marriages are delayed by the need for a dowry, or by the costs of setting up a household, rising incomes permit earlier marriage and earlier childbearing—and thus higher fertility. But these effects are transitory and may be avoided altogether. They can be offset by the social changes that accompany economic growth—such as education and family planning programs—and that work to lower fertility.

This relation adds up to a well-established fact: in the long run, people with more income want fewer children. Alternative uses of time—earning money, developing and using skills, enjoying leisure—become more attractive, particularly to women who are primarily responsible for bringing up children. Parents start to want healthier and better-educated but fewer children. Education of children becomes more attractive as job opportunities depend less on traditional factors—class origin or family background—and more on education and associated skills. And children's work becomes less important to family welfare. Higher income means an increased surplus to invest in land or other assets, a greater awareness of alternative investments, and the spread of social security and pension schemes that guard against destitution in emergencies or in old age. In short, it is not higher

Box 6.1 Landholding and fertility

Land reform provides farmers with greater security, improves income distribution in rural areas, and lays the base for subsequent agricultural progress. But careful studies of fertility behavior in rural areas suggest land reform can have two contradictory effects on fertility.

• With more land, farmers need more labor to work it, so the contribution of children becomes more valuable. With higher incomes, farmers are also able to afford larger families. Studies in Bangladesh, India, Iran, Nepal, the Philippines, and Thailand all show that fertility rises as farms get bigger. In an anthropological study in Guatemala, farmers with irrigated land—who were usually engaged in multiple cropping, with high labor demands—had higher fertility than farmers with rainfed land. In a survey in Thailand, 50 percent of families with large landholdings cited children's help as an advantage of having many children, compared with only 4 percent of families with no farm or business.

• A tenant who becomes a landowner gains extra income from ownership that is not dependent on his being able to work or manage the farm. This gives him some security for old age, making him less dependent on his children. One study in northwestern Iran found that landowners wanted smaller families and had had fewer children than villagers who owned no land. Wives of landowners had married earlier, but they were also more inclined to use contraceptives, so on balance their fertility was lower. The same conclusion was reached by studies in Thailand and the Philippines. But arrangements short of ownership do not have the same effect. In some of the Mexican agricultural communities called *ejidos*, farmers were granted usufruct rights instead of ownership. This led to higher fertility, not only because their landholdings increased, but also because of the uncertainty over future use of the land and the advantages of having a large family in order to retain control.

A study in southern Egypt showed the conflicting effects of land reform. The number of children was estimated by ownership status and farm size, making allowance for wife's age (the mean was thirty-five), age at marriage, education, and employment. The number of children was high for all groups (at least five per family) and increased with farm size. But it was lower, at each level of farm size, among those who owned their land than among tenants.

---

income itself, but the changes it brings to people's lives, that lowers fertility.

The association of income and fertility varies according to absolute levels of income. Below some minimum income, increases in income are associated with higher fertility (see Figure 6.2). In the poorest countries of Africa and South Asia, many families are below that threshold. Above that threshold, further increases in income are associated with lower fertility—for a given increase in income, the reduction is greater for low-income groups. Raising the incomes of the rich (be it of rich countries or of rich groups within countries) reduces fertility less than does raising the incomes of the poor. There is, however, no good evidence that the distribution of income has an independent effect on fertility; it is influential only to the extent that poor households usually have higher absolute incomes if their share of the total is higher.

Educating parents

More education for women is one of the strongest factors in reducing fertility. It is true that, in poorer countries, women with a few years of primary schooling have slightly higher fertility than do women with no education at all, especially in rural areas. Some education may be associated with a lower rate of sterility, and it often leads to a decline in breastfeeding not offset by greater use of contraceptives.

In time, however, the effect of education in reducing fertility becomes increasingly clear. In all countries, women who have completed primary school have fewer children than women with no education, and everywhere the number of children declines regularly (and usually substantially) as

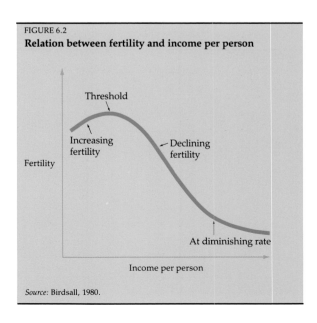

FIGURE 6.2
Relation between fertility and income per person

Source: Birdsall, 1980.

the education of mothers increases above the primary-school level. The differences can be large—about four children between the highest and lowest educational groups in Colombia, for example (see Figure 6.3).

Studies also show that educating women makes a greater difference than does educating men in reducing family size. There are several plausible reasons for this. Children cost women more than they do men, in time and energy (see Box 6.2). The more educated the woman, the more opportunities she gives up if she chooses to stay at home to raise children. Education delays marriage for women, either because marriage is put off during schooling or because educated women are more likely to work or to take more time to find suitable husbands. In ten out of fourteen developing countries studied, a woman with seven or more years of education marries at least 3.5 years later than a woman who has never been to school.

Educated women are also more likely to know about and adopt new methods of birth control. In Kenya 22 percent of those with nine or more years of education use contraception, as opposed to only 7 percent of those with five or fewer years of education. In Mexico the comparable figures are 72 percent and 31 percent. Such differences among education groups are only slightly reduced when other socioeconomic characteristics are taken into account. The contrast between these countries is due to other factors, including access to family planning methods. The differences in contraceptive use among education groups tend to be small in countries where average use is either very low (Bangladesh, Kenya, Nepal, and Pakistan) or very high (Costa Rica, Fiji, and Korea).

Women's employment and status

To women in developed countries it may seem that employment leaves little time for childcare. This is seldom true for peasant women in developing countries. Family agriculture and cottage industries keep women close to the home and allow considerable flexibility in working arrangements. In addition, village life often ensures that there are many other people, young and old, who can look after babies while mothers are working. But these conveniences do little to modernize a woman's outlook or to develop a commitment to continued employment that would discourage high fertility.

In towns and cities women have less scope for resolving the conflict between childcare and work. Although there are many exceptions, research tends to show that urban women who work full time, particularly in "modern" jobs, have fewer children. They restrict fertility in part by using contraceptives. But of equal significance is that they delay marriage—by one and a half to two years, according to one study of five Asian countries. Delay seems to affect even informal unions: a study of Jamaica confirmed that women who experienced no prolonged unemployment on leaving school entered informal unions later than did other women. Even if they eventually end up with the same number of children (which is generally not the case), the delay in the start of childbearing reduces population growth by extending the interval between generations.

Although employment seems to have an independent effect on fertility only for women in well-paid, modern jobs, more job opportunities should affect the fertility of all women indirectly, by

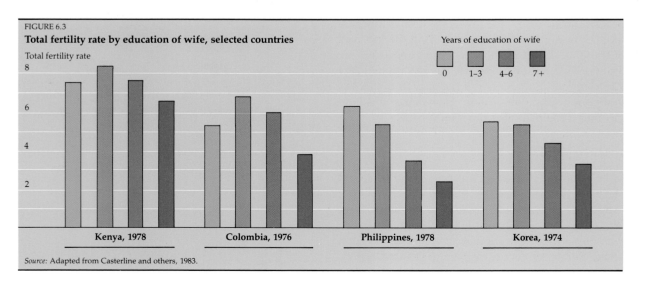

FIGURE 6.3
Total fertility rate by education of wife, selected countries

Years of education of wife

0   1-3   4-6   7+

Total fertility rate

Kenya, 1978   Colombia, 1976   Philippines, 1978   Korea, 1974

Source: Adapted from Casterline and others, 1983.

Box 6.2 Women's use of and control over their time

Women with young children face considerable demands on their time. In one village in Bangladesh, women spend nine to ten hours every day of the week doing housework or market work. Having to care for a young child reduces the time available to earn income, particularly among poorer women. The first baby is an especially heavy burden. Once children reach the age of nine or so (and particularly if they are daughters), they free a woman from some responsibilities at home and increase the time she can work in the market.

The greatest demands are made by children under one. Women in rural Laguna in the Philippines average an hour a day of market work if they have a child under one at home, as opposed to two hours a day among all other women. The chart shows how women in Laguna divide the twenty-four hours in their

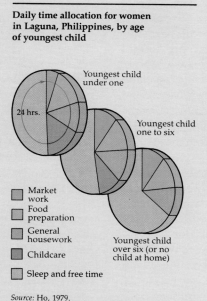

Daily time allocation for women in Laguna, Philippines, by age of youngest child

- Youngest child under one
- 24 hrs.
- Youngest child one to six
- Market work
- Food preparation
- General housework
- Childcare
- Sleep and free time
- Youngest child over six (or no child at home)

Source: Ho, 1979.

day. Childcare does not cut into other household work and reduces market work only when the child is under one. What it does do is reduce the time a woman has to herself, by three to four hours a day, as long as the child is under seven. Similarly, when a woman works outside the home, the time required does not come out of housework or child care, but out of her leisure time. The average working woman in this sample had four hours less leisure time than the average nonworking woman.

---

increasing the incentive to educate girls. The proportion of girls enrolled in school is low in many countries of the Middle East, where employment and other activities outside the home are extremely limited for women. In other Muslim countries—for example, Indonesia—female education and female employment tend to rise together. Once they are able to earn an income, women may acquire higher status in the home, thus enabling them to talk more openly about birth control with their husbands. Although a significant number of women use contraception without the knowledge of their husbands, open discussion leads to longer and more effective contraceptive use.

The "status of women" is a phrase covering numerous social and economic characteristics that affect a woman's life. In northern India, Pakistan, Bangladesh, and many countries of the Middle East, a woman is separated from her own family at marriage and required to develop new allegiances to her husband's family. This ensures that she will not become a liability to her own family. Her personal contacts and relations with strangers are limited. Typically, she cannot inherit property from her husband's family, nor can she pass it on. Often, her chief role is to produce sons; in that way she most effectively secures her own position in her new family.

Economic dependence on men entails special risks for these women, risks that go beyond the natural disasters or the process of aging to which both men and women are exposed. Widowhood, divorce, separation, incapacitating illness of the husband—these are serious threats when women have few ways to provide for themselves. The most obvious insurance against the risk of losing the economic support of a husband is to have several sons. Such a preference is likely to raise fertility, particularly if a target number of sons is considered essential.

In addition to encouraging better education and work opportunities for women, each government can lay the groundwork for improvements in women's status by guaranteeing women certain rights—of inheritance, marriage, divorce, litigation, and property. In other areas, too—such as the right to participate in the choice of a husband— much remains to be done to reshape deep cultural beliefs so that women can play their full part in the economic and social life of their countries. In the process, much will be done to reduce fertility.

Urban residence

Urban dwellers generally enjoy many advantages over their rural counterparts. They have access to

111

better education and health services, a wider range of jobs, and more avenues for self-improvement and social mobility. They also face higher costs in raising children. As a result, urban fertility is lower than rural fertility, on average by between one and two births per mother. This is true of migrants from rural areas as well as of long-term urban residents. Indeed, recent evidence shows that migrants in Colombia, Korea, and Thailand (and immigrants in the United States) often have even lower fertility than that of their urban counterparts of comparable education, perhaps because they are particularly interested in providing education for their children.

Apart from these advantages, is there a purely urban effect on fertility? One feature of urban life is wider and more varied personal contacts. These encourage people to search more widely before opting for a marriage partner. In ten out of fourteen developing countries studied, the urban woman marries on average at least one and a half years later than does the rural woman; the gap is shortened, but not eliminated, when socioeconomic differences between urban and rural women are taken into account. In addition, in urban areas the idea of controlling fertility and the means of doing so is spread more quickly. And, by being exposed to new consumer goods, urban people are encouraged to delay or limit their childrearing to increase their incomes.

But living in towns and cities is certainly not a sufficient condition for lower fertility. Nor is it even necessary, to judge by the declines in fertility in rural areas of China, Colombia, Indonesia, and Sri Lanka. The changes that do lower fertility—increased education, better opportunities for children, and so forth—can occur just as well in the countryside. In largely agricultural countries, differences in fertility between urban and rural areas are small anyway. In much of Africa and South Asia, which are largely rural, it is clearly futile to wait for urbanization alone to reduce fertility. It is only in the already more urbanized societies of Latin America and East Asia that further urbanization will lower fertility quickly.

Markets, security, and fertility

One feature of development is that markets become more efficient. Markets for labor, for capital, for land, and for many goods enlarge and diversify. Better transport helps this process along, as does the increasing scale and interpenetration of rural and urban life. Local moneylenders who charge exorbitant rates are undersold by banks and credit unions so that the price of credit comes down. Trustworthy institutions gradually establish themselves and offer means to save and borrow. The benefits of education in leading to higher income emerge; contacts and kin matter less as guarantors of jobs and of help with the harvest.

Greater market efficiency affects fertility in several ways. First, the logic of investing in children, especially in their education, becomes clearer. Second, children become less important as safeguards in times of disaster and as old-age security. Their greater regional mobility makes them less dependable as a source of support, and other instruments for old-age security, such as provident funds and social insurance, come into the picture. A study of a rural area of southern Mexico where a social security program was extended to cover sugarcane workers demonstrated that program coverage of half the working population led to a 10 percent decline in fertility. In India participation in a provident fund is associated with later marriage and, in nuclear households, with lower fertility. In both India and Malaysia, women more so than men look to children for support in old age. Information about programs to provide insurance and security should probably be directed more to women than it is currently.

There is little question that socioeconomic change in the long run lowers fertility and slows population growth. At the same time, the evidence is that socioeconomic gains from a low level do not slow population growth much—and can even raise it. A small drop in infant and child mortality results in more mouths to be fed. In some settings, a couple of years of primary education lead to slightly larger families. Employment of women in cottage industries or in other low-paying part-time jobs permits households to support additional children. Living in small towns does less to reduce fertility than does living in larger cities. That many of these changes take time to have an effect only underlines the need to begin them now. At the same time, other measures that complement and speed socioeconomic change can hasten a decline in fertility.

Marriage, breastfeeding, and contraception

Where fertility has fallen significantly, it has been regulated significantly—by methods that have included contraception and abortion. In the early stages of falling fertility, however, marriage timing and breastfeeding practices can reduce fertility.

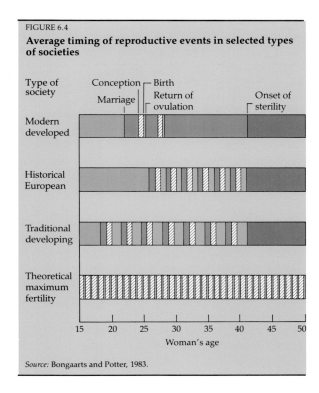

FIGURE 6.4

Average timing of reproductive events in selected types of societies

Type of society

Conception — Birth
Marriage | Return of ovulation | Onset of sterility

Modern developed

Historical European

Traditional developing

Theoretical maximum fertility

15   20   25   30   35   40   45   50
Woman's age

Source: Bongaarts and Potter, 1983.

Even without directly altering desired family size, they can help make the goals of individuals more compatible with those of society at large. Breastfeeding reduces fertility by suppressing fecundity; it also reduces high infant mortality. Later marriage reduces population growth by lengthening the interval between generations; it also fosters a climate that encourages women to expand their horizons beyond the family.

Figure 6.4 illustrates how the childbearing span is affected by age at marriage, breastfeeding, and fertility regulation. Traditional developing societies achieve high fertility through marriage that is relatively early and waiting times to conception that are mostly short. Fertility would be even higher except for lengthy breastfeeding, complemented in some instances by sexual abstinence. Today's developed economies achieve low fertility by later marriage and long periods between births, made possible by contraception and abortion.

All these factors have played some part in reducing the number of babies per mother from the theoretical maximum of seventeen. Their respective contributions have been calculated for twenty-nine countries covered by the World Fertility Survey (see Table 6.1). In the five African countries, where total fertility is high, breastfeeding accounts for the bulk of forgone fertility (sexual abstinence was not

measured), delayed marriage contributes little, and contraception virtually nothing. In Bangladesh, Pakistan, and Nepal the pattern is similar. Bangladesh has the longest period of breastfeeding (twenty-nine months) and the youngest average age at marriage for women (sixteen years). In other countries, such as Thailand, Korea, and Mexico, breastfeeding does not last so long, but later marriage partly compensates. In Costa Rica and Sri Lanka delayed marriage accounts for a substantial part of the low fertility rates, which are below four; in Sri Lanka breastfeeding is also important.

Over time, reductions in breastfeeding have slowed the decline in fertility in India, Indonesia, Korea, and Thailand. Delays in marriage have contributed to the decline, roughly offsetting the effect of less breastfeeding. The major factor in fertility decline in all four countries, however, has been an increase in contraceptive use. Averaging indices for many countries provides a composite picture of change over a long period (see Figure 6.5). Of the reduction in total fertility of almost 5 children over the whole period, delay in marriage contributes a reduction of about 1.4 children; reduced breastfeeding works in the opposite direction, raising fertility by about 1.5 children. Increased use of contraception contributes the most, about 4.5, and increased abortion contributes about 0.5.

Raising age at marriage

The younger women marry, the earlier they start childbearing and the longer they are exposed to the risk of conception. They lose the chance of longer schooling and of employment, and they enter marriage with less motivation and fewer personal resources to plan their families successfully. In addition, early marriage means a shorter gap between successive generations, significantly increasing the birth rate.

In South Asia and sub-Saharan Africa about half of all women aged between fifteen and nineteen are, or have been, married; in the Middle East and North Africa the proportion is close to a quarter. It falls to less than 20 percent in Latin America and in East Asia, and to less than 5 percent in Hong Kong and Korea. Still, variations among the countries in each region are considerable. In Tunisia only 5 percent of women aged fifteen to nineteen have been married, in Libya more than 70 percent. In Bangladesh the mean age at marriage for women is sixteen; in Sri Lanka it is twenty-five. If Bangladesh could immediately adopt the Sri Lankan marriage pattern, with no other change in fertility practices,

TABLE 6.1
Total fertility rates and reduction from total potential fecundity due to different determinants of fertility, selected countries and years

Country and year	Total fertility rate	Reduction from total fecundity due to			
		Marriage delay	Breast-feeding	Contra-ception	All other factors
Sub-Saharan Africa					
Ghana (1979–80)	6.22	2.16	4.31	0.86	3.45
Kenya (1977–78)	7.40	2.69	4.22	0.67	2.02
Lesotho (1977)	5.27	3.05	4.34	0.47	3.87
Senegal (1978)	6.90	1.72	4.65	0.20	3.54
Sudan, North (1979)	5.93	2.88	3.87	0.44	3.99
Latin America and Caribbean					
Colombia (1976)	4.27	4.71	1.53	4.20	2.29
Costa Rica (1976)	3.17	4.70	0.83	6.92	1.52
Dominican Republic (1975)	5.39	3.72	1.63	3.60	2.55
Guyana (1975)	4.78	2.93	1.10	3.18	5.01
Haiti (1977)	5.15	4.38	3.20	1.42	2.84
Jamaica (1975–76)	4.67	2.59	1.60	4.19	3.95
Mexico (1976–77)	6.27	3.43	1.82	3.43	2.04
Panama (1976)	3.84	4.21	1.45	6.71	1.18
Paraguay (1979)	4.56	4.48	1.99	3.23	2.74
Peru (1977–78)	5.35	4.66	2.68	2.80	1.51
Trinidad and Tobago (1977)	3.18	2.90	0.97	4.70	5.25
Venezuela (1977)	4.36	4.17	1.39	5.06	2.02
South Asia					
Bangladesh (1975–76)	5.96	1.21	6.84	0.77	2.32
Nepal (1976)	6.12	1.74	6.09	0.22	2.83
Pakistan (1975)	6.24	2.26	4.52	0.43	3.55
Sri Lanka (1975)	3.70	5.05	4.26	2.26	1.73
East Asia and Pacific					
Fiji (1974)	4.14	3.47	1.67	3.60	4.24
Indonesia (1976)	4.51	2.62	5.25	2.50	2.12
Korea, Rep. of (1974)	4.23	4.72	3.32	2.55	2.17
Malaysia (1974)	4.62	4.33	0.99	2.97	4.09
Philippines (1978)	5.12	4.99	2.61	2.97	1.31
Thailand (1975)	4.55	3.98	3.86	3.49	1.12
Middle East and North Africa					
Jordan (1976)	7.63	3.28	2.53	2.62	0.94
Syria (1978)	7.46	3.43	2.77	2.10	1.24

Source: Computed from WFS data.

families would have an average of 2.2 fewer children.

Marriage practices vary widely from country to country. Parentally arranged child marriages, still common in parts of South Asia, contribute to higher fertility; though consummation is often delayed and fecundity is lower among very young girls, the long-run effect of these arranged marriages is to reduce young women's exposure to opportunities outside the family and to encourage them to have many children. Polygamy, practiced in parts of Africa, has a mixed effect on fertility. Informal unions, common in the Caribbean, are

typically transitional stages preceding legal marriage; while in such unions, women tend to have few children.

Among developing regions in the recent past, age at marriage has changed most in Asia. Korea provides a striking example. Between 1925 and 1975 the average age for a woman at marriage rose from 16.6 to 23.7 years. This rise started slowly and gradually picked up speed, especially in the years between 1955 and 1966, when mean age at marriage was rising at a rate exceeding two months a year. In Korea the tradition of early marriage was substantially undermined by considerable migration into and out of the country and from rural to urban areas, as well as by the social unrest connected with World War II, liberation, the partitioning of Korea, and the Korean War. Increasing educational opportunities for both men and women and compulsory military conscription also played a part. Manufacturing has provided more and more jobs for women, in a society where factory work has been considered incompatible with marriage but quite compatible with continuing to live at home to contribute to the support of parents.

Development itself serves to raise the age of marriage, as does improvement in the status of women. Those governments which have tried to raise the legal minimum age for marriage have usually done so in conjunction with other measures that would work in that direction anyway. Tunisia introduced legal minimums of fifteen for women and twenty-one for men in 1956 and raised the minimum age for women to seventeen in 1964.

These changes were accompanied by legal and social measures affecting women: polygamy and repudiation of wives were outlawed, family planning services were gradually provided, and educational opportunities for women were expanded, so that the proportion of girls enrolled in primary and secondary schools rose from 27 to 47 percent during the 1960s. The president was a strong supporter of these reforms and a stern critic of keeping women in seclusion. These and other factors, such as heavy emigration of male workers, contributed to a decline from 42 percent in 1956 to 6 percent in 1975 in the proportion of women married in the age group fifteen to nineteen.

China legislated minimum ages for marriage of eighteen for women and twenty for men in 1950 as part of an overhaul of marriage laws and an attempt to provide equal rights for men and women. The Chinese considered raising the minimums again in 1957 but, recognizing the limited

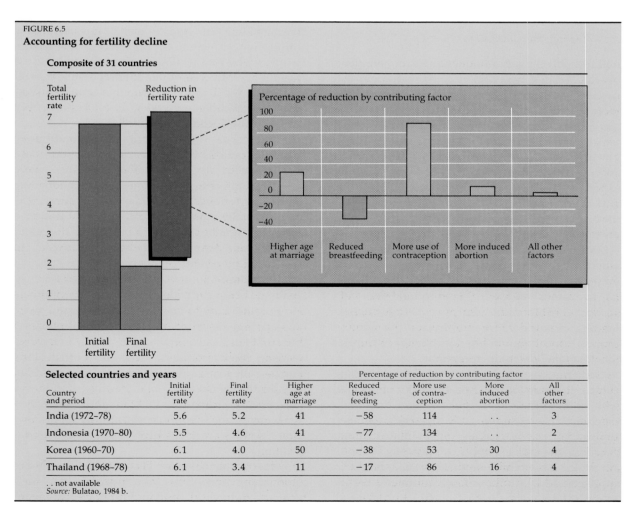

FIGURE 6.5

Accounting for fertility decline

Composite of 31 countries

Selected countries and years			Percentage of reduction by contributing factor				
Country and period	Initial fertility rate	Final fertility rate	Higher age at marriage	Reduced breast-feeding	More use of contra-ception	More induced abortion	All other factors
India (1972–78)	5.6	5.2	41	−58	114	. .	3
Indonesia (1970–80)	5.5	4.6	41	−77	134	. .	2
Korea (1960–70)	6.1	4.0	50	−38	53	30	4
Thailand (1968–78)	6.1	3.4	11	−17	86	16	4

. . not available
Source: Bulatao, 1984 b.

effectiveness of existing laws, instead increased institutional and community pressure for later marriage. In 1980 the government raised the legal minimum ages to twenty and twenty-two—less than the widely and officially propounded minimums of twenty-three and twenty-five. This was interpreted as a relaxation of controls on marriage, and it may have contributed to a recent increase in marriage and a spurt in the birth rate.

With the possible exception of China, efforts to raise the age at marriage by persuasion and edict have not been particularly successful. Legislation, however, is a way for governments to encourage social support for later marriage; and governments can link the idea to specific programs, especially schooling for girls, which affect fertility indirectly. In countries where early marriage is common, governments need to go further, giving women more rights and encouraging men and women to support expanded women's opportunities within the household as well as in society at large.

Providing information about breastfeeding

Full breastfeeding and frequent suckling are good guarantees that resumption of menstruation will be delayed, though protection decreases with each month after childbirth. Failure to menstruate is a good, but not an absolute, guarantee against pregnancy; about 7 percent of women conceive without having resumed menstruation. As a basic form of contraception, breastfeeding has a well-established reputation in developing countries. In one study three-quarters of Guatemalan mothers knew that it could postpone conception; in another, 60 percent of Malaysian women knew it made conception more difficult, and 20 percent thought it made it impossible. Women who breastfeed and who want to avoid pregnancy are 10 percent of all married women in Mexico, 15 percent in Peru, and 16 percent in Honduras. Only ten years ago breastfeeding provided more months of protection against conception in the developing countries than did family planning programs.

Aside from its effect on fecundity, breastfeeding avoids the considerable health risks connected with bottlefeeding—particularly where the powdered milk may be improperly prepared, adequate sterilization is not possible, and families cannot afford an adequate supply of powder. Though after four to six months mother's milk should be supplemented with other food, continued breastfeeding still benefits a baby's health. In Malaysia

declines in breastfeeding in the last three decades slowed the decline in infant mortality.

At least 70 percent of women in developing countries initially breastfeed their children, although this proportion is falling. How long they continue to do so varies widely, from two months in metropolitan Malaysia to twenty-nine months in rural Bangladesh. The trend is toward less breastfeeding: in Thailand, for example, between 1969 and 1979 mothers reduced the average length of breastfeeding from 22.4 to 17.5 months in rural areas and from 12.9 to 8.4 months in the cities. In Malaysia the percentage of infants initially breastfed dropped from 89 to 74 percent between 1960 and 1974, and the percentage breastfed more than three months dropped from 75 to 53 percent.

Some decline in the duration of breastfeeding is a natural consequence of economic development and may be a reasonable choice—if for example, a working mother's income more than compensates in improved health care and nutrition for the family. Studies show that mothers' employment in itself does not affect whether mothers initiate breastfeeding, but employment may affect how long they continue to breastfeed. Malaysian women who had recently been employed off the farm tended to wean their children completely at an earlier age. Filipino women in a semiurban setting breastfed if they worked close to home, but started mixed feeding earlier if they worked in a different area. In addition, employment may lengthen periods between sucklings, leading to a briefer amenorrheic period. But especially where breastfeeding is being shortened only moderately from long periods, say, of a year or more, the mother's and infant's health is unlikely to suffer—as long as families can afford proper nutrition and couples can use contraception to avoid an unwanted immediate pregnancy.

But evidence shows that in many cases breastfeeding is being curtailed simply because mothers do not know how to do it; the chief reason given for stopping breastfeeding is insufficient milk, yet that is biologically implausible for all but a few women. Some mothers switch to bottlefeeding because they lack guidance and information about the health benefits of breastfeeding, and they believe bottlefeeding is more "modern." In Malaysia women who live with parents, in-laws, or other adult relatives are less likely to abandon breastfeeding.

Evidence that behavior will change in the light of information comes from the industrialized countries, where medical opinion did not clearly favor breastmilk until the late 1960s. As the advantages of breastfeeding became better known, breastfeeding increased among better-educated women. In the United States, for example, college-educated women are now most likely to start breastfeeding and continue it for the longest periods.

Apart from providing more information on the advantages of breastfeeding, medical authorities in developing countries can restructure hospital and clinic routines that discourage breastfeeding by separating mother and child and offering unnecessary supplementary bottlefeedings. In Malaysia government family planning clinics that encourage breastfeeding have a positive effect; women who give birth in nearby private maternity clinics are less likely to breastfeed, all other things being equal. Legislation to control the promotion of powdered milk can also be effective. In Port Moresby, Papua New Guinea, changes in hospital practices and restrictions on the advertising and distribution of powdered milk increased the proportion of breastfed children under two years old from 65 to 88 percent in just two years, between 1975 and 1977.

Without such efforts, breastfeeding seems likely to go on declining. In this case—unless contraceptives are used more widely—fertility will rise. As an example, reducing the duration of breastfeeding from an average of three years to one month could double a mother's fertility from five to ten children. In the mid-1970s, if all mothers in Thailand had started menstruating three months after each baby was born, contraceptive use there would have had to double to prevent fertility from rising. In Indonesia, contraceptive use would have had to more than double; in Bangladesh it would have had to increase sixfold, and in Pakistan eightfold.

Making contraception easier

As shown in Figure 6.5, fertility declines everywhere have been eventually tied to increasing use of contraception. Use of contraception is partly a function of a couple's wish to avoid (or to postpone) additional children; the number of children desired is related to the social and economic factors discussed above. But use of contraception is also related to its costs, that is, to the costs of limiting or postponing births. People have regulated family size for centuries—through abortion, withdrawal, sexual abstinence, and even infanticide. But these methods are all costly in terms of reduced emotional, psychological, and, in the case of traditional abortion, physical well-being. Moreover, except for complete abstinence and infanticide, they do not always work. Under these circumstances, risking an additional child may seem less costly than preventing a birth, and even the stated "desired family size" may be higher than it would be if birth control were easier.

It follows that programs to provide publicly subsidized information and access to modern methods of contraception can reduce fertility. They do so in several ways: by making it easier for couples to have only the children they want; by spreading the idea of birth control as something individuals can do; and by providing information about the private and social benefits of smaller families, which may itself alter desired family size. The next chapter looks at how family planning programs can be run to best meet people's needs for safer and more effective contraception. The rest of this chapter examines the evidence that support for family planning services (delivered by both public and private agencies) has helped to reduce fertility.

EFFECTS OF FAMILY PLANNING PROGRAMS ON FERTILITY. Measuring the impact of family planning programs is less straightforward than it seems. To distinguish the specific impact of a program, analysts must estimate how fertility would have changed in its absence. That requires systematically eliminating other possible causes of a country's fertility decline—such as increases in income, education, and life expectancy in the same period. In addition, information on the change in the *availability* of family planning services is needed (not on change in the *use* of services, since use is related to people's fertility goals and does not indicate the difference services alone would make to people who now have no access to them). Such information has, until recently, been patchy and inadequate.

Given these analytical difficulties and the lack of good information, it was not surprising that a decade ago policymakers and planners could not completely agree on the relative importance to a fertility decline of the supply of family planning services versus the "demand" factors—increasing education, lower infant mortality, and the like. Early family planning programs in Korea, Hong Kong, and other areas of East Asia had been established in countries where a marked fall in fertility was already in progress; some of the continued decline might have occurred even without official programs. In other countries (such as India and Pakistan), where programs were also established in the 1950s and 1960s, fertility was changing little during the late 1960s.

But family planning programs spread rapidly in the late 1960s and early 1970s, and more systematic information on them is now available.

• A country-level family planning index was developed in the mid-1970s. It was based on countries' performance in 1972 on fifteen criteria, such as the availability of many contraceptive methods, either through government programs or commercially; inclusion of fertility reduction in official policy; adequacy of the family planning administrative structure; and use of mass media and fieldworkers. The index has been updated for this Report to 1982; countries are classified into groups by this index as of 1972 and 1982 in Table 6 of the Population Data Supplement.

• Household and community surveys conducted within countries during the 1970s provided information on the distance and travel time to services for household members. Those carried out as part of the World Fertility Survey (WFS) project in over forty countries, and of the Contraceptive Prevalence Survey (CPS) project in about fifteen countries, have several advantages: most are representative, nationwide samples and, because similar questions were asked everywhere, are largely comparable among countries.

These two sources, supplemented by the results of small experimental field studies, have provided the basis for careful analyses of the effects of family planning programs. They leave little doubt that the programs work.

CROSS-COUNTRY STUDIES. Using the family planning index, along with indicators such as literacy, life expectancy, and GNP per capita in about 1970, research in the late 1970s found that birth rates declined most (29 to 40 percent) between 1965 and 1975 in countries such as Costa Rica, Korea, and Singapore, where socioeconomic development was relatively advanced and family planning programs were strong. There was a modest decline in birth rates (10 to 16 percent) where development was relatively strong but the family planning index was weak, as in Brazil and Turkey. There was also a modest decline where development levels were low but the family planning index was moderately strong, as in India and Indonesia. (Indonesia's family planning program, now one of the world's strongest, had been operating for only two years by 1972, the reference year for the family planning index.) The same results emerged from using measurements of socioeconomic change from 1970 to 1977 rather than levels at one point in time during the period.

One objection to this type of study is that the family planning index may itself be the result of a demand for contraception that already existed as a byproduct of development. In this case, family planning services provided by the government may simply displace traditional methods of contraception or modern methods already available through the private sector. Indeed, analysis does show that in the early 1970s family planning programs were more likely to be instituted and were more successful where demand for contraception already existed: Korea, Hong Kong, and Singapore. The existence and strength of early programs is closely related to the proportion of educated women (itself a measure of demand for services), and to the degree to which fertility had declined in the late 1960s. But these factors do not completely explain differences in the family planning index; to some extent, indices were stronger or weaker because of other factors—political leadership, for example. And the *change* in country effort between 1972 and 1982 is not at all related to earlier declines in fertility or to levels of development; it has been more clearly the result of government initiatives.

Furthermore, although family planning programs are in part a response to preexisting demand, recent studies show that such programs do have an independent effect on fertility. Cross-country analysis shows that, for the average country, previous fertility decline accounted for 33 percent of the total fall in fertility between 1965 and 1975; socioeconomic change accounted for 27 percent; the family planning index accounted for more than either: 40 percent.

STUDIES WITHIN COUNTRIES. The cross-country studies are complemented by several examples of apparent family planning success in individual countries. In China and Indonesia, per capita income is low and the population still overwhelmingly rural, but governments have made a concerted effort to bring family planning services to the villages. In China the birth rate at the end of 1982 was estimated to be nineteen per 1,000 people, down from forty in the 1960s. The current figure, based on birth registrations rather than on a census, may slightly understate the actual birth rate; but it would still be well below current rates in South Asia, Africa, and most of Latin America. Up to 70 percent of Chinese couples of childbearing age are estimated to be using modern contraceptives. The government believes that its family planning program is critical to reducing fertility.

Indonesia's current birth rate is estimated at thirty-four per 1,000 people, which is a notable drop from an estimated forty-four in 1960. In Java and Bali, the two most densely populated islands of the country, the percentage of married women of reproductive age currently using modern contraception more than doubled between 1974 and 1976 (11 to 24 percent), nearly doubled again to 42 percent by 1980, and by 1983 had reached an estimated 53 percent.

Other developing countries and regions have also had remarkable increases in contraceptive use and rapid fertility declines, even among women with little or no education. In Colombia a strong private family planning program was under way by the late 1960s, and the government began supporting family planning in 1969. In urban areas the proportion of married women using contraception increased from 43 to 53 percent between 1969 and 1976, with a big switch from less effective methods, such as rhythm and withdrawal, to pills and IUDs (although the increase since then has slowed); in rural areas the proportion doubled, from 15 to 30 percent. As Figure 6.6 shows, the drop in fertility for Colombian women with little schooling has paralleled that of better-educated women, although fertility levels are still higher among those with less education. Fertility had begun to fall by 1965, before family planning services became widely available, but it declined faster in Colombia in the early 1970s than it did in Brazil or Mexico, where family planning services were less widely available. (Colombia has a somewhat lower per capita income than does Brazil or Mexico, and similar literacy and urbanization rates.)

In Mexico, as in Colombia, fertility began to fall a few years before the establishment of extensive family planning programs, both private and government-sponsored; but as those programs gained momentum, the fall in fertility accelerated. The government adopted a policy to reduce population growth at the end of 1973—an abrupt shift from its earlier pronatalist position. Rates of contraceptive use among married women aged fifteen to forty-nine more than doubled between 1973 and 1976, from 11 to 29 percent; by 1982 they had reached an estimated 48 percent. Public programs accounted for virtually all of the increase. The total fertility rate fell from 6.7 in 1970 to about 4.6 in 1982.

Of course, the availability of family planning services has not been the only reason for falling fertility in these countries. In China the government has exerted considerable social pressure and adopted economic incentives to reduce fertility; family planning services have provided couples with the means to respond. In Colombia and Mexico work opportunities and household incomes of women with little education were probably increasing in the 1960s and 1970s, which also encouraged the use of contraception.

In several low-income countries family planning programs have not been effective in reducing fertility—for example, Ghana, Kenya, and Pakistan. Lack of demand has been a factor, but so has limited availability of services and weak government support for the programs. Comparisons within countries show the difference actual availability can make. In Mexico, Korea, Thailand, and India contraceptive use is higher in communities with more sources of family planning supplies, even when differences in development levels are taken into account. In one district in India a 10 percent increase in the number of clinics per hundred thousand people was associated with a 3 to 4 percent increase in the combined acceptance rates of intrauterine devices (IUDs) and sterilization; similarly, a 10 percent increase in the number of extension workers raised acceptance rates by 4 to 6 percent.

FIELD PROJECTS. Experiments conducted in widely different communities have also revealed numerous examples of the effectiveness of family planning programs.

- In Matlab, a largely inaccessible part of Bangladesh, trained local women provided comprehensive family planning services in seventy villages. For the four years prior to the project, fertility rates for these villages were comparable with those for seventy-nine other Matlab villages; over the two subsequent years, rates were 22 percent lower (see Box 7.6).
- In San Pablo Autopan, Mexico, maternal and child health services and contraceptives were delivered to individual households in 1976–77. Contraceptive use rose from 5 to 9 percent in the surrounding areas, and from 7 to 25 percent in the area covered by the project.
- On the island of Cheju, Korea, family planning staff distributed oral pills and condoms through home visits in 1976–79 and also referred to clinics women who wanted IUDs and subsidized sterilization. Over the period, fertility in the surrounding areas fell by 29 percent; in Cheju it fell by 35 percent, mainly because of sterilization.
- In some parts of the island of Bohol, Philippines, village workers (including midwives and

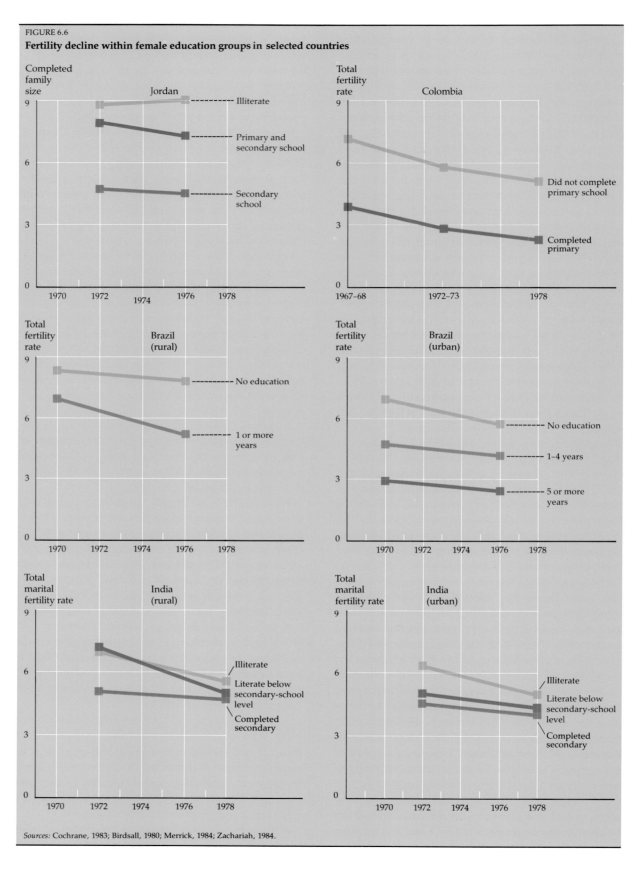

FIGURE 6.6

Fertility decline within female education groups in selected countries

Completed family size — Jordan
9 — 9 ------- Illiterate
— Primary and secondary school
6
— Secondary school
3
0
1970 1972 1974 1976 1978

Total fertility rate — Colombia
9
6 ------- Did not complete primary school
3 — Completed primary
0
1967–68 1972–73 1978

Total fertility rate — Brazil (rural)
9
— No education
6 ------- 1 or more years
3
0
1970 1972 1974 1976 1978

Total fertility rate — Brazil (urban)
9
6 ------- No education
------- 1–4 years
3 ------- 5 or more years
0
1970 1972 1974 1976 1978

Total marital fertility rate — India (rural)
9
6 — Illiterate
— Literate below secondary-school level
3 — Completed secondary
0
1970 1972 1974 1976 1978

Total marital fertility rate — India (urban)
9
6 — Illiterate
— Literate below secondary-school level
3 — Completed secondary
0
1970 1972 1974 1976 1978

Sources: Cochrane, 1983; Birdsall, 1980; Merrick, 1984; Zachariah, 1984.

traditional birth attendants) provided maternal and child health care, as well as family planning services in 1974–79. In those areas, fertility declined by 15 percent; elsewhere on the island, it fell by 9 percent.

• A comprehensive rural health program was undertaken in an area in Maharashtra, India, from 1971 to 1978. In a nonprogram area, fewer than 10 percent of eligible couples used contraceptives in 1976, and the crude birth rate was thirty-seven per thousand. In the program area, contraceptive use rose from 3 to 51 percent, and the crude birth rate in 1976 was twenty-three per thousand.

Unfortunately, experiments such as these are difficult to replicate. They often cost more than a government could spend on a nationwide effort; more important, they may work because of the intense involvement of research and other staff. Indeed, not all field projects work well; effects of projects were small in a condom-marketing scheme in Kenya, and nonexistent in one in Rio de Janeiro, Brazil (the only project conducted exclusively in an urban area, where contraceptives were easily available). But the results still suggest that good services reduce fertility significantly, by closing the gap between actual and desired family size.

COST EFFECTIVENESS OF FAMILY PLANNING PROGRAMS. By increasing the supply of services, family planning programs reduce the cost of using contraception to potential users. By contrast, increased education, lower mortality, and other social changes increase the demand for contraception. For the single goal of reducing fertility, spending on family planning services turns out to be more cost effective (that is, it leads to the same fertility reduction at lower cost) than does spending on education, health (which reduces fertility by reducing infant mortality), and other programs. Of course, this comparison does not take into account (1) that education and health programs have other objectives in their own right, independent of effects in fertility; (2) that family planning has other benefits—including reducing mortality; and (3) that these different approaches are not really alternatives but complement and reinforce each other. At low levels of education and high levels of mortality, the underlying demand for family planning will be low. The same amount spent on a program in a high-education, low-mortality setting will induce a greater increase in contraceptive use.

One reason family planning is cost effective is that it has an immediate impact—at least where there is underlying demand. Similarly, the effect of

reducing infant mortality and of providing more schooling for children can be rapid—but these cost more in most settings to produce the same effect on fertility. With respect to the single goal of reducing fertility, one study concluded that family planning programs were at least seven times as cost effective in reducing fertility as were nutrition programs or education schemes for rural women. In Bangladesh, Korea, and the Philippines family planning programs are estimated to be five times as cost effective as health programs that reduce fertility through reducing mortality. But where mortality is high and demand for family planning is limited, as in Kenya, reducing infant mortality is a more cost-effective way to lower fertility.

Emphasis on the cost effectiveness of family planning should not obscure the third point noted above: that family planning and social development complement each other. Analysis of fertility change across countries done for this Report shows that between 1972 and 1982 family planning programs have had minimal effect where female education is low, in part because it is difficult to operate such programs without some educated women to staff them, and in part because of lack of demand for contraception. Equally, female education has had minimal effect where family planning services have been unavailable. However, the effect of the two together has been powerful. The decline in fertility in Kerala, India, provides a good illustration. Education levels have been higher in Kerala than in most other Indian states for many years, and infant and child mortality rates have been lower. Around 1980 the literate proportion of Kerala's population was twice that of India's as a whole, and the infant mortality rate less than half the national rate. The fertility rate fell from 4.1 to 2.7 between 1972 and 1978 in Kerala (compared with a fall from 5.8 to 4.9 for India as a whole), in part because investment per capita in family planning in Kerala has been high, at times almost as great as in Hong Kong. But this investment would have had much less impact in less favorable conditions of education and health.

Incentives and disincentives

To complement family planning services and social programs that help to reduce fertility, governments may want to consider financial and other incentives and disincentives as additional ways of encouraging parents to have fewer children. Incentives may be defined as payments given to an individual, couple, or group to delay or limit child-

Box 6.3 Measuring the value of children

Potential parents trying to estimate the cost of children would need to consider the following:

- Goods and services (food, shelter, clothing, medical care, education, and the like) needed in raising children, and specifically the amount required in each future year, and the expected prices, year by year, for goods and services.
- The amount of time they will put into caring for children, year by year, and the expected wages they will thereby lose.
- The amount of time children would put into earning for the household, and the wages the household can expect to receive.
- The probability that children will survive to any given age, which should be used to weight the probable costs for each year.
- The weight to attach to future costs and benefits from children, such as security for old age, in contrast to immediate costs and benefits.

Few parents explicitly make such calculations, but illustrative examples suggest what the results of such calculations would be.

For a rural sample in the Philippines, three-quarters of the costs involved in rearing a third child come from buying goods and services; the other quarter comes from costs in time (or lost wages). But receipts from child earnings, work at home, and old age support offset 46 per-cent of the total. The remaining 54 per-cent, the net cost of a child, is equivalent to about 6 percent of a husband's annual earnings.

By contrast, a study of an urban area of the United States in 1960 showed that almost half of the costs of a third child are time costs. Receipts from the child offset only 4 percent of all costs.

Only economic costs and benefits are taken into account in these calculations. To investigate social and psychological costs, other researchers have examined how individuals perceive children.. The figure shows the variety of values and drawbacks of children mentioned by mothers in the Philippines, Korea, and the United States. Economic contribu-tions from children are clearly more important in the Philippines, where fer-tility is higher than in the Korea or the United States; concern with the restric-tions children impose on parents, on the other hand, is clearly greatest in the United States.

In all three countries, however, couples demonstrate a progression in the values they emphasize as their families grow. The first child is important to cement the marriage and bring the spouses closer together, as well as to have someone to carry on the family name. Thinking of the first child, couples also stress the desire to have someone to love and care for and the child's bringing play and fun into their lives.

In considering a second child, parents emphasize more the desire for a compan-ion for their first child. They also place weight on the desire for a child of the opposite sex from the first. Similar val-ues are prominent in relation to third, fourth, and fifth children; emphasis is also given to the pleasure derived from watching children grow.

Beyond the fifth child, economic con-siderations predominate. Parents speak of sixth and later children in terms of their helping around the house, contri-buting to the support of the household, and providing security in old age. For first to third children, the time taken away from work or other pursuits is the main drawback; for fourth and later chil-dren, the direct financial burden is more prominent than the time costs. Like the economic evidence, this account high-lights the economic contributions that children in large families make and, once family size has declined somewhat, the significance of time costs in producing one- and two-child families.

These studies focus on the advantages and disadvantages to couples of having one or more children. But society as a whole bears many of the costs of popula-tion growth. Do couples limit their own childbearing for essentially altruistic rea-sons? One small study, conducted a decade ago in the Philippines, suggests they might.

About 300 people from Manila and sur-

bearing or to use contraceptives. They extend fur-ther the subsidy governments provide when they use public resources to deliver family planning services. Disincentives are the withholding of social benefits from those whose family size exceeds a desired norm.

Incentives and disincentives serve three main purposes.

- They encourage birth control by calling atten-tion to family planning, spreading information about its availability, motivating individuals to consider it more seriously, and compensating for costs and inconvenience that might discourage potential users.
- They alter the costs and benefits of children and may therefore affect desired family size (see Box 6.3). Incentives offer alternative ways to ensure the benefits children might otherwise pro-vide; disincentives raise the costs of children. Where large families are not in the interests of soci-ety as a whole, society may benefit more by pro-viding incentives that lower fertility than by bear-ing the social costs of high fertility.
- They help inform people about society's pop-ulation goals and the damaging effects of rapid population growth and large families.

Payments to people who volunteer for steriliza-tion are usually meant to compensate for travel and work time lost; like incentives and free family planning services, they provide a subsidy that

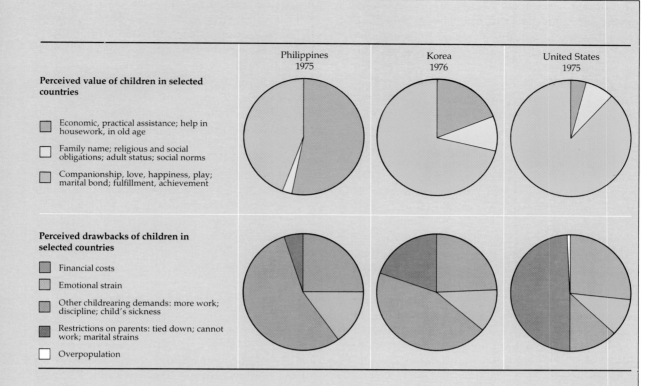

Perceived value of children in selected countries

Philippines 1975 · Korea 1976 · United States 1975

- ☐ Economic, practical assistance; help in housework, in old age
- ☐ Family name; religious and social obligations; adult status; social norms
- ☐ Companionship, love, happiness, play; marital bond; fulfillment, achievement

Perceived drawbacks of children in selected countries

- ☐ Financial costs
- ☐ Emotional strain
- ☐ Other childrearing demands: more work; discipline; child's sickness
- ☐ Restrictions on parents: tied down; cannot work; marital strains
- ☐ Overpopulation

rounding rural areas were asked questions about various hypothetical crises that might arise and how they would be willing to respond to them. For example, in the case of a severe rice shortage, 60 percent said they would be "very willing" or "moderately willing" to eat corn instead of rice at least once a day. In case of an invasion, 82 percent would be willing to send a son into the army.

This question was also posed:

Supposing the government determined that the population was growing too fast and there were not enough jobs for the adults, not enough schools for the children, not enough hospitals for everyone, and not enough money to pay for these things. Would you be willing to stop having children (and to stop at two children, if you had no children yet) in

order to help solve the problem?

Eighty-four percent of respondents said they would be willing to stop at two children (if they had none to begin with), and 86 percent said they would be willing to stop at the number they had. The social costs of population growth, for this small sample, appeared real enough to generate some sacrifice from almost everybody.

encourages smaller family size (though they are usually offered to all clients regardless of family size). Some population programs also provide bonus payments as incentives to family planning workers; they are meant not to increase demand for services but to improve supply, and are discussed in the next chapter.

Incentives and disincentives give individuals a choice. They provide direct and voluntary trade-offs between the number of children and possible rewards or penalties. But choice will be preserved only if programs are well designed and carefully implemented. The ethical questions raised by incentives and disincentives are touched on here but discussed more in Chapter 8.

Examples and experience

Although various forms of incentives and disincentives now exist in over thirty countries in the developing world, it is still not possible to estimate exactly how much influence they have had on fertility. In countries in which they have been tried, they have been accompanied by social change, family planning services, and (in the case of China) various social pressures that make it impossible to distinguish their separate effects.

Disincentives built into benefit or tax systems are the most common. Ghana, Malaysia, Pakistan, and the Philippines limit income tax deductions, child allowances, and maternity benefits beyond a few births; to encourage spacing, Tanzania allows working women paid maternity leave only once every three years. But these policies affect only the small minority who are public employees or who pay taxes. Singapore has disincentives which affect more people because of the country's higher income, comprehensive health services, urbanized setting, and extensive public housing. Singapore's disincentives include limitation of income tax relief to the first three children, restriction of paid maternity leave to the first two pregnancies and an increase in childbirth costs after the first two deliveries. Singapore also gives children from smaller families priority in school admission and ignores family size in the allocation of state housing, so smaller families enjoy more space per person. Attitudinal studies suggest that these disincentives, particularly the school admission policy, are much more influential in Singapore than are the more common tax disincentives. Disincentives were introduced gradually in Singapore beginning in 1969, more than a decade after fertility had started to fall. The timing and pattern of the fertility decline thereafter suggests that they have had some impact.

In 1984 the Singapore government shifted the emphasis of its population policy. While it still encourages most women to have only two children, women university graduates are encouraged to have more. If graduates have more than two, the government will now give their children priority admission to state schools. This approach is based on a belief that highly educated parents are more intelligent than those with less education, and that children inherit intelligence from their parents. Were this the case—since better-educated parents have typically had fewer children, at least for the past 100 years—the average intelligence of humankind would be falling. But it does not appear to be. In any event, local newspaper polls indicate that the policy is not popular, even among women who could benefit from it. Many such women have said that priority in school admission is not enough to persuade them to have more than one or two children.

China has the most comprehensive set of incentives and disincentives, designed (most recently) to promote the one-child family. Since the early 1970s women undergoing various types of fertility-related operations have been entitled to paid leave: in urban areas fourteen days for induced abortion; ten days for tubal ligation; two to three days for insertion or removal of an IUD; and in the case of postnatal sterilization, seven extra days over the normal fifty-six days of paid maternity leave. Since 1979 the central government has been encouraging, even requiring, each area and province to draw up its own rewards and penalties. Sichuan, for example, provides for a monthly subsidy to one-child families of five yuan (8 percent of the average worker's wage) until the child is fourteen years old. The child will have priority in admission to schools and in obtaining a factory job. In rural areas in Hunan, parents of only one child receive annual bonuses until their child is fourteen years old and private plots and housing lots big enough for a two-child family. In some urban areas, a single child is allotted adult food rations. Most factories and other work units give preference in the allocation of scarce housing to single-child families. In some cases, medical and educational entitlements are granted preferentially to parents whose only child is a girl—one way, the government hopes, of overcoming the preference for sons.

Penalties for excessive fertility also vary by area in China. In some places, couples who have a second child must return any bonuses obtained for the first child. A couple having a second child may be required to pay for the privilege. (In one brigade in Beijing studied by foreign researchers, several couples have been willing to pay more than twice the annual collective income distributed to each brigade member in order to have a second child.) Parents may have to pay a higher price for grain that they buy for a second child whose birth has not been authorized under the planned-birth program. Some areas and provinces impose taxes, which can be as high as 10 percent of family income, only on third and later-born children. Similarly, mothers may not be entitled to paid maternity leave for a third child, and parents may have to pay all its medical expenses. In 1983 the State Family Planning Commission proposed a tax of 10 percent of family wages on urban dwellers with two or more children, unless one or the other partner is sterilized.

In addition to China and Singapore, Korea is the only other country with a national system of rewards and penalties for individuals to encourage parents to have few children. Korea offers free medical care and education allowances to two-child families provided one of the parents has been sterilized.

Incentives do not have to be provided just by the state. A private group in Thailand offers technical assistance in farm production and marketing to contraceptive users or to those who commit themselves to birth control. Rates of contraceptive use have risen to as high as 80 percent in some villages that receive, or hope to receive, the benefits of this program. Qualifiers have been given credits for livestock, feed, and construction materials, and have been offered lower prices for fertilizer, seed, garlic, dressmaking, hairdressing, and medical treatment. Some communities have also been allowed to use a "family planning bull" for servicing their cattle. The scheme also offers pig-rearing contracts: a woman acceptor gets a piglet to fatten over a period of eight to nine months and is given a share of the profits. Should she become pregnant, the pig is not taken away, but she may lose the opportunity to get another one in the future.

In the past decade, a few countries have started offering small-family incentives to communities. The Indonesian program gives prizes and popular recognition for meeting fertility targets or for performing better than other communities. In Thailand the government rewards villages that achieve certain targets with anything from a biogas plant to a cooperative store. Community incentives work where there is a well-organized, community-based family planning system and where the village or hamlet is an important social or political unit.

Several other countries, including Bangladesh, India, and Sri Lanka, have offered rewards to people who volunteer to be sterilized, primarily to compensate them for the cost of travel and loss of work time. These programs are easier to administer than incentive systems tied directly to lower family size. In most cases, volunteers have been carefully screened to avoid any possibility of coercion or of changing their minds when it is too late. In Sri Lanka, for example, the couple must have at least two children, the youngest at least a year old. These facts must be certified by the village head and reviewed by a medical officer at the clinic where the operation will be performed. The volunteer must sign a statement of consent; he or she receives the equivalent of $20. At their peak in 1980–81, sterilization payments cost an amount equal to 3 percent of total government spending on health; that much could easily have been saved in the costs associated with abortion and unwanted births.

Unresolved issues

Payments and penalties raise a host of issues not yet resolved. Some people may be willing to defer pregnancy or to have fewer children even without an incentive, yet they cannot be stopped from claiming it; and they may be those least in need of an incentive. Disincentives that work through tax and benefits systems affect only a few people, yet broader disincentives might unfairly burden the poor, who gain most from children. Disincentives tied to school admissions may affect children who have no control over parental decisions. Verification (was a child born and not reported?) can be administratively difficult, and the money to reward compliance may be improperly used. Payments for sterilization have little impact on fertility if families have already had four or more children.

The cost of incentives is also a consideration in judging their effectiveness. From a national accounting point of view, incentives are transfer payments and in themselves do not use up resources. Their economic impact will depend on the savings and consumption patterns of those who are taxed and those who receive payments. The principal question is likely to be a budgetary one for the government: is money available and might it be better spent in other ways? If conventional incentive schemes absorb funds that might better go to investments, the cost to an economy in terms of long-run investment and growth may also matter. This is clearly a problem in China, where incentives large enough to ensure one-child families would become a heavy burden on the economy, unless those who received them in turn used the incentives for saving, say, for their own old age.

Deferred incentives

Deferred incentive schemes overcome some, though not all, of the difficulties of conventional incentives. They have not been tried on a national level, but two local experiments demonstrate their feasibility. A township in China began a deferred bonus scheme in 1971, offering to pay the high-school education of children of two-child families. No specific family planning service was involved, but parents had to show that they agreed with the terms of the entitlement when their children were ready to enter high school. Two-thirds of families enrolled in the program; its effects on fertility could not, however, be differentiated from a general decline in fertility.

A no-birth bonus scheme developed on three tea estates in India also provided a deferred payment. Each woman worker had an extra day's pay credited to an account for every month she was not pregnant. Her benefits were suspended for a year for each pregnancy and she forfeited a part of her account for each birth beyond two. She could claim the proceeds when she retired. An evaluation conducted several years after the start of the program showed that it had helped to accelerate the declining trend in fertility.

Both these programs were designed to cover their costs and to produce some saving—through lower educational expenses in the first case, and through lower child care, medical, and work-loss expenses in the second.

Deferred incentives have an immediate financial advantage: the payments by government to bondholders come in the future, at the time when the saving to society from fewer births is being reaped. However, they can still be costly. For example, an incentive scheme proposed in Bangladesh would provide a bond for all couples who agreed to sterilization and who had only two or three living children. To fully fund the scheme nationwide, the government would have to set aside a substantial proportion of its budget now (see Box 6.4).

There are also practical arguments in favor of deferred schemes, especially for sterilization. The first, alluded to above, is that a deferred payment avoids the risk of people volunteering simply because they need money immediately. If they later regret their decision, they can do nothing about it. If many people were do this, they might provoke a general reaction against sterilization. The second merit of a system with delayed payments is that it avoids the need for a large number of cash payments to be made by junior officials and thus minimizes the potential for corruption.

Deferred incentives, however, are not without their own problems. For example, it is not certain that potential recipients would trust the government's ability and willingness to provide benefits in the future. The administrative requirements of a deferred system are also considerable. For schemes not tied to sterilization, individuals would have to be registered and their births monitored. For many developing countries, keeping track of all births in circumstances where parents may wish to conceal them would require a more effective administrative system than now exists.

Despite these possible shortcomings, deferred incentives have much potential. If they could be made to work, they could provide for a transfer of income to the poor that would reduce fertility. Nepal is trying deferred incentives in a few areas, and Bangladesh is now considering such schemes. They could also be tried in those rural areas of India and Indonesia where family planning services and administrative systems are adequate.

7 Family planning as a service

Some eighty-five countries in the developing world, representing about 95 percent of its population, now provide some form of public support to family planning programs. Tremendous progress has been made in improving couples' access to information and services. But in all countries more could be done. Nearly all programs still fail to reach most rural people; even in the towns and cities the quality of services is often poor and discontinuation rates high. In many countries the potential of the private sector to provide family planning services has hardly been tapped; in others the gap in services provided privately can be filled only by enlarging public programs. Twenty-seven countries have yet to introduce family planning programs. Almost half of these are in Africa, where incomes are the lowest in the world, population growth is the highest, and the potential benefits from family planning may be greatest.

The benefits of family planning, moreover, do not depend on the existence of demographic objectives.

● Family planning improves the health of mothers and children. Both infant and maternal mortality in developing countries could be substantially reduced if pregnancies were spaced at least two years apart, and if pregnancies among teenagers and women over forty were prevented (see Box 7.1). Couples with access to family planning services can prevent unwanted pregnancies that might otherwise result in poorly performed abortions and the risk of serious, even fatal, complications. Family planning services were recognized as one of eight essential components of primary health care by the International Conference on Primary Health Care in Alma-Ata in 1978.

● Family planning makes responsible parenthood easier. Parents can have the number of children for whom they know they can provide adequate food, health care, and education.

● Family planning enlarges the choices available to people, a central purpose of economic and social development. This is particularly true for women,

who are often caught in a vicious circle in which too many children mean too few opportunities for other kinds of activity, and vice versa. By enabling women to control their fertility, family planning frees them to become better educated and to increase their own and their children's contribution to development.

● Family planning offers the greatest potential benefits for the poorest people, whose mortality and fertility rates are usually the highest of any group.

For all these reasons, programs to support family planning deserve a central role in the social and economic strategies of governments throughout the developing world. Properly designed, programs need not be particularly expensive. But lack of finance is one of the reasons family planning is

TABLE 7.1

Percentage of currently married women aged 15 to 49 using contraception, by region and for selected countries

Region and country	Total	Urban	Rural
Sub-Saharan Africa	(6)[a]		
Ivory Coast (1980–81)	3	4	2
Kenya (1977–78)[b]	7	12	6
Middle East and North Africa	(22)[a]		
Egypt (1980)	24	40	12
Syria (1978)	20	34	5
East Asia	(65)[a]		
Philippines (1978)	36	47	31
Thailand (1981)	57	64	55
Latin America and Caribbean	(40)[a]		
Colombia (1980)	49	54	37
Mexico (1979)	39	51	27
South Asia	(25)[a]		
Bangladesh (1983–84)	19	36	17
Sri Lanka (1982)	55	57	54

Note: Numbers are based on recent surveys, except for India and Indonesia, which are based on recent program statistics.
a. Average weighted by population for all countries in region with recent surveys.
b. Ever-married women aged 15 to 50.
Source: World Development Indicators, Table 20.

Box 7.1   Family planning for health

Early and frequent childbearing contributes substantially to illness and death of infants, young children, and mothers in developing countries. Family planning programs can tackle these problems through four main mechanisms:

• Lengthening the interval between pregnancies (child spacing). The interval between pregnancies is an important determinant of survival for both the newborn baby and his or her older sibling. Infants and children at highest risk of death are those born less than two years apart (see first chart). This relation holds even when allowance is made for birth order, mother's age, mother's education, urban or rural residence, and the sex of the child.

There are two main explanations for the link between mortality and spacing. The first is that the youngest and next youngest child must compete for the resources of the family and for the attention of the mother. When a woman becomes pregnant again soon after giving birth, the young child may be prematurely weaned, increasing the risk that he or she will suffer from malnutrition, gastrointestinal infection, diarrhea, and other illnesses. Second, a rapid succession of pregnancy, breastfeeding, and then another pregnancy weakens the mother and is linked to low birth weight

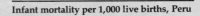

Infant mortality per 1,000 live births, Peru

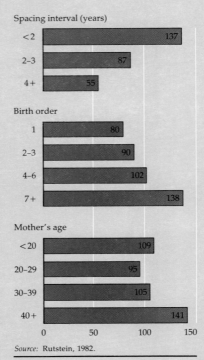

Source: Rutstein, 1982.

in the newborn baby. One study of twenty-five developing countries suggested that, if births were spaced two to six years apart, infant mortality would decline by an average of 10 percent, and

child mortality would decline by 16 percent. In Pakistan infant mortality (currently 140 per thousand) would fall by 30 percent if all birth intervals of less than thirty-six months could be lengthened to thirty-six to forty-seven months.

• Preventing births for women under twenty and over thirty-four years of age. In these age groups, women who become pregnant carry a greater risk of illness and death, both for themselves and their children. Infant and maternal mortality are highest among teenage mothers. In Pakistan, for example, babies born to teenage mothers have a 50 percent greater chance of dying than do those whose mothers are aged twenty to twenty-nine; in Peru the chance is 15 percent greater. There were 860 maternal deaths per 100,000 live births among teenage mothers in Matlab Thana, Bangladesh in the mid-1970s, compared with 450 for women aged twenty to twenty-nine (see second chart). Part of the explanation for these contrasts is that teenage mothers may not be physically mature enough for a safe pregnancy; in addition, most of their births are first births, which often carry a higher risk of infant and maternal death. As for mothers over thirty-five years old, their babies run an increased risk of congenital defects such as Down's syndrome, cleft

---

being neglected in some countries and is making only slow progress in others. Aid donors have a major contribution to make in ensuring that family planning programs receive the money they need to be effective.

The use of contraception

Surveys of married women of reproductive age (fifteen to forty-nine) show wide variations in contraceptive use among developing regions (see Table 7.1). In East Asia nearly two-thirds of the married women in that age group use contraception; in China, Hong Kong, and Singapore the proportion is 70 percent or more, as high as in the United States and western Europe. Latin America has reached about 40 percent, whereas the proportion in the Middle East and South Asia is only

about 25 percent. Contraceptive use is lowest in sub-Saharan Africa, at less than 10 percent of married women, and this estimate excludes many countries in which use is negligible but data are unavailable.

Contraceptive use varies widely within countries as well. In most, a higher proportion of urban than rural couples use contraception; the distinction is particularly stark in Syria, where 34 percent of urban, but only 5 percent of rural, women were using contraception in 1978. In the Ivory Coast, Kenya, and Mexico, contraceptive use in rural areas is roughly half the rate in urban areas, and in Egypt it is less than a third. Regional differences are also great: in Indonesia, contraceptive use ranged from 53 percent of couples on the islands of Java and Bali to only 16 percent in some of the outer islands in 1983. In Maharashtra and Gujarat palate, and heart disorders. Infant and maternal mortality also increase for mothers in their thirties and forties.

• Because most births are already to women in the twenty to thirty-four age group, confining all births to that group would have only a modest effect on overall infant and child mortality rates. For example, both rates would decline by only 2 to 6 percent in Indonesia, Pakistan, and the Philippines. The effect on

Maternal mortality per 100,000 live births, Matlab, Bangladesh

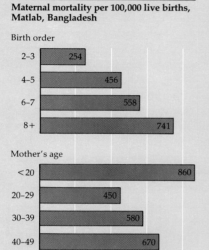

Birth order

Mother's age

Source: Chen and others, 1974.

maternal mortality is potentially greater. A study in the mid-1970s estimated that maternal mortality would be reduced by 24 percent in the Philippines, by 23 percent in Colombia and France, and by 19 percent in Mexico, Thailand, Venezuela, and the United States. The effect on maternal and child illness has not been estimated, but it would certainly be greater than on mortality.

• Allowing couples to have fewer children. Depending on the country, the risks of infant and maternal mortality increase rapidly after the third, fourth, or fifth child. In El Salvador, for example, infant mortality for fifth and later children is more than twice the level for the second and third child. In Matlab Thana, Bangladesh, maternal mortality is about 250 per 100,000 live births for the second and third births but is about 450 per 100,000 for the fourth and fifth births. These relations hold even when allowance is made for differences in the age of mothers. If all births of fourth and later children were prevented, infant mortality would decline by between 5 and 11 percent in Indonesia, Pakistan, the Philippines, and Sri Lanka.

• Preventing illness and death resulting from unsafe abortion. Abortion is extremely safe when performed in the first three months of pregnancy by trained personnel in sanitary conditions. But in most developing countries the procedure is illegal, and therefore more likely to be self-induced or performed unhygienically by untrained people. Such abortions carry with them a high incidence of complications, such as incomplete abortion, pelvic hemorrhage, lacerations of the cervix, perforation of the uterus, and tetanus. These complications may require hospitalization and may damage the mother's fertility; in the worst cases, they can kill her.

Because abortion is illegal in many countries, the number of women affected is difficult to estimate. In twenty-four countries during 1970–78, complications of abortion were cited as a cause of between 6 and 46 percent of all registered, maternity-related deaths. Scattered evidence from Africa suggests that hospital admissions for complications after induced abortion are increasing, and that a disproportionate number of admissions are teenagers. The International Planned Parenthood Federation (IPPF) estimated in the late 1970s that 84,000 women die annually from complications of abortion in sixty-five developing countries. Provision of safe, effective, and convenient contraception could prevent many unwanted pregnancies that are aborted.

states of India, 35 percent of couples were using contraception in 1981–82, compared with only 11 percent of couples in the states of Uttar Pradesh and Jammu and Kashmir.

Among countries for which more than one survey estimate is available, contraceptive use has increased fastest in East Asia and Latin America (see Figure 7.1). In Thailand, for example, the proportion of married women aged fifteen to forty-four using contraception rose from 15 percent in 1970, the year the official family planning program was launched, to 59 percent in 1981. Progress in South Asia has been slower, with contraceptive use increasing by about 1 percent of couples a year in Nepal, more quickly in Bangladesh, but not at all in Pakistan. In Egypt and Kenya contraceptive use has remained unchanged, despite longstanding public programs.

These survey-based estimates may underestimate contraceptive use because they do not include use among unmarried men or women and sometimes exclude use among couples in informal unions. There may also be underreporting by some women of the use of contraception by husbands, and some respondents may be reluctant to admit to using contraception themselves. At the same time, these figures may overstate the number of people protected by contraception because not all couples using a method are equally protected from the risk of pregnancy. Some are using "efficient" contraceptive methods such as sterilization, the pill, the IUD, injectable contraceptives, condoms, spermicidal foam, and the diaphragm. But others are using less effective methods, such as douche, rhythm, and withdrawal, or are abstaining (see Box 7.2). In Peru, 53 percent of those using

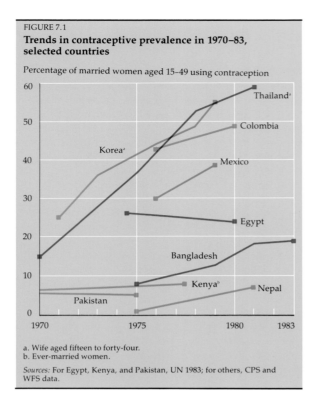

FIGURE 7.1

Trends in contraceptive prevalence in 1970–83, selected countries

Percentage of married women aged 15–49 using contraception

a. Wife aged fifteen to forty-four.
b. Ever-married women.

Sources: For Egypt, Kenya, and Pakistan, UN 1983; for others, CPS and WFS data.

88 in Romania (1979). Resort to both legal and illegal abortion often results from lack of information about, and access to, safe and effective contraceptive methods.

Unmet need

In the surveys from which data on contraceptive use have been drawn women were also asked whether they would like to have more children. Forty to 75 percent of married women of childbearing age in East and South Asian countries and in Latin American and Caribbean countries want no more children. In a few countries women were also asked whether they wished to delay their next pregnancy for a year or more. Nineteen percent of women of childbearing age in Bangladesh and Thailand, 25 percent in El Salvador, and 32 percent in Guatemala said yes. In countries where both questions have been asked, from 50 to 90 percent of women want either to limit or to space births.

In virtually all countries surveyed, the number of women of childbearing age who want no more children exceeds the number using some kind of contraception. Some of the women who want no more children or who wish to delay a pregnancy are not using a method because they are currently pregnant or because they have been breastfeeding for less than one year and therefore are afforded some (but not total) protection. Others are unable to conceive, or their husbands are away. These women are not ''exposed'' to the risk of pregnancy, so they do not need contraception, at least not immediately.

The remaining women—those who would like to space or to limit births, who are not using contraception, and who are exposed to the risk of pregnancy—are said to have ''unmet need'' for contraception. By this definition, 6 to 12 percent of women of childbearing age in Egypt, Kenya, and the Philippines have unmet need for contraception to limit births (see Figure 7.2, low estimate). In Bangladesh, Korea, and Peru, where both limiting and spacing questions were asked, 16 to 33 percent of women of childbearing age have unmet need for contraception. If women who are breastfeeding and those using inefficient methods of contraception are also considered to have unmet need, more than 40 percent of women in Bangladesh and Peru have unmet need for limiting and spacing births; 22 percent of women in Egypt, 10 percent in Kenya, and 29 percent in the Philippines have unmet need for contraception only to limit births (Figure 7.2, high estimate). Estimates for other

rhythm or withdrawal had an unwanted pregnancy within three years after a birth, compared with only 29 percent of women who used the pill, the IUD, or injectable contraceptives. The 1978 Philippines Fertility Survey found that 36 percent of married women of reproductive age used some method, but only 16 percent used an efficient method. In contrast, in the Dominican Republic in 1975, contraceptive use was 32 percent for all methods and 26 percent for efficient methods.

Contraception is not the only method of birth control. Induced abortion is widespread, even where it is illegal. There may be as many as 30 million to 50 million induced abortions performed annually worldwide; this wide range is due to uncertainty about the number of illegal abortions. Illegal abortion carries with it a high risk of complications and death and can affect future fertility. In many developing countries abortion is illegal under any circumstances or is permitted only to save the life of the mother; China and India are major exceptions. Elsewhere legal abortion is an important method of birth control—in Cuba, Japan, Korea, the USSR, and eastern Europe. Legal abortion rates per thousand women of childbearing age range from 11 in Canada (1981) and 25 in the United States (1980) to 84 in Japan (1975) and

FIGURE 7.2

Contraceptive use and unmet need for contraception, selected countries, 1977–81

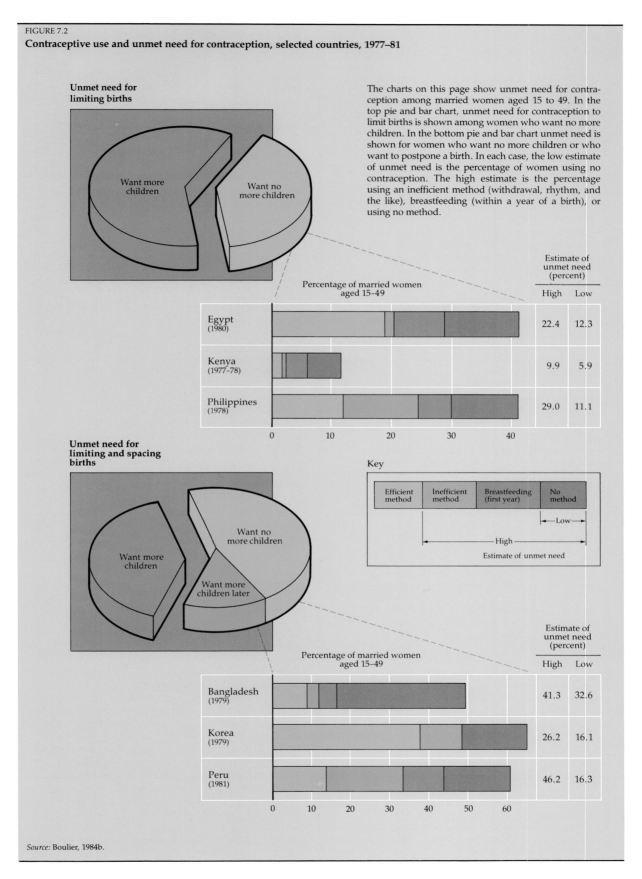

Unmet need for limiting births

Want more children

Want no more children

The charts on this page show unmet need for contraception among married women aged 15 to 49. In the top pie and bar chart, unmet need for contraception to limit births is shown among women who want no more children. In the bottom pie and bar chart unmet need is shown for women who want no more children or who want to postpone a birth. In each case, the low estimate of unmet need is the percentage of women using no contraception. The high estimate is the percentage using an inefficient method (withdrawal, rhythm, and the like), breastfeeding (within a year of a birth), or using no method.

Percentage of married women aged 15–49

		Estimate of unmet need (percent)	
		High	Low
Egypt (1980)		22.4	12.3
Kenya (1977–78)		9.9	5.9
Philippines (1978)		29.0	11.1

0   10   20   30   40

Unmet need for limiting and spacing births

Want more children

Want no more children

Want more children later

Key

Efficient method	Inefficient method	Breastfeeding (first year)	No method

←Low→

High

Estimate of unmet need

Percentage of married women aged 15–49

		Estimate of unmet need (percent)	
		High	Low
Bangladesh (1979)		41.3	32.6
Korea (1979)		26.2	16.1
Peru (1981)		46.2	16.3

0   10   20   30   40   50   60

Source: Boulier, 1984b.

Box 7.2 Birth planning technology

Several methods of birth control have been practiced throughout human history—abstinence, abortion, prolonged breastfeeding, and coitus interruptus (withdrawal)—but with uncertain effectiveness, and psychological and health damage. Contraceptive research in the past thirty years has made possible a much greater variety of more effective methods. Combined estrogen and progestin oral contraceptives (the "pill") and various intrauterine devices (IUD) were the first major breakthroughs in the late 1950s and early 1960s. Since then other methods have been developed: injectable contraceptives effective for two to three months; more effective copper and hormone-releasing IUDs; menstrual regulation (vacuum aspiration of the uterus within seven to fourteen days of a missed period); male sterilization; simplified female sterilization by laparoscopy and minilaparotomy; low-estrogen pills with fewer side effects; and a progestin-only "minipill." Barrier methods, such as the condom, diaphragm, and spermicides, have also been improved.

In 1980 the most commonly used methods of birth control worldwide were sterilization and the pill. Among developed countries the pill is the most used method, but sterilization has gained in popularity in the United States and in Great Britain, where it accounts for about a quarter of total use among married couples of childbearing age. The major exceptions to this pattern are Spain, Italy, and the Eastern European countries (except Hungary), where withdrawal, rhythm, or abstinence are still the most prevalent methods.

Among developing countries, sterilization is the most common modern method in Bangladesh, El Salvador, India, Korea, Nepal, Pakistan, Panama, Sri Lanka, Thailand, and Tunisia. The pill is the most favored method in Egypt, Jordan, Syria, much of Latin America, Malaysia, and Indonesia. Injectable contraceptives are widely used in Jamaica (11 percent of eligible women), Thailand (7 percent), Trinidad and Tobago (5 percent), and Mexico (3 percent); this method is convenient to use for rural women and, unlike the pill, does not interfere with lactation. Both the World Health Organization and IPPF have approved injectables—legal in more than 100 countries—but greater use in developing countries is partly constrained by the method's limited availability. The United States, the major contraceptive donor worldwide, cannot donate injectables because US assistance policy prohibits supply of drugs not approved for domestic use.

Despite the greater variety of contraceptive methods now available, all have shortcomings:

- *Effectiveness*. Under the ideal conditions of controlled studies in developed countries, existing methods can be highly effective in preventing pregnancy: nearly 100 percent for sterilization, the pill, and injectables; 98 percent for the IUD; and as much as 97 percent for the condom and the diaphragm after one year of use. But outside these controlled studies, some methods can be significantly less effective owing to incorrect or inconsistent use. In the United States, one in 100 couples using the pill will have a pregnancy within one year, more than two couples using the IUD, twelve using the condom or diaphragm, and twenty using rhythm. In the Philippines more than three women out of 100 using either the IUD or the pill and thirty-three using rhythm will become pregnant within a year. The motivation of couples to prevent pregnancy is important in the effectiveness of contraceptives. Couples who want no more children are likely to use methods more effectively than those who are spacing births.
- *Side effects*. Physical side effects are a main reason that people switch, or stop using, contraceptives. For some methods, the long-term health risks of prolonged use are unknown. Methods such as the IUD and injectables, which alter bleeding patterns—by spotting between periods, increased or decreased flow, or amenorrhea—may be culturally unacceptable or restrict the activities of users.

Box 7.3 Measuring unmet need for family planning

The concept of "unmet need" used in this Report is based on two questions asked of married women in representative nationwide surveys during the past decade. In more than forty countries women were asked, "Do you want additional children?" Among women who were exposed to the risk of pregnancy (that is, they were neither pregnant nor infertile), some said that they did not want more children. Of them, those who were not using any contraceptive method were defined as having unmet need for *limiting* births. In some surveys (in fewer countries), women were also asked, "Do you wish to delay pregnancy for a year or more?" Among women at risk of pregnancy, some said yes. Of them, those who were not using any contraceptive method were defined as having unmet need for *spacing* births.

Some investigators have suggested that responses to such questions are meaningless or, at best, unreliable. They argue that many women in developing countries are not accustomed to planning their families or are uninformed about how to affect the number of births they will eventually have. These criticisms apply most strongly to questions on preferred family size ("Suppose you were recently married and were able to have just the number of children you wanted, how many would that be?") and desired family size ("If you could choose exactly the number of children you have in your life, how many would that be?") These questions contain significant hypothetical components, since women cannot costlessly choose family size, cannot have fewer children than they already have, and must imagine alternative life cycles involving different family sizes. Responses to such questions are not consistent even when women are asked the same question at different dates. For example, in Indonesia only 46 percent of women reinterviewed four months after an initial survey gave an identical response to a question on desired family size. In a similar study elsewhere, only

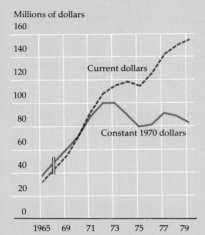

Worldwide expenditure on reproductive research and contraceptive development, 1965–79

Millions of dollars

Current dollars

Constant 1970 dollars

Source: Atkinson and others, 1980.

- *Inconvenience.* Barrier methods (condom, diaphragm, spermicides) have to be used each time couples have intercourse. In households in developing countries, pills and diaphragms are difficult to store and condoms difficult to dispose of.
- *Reversibility.* Sterilization is highly effective but rarely reversible. Injectables

are completely reversible but delay the return to fertility for several months.

- *Acceptability.* To some couples, abortion and sterilization are religiously or culturally unacceptable; some may regard only abstinence or rhythm as acceptable.
- *Delivery.* Sterilization (of both men and women) requires skilled medical or paramedical staff, who are often scarce in developing countries. The IUD, injectables, and the pill require medical backup for treatment of complications and side effects. Programs which promote the condom, pill, and spermicidal foam require a good network of supply points.

No single method of contraception is appropriate to the needs of all people nor is there one that is completely safe, reversible, effective, and convenient. Nor is such an "ideal" method likely to be developed in the next twenty years. Family planning programs will have to rely on a mix of existing methods and a few new ones whose development is already well advanced.

Research is being concentrated in two areas: improving the safety, convenience, and life span of existing methods, such as the IUD, pill, injectables, and female barrier methods; and developing new methods, such as a monthly pill to induce menstruation, long-lasting biodegradable hormonal implants for women,

nonsurgical chemical sterilization for men and women, a male "pill," and an antipregnancy vaccine for women. Some of these new methods—such as the hormonal implant (in the arm), improved IUDs, the vaginal sponge, cervical cap, and diaphragms which release spermicide—may be widely available in the near future. Others, such as new male methods and an antipregnancy vaccine, require much more research and are unlikely to be marketed before the end of this century.

Compared with the past few decades, the pace of technological development is slowing. Worldwide funding for contraception-related research was $155 million in 1979, but has been declining in real terms since 1972–73 (see chart). About 30 percent of the total is spent on contraceptive development and safety studies; the rest goes to training and basic research on human reproduction. Some 72 percent of the total was spent in the United States. Over 80 percent of the total was financed by the public sector; industry's share has shrunk from 32 percent in 1965 to less than a tenth. Special testing and regulatory requirements, combined with product-liability problems, have lengthened the time between product development and marketing, increased the cost of developing new products, and made the future profitability of research more uncertain for private firms.

67 percent of those reinterviewed after one month gave an identical response to a question on preferred family size.

In contrast, women respond consistently over time to a question on whether or not they want additional children, and their replies are reasonably good predictors both of contraceptive use and of future fertility. (The Population Data Supplement gives country-level information on responses to this question.) In the study in which two-thirds of responses to a question on preferred family size were inconsistent, 90 percent of women were consistent in answering a question about wanting additional children. In countries surveyed as part of the

World Fertility Survey, contraceptive use among women who said they wanted no more children consistently exceeded use among women wanting more children.

Obviously, not all women who want no more children use contraception, and not all women who want to limit their family size cease bearing children. Several factors may account for these discrepancies between attitudes and behavior. First, some women may not consider the costs of birth control in answering questions on family size. If the benefits of avoiding births are small in relation to the costs of contraception, women who want no more children have little motivation to use contraception. Second, the

surveys inquire only about women's, not men's, attitudes. Where both spouses have been interviewed, the difference between them tends to be small, but there are differences. Third, growing experience with children, plus unanticipated events—a child dying, illness of husband or wife—may lead couples to alter their plans. Fourth, even modern contraceptive methods can fail, so that some women will have more babies despite their intention not to increase family size.

TABLE 7.2
Percentage of married women aged 15 to 49 practicing efficient contraception among those who want no more children

| | Residence and education | | | |
| | Urban | | Rural | |
Country and family planning index[a]	No education	Seven years' education or more	No education	Seven years' education or more
Strong or very strong				
Korea, Rep. of, 1979	58	62	61	63
Colombia, 1980	35	69	30	52
Moderate				
Malaysia, 1974	37	..	27	49
Thailand, 1981	72	83	53	58
Philippines, 1978	22	45	15	38
Tunisia, 1979	50	60	45	..
Bangladesh, 1979	21	55	16	37
Mexico, 1978	40	71	17	53
Weak or very weak				
Nepal, 1981	40	71	15	45
Egypt, Arab Rep., 1980	53	72	24	70
Ecuador, 1979	17	60	6	58
Pakistan, 1975	17	35	6	17
Venezuela, 1976	53	67	18	54
Kenya, 1977–78	13	44	12	32
Honduras, 1981	53	58	15	49
Ghana, 1979–80	11	30	8	25

Note: Efficient contraception includes male and female sterilization, pills, IUD, injectables, diaphragm, and condoms. Women who are pregnant or infecund are excluded from this table.
.. Not available.
a. Family planning index is interpolated from 1972 and 1982 data to year shown. See notes for Table 6 of the Population Data Supplement.
Sources: CPS and WFS data; Lapham and Mauldin, 1984.

countries are shown in the Population Data Supplement, Table 3.

These high and low calculations of unmet need provide rough estimates, given existing preferences for family size, of the potential for additional contraceptive use. Some analysts, however, have questioned the validity of estimates based on the responses of married women to survey questions (see Box 7.3). Others have noted that even women who are pregnant may have had unmet need in the past that resulted in an unplanned pregnancy, and that such women may shortly be in need again. Nor do these surveys include unmet need among unmarried people. Clearly, use of contraception depends not only on accessibility and cost, but also on how intensely a couple wishes to avoid a birth. This factor is difficult to measure in surveys. Whether unmet need can ever be completely satisfied is debatable. But in the United States, where contraception is widely available, unmet need for limiting births was estimated at only 4 to 8

percent of married women of childbearing age in 1976.

The concept of unmet need is not static. Unmet need may decline as more people have access to contraception or as the nature of services changes. It may increase as people want fewer children, or as the better availability of services raises interest in regulating fertility faster than new services can meet new need. Many women who say they want more children might be potential users of services if given the chance to plan their births. To some extent family planning programs do more than simply satisfy unmet need; they actually generate and then fill such need. In this sense "demand" for contraceptive services is not easily measured; it is partly a function of their supply.

In most countries women in rural areas and with less education are less likely to want to stop childbearing than are urban and more educated women. But of the former, those who do want to stop are less likely than their urban and educated counterparts to be practicing contraception. Government plays a central role in narrowing these gaps, especially between urban and rural areas (see Table 7.2). In Colombia and Korea, which have strong family planning programs, rural women who want no more children are as likely as urban women to be practicing contraception. In Kenya, Nepal, and Pakistan, which have weaker programs, the contrast between rural and urban areas is much greater.

Reasons for not using contraception

Couples who wish to plan their families face certain costs—financial, psychological, medical, and time-related costs. If these exceed the net costs of additional children, couples will not regulate their fertility, even if, ideally, they would prefer to postpone or to prevent a pregnancy. To individuals, the costs of contraception include:

• Information—the effort to find out where contraceptive methods can be obtained and how they are properly used. In Kenya 58 percent of married women aged fifteen to forty-nine who are exposed to the risk of pregnancy do not know where they can obtain a modern method of contraception; in Mexico the figure is 47 percent.

• Travel and waiting time—the money and time needed to go to and from a shop or clinic and to obtain family planning services. Average waiting times are as high as three hours in hospitals and family planning clinics in El Salvador. Family planning programs in Bangladesh, India, and Sri Lanka compensate sterilization clients for their transport costs and lost wages.

• Purchase—the financial cost of either contraceptive supplies (condoms, pills, injections) or services (sterilization, IUD insertion and periodic checkups, menstrual regulation, and abortion). Most public family planning programs provide supplies and services free of charge or at highly subsidized rates. Purchase costs from private suppliers and practitioners may be substantially higher.

• Side effects and health risks—the unpleasant and sometimes medically serious symptoms that some women experience while practicing contraception. Users of the pill may gain weight or feel ill. The IUD may cause excessive menstrual bleeding, persistent spotting, and painful cramps. In addition, in some countries women are forbidden for religious or cultural reasons from cooking during their menstrual periods; spotting and heavier menstrual flow caused by the IUD can further

restrict their activities. Some methods increase the risk of developing serious health problems; higher risk of pelvic inflammatory disease among IUD users and of cardiovascular disease among users of the pill have been reported. (These risks, however, are small compared with those associated with pregnancy and childbirth.)

• Social disapproval—the private nature of family planning and the difficulty of discussing it with providers of services or even with spouses. Family planning may violate personal beliefs, create marital disharmony, or be socially, culturally, or religiously unacceptable.

Surveys of contraceptive use in ten countries asked married women not practicing contraception why they were not doing so. Unless they wanted another child or were pregnant, their reasons included lack of knowledge of a source or method of contraception, medical side effects of methods, religious beliefs, opposition from husbands, and financial costs. In Nepal lack of knowledge of a source was the main reason. In Honduras, Mexico, and Thailand half of the women who did not practice contraception but were exposed to the risk of pregnancy either knew of no source of contraception or feared side effects. In Bangladesh, Barbados, and Nepal as much as a quarter to a third of all married women were not using contraception for these reasons. Contraceptive prevalence clearly could be increased by better information and services—directed to men as well as to women.

Discontinuation rates tell a similar story. According to surveys in thirty-three countries, as many as 30 percent of married women of childbearing age have used contraception in the past but are no longer doing so (see Table 7.3). When contraception is being used to space births, some discontinuation is normal. But many who discontinue contraceptive use do not want more children. As the second column of Table 7.3 shows, as many as 10 percent of all married women are discontinuers who want no more children and are at risk of getting pregnant. In Barbados, Guyana, Jamaica, Korea, and Pakistan, the proportion exceeds one-third (column 3). Follow-up surveys of women who have accepted contraception typically find that much discontinuation is due to medical side effects. In a follow-up survey in the Philippines, for example, this reason was cited by 66 percent of those who stopped using the pill and 43 percent of those who stopped using the IUD. Reducing discontinuation among women who want no more children could increase contraceptive use by at least one-fifth in eight countries (column 4).

TABLE 7.3
Discontinuation of contraception, recent surveys

Country	Percentage of married women aged 15 to 49		Percentage of all discontinuers who are exposed and want no more children (2 divided by 1) (3)	Discontinuers who are exposed and want no more children (2), as a percentage of current users (4)
	Used contraception but are not current users ("discontinuers") (1)	Discontinued use, exposed[a] and want no more children (2)		
Sub-Saharan Africa				
Cameroon (1978)	6	(.)	1	2
Ghana (1979–80)	30	2	7	23
Kenya (1977–78)	25	2	7	24
Lesotho (1977)	18	2	10	33
Sudan (1979)	8	1	8	15
Middle East and North Africa				
Egypt (1980)	17	4	25	18
Jordan (1976)	22	3	12	10
Syria (1978)	14	1	9	6
Tunisia (1978)	15	3	18	9
South Asia				
Bangladesh (1979)	9	3	30	21
Nepal (1981)	2	(.)	8	2
Pakistan (1975)	5	2	43	42
Sri Lanka (1975)	14	4	29	12
East Asia				
Indonesia (1976)	12	2	16	7
Korea, Rep. of (1979)	24	8	33	16
Philippines (1978)	23	4	19	12
Thailand (1981)	21	5	26	9
Latin America and Caribbean				
Barbados (1981)	28	10	36	21
Colombia (1980)	20	4	22	9
Costa Rica (1980)	23	3	14	5
Dominican Republic (1975)	18	3	17	8
Ecuador (1979)	20	4	20	12
Guyana (1975)	22	8	34	22
Haiti (1977)	17	3	15	14
Honduras (1981)	15	2	10	6
Jamaica (1975–76)	26	9	36	24
Mexico (1978)	15	3	20	8
Panama (1976)	21	4	17	7
Peru (1981)	20	3	14	7
Paraguay (1979)	21	3	12	7
Trinidad and Tobago (1977)	27	8	28	14
Venezuela (1977)	20	4	19	8

Note: Figures in columns 1 and 2 were rounded after computing columns 3 and 4.
(.) Less than half of 1 percent.
a. Not pregnant or infecund.
Source: Ainsworth, 1984.

Supplying family planning services

Family planning programs have evolved in various ways, but a typical pattern begins with services being provided only by private family planning associations and a few concerned doctors and nurses. These groups gradually show that family planning is feasible and acceptable and start press-ing for government support. Once persuaded, governments typically provide family planning through the public health system. But because health care is often underfinanced and concentrated in urban areas, and because family planning competes with other medical priorities, the quality of services is uneven and available to only a small proportion of people. Eventually programs are extended to the countryside, often by paramedical and semiskilled staff with backup support from health centers. More attention is paid to increasing the range of contraceptive methods, providing follow-up services to clients, and working with community leaders to encourage local support. Commercial organizations are also encouraged to provide family planning. Private associations are delegated major responsibilities within the national program for certain services or target groups and continue to test new ways of providing services.

Public family planning programs are now at different stages of development in different regions.

• *East Asia.* Governments have a longstanding commitment to reduce population growth. They have been extremely successful in improving access to family planning services and in widening the range of contraceptive methods available. Large numbers of field workers have been recruited to provide family planning, and sometimes basic health care, in villages in China, Indonesia, and Thailand. Contraceptive use has increased dramatically during the past decade.

• *South Asia.* Official commitment to reduce fertility is strong, but results have been mixed. Contraceptive use is highest in Sri Lanka and several states in southern India, and is lowest in Nepal and Pakistan. The demand for contraception is still constrained by high infant mortality and by a preference for large families. At the same time, recent surveys have revealed substantial unmet need for both limiting and spacing births. Most programs have yet to achieve the rural spread found in East Asia and have tended to emphasize sterilization. Other methods have been largely supplied through subsidized commercial outlets.

• *Latin America and the Caribbean.* At first, widespread demand for family planning was met largely by private doctors, pharmacies, and nonprofit organizations, primarily in urban areas. Government support was weak, in part because of opposition from some religious authorities. The 1970s saw a growing interest on the part of governments and a greater tolerance by religious authorities. Most governments now support family planning services for health and humanitarian purposes; Barbados, Colombia, the Dominican Republic, El Salvador, Guatemala, Haiti, Jamaica, Mexico, and Trinidad and Tobago do so to reduce fertility as well. In rural areas, access to services is still inadequate in most countries.

• *Middle East and North Africa.* Some countries in North Africa—Egypt, Morocco, and Tunisia, for example—have long-established programs to reduce fertility. About half the countries in the Middle East provide family planning to improve child spacing and to promote health; only Turkey's program seeks to reduce fertility. In a few Middle Eastern countries, contraception is illegal. In others, cultural practices often confine women to their households, which makes it difficult for them to seek out family planning services. Programs that include home visits by family planning workers are not well developed.

• *Sub-Saharan Africa.* Of forty-one governments for which data are available, only nine have demographic objectives. Most governments that support family planning do so for health reasons, and twelve countries still provide no official backing for family planning. Where services exist, they are provided through health care systems that have only limited coverage, particularly in rural areas. Throughout Africa couples want large families, and infant mortality is high. There is some demand for family planning but it is poorly met by existing programs. As traditional ways of child spacing (prolonged breastfeeding and sexual abstinence) erode, the demand for modern contraception increases. Private organizations have helped to demonstrate that demand and to press for government support.

The management of family planning programs

Perhaps more than any other social programs, family planning programs can be effective only to the extent that they meet the needs of individuals, both for better information about the benefits of controlling fertility and for better services to facilitate doing so. At the same time family planning programs, like all public programs, operate within certain constraints: the availability of manpower and finance, the capacity for training and supervision, and the transport and communications infrastructure. Medical backup is necessary to deliver some contraceptive methods. The challenge for family planning managers is to address individual needs within the confines of these constraints, and in the longer term to ease such limitations.

The personal nature of family planning services has several important implications for designing and managing programs. First, programs must be able to accommodate local and individual needs and a variety of users. Potential clients include men and women; those who are married and unmarried; those of different social, economic, cultural, or religious backgrounds; and those who may be delaying a first pregnancy, spacing between children, or preventing additional pregnancies. Staff must be discreet, sensitive to the individual needs of clients, and familiar with local customs and beliefs. This requirement has been addressed in several ways: by selecting staff from local communities, by training staff in the environment in which they will work, and by making special efforts to hire female workers. Special services have also been targeted for specific client groups: adolescents, women who have just given birth, and mothers with young children.

Second, programs must encourage clients not only to accept a method of contraception but also to use it effectively and continuously. In societies in which people marry young, couples who are spacing and limiting births may have to use contraception for twenty years. Prolonged, effective use is easier if information and support regarding side effects are assured, resupply is convenient, and the opportunity to switch methods is available. Medical backup and referral is critical, as is the capacity to follow up on clients. Managers need information not only on new acceptors but also on continuing users, dropouts, and nonparticipants (see Box 7.4). Indonesia is one country with an effective monitoring system, including acceptor records, quarterly follow-up surveys of acceptors, and periodic sample surveys of households in which information on fertility and contraceptive use is collected.

Third, because information about the benefits of family planning and of small families may not be widespread, programs must create an awareness of services and their benefits, as well as spread information about the proper use of methods. Information and education activities are necessary both within and outside the system for delivering

---

Box 7.4 Management information systems for improved service delivery

The arrangements for providing family planning services in many countries are plagued by lack of reliable information on which to base management decisions. Requirements for data collection are imposed on overburdened staff and supervised by medical or other technical personnel untrained to make use of the information. Much time is spent collecting information that is never used.

A management information system (MIS) is any system which organizes the collection and interpretation of data needed by managers to make decisions. The rural health supervisor reviewing a worker's records to assess performance, and the health minister reviewing information on hiring and deployment of staff are both using an MIS. For a family planning program, an MIS could include information on target group size and characteristics, new and continuing acceptor rates and characteristics, numbers and types of follow-up visits, birth rates, staffing patterns, and availability of supplies. These data allow managers to make decisions based on up-to-date and reliable information that is collected as a matter of routine.

Studies in two states in India, Karnataka and Uttar Pradesh, in the mid-1970s showed that fieldworkers providing health and family planning services were spending as much as 60 percent of their time on activities not directly related to delivering their services. Keeping records and attending meetings were the most common extraneous activities. A total of forty-six registers were maintained by five types of fieldworkers, relating to a range of subjects (family planning, maternal and child health, immunization, malaria control) and with considerable overlap of the data they recorded. An assistant nurse-midwife alone maintained twenty-two records and prepared twelve reports a month. The information was not used by supervisors and managers, nor did workers receive any systematic feedback on their performance compared with others. There was little incentive to maintain good records and to report regularly and on time.

Following a review of the system, recordkeeping and reporting were streamlined. The number of registers kept by fieldworkers was reduced from forty-six to six: a register of eligible couples and children, a maternal and child health register, a report on blood smears for malaria, a birth and death register, a stock and issue register, and a diary of daily activities. The various separate reports forwarded to program managers were replaced by a single monthly report by each fieldworker, a single report by each supervisor, and a single report from each primary health center. Family planning staff were told immediately how they were measuring up to predetermined targets. To encourage competition, feedback reports from the district to the primary health centers also ranked centers on the basis of ten indicators, such as the number of immunizations and the number of sterilizations as a percentage of annual targets.

In three districts in the state of Andhra Pradesh where this system was introduced, the time spent on recordkeeping and reporting has been reduced considerably. An assistant nurse-midwife, for example, now spends only about half an hour a day with the new system compared with two hours before. Reports are complete and are submitted on time (in other districts reporting is about three months behind schedule), and managers are responding better to local needs. Steps to expand the system for statewide use are now being taken in Andhra Pradesh, and the government of India is recommending that all states adopt the new MIS.

services. Program staff recruit potential clients and offer information on proper use of methods. The mass media can be used to inform people of the benefits of small families and how to obtain contraceptive methods. Instruction on human reproduction, family planning, responsible parenthood, and problems of rapid population growth as part of school curricula can inform young people before they marry; such instruction can also be offered through nonformal education, such as adult literacy programs. These efforts complement other economic and social policies, discussed in Chapter 6, to create demand for smaller families.

Because of the need for medical services for provision or follow-up of many contraceptive methods, most family planning programs are linked to the public health system. The nature of these links varies among countries and has often changed. In some programs, family planning workers provide services through clinics administered by the ministry of health, but are responsible to some other body. In Pakistan primary responsibility for family planning lies with the Population Welfare Division of the Ministry of Planning and Development, using the division's own specialized facilities and workers. Elsewhere family planning is directly administered by the ministry of health, through a special department of family planning (as in Egypt) or as part of preventive or maternal and child health services (as in Botswana, Kenya, and Malawi). Staff may specialize in family planning (that is, as "single-purpose" workers), as in Kenya, Pakistan, and Indonesia; or they may be responsible for general health or maternal and child health services in addition to family planning (that is, as "multipurpose" workers), as in Bangladesh, Botswana, and India.

There have been obvious advantages in integrating health and family planning in the delivery of services. The health benefits for mothers and children of spacing and limiting births clearly establish family planning as a valuable component of maternal and child health services. For both services the main target group—married women of childbearing age—is the same. Joint delivery can reduce unit costs, and in countries where family planning is controversial, integrated services make the program more acceptable.

But integrated services also present difficulties. Health ministries are often understaffed and underfunded; they cannot always mobilize the political and administrative wherewithal to implement an effective family planning program. Heavy demands for health care may eclipse the provision of family planning services, and medical staff may give priority to curative rather than preventive services. Multipurpose workers who are overloaded with responsibilities will do none of their tasks well. If an integrated delivery system employs single-purpose workers, friction may arise over differences in training, seniority, salaries, and promotion. For example, in addition to their salaries, family planning workers have sometimes received incentive payments based on the number of acceptors they recruit, whereas health workers receive only salaries. In Kenya family health field educators (with family planning responsibilities) were paid more than the enrolled community nurses to whom they were to report. These personnel issues can seriously affect worker morale and performance.

Although family planning programs need some link with health systems, family planning services need not be confined to them. When services are provided through a maternal and child health program, important client groups may be overlooked: men, adolescents, unmarried women, and nonpregnant women. Ministries of health may be poorly equipped to organize social marketing schemes (for subsidized commercial distribution of contraceptives, discussed below), to develop mass media programs, or to coordinate public, private, nongovernmental, and commercial activities. Some of these responsibilities are often delegated, for example, to information or education ministries. Many programs have boards within or outside a ministry to coordinate the wide range of family planning activities. In Mexico the semi-autonomous Coordinacion General del Programa Nacional de Planificacion Familiar monitors and coordinates all family planning activities; it is located within the Ministry of Health but has direct access to the president and works closely with the National Population Council (CONAPO), a separate body responsible for population policy. In Indonesia the National Family Planning Coordinating Board (BKKBN) is an autonomous body that collects data, produces information and education programs, coordinates activities, and has its own fieldworkers who promote family planning, refer clients, and set up community distribution points. In some countries these family planning boards are also responsible for overall population policy—a role discussed more fully in Chapter 8.

In conclusion, there is no simple formula for the best organization of family planning programs. Programs that differ widely in structure can be equally successful. Workers in India deliver both family planning and maternal and child health services and are under the general guidance of the Division of Family Welfare within the central Ministry of Health and Family Welfare. Indonesia provides family planning as part of maternal and child health services within the health system, but also uses single-purpose fieldworkers responsible to the BKKBN. The Chinese program relies on joint personnel in the health system but has a separate policymaking body for family planning and overall population policy. No matter how service delivery is organized, all programs need some health backup.

Other significant factors in the success of programs are the degree of political commitment and the overall administrative capacity of government to coordinate the deployment, training, supervision, and availability of staff. These influence the effectiveness of three program strategies for expanding contraceptive use: increasing access to services, improving service quality, and ensuring social acceptability.

Increasing access

Perhaps the greatest achievement of family planning programs in the past decade has been to make information and services more accessible to those who need them. In twenty-three of twenty-nine developing countries in which surveys have taken place, more than 80 percent of married women are aware of at least one effective method of contraception. In urban areas of almost all of thirty-six countries examined by the World Fertility Survey (WFS), family planning methods are available within an hour's travel from home. In Costa Rica and Thailand most people in rural areas are also less than an hour away from services. Furthermore, most public programs provide services free of charge or at heavily subsidized rates.

But there are still many countries and areas in which information and travel costs are major obstacles to satisfying the unmet need of clients. According to household surveys in Guatemala and Piauí State, Brazil, 15 percent of married women of childbearing age said that they would like to use contraceptives but did not know where to get them. In Nepal half of married women do not know of a method of contraception; about 15 percent know of a method but not of an outlet. In Honduras about a quarter of women are unaware of either method or outlet. Of those women in rural areas who know where to obtain contraceptives, 32 percent in Colombia, 42 percent in Honduras, and 62 percent in Nepal live more than an hour away from the source of supply. These barriers—lack of information and distance—are particularly high in sub-Saharan Africa: more than half the eligible women in Senegal and Sudan are unaware of modern contraceptive methods, and in most African countries contraceptives are available only in urban areas.

To reach the rural areas, family planning programs have placed special emphasis on extending the work of health centers into communities and households through the use of fieldworkers and other outreach staff. Access has also been increased in many countries by encouraging the private sector to provide family planning services.

EXTENDING PUBLIC SERVICES THROUGH "OUTREACH." Until a decade ago almost all public family planning programs provided services from centers—usually clinics—and relied heavily on medical staff. Because health services were not well established in rural areas and medical staff were scarce, access to family planning as well as to medical care was limited.

Today many large family planning programs have succeeded in using their health centers as a springboard for taking services and supplies into the villages.

• Paramedical workers have been trained to provide many methods formerly provided only by physicians. In Thailand, for example, auxiliary midwives insert IUDs and administer injectable contraceptives. Elsewhere nonmedical workers distribute the pill; they receive careful training on screening for contraindications, proper use, how to deal with side effects, and referral procedures.

• Staff based in clinics have been supplemented with fieldworkers who provide a link between the clinic and the community (see Box 7.5). Fieldworkers periodically visit homes and outlying communities to refer clients to service outlets; to distribute nonclinical methods such as the pill, condom, and spermicidal foam; and to reassure users. In some cases fieldworkers also supervise local volunteers.

• Official outlets have been increased by organizing local supply depots for nonclinical methods. Such local outlets in Mexico and Indonesia assist the work of field staff and reduce costs to clients.

The advantages of outreach are considerable: fieldworkers take less time and money to train than do medical professionals; health staff can spend more time on health care than they other-

Box 7.5 Family planning fieldworkers

Outreach systems using fieldworkers have been a key to success in effective national family planning programs—overcoming the relative inaccessibility of physicians and lowering the costs of contraceptive use by bringing services directly to beneficiaries. Experience in different countries illustrates a diversity of approaches to the training, duties, and coverage of fieldworkers.

• *India*. Family planning services are delivered by male and female multipurpose workers. Female workers provide pre- and post-natal services to mothers, spread family planning information, distribute condoms, and deliver babies. The government has recently sanctioned the distribution of oral contraceptives by female workers; workers are trained to screen clients for contraindications, and each acceptor must be examined by a doctor within three months. Male workers concentrate mainly on environmental sanitation but also provide family planning information and distribute condoms. Between them they are expected to cover a population of 5,000 (3,000 in remote hilly and tribal areas), although in many parts of India, this coverage has not yet been achieved.

• *Indonesia*. On the islands of Java and Bali, there is about one family planning fieldworker to every 2,000 eligible couples. The fieldworkers, who are normally secondary school graduates, recruit new acceptors, provide door-to-door supplies, and provide the managerial link between health clinics and part-time local volunteers who run village and sub-village contraceptive resupply centers. Financing constraints have precluded reliance on paid fieldworkers in recent extensions of the program into the other islands.

• *Kenya*. The privately run Chogoria hospital project in the Meru district has used volunteer workers selected by local health committees to provide pills, condoms, and other basic health services to villages. Volunteers are supervised by paid workers attached to local health centers. Contraceptive prevalence has reached 28 percent, compared with a rate of 7 percent in the rest of the country.

• *Korea*. Full-time paid family planning fieldworkers—nurses, midwives, and nurse aides—are assigned to health subcenters from which they spend at least fifteen days each month making home visits and organizing group meetings to recruit eligible couples. They also distribute condoms and pills and refer IUD and sterilization clients to designated family planning clinics. Coverage averages one fieldworker per 2,600 married women of reproductive age nationwide but is greater in rural areas (one per 1,200 couples), than in urban (one per 6,900 couples) because of greater distances in rural areas.

• *Mexico*. The national program provides outreach services through four different government agencies. The Secretariat of Health and Welfare trains multipurpose fieldworkers who concentrate mainly on family planning. They are local volunteers who receive small incentive payments. The Social Security Institute runs a program to reach isolated areas by training traditional midwives and other local volunteers to provide information and supplies in exchange for a modest payment. The Secretariat of Agrarian Reform and the National System for Integrated Family Development also provide services through outreach workers.

• *Pakistan*. In 1981 the government reorganized its program to include a system of fieldworkers and community volunteers. The earlier system was based entirely on paid fieldworkers, which proved costly and ineffective. The new program uses locally recruited male and female volunteers—including satisfied clients, barbers, and teachers—to inform couples about available services, teach them the advantages of family planning, encourage breastfeeding and childspacing, distribute nonclinical methods, and refer clients to family welfare centers for other methods. The volunteers are trained and supervised by one male and one female worker at the family welfare center.

• *Philippines*. About 3,000 outreach workers—one to every 2,000 eligible couples—work as full-time government employees. Each worker recruits, trains, and supervises about sixteen community volunteers who provide information to couples, supply condoms and pills to current users, and make referrals to government health clinics. Some 50,000 volunteers serve almost three-quarters of the nation's eligible couples. The future of the outreach program is uncertain because external funding will terminate in 1985 and local governments have not been able to absorb the cost of the fieldworkers' salaries as rapidly as expected.

• *Thailand*. Until recently, the Thai national program has been clinic based. Now multipurpose village health volunteers—serving nearly half of the nation's villages—have been trained to provide family planning information and are authorized to resupply pill and condom acceptors. They also serve as referral agents for a mobile sterilization service.

• *Zimbabwe*. The Child Spacing and Family Planning Council, a parastatal under the Ministry of Health, provides many of the services and has about 300 full-time, single-purpose outreach workers who supply oral contraceptives to rural couples through regular home visits. A new project will train another 500 to 600 fieldworkers by 1987.

---

wise would; and community-based fieldworkers are often most aware of local needs. But the extensive use of fieldworkers requires regular, supportive supervision. They must be trained well at the outset and must receive periodic refresher courses to maintain the quality of services. They should concentrate on a few main tasks; additional responsibilities must be introduced only gradually. Fieldworkers also require a good medical backup and referral system so that any side effects that clients may develop can be promptly treated. Finally, supervisors and fieldworkers must travel frequently, and contraceptive supplies must be made available in an increasing number of remote outlets. Money for transport is often first to be sacrificed when budgets are cut, yet the whole strategy depends on extensive travel and good logistics.

ENCOURAGING PRIVATE SUPPLIERS. Another way in which governments have increased access to family planning services is by encouraging wider private involvement. This strategy makes fewer demands on scarce public funds and on administrative capacity. Policies include subsidizing commercial distribution of contraceptives, coordinating with and encouraging private nongovernmental organizations (NGOs), and removing legal and other barriers to private and commercial provision of contraception.

Subsidized provision of contraception through commercial outlets—often called social marketing—has been tried with some success in at least thirty countries. Social marketing programs use existing commercial distribution systems and retail outlets to sell, without prescription, contraceptives that are provided free or at low cost by governments or external donors. The first social marketing scheme was in India, selling subsidized ''Nirodh'' condoms. Almost all countries with such schemes sell condoms, and at least seventeen are known to sell oral contraceptives, sometimes several brands. Spermicides, in the form of suppositories, creams, pressurized foam, and foaming tablets are also commonly sold. Until recently, social marketing schemes have been limited to methods that do not require clinical services for distribution. But Egypt now sells subsidized IUDs through private doctors and pharmacies. And in Bangladesh there are plans to test-market injectable contraceptives through social marketing arrangements.

Social marketing makes family planning supplies more easily accessible by increasing the number and variety of outlets through which they can be obtained: pharmacies, groceries, bazaars, street hawkers, and vending machines. In Sri Lanka some 6,000 commercial outlets sell subsidized condoms and pills—more than five times the number of government family planning outlets. In the late 1970s social marketing schemes accounted for more than 10 percent of total contraceptive use in Jamaica, Colombia, Thailand, and Sri Lanka. In Bangladesh the social marketing program supplied about one-

quarter of couples who used contraception in 1983: it accounted for 67 percent of total condom use, 12 percent of oral contraceptive use, and 70 percent of spermicide use. In 1981 about half of all pill users and 80 percent of condom users in Sri Lanka obtained supplies from the social marketing program.

Reliance on commercial distributors does not lift all the burden off the public sector, however. The public sector still has to provide advertising, promotion, contraceptive supplies, distribution, and medical backup. Some training is necessary for commercial suppliers to dispense oral contraceptives and to advise clients how to use them properly, as has been done in Jamaica, Korea, Nepal, and Thailand. Failing that, some system of referral or prescriptions must be developed.

Although government subsidies to the commercial sector are usually provided for contraceptive supplies only, some governments also subsidize IUD insertion, abortion, and sterilization by private physicians. In Korea more than 2,300 physicians have been trained and authorized by the government to provide family planning services. The government pays the entire cost of sterilization, but the cost of IUD insertion is shared—two-thirds by the government, one-third by the client. The involvement of private physicians has been a crucial factor in the success of the Korean program, although in 1978 about 60 percent of rural townships still had no authorized physician.

Access to services has also been increased by collaborative efforts between government and NGOs. This collaboration has taken many forms: subsidization of or grants to NGO services, coordination of NGO and government services to assure maximum coverage and allocation of responsibilty for critical functions or services in certain regions to NGOs. In Bangladesh and Indonesia, for example, government services are allocated to rural areas, leaving NGOs to provide a large share of urban services. Since 1973 the Brazilian Family Planning Association (BEMFAM) has worked with the governments of several states in Brazil to establish community-based programs for low-income groups in the Northeast. The private nonprofit program in Thailand acts as an extension of the government's rural health service and recruits local distributors to promote family planning and sell subsidized contraceptives donated by the government and international agencies. By mid-1978 there were some 10,000 distributors covering one-quarter of the 600 districts in Thailand. In Kenya in 1980, NGOs were operating 374 out of 1,204 rural health facilities. But less than 1 percent of the NGO facilities offered daily family planning services, and only 7 percent offered part-time services. A new project is creating family planning service delivery points in at least thirty of the NGO facilities. In addition, both government and NGO representatives will sit on a National Council on Population and Development that will coordinate national efforts in population information, education, and communications.

Governments have also removed legal and regulatory obstacles that restrict commercial distribution. In Egypt the sale of oral contraceptives through private pharmacies does not require a physician's prescription, although their provision through government clinics serving rural areas does. Several countries—including China, Mexico, Morocco, the Philippines, and Thailand—allow pills to be distributed in facilities other than pharmacies or health centers. Other options for stimulating the private sector include removal of import tariffs on contraceptive supplies (Korea recently eliminated a 40 percent tariff on raw materials for domestically produced contraceptives); active government promotion of condoms, spermicides, and pills that can be easily supplied through commercial outlets; and training of private pharmacists and physicians who frequently have little knowledge of modern family planning methods.

Improving quality

The quality of family planning services matters in all phases of program development. In the early stages services are new, and contraception still lacks social legitimacy. Once programs are well established and accessible, quality counts because other costs of family planning—such as physical side effects—have replaced access as the factor limiting the success of the program. Three ingredients of quality—the mix of contraceptive methods, the information and choice provided, and program follow-up—have contributed much to program success (see Box 7.6).

THE METHOD MIX OF PROGRAMS. The number and characteristics of available contraceptive methods affect the ability and willingness of clients to practice birth control. Additional options are likely to increase acceptance, permit switching, and reduce discontinuation rates.

- Some women have medical conditions that rule out certain methods. Oral contraceptives should not be prescribed for women who are over forty years old, who smoke and are over thirty-five years old, who are breastfeeding, or who have a history of stroke, thromboembolism, cancer, liver damage, or heart attack. The IUD is undesirable for women with pelvic infection or a history of ectopic pregnancy. Some women cannot be properly fitted with diaphragms.

- If the side effects of one method cannot be tolerated, the availability of other methods improves the chance that couples will switch rather than stop using contraception altogether. For example, in Matlab Thana, Bangladesh, 36 percent of women had switched methods within sixteen to eighteen months after initial acceptance. And a study in the United States showed that married white women aged twenty-five to thirty-nine had used an average of more than two methods; more than a third of those aged twenty-five to twenty-nine had used three or more.

- Couples' preferences are influenced by their fertility goals—postponing a first birth, spacing between children, or limiting family size. Women using the pill tend to be younger and to have had fewer births than those protected by sterilization; many of the former are spacing births, while the latter have completed their families.

- Some methods of fertility control may be religiously or culturally unacceptable. Two-fifths of the world's countries, comprising 28 percent of its population, either prohibit abortion completely or permit it only to save the life of the mother. For religious reasons, sterilization is illegal in several countries. When couples regard periodic abstinence as the only acceptable form of birth control, programs should provide information on proper timing of abstinence, although this method carries higher risks of unwanted pregnancy.

Due to sheer lack of alternatives, early family planning programs offered only a limited range of contraceptive methods. In the late 1950s and early 1960s, the Indian program had to rely on rhythm, the diaphragm, and the condom. Today, most national programs offer a wider variety of methods, although the number available at any given outlet is often fewer than that implied by official statements. Some governments still promote a single method because such an approach is easier to administer or because certain methods, such as sterilization and the IUD, are viewed as more ''effective'' and require less follow-up over the long run than do other methods. For example, India, Korea, and Sri Lanka continue to emphasize sterilization. Until recently, Indonesia had almost

Box 7.6   The impact of service quality: Matlab Thana, Bangladesh

Matlab Thana is an administrative division of 280,000 people in a rural area of Bangladesh. Its population density is 2,000 people per square mile. Transport is difficult—mostly by boat—and incomes are low. Fishing and farming are the main activities.

Between 1975 and 1981 the International Centre for Diarrhoeal Disease Research, Bangladesh conducted two experiments in Matlab Thana to measure the effect that availability, access, and quality of family planning services had on contraceptive use. Before 1975 family planning services were based in a government-run center in Matlab town. A small staff provided a conventional range of contraceptives and IUD insertions but, with the exception of two brief house-to-house campaigns conducted nationally, made little attempt to reach out to the villagers. Throughout Bangladesh, unmet need for contraception clearly existed. A national survey in 1968 showed that 55 percent of rural married women wanted no more children and that 13 percent would consider using contraception, but that only 1.9 percent were currently using a method.

The Contraceptive Distribution Programme (CDP). The first of two experiments, from 1975 to 1978, tested the effect of house-to-house distribution of oral contraceptives and, one year later, of condoms. Female workers were given six half-days of training on the proper use of the condom and the pill, adverse symp-

Comparison of the cumulative contraceptive acceptance and user rates in the first 18–24 months, for the simple household Contraceptive Distribution Project (CDP) and the Family Planning—Health Services Project (FPHSP)

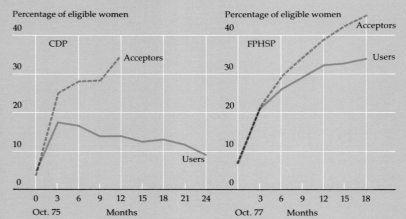

Source: Reprinted with the permission of the Population Council from Shushum Bhatia and others, ''The Matlab Family Planning-Health Services Project,'' *Studies in Family Planning* 11, no. 6 (June 1980): 210.

toms, expected side effects, and simple treatments for them. These workers were mostly elderly, widowed, and illiterate women, with almost no personal experience of contraceptives. Beginning in October 1975, they visited each household in the project area of 150 villages. During a 5–10-minute visit, women were told about the benefits of spacing and limiting births, proper use of the pill, and possible side effects. Those who were interested were given a six-month supply of pills. For thirty months, workers were responsible for continuing to

recruit acceptors, resupplying users, and advising on side effects.

The impact of the CDP was great but shortlived. Contraceptive use in the project area jumped from 1.1 to 17.9 percent in three months, but declined to 11 percent after two years. During the same period, the rate of contraceptive use outside the project area increased from 2.9 to 3.8 percent. After a year, 34 percent of married women in the project area had accepted contraception, but only 42 percent of these women were continuing to use it (see chart). Some ten to fourteen

exclusively promoted the pill but now is giving more emphasis to the IUD.

Supply constraints also limit the availability of different methods. Most contraceptives are imported and are often provided free or cheaply by donors; China, India, and Korea, which produce most of their own contraceptives, are major exceptions. Heavy reliance on one donor can cause problems, since some donors can supply only certain types of contraceptives. The United States Agency for International Development (USAID) is legally prevented from financing abortion training or services and does not finance Depo-Provera, an injectable contraceptive, because it has not been

approved for use in the United States. Because of the limited number of donors that supply injectable contraceptives, Thailand almost exhausted its supplies in 1982, raising the prospect that many clients would have to switch methods or discontinue altogether. Difficulties can also arise if donors change suppliers, since the hormonal makeup of oral contraceptives varies from one manufacturer to another. Other factors restricting method mix include shortages of trained staff to perform sterilizations, poor transport and logistics for timely resupply, and the great distances that clients must travel to obtain some methods.

To improve the method mix of programs, male

months into the program, fertility had declined by 11 to 17 percent, but this effect lasted only one year. The project's limited impact was attributed to poor management of side effects, inadequate training of staff, insufficient information provided to clients, the narrow range of contraceptive methods (which discouraged method switching), and too little supervision.

The Family Planning-Health Services Project (FPHSP). In October 1977 a second experiment also tested house-to-house distribution of contraception, but with much better quality of services. Female village workers were recruited locally and received seven weeks of preservice training and weekly in-service training sessions. They were literate, married with children, had contraceptive experience, and came from respected families. Eighty workers—one per 1,000 people— received technical supervision and medical backup from four clinics staffed by qualified women paramedics, and administrative supervision from a male senior health assistant.

The FPHSP provided comprehensive services for the special needs of each current and prospective client. The methods offered included not only pills and condoms, but foam tablets and injectables. In addition, women were referred to centers where tubectomy, IUD insertion, and menstrual regulation could be performed, and where their husbands could get vasectomies. All households were visited once a fortnight, regardless of whether couples were using contraceptives. Side effects were managed through reassurance, frequent method-switching, and medical referral for treatment. Workers also offered aspirin, vitamins, and iron tablets, thereby gaining access to households that had previously rejected family planning.

In the first three months contraceptive use in the project area rose from 7 to 21 percent. Unlike the trend in the CDP, however, the rate continued to climb slowly to 34 percent. Continuation rates were dramatically improved: after a year, 39 percent of eligible women in the FPHSP had accepted contraception and 81 percent of these women were continuing to use it (see chart). During the first two project years, fertility declined by 22 to 25 percent compared with villages outside the project area. After a three-year plateau at 34 percent, contraceptive use began to rise and now stands at 41 percent—almost exclusively modern methods. The injectable, Depo-Provera, accounts for almost half of contraceptive use. In the rest of the country in 1983, modern methods account for only 14 percent of contraceptive use. Tetanus, toxoid, and oral rehydration therapy have been added to the Matlab project's service package but were apparently not responsible for increased contraceptive prevalence.

Replicability. The FPHSP has been highly effective in increasing contraceptive use in field conditions typical of rural Bangladesh. But it may be hard to replicate on a larger scale because the FPHSP was able to draw on extra resources unavailable to the national family planning program. For example, although fieldworkers in the project receive salaries equivalent to workers in the national program, their supervisors' salaries are much higher. The project also used costly speedboats to move supervisors and research staff around the area. And management was decentralized to an extent rarely found in national programs. The managerial and organizational structure that guaranteed close, supportive supervision, worker accountability, continuous training, good recordkeeping, and continuous feedback to workers should take much of the credit for the project's success.

The government of Bangladesh and the International Centre are now embarking on an extension project to transfer some of the management techniques of the Matlab project to government health and family planning workers in several thanas in North Bengal and to measure the impact of these changes on fertility, mortality, and contraceptive use. The project will make minimal changes in the existing program structure and there will be no special inputs other than for training, organization-building, and research.

and female sterilization and IUDs can be made more readily available through mobile facilities (such as sterilization vans in Thailand) or periodic ''camps'' (such as vasectomy and tubectomy camps in India and IUD ''safaris'' in Indonesia). Careful attention must be paid to providing follow-up services in the case of complications, however. Paramedical workers can be trained to provide the IUD and injectable contraceptives in clinics and even in homes. Referral procedures can be strengthened so that clients are informed about all methods available from public, private, and commercial sources. Private suppliers can be encouraged to offer contraceptive methods that are in short supply or that cannot be offered by the official program. Finally, governments can sponsor local research on the effectiveness, side effects, and acceptability of methods that might be introduced into the national program.

INFORMED CHOICE. Although family planning workers may know more about the advantages and disadvantages of each method, clients are best equipped to choose what suits them—provided they have information on effectiveness, side effects, reversibility, and proper use. In the early stages of the Indian and Pakistani programs, the side effects of the IUD were not fully explained, a medical examination was not always conducted before insertion, and there was little in the way of treatment or referral for side effects. For years afterward, IUDs were shunned. With a fuller explanation of side effects and greater care paid to screening and medical backup, the IUD is now regaining popularity. When private pharmacies in Colombia provided their customers with pamphlets explaining effectiveness, proper use, and side effects, sales of contraceptives increased.

Virtually all family planning programs provide some information to clients about methods, but fully informed choice is still only an ideal in many countries. Family planning workers still tend to doubt the ability of couples to use effectively methods such as the condom and pill, thereby discouraging their use. Staff may also fail to mention methods of which they disapprove, such as the pill, abortion, or sterilization. When incentives are offered to staff for recruiting acceptors of some methods but not of others, the information provided to clients may be biased. Sometimes clients are given inaccurate or incomplete information because family planning staff are themselves not properly informed about methods and their side effects. A survey of the Dominican Republic, Kenya, and the Philippines by the United Nations Fund for Population Activities (UNFPA) in the mid-1970s found that workers felt that their training in methods had been inadequate. A study in India, Korea, the Philippines, and Turkey demonstrated the strong influence of providers of services on clients' choice of method: clients given a thorough explanation of all available contraceptive methods chose a very different mix of methods than did those prior to the study, who had not been given this information.

From the manager's viewpoint, what are the critical requirements for better information? First is appropriate training. Workers must be trained to explain properly the methods available to clients and to encourage them to participate in the choice. Informal explanation works better than formal presentations that use technical or anatomical terms. As new contraceptive methods are included in programs, staff must receive prompt training. Second is more and better supervision of workers to ensure that they are not holding back information on methods because of their own prejudices or because they are receiving financial incentives for encouraging some but not all methods. The incentive structure might also be altered by offering financial or other awards (such as educational opportunities or additional training) to the worker

who attracts and retains the most clients for a variety of different methods.

FOLLOWING UP ACCEPTORS. In their early stages, family planning programs devoted much time to recruiting new clients. It is now obvious that sustained use cannot be assumed—follow-up support is needed. Follow-up support includes medical backup and referral for side effects; encouraging clients to change contraceptive methods if their initial choice has caused problems or if their needs have changed; reassuring them that they are using contraceptives properly; and reminding them of the benefits.

Follow-up is most important in the first few months after acceptance, since this is when side effects are first experienced, when clients are learning to use methods properly, and when they need reassurance in the face of social disapproval. A study in Calabar State, Nigeria, found that 11 percent of pill acceptors never took even the first month's allotment of pills, and only 53 percent were using the pill three months later. A lack of concern with follow-up is believed to be the major contributory cause of the low continuation rates among IUD and pill users in Korea. According to a survey of contraceptive acceptors, only 24 percent were followed up at home or returned to health centers for consultation on side effects. Korea's program sets targets for the number of acceptors, but none for follow-up work.

Follow-up cannot be left to clients, who are likely to return to the family planning center only if they are living close by or if they experience severe side effects that they cannot correct even by abandoning contraception. Follow-up is best provided by fieldworkers and by community-based services. But in areas in which family planning is still regarded with suspicion, some clients would like to be spared the embarrassment of a follow-up visit from a family planning worker. Some programs have managed this by having fieldworkers deliver health services as well.

With or without an extensive field network, family planning programs can improve follow-up.

• They can change policies that encourage staff to recruit new acceptors but not to follow up on them. Targets and incentives can be offered to staff on the basis of the number of current users of contraception or of the number of checkups, rather than only on the basis of the number of new acceptors. Training must also emphasize follow-up procedures.

- Where the burden of follow-up rests on clients, programs can experiment with various ways of encouraging clients to seek appointments. For example, financial incentives might be offered to clients who return for a follow-up visit within a specified period of time, just as South Asian programs offer compensation to acceptors of sterilization for the costs of transport, food, and work time lost. The media can also be used to reassure acceptors about side effects and to encourage them to return for checkups.

- The quality of follow-up can be monitored by periodic sample surveys of acceptors.

Ensuring social acceptability

To be successful, family planning programs must have the support of the clients and communities they serve. But in communities in which modern family planning has never been provided, there may be little evident demand because potential clients are not aware of the benefits of the service, of smaller families, or of longer child spacing intervals. Services introduced by an "outside" agency with few local links and little appreciation of local customs and needs may not be readily accepted. The absence of links to the local community can be a weakness for family planning in particular, because it is a personal matter and may conflict with social norms that favor high fertility.

Private family planning associations and NGOs have led in experimenting with new ways to involve clients and communities. Their strategies have included consultation with local leaders, training local people as paid or volunteer workers, consulting and training traditional midwives and healers, establishing local management or review committees, encouraging local contributions of money and labor, and organizing groups of family planning acceptors to reinforce effective use and to engage in other community development projects.

In communities where there is no apparent demand for family planning, it can be introduced jointly with services in greater demand. The Honduras Family Planning Association includes a planned parenthood theme in its community-based adult literacy program. In Awutu, Ghana, family planning is promoted for child spacing as part of a maternal and child health project. Family planning is provided with agricultural extension to a population of 100,000 in Allahabad (in the state of Uttar Pradesh, India) and as part of the nationwide Integrated Rural Development Project in Pakistan. It has been offered through the resettlement schemes of the Federal Land Development Authority in Malaysia and through women's rural credit cooperatives and vocational training in Bangladesh. Profamilia, the private family planning organization in Colombia, extended its services to the countryside through the National Federation of Coffee Growers. In China, India, and the Philippines family planning services are organized in factories. Both the Indonesian and Chinese programs have used strong political organizations, which extend into rural areas, to provide many economic and social services, including family planning.

Private family planning associations are well suited to implement these approaches: they are small, decentralized, well staffed, highly motivated; have greater control over service quality; and are less confined by the bureaucratic constraints of government. But many of these approaches have also been tried on a larger scale. For example, the Planned Parenthood Federation of Korea pioneered the highly successful mothers' club program. At first these clubs served as sources of contraceptives, of reassurance for acceptors, and of information on the benefits of family planning. They now have merged with the Saemaul Women's Association and are also involved in agricultural cooperatives and community construction projects. Mothers' clubs have also been used by programs in Indonesia and Bangladesh. The national program in Indonesia has successfully involved village headmen, religious leaders, and local volunteers on the islands of Java and Bali, where more than two-thirds of Indonesia's population lives. In the Philippines some outlets for contraceptives are organized and run by local volunteers.

Where communities and clients are involved, they are less likely to see family planning as being imposed by outsiders. Use of traditional midwives and volunteers, and local contributions in cash or in kind also reduce the cost of services. But these strategies require certain managerial qualities not always found in larger public programs: decentralized decisionmaking; technical and organizational expertise to support local organizations, volunteers, and clients; skilled managers and fieldworkers who can identify local leaders, stimulate community activities, supervise volunteers, and reconcile local needs with program capabilities; and, sometimes, workers who are technically competent in more than one field. Finally, social acceptance of family planning takes time and is a continuous process. There is no benchmark for measuring social acceptability, or easy formula for ensuring it.

Financing family planning

Public family planning programs, like programs in education and health, are heavily subsidized, and services are often offered free of charge. Although the private sector makes a significant contribution to providing services in some countries, public finance will continue to be critical, especially in low-income countries and in backward regions, where contraceptive demand is limited and health services are weak.

Public spending

China and India—the two most populous countries in the developing world, with approximately half its population—spent roughly $1.00 and $0.30 per capita, respectively, on population programs in 1980. In most of three dozen developing countries for which rough estimates are available, spending fell within this range (see Table 7.4). If other developing countries with programs were spending equivalent amounts, the total spent on population activities in all developing countries in 1980 must have been about $2 billion.

Practically all spending on population in China, and close to 80 percent of the total in India, is financed from domestic resources. For all other developing countries combined, government and foreign donors each contribute about 50 percent. The government share tends to rise the longer a program has been in existence. Three out of four countries with programs less than five years old were contributing less than 10 percent of the costs of their programs, in contrast to an average of 54 percent among twenty-seven countries with programs at least ten years old. Nepal is one of the rare exceptions: the share of domestic government financing fell from 80 percent of its spending on population in 1975 to 40 percent in 1980.

Even among well-established programs there is wide variation in government spending. Domestic budgetary outlays in 1980 are estimated to have been $0.42 per capita in Sri Lanka, about $0.71 per capita in Korea, and $1.45 per capita in Costa Rica. But these estimates probably understate the true government contribution. The cost of health workers, whose functions often include family planning, is not always imputed to the population program—nor are contributions by local government.

The estimate for China of $1 per capita includes the amount spent by its formal layers of government—central, provincial, prefectural, and county—on providing contraceptive supplies free to users; reimbursing service fees for sterilization, abortion, and IUD insertion; and providing training and information on family planning. These costs amount to $213 million annually, about $0.21 per capita. In addition, the rural collective system finances the family planning staff at the commune or brigade level (at an estimated cost of $0.34 per capita) and pays incentives, in the form of food supplements and reimbursement of travel costs, to holders of one-child certificates ($0.25 per capita) and to individuals undergoing sterilization ($0.15 per capita). Finally, additional time is spent by barefoot doctors on family planning work (though not much: in Shandong Province they allocate an average of 1.5 percent of their time to family planning, valued at approximately $3 million). Health workers and midwives probably spend more time on family planning. Adding all these contributions together produces a figure for family planning expenditure in China of nearly $1 per capita.

Although governments finance a large share of their population programs, the amounts spent are still trivial—both in absolute terms and in relation to other government outlays (see Box 7.7). In China the state budget for the family planning program absorbs only 0.4 percent of total current spending, compared with 5.2 percent for health and 13.1 percent for education. In India and Mauritius spending on family planning in 1981 accounted for only 0.5 percent of total government expenditure. The figures are even lower in Korea (0.2 percent) and in Malaysia (less than 0.1 percent).

Foreign donors spent an estimated $491 million for population programs in developing countries in 1981; about two-thirds of this amount was for family planning and related programs. In real terms, population assistance grew at almost 6 percent a year during the 1970s but fell 3 percent in 1980 and 6 percent in 1981. The prospects for increased assistance are not good: UNFPA, a major channel for population assistance, expects its spending to rise by barely 1 percent over the next four years. Population assistance from donors is discussed further in the next chapter.

Private spending

Important constraints limit the growth of private suppliers of family planning, especially in rural areas. The most severe constraint is the need for

TABLE 7.4
Public expenditure on population programs, selected countries, 1980

Region and country	Total public expenditure (millions of dollars)	Per capita public expenditure (dollars)	Expenditure per current contraceptive user (dollars)
Sub-Saharan Africa			
Ghana	2.8	0.24	16
Kenya	11.8	0.71	68
Liberia	2.3	1.22	a
Mauritius	1.7	1.81	24
Sierra Leone	1.5	0.44	a
Swaziland	1.8	2.89	a
Tanzania	3.3	0.18	a
Zaire	1.8	0.06	a
Zimbabwe (1978)	1.9	0.27	13
Middle East and North Africa			
Egypt, Arab Rep.	34.1	0.81	22
Iran, Islamic Rep. (1976)	50.6	1.30	38
Jordan	2.5	0.78	21
Morocco	13.3	0.66	a
Tunisia	8.3	1.31	32
South Asia			
Bangladesh	45.1	0.51	26
India	226.9	0.34	10
Nepal	10.6	0.72	69
Pakistan	24.5	0.30	33
Sri Lanka	6.2	0.42	7
East Asia			
China	979.6	1.00	10
Hong Kong	2.0	0.40	3
Indonesia	86.2	0.59	11
Korea, Rep. of	27.1	0.71	9
Malaysia	16.4	1.18	19
Philippines	37.6	0.78	11
Singapore	1.8	0.74	7
Thailand	28.1	0.60	7
Latin America and Caribbean			
Bolivia (1977)	0.1	0.03	a
Brazil	10.6	0.09	a
Colombia	8.1	0.31	4
Costa Rica	3.3	1.45	15
Dominican Rep.	3.8	0.70	11
Ecuador	6.3	0.75	15
El Salvador	8.1	1.77	35
Guatemala	9.3	1.28	47
Haiti	3.9	0.77	27
Honduras	3.0	0.81	20
Jamacia	4.8	2.19	27
Mexico	61.3	0.88	15
Panama	4.4	2.42	26
Paraguay	2.1	0.69	13
Peru	5.3	0.32	5

Note: Expenditure includes funding from domestic and foreign sources on population activities, including (but not limited to) family planning services.
a. Contraceptive prevalence rate unavailable or close to zero.
Source: Bulatao, 1984a.

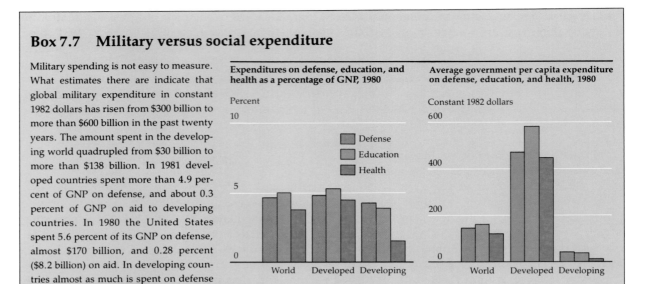

Box 7.7 Military versus social expenditure

Military spending is not easy to measure. What estimates there are indicate that global military expenditure in constant 1982 dollars has risen from $300 billion to more than $600 billion in the past twenty years. The amount spent in the developing world quadrupled from $30 billion to more than $138 billion. In 1981 developed countries spent more than 4.9 percent of GNP on defense, and about 0.3 percent of GNP on aid to developing countries. In 1980 the United States spent 5.6 percent of its GNP on defense, almost $170 billion, and 0.28 percent ($8.2 billion) on aid. In developing countries almost as much is spent on defense as on education and health combined (see chart).

Expenditures on defense, education, and health as a percentage of GNP, 1980

Percent

- Defense
- Education
- Health

World   Developed Developing

Average government per capita expenditure on defense, education, and health, 1980

Constant 1982 dollars

World   Developed Developing

Source: Sivard, 1983.

medical backup for providing contraceptives. Although prescription regulations have been liberalized in nineteen countries, making condoms and oral contraceptives available through nonclinical suppliers such as pharmacies, the demand for IUDs, male and female sterilization, and abortion can be met only by trained health workers. Very few of them work in the private sector. In addition, the cost of providing family planning services is high in rural and marginal urban areas, whereas the ability to pay for commercial services is low. Private suppliers cannot appeal to the national interest the way governments can to stimulate demand for contraception and cannot use community institutions and pressures to spread family planning. Finally, the development of private supply is often inhibited by a combination of government policies, including price controls; prohibition of, or tariffs on, the import of contraceptives; and restrictions on certain kinds of family planning services, especially sterilization and abortion in Muslim and Catholic countries.

Despite these constraints, private suppliers provided more than 20 percent of all family planning services in more than two-thirds of the countries studied in recent surveys (see Table 7.5). In some countries private suppliers play a major or even dominant role, especially among urban consumers. In Korea 42 percent of all contraceptive users are supplied by pharmacies or physicians; in the state of Sao Paulo, Brazil (a country with some state, but no central government, programs), the proportion is as high as 63 percent.

Private spending on family planning services as a consequence equals about a fourth of public spending on these services in the developing world. In some regions private spending is greater: in Latin America it may in fact be slightly above public spending.

In urban areas some commercial suppliers may be displaced by publicly subsidized contraceptives: half of the initial users of an official program of oral contraception in Piaui State, Brazil, in 1979 had shifted over from the private sector. Yet private suppliers do benefit from family planning advertising financed by the government. It is probably not a coincidence that they flourish in several countries, such as Korea, Mexico, and Thailand, where government strongly supports birth control.

The activities of private suppliers demonstrate that many people in developing countries are willing to pay for contraceptive services. Although charges for publicly subsidized services are usually low or nonexistent, data for twenty developing countries show that private sector prices can be high enough to absorb a significant fraction of household income. The cost of a year's supply of oral contraceptives averaged $25 in 1980, ranging from $5 in Mexico and $6 in Egypt to as much as

$90 in Nigeria. Across countries, the various forms of contraception cost an average of $20 to $40 a year.

In the better-off developing countries, the cost of buying commercially available contraceptives is small in relation to average income per capita (although even in those countries the cost may be relatively large for the poor). For example, the retail price of a year's supply of oral contraceptives in 1979 was equivalent to only 0.3 percent of per capita income in Mexico and to 0.5 percent in Brazil. But in low-income countries the cost can be prohibitive—equivalent to 17 percent of per capita income in Bangladesh, for example, and 18 percent in Zaire, or about 3 percent of total income for the average household. All these figures understate the real cost of obtaining family planning services, whether private or public, because people also have to pay for the time and travel needed to obtain their contraceptives.

In Korea some 1.2 million users bought contraceptives commercially in 1979 at an average annual cost of about $12—a total outlay of $15 million, about $0.40 per capita for Korea's entire population, and roughly equivalent to the $0.42 per capita spent on the domestic government budget, exclusive of foreign donor contributions. In Peru about 300,000 users of commercial sources of contraception spent an average of $30 each in 1981, their total outlay being several times what the government spent. Private spending on this scale—which understates the total because it excludes access costs—is not typical of all developing countries, but it shows a widespread willingness to pay for contraception.

Allocation of public expenditures

The bulk of public spending on population—almost 50 percent in seventeen countries reporting details of expenditures—goes directly to providing contraceptive services. Progressively smaller shares are taken up by general program administration, information-education-communication activities, research and evaluation, and personnel training.

With all public spending on family planning taken into account, expenditure averages about $0.70 per capita across all developing countries. For each contraceptive user, spending is much higher—around $21 a year. But most users are in China and India, where programs spend less per user, so the weighted average is lower at $11. Adding private expenditures could easily double the

TABLE 7.5
Source of contraception among currently married women aged 15 to 44 and their husbands
(percentage distribution of current contraceptive users)

Region and country	Government programs	Other publicly funded or subsidized programs	Private sector	No source or other[a]
East Asia				
Korea, Rep. of (1979)	36	0	42	22
Thailand (1978)	37	35	18	10
Latin America and Caribbean				
Brazil				
Piauí (1979)	59	0	23	18
Sao Paulo (1978)	16	0	63	21
Bahia (1980)	27	1	48	24
Rio Grande do Norte (1980)	57	0	22	21
Colombia (1978)	21	27	33	19
Costa Rica (1978)	57	0	28	15
El Salvador (1978)	73	8	12	6
Guatemala (1978)	44	11	26	18
Jamaica (1979)	63	27	7	3
Mexico (1978)	42	2	36	20
Panama (1979–80)	71	0	19	10
Paraguay (1977)	41	8	28	22
North Africa				
Tunisia				
Jendouba (1979)	91	0	5	4

a. Applies to rhythm or withdrawal; other may include contraceptives obtained from a friend or in a foreign country.
Sources: Morris and others, 1981; Merrick, 1984.

costs per user. Public cost per user varies among countries, as Table 7.4 shows, depending on many factors, including local salaries and program efficiency and quality.

Cost per user tends to be very high in the first few years of a family planning program; it then falls sharply as the rate of contraceptive use rises above 5 percent. At higher rates the cost per user tends to stabilize, or perhaps to rise slightly. Between 1965 and 1980, while contraceptive use in Korea rose from 12 to 30 percent, cost per user fluctuated (with little apparent trend) between $7 and $13 (in constant 1982 dollars).

In any country with contraceptive use of at least 5 percent, current cost per user is a conservative guide to costs at higher levels of use. Marginal costs could rise if new users are in inaccessible rural areas with high delivery costs, though they could also fall if services are more intensively used.

Future financial requirements

What would it cost to satisfy the unmet need for limiting births? Some idea can be obtained by extrapolating levels of unmet need—the proportion of women exposed to the risk of pregnancy who want no more children—in thirty-five developing countries in the mid-1970s to cover the developing world as a whole. That extrapolation suggests a possible increase in the rate of contraceptive use of 13 percentage points. If the public cost for each additional user were the same, country by country, as the cost per user in 1980, such an increase would require another $1 billion in public spending (see Table 7.6).

In the next two decades total spending for family planning programs will need to increase because of the growing number of women of childbearing age and the increasing proportion of them who are likely to want modern contraceptives. World Bank projections indicate that the number of married women of reproductive age in all developing countries will increase from about 500 million to more than 700 million between 1980 and 2000. About 40 percent of these women used contraception in 1980.

The "standard" projections in Chapter 4 imply an average total fertility rate of 3.3 in developing countries in the year 2000. If it is assumed that the fertility effects of later marriage and of shorter breastfeeding will largely cancel each other out and that the abortion rate will stay constant, achieving this fertility decline will require an increase in the rate of contraceptive use to 58 per-

cent. For the projections of a "rapid" decline in fertility, which imply a total fertility rate of 2.4 in 2000, contraceptive use would need to reach 72 percent.

How much would this cost? To achieve the standard decline in fertility, and assuming 1980 costs per user, total public spending on population programs would need to reach $5.6 billion (in constant 1980 dollars) by the year 2000—a rise in real terms of 5 percent a year. To ensure the rapid decline, spending would need to total $7.6 billion by 2000, a rise of 7 percent a year in real terms.

Growth in spending will have to be much greater in some regions than in others. Average real increases in spending of 2.5 percent a year would be enough to meet targets in East Asia as a whole (though not for individual countries), and 5 percent would be enough for Latin America and the Caribbean. In South Asia, the Middle East and North Africa, and sub-Saharan Africa, however, population spending would have to grow 8 to 10 percent every year to achieve a standard decline in fertility, and in sub-Saharan Africa as much as 16 percent every year to support a rapid decline.

Because spending on population currently represents less than 1 percent of government budgets, small increases could go a long way toward meeting the requirement for higher spending. The same is true for external assistance. Only about 1 percent of official aid now goes for population assistance (and only a part of that for family planning). Increasing spending by 50 percent could fill "unmet need" today, but larger increases will be needed in the future. In many countries the required increase in public expenditure for family planning would be more than offset by reductions in public expenditure in other sectors. With constant enrollment rates, rapid fertility decline would generate per capita savings in education expenditure in the year 2000 of $1.80 in Egypt, $3.30 in Kenya, $6.00 in Korea, and $6.60 in Zimbabwe.

Obstacles to program expansion

If the financial resources to expand family planning services were made available, could they be put to good use? Program expansion may be difficult for a variety of reasons, including administrative and logistical obstacles, scarcity of personnel, and limited demand. These tend to limit the rate at which a good program can be expanded, but not expansion itself.

The administrative and logistical obstacles include many of the same constraints that hamper

TABLE 7.6
Fertility targets and estimates of population program expenditures, 1980 and 2000

Region and scenario	Year	Fertility targets		Expenditures	
		Total fertility rate	Contraceptive prevalence (percent)	Per capita (constant 1980 dollars)	Total (millions of constant 1980 dollars)
All developing countries					
Current estimate	1980	4.36	39	0.62	2,016
With unmet need filled	1980	3.54	52	0.90	2,961
Under standard decline	2000	3.30	58	1.14	5,569
Under rapid decline	2000	2.32	72	1.66	7,591
Sub-Saharan Africa[a]					
Current estimate	1980	6.59	11	0.29	112
With unmet need filled	1980	6.03	20	0.76	297
Under standard decline	2000	5.81	24	1.07	791
Under rapid decline	2000	2.69	73	3.72	2,353
Middle East and North Africa					
Current estimate	1980	5.70	24	0.66	142
With unmet need filled	1980	4.98	35	1.04	222
Under standard decline	2000	3.73	59	1.94	726
Under rapid decline	2000	2.39	74	2.43	812
South Asia[b]					
Current estimate	1980	5.22	20	0.35	315
With unmet need filled	1980	4.15	38	0.77	688
Under standard decline	2000	3.43	51	1.10	1,517
Under rapid decline	2000	2.42	67	1.50	1,873
East Asia					
Current estimate	1980	3.02	61	0.87	1,238
With unmet need filled	1980	2.27	72	1.04	1,480
Under standard decline	2000	2.28	75	1.09	2,022
Under rapid decline	2000	2.16	74	1.08	2,015
Latin America and Caribbean					
Current estimate	1980	4.28	40	0.59	209
With unmet need filled	1980	3.53	51	0.77	274
Under standard decline	2000	2.80	63	0.95	513
Under rapid decline	2000	2.17	72	1.07	538

Note: The fertility targets and per capita expenditure figures are population-weighted means. Because of lack of data on contraceptive prevalence for many countries, regional estimates include country rates which were estimated based on various social and economic data.
a. Includes Republic of South Africa.
b. Includes Afghanistan.
Source: Bulatao, 1984a.

other development programs. For example, a family planning program requires a system for obtaining, storing, and distributing contraceptives. If a program attempts to provide a mix of methods, this system can become complicated; it may require more than one distribution network—commercial, clinical, and nonclinical. Where overall government administration is weak, roads are poor, and communications slow, even the best-run programs will appear inefficient and incapable of sustained expansion. These limits may not be evident in small pilot projects, but they can become important when an attempt is made to extend services on a larger, national scale. In areas where health services are scant or nonexistent, a family planning program will be extremely difficult to implement.

The personnel requirements for an extensive family planning program are not large in relation to the supply of educated people. Desirable ratios are about 1 fieldworker to 300 families, and 1 supervisor for every 8 fieldworkers. For Upper Volta, a country with extremely low literacy, a program could be fully staffed at these ratios by about a tenth of a single year's primary and secondary school graduates. The conclusion becomes less sanguine, however, as soon as one takes into account specific requirements for fieldworkers: for instance, they should be village-based rather than city-based, belong to the appropriate ethnic, linguistic, or caste group, and be favorably disposed to contraception. The Pakistani program has faced recruitment problems of this sort. In the late 1960s only a seventh of the midwives assigned as fieldworkers believed in the efficacy of modern contraceptives. In the early 1970s they were replaced by a group including many unmarried women from urban areas who did not have the confidence of the villagers. If finding appropriate fieldworkers in each area is difficult, finding higher-level supervisors can be even more of a problem.

Program expansion also depends on the demand for contraceptive services. A principal task of programs is to generate some of this demand itself, but where initial interest is low or nonexistent this task can take time.

Taken together, these limits to rapid expansion might seem to suggest that programs could not make good use of more money. But such a view would be wrong. During the 1970s India, Pakistan, Bangladesh, and Sri Lanka were spending as much as $2.50 per married woman on family planning programs and were still producing contraceptive users at acceptable cost—under $20 each, in some years much less. Despite the unpromising conditions—per capita GNP between $100 and $300, adult literacy rates as low as 20 percent, and infant mortality rates as high as 150 per thousand—spending on family planning was effective and economical.

Furthermore, many of the factors that hamper effectiveness can be overcome as a program develops. Culturally acceptable solutions to administrative and personnel problems, and to limited public interest, take time to develop, as do the quality improvements discussed above. But in every part of the world where an effort has been made, there has been progress.

Foreign funding has been largely absent in the early stages of some family planning programs, as it continues to be in China. In other programs it has played a catalytic role—for instance, through stimulating pioneering research of demographic problems. Local finance, however, eventually becomes critical; most of the older, more effective programs in 1980 had 40 percent or less foreign funding. For one thing, local finance demonstrates political commitment to family planning, the subject of the next chapter. Many of the obstacles to expansion of family planning can be overcome with sufficient commitment, and most of them cannot be overcome without it.

8 The policy agenda

"Population policy" is the province of government. By choosing how many resources and how much political authority to invest in a policy, a government determines the policy's effectiveness. In its broadest sense, population policy is concerned with population distribution as well as with population growth. This chapter discusses population policy to reduce population growth. In the area of fertility reduction, inaction is itself a choice which has implications for both future policy and the room for maneuver that a government will later have. Religious and cultural conditions cannot be ignored in designing an effective policy to reduce fertility; actions culturally and politically acceptable in one country might be rejected in others. But religious and cultural characteristics do not rule out effective action. In every part of the developing world during the past decade some governments have made significant progress in developing a policy to reduce population growth.

Choosing from policy options is a matter for local decision. But foreign aid for population programs can help developing countries meet their population policy objectives and can increase the impact of aid in other parts of the economy. This chapter examines the elements of an effective population policy, the main policy issues in each region of the developing world, and how aid donors can complement the efforts of developing countries.

Population policy

A population policy to lower fertility needs to be distinguished from public support for family planning services. Family planning support has wider social goals than fertility reduction but more limited population goals than overall population policy. Family planning programs provide information and services to help people achieve their own fertility objectives. By contrast, population policy involves explicit demographic goals. It employs a wide range of policies, direct and indirect, to change the signals that otherwise induce high fertility. Effective policy requires action by many ministries, and thus an interministerial approach to setting policy and monitoring its results. And it requires clear direction and support from the most senior levels of government.

Family planning programs and other socioeconomic policies that can reduce fertility are often pursued by governments to achieve overall development objectives, irrespective of their effect on fertility. What distinguishes countries with a population policy from those without one is an explicit demographic objective and the institutional mechanisms to translate that objective into effective policy.

Policy steps

Table 8.1 summarizes the current state of population policy in twenty-six developing countries with 15 million people or more. In the table, an *x* shows those countries which have already taken a particular policy step. Countries are listed by region, and within regions in order of their 1982 family planning "index," explained in Chapter 6.

Developing a population policy takes time. Countries in which the policy to reduce population growth is recent tend to have taken fewer of the policy steps listed in the table. Others—China, India, Korea, and Sri Lanka, for instance—have had longstanding policies and tend to have taken more steps. But there are important exceptions. Countries such as Indonesia and Mexico have developed strong programs in a short period. In contrast, programs in Egypt, Kenya, Morocco, and Pakistan have made little progress for more than a decade. Progress can also be reversed. In five countries not shown in the table—Chile, Costa Rica, Fiji, Jamaica, and Panama—family planning indices have declined by as much as half in the past decade. In some countries population policy aims to *increase* population growth (see Box 8.1).

155

TABLE 8.1
Population policy indicators for selected countries with populations of 15 million or more

Region and country	TFR 1982	Family planning index 1982	Demo-graphic data A	Politi-cal com-mitment B	Institu-tions C	Institu-tions D	Family planning E	Family planning F	Family planning G	Family planning H	Family planning I	Incentives and disincen-tives J	Incentives and disincen-tives K	Incentives and disincen-tives L	Birth quotas M
Sub-Saharan Africa															
Kenya	8.0	□	x	x	x		x	x							
Tanzania	6.5	□					x	x							
Nigeria	6.9	□					x								
Zaire	6.3	□													
Sudan	6.6	□	x				x								
Ethiopia	6.5	□													
Middle East and North Africa															
Egypt	4.6	□	x	x	x	x	x	x				x	x		
Morocco	5.8	□	x	x				x							
Turkey	4.1	□	x	x			x	x							
Algeria	7.0	□	x				x								
Latin America and Caribbean															
Colombia	3.6	■	x	x	x		x	x							
Mexico	4.6	■	x	x	x	x	x	x	x	x					
Brazil	3.9	■	x				x	x							
Venezuela	4.3	□	x				x	x							
Peru	4.5	□	x	x	x		x	x							
South Asia															
Sri Lanka	3.4	■	x	x	x	x	x	x	x		x				
India	4.8	■	x	x	x	x	x	x	x	x	x				
Bangladesh	6.3	■	x	x	x	x	x	x	x	x	x				
Pakistan	5.8	■	x	x	x	x	x	x							
Nepal	6.3	□	x	x	x	x	x	x	x	x	x				
East Asia															
China	2.3	■	x	x	x	x		x	x	x		x	x	x	x
Korea, Rep. of	2.7	■	x	x	x	x	x	x	x	x		x	x		
Indonesia	4.3	■	x	x	x	x	x	x	x	x		x			
Malaysia	3.7	■	x		x	x	x	x	x	x					
Thailand	3.6	■	x	x	x	x	x	x	x	x					
Philippines	4.2	■	x	x	x	x	x	x	x	x			x		

Note: The following countries with greater than 15 million population were omitted because of lack of data: Afghanistan; Argentina; Burma; Islamic Republic of Iran; Democratic Republic of Korea; South Africa; Venezuela; and Viet Nam.

TFR = Total fertility rate.

Key: ■ = very strong index; ■ = strong; ■ = moderate; □ = weak; □ = very weak or none. For explanation of index, see Population Data Supplement Table 6 and notes.

A Published census data and data from other household surveys on fertility, mortality, and contraceptive use (such as WFS or CPS) less than ten years old. **B** Official policy to reduce population growth expressed by high officials and in a national development plan, sometimes including specific demographic targets. **C** Existence of a population planning unit that integrates demographic projections into current economic plans and considers the effect of policies on demographic parameters. **D** Existence of a high-level coordinating body, such as a population commission, to set population policy, oversee implementation, and evaluate results of multisectoral policies. **E** Government financial support of private family planning associations. **F** Public family planning services. **G** Family planning outreach, including community-based distribution systems and/or fieldworkers. **H** Active use of mass media for information and education to promote family planning and small family norms. **I** Publicly subsidized commercial sales of contraceptives. **J** Elimination of all explicit and implicit subsidies that encourage large families (tax reductions for each child, family allowances, free or subsidized health and education services). **K** Incentives to individuals or communities to have small families. **L** Strong disincentives to discourage more than two births per woman, such as reduced services or an income tax for third and later-born children. **M** Policy to set quotas on the number of births permitted annually in a community under which couples must obtain permission to have a child.

Box 8.1 Pronatalist policies

In some countries governments feel that fertility rates are too low. This is so in several European countries such as France, Hungary, and Romania, as well as in Argentina, Bolivia, Burma, Chile, Guinea, Israel, Ivory Coast, and Kampuchea.

Hungary

Hungarian leaders have set a target of replacement-level fertility by 2000. They are relying on economic incentives that reduce the private costs of children. The incentives for childbearing are numerous: monthly payments for children (with a larger increase for the second child; in 1981 payment for each child was equivalent to 11.7 percent of the average wage); five months' maternity leave at full pay and up to two and a half years at one-third of the average wage; a birth bonus equal to about one month's salary, provided the mother attends prenatal consultations; unlimited sick leave (which is always at 75 percent of salary) for child care for the first year, sixty days up to the third year, then thirty days up to the age of six; partial downpayment for a house, depending on the number of children planned; subsidies on children's clothing, milk, baby-care products, and school supplies; two additional paid holidays a year for one child under fourteen, five days for two, and nine days for three; and guaranteed job security for mothers.

Hungary placed restrictions on legal abortion in 1974, allowing it only for single, divorced, separated, and widowed women, married women over the age of forty, those who have had three children, and those without adequate housing. These restrictions occurred when access to modern methods of contraception had been much improved and their use had been encouraged. In 1977, 74 percent of married women of childbear-ing age were using contraception and 71 percent of all people practicing contraception were using an efficient method such as the pill and IUD.

Hungary's pronatalist policies have affected the timing but not the number of births: couples are having the same number of children, but sooner. The total fertility rate increased from 1.8 in 1965 to 2.4 in 1975, the year after abortion was restricted. But it had fallen back to 1.9 by 1980. Economic incentives evidently do not offset the increased private costs—in money and time—of larger families. Incentives have created a fiscal burden, however. In 1982, maternity payments and family allowances amounted to 2.4 percent of GDP.

Romania

Romania has attempted to raise fertility by placing limits on both abortion and contraception. Abortion on demand was legalized in 1957 and was an important backup to withdrawal and rhythm, since no other contraceptive methods were available. By 1965 there were four times more abortions than live births. In November 1966 the government limited access to abortion to women over age forty-five, those with four or more children, those whose life was endangered, and those whose pregnancy was the result of rape. Restricted abortion was not accompanied by improved access to contraception. Modern contraceptives are available only for medical reasons. According to the 1978 World Fertility Survey, 58 percent of Romanian couples are using a method of family planning, almost all rhythm and withdrawal. Economic incentives for childbearing are relatively limited. In 1979 the child allowance was about 9 percent of the average wage, the maternity grant of $85 was paid only for third and later births, and maternity leave of sixteen weeks was the

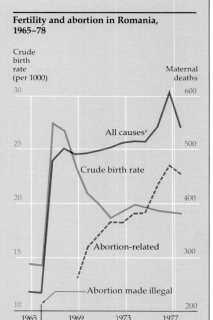

Fertility and abortion in Romania, 1965–78

a. Deaths due to complications in pregnancy and delivery, and abortion-related deaths.

Source: UN, 1966 and 1980.

shortest of any country in central or eastern Europe. However, part-time work is being made more readily available to mothers of young children and creche facilities are being expanded.

The immediate effect of limiting access to abortion in Romania was to increase total fertility from 1.9 in 1965 to 2.9 in 1970; the birth rate rose from 14 to 27 per thousand between 1966 and 1967. But total fertility had gradually declined to 2.5 by 1980 and the birth rate to 19. Fertility is now above replacement level, but on a falling trend. As in Hungary, pronatalist policies in Romania have not been without cost; the cost, however, is not so much in financial as in health terms. Maternal mortality due to illegal abortion in 1977 was triple the rate of 1966 and continues to rise (see chart).

The development of population policy includes the following steps:

DATA COLLECTION AND ANALYSIS. Reliable data on population size, fertility, and mortality document the existence of rapid growth and allow projec-tions of its consequences. This information is critical to generating and sustaining the political commitment of leaders to slower growth. Demographic data are also vital inputs for economic planning, policy formulation, and evaluation (see Box 8.2). Data needs include published

Box 8.2 China's census: counting a billion people

China is rich in historical population statistics, having fairly good estimates stretching back to the Zhou dynasty, a thousand years before the Roman censuses. But census taking deteriorated in the modern era. There was a head count of just over 600 million Chinese in 1953. Data from the 1964 census, only recently released, showed a population of just under 700 million.

In the first two weeks of July 1982, the Chinese government marshalled a force of 6.3 million census takers and their supervisors to carry out a new census, the largest ever executed anywhere in the world. With rapid hand-processing, the government published initial results in October 1982, far more quickly than most census organizations in low-income countries. Total population exceeded one billion persons. By using advanced computer technology supplied with the

assistance of UNFPA, the government expects to publish complete results for local administrative units before the end of 1984.

With such a large undertaking some compromises had to be made between rapid feedback of results and complete coverage. For example, census takers did not visit residences but relied instead on responses at places of work and other central locations, a less satisfactory data collection method. A subsequent survey (see below) suggests that about 17 million women may have been missed in the census count.

In September 1982, less than three months after completing the census, the Chinese government conducted a retrospective fertility survey of over one million persons, many of whom were visited in their homes by interview teams. The survey found that fertility rose by 25

percent between 1940 and 1968, with ups and downs in famines and recoveries, before beginning the transition to lower fertility in 1969. Fertility had reached a low of about 2.2 in 1980, then rose by 18 percent in 1981. In that year more than a third of women were not using contraception and, despite the one-child policy, over half of all births were second or higher order. The survey thus identified possible problems with the execution of population policy.

The above-mentioned findings from the census and the survey complement each other and provide overall policy guidance for Chinese population policy. These data collection efforts are remarkable achievements, in part because China lacks the many years of experience that countries such as India have in such activities.

and analyzed census data not more than ten years old and other national sample surveys documenting current fertility, mortality, and contraceptive use at more frequent intervals (item A in Table 8.1). Lack of reliable demographic data has hampered the growth of political support for population policies in sub-Saharan Africa. Data collection and analysis is a continuous process, necessary to monitor trends and the effect of policies over time.

POLITICAL COMMITMENT. Support for slowing population growth has been expressed in public statements by the head of state and other national leaders, and in written statements of national priorities, such as a national development plan (item B). These statements can range from a general commitment to reducing population growth to specific demographic targets (see Box 8.3). Countries with strong policies have been able to mobilize visible and sustained political commitment, not only at the highest levels of government but throughout the political and administrative hierarchy, down to those who are in immediate touch with the public. This commitment helps to forge cooperation among the numerous sectors and ministries involved in population policy.

INSTITUTIONS. The role of institutions is to translate political commitment into effective policy. The

experience of countries shown in Table 8.1 suggests the importance of institutionalizing two functions:

- Relating demographic targets to the policies and resources necessary to achieve them. A population policy should include consideration of the demographic benefits of a wide range of social policies, in education, health, and social security, as well as in family planning. It should also consider the complementarities among these policies. This is fundamentally a planning function, one which relates demographic variables and policy alternatives (item C). It is usually the responsibility of a specialized unit within a planning ministry, such as the Manpower Board of the Ministry of Finance and Plan in Ghana, and the Population Planning Section within the Planning Commission in Bangladesh.

- Coordinating and evaluating the implementation of population policy. This may require few new institutional arrangements if the scope of population policy is limited to, say, wider provision of family planning. In this case, the policy coordinating body may be the one that also coordinates multisectoral family planning activities. But as population policy becomes more complex, it is likely to involve the joint efforts of other ministries: education (for population education and female literacy); information (to encourage breast-

Box 8.3 Demographic policy objectives

At least forty-two developing countries—comprising more than three-quarters of the total population of developing countries—have adopted official policies to reduce the rate of population growth. Some countries have quantitative targets in terms of achieving a particular total fertility rate, crude birth rate, net reproduction rate, rate of population growth, or population size in a given year. The table summarizes current demographic targets for sixteen countries and compares them with the demographic outcomes implied by projections using World Bank estimates of standard and rapid declines in fertility (see Chapter 4). The policy targets are expressed in terms of the total fertility rate (TFR) or the crude birth rate (CBR).

Five of the countries shown have specified their targets in different ways. Bangladesh and Jamaica hope to achieve a net reproduction rate of 1 by the year 2000; for Ghana the goal is a population growth rate of 2.0 percent in 2000; for Uganda a growth rate of 2.6 percent in 1995; the official target in China is a population size of 1.2 billion in 2000. For these countries the TFR or CBR given in the table approximates what would be required to attain these objectives. In most countries the government's official policy objectives are comparable to, or even more ambitious than, those required to achieve a "rapid" decline in fertility.

Demographic targets and projections of fertility declines, selected countries and years

| | | Policy target | | Fertility decline | | | |
| | | | | Standard | | Rapid | |
	Year	TFR[a]	CBR[b]	TFR[a]	CBR[b]	TFR[a]	CBR[b]
Asia							
Bangladesh	2000	2.5	..	4.9	36	2.8	23
China	2000	2.0	..	2.0	..	2.0	..
India	1996	..	21	3.5	28	2.5	21
Indonesia	1990	2.7	22	3.7	30	2.9	24
Korea, Rep. of	1988	2.1	..	2.6	24	2.2	20
Nepal	2000	2.5	..	5.3	38	2.9	24
Pakistan	1988	..	36	6.4	45	5.2	38
Philippines	1987	..	28	4.0	31	3.5	28
Thailand	1986	2.6	..	3.4	28	3.0	25
Africa and Middle East							
Egypt	2000	..	20	3.1	25	2.3	20
Ghana	2000	3.3	..	6.0	43	3.2	27
Mauritius	1988	2.3	..	2.7	25	2.3	21
Tunisia	2001	..	22	3.1	25	2.2	20
Uganda	1995	5.0	..	6.7	49	4.3	34
Latin America and Caribbean							
Haiti	2000	..	20	3.4	29	2.4	22
Jamaica	2000	2.1	..	2.2	20	2.1	20
Mexico	1988	..	25	4.1	32	3.6	29

.. Not available.
a. TFR equals total fertility rate.
b. CBR equals crude birth rate.

feeding and use of family planning); justice (age at marriage, incentives and disincentives); women's affairs, rural development, and cooperatives (integrated population and development projects). For example, very few countries now give much priority to raising the legal age of marriage as part of demographic policy—more likely because the institutional framework to do so is poor than because the costs of implementing such a policy are high.

As the task of coordination becomes more complicated, the responsible body may need an independent base in the government (item D), separate from the delivery system for family planning. The institutional arrangements vary: a unit within an existing ministry of health or planning but with representatives from many ministries (Tunisia, Panama); an extraministerial committee (Egypt, Mexico); or a separate ministry devoted entirely to multisectoral population policies (Indonesia). There is no consensus on what works best; sustained political commitment seems to matter more to the outcome than organizational structure.

FAMILY PLANNING. In many countries—such as Brazil, Nigeria, Sudan, and Tanzania—subsidized family planning is provided as a basic health measure for mothers and children although the government has not formally adopted a policy to reduce population growth. But once the objective of reduced population growth has been established, support for family planning services intensifies. As noted in Chapter 7, family planning policies tend to evolve in similar ways. Government programs are often preceded by private family planning organizations which eventually receive government financial support (item E). As political commitment increases, government assumes a bigger role, providing public services (item F), family planning outreach (item G), educational and informational activities (item H), and subsidized commercial distribution of contraceptives (item I).

Policy steps E to I help couples have the number of children they want. Virtually all countries in the table could reduce their fertility by increasing the availability and quality of family planning services. Countries with moderate and weak programs have yet to generate any outreach services; many with stronger programs, including outreach, fail to cover the entire population. Subsidized commercial distribution of contraceptives is not widely used, even among countries with relatively strong programs. Based on estimates of "unmet need" described in Chapter 7, there are about 65 million couples in developing countries who want to limit or space births but do not have effective access to family planning services.

INCENTIVES AND DISINCENTIVES. By ensuring that people have only as many children as they want, governments can slow population growth. However, this might not be enough to bring privately and socially desired fertility into balance. If a private-social gap still exists, it cannot be reduced simply by providing more family planning. Economic and social policies are indispensable to reduce this gap in the long run. They may take some time to have an impact on fertility, however. Items J to L are policies that close the gap more quickly: eliminating all implicit subsidies for large families (item J), offering financial or other incentives for small families (item K), and imposing disincentives for large families (item L). A large number of countries have disincentives built into their tax system and their benefits system for public employees, but these are generally mild and affect only a small part of the population. Only a handful of countries, even among those with the strongest programs, have more broad-ranging incentives and disincentives.

BIRTH QUOTAS. China is the only country to have implemented a system of assigning to communities (sometimes employees of a particular factory) a quota of births to be permitted each year (item M). Individual couples within communities are then given permission to have a child, with priority given to couples who have followed the recommendations for marrying only after a certain age, and who are older. The system of quotas, and the accompanying pressure to have an abortion when a woman becomes pregnant without permission, are an additional policy "step" over and above the extensive system of incentives and disincentives.

Policy and ethics

Birth control is not just a technical and demographic issue; it has a moral and a cultural dimension. Becoming a parent is both a deeply personal event and—in virtually all societies—central to community life as well. Procreation is held by many to be a right which is personal and fundamental, superior to any "good" which might be bought and sold, and subject to challenge only by some other right. The tradeoff between the rights and welfare of the current generation and those of future generations, insofar as a tradeoff exists, will differ in different settings. But regardless of setting, a public policy to reduce fertility must be sensitive to individual rights today as well as to long-run social goals, and must recognize the distinction between encouraging lower fertility (by changing the "signals" which influence people) and coercion. Governments need to recognize that once they are actively involved in reducing fertility, the methods they use require careful and continuous scrutiny.

Virtually all the programs to lower fertility recommended in this Report would also improve individual welfare; they pose no obvious tradeoff between present and future welfare. Programs to raise education and reduce mortality raise welfare. Family planning programs expand the options available to people, allowing couples to realize their own fertility objectives and improving the health of mothers and children. In many countries current fertility exceeds desired family size; within most countries, there is "unmet need" for family planning. Incentives and disincentives, carefully designed, can also meet the criteria of improving welfare and allowing free choice. Incentives compensate individuals for the economic and social losses of delaying births or of having fewer children. Those who accept payment for not having children do so because they find this tradeoff worthwhile; they are compensated for some of the public savings from lower fertility. Similarly with disincentives: those who elect to pay the higher costs of additional children compensate society as a whole for the private benefits of more children.

But incentive and disincentive programs require extra care to avoid unfairness and abuse, not only in their implementation but also in their design. Some benefits from an incentive program are bound to go to people who would have deferred pregnancy or limited births anyway; public subsidies may therefore benefit the rich unnecessarily. When payments are offered as an inducement to sterilization—which is usually irreversible—care must be taken that the poor are not being tempted to act out of short-term economic necessity contrary to their long-term interests. Such payments are usually quite small, since they are meant to compensate for time and travel costs. Governments that offer them have generally established procedures that make written consent mandatory, and have imposed criteria that potential clients must fulfill (such as having several children already). A waiting period between the decision, the sterilization, and the payment can also be a safeguard—though in inaccessible rural areas a waiting period may be impractical, since those seeking sterilization may find it hard to make even one trip to a clinic. Deferred incentives, as in the case of educational bonds or an old-age security payment, have the advantage of building in such a safeguard.

Incentives that offer schools, low interest loans, or a tubewell to communities where contraceptive use is high also directly link lower fertility to increased welfare. To the extent that all members can benefit from community incentives, individual welfare is improved. Care must be taken that the benefits of community incentives are distributed equitably, however. There is the danger that, in closely knit communities, some couples will be pressured to use contraception against their will. But community pressure always exists, and usually influences couples to have many children even when they would prefer not to. In Indonesia and Thailand community incentives are only loosely tied to actual use of contraception and are thus primarily promotional.

Like incentives and various socioeconomic programs, disincentives alter the balance of costs and benefits of having children. Rather than raise the benefits of having fewer children, however, they increase the cost of having many. They have therefore the disadvantage that they might unfairly penalize the poor. The rich will find it easier to accept the additional costs of more children, yet the poor may have greater need of children. And children, who have no choice in the matter, bear the costs of certain disincentives—those which give preference in schooling to the first born and which heavily tax family income. It is essential to design disincentives so that they avoid inequality; with care, however, they need be no more objectionable than any other taxes or subsidies.

Even policies that are theoretically voluntary can be implemented in a coercive fashion if not properly monitored. Many countries set performance targets for family planning workers in recruiting new acceptors. While some criteria for evaluating workers' performance are clearly necessary, excessive pressure to achieve unrealistic targets threatens the voluntaristic nature of programs. This is the lesson of the Indian Emergency of 1976–77, when workers were subject to extreme pressure to achieve high sterilization quotas and many people were pressured to be sterilized against their will. Consequently, the party in power lost the next election. In more recent years, this program, operating on a strictly voluntary basis, has proved very successful.

To repeat an important point noted in Chapter 1, the ultimate goal of public policy is to improve living standards, to enhance individual choice, and to create conditions that enable people to realize their potential. Lower fertility is only an intermediate objective; a commitment to achieve lower fertility must not mean a willingness to achieve it at any cost. The successful experience of many countries already indicates that it need not.

Policy priorities in developing regions

The differences among developing countries, both in their demographic situation and in the evolution of their population policies, are profound. In sub-Saharan Africa, few countries have yet to take the first steps in developing a population policy. At the other extreme, in East Asia family planning services are accessible, political commitment is high, and governments offer incentives for couples to have small families. In all regions there is scope for reducing mortality, increasing literacy, and improving the availability of family planning services. But in taking the next steps in population policy, each region faces a different set of issues.

Sub-Saharan Africa: how to increase public commitment

Sub-Saharan Africa has the fastest population growth rate and the highest fertility in the world. Between 1970 and 1979 population increased at 2.7 percent a year, up from 2.5 percent a year during the 1960s. In a few East African countries population is growing at 4 percent or more a year. Of the thirty-three sub-Saharan countries with more than 1 million people, thirty have a total fertility rate of 6 or more. Kenya, Rwanda, and Zimbabwe have fertility rates of 8 or more. Probably fewer than 10 percent of married women of reproductive age are using modern contraception. Sub-Saharan Africa is the only region in which fertility has not begun to fall, and in which population growth is expected to accelerate in the next decade.

Africa is also the poorest region, with a per capita income averaging only $482 in 1982—or $354 if Nigeria is excluded. During the 1970s per capita income grew in real terms by just 0.8 percent a year; if Nigeria is excluded, it declined. The region's gross domestic product stagnated in 1981 and 1982, while population rose 2.7 percent in each year. Fertility in most countries is higher than income alone would predict (see Figure 8.1). But when Africa's high mortality, low literacy, and largely rural population are taken into account, fertility is not unusually high. About a third of the adult population are literate in sub-Saharan countries, compared with half of adults in all low-income countries and two-thirds in all middle-income countries (see Table 8.2). Life expectancy at birth is forty-nine years, ten years less than in other countries at the same income level.

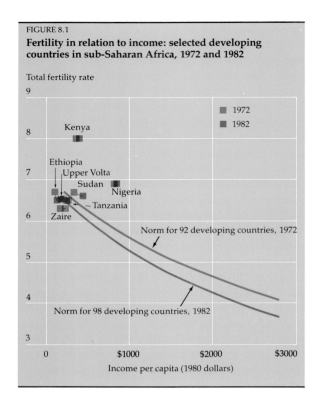

FIGURE 8.1

Fertility in relation to income: selected developing countries in sub-Saharan Africa, 1972 and 1982

The poor economic performance of sub-Saharan Africa cannot be blamed on rapid population growth alone, nor will slower population growth solve all its economic problems. External economic shocks, as well as inappropriate domestic policies, have contributed to the region's economic crisis. But rapid population growth is creating severe strains in some countries and, throughout the region as a whole, it is holding back improvements in living standards.

The strains are acute in a few countries and areas that are already overcrowded—Burundi, Kenya, Malawi, eastern Nigeria, Rwanda, and parts of the

TABLE 8.2

Development indicators: Africa compared with all developing countries

Country group	Per capita income 1982 (dollars)	Adult literacy 1980 (percent)	Life expectancy 1982 (years)	Primary-school enrollment ratio, female[a] 1981 (percent)
Sub-Saharan Africa				
Low-income	249	38	49	57
Middle-income	777	35	50	70
All low-income countries	280	52	59	81
All middle-income countries	1,520	65	60	95

Note: Averages are weighted by 1982 population.

a. Number of females enrolled in primary school as a percentage of all females of primary-school age.

Sahelian countries (see Box 8.4). These and other countries, such as Ethiopia and Upper Volta, have neither the physical capital nor the skills to compensate for a shortage of natural resources. A few countries—such as Angola, Ivory Coast, Nigeria, Zaire, and Zambia—are rich in natural resources, but need extra skills, as well as heavy investment in roads and storage and distribution systems to exploit those resources.

In all sub-Saharan countries, the labor force is growing rapidly, by more than 3 percent a year in most countries, meaning a doubling about every twenty years. Government revenues are growing slowly as a result of slow or no economic growth, so countries have had to struggle not only to provide jobs but to provide basic services such as education. In 1978 education was taking 16 percent of national budgets, but reached less than two-thirds of primary-school-age children. Only a tiny fraction of the people can obtain modern medical care. Human development in all its forms is essential to future economic progress but, as Chapter 5 showed, population growth makes it hard to achieve. These difficulties will remain, because sub-Saharan Africa's current population of 385 million seems set to double by the year 2005. That much is almost inevitable. The real question is whether populations will merely triple in size in the next half-century or increase even more rapidly, to five or six times their current size.

Few sub-Saharan countries have explicit policies to reduce rapid population growth. Kenya was the first to adopt such policies in 1967, Ghana followed in 1969, and Mauritius in the early 1970s. There are recent indications of heightened concern about rapid population growth in Burundi, the Comoros, Malawi, Rwanda, Senegal, and Zimbabwe. About half the governments in sub-Saharan Africa provide family planning services for health and human rights reasons, but without any explicit demographic purpose. Limited services are provided by a few private associations and through an already overstretched public health system, with poor coverage of rural areas. Twelve sub-Saharan countries neither have population policies nor support family planning. Most are in Francophone Africa—Chad, Gabon, Guinea, Ivory Coast, Madagascar, Mauritania, Niger, and Upper Volta—where anticontraception laws from the colonial period are still in effect. These countries have no tradition of private family planning associations, which are elsewhere active in lobbying governments for public involvement.

What explains the limited development of popu-lation policy in sub-Saharan Africa? Population control is a sensitive political issue wherever religious and tribal groups are competing for resources. And much of the pressure for smaller families has come from (or is perceived to come from) western aid donors; this pressure can cause local resentment.

Even if these factors were less important, politicians would still be hesitant to propose smaller families when the demand for children is extremely high. Recent surveys in six countries found that women wanted between six and nine children in their completed families. Depending on the country, only 4 to 17 percent of currently married, fecund women wanted no more children, and most of them had already had at least six. In much of the region the concept of self-determined family size is unknown. Modern contraception is poorly understood and lacks social legitimacy. In this atmosphere couples who wish to use family planning services are discouraged from doing so. And, compared with other regions, infertility affects a disproportionate number of Africans, tragically depriving some women of any children (see Box 8.5). The threat of infertility discourages couples from controlling their childbearing through modern contraception.

Policy development and political commitment are constrained throughout the region by a lack of recent and reliable demographic data needed to demonstrate the magnitude and consequences of rapid population growth. Many African countries, particularly in Francophone Africa, do not have a long history of census-taking. In some countries where censuses have been conducted, the results have never been published because of political controversy. As a result, the size and growth rate of population for countries such as Ethiopia, Guinea, Nigeria, and Zaire are not known within a reasonable degree of certainty.

Yet census results are important in demonstrating to political leaders the need for population policy. The results of the 1976 Senegalese census implied a population growth rate of 2.9 percent a year, much higher than the 2.2 percent annual rate in the 1960s. This prompted the president to create the National Population Commission in 1978 to consider a population policy and family planning services. The 1960 census was a catalyzing factor for population policy in Ghana. The World Fertility Survey, conducted in Benin, Cameroon, Ghana, the Ivory Coast, Kenya, Lesotho, Mauritania, Nigeria, Senegal, and Sudan, has made an important contribution to improving demographic data

Box 8.4 Africa: how much land, how many people?

Africa is often portrayed as an underpopulated region with vast acres of untapped land. It is true that its average population density is low—less than one-fifth of Asia's. But considering the rudimentary farming practices in most of Africa, some countries are becoming crowded, at least in the sense of limited food production potential. This is one of the main findings of the FAO's recently completed project, Land Resources for the Future.

Of course, the goal of self-sufficiency in food production cannot be recommended for all countries. But those which do not manage it must generate enough foreign exchange outside of agriculture to import food (or face the prospect of continuing dependence on food aid or rising malnutrition). For many African countries nonagricultural exports are unlikely to provide a viable short-term source of foreign exchange.

The FAO compared potential population-supporting capacities—determined by soil and climatic conditions and levels of farm technology—to actual and projected populations. The calculations for Africa as a whole confirm the conventional wisdom: even at subsistence farming levels (that is, no use of fertilizers or pesticides, traditional seed varieties and

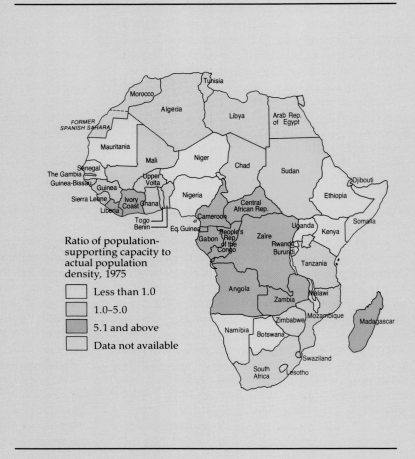

Ratio of population-supporting capacity to actual population density, 1975

- ☐ Less than 1.0
- ☐ 1.0–5.0
- ▓ 5.1 and above
- ☐ Data not available

in the region, but periodic sample surveys have generally not been institutionalized.

In the long run, social development—especially the education of women—is essential to reduce desired family size. More and better schooling for women will help to lower infant mortality, reducing the uncertainty about child survival which keeps family size high. An all-out attack on infant and child mortality and on infertility is imperative; as long as fate seems to govern family size, pronatalist norms will be reinforced and individual choice discouraged.

In the short run, family planning services could do more on two fronts, even in the face of relatively little unsatisfied demand for birth control:

- *Childspacing.* Extended breastfeeding and sexual abstinence have long been practiced in Africa to guarantee two to three years between each

child. The principal aim is to protect the health of children and maximize the number who survive. Throughout Africa, there is potential demand for contraception to space births in both urban and rural areas. But spacing practices appear to be declining most rapidly in urban areas—where desired family size is likely to fall first. In Senegal, for example, both breastfeeding and postpartum amenorrhea are six months shorter in the capital city of Dakar than in rural areas. In Lagos, Nigeria, traditional childspacing practices are in decline and intervals between births are shortening. Unless contraception becomes a more readily available substitute, total fertility may increase and the health of mothers and children may worsen.

Programs in Rwanda, Tanzania, and Zaire have recently been set up to promote contraception for childspacing. In Zimbabwe, the Child Spacing and cropping patterns, and no conservation measures), there is enough land to allow food self-sufficiency for a population 2.7 times larger than the actual population in 1975. When the results are tabulated by country, however, a much more complex picture emerges.

Of forty sub-Saharan countries (excluding Djibouti and the smaller island nations), fourteen do not have enough land—assuming subsistence level farming—to support on a sustainable basis populations as large as those already reached in 1975. The fourteen are Botswana, Burundi, Ethiopia, Kenya, Lesotho, Malawi, Mauritania, Namibia, Niger, Nigeria, Rwanda, Senegal, Somalia, and Uganda (see map); as a group, they account for one-third of the land area of sub-Saharan Africa and about half of its 1981 population.

In some areas of these countries—parts of Kenya, Ethiopia, and Nigeria, and much of Rwanda and Burundi—higher levels of inputs in denser areas mean more people are being supported. But these countries will face increasing difficulties as populations double again in the next twenty to thirty years. Small landlocked countries such as Rwanda and Burundi face particularly serious problems. Population pressure has led to

more intensive farming methods, based on higher and higher labor inputs. But the remoteness of the countries and their terrain make it expensive to use advanced technologies; they also limit agricultural and nonagricultural export opportunities, and thus the scope for importing food. Low rainfall and remoteness also create considerable problems for Sahelian countries like Niger.

Nevertheless, there are eleven countries, largely in central Africa, still possessing extensive areas of underused land. According to the FAO, the land of the Congo and the Central African Republic is capable of supporting populations more than twenty times larger than they had in 1975; in the case of Gabon, the multiple reaches almost 100. Together, the land-abundant countries of sub-Saharan Africa occupy about 30 percent of the region's land, but account for only one-fifth of its 1981 population.

As populations increase further in the land-scarce countries of sub-Saharan Africa, the pressure for people to migrate to land-abundant countries will mount, particularly where they share a common border. Migration already brings mutual benefits to countries such as the Ivory Coast and Upper Volta. As pointed out in Chapter 5, however, the opportunities

for accommodating population growth through international migration do have limits political and social factors introduce uncertainty even where economic benefits for both sending and receiving countries could be great. The recent expulsion of Ghanaians from Nigeria provides an example.

Throughout Africa, traditional methods of farming require more land per capita than in regions such as Asia, where irrigation and double-cropping are more common. To avoid a fall in agricultural output per worker, land-scarce countries will require new technologies—fertilizers, improved seed, and different farming techniques—supported by pricing policies to encourage production. But such measures alone might not be enough. According to the FAO's calculations, seven sub-Saharan countries—Burundi, Kenya, Lesotho, Mauritania, Niger, Rwanda, and Somalia—would not achieve self-sufficiency in food in the year 2000 (when their combined population is expected to reach about 80 million) even if their agricultural techniques were to match those now found on commercial farms in Asia and Latin America.

Family Planning Council provides 40 percent of national childspacing services, in addition to in-service training and contraceptive supply procurement for the Ministry of Health's childspacing program. Among women of childbearing age, contraceptive use is estimated at 15 percent. Formerly a private association, although heavily subsidized by government, the Council recently became a parastatal under the Ministry of Health and is intensifying its activities with funding from USAID; a doubling of field staff, recruitment of a full-time information and education staff, and expanded research capability are planned.

The emphasis on spacing means that programs throughout Africa must offer effective, reversible methods of contraception. Since most people will never have tried modern contraception, careful explanation, reassurance, and treatment of side

effects will be critical. Such programs also provide an opportunity to encourage breastfeeding, which is still almost universal in Africa but declining in urban areas.

● *Adolescents.* In many countries—not just in Africa—there has been a sharp rise in premarital adolescent pregnancy, abortion, and sexually transmitted disease (see Box 8.6). Family planning services and advice can avert these unwanted births, abortions, and health risks. In Ghana education about family life is now part of the school curriculum. Eight other sub-Saharan countries are considering this step.

Middle East and North Africa:
rural outreach and expanding women's opportunities

The countries of the Middle East and North Africa

Box 8.5   Infertility: a challenge to programs in sub-Saharan Africa

Surveys in the 1950s and 1960s found that an average of 12 percent of women who had passed their childbearing years in eighteen sub-Saharan countries were childless, compared with a rate of 2 to 3 percent in other developing countries. Childlessness—"primary" infertility—was greatest in the Central African Republic (17 percent), Cameroon (17 percent), Zaire (21 percent), Congo (21 percent), and Gabon (32 percent). In parts of Zaire, as many as 65 percent of women aged forty-five to forty-nine were childless. Childlessness in younger age groups is less common (presumably due to improved medical care) but still high. In Cameroon 10 percent of women aged thirty to thirty-four are childless; in the Congo the figures are 12 to 13 percent. In addition, large numbers of people suffer from "secondary" infertility—the inability to conceive or give birth again following an earlier birth. Studies in Kenya have shown that primary and secondary infertility occur with approximately equal frequency, while in much of West Africa secondary infertility accounts for up to two-thirds of diagnosed cases. Secondary infertility afflicts 14 to 39 percent of women aged fifteen to fifty in different regions of Cameroon.

The consequences of infertility are particularly severe for women, who may be ostracized, abandoned, or divorced. Fear of infertility makes couples reluctant to practice modern contraception. Thus, although high infertility keeps fertility lower than it otherwise would be—every 9 percent increment in childlessness reduces total fertility by about 1—it also inhibits contraceptive use and slows eventual fertility decline.

What causes high levels of infertility? Sexually transmitted diseases, particularly gonorrhea and syphilis, are major causes of both primary and secondary infertility. Gonorrhea, if left untreated, can lead to irreversible blockage of the fallopian tubes in women and of the vas deferens in men. Because the symptoms are not readily noticeable in women, it may go for several years without treatment. Syphilis causes miscarriage and stillbirth. Poor obstetrical care and unhygienic abortion are additional causes of secondary infertility. Malnutrition, congenital defects, genital tuberculosis, and various uterine, vaginal, and urethral infections also contribute.

Treatment for infertility is costly and difficult; even then, the outcome is uncertain. Depending on the cause, only one-quarter to one-half of couples treated may subsequently have a live birth. Three major causes—sexually transmitted disease, poor obstetrical care, and illegal abortion—can be prevented at less cost. Public campaigns can inform couples of the causes of infertility, the symptoms of sexually transmitted disease, its prevention through limiting sexual partners and use of barrier methods of contraception (especially condoms), and the availability of treatment. These informational efforts need to be directed to men in particular, since they are more reluctant to submit to infertility tests and treatment. Though women are usually held responsible for childlessness, in fact they account for about 40 percent of infertility cases. Men account for another 40 percent, with both part-

ners being infertile in the remaining 20 percent of cases. When the infertility is caused by sexually transmitted disease, it is essential that both partners be medically treated. Other causes of infertility can be prevented by improving the quality of obstetrical care, such as by training traditional midwives, and by increasing the availability of contraception so that couples can prevent unwanted pregnancies that might result in abortion.

There are few specialists or centers for diagnosis and treatment of infertility in sub-Saharan Africa. Since 1973 infertility clinics have been set up in Cameroon, Kenya, Tanzania, and Uganda. Programs to control the spread of sexually transmitted disease have been launched in the Central African Republic, Ethiopia, and Zambia. The Association for Voluntary Sterilization has provided grants for research, treatment, training, and public education on infertility in Nigeria, Sierra Leone, and Sudan.

Resources are needed for research into the causes and treatment of infertility, as well as for better data on its prevalence. About $4 million of a total of $6 million spent by the public sector on infertilty research worldwide in 1982 went for research into unexplained causes of infertility; the bulk of this work was conducted by the Center for Population Research in the United States. Total spending on infertility research by the World Health Organization in 1982 was only $900,000. The United Nations Development Programme has proposed increasing this amount to $2–4 million a year over the next five to seven years.

---

are quite diverse, ranging from one of the world's poorest (Afghanistan) to five of the wealthiest (Kuwait, Libya, Oman, Saudi Arabia, and the United Arab Emirates). But 90 percent of its 260 million people live in thirteen middle-income countries. All share a common cultural heritage and are predominantly Islamic. Countries in the Middle East and North Africa have the second highest rates of population growth and fertility in the world, after sub-Saharan Africa. Between 1970 and 1982 their population grew at an average 2.9

percent a year; the total fertility rate in 1982 was 5.4. Migration is common, both into and out of the region and among countries within it.

In most countries fertility is higher than would be expected given per capita income (see Figure 8.2). Five high-income oil exporters, with per capita incomes of $14,820, had a fertility rate of 6.9 in 1982. In the past decade incomes in Jordan, Syria, and Algeria have risen strongly but total fertility has remained at more than 7. Income growth in these countries is recent and social development has come more slowly. Low literacy (particularly among women) and high infant mortality help to explain high fertility. Also responsible are cultural, religious, and legal pressures that confine women to the home and restrict their property rights, rights within marriage, and ability to seek work outside the home.

Three countries in Figure 8.2—Egypt, Tunisia, and Turkey—have had a marked fall in fertility in the past decade; in all three, fertility is now below what would be expected for their income levels. In Morocco, fertility has declined more modestly. Unlike most other countries in the region, these four have policies to reduce population growth.

Government family planning programs began in 1964 in Tunisia, in 1965 in Egypt and Turkey, and in 1966 in Morocco. According to recent surveys, 24 percent of married women of childbearing age in Egypt, 38 percent in Turkey, and 41 percent in Tunisia are practicing contraception. Later marriage has also contributed to fertility decline. The change has been most dramatic in Tunisia, where the proportion of women aged fifteen to nineteen who are married fell from 42 percent in 1956 to 6 percent in 1975. In Egypt the proportion fell from 32 percent in 1960–61 to 21 percent fifteen years later; in Turkey, the decline was from 33 percent to 22 percent.

Box 8.6 Teenage pregnancy

Teenage pregnancy is common in both developed and developing countries, accounting for about 10 to 15 percent of births worldwide. And this understates the problem since many teenage pregnancies are terminated by legal and illegal abortion. Because couples in developing countries tend to marry earlier, most teenage pregnancy is within marriage. In developed countries, with later age of marriage, more teenage pregnancy occurs outside marriage. In 1979, for example, almost two-thirds of live births to American teenagers were to unwed mothers. As the age at marriage rises and urbanization loosens traditional social restraints on sexual activity, the incidence of premarital teenage pregnancy may increase in developing countries. In a Bombay hospital in the early 1970s, 12 percent of women admitted for abortions were younger than eighteen; of these, 92 percent were unmarried. In a major Lagos hospital the number of teenage pregnancies and abortions increased over a recent five-year period; 93 percent of the teenagers admitted were single girls of school age.

Teenage pregnancy—within or outside marriage—has adverse consequences for mothers and children:

• Childbirth poses greater health dangers for teenage mothers than for older women, and for their children. Children of teenage mothers are more likely to be premature, have low birth weight, and have a greater risk of death. As was

shown in Box 7.1, postponing giving birth until the age of twenty or older would significantly reduce maternal and infant mortality rates.

• Many teenage pregnancies—particularly when outside marriage—end in abortion. If poorly performed, abortion is highly risky and may impair future fertility. Nearly 40 percent of adolescent pregnancies in the United States ended in legal abortion in 1978.

• Pregnancy and childbirth disrupt the education and career opportunities of young women. Teenage mothers frequently do not complete primary or secondary school. The time demands of childrearing can restrict their current employment possibilities, while limited education affects their future income-earning potential.

• The children of adolescent mothers are also worse off. Teenage couples are likely to have fewer economic assets than are somewhat older couples to support children, and single teenage mothers have even less. It is believed that many abandoned children—in Brazil, an estimated 16 million children or one-third of its youth—have young mothers who are unwed or in unstable unions. Studies in developed countries show deficits in the cognitive development of children of adolescent mothers that are partly attributable to the social and economic consequences of early childbearing; children of teenage mothers are likely to spend a considerable part of their childhood in

one-parent households, and they are more likely themselves to have children while still adolescents.

Teenage pregnancy can be averted. When family planning services are combined with maternal and child health programs, information about family planning may reach only married women who already have children. To have an impact on teenage pregnancy, young people—with and without children, male and female, in and out of school—must also be reached. Family life education, including human reproduction, family planning, and responsible parenthood, is taught in schools in the Dominican Republic, Ghana, Korea, Mexico, and the Philippines. Kenya and Sierra Leone are developing similar curricula. Posters, radio, and television messages can be used to reach out-of-school youth.

For teenagers who are already pregnant the consequences can be minimized by providing continued educational and employment opportunities. A women's center run by the Jamaican Women's Bureau provides support and classroom instruction for pregnant women aged twelve to sixteen with the goal of returning them to school. Of the students registered at the center in 1978–79, almost two-thirds were placed in secondary schools, high schools, or vocational training schools, and 92 percent had not become pregnant again by the end of 1981.

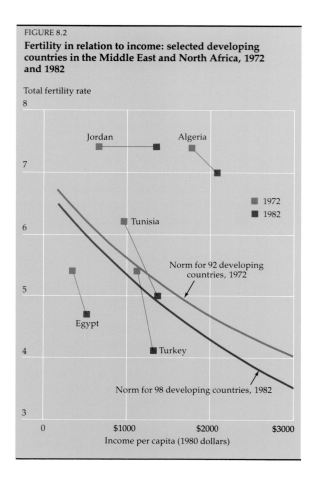

FIGURE 8.2

Fertility in relation to income: selected developing countries in the Middle East and North Africa, 1972 and 1982

Total fertility rate

- Jordan
- Algeria
- Tunisia
- 1972
- 1982
- Norm for 92 developing countries, 1972
- Egypt
- Turkey
- Norm for 98 developing countries, 1982

Income per capita (1980 dollars)

Despite these achievements, population growth remains rapid and acceptance of family planning slow. Total fertility, although reduced, is still 4 to 5 in Egypt, Tunisia, and Turkey, and about 6 in Morocco. In Egypt and Tunisia, an increase in the proportion of women of childbearing age has kept the birth rate high. Mortality has declined, and the rate of population growth has changed little. Population pressure has been eased in both countries by emigration, but poor economic conditions in Europe have reduced emigration from Tunisia and caused many emigrants to return. The rate of contraceptive use has remained at about 25 percent in Egypt for several years; increases have been slow in Turkey and Morocco. The number of new acceptors of family planning has barely risen in Tunisia for about five years.

There is ample evidence of unmet need for family planning services. Low and high estimates in Egypt ranged from 12 to 22 percent of married women of childbearing age in 1980. In certain areas unmet need is even higher. One study found that 82 percent of married women in rural areas of upper Egypt want no more children but are not using contraception, and that more than half of these women would like to use a method. In Jendouba, Tunisia, 46 percent of women who were not using contraception wanted no more children, and 22 percent said that they would like to space the next birth. When women in Marrakech, Morocco, were offered supplies of oral contraceptives through home visits, the rate of contraceptive use rose from 18 to 43 percent. In the Sfax region of Tunisia, household distribution increased the rate from 7 to 18 percent.

Continued progress in reducing fertility in these countries will depend both on better family planning services and on measures to improve the status of women.

● *Family planning programs.* Access to services in rural areas is still restricted. The Tunisian program has had difficulty reaching a dispersed rural population, which includes half of the married women of reproductive age. Services in Morocco and Egypt rely heavily on physicians and are clinic-based with little outreach. In Egypt only physicians may prescribe the pill and insert the IUD. The few outreach workers in place are not permitted to distribute contraceptives and are supposed to motivate only women who already have three children. In Morocco, nurses were only recently authorized to insert IUDs, and nonclinical distribution of the pill is still frowned upon. Yet experience in South and East Asia as well as in Latin America indicates that carefully trained paramedical fieldworkers can deliver many methods and increase contraceptive prevalence dramatically. Use of the media to promote family planning and small families has been limited in Morocco: not until 1982 were the Ministry of Public Health and the private family planning association permitted to broadcast family planning messages and show films.

The limited range of contraceptives available in Egypt and Morocco also restricts their use. Although the IUD and condoms are theoretically available, both programs favor the pill. Only one-quarter of outlets in Egypt are staffed or supplied to provide IUD insertions. Only one brand of pill is offered. Sterilization is legal but not promoted by the official program; abortion is prohibited. In contrast, the Tunisian program has made the pill, IUD, female sterilization, and abortion (in the first three months of pregnancy) more widely available.

● *The status of women.* Increasing the number of educated women could do much to reduce fertility in the region. Enrollment rates for girls in 1980

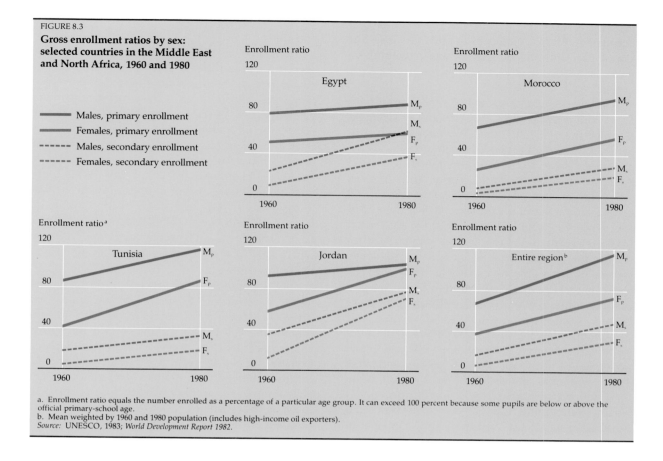

FIGURE 8.3

Gross enrollment ratios by sex: selected countries in the Middle East and North Africa, 1960 and 1980

Males, primary enrollment
Females, primary enrollment
Males, secondary enrollment
Females, secondary enrollment

Egypt

Morocco

Tunisia

Jordan

Entire region[b]

a. Enrollment ratio equals the number enrolled as a percentage of a particular age group. It can exceed 100 percent because some pupils are below or above the official primary-school age.
b. Mean weighted by 1960 and 1980 population (includes high-income oil exporters).
Source: UNESCO, 1983; *World Development Report 1982.*

were still only two-thirds the rates for boys at both primary and secondary schools (see Figure 8.3); in twenty years the gap has not narrowed. An important exception is Jordan, where primary-school education is now universal and about three-quarters of secondary-school-age children of both sexes are enrolled. In Egypt, Morocco, and Tunisia universal primary schooling for girls has yet to be achieved. Female primary enrollment has increased steeply in Tunisia, and the male-female gap has been somewhat reduced. In Egypt the increase in primary-school places has barely kept pace with population growth; the primary-school enrollment rate has remained low and access is particularly limited in rural areas, where fertility is high. At the same time, much has been invested in expanding secondary schooling.

Women's status can also be improved by raising the minimum age of marriage and by changing laws that restrict women's social and financial rights. The legal minimum age of marriage for women in Tunisia was raised to fifteen in 1956, and then to seventeen in 1964. The legal minimum age in Morocco and Turkey is still fifteen. In Turkey

other legal changes are under discussion: the repeal of a husband's automatic status as head of the family in favor of a system of "joint responsibility of spouses" and abolition of a husband's right of consent for his wife to be gainfully employed.

Latin America and the Caribbean: reducing social inequities

Almost all of the countries in Latin America and the Caribbean are middle-income, but with great demographic diversity. In four countries with per capita incomes exceeding $2,500—Argentina, Chile, Trinidad and Tobago, and Uruguay—population growth has slowed to below 2 percent a year and total fertility is nearing replacement level. The highest fertility in the region is in six lower-middle-income countries: Bolivia, Ecuador, El Salvador, Guatemala, Honduras, and Nicaragua. Total fertility in these countries exceeds 5 and population growth ranges from 2.5 to 3.4 percent. Fertility is high in the Caribbean, with the exception of Cuba, but emigration moderates population growth. Fertility has declined in the three largest countries—Brazil, Colombia, and Mexico—but population will still double in about twenty-five years in Mexico and in about thirty years in the others.

In short, population growth is rapid throughout Latin America and the Caribbean and will remain so until the 1990s at least. Populations are projected to grow by at least 2 percent a year in most countries, closer to 3 percent in much of Central America. Only in Argentina, Chile, and Uruguay will growth rates be lower. The labor force will grow by more than 2 percent a year until the end of the century. Urbanization will slow somewhat from its recent fast pace, but in some countries (Argentina, Chile, Uruguay, and Venezuela) 80 percent of the people are already living in cities.

No single issue is so important in Latin America as the manner in which opportunity and access are shared. Because of inequalities of income and wealth, and despite rapid economic growth in the past quarter century, millions of people still live in poverty. As economic growth accelerated after 1950, some areas and socioeconomic groups benefited more than others, widening income and wealth differentials. As development proceeds, those differences may start to narrow. One aim of public policy, particularly in health and education, is to promote equality of opportunity. Population programs have a related role to play: they can improve the chances of the poor by making it possible for them to devote more resources to each child.

Three countries, Brazil, Colombia, and Mexico, account for 60 percent of the region's 370 million people. Economically and demographically they are more advanced than the northern Andean countries, most of Central America and the Caribbean, but (except for central and southern Brazil) less advanced than Argentina, Chile, and Uruguay.

As is true elsewhere in Latin America, a major characteristic of these countries is their urban-rural contrast. In Colombia health facilities are concentrated in the urban areas; per household, public subsidies to rural health are less than one-seventh the national average. Life expectancy for urban Colombians is sixty-four compared with fifty-eight for those in the countryside. In Brazil current spending on education is as much as ten times greater per child in urban than in rural areas; urban teachers have on average more than eleven years of education, compared with six years for rural teachers. Literacy rates in rural Brazil are 48 percent, compared with 78 percent in the towns and cities.

Provision of family planning services is also greater in urban areas, especially in Brazil. The national government has not assisted or promoted family planning services, so most users rely on private suppliers. In the well-to-do southern state of Sao Paulo, 63 percent of women obtain contraceptives through a private doctor or a drugstore. This is difficult or impossible in rural areas. The Brazilian Family Planning Association (BEMFAM), a private nonprofit organization, does provide services to the poor. In the poor states of Rio Grande do Norte and Piaui, where BEMFAM is active, almost 60 percent of women use contraceptives. In Bahia, where BEMFAM does not operate, only 40 percent use contraceptives.

How is population growth related to inequality in these countries? Fertility is consistently and inversely related to household income and to education. Surveys in Brazil indicate that poor rural women bear twice as many children as do women from the upper 40 percent of urban households. Brazilian women who neither have paid jobs nor have completed primary school have more than twice as many children as working women who completed secondary school. Similar differentials occur in Mexico and Colombia. The well-to-do are able to spend more per child than are the poor and they have fewer children.

The extent of these differences was described in Chapter 4. In both Brazil and Colombia, the poorest 20 percent of households have almost one-third of all children—but only 4 percent of total income in Colombia and 2 percent in Brazil. The richest 20 percent of households, in contrast, have 10 percent of the children and 60 percent of the income in Colombia, 8 percent of the children and 64 percent of the income in Brazil. These differences are far greater than those in such countries as India, Thailand, and Malaysia.

Population policies have helped to reduce fertility in Latin America. In 1966 Colombia's Ministry of Health signed an agreement with a private medical association to provide a program of training and research that included family planning. By combining low-key public support with private family planning programs, the Colombian government has helped facilitate a rapid fertility decline.

The Mexican government adopted a population policy to reduce fertility in 1973 and began providing family planning services in 1974. By 1976 contraceptive use had doubled, almost entirely because of public programs. Between 1970 and

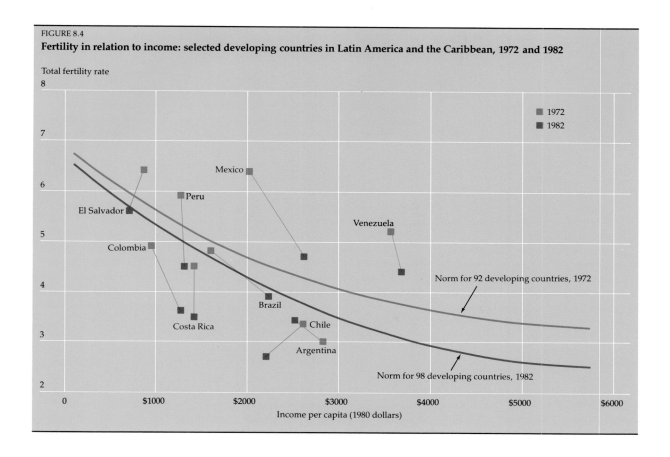

FIGURE 8.4

Fertility in relation to income: selected developing countries in Latin America and the Caribbean, 1972 and 1982

Total fertility rate

- 1972
- 1982

El Salvador

Colombia

Peru

Mexico

Venezuela

Norm for 92 developing countries, 1972

Costa Rica

Brazil

Chile

Argentina

Norm for 98 developing countries, 1982

Income per capita (1980 dollars)

1980 fertility fell in both Mexico and Colombia by about one-third; in contrast, it declined by less than 20 percent in Brazil, a country in which the national government had not committed itself to a population policy or program (see Box 8.7).

This contrast becomes even sharper when it is noted that per capita real incomes nearly doubled in Brazil but were up by only 50 percent in Colombia and Mexico. Whereas Colombia and Mexico managed a sharp decline in fertility in relation to income growth, Brazil's fertility decline was more modest (see Figure 8.4). If Brazil had followed the pattern of Colombia and Mexico, its total fertility rate would have fallen to 3.0 by 1982 given its income growth; in fact it was 3.9. With a population policy no more vigorous than that of Colombia and Mexico during the 1970s, Brazilian fertility might now be one-quarter lower than it is. Most of the difference would come from lower fertility among the poor, since it is they who would be assisted most by a public policy.

The advantages of lower fertility are already becoming apparent in some Latin American countries. In Colombia the number of enrolled primary-school students increased by 1.6 million between 1965 and 1975; in the 1980s the number of children in the primary-age group will grow by less than a million, easing the strain on the education budget. By 1990 the Colombian labor force will be growing by 2.2 percent a year, well below the 3.5 percent rate of the 1970s. With fewer new entrants to the labor force, a larger proportion of them can expect to qualify for high-wage jobs.

Looking ahead, Colombia and Mexico need to extend public family planning programs to the rural poor, and to do more to integrate population policy into the overall framework of development planning. Brazil's popular private sector programs, long tolerated by the government, do not have adequate resources. There is significant unmet need for family planning in the poor Northeast. Brazil spends more than 4 percent of its GDP on health; by devoting a tiny share of that budget to family planning, it could extend family planning coverage to the 40 million people of its poorer regions.

Brazil, Colombia, and Mexico are not the only countries in Latin America where population policies could be effective against poverty and inequality. Ecuador, Paraguay, Peru, and the Central

Box 8.7 Changing policies and attitudes toward family planning in Brazil

Official Brazilian policy on population was, until 1974, implicitly pronatalist. The traditional official view, dating from colonial times, had been that Brazil would benefit from a large growing population to complement its vast territory and natural resources.

The first perceptible change from a pronatalist to a laissez-faire stance occurred during the 1974 World Population Conference, and at about the same time in the Second National Development Plan. Official statements maintained that Brazil's 2.5 percent annual rate of population growth was not a serious threat to economic development, but they went on to recognize the responsibility of the government to provide family planning services to those who want, of their own free choice, to plan their families but are too poor to pay for the services that are available privately. Federal authorities gave tacit approval to a number of state-level family planning programs organized by the Brazilian Family Planning Association (BEMFAM), the Brazilian affiliate of the International Planned Parenthood Federation.

In 1977 the federal government took the first step to provide family planning services for the poor. It announced that the 1978–81 plan for maternal and child health would include family planning services for women for whom pregnancies would involve a high health risk. Then in October 1983 the minister of health announced that a broad new health program for women would be implemented beginning in 1984, with family planning assistance being included as part of a full range of maternal and child health care.

Underlying this more active involvement in family planning are three trends, not entirely unrelated: growing public awareness of Brazil's population problem, including among important elites formerly opposed to family planning programs; a growing social demand for (and practice of) family planning; and the economic recession, which has heightened social tensions because of growing unemployment and underemployment and falling real incomes.

In March 1983 Brazil's president told Congress that the country's rapid population growth was capable of causing "social, economic, cultural and political imbalances" and proposed opening a broad debate which could lead to specific policy measures to deal with this threat. Fifteen days later, a Parliamentary Commission of Inquiry on problems associated with Brazil's population growth was established in the Senate, and in mid-May the Ministry of Health sent the president a preliminary document on the proposed health program for women.

A recent military report showed that half of the young men who enrolled for military service in 1982 were rejected for medical reasons, and of these, 60 percent were likely to be unfit for service in the future because their physical and mental capacity had been permanently stunted. Statements by the Chief of Staff of the Armed Forces, in a newspaper interview in June 1983, differed from the traditional military view that Brazil needed rapid population growth to fill up its vast territory. Noting that the quality of recruits had been falling for some time, he said, "What we need in this country is a well-qualified and capable population. We do not need numbers of people . . . . A child who is not well fed in the first year of life suffers permanent mental damage, can never again be productive, and will always be dependent on society."

The official position of the Catholic Church is to promote responsible parenthood only by natural means. But at least one theologian has publicly argued that "only the couple has the right to choose the means most appropriate for practicing responsible parenthood." Increasing concern with social justice is likely to weaken further the church hierarchy's opposition to government-supported family planning programs, as long as the state does not try to dictate how many children a couple should have or the means to be used to achieve their goal.

The taboo on public discussion of family planning in Brazil has now ended. A report on vasectomy was featured in a fifteen-minute program in prime television time on a Sunday evening in December 1983. A recent poll in the city of Sao Paulo found that 75 percent of those interviewed believed that couples should plan the number of children that they have. Civilian politicians in both opposition and government parties increasingly express the strong social demand for "democratization of access to family planning" and some opposition parties have called for legalization of abortion. (It is estimated that between 3 million and 5 million illegal and clandestine abortions are performed every year in Brazil, or roughly one for each live birth.)

A growing number of Brazilian politicians belong to an association of legislators favoring an active family planning policy, which hosted the first "Western Hemisphere Conference of Parliamentarians on Population and Development" in Brasilia in December 1982. A private organization, Pro Familia, recently organized a three-day "First National Conference on Maternal and Child Protection and Family Planning" with some 1,200 participants (80 percent of them women) in the auditorium of the federal senate. The conference recommended that family planning should cease to be a privilege of the well-to-do, and that the state, complemented by private institutions, should provide family planning information and services. The conference also recommended the creation of a new agency to coordinate a National Family Planning Program, revision of existing laws to allow the use of all means of contraception approved by the international scientific community, and inclusion in primary and secondary school curricula of material on human sexuality and the physiology of reproduction. The closing session of the conference was attended by the president of Brazil, the ministers of social welfare and the interior, the acting minister of health, a number of federal senators and deputies, and the chief of staff of the armed forces.

American countries could all benefit from stronger policies. Rapid population growth in El Salvador has been identified by many as a partial cause of its civil war. In Bolivia and Haiti, the poorest countries in the region, initiatives to slow population growth are among the most urgent policy needs to combat poverty.

South Asia: expanding and improving programs

The 930 million people of Bangladesh, India, Nepal, Pakistan, and Sri Lanka comprise one-fifth of world population and one-quarter of the population of developing countries. Although incomes in South Asia are among the lowest in the world, the region's fertility has already fallen substantially (see Figure 8.5). In Sri Lanka, for example, the total fertility rate fell from 5.5 in 1960 to 3.5 in 1974; in India it dropped from 6.5 in the 1950s to 4.8 in 1982. The rate of contraceptive use (both modern and traditional methods) is 55 percent in Sri Lanka, the highest in the region. About 28 percent of couples in India use modern contraceptives. No other country at India's level of socioeconomic development—measured by low literacy and per capita income and high infant mortality—has a lower level of fertility. Bangladesh and Pakistan have had more modest declines. In Bangladesh 19 percent of couples use either modern or traditional methods (see Figure 8.6).

What accounts for this impressive record? Continued progress in raising female literacy and lowering infant mortality, as well as a concerted effort to expand access to family planning, have both been important. Within India there is wide variation in fertility and in contraceptive use, a variation which closely corresponds to patterns of social development. For example, in the state of Kerala, which has the lowest total fertility (2.7 in 1978), 75 percent of rural women are literate, infant mortality is 47 per thousand live births, and 32 percent of couples are protected by modern contraception. In contrast, in the state of Uttar Pradesh total fertility was 5.6 in 1978, infant mortality is almost four times higher (171 per thousand), and female literacy and contraceptive use are, respectively, one-seventh and one-third the levels found in Kerala.

The experience in Sri Lanka is similar. Despite a per capita income of only $320 in 1982, infant mortality had been reduced to 41 per thousand and virtually all primary-school-age girls were enrolled in school. Of a contraceptive use rate of 55 percent, almost two-thirds comprised modern methods; total fertility had declined to 3.4.

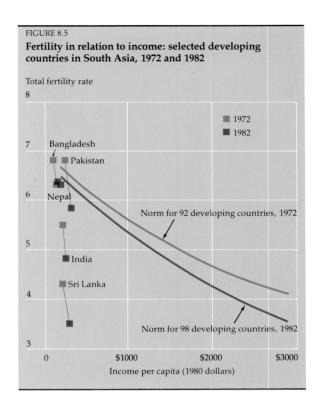

FIGURE 8.5

Fertility in relation to income: selected developing countries in South Asia, 1972 and 1982

Progress in South Asia has not been uniform, however, and rapid population growth is a source of continuing concern. In India and Sri Lanka mortality has declined as fast as, or faster than, fertility. As a result, population growth has increased in India—its population is now increasing by 16 million a year, more than in any other country, including China. India's birth rate has remained at 33 to 34 per thousand since 1976; contraceptive use, steady at 23 to 24 percent since 1976, has only recently begun to rise again. Total fertility has stopped falling in Sri Lanka, and has been fluctuating between 3.4 and 3.7 since 1974. In Bangladesh contraceptive use increased from 8 percent in 1975 to 19 percent in 1981, but appears to have made slow progress since then (though the share of modern methods has apparently risen). In Pakistan only about 5 percent of couples practice contraception, and in Nepal only 7 percent. Both of these countries lag behind others in providing health and family planning services, although both show signs of a renewed political commitment to curb population growth.

The experience in Sri Lanka and in some Indian states suggests that much more could be done to bring about fertility decline. In every country there is considerable scope for reducing infant mortality, raising the legal marriage age, and increasing

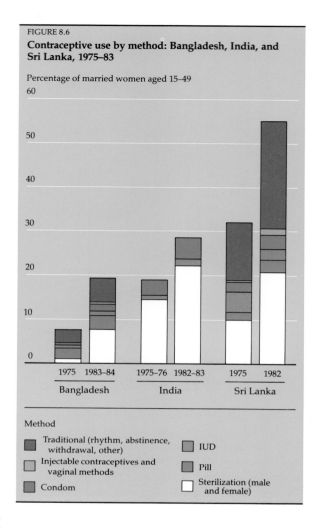

FIGURE 8.6

Contraceptive use by method: Bangladesh, India, and Sri Lanka, 1975–83

Percentage of married women aged 15–49

Method

- Traditional (rhythm, abstinence, withdrawal, other)
- Injectable contraceptives and vaginal methods
- Condom
- IUD
- Pill
- Sterilization (male and female)

childbearing age have unmet need for contraception to limit or space births. Pilot projects there have achieved rates of contraceptive use of 35 to 40 percent with modern methods, three to four times the prevalence of these methods nationwide. In Sri Lanka 44 percent of women of childbearing age who want no more children are nevertheless not practicing contraception.

To satisfy unmet need, family planning programs must resolve important issues of access and quality.

- *Access*. Better family planning outreach could go a long way to increase contraceptive use throughout the region. Access is most restricted in Nepal and Pakistan. In Nepal there is unmet need for contraception among 22 to 27 percent of eligible women. About half of currently married women in Nepal are unaware of a modern contraceptive method, and an additional 15 percent who are aware do not know where a method can be obtained. In Pakistan, three-quarters of married women of childbearing age knew of a modern method in 1975, but only 5 percent were using one. A quarter to a half of these women had unmet need for contraception to limit births. Since then contraceptive use has stagnated. The government plans to meet the need for contraception by greatly expanding and upgrading services.

- *Method mix*. Family planning programs in South Asia have continued to emphasize sterilization to the neglect of reversible methods of contraception, particularly in India and Sri Lanka (see Figure 8.6). Sterilization accounts for more than three-quarters of modern contraceptive use in India and Nepal, two-thirds in Sri Lanka, and about half in Bangladesh. Sterilization is clearly in demand among couples who want no more children. But other forms of contraception are used less, largely because they are not widely available. Given the high rate of child mortality in South Asia, reversible contraceptive methods may be more desirable for couples who have had two or three children but who do not wish to be sterilized immediately. To maximize contraceptive use, both reversible methods and sterilization need to be made available.

The only widely available reversible method in India is the condom, which is provided through 400,000 retail outlets in the social marketing program as well as in family planning program outlets. The pill, important in countries such as Indonesia, is not offered through social marketing arrangements, and in 1981–82 was being distributed through only 4,500 rural and 2,500 urban out-

female education—all of which would have a profound effect on fertility. In Bangladesh family planning and greater economic independence of women are jointly promoted through credit cooperatives for women (see Box 8.8). A few countries are moving beyond schemes that compensate those who adopt contraception to consider positive incentives for small families. Bangladesh has contemplated offering bonds to sterilization clients with two to three children and to couples who postpone a first pregnancy or space children at long intervals (see Box 6.4). India is considering a scheme to give "green cards" to couples sterilized after two children; these cards would entitle them to preferential access to social services.

Desired family size in Bangladesh is now about four; actual size averages about 5.5. Sri Lankan women are having on average one child more than they want. According to a 1979 survey in Bangladesh, as many as 41 percent of married women of

Box 8.8 Family planning and women's credit cooperatives in Bangladesh

The Bangladesh Rural Development Board has been sponsoring credit cooperatives for rural women since 1975, funded by IDA and bilateral cofinanciers as a component of two population projects. By providing training and income-earning opportunities, the program seeks to reduce women's dependence on childbearing for their short- and long-term security. Cooperatives have also been used to transmit information about family planning. They provide a social setting that encourages acceptance and continued use of contraception.

Membership is open to all women who purchase a share in the cooperative, at ten taka (roughly $0.40). Members must save regularly and attend weekly cooperative meetings in their village. In some societies all members are loaned the same amount; in others the amount varies, depending on the number of shares, total savings, or length of membership. Credit is offered to individuals as well as to group enterprises. Loans carry an interest rate of 12.5 percent. Thana-level project officers review each cooperative's loan program. All deputy project officers are women who have received 4 to 6 months' special training.

Each cooperative sends one woman to a weekly thana-level training and development center several miles from the village. These representatives are trained in poultry raising, horticulture, health and family planning, loan policy, and cooperative law and procedure. They pass on this new information to society members during their weekly meetings and, in turn, take their members' problems and questions to the training session.

As of July 1983 the program had established 1,215 cooperatives with 49,368 members, share capital of about $50,000, and savings of about $104,000. The demand for loans far outstrips the amount available, although the Sonali Bank has recently agreed to provide new capital. The repayment rate has been extremely high, always over 90 percent, often near 100 percent. Women have taken loans for processing paddy, muri, turmeric, mustard oil, dal, chili, fish, and peanuts; for buying livestock to raise and sell; for small enterprises, such as pottery, jute goods, or bamboo mats; and in a few cases for buying water to irrigate a rice crop or lease land for cultivation. Initially, most loans have gone to individuals to generate an immediate return on a traditional skill (such as paddy processing). As time passes, however, a higher proportion is going to groups of members for activities that provide a longer-run return, such as fish breeding, commercial poultry, and market gardening.

Family planning is on the agenda of cooperatives' weekly meetings: the methods available, side effects to be expected, and how to obtain contraceptives and medical attention. Those interested in receiving services are referred to local family planning and health clinics. Cooperative leaders keep track of the contraceptive status of members, problems they may have in common, the need to switch methods, and special arrangements that need to be made for

women who want to be sterilized or need other medical help.

A study by the Bangladesh Planning Commission in 1978 compared the knowledge and practice of family planning among cooperative members and nonmembers with similar socioeconomic backgrounds in the project area. In both groups, most women had positive attitudes to family planning. But cooperative members knew more about the different methods and a larger proportion were practicing contraception. Among all members, regardless of age, pregnancy, or marital status, 31 percent were using family planning. Of those who would otherwise be at risk of pregnancy (married, exposed, in the childbearing ages), two thirds were using a method. In contrast, about 19 percent of married women of childbearing age were practicing contraception in Bangladesh as a whole in 1981.

Another project combining work for women and family planning is in Maros Regency, South Sulawesi, Indonesia. It has generated income from poultry raising and tripled contraceptive use among members. Private family planning associations in thirteen African countries (Benin, the Gambia, Ghana, Kenya, Lesotho, Madagascar, Mali, Nigeria, Sierra Leone, Tanzania, Togo, Uganda, and Zaire) are also sponsoring pilot projects that promote planned parenthood alongside development programs for women.

lets. There are plans to train health and family planning workers to insert IUDs; they are not yet permitted to prescribe pills. Although access to abortion was liberalized as a backup service for contraceptive failure more than ten years ago, safe abortion is still difficult to obtain. An estimated 4 million to 6 million abortions were performed illegally by unauthorized persons in 1981, compared with 376,000 performed legally.

In Sri Lanka 25 percent of married couples of childbearing age were using traditional methods of fertilty regulation (rhythm, withdrawal, and so on) in 1981, a doubling of the percentage since 1975. Such an increase in use of traditional methods attests to growing unmet need for more effective spacing methods. Only 664 centers offer the IUD; public health midwives have not yet been trained to perform insertions. Injectable contraceptives are popular in rural areas because of their convenience, but are available at only 120 centers.

Although Bangladesh continues to stress sterilization, its social marketing project has made available several types of condoms, pills, and spermicides. And the program has recently put more emphasis on IUDs by offering financial incentives to staff and compensation for travel and lost wages to acceptors. There are plans to train more fieldworkers in IUD insertions and menstrual regulation, but not all fieldworkers are in place, and not all of those who are have received adequate training. Injectable contraceptives have proved popular in pilot projects, but are available on only a limited basis under the supervision of a physician.

• *Follow-up.* As South Asian programs try to meet the demand for a wider range of reversible methods, following up acceptors will become even more critical. The emphasis on sterilization has meant that staff have had little continuing contact with clients. Lack of follow-up services greatly reduced the acceptability of the IUD throughout South Asia in the 1960s; it has only recently regained public approval. At present, family planning staff are judged (and are rewarded) according to the number of acceptors they recruit, not by the number of users they assist. Programs will have to adopt new performance criteria and incentive arrangements to stress regular contact with clients.

Certain administrative and operational difficulties also need to be resolved. Family planning services have undergone major reorganization in some countries. In Bangladesh, for example, health and family planning services were initially separate, then integrated, then divided, and are now reintegrated. The program in Pakistan has also recently undergone a major reorganization. Whenever there are such upheavals, staff morale and performance suffer. Other problems are manifest in all programs. In some cases salaries are so low that staff have to take on other work to support their families. Inadequate training, incomplete staffing patterns, and lack of supervision have also lowered morale and performance. Where it exists, supervision takes the form of enforcing accountability and targets rather than supportive training and advice.

Program managers have tried to overcome problems of morale and supervision in two ways: by paying workers according to their performance in recruiting acceptors, but this system carries the risk that follow-up services will be neglected; and by setting high program targets. But neither incentives nor targets can substitute for better training and supervision—the two requirements that are critical to improving the performance of family planning programs in South Asia.

East Asia: incentives for small families

The countries of East Asia have experienced marked declines in fertility in the last decade (see Figure 8.7). Total fertility (less than 3) and rates of natural increase (about 1.5 percent a year, 2.2 percent excluding China) are the lowest of any developing region. For the most part, recent declines in fertility have occurred in countries where fertility was already lower than would be expected, given the region's income. The most dramatic reductions have been in China: total fertility dropped from 7.5 to 2.3 over the past two decades, despite a per capita income of only $310 in 1982. Indonesia, the Philippines, and Thailand have also experienced remarkably rapid falls in fertility with only modest increases in income.

Population policy is more developed in East Asia than in any other region. In most countries, political commitment to reduce rapid population growth is high. Family planning programs are well established, with outreach to rural areas and a reasonable mix of contraceptive methods. Many governments, irrespective of level of income, have been highly successful in improving socioeconomic conditions favorable to fertility decline. Ninety percent or more of all girls of primary-school age are enrolled in China, Hong Kong, Indonesia, Korea, Malaysia, the Philippines, Singapore, and Viet Nam. Overall, secondary-school enrollments are also high in a few countries—53 percent in Malaysia, 63 percent in the Philippines, and 85 percent in Korea. Life expectancy in China, Hong Kong, and Singapore has risen to seventy years or more and in most other countries exceeds sixty. In almost all countries, infant mortality has been reduced by half or more over the past twenty years. Nevertheless, further substantial reductions could be made in Indonesia (where the rate exceeds 100 per thousand live births), China (with a rate of 67), and Thailand, the Philippines, and Viet Nam (about 50).

Despite dramatic declines in fertility, population in the region will double in about forty-five years. Burma, Indonesia, Malaysia, the Philippines, Thailand, and Viet Nam all have annual rates of population growth of at least 2 percent a year. At its current growth rate of 2.4 percent a year, the population of the Philippines will increase by half (25 million people) by 2000. Even in China, with an annual increase of 1.2 percent, population will continue to grow rapidly for a long time because of the momentum of past growth. According to the standard projection, China's population will

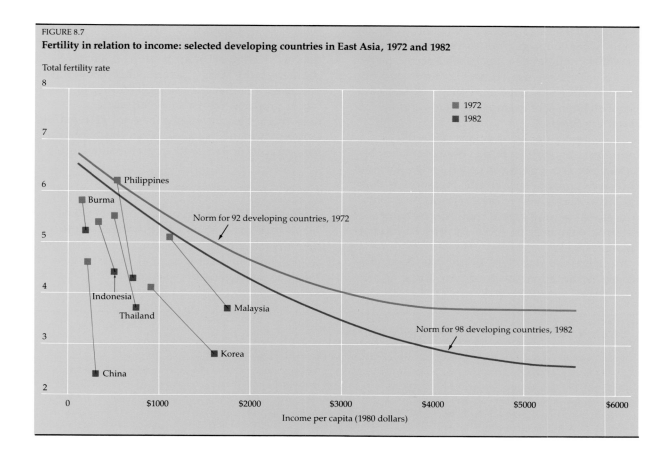

FIGURE 8.7
Fertility in relation to income: selected developing countries in East Asia, 1972 and 1982

Total fertility rate

■ 1972
■ 1982

Norm for 92 developing countries, 1972

Philippines
Burma
Indonesia
Thailand
Malaysia
Korea
China

Norm for 98 developing countries, 1982

Income per capita (1980 dollars)

increase by almost half, to 1.45 billion by 2050. Replacement-level fertility is still a long way off for Burma, Indonesia, Malaysia, the Philippines, Thailand and Viet Nam, with total fertility rates of at least 3.6; total fertility in Korea, at 2.7, is also still above replacement level.

Though contraceptive use is higher in East Asia than in most other developing regions, there is still considerable unmet need for contraception. Low and high estimates of unmet need are 19 to 49 percent of married women of childbearing age in the Philippines (1978), 20 to 31 percent in Indonesia (1976), 15 to 26 percent in Thailand (1981), and as much as 30 percent in Korea (1979). Actual family size exceeds desired family size by one child in the Philippines. More than half of eligible couples who want no more children are not using any method of birth control. And among the 36 percent of Filipino couples using a method, more than half are using less effective methods such as withdrawal and rhythm. In some countries family planning programs have not achieved complete geographic coverage. In Indonesia, for example, contraceptive use in the outer islands, where one-third of the country's population lives, is less than

half the level on Java and Bali—in some places much less. There are also marked regional disparities in access to services in the Philippines.

In addition, some countries have overlooked potentially important methods. The Indonesian program, for example, does not offer sterilization. Yet this method has been very popular in South Asia, Korea, Thailand, and some Latin American countries. Injectable contraceptives have been much favored in Thailand but are only recently gaining ground in Indonesia. The Korean program has emphasized sterilization; wider promotion of spacing methods might also lower fertility. The potential demand for spacing methods is demonstrated by the high resort to abortion in Korea. In the Philippines, improving the effectiveness of traditional methods and promoting more effective alternatives could have a substantial effect.

Given the relatively advanced state of population policies, more use could be made of incentives and disincentives. Among the countries of East Asia, China, Singapore, and to a lesser extent Korea, have made greatest use of measures to promote small families. Sometimes they have relied on individual incentives (such as giving priority in

177

housing schemes to parents with only two children). Some countries have also offered incentives to whole communities that reach specific targets for contraceptive use. Some governments also penalize those who have more than a certain number of children—for example, by the withdrawal of maternity benefits.

China has a complex structure of incentives, disincentives, and birth quotas to promote a one-child family (see Box 8.9). Most governments have not chosen to promote such drastic measures as those in China. And few have the administrative control necessary to implement national schemes of deferred payments or social security to promote smaller families.

In China the one-child policy has been challenged by an apparent preference for sons. The same bias in favor of sons exists in Korea, and has been partly responsible for keeping total fertility, now at 2.7, from declining to replacement level. To counteract this bias, governments need public information campaigns and legal reforms of inheritance, property rights, and employment. Incentives might also be offered to one- or two-child families with girls, such as lower educational and medical costs or preferred access to schooling.

Donor assistance policies

International aid for population programs has two major objectives: to assist governments and private organizations in providing family planning, information, and services, and to assist governments in developing population policies as part of

---

Box 8.9   China's one-child family policy

Birth control has been a national priority in China since 1971 when the government launched a new program to promote later marriage, longer spacing between births, and fewer children. In the late 1970s it became clear that, with the large number of women entering childbearing age as a result of past high fertility and falling mortality, even compliance with a two-child family norm would not reduce the rate of population growth enough to meet the national goal of 1.2 billion people by the year 2000. In 1979 Sichuan province instituted a policy designed to persuade married couples to have no more than one child. This policy was backed by a system of economic rewards to parents with more than one child who committed themselves to have no more, and penalties for those who had more than two. This soon became a national policy and individual provinces are all expected to implement such systems. In 1980 the vice-premier stated as specific goals that 95 percent of married couples in the cities and 90 percent in the countryside should have only one child. By 1982 most provinces and municipalities had introduced incentives and disincentives to promote the one-child norm.

Early results of the one-child campaign seem striking. The proportion of first births out of total births increased from 21 percent in 1970 to 42 percent in 1980 and 47 percent in 1981. By 1982 the proportion of first births exceeded 80 percent in each of the three large urban municipalities—Beijing, Shanghai, and Tianjin—and in five other provinces.

But several factors are working against the one-child policy.

• *Old-age security*. A compulsory pension system applies only to employees of state enterprises in urban areas, who constitute at most 15 percent of the labor force. A 1982 survey of rural production brigades in eleven provinces and municipalities found that only 1 percent of men over sixty-five and women over sixty received monthly pensions paid by welfare funds. For the rural majority, children remain the main source of old-age security.

• *The responsibility system*. The widespread introduction of the production responsibility system has given families a direct economic incentive to have more children, for two reasons. In some areas land for household use is allocated on a per capita basis, so more children ensures access to more land. In addition, whatever security for the elderly is provided on a collective basis will be reduced as collective income declines. In an effort to combat this, some brigades have introduced a double contracting system under which households are required both to deliver their quota of farm output to the state and to refrain from having an unauthorized birth.

• *Persistent male preference*. A preference for sons is a strong cultural impediment to having only one child. A 1980 survey of one-child families in Anhui Province found that 61 percent of the children of one-child certificate holders were boys. The pressure to have one child (and the desire for a boy) may have led to a revival of the practice of female infanticide, about which the Chinese government has expressed considerable concern. The 1982 census data on births in 1981 showed that there were 108.5 boys for every 100 girls at birth, an abnormally high figure.

• *Financing incentives*. Responsibility for financing incentives falls on local areas, not the central government. As a result there is great variation in the type and value of incentives. In a model county in Jilin Province in 1981 families pledging to have only one child were granted annual bonuses of almost fifty yuan—equivalent to 7 percent of average rural income—to last for fifteen years, and received a double-size private plot. For their single child they received an adult grain allowance and a special health care allowance. Yet in Hofei city in Anhui province, bonuses paid to parents were much lower—a one-time payment of ten or twenty yuan, a few towels, a thermos bottle, some toys, a wash basin, or even nothing at all.

their overall development strategy. Population assistance now amounts to nearly $500 million a year, equal to about 1.9 percent of OECD aid and about 1.5 percent of OPEC aid. At its peak, the population assistance share of aid was considerably larger—2.2 percent of OECD aid.

Since Sweden's first population grant in 1968, donors have transferred more than $7 billion in population aid (in 1982 prices). In terms of per capita receipts in the developing countries, assistance for population programs was lower in 1981 (the latest year for which complete data are available) than in 1974, the year of the World Population Conference in Bucharest (see Figure 8.8). The United States remains the biggest supporter of population programs—its government, along with private American foundations, provides about 40 percent of all aid for population. But its contribution has been falling in real terms since 1972. Japan is the second largest donor. Japan and other donors, including Canada, the Federal Republic of Germany, the Netherlands, Norway, and Sweden, have increased their share of the total. All gave $10 million or more in population assistance in 1982.

The main role of donors has been to provide supplies and training for family planning and related health programs; about two-thirds of population aid is devoted to family planning and related maternal and child-health programs. Donors also support basic data collection, operations and social and economic research, information and education activities, and policy and institutional development. In Asia and the Middle East, over 80 percent of assistance goes toward family planning services, in Latin America and Africa about 60 percent. In sub-Saharan Africa, almost a fifth of assistance is used to finance data collection; as Table 8.1 showed, data development is often an early step in heightening consciousness about population issues. As shown in Chapter 7, program development is often constrained by limited training, the absence of local institutions, and poor demographic information. Development of local capability must continue to be a priority for donors.

About $150 million is spent by donor governments for research on reproductive biology and contraceptive technology; such research contributes to methods that can be adopted in developing countries as well. Developing countries could benefit from larger sums spent on research and product development. Support by donors is critical since spending by the private sector in developed countries has fallen (see Box 7.2). Donor support could hasten development of institutions to pro-

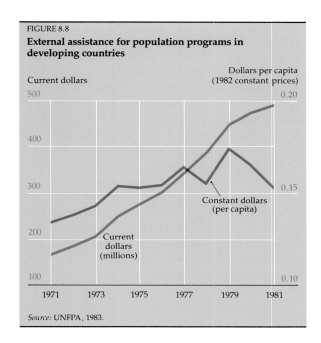

FIGURE 8.8

External assistance for population programs in developing countries

Source: UNFPA, 1983.

vide a local base for social and economic research as well as for contraceptive research.

Donor assistance is provided both directly to country programs and through multilateral and nongovernmental organizations. The two largest organizations are:

• *The United Nations Fund for Population Activities (UNFPA).* More than 130 countries contribute to its annual budget of about $140 million. About 100 developing countries have requested and received UNFPA assistance. To guide its programming, UNFPA has assessed the needs of more than seventy countries. It receives requests for assistance that far exceed the money it has available.

• *The International Planned Parenthood Federation (IPPF).* A nongovernmental body of more than one hundred national family planning associations, IPPF had a 1983 program budget of $90 million, over half of which came as contributions from OECD countries. About one-third of its budget support is raised by member associations in their own countries. Countries receiving its largest grants in recent years are Brazil, Colombia, India, Mexico, and Korea.

About one-quarter of the population aid from the US government is administered through more than twenty nongovernmental organizations in the United States, particularly universities and research institutions. They cooperate with organizations in developing countries in service delivery and training, data collection and analysis, special projects, and biomedical and operations research. Family Planning International Assistance, a branch of The Planned Parenthood Federation of America, the American affiliate of IPPF, provides population assistance in more than forty countries. The Population Council, with a budget of $16 million from both public and private sources, provides technical assistance and supports social science and contraceptive research. The Pathfinder Fund is an example of smaller nongovernmental organizations. Pathfinder manages about $7 million in public and private funds, which are spent on innovative family planning services, women's programs, and population policy development. These small programs, and similar programs in other countries, add to the flexibility and responsiveness of population assistance.

The World Bank supports population activities through IDA credits and loans to borrowers. Over a period of fourteen years, the Bank has committed $355 million for population projects, and had disbursed $215 million by the end of 1983 (including $38.4 million in fiscal year 1983 itself). World Bank finance is not available on terms as easy as most population assistance, much of which is given in the form of grants; nonetheless, Bank operations grew in real terms by more than 5 percent a year between 1977 and 1983. Over the past three years the largest disbursements have gone to Bangladesh, Egypt, India, Indonesia, the Philippines, and Thailand, which together accounted for more than 90 percent of Bank lending for population.

The World Bank also supports an active program of economic and sector work aimed at enhancing understanding of how population growth affects development prospects and how population programs can contribute to overall development. The Bank cooperates with other UN organizations, especially UNFPA and the World Health Organization, in research and analysis requested by member governments.

The predominance of foreign assistance within the population sector in many countries means that the attitudes and priorities of donors become significant. At the same time, the great number of donors—private, official, bilateral, and multilateral—means that their priorities may not always coincide. They may send conflicting signals to host governments, fueling internal controversies. Further, their numerous activities may not be complementary or represent the most efficient allocation of resources. Coordination among donors and with the host government is therefore extremely important for effective use of population assistance.

One sign of the success of international assistance is that many local governments now help pay for programs that only a few years ago were supported by international grants. Colombia, Indonesia, Korea, and Thailand are picking up a progressively larger share of the costs of their population programs. India has for many years paid for a large share of its program, and China has always completely financed its own program. This trend toward self-financing makes it possible to reallocate aid budgets to countries that are only starting to develop their population programs. For example, the share of the UNFPA's budget going to Africa rose from about 12 percent during the 1970s to 23 percent in 1983.

Asia continues to receive the bulk of population assistance (51 percent of the total), followed by Latin America (20 percent), Africa (15 percent), and the Middle East (14 percent). Given the emerging pattern of needs described in Chapter 7, a substantial increase in assistance is needed, especially for Africa and South Asia. To meet unmet need in all regions in 1980 would have required spending $3 billion rather than the $2 billion that was actually spent (see Chapter 7, Table 7.6). By the same yardstick, spending for population programs in sub-Saharan Africa and South Asia should have been more than double what it was. Since Africa and South Asia are the poorest regions and most in need of external assistance, the bulk of the extra program support would have had to have come from international aid.

The analysis in Chapter 7 led to two estimates of required public spending for population programs by the year 2000. If developing countries are to achieve a "rapid" decline in fertility, $7.6 billion (in 1980 dollars), almost a quadrupling of 1980 spending, would be needed. The "standard" decline would require $5.6 billion. With two-thirds of external population assistance going to support family planning, foreign aid now supports about 25 percent of all family planning costs in developing countries. Assuming these proportions do not change, population assistance will need to triple (standard decline) or quadruple (rapid decline) its current level. A quadrupling would raise population assistance to an annual level of $2 billion (1980 dollars) by the year 2000. With no other changes in official development assistance, total aid for all assistance programs would increase by 5 percent, by no means an unmanageable addition to aid budgets. With the expected growth of industrial countries as outlined in Chapters 2 and 3, and aid as a constant share of their GNP, expanded population assistance would by the year 2000 need to equal 3.3 percent (to achieve standard fertility decline) or 4.3 percent (to achieve rapid fertility decline) of total concessional assistance.

Thus, small differences in financial assistance from donors can, given effective policies in recipient countries, make a big difference in population change. Sustained progress, however, requires not just donor funds; it also requires a commitment by the international community to population programs as a critical part of the effort to improve people's lives.

9 Ten years of experience

Much that is new about the two themes of this Report has been revealed in the past ten years. In 1974, with oil prices quadrupled and the world sliding into recession, there was pessimism about the economic prospects of the non-oil developing countries. In 1974, at the World Population Conference in Bucharest, there was debate about the relative merits of development and family planning programs as alternative ways of slowing down population growth. Today, both these issues are viewed in a different light; neither economic pessimism nor the development-family planning dichotomy captures what has actually happened in developing countries. The achievements of the developing countries have been much more varied, but they do point to one general conclusion of great importance. In both economic growth and population, differences among countries are largely attributable to differences in policy.

Economic adjustment

Much attention has been paid to the difficulties of developing countries that borrowed heavily in the 1970s but then found that they could not service their debts. Many of those countries have had to seek the support of the IMF and the collaboration of banks and governments in rescheduling debts and arranging new credits. Most have also cut back on imports, a reduction that has improved their external accounts but at considerable cost to economic growth, investment, and employment. This short-term cost has underlined the priority of their longer-term task—to redirect their economies to earn more foreign exchange so that growth, along with external accounts, can be restored to healthy levels. Their efforts deserve the support of the international community, both in providing aid and trade credits and, above all, in resisting any protectionist measures that would hamper the debtor countries' exports.

Prominent though they are, the problems of big debtors should not obscure the achievements of another group of middle-income countries. Many of them, principally in East Asia, have managed to maintain rapid economic growth without running into serious balance of payments difficulties. The most successful—Korea and Hong Kong, for example—had GDP growth of more than 10 percent a year in 1974–79, slowing down to about 6 percent a year in 1980–83. Although they increased their external debt in the past ten years, they expanded their exports so rapidly that their debt service ratios never rose as much as did some in Latin America.

The contrasting performance of these two groups of middle-income countries is the result of their contrasting policies. East Asian countries have in general adopted policies to promote exports, largely by maintaining competitive exchange rates. This has enabled them to expand their exports rapidly, has restricted imports on the basis of price rather than by quota, and has not made foreign loans seem attractively cheap in domestic currency terms. East Asian countries have also tended to maintain positive real interest rates, which have encouraged domestic saving and have ensured that investment has been directed to the areas of highest return. Their future prospects depend largely on their maintaining the same successful mix of policies. But those policies will achieve their full potential only if the industrial countries eschew the trade barriers that would hold back exports.

A third group of developing countries has experienced only slow economic growth in the past ten years, and its future looks little brighter than its past. This group includes many of the poorest countries in the world, mainly in sub-Saharan Africa. These countries have been badly affected by slow growth in the industrial world, which has weakened the prices of many of the primary commodities on which they still depend for about 90 percent of their export earnings. They have had difficulties in servicing the little commercial debt they have; their capital inflows are largely in official aid, which has risen in real terms at only 6.5 percent a year in the past ten years, not much above the rate of growth of population.

The problems of sub-Saharan Africa are of a different order from those faced by the middle-income countries. Most African countries still lack the institutions and human skills that are prerequisites for rapid economic growth. These resources need to be developed as a matter of urgency, and substantial foreign assistance must be forthcoming to finance the effort. Nevertheless, African countries could do much to improve their prospects by reforming their policies. Even among the poorest countries, some have done better than others, largely by raising producer prices to farmers, by maintaining competitive exchange rates, and in general by using prices rather than government directives to allocate resources.

The need for adjustment is not confined to the developing countries. Part I of this Report argued that many of the failings in the world economy have their roots in the industrial countries, whose financial and economic weight greatly influences economic prospects in the developing world. To varying degrees, the industrial countries have been unwilling to tackle the rigidities in their economies. They have maintained capacity in obsolescent industries, by subsidies or by restricting imports. Their macroeconomic policies caused, first, a rapid inflationary buildup in the 1970s and then, in the past three years of disinflation, high real interest rates resulting from the conflict between monetary restraint and relative fiscal laxity.

Until the industrial countries correct these underlying weaknesses, the prospects for the world economy will remain clouded. Some scenarios presented in Chapter 3 suggest that, without an improvement in the performance of the industrial countries, GDP in the developing world as a whole would grow at only 4.7 percent a year in 1985–95. Within that total, growth in sub-Saharan Africa would be as low as 2.8 percent a year. This is less than the likely rate of population growth, so that people in many of the world's poorest countries would get steadily poorer. Among developing countries as a group, improvement in domestic policies could raise growth to 5.1 percent a year if industrial-country growth is weak. Even with faster growth in the industrial countries (and no change in domestic policies), Africa's prospects would not brighten much; GDP growth of 3.2 percent a year in that region in 1985–95 would not be enough to raise per capita incomes. At the other end of the scale, middle-income major exporters of manufactures would enjoy GDP growth averaging 6.3 percent a year in 1985–95. The diversity that has been such a prominent feature of the world economy in the past ten years seems likely to persist.

Population change: success and new challenge

The accumulating evidence on population change in developing countries underscores the strong link between fertility decline and the general level of socioeconomic development, and the contribution that family planning programs can make to slowing population growth. Differences in fertility among and within countries are related less to income per person than to life expectancy, female literacy, and the income of poorer groups. They are also related to availability of family planning services. Thus Sri Lanka has lower fertility than India, and India has lower fertility than Pakistan. Colombia has lower fertility than Brazil, and Brazil has lower fertility than Peru. Egypt has lower fertility than Morocco. Countries which have made a substantial and sustained effort in family planning have achieved remarkable success; where education is widespread, the success is even more striking. The evidence accumulated in the past decade is especially convincing. Contraceptive use tripled and fertility fell by 30 percent in Mexico between 1974 and 1979. In Java, Indonesia, contraceptive use rose from 11 percent to more than 50 percent and total fertility fell from almost 5 to about 4 between 1974 and 1980. In Kerala state of India, the total fertility fell from 4.1 in 1972 to 2.7 in 1978; per capita income is low, but female literacy is high and family planning services are widespread.

But there is also evidence that further fertility decline, and the initiation of decline where it has not begun, will not come automatically. There are two points to bear in mind. One is that in most developing countries desired family size is about four. It is higher in rural areas and among the less educated. Without sustained improvements in living conditions, desired family size could remain around four—implying population growth rates at or above 2 percent. The second is that family planning programs, successful as they have been, have by no means reached their full potential. In virtually every country surveyed, many couples who say they want no more children do not use contraception—usually because they have poor access to modern services. In many areas where services are available, discontinuation rates are high—often because few effective methods are offered, and because follow-up services are limited.

It has been almost two decades since the peak of population growth in developing countries was passed. But the turnaround to slower growth has been slow and has not occurred everywhere. Increases in population size are projected to mount for another two decades, and in many countries of the developing world, populations will triple in size by the year 2050, even assuming substantial declines in fertility. Two decades after the turn-around, the slow pace of change and its uneven incidence point more than ever to rapid population growth as a central development concern.

A development problem

The focus of this Report has been different from neomalthusian descriptions of population as a problem. World population has grown faster, to higher numbers, than Malthus would have imagined; world production and income have grown too. The future may be more difficult; in the very long run, history may seem to vindicate Malthus and the problem of population may indeed be one of numbers outrunning world resources. But for the next five or six decades, the problem goes beyond one of global resources and is less easily amenable to any technological fix. It is a mismatch between population and income-producing ability, a mismatch that leaves many of the world's people in a vicious circle of poverty and high fertility. In this Report rapid population growth is associated, at household and national levels, with slower progress in raising living standards, especially of the poor. At the national and the family level, rapid population growth exacerbates the difficult choice between higher levels of living now and investment, for example in children's schooling, to bring higher levels of living in the future. It is the poor who have many children; caught by the poverty of their parents, those children carry their disadvantages into the next generation. Still rapid population growth in most countries—2 percent to more than 4 percent a year—means up to 50 percent of populations are under age fifteen, so job creation for many years will be a formidable task. For some countries and many rural families, high fertility means extra resources must go into agriculture just to keep pace with food requirements. In many countries still largely dependent on agriculture, there is little or no unused land that can be cheaply brought under cultivation; raising production means increasing yields on existing land,

which in turn means new investments just to maintain per capita output. In cities, rapid population growth heightens the organizational and administrative difficulties of managing urban growth; redistribution policies offer little relief at high cost.

Population growth would not be a problem if economic and social adjustments could be made fast enough, if technical change could be guaranteed, or if rapid population growth itself inspired technical change. But rapid population growth, if anything, makes adjustment more difficult. It brings at best only the gradual adaptation that is typical of agriculture, maintaining but not increasing per capita output. The money and research skills needed for modern technological change are overwhelmingly in the rich countries, where population growth is slow. If anything they produce labor-saving, not labor-using, innovations. In today's developed countries fertility was never as high as in developing countries now, and mortality fell more slowly. Population growth rarely exceeded 1.5 percent a year; rural population growth had virtually ended by the beginning of the twentieth century.

Appropriate policies

Part II of this Report dwells at length on the meaning and implications of a paradox. On the one hand, the social costs of large families are high, and in some families children suffer directly from having many siblings. On the other hand, poor parents make a reasonable choice in having many children. High infant and child mortality and poor educational and job opportunities mean that parents with few children cannot feel secure about their own future until they have had four or five babies—including, in some settings, two or three sons. The very idea of planning pregnancies may be unknown, and modern contraceptives may be unavailable or expensive. In such a context, each individual family's decision to have another child seems rational. Yet added together, these separate decisions make all families, and especially children, worse off in the end. There is a gap between the private and social gains to large families. The gap is caused in large part by poverty and the resulting lack of access to opportunities that would encourage small families.

The process of economic development itself generates new signals that lower fertility. Decisions change as women become more educated, as more children survive childhood disease, as children become less valuable as workers and sources of old-age security, and as information about the possibility of birth control spreads. Parents time the births of children, have fewer of them, and spend more on their health and schooling.

The gap between the private and social gains to high fertility provides additional justification for governments to act in areas that already merit government action. This Report has emphasized policy measures to increase people's welfare as well as (and as a means) to reduce fertility: education (particularly for girls) and more primary health care for mothers and children. But it has also noted that measures to raise living standards take time to lower fertility. On the one hand, this underscores the need to act now to improve education, to reduce mortality, and to improve women's opportunities, so that a sustained decline in fertility can be realized in the long run. On the other hand, it also means that other actions with a more immediate payoff are desirable. Virtually no developing country is yet doing all it might to promote later marriage and to inform people of the health and fertility benefits of breastfeeding. And in countries in which parents have only as many children as they want, but the desired number of children is still high, carefully designed financial incentives provide an additional mechanism to encourage lower fertility.

At the same time, new data on fertility and contraceptive use show that many couples still have more children than they want and do not benefit from adequate family planning services. The gap between actual and desired family size means that a public policy to provide family planning information and services will bring fertility closer to socially desirable levels at the same time that it helps couples have the number of children they want. Though the private sector might be expected to fill this need, and has done so to some extent in urban areas, it cannot make much progress in rural areas, where backup health systems are poor and information about birth control spreads only slowly.

As Chapter 7 showed, if current public expenditures on family planning in developing countries were increased by 50 percent, it would be possible to meet the need that more than 65 million couples now have for family planning services. Quadrupling the funds by the year 2000 is necessary to bring the "rapid" fertility decline described in Chapter 4. These targets are ambitious but not hugely expensive: quadrupling the foreign aid spent on population programs would mean spending a total of about $2 billion (in 1980 dollars), equivalent to about 5 percent of all aid programs in 1982. A new generation of programs is now building on the past, emphasizing easier access through outreach programs, and, to reduce discontinuation, greater choice of methods, follow-up of clients, and better communication between providers and clients. These programs are not expensive but will require new financing to reach growing numbers of users.

This Report has shown that economic and social progress helps slow population growth; but it has also emphasized that rapid population growth hampers economic development. It is therefore imperative that governments act simultaneously on both fronts. For the poorest countries, development may not be possible at all, unless slower population growth can be achieved soon, even before higher real incomes would bring down fertility spontaneously. In middle-income countries, a continuation of high fertility among poor people could prolong indefinitely the period before development significantly affects their lives. No one would argue that slower population growth alone will ensure progress; poor economic growth, poverty, and inequality can persist independently of population change. But evidence described in this Report seems conclusive: because poverty and rapid population growth reinforce each other, donors and developing countries must cooperate in an effort to slow population growth as a major part of the effort to achieve development.

Population data supplement

The six tables and two maps in this Supplement provide demographic and policy-related data in addition to those presented in the World Development Indicators, Tables 19–25. In the tables of this Supplement, countries are listed in ascending order of 1982 income per capita, except for those for which no GNP per capita can be calculated. These are listed in alphabetical order, in italics, at the end of the per capita income group into which they probably fall. An alphabetical listing of countries and the reference numbers indicating this order can be found in the key to the Indicators.

Tables 1 and 3 through 6 include only low- and middle-income countries for which data are available. In Tables 3 through 6, countries with fewer than one million inhabitants are listed under a separate heading in ascending order of 1982 income per capita, except for those for which no GNP per capita can be calculated. The latter are listed in alphabetical order, in italics, at the end of the table.

Figures in the colored bands are summary measures for groups of countries. The letter *w* after a summary measure indicates that it is a weighted average, the letter *t* that it is a total. Figures in italics are for years other than, but generally within, two years of those specified. The symbol (.) indicates less than half the unit shown, . . not available, and n.a. not applicable. All data are subject to the same cautions regarding reliability and cross-country comparability that are noted in the World Development Indicators.

Table 1. Population projections

The population projections here as well as in Table 19 of the World Development Indicators were made on the basis of a World Bank computer program that uses a modified cohort-component method to simulate the effects of various fertility, mortality, and migration assumptions on future population size and age structure in successive five-year periods. Births for each period were cal-

culated by applying a schedule of age-specific fertility rates, scaled to agree with the given total fertility rate, to the female population, classified by age group, for the period. These births enter the population as the youngest cohort; each cohort grows older in accordance with assumed mortality conditions.

The fertility assumptions were entered in the form of total and age-specific fertility rates, and mortality assumptions in the form of expectations of life at birth or mortality levels based on standardized life tables. Migration assumptions were entered in the form of the number of net migrants in each five-year period by sex and age; the age distribution of migrants was obtained from a model on the basis of their overall sex ratio. Migration assumptions do not vary for alternative fertility and mortality scenarios, but for most countries net migration was assumed to reach zero by 2000. The sources of data for base-year population estimates are discussed in the technical note to Table 19 of the World Development Indicators.

For the *standard projection,* the future path for fertility is based on the experience of a group of countries for which a judgment regarding the future year of reaching replacement-level fertility could be made with relative confidence. The assumed year for replacement-level fertility in these countries was regressed on several predictors: the current total fertility rate for each country, the change in this rate over the previous ten years, the proportion of couples using contraception, and the current female life expectancy. On the basis of this regression, a year for reaching replacement-level fertility (constrained to fall between the years 2000 and 2050) was calculated for every country. (Fertility in industrial countries already below replacement level was assumed to rise to replacement by 2000.) For each country a curve was mathematically fitted for the course of the total fertility rate between the current year and the year of replacement-level fertility. The curves were chosen to provide accelerating decline early on (in some cases after a few years of constant fertility), followed by decelerating decline as fertility approaches replacement level. Fertility is assumed to remain at replacement level once it has been reached.

The future path for mortality is based on the assumption that increments to life expectancy depend on the level reached. Changes in female life expectancies between 1965–69 and 1975–79 were regressed on the initial life expectancies, separately for two groups of countries: those with female primary-school enrollment percentages under 70, and those with percentages of 70 or more (including developed countries). Estimates of one-year increments were obtained by dividing the estimated ten-year increments from these two equations by ten.

Alternative projections build in more rapid fertility and mortality decline. For *rapid fertility decline* the future path of fertility is based on the experience of eleven developing countries, including China, Colombia, and Thailand, that have had rapid fertility decline since World War II. Once fertility decline began in these countries, the total fertility rate fell by a roughly constant amount—about 0.2—every year. A constant linear decline at the average pace of these eleven countries provides the path for rapid fertility decline, with the added proviso that decline ends when replacement level is reached and fertility thereafter stays at replacement level.

Summary measures for country groups may differ from those in Table 19 of the Indicators because projections were not computed for all countries.

For *rapid mortality decline*, a logistic curve was derived to represent the trend in life expectancy among developing countries between 1960 and 1980 (see the chart in Box 4.5). Fourteen countries that substantially outperformed this curve (and had initial life expectancies above forty) were used to derive a second logistic curve. This second curve provided the time path for rapid mortality decline.

The *rate of natural increase* is the difference between births and deaths per hundred population. Summary measures are weighted by population in 1982.

The *total fertility rate* represents the number of children that would be born to a woman if she were to live to the end of her childbearing years and were to bear children at each age at prevailing age-specific fertility rates. The rate for 2000 is given under the assumptions of both standard and rapid fertility decline. Summary measures are weighted by 1982 population.

Table 2. Population composition

The *dependency ratio* is the combined population under fifteen and over sixty-four years as a percentage of the population between those ages. The dependency ratio for 2000 is derived from the standard World Bank population projections used in Table 1 of this Supplement and in Table 19 of the World Development Indicators.

Table 3. Contraceptive use and unmet need

Current use of contraception is expressed as the percentage of currently married women aged 15–49 using each method of contraception. For El Salvador, Thailand, Guatemala, Jamaica, Korea, Panama, and Venezuela the base is currently married women aged 15–44; for Kenya and Sudan it is ever-married women aged 15–50. *Sterilization* includes both male and female sterilization. *Vaginal methods* include spermicides and the diaphragm. *Other methods* include rhythm, withdrawal, abstinence, and in some cases douche and folk methods. The sum of prevalence for each method may not add to the total because of rounding.

Low and high estimates of *unmet need* for contraception are calculated only for women who want no more children; they do not include women who wish to delay a birth. The *low* estimate includes married women of reproductive age who want no more children, are not using any method of contraception, and are exposed to the risk of pregnancy (that is, are fecund, not pregnant, not breastfeeding, or breastfeeding more than a year). The *high* estimate includes, in addition to the above, those who are using less effective contraceptive methods (rhythm, withdrawal, and the like), as well as those breastfeeding less than one year.

Data for contraceptive prevalence and unmet need are all from nationally representative World Fertility Surveys (WFS) and Contraceptive Prevalence Surveys (CPS) for the years specified. The figures for contraceptive use may differ from figures in Table 20 of the World Development Indicators because more recent estimates, based not on surveys but on family planning program statistics, are included there. Figures in italics refer to earlier years than stated: Bangladesh (1979), Sri Lanka (1975), Tunisia (1978), Jamaica (1975–76), Panama (1976), and Mexico (1978). Surveys in three countries did not achieve national coverage: Sudan (northern population only); Mauritania (sedentary population only); and Malaysia (peninsula only).

Table 4. Factors influencing fertility

The *mean number of living children* includes children living at the time of the survey. *Desired family size* is based on the response to the question: "If you could choose exactly the number of children to have in your whole life, how many would that be?" Figures are the means for survey respondents who gave numerical answers.

Both the number of living children and desired family size generally pertain to all ever-married women aged 15–49, with the exception of Sudan and Kenya (aged 15–50), Costa Rica and Panama (aged 20–49), Venezuela (aged 15–44), and Mauritania (aged 12–50). Desired family size figures for Ghana and Turkey are for currently married women, and for Barbados for all women of childbearing age. Living children data for Barbados, Kenya, and Nigeria are for all women of childbearing age.

The *percentage of women aged 15–19 ever married* includes common-law and consensual unions, as well as legal marriages.

Mean duration of breastfeeding is the number of months a woman would breastfeed, on average, if she followed current practice. It is derived using life-table techniques and survey data on current breastfeeding status for all births.

Sources for this table are WFS and CPS surveys for the years specified, as reported in country reports and in the following publications: Maryson Hodgson and Jane Gibbs, "Children Ever Born," *WFS Comparative Studies* no. 12, 1980; Robert E. Lightbourne and Alphonse L. MacDonald, "Family Size Preferences," *WFS Comparative Studies* no. 14, 1982; Benoit Ferry and David P. Smith, "Breastfeeding Differentials," *WFS Comparative Studies* no. 23, 1983; Hazel Ashurst and John B. Casterline, "Socioeconomic Differentials in Current Fertility," *WFS Comparative Studies: Additional Tables*, forthcoming; David P. Smith, "Age at First Marriage," *WFS Comparative Studies* no. 87, 1980; and Sundat Balkaran and David P. Smith, "Marriage Dissolution and Remarriage," *WFS Comparative Studies: Additional Tables*, forthcoming. Figures in italics are for years other than those specified: Bangladesh (1975–76), Indonesia (1979), Korea (1974), and Tunisia (1980). The figure on percentage of women aged 15–19 ever married for Indonesia is from the 1979 National Socioeconomic Survey.

Table 5. Status of women

The *ratio of adult male to adult female literacy* is the

percentage of males aged fifteen and over who can read and write divided by the percentage of females aged fifteen and over who can read and write. Data are from UNESCO, WFS, and CPS.

The *percentage aged 15–49 ever enrolled in primary school* was estimated by assigning past primary-school enrollment rates to five-year age groups of the 1980 population aged 15–49 and weighting these rates by the proportion of each five-year age group in the total 1980 population aged 15–49.

The *singulate mean age at marriage* is the mean age at first marriage among people who marry by age 50. It is calculated using data on the proportion ever married in each age group of the current population, and thus does not reflect the experience of any particular age cohort. The sources for this column are Smith (1980) and Balkaran and Smith (forthcoming), as cited in the notes for Table 4, and various WFS country reports.

The *economically active* population includes the armed forces and the unemployed but excludes housewives, students, and other inactive groups. Data are from the US Bureau of the Census.

Table 6. Family planning policy

Support for family planning exists if a government subsidizes family planning services. Governments are characterized as providing support for *demographic and other reasons* (that is, specifically to reduce population growth, as well as for other reasons), support for *health and human rights reasons*, or *no support*.

Indicators of support and *year the official family planning program started* are based on the following sources: Dorothy Nortman and Joanne Fisher, *Population and Family Planning Programs: A Compendium of Data through 1981* (New York: Population Council, 1982); John A. Ross, ed., *International Encyclopedia of Population* (New York: The Free Press, 1982); United Nations, Department of International Economic and Social Affairs, Population Division, "Population Policy Briefs: Current Situation in Developing Countries and Selected Territories, 1982"; and World Bank sources.

The *family planning index* for 1972 and 1982 is adapted from the background paper by Robert Lapham and W. Parker Mauldin. They assigned a numerical index to countries on the basis of responses to detailed questionnaires of individuals familiar with family planning activities in each country. An average of three respondents per country assessed such factors as official political commitment, availability and quality of family planning services (public and commercial), method mix, outreach, use of mass media, local financial support, and record keeping and evaluation. Countries that received 80 percent or more of the maximum possible index are recorded as *A*, 60 to 79 percent as *B*, 40 to 59 percent as *C*, 20 to 39 percent as *D*, and 0 to 19 percent as *E*.

Contraceptive prevalence

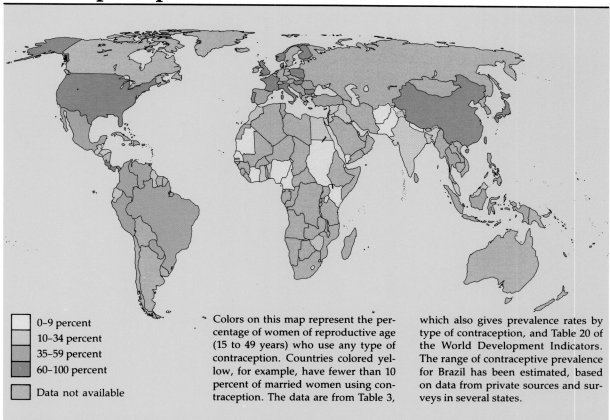

0–9 percent
10–34 percent
35–59 percent
60–100 percent

Data not available

Colors on this map represent the percentage of women of reproductive age (15 to 49 years) who use any type of contraception. Countries colored yellow, for example, have fewer than 10 percent of married women using contraception. The data are from Table 3, which also gives prevalence rates by type of contraception, and Table 20 of the World Development Indicators. The range of contraceptive prevalence for Brazil has been estimated, based on data from private sources and surveys in several states.

These charts show the prevalence of specific contraceptive methods in three developing countries. The method mix varies greatly across countries, though effective modern methods generally predominate. Similar variability exists across developed countries.

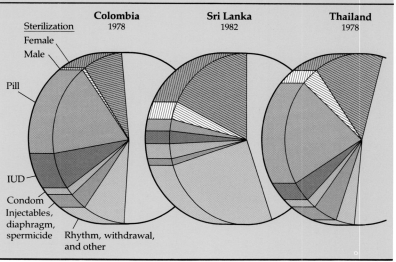

Sterilization
Female
Male
Pill
IUD
Condom
Injectables, diaphragm, spermicide
Rhythm, withdrawal, and other

Colombia 1978
Sri Lanka 1982
Thailand 1978

Births and total fertility

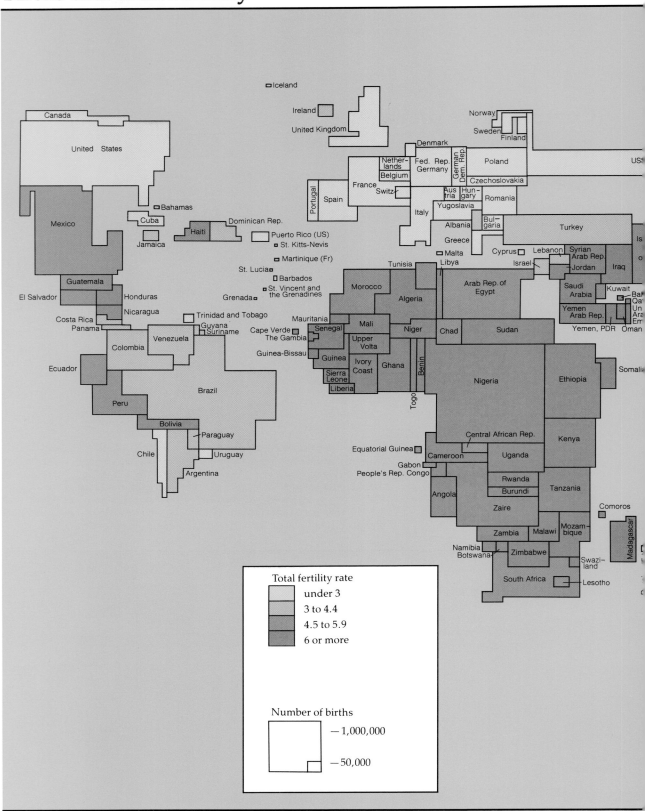

Total fertility rate
- under 3
- 3 to 4.4
- 4.5 to 5.9
- 6 or more

Number of births
— 1,000,000
— 50,000

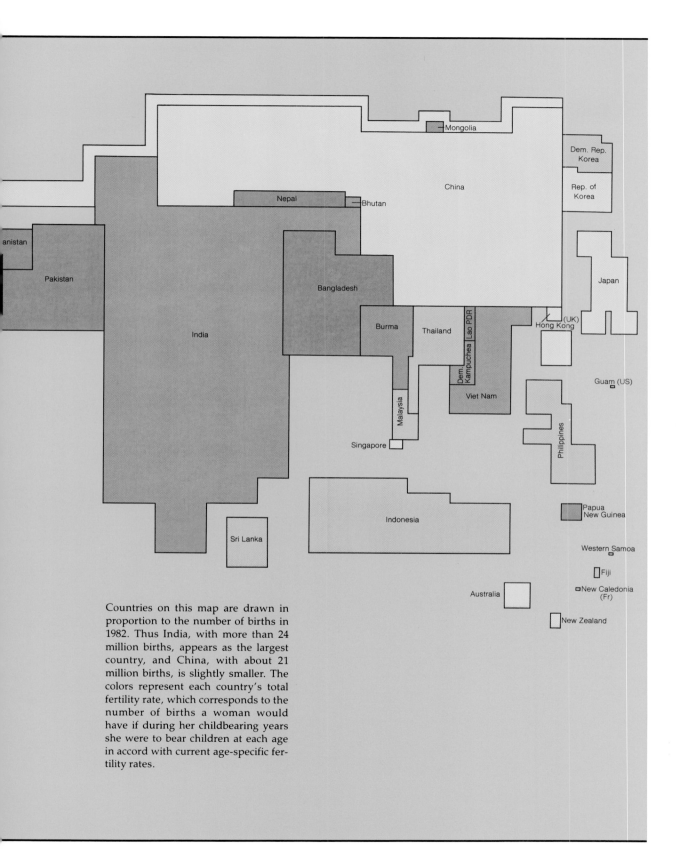

Countries on this map are drawn in proportion to the number of births in 1982. Thus India, with more than 24 million births, appears as the largest country, and China, with about 21 million births, is slightly smaller. The colors represent each country's total fertility rate, which corresponds to the number of births a woman would have if during her childbearing years she were to bear children at each age in accord with current age-specific fertility rates.

Table 1. Population projections

	Population (millions) mid-1982	Projected population (millions)						Rate of natural increase, 2000		Total fertility rate, 2000	
		Standard projection		Rapid fertility decline only		Rapid fertility and mortality decline		Standard projection	Rapid fertility decline	Standard projection	Rapid fertility decline
		2000	2050	2000	2050	2000	2050				
Low-income economies	**2,276 t**	**3,107 t**	**5,092 t**	**2,917 t**	**4,021 t**	**2,931 t**	**4,225 t**	**1.6 w**	**1.1 w**	**3.0 w**	**2.3 w**
China	**1,008**	**1,196**	**1,450**	**1,196**	**1,450**	**1,185**	**1,462**	**1.0**	**1.0**	**2.0**	**2.0**
Other low-income	**1,268 t**	**1,911 t**	**3,642 t**	**1,721 t**	**2,571 t**	**1,746 t**	**2,763 t**	**2.0 w**	**1.2 w**	**3.9 w**	**2.6 w**
1. Chad	5	7	17	6	8	6	9	2.4	1.0	5.6	2.7
2. Bangladesh	93	157	357	136	212	139	230	2.6	1.3	5.1	2.8
3. Ethiopia	33	57	164	48	77	50	84	3.0	1.3	6.1	2.9
4. Nepal	15	24	54	21	31	22	35	2.4	1.1	5.3	2.8
5. Mali	7	12	31	10	16	10	17	3.0	1.3	6.0	2.9
6. Burma	35	53	99	48	73	48	77	2.0	1.2	3.6	2.3
7. Zaire	31	55	136	45	73	46	79	3.1	1.4	5.8	2.7
8. Malawi	7	12	35	10	17	10	19	3.3	1.9	7.1	4.0
9. Upper Volta	7	10	25	8	13	9	15	2.9	1.3	6.0	2.9
10. Uganda	14	25	67	21	35	21	39	3.3	1.7	6.4	3.2
11. India	717	994	1,513	927	1,313	938	1,406	1.5	1.1	2.9	2.4
12. Rwanda	6	11	34	9	17	9	19	3.8	2.2	7.6	4.5
13. Burundi	4	7	20	6	10	6	11	3.0	1.3	6.0	2.9
14. Tanzania	20	36	93	31	51	31	55	3.2	1.5	5.8	2.8
15. Somalia	5	7	16	6	8	6	10	2.5	1.1	6.1	3.1
16. Haiti	5	7	13	7	10	7	10	1.9	1.4	3.4	2.4
17. Benin	4	7	18	6	9	6	10	3.1	1.5	5.9	2.9
18. Central African Rep.	2	4	10	3	5	3	5	2.7	1.1	5.6	2.5
19. China	1,008	1,196	1,450	1,196	1,450	1,185	1,462	1.0	1.0	2.0	2.0
20. Guinea	6	9	20	7	11	8	12	2.4	1.0	6.1	3.1
21. Niger	6	11	29	9	15	9	16	3.1	1.5	6.4	3.2
22. Madagascar	9	16	42	14	22	14	24	3.0	1.4	5.9	2.8
23. Sri Lanka	15	21	31	20	28	20	28	1.4	1.3	2.3	2.1
24. Togo	3	5	13	4	7	4	7	3.1	1.4	5.9	2.9
25. Ghana	12	24	66	20	36	21	39	3.5	1.9	6.3	3.2
26. Pakistan	87	140	302	120	181	122	197	2.5	1.2	4.8	2.5
27. Kenya	18	40	120	34	69	35	73	4.1	2.7	7.1	4.2
28. Sierra Leone	3	5	11	4	6	4	7	2.4	1.0	6.1	3.1
29. *Afghanistan*	17	25	55	24	38	25	42	2.1	1.5	5.6	4.2
30. *Bhutan*	1	2	3	2	2	2	2	2.0	0.9	5.1	2.9
31. *Kampuchea, Dem.*	7	10	17	9	12	9	13	1.4	0.7	3.9	2.7
32. *Lao PDR*	4	6	14	5	8	5	8	2.9	1.3	5.9	2.9
33. *Mozambique*	13	24	63	20	33	20	35	3.1	1.5	5.9	2.8
34. *Viet Nam*	57	88	154	81	125	81	130	2.0	1.4	3.1	2.1
Middle-income economies	**1,120 t**	**1,695 t**	**3,144 t**	**1,542 t**	**2,321 t**	**1,556 t**	**2,437 t**	**2.0 w**	**1.4 w**	**3.5 w**	**2.4 w**
Lower-middle-income	**673 t**	**1,023 t**	**1,993 t**	**927 t**	**1,406 t**	**937 t**	**1,490 t**	**2.1 w**	**1.4 w**	**3.7 w**	**2.5 w**
35. Sudan	20	34	86	29	46	30	50	3.0	1.3	6.0	2.9
36. Mauritania	2	3	6	2	3	2	3	2.8	1.1	5.9	2.7
37. Yemen, PDR	2	3	9	3	5	3	5	3.2	1.5	6.3	3.1
38. Liberia	2	4	10	3	5	3	6	3.2	1.6	6.2	3.1
39. Senegal	6	10	26	9	14	9	15	2.8	1.3	6.0	2.9
40. Yemen Arab Rep.	8	12	32	11	17	11	19	3.0	1.4	6.2	3.1
41. Lesotho	1	2	5	2	3	2	3	2.7	1.2	5.2	2.4
42. Bolivia	6	9	18	8	13	9	14	2.2	1.4	4.2	2.7
43. Indonesia	153	212	330	197	285	198	298	1.5	1.2	2.8	2.3
44. Zambia	6	11	29	10	16	10	18	3.3	1.6	6.1	3.0
45. Honduras	4	7	14	6	11	6	12	2.6	1.7	4.1	2.7
46. Egypt, Arab Rep.	44	63	102	58	84	58	88	1.7	1.2	3.0	2.3
47. El Salvador	5	8	15	8	12	8	13	2.2	1.5	3.3	2.2

	Population (millions) mid-1982	Projected population (millions)						Rate of natural increase, 2000		Total fertility rate, 2000	
		Standard projection		Rapid fertility decline only		Rapid fertility and mortality decline		Standard projection	Rapid fertility decline	Standard projection	Rapid fertility decline
		2000	2050	2000	2050	2000	2050				
48. Thailand	49	68	102	64	89	64	92	1.5	1.3	2.6	2.2
49. Papua New Guinea	3	5	8	4	6	4	7	2.0	1.3	3.6	2.4
50. Philippines	51	73	116	68	100	68	103	1.7	1.4	2.7	2.1
51. Zimbabwe	8	16	49	14	28	14	30	4.0	2.7	7.1	4.2
52. Nigeria	91	169	471	143	243	147	265	3.3	1.7	6.3	3.1
53. Morocco	20	31	59	29	45	29	49	2.2	1.4	3.8	2.5
54. Cameroon	9	17	50	14	23	14	25	3.4	1.5	6.4	2.8
55. Nicaragua	3	5	10	5	8	5	8	2.5	1.7	4.0	2.6
56. Ivory Coast	9	17	44	15	23	15	26	3.0	1.5	6.4	3.2
57. Guatemala	8	12	22	11	17	11	18	2.2	1.4	3.4	2.2
58. Congo, People's Rep.	2	3	8	3	4	3	5	3.3	1.5	5.7	2.5
59. Costa Rica	2	3	5	3	5	3	5	1.5	1.4	2.3	2.1
60. Peru	17	26	44	23	34	24	36	1.9	1.3	3.2	2.2
61. Dominican Rep.	6	8	14	8	12	8	12	1.8	1.5	2.7	2.2
62. Jamaica	2	3	4	3	4	3	4	1.5	1.4	2.3	2.1
63. Ecuador	8	13	24	12	19	12	19	2.2	1.4	3.5	2.2
64. Turkey	47	65	101	60	86	61	89	1.6	1.2	2.7	2.2
65. Tunisia	7	10	17	9	14	9	15	1.9	1.3	3.1	2.2
66. Colombia	27	38	57	35	49	35	51	1.6	1.3	2.6	2.2
67. Paraguay	3	5	8	4	6	4	7	1.8	1.4	2.7	2.1
68. Angola	8	13	32	11	17	12	19	2.7	1.2	6.0	3.0
69. Cuba	10	12	14	12	15	12	15	0.9	1.0	2.0	2.1
70. Korea, Dem. Rep.	19	27	42	25	36	25	37	1.6	1.3	2.6	2.1
71. Lebanon	3	3	5	3	5	3	5	1.5	1.4	2.4	2.1
72. Mongolia	2	3	5	3	4	3	4	2.0	1.4	3.1	2.1
Upper-middle-income	**447 t**	**672 t**	**1,151 t**	**615 t**	**915 t**	**619 t**	**947 t**	**1.8 w**	**1.3 w**	**3.1 w**	**2.3 w**
73. Syrian Arab Rep.	10	17	37	17	32	17	33	2.7	2.3	4.0	3.4
74. Jordan	3	6	14	6	10	6	11	3.2	2.4	5.2	3.6
75. Malaysia	15	21	31	19	28	19	28	1.5	1.3	2.4	2.1
76. Korea, Rep. of	39	51	67	49	63	50	65	1.1	1.1	2.1	2.1
77. Panama	2	3	4	3	4	3	4	1.5	1.4	2.3	2.1
78. Chile	12	15	20	14	19	14	19	1.1	1.1	2.2	2.1
79. Brazil	127	181	279	168	239	169	247	1.5	1.3	2.6	2.2
80. Mexico	73	109	182	101	155	101	160	1.9	1.5	2.8	2.1
81. Algeria	20	39	97	33	58	34	62	3.5	1.9	6.1	3.2
83. Argentina	28	36	50	34	43	34	44	1.0	0.8	2.5	2.1
84. Uruguay	3	3	4	3	4	3	4	0.7	0.6	2.2	2.1
85. South Africa	30	52	106	44	67	44	69	2.6	1.2	4.4	2.1
87. Venezuela	17	26	43	24	36	24	37	1.8	1.4	2.7	2.1
89. Israel	4	5	8	5	7	5	7	1.2	1.1	2.3	2.1
90. Hong Kong	5	7	8	7	8	7	8	0.7	0.7	2.1	2.1
91. Singapore	3	3	3	3	4	3	4	0.8	0.8	2.1	2.1
92. Trinidad & Tobago	1	2	2	1	2	1	2	1.4	1.1	2.4	2.1
93. Iran, Islamic Rep.	41	70	139	61	97	62	102	2.5	1.4	4.2	2.3
94. Iraq	14	26	57	23	39	23	41	2.9	1.8	4.9	2.9
High-income oil exporters	**17 t**	**33 t**	**77 t**	**30 t**	**46 t**	**30 t**	**49 t**	**3.0 w**	**1.7 w**	**5.7 w**	**3.2 w**
95. Oman	1	2	3	2	3	2	3	2.1	1.7	4.0	3.3
96. Libya	3	7	17	6	10	6	11	3.4	1.9	6.3	3.4
97. Saudi Arabia	10	19	49	17	27	17	29	3.3	1.7	6.3	3.3
98. Kuwait	2	3	5	3	4	3	4	1.9	1.4	3.0	2.3
99. United Arab Emirates	1	2	3	2	2	2	2	2.2	1.0	4.8	2.4

193

Table 2. Population composition

	Dependency ratio (percent)			Index numbers for relative sizes of age groups (size of age group in 1980=100)					
				Aged 0–14		Aged 15–64		Aged 65 and over	
	1960	1980	2000	1960	2000	1960	2000	1960	2000
Low-income economies									
1. Chad	76	78	87	64	151	71	171	66	178
2. Bangladesh	90	83	86	63	159	58	191	74	184
3. Ethiopia	87	93	95	63	167	66	198	64	209
4. Nepal	74	85	85	59	147	68	178	75	205
5. Mali	86	100	99	56	158	64	186	57	196
6. Burma	69	82	71	61	137	70	173	47	188
7. Zaire	89	93	99	61	170	62	207	67	222
8. Malawi	92	96	108	56	191	59	200	35	134
9. Upper Volta	84	96	95	65	147	70	173	69	183
10. Uganda	86	102	104	55	172	60	215	53	208
11. India	84	78	60	64	116	61	162	97	204
12. Rwanda	89	94	114	55	208	56	203	56	223
13. Burundi	83	89	96	69	164	73	191	67	200
14. Tanzania	84	99	100	51	178	59	212	55	212
15. Somalia	87	88	87	58	158	57	164	58	187
16. Haiti	81	89	63	68	123	75	160	81	157
17. Benin	87	99	102	57	188	62	194	55	201
18. Central African Rep.	73	83	95	66	164	74	179	63	189
19. China	78	68	41	82	75	64	141	64	203
20. Guinea	81	89	86	68	145	73	170	69	157
21. Niger	90	92	101	50	182	54	196	54	211
22. Madagascar	81	96	98	60	170	65	196	61	202
23. Sri Lanka	84	70	56	78	117	61	155	58	200
24. Togo	87	98	101	55	169	61	207	57	215
25. Ghana	89	101	106	56	188	62	230	57	238
26. Pakistan	93	89	82	53	146	57	191	87	178
27. Kenya	101	117	120	47	231	51	245	53	229
28. Sierra Leone	82	82	86	66	146	73	172	71	175
29. *Afghanistan*	82	89	82	58	143	66	175	81	183
30. *Bhutan*	79	77	77	74	135	77	167	80	170
31. *Kampuchea, Dem.*	89	55	71	. .	. .	. .	. .	. .	. .
32. *Lao PDR*	77	98	91	60	135	77	194	63	215
33. *Mozambique*	78	90	100	50	179	58	207	51	217
34. *Viet Nam*	. .	87	68	. .	133	. .	185	. .	175
Middle-income economies									
Lower-middle-income									
35. Sudan	88	91	93	58	164	59	191	65	207
36. Mauritania	87	88	99	61	161	67	172	62	183
37. Yemen, PDR	91	95	98	63	151	67	207	74	237
38. Liberia	92	81	102	52	180	53	214	54	260
39. Senegal	84	90	93	59	175	63	188	66	207
40. Yemen Arab Rep.	84	96	97	55	147	63	200	60	212
41. Lesotho	76	83	92	61	161	67	182	68	185
42. Bolivia	83	88	74	59	140	64	179	65	187
43. Indonesia	78	82	60	66	124	64	157	65	199
44. Zambia	90	103	102	54	194	59	207	54	214
45. Honduras	91	102	80	50	152	56	210	42	226
46. Egypt, Arab Rep.	83	76	62	65	120	59	166	54	202
47. El Salvador	92	95	71	53	132	54	198	52	222
48. Thailand	90	77	55	62	107	55	172	51	207
49. Papua New Guinea	77	90	67	62	134	67	166	57	177
50. Philippines	91	82	58	57	117	56	179	56	180
51. Zimbabwe	93	113	121	50	207	54	261	56	278
52. Nigeria	. .	99	103	58	177	64	219	59	240
53. Morocco	90	96	72	59	133	63	187	49	185
54. Cameroon	75	91	106	58	174	65	216	57	194
55. Nicaragua	. .	99	78	53	145	53	215	56	222
56. Ivory Coast	86	87	94	41	186	42	218	55	339
57. Guatemala	96	88	69	58	141	52	185	49	222
58. Congo People's Rep.	79	95	108	54	200	63	210	59	230
59. Costa Rica	102	73	55	69	117	48	173	46	228
60. Peru	92	85	65	60	133	56	172	72	175
61. Dominican Rep.	103	88	61	59	120	53	182	61	206
62. Jamaica	85	87	62	77	101	76	155	54	137
63. Ecuador	92	92	70	58	137	58	193	60	190
64. Turkey	81	76	61	65	113	61	167	49	195
65. Tunisia	91	82	67	69	115	63	183	75	224
66. Colombia	99	75	57	78	115	51	159	54	213

	Dependency ratio (percent)			Index numbers for relative sizes of age groups (size of age group in 1980 = 100)					
				Aged 0–14		Aged 15–64		Aged 65 and over	
	1960	1980	2000	1960	2000	1960	2000	1960	2000
67. Paraguay	97	86	59	62	126	58	180	59	191
68. Angola	80	89	91	60	160	67	185	59	200
69. Cuba	64	63	49	76	94	73	133	50	151
70. Korea Dem. Rep.	89	78	59	64	122	56	170	54	191
71. Lebanon	87	84	62	71	102	67	143	83	149
72. Mongolia	84	86	66	54	115	57	197	70	224
Upper-middle-income									
73. Syrian Arab Rep.	93	102	82	48	162	55	233	53	180
74. Jordan	94	111	100	55	172	59	246	89	260
75. Malaysia	95	74	55	65	105	55	176	63	205
76. Korea, Rep. of	86	60	49	82	103	57	144	56	206
77. Panama	93	79	54	64	109	57	169	60	191
78. Chile	77	61	50	82	103	62	143	55	189
79. Brazil	86	72	58	63	123	58	165	46	212
80. Mexico	96	93	63	54	123	53	186	52	187
81. Algeria	91	104	104	53	178	62	237	63	184
82. Portugal	59	57	54	99	101	90	116	72	126
83. Argentina	57	62	58	81	109	74	132	48	181
84. Uruguay	56	59	58	91	101	89	116	66	150
85. South Africa	81	75	83	61	179	60	184	62	197
86. Yugoslavia	58	52	50	102	101	78	113	59	155
87. Venezuela	95	82	60	53	135	45	188	39	247
88. Greece	53	57	57	100	102	88	108	56	127
89. Israel	69	72	53	59	116	55	151	32	148
90. Hong Kong	78	46	48	88	120	52	133	27	200
91. Singapore	83	45	42	101	102	56	127	31	191
92. Trinidad and Tobago	89	65	59	101	112	67	150	66	225
93. Iran, Islamic Rep.	96	91	81	52	141	52	216	71	190
94. Iraq	94	97	89	51	160	52	224	51	256
High-income oil exporters									
95. Oman	..	87	70	49	154	54	202	50	214
96. Libya	90	96	94	42	193	47	265	80	336
97. Saudi Arabia	85	86	92	42	180	46	233	41	239
98. Kuwait	59	79	55	16	168	26	227	34	506
99. United Arab Emirates	..	45	58	..	183	..	241	..	200
Industrial market economies									
100. Ireland	73	70	55	84	105	83	136	85	111
101. Spain	55	58	55	85	101	83	116	63	138
102. Italy	52	55	52	100	95	91	103	64	118
103. New Zealand	71	58	49	89	96	70	118	72	124
104. United Kingdom	54	56	53	103	100	95	101	75	108
105. Austria	52	56	50	99	96	96	104	74	97
106. Japan	56	48	48	103	90	76	109	54	174
107. Belgium	55	53	51	106	98	92	102	80	111
108. Finland	60	52	46	137	97	85	102	58	121
109. Netherlands	64	51	46	108	96	75	109	65	123
110. Australia	63	54	50	82	106	67	125	65	150
111. Canada	70	46	46	105	110	66	121	63	153
112. France	61	55	52	100	99	82	110	74	111
113. Germany, Fed. Rep.	47	51	49	101	95	92	98	66	104
114. Denmark	56	55	48	107	94	89	104	68	104
115. United States	67	51	48	108	105	72	116	68	125
116. Sweden	51	56	53	100	97	92	104	68	103
117. Norway	59	58	51	101	96	87	108	68	103
118. Switzerland	51	49	55	99	94	84	101	64	113
East European nonmarket economies									
119. Hungary	52	55	52	111	97	93	102	64	116
120. Romania	57	59	55	93	100	83	115	58	145
121. Albania	86	73	52	64	110	55	164	62	177
122. Bulgaria	51	52	56	105	99	89	103	57	141
123. Czechoslovakia	56	58	52	103	99	90	113	62	112
124. German Dem. Rep.	53	54	51	109	101	105	106	88	94
125. Poland	65	52	51	115	104	76	116	49	141
126. USSR	60	52	52	100	105	77	114	58	147

.. Not available.

Table 3. Contraceptive use and unmet need

(Percentage of currently married women aged 15–49)

		Current use of contraception						Percentage who want no more children	Unmet need for contraception	
	Year	Sterili-zation	Pill and injectables	IUD	Condom and vaginal methods	Other methods	Total		Low estimate	High estimate
Low-income economies										
2. Bangladesh	1983–84	7	4	1	2	5	19	50	25	28
4. Nepal	1981	5	1	(.)	(.)	(.)	7	41	22	27
16. Haiti	1977	(.)	4	(.)	1	14	19	50	13	30
17. Benin	1981–82	(.)	(.)	(.)	(.)	17	17	. .	. .	. .
23. Sri Lanka	1982	21	4	3	3	25	55	67	18	31
25. Ghana	1979	1	3	(.)	2	4	10	20	5	8
26. Pakistan	1975	1	1	1	1	1	5	50	17	27
27. Kenya[a]	1977–78	1	3	1	(.)	2	7	25	6	10
Middle-income economies										
Lower-middle-income										
35. Sudan[a]	1979	(.)	3	(.)	(.)	1	5	27	6	9
36. Mauritania	1981	. .	. .	. .	. .	. .	1	. .	. .	. .
39. Senegal	1978	(.)	(.)	(.)	(.)	3	4	. .	. .	. .
40. Yemen Arab Rep.	1979	(.)	1	(.)	(.)	(.)	1	29	8	12
41. Lesotho	1977	1	1	(.)	(.)	3	5	26	5	9
43. Indonesia	1976	(.)	15	6	2	3	26	49	10	15
45. Honduras	1981	8	12	2	1	3	27	48	9	21
46. Egypt, Arab Rep.	1980	1	17	4	1	1	24	58	12	22
47. El Salvador[a]	1978	18	9	3	2	2	34	. .	. .	. .
48. Thailand[a]	1981	23	27	4	2	3	59	68	13	17
50. Philippines	1978	6	5	2	4	20	36	59	11	29
52. Nigeria	1982	. .	. .	. .	. .	. .	6	. .	. .	. .
53. Morocco	1980	. .	. .	. .	. .	. .	19	. .	. .	. .
54. Cameroon	1978	(.)	(.)	(.)	(.)	2	2	23	1	1
56. Ivory Coast	1980–81	(.)	(.)	(.)	(.)	2	3	12	2	3
57. Guatemala[a]	1978	6	7	1	1	3	18	. .	. .	. .
59. Costa Rica	1981	18	23	6	10	9	65	55	6	11
60. Peru	1981	5	6	4	2	24	41	75	13	41
61. Dominican Rep.	1975	12	8	2	4	6	32	56	21	12
62. Jamaica[a]	1979	10	35	2	7	1	55	67	21	25
63. Ecuador	1979	8	10	5	3	8	34	59	13	26
64. Turkey	1978	(.)	7	3	3	25	38	. .	. .	. .
65. Tunisia	1983	14	5	13	3	6	41	56	10	19
66. Colombia	1980	11	19	8	3	8	49	69	7	24
67. Paraguay	1979	2	14	5	2	12	36	39	9	17
Upper-middle-income										
73. Syrian Arab Rep.	1978	(.)	12	1	2	5	20	44	7	15
74. Jordan	1976	2	12	2	1	7	25	48	7	17
75. Malaysia	1974	3	16	1	3	10	33	51	15	23
76. Korea, Rep. of[a]	1979	20	7	10	6	11	54	77	. .	23
77. Panama[a]	1979–80	30	20	4	3	4	61	66	9	18
80. Mexico	1979	9	16	6	2	6	39	61	14	22
87. Venezuela[a]	1977	8	16	7	6	12	49	56	10	22
90. Hong Kong	1977	19	25	3	17	9	72	. .	. .	. .
92. Trinidad and Tobago	1977	6	18	3	20	6	52	58	14	19
Countries with less than one million population										
Guyana	1975	9	9	6	(.)	7	31	62	23	29
Fiji	1974	16	8	5	6	5	41	55	10	15
Barbados	1981	14	18	4	8	2	46	53	. .	19

Note: Figures in italics are for earlier years than specified; see technical notes.

. . Not available.

(.) Less than half of 1 percent.

a. Age or marital status differs from that specified; see technical notes.

Table 4. Factors influencing fertility

	Year	Among ever-married women of childbearing age		Percentage of women aged 15–19 ever married	Mean duration of breastfeeding (months)	Total fertility rate among women with	
		Mean number of living children	Desired family size			No schooling	Seven years' schooling or more
Low-income economies							
2. Bangladesh	1981	3.0	4.1	63	29	6.1	5.0
4. Nepal	1976	2.4	3.9	59	25	..	..
16. Haiti	1977	2.7	3.5	16	16	6.1	2.9
17. Benin	1981–82	2.5	..	44	19	7.3	4.3
23. Sri Lanka	1975	3.5	3.8	7	21	..	..
25. Ghana[a]	1979	..	6.1	31	18	6.8	5.5
26. Pakistan	1975	3.2	..	38	19	6.5	3.1
27. Kenya[a]	1978	3.2	7.2	28	16	8.3	7.3
Middle-income economies							
Lower-middle-income							
35. Sudan[a]	1979	3.5	6.3	23	16	6.5	3.4
36. Mauritania[a]	1981	3.1	9.2	39	16	..	..
39. Senegal	1978	2.9	8.8	59	..	7.3	4.5
40. Yemen Arab Rep.	1979	..	..	61	11	8.5	..
41. Lesotho	1977	2.6	5.9	32	20	6.2	4.8
43. Indonesia	1976	2.8	4.1	29	24	..	..
46. Egypt, Arab Rep.	1980	3.1	4.1	22	19	..	..
48. Thailand	1975	3.4	3.7	16	19	..	..
50. Philippines	1978	4.1	4.4	7	13	5.5	3.8
52. Nigeria[a]	1982	2.5	..	44	18	..	..
53. Morocco	1980	..	..	22	15	6.4	4.1
54. Cameroon	1978	2.7	..	53	..	6.4	5.2
56. Ivory Coast	1980–81	..	..	56	17	7.5	5.8
59. Costa Rica[a]	1976	3.8	4.7	15	5	4.5	2.5
60. Peru	1977–78	3.7	3.8	14	13	7.3	3.3
61. Dominican Republic	1975	3.5	4.6	28	9	7.0	3.0
62. Jamaica	1975–76	3.3	4.0	27	8	6.2	4.8
63. Ecuador	1979	..	..	19	12	7.8	2.7
64. Turkey[a]	1978	3.1	3.0	16	..	..	..
65. Tunisia	1983	3.8	..	5	14	..	..
66. Colombia	1976	3.7	4.1	15	9	7.0	2.6
67. Paraguay	1979	3.5	5.1	17	11	8.2	2.9
Upper-middle-income							
73. Syrian Arab Rep.	1978	4.2	6.1	23	12	8.8	4.1
74. Jordan	1976	4.7	6.3	19	11	9.3	4.9
75. Malaysia	1974	3.8	..	11	6	5.3	3.2
76. Korea, Rep. of	1979	3.1	3.2	3	16	5.7	3.3
77. Panama[a]	1975–76	3.7	4.2	20	7	5.7	2.7
80. Mexico	1976–77	4.0	4.5	19	9	8.1	3.3
87. Venezuela[a]	1977	3.3	4.2	20	7	7.0	2.6
90. Hong Kong	1976	2.9	..	4	..	..	..
92. Trinidad and Tobago	1977	2.9	3.8	20	8	4.6	3.2
Countries with less than one million population							
Guyana	1975	3.6	4.6	28	7	6.5	4.8
Fiji	1974	3.5	..	12	10	..	..
Barbados	1981	1.7	2.4	52	..	..	..

Note: Figures in italics are for years other than specified; see technical notes.
.. Not available.
a. See technical notes.

Table 5. Status of women

	Ratio of adult male to adult female literacy, 1980	Number enrolled in secondary school as percentage of age group, 1981		Percentage aged 15–49 ever enrolled in primary school 1980		Singulate mean age at marriage 1977		Percentage economically active among urban population aged 10–64 1978	
		Male	Female	Male	Female	Male	Female	Male	Female
Low-income economies									
2. Bangladesh	..	24	6	68	32	24	16	..	.
3. Ethiopia	..	16	8	21	9	..	..	..	..
4. Nepal	6.3	33	9	40	9	21	17	..	..
5. Mali	..	..	..	..	..	..	..	61	8
6. Burma	1.4	..	..	..	..	..	..	..	..
7. Zaire	2.0	..	..	..	..	..	..	..	..
8. Malawi	..	6	2	..	..	..	..	69	23
9. Upper Volta	..	4	2	15	8	..	..	..	..
10. Uganda	..	7	3	..	..	..	..	..	..
11. India	1.9	39	20	84	48	..	..	..	..
12. Rwanda	1.6	3	1	75	49	..	..	..	..
13. Burundi	1.6	4	2	32	14	..	..	..	..
14. Tanzania	1.1	4	2	47	32	..	..	..	..
15. Somalia	3.7	16	6	17	7	..	..	..	..
16. Haiti	..	13	12	..	..	..	..	..	..
17. Benin	2.4	26	10	50	22	..	18	..	..
18. Central African Rep.	2.5	20	7	70	26	..	..	..	..
19. China	..	53	35	..	..	..	..	..	..
20. Guinea	..	23	9	44	19	..	..	..	..
21. Niger	2.3	..	..	..	..	..	..	83	11
23. Sri Lanka	1.1	49	54	100	92	28	25	..	..
24. Togo	..	46	16	85	39	..	..	..	..
25. Ghana	..	44	27	..	..	27	19	..	..
26. Pakistan	..	27	7	54	19	25	20	..	..
27. Kenya	1.7	23	15	74	48	..	20	..	..
29. Afghanistan	5.5	17	4	..	..	..	..	..	..
30. Bhutan	..	2	1	..	..	..	..	..	..
32. Lao PDR	1.4	22	14	..	..	..	..	..	..
33. Mozambique	1.9	9	4	..	..	..	..	..	..
34. Viet Nam	..	53	43	..	..	..	..	..	..
Middle-income economies									
Lower-middle-income									
35. Sudan	..	20	15	42	23	..	21	..	..
36. Mauritania	..	16	4	19	7	28	19	..	..
37. Yemen, PDR	..	24	11	..	..	..	..	..	..
38. Liberia	..	29	11	58	27	..	..	..	..
39. Senegal	..	16	8	..	..	..	..	..	..
40. Yemen Arab Rep.	18.0	9	2	..	..	22	17	..	..
41. Lesotho	0.7	13	20	..	..	25	20	..	..
42. Bolivia	..	37	31	84	58	..	..	65	25
43. Indonesia	..	36	24	89	68	24	19	63	25
44. Zambia	..	21	11	..	..	..	..	..	..
45. Honduras	..	29	30	79	79	..	..	..	..
46. Egypt, Arab Rep.	1.3	64	39	84	55	27	21	..	..
47. El Salvador	..	19	21	83	80	..	..	..	..
48. Thailand	..	30	27	..	..	25	23	66	46
49. Papua New Guinea	..	17	8	..	..	..	..	..	..
50. Philippines	..	58	68	..	..	26	25	73	45
51. Zimbabwe	1.3	18	13	..	..	..	..	..	..
52. Nigeria	2.0	..	..	..	..	..	..	..	..
53. Morocco	..	31	20	71	34	26	21	..	..
54. Cameroon	..	25	13	..	..	26	18	56	22

	Ratio of adult male to adult female literacy, 1980	Number enrolled in secondary school as percentage of age group, 1981		Percentage aged 15–49 ever enrolled in primary school 1980		Singulate mean age at marriage 1977		Percentage economically active among urban population aged 10–64 1978	
		Male	Female	Male	Female	Male	Female	Male	Female
55. Nicaragua	..	38	45	76	78	..	..	..	..
56. Ivory Coast	1.9	25	9	..	..	27	18	..	..
57. Guatemala	..	17	15	57	46	..	..	..	..
59. Costa Rica	..	44	51	100	100	26	23	71	31
60. Peru	..	62	52	100	86	26	23	..	..
61. Dominican Rep.	..	..	..	98	98	25	21	..	..
62. Jamaica	..	54	62	..	..	..	19	..	..
63. Ecuador	..	39	41	..	..	26	22	..	..
64. Turkey	1.6	57	28	100	77	..	..	..	..
65. Tunisia	..	37	23	100	63	28	24	..	..
66. Colombia	..	45	51	96	97	26	22	72	38
69. *Cuba*	1.0	72	77	..	..	..	..	..	..
71. *Lebanon*	..	60	56	..	..	..	..	..	..
72. *Mongolia*	..	85	92	..	..	..	..	..	..
Upper-middle-income									
73. Syrian Arab Rep.	..	59	37	95	53	26	22	..	..
74. Jordan	..	79	76	..	..	26	22	..	..
75. Malaysia	..	56	53	99	84	..	..	..	..
76. Korea, Rep. of	..	89	80	100	97	..	..	74	36
77. Panama	1.0	60	69	100	99	26	21	..	..
78. Chile	..	53	62	100	100	..	..	..	..
79. Brazil	1.1	..	..	..	..	..	..	..	..
80. Mexico	1.1	54	49	97	92	24	22	..	..
81. Algeria	..	42	29	79	51	..	..	..	..
83. Argentina	..	54	63	..	..	..	..	..	..
84. Uruguay	..	54	61	100	100	..	..	..	..
87. Venezuela	..	41	38	..	..	..	..	..	..
89. Israel	..	69	80	..	..	..	..	63	34
90. Hong Kong	..	62	68	100	97	..	..	..	..
91. Singapore	1.2	65	65	100	100	..	..	..	..
93. *Iran, Islamic Rep.*	..	54	35	..	..	..	..	64	9
94. *Iraq*	..	78	40	..	..	..	..	62	8
High-income oil exporters									
95. Oman	..	*30*	*13*	..	..	..	..	..	..
97. Saudia Arabia	2.9	*37*	*24*	..	..	..	..	..	..
98. Kuwait	..	80	71	..	..	..	..	..	..
99. United Arab Emirates	..	57	66	..	..	..	..	..	..
Countries with less than one million population									
Guinea-Bissau	1.9	33	7	..	..	..	..	..	..
Comoros	..	33	*17*	..	..	..	..	..	..
Gambia	2.4	19	8	..	..	..	..	..	..
Guyana	..	57	*61*	..	..	..	*20*	..	..
Botswana	..	21	25	..	..	..	..	..	..
Swaziland	..	41	40	..	..	..	..	..	..
Mauritius	1.2	52	49	..	..	..	..	..	..
Fiji	..	*60*	*64*	..	..	..	..	..	..
Barbados	..	81	90	..	..	..	..	..	..
Bahrain	*1.1*	61	54	..	..	..	..	..	..
Qatar	..	63	75	..	..	..	..	..	..
Suriname	1.1	..	..	..	..	..	..	..	..

Note: Figures in italics are for years other than specified; see technical notes.
.. Not available.

Table 6. Family planning policy

	Support for family planning			Year official family planning program started	Family planning index[a]	
	Demographic and other reasons	Health and human rights reasons only	No support		1972	1982
Low-income economies						
1. Chad			x	n.a.	E	E
2. Bangladesh	x			1971	E	C
3. Ethiopia		x		1981	E	E
4. Nepal	x			1966	D	D
5. Mali		x		1972	E	E
6. Burma			x	n.a.	E	E
7. Zaire		x		1973	E	E
8. Malawi			x	n.a.	E	E
9. Upper Volta			x	n.a.	E	E
10. Uganda	x			1971	E	E
11. India	x			1952	B	B
12. Rwanda	x			1981	E	D
13. Burundi			x	n.a.	E	E
14. Tanzania		x		1970	E	D
15. Somalia		x		1977	E	E
16. Haiti	x			1982	E	D
17. Benin		x		1969	..	..
18. Central African Rep.		x		1978	E	E
19. China	x			1962	A	A
20. Guinea			x	n.a.	E	E
21. Niger			x	n.a.	E	E
22. Madagascar			x	n.a.	E	E
23. Sri Lanka	x			1965	C	B
24. Togo		x		1975	E	E
25. Ghana	x			1969	E	E
26. Pakistan	x			1960	D	C
27. Kenya	x			1967	D	D
28. Sierra Leone		x		1978	E	E
29. *Afghanistan*		x		1970	E	E
30. *Bhutan*		x		1979	..	..
31. *Kampuchea, Dem.*			x	1977[b]	E	E
32. *Lao PDR*			x	1976[b]	E	E
33. *Mozambique*		x		1977	E	E
34. *Viet Nam*	x			1977	B	C
Middle-income economies						
Lower-middle-income						
35. Sudan		x		1970	E	E
36. Mauritania			x	n.a.	E	E
37. Yemen, PDR		x		1973	E	E
38. Liberia		x		1973	E	D
39. Senegal	x			1976	E	E
40. Yemen Arab Rep.			x	n.a.	E	E
41. Lesotho		x		1974	E	E
42. Bolivia			x	1976[b]	E	E
43. Indonesia	x			1968	C	B
44. Zambia		x		1974	E	E
45. Honduras		x		1966	D	D
46. Egypt, Arab Rep.	x			1965	D	D
47. El Salvador	x			1974	C	B
48. Thailand	x			1970	D	C
49. Papua New Guinea		x		1968	E	D
50. Philippines	x			1970	C	C
51. Zimbabwe		x		1968	E	D
52. Nigeria		x		1970	E	E
53. Morocco	x			1966	E	D
54. Cameroon			x	n.a.	E	E
55. Nicaragua		x		1967	E	E
56. Ivory Coast			x	n.a.	E	E
57. Guatemala	x			1975	D	D
58. Congo, People's Rep.		x		1976	E	E
59. Costa Rica		x		1968	B	D

	Support for family planning			Year official family planning program started	Family planning index[a]	
	Demographic and other reasons	Health and human rights reasons only	No support		1972	1982
60. Peru		x		1976	E	D
61. Dominican Rep.	x			1968	C	C
62. Jamaica	x			1966	B	C
63. Ecuador		x		1968	D	C
64. Turkey	x			1965	D	D
65. Tunisia	x			1964	C	C
66. Colombia	x			1970	C	B
67. Paraguay		x		1972	E	E
68. *Angola*			x	n.a.	. .	. .
69. *Cuba*		x		. .	C	C
70. *Korea, Dem. Rep.*		x		. .	. .	. .
71. *Lebanon*		x		1970	E	D
72. *Mongolia*			x	n.a.	E	E
Upper-middle-income						
73. Syrian Arab Rep.		x		1974	E	E
74. Jordan		x		1976	E	E
75. Malaysia	x			1966	C	B
76. Korea, Rep. of	x			1961	A	A
77. Panama		x		1969	C	B
78. Chile			x	1979[b]	C	C
79. Brazil		x		1974	E	C
80. Mexico	x			1974	E	B
81. Algeria		x		1971	E	D
83. Argentina			x	n.a.	. .	. .
84. Uruguay			x	n.a.	. .	. .
85. South Africa		x		1966	. .	. .
87. Venezuela		x		1968	D	D
89. Israel		x		. .	. .	. .
90. Hong Kong	x			1973	B	B
91. Singapore	x			1965	A	A
92. Trinidad and Tobago	x			1967	C	C
93. *Iran, Islamic Rep.*				. .	. .	. .
94. *Iraq*		x		1972	E	E
High-income oil exporters						
95. Oman			x	n.a.	. .	. .
96. Libya			x	n.a.	E	E
97. Saudi Arabia			x	n.a.	. .	. .
98. Kuwait			x	n.a.	E	E
99. United Arab Emirates			x	n.a.	. .	. .
Countries with less than one million population						
Guinea-Bissau		x		1976	. .	. .
Cape Verde		x		1978	. .	. .
Gambia		x		1969	. .	D
St. Vincent and Grenadines	x			1972	. .	. .
Solomon Islands	x			1970	. .	. .
Guyana		x		1977	. .	D
St. Lucia	x			1975	. .	. .
Grenada	x			1974	. .	. .
Botswana	x			1970	. .	D
Swaziland	x			1975	. .	. .
Mauritius	x			1965	B	B
Fiji	x			1962	B	C
Barbados	x			1967	. .	. .
Cyprus			x	n.a.	. .	D
Gabon			x	n.a.	. .	. .
Seychelles	x			1975	. .	. .
Western Samoa	x			1970	. .	D

. . Not available.

n.a. Not applicable.

a. A = very strong; B = strong; C = moderate; D = weak; E = very weak or none. For explanation of the index, see technical notes.

b. Year in which previously existing program was canceled.

Bibliographical note

This Report has drawn on a wide range of World Bank work as well as on numerous outside sources. World Bank sources include ongoing economic analysis and research, as well as project, sector, and economic work on individual countries. Outside sources include research publications and the unpublished reports of other organizations working on global economic and population and development programs and issues. Selected sources are briefly noted by chapter below and listed alphabetically by author in two groups. The first includes background papers commissioned for this Report; these reports synthesize relevant literature and Bank work. Most include extensive bibliographies; the sources cited in these papers are not listed separately. Those issued as World Bank Staff Working Papers are available from the Bank's Publications Sales Unit. The views they express are not necessarily those of the World Bank or of this Report. The second group consists of selected other sources used in the preparation of this Report.

Selected sources, by chapter

Chapter 1

Historical population data are based on Durand and, for this century, United Nations data to 1950 and World Bank data thereafter. Historical data on income are reviewed in McGreevey; demographic and social data are from Tan and Haines.

Chapters 2 and 3

Data used in these chapters draw on GATT, IMF, OECD, and UNCTAD publications as well as World Bank data. For analysis of the extent and effects of labor market rigidities in the economic performance of OECD countries; the causes of the productivity slowdown; and the effects of protection, see Lal and Wolf. The discussion of debt problems is based on papers by Kindleberger, Lawrence, and by Sjaastad and others. The discussion of the problems faced by developing countries in a volatile world economy is based on internal Bank documents and *Sub-Saharan Africa: Progress Report on Development Prospects and Programs*. Quantitative analysis of the link between budget deficits in industrial countries and global "crowding out" is in Lal and van Wijnbergen. Alternative views on macroeconomic stabilization are surveyed in Haberler. For a review of public expenditures and budget deficits in OECD countries, see Hakim and Wallich.

Box 2.1 comparing the 1930s to the present draws on Maddison. Box 2.2 on protection in industrial countries is based on UNCTAD data. The analysis for Box 2.3 is in Mitra. Box 2.4 and Box 3.3 are based on Bank macroeconomic modeling work summarized in Sanderson and Williamson. Box 2.5 on Latin American debt problems made use of the background papers by Sjaastad and others, and by Lawrence. Box 3.1 is based on Wolf and others. Box 3.2 on the engine of growth is based on Riedel and on Lal. Box 3.3 is based on Lal and unpublished work by Srinivasan. The discussion of IDA lending in Box 3.4 draws on the Bank report *IDA in Retrospect*.

Chapter 4

The description of the setting for high fertility is from Birdsall (1980). For additional sources and evidence on the advantages of children in poor communities, see Cain.

The historical discussion is based on sources cited in Cassen and in McGreevey. The discussion of present trends is based primarily on World Bank and United Nations data. Mortality trends are analyzed in Hill; Preston; and Bulatao and Elwan. Work on causes of mortality decline includes DaVanzo and Habicht; and Cochrane and others. The stall in fertility decline in selected countries is analyzed in Gendell. The evidence on international migration is surveyed in Swamy.

Box 4.1 on the isolation paradox draws on the writings of Sen and of Cassen. Box 4.2 was assembled with the help of Peter Lindert and members of the Graduate Group in Demography at the University of California, Berkeley and Davis. Box 4.3 draws on data assembled by the European Fertility

Transition project at Princeton University, which resulted in the book edited by Coale and Watkins.

Chapter 5

The literature on macroeconomic effects of population growth, including effects on income distribution, is surveyed and reviewed in McNicoll. On the relation between fertility and savings, see Hammer. Projections of schooling costs are based on Bank data on current costs and a projection model of The Futures Group. The structural transformation discussion is based on Porter and on Johnston and Kilby. The discussion of food and agriculture is based on the FAO study *Agriculture: Toward 2000*; Bank work on Africa; Porter; and Pingali and Binswanger. Kirchner and others analyze the links between population and natural resources; for related discussion, see Muscat. Urban population growth and migration are discussed in Linn and in Standing. Redistribution policies (including Box 5.5) are analyzed in Mahar. Work on the international economy as it relates to population is in Sapir and in Swamy.

Box 5.1 discusses the works of Meadows and others, who prepared the book ascribed to the Club of Rome, and of Simon. The analysis used for Box 5.2 is described in Kamin.

Chapter 6

The discussion of socioeconomic and proximate determinants of fertility is based on recent reviews, including the background paper by Bulatao; the compilation of Bulatao and Lee; unpublished papers produced by the Fertility Determinants Group at Indiana University; and Birdsall, 1980. Important conceptual contributions include those of Becker, Bongaarts, Easterlin, Freedman, and Schultz. Essential data were obtained from the World Fertility Survey Comparative Studies series, especially the paper by Casterline and others. The links between fertility and mortality are reviewed in Bulatao and Elwan and in Gwatkin. Cain analyzes the link between the status of women and fertility. Policy recommendations affecting marriage are discussed especially in Henry and Piotrow and on breastfeeding in McCann and others. For analyses of the effects of family planning on fertility see Boulier; Wheeler; and Lapham and Mauldin. Merrick presents evidence on family planning and other factors influencing fertility for Latin America, and Zachariah presents such evidence for India. The incentives section draws on Bank sector work on

China, on Jacobsen, and on the 1974 World Bank publication by King and others. Boxes in this chapter discuss articles by Stokes and Schutjer (Box 6.1), Ho (Box 6.2), Lindert, and Bulatao, 1981 (Box 6.3).

Chapter 7

On contraceptive use and unmet need see the papers by Ainsworth and by Boulier (a). Data used in this section are from World Fertility Survey and Contraceptive Prevalence Survey data tapes prepared for this Report. Some of the information is available in publications of the World Fertility Survey (published by the International Statistical Institute, The Netherlands). Program issues—management, access, and quality—are discussed in Ainsworth and in Jones. Bulatao analyzes the costs of family planning programs. Examples throughout the chapter come from World Bank sector reports, other background papers, and materials furnished by the International Planned Parenthood Federation, the Pathfinder Fund, and the United States Agency for International Development.

Box 7.1, on the health benefits of family planning, is based on Trussell and Pebley and other analyses surveyed in Ainsworth. Sources for Box 7.2, on contraceptive technology, include Atkinson and others; and the US Congress Office of Technology Assessment study. Sources for Box 7.6, on the Matlab projects, are cited in Ainsworth. Box 7.7 on military expenditures is based on Sivard and World Bank data.

Chapter 8

This chapter draws heavily on Bank operational experience and sector work. The discussion of population policy uses information gathered and summarized by Lapham and Mauldin. The African section is based in part on the papers by Ascadi and Johnson-Ascadi; and by Faruqee and Gulhati. The background papers by Gendell, Jones, and Zachariah contributed to the section on South Asia, and that of Merrick to the section on Latin America. Herz summarizes information on donor assistance.

Box 8.1, on pronatalist policies, is based on Denton. Demographic policy objectives in Box 8.2 are drawn largely from official government statements and development plans. The FAO report by Higgins and others is the main source for Box 8.3. Studies on infertility in Africa (Box 8.4) include that of Frank. Box 8.7 was prepared with help from Judith Bruce of The Population Council.

Background papers

Note: Source references to these papers carry the publication year 1984.

* An asterisk after a citation indicates a background paper that will be published in a volume provisionally entitled "Perspectives on the Global Economy."

† A dagger after a citation indicates a background paper that is forthcoming as a World Bank Staff Working Paper.

Ainsworth, Martha. "Family Planning Programs: The Client's Perspective." In Ainsworth and Jones.

Ainsworth, Martha, and Huw Jones. "Family Planning Programs: Client and Management Perspectives."†

Birdsall, Nancy, ed. "Three Cross-country Analyses of the Effects of Organized Family Planning Programs on Fertility."†

Boulier, Bryan. a. "Family Planning Programs and Contraceptive Availability: Their Effects on Contraceptive Use and Fertility." In Birdsall, ed.

Boulier, Bryan. b. "Unmet Need for Contraception: Evaluation of Measures and Estimates for Thirty-six Developing Countries."†

Bulatao, Rodolfo A. a. "Expenditures on Population Programs in Major Regions of the Developing World: Current Levels and Future Requirements."†

Bulatao, Rodolfo A. b. "Reducing Fertility in Developing Countries: A Review of Determinants and Policy Levers."†

Bulatao, Rodolfo A., and Ann Elwan. "Fertility and Mortality Transition in Developing Countries: Patterns, Projections, and Interdependence."†

Cain, Mead. "On Women's Status, Family Structure, and Fertility in Developing Countries."†

DaVanzo, Julie, and others. "Quantitative Studies of Mortality Decline in the Developing World."†

DaVanzo, Julie, and Jean-Pierre Habicht. "What Accounts for the Decline in Infant Mortality in Peninsular Malaysia, 1946-75?" In DaVanzo and others.

Denton, Hazel. "The Declining Growth Rates of the Population of Eastern Europe."†

Gendell, Murray. "Factors Underlying Stalled Fertility in Developing Countries."†

Gwatkin, Davidson. "Mortality Reduction, Fertility Decline, and Population Growth."†

Haberler, Gottfried. "The Slowdown of the World Economy and the Problem of Stagflation: Some Alternative Explanations and Policy Implications."*

Hakim, Leonardo, and Christine Wallich. "OECD Deficits, Debts, and Savings: Structure and Trends, 1965-80."*

Hammer, Jeffrey S. "Population Growth and Savings in Developing Countries."†

Herz, Barbara. "Official Development Assistance for Population."†

Hill, Ken. "The Pace of Mortality Decline since 1950." In DaVanzo and others.

Jones, Huw. "National Family Planning Programs: A Management Perspective." In Ainsworth and Jones.

Kamin, Steve. "New Poverty Projections for the Developing Countries."

Kindleberger, Charles. "Historical Perspective on Today's Third-World Debt Problem."†

King, Timothy, and Robin Zeitz. "Taking Thought for the Morrow: Prospects and Policies for Aging Populations."†

Kirchner, J. W., and others. "Two Essays on Population and Carrying Capacity."†

———. "Carrying Capacity, Population Growth, and Sustainable Development." In Kirchner and others.

Lal, Deepak, and Martin Wolf. "Debt, Deficits, and Distortions: Problems of the Global Economy."*

Lal, Deepak, and Sweder van Wijnbergen. "Government Deficits, the Real Interest Rate, and LDC Debt: On Global Crowding Out."*

Lapham, Robert J., and W. Parker Mauldin. "Conditions of Fertility Decline in Developing Countries, 1965-80." In Birdsall, ed.

Lawrence, Robert. "Systemic Risk and Developing Country Debt."*

Lluch, Constantino. "Investment Cycles, Saving, and Output Growth."*

Maddison, Angus. "Developing Countries in the 1930s: Possible Lessons for the 1980s."*

Mahar, Dennis. "The Settlement of Tropical Frontiers: Some Lessons from Brazil and Indonesia."†

McGreevey, William. "Economic Aspects of Historical Demographic Change."†

McNicoll, Geoffrey. "Consequences of Rapid Population Growth: An Overview and Assessment."†

Merrick, Thomas W. "Recent Fertility Declines in Brazil, Colombia, and Mexico."†

Muscat, Robert. "Carrying Capacity and Rapid Population Growth: Definition, Cases, and Consequences." In Kirchner and others.

Porter, Ian. "Population Growth and Agricultural Transitions."†

Prescott, Nicholas. "Financing Family Planning Programs."†

Preston, Samuel H. "Mortality and Development Revisited." In DaVanzo and others.

Sanderson, Warren C., and Jeffrey G. Williamson. "How Should the Developing Countries Adjust to External Shocks in the 1980s? Looking at Some World Bank Macromodels."†

Sapir, Andre. "Some Aspects of Population Growth, Trade, and Factor Mobility."†

Sjaastad, Lawrence, Aquiles Almansi, and Carlos Hurtado. "The Debt Crisis in Latin America."*

Standing, Guy. "Population Mobility and Productive Relations: Demographic Links and the Evolution of Policy."†

Swamy, Gurushri. "Population, International Migration, and Trade."†

Tan, Jee-Peng, and Michael Haines. "Schooling and Demand for Children: Historical Perspectives."†

Trussell, James, and Anne R. Pebley. "The Impact of Family Planning Programs on Infant, Child, and Maternal Mortality."†

Wheeler, David. "Female Education, Family Planning, Income, and Population: A Long-run Econometric Simulation Model." In Birdsall, ed.

Zachariah, K. C. "Determinants of Fertility Decline in India."†

Selected bibliography

Ascadi, George T., and Gwendolyn Johnson-Ascadi. 1983. ''Demand for Children and Spacing in Sub-Saharan Africa.'' Background paper for the ''Report on Population Strategies for Sub-Saharan Africa.'' Washington, D.C.: World Bank.

Atkinson, Linda, and others. 1980. ''Prospects for Improved Contraception.'' *Family Planning Perspectives* 12, 4.

Becker, Gary S. 1980. ''An Economic Analysis of Fertility.'' In *Demographic and Economic Change in Developed Countries*. Universities-National Bureau Conference Series, no. 11. Princeton, N.J.: Princeton University Press.

Bhatia, Shushum, and others. 1980. ''The Matlab Family Planning-Health Services Project.'' *Studies in Family Planning* 11, 6.

Birdsall, Nancy. 1980. ''Population Growth and Poverty in the Developing World.'' *Population Bulletin* 35, 5. (Also available as World Bank Staff Working Paper no. 404, 1980.)

Bongaarts, John. 1978. ''A Framework for Analyzing the Proximate Determinants of Fertility.'' *Population and Development Review* 4:105-32.

Bongaarts, J., and R. G. Potter. 1983. *Fertility, Biology and Behavior: An Analysis of the Proximate Determinants*. New York: Academic Press.

Bulatao, Rodolfo A. 1981. ''Values and Disvalues of Children in Successive Childbearing Decisions.'' *Demography* 18:1-25.

Bulatao, Rodolfo A., and Ronald D. Lee, eds. 1983. *Determinants of Fertility in Developing Countries*. 2 vols. New York: Academic Press.

Cassen, Robert H. 1978. *India*. New York: Holmes and Meier.

Casterline, John B., and others. 1983. ''The Proximate Determinants of Fertility.'' Unpublished paper. World Fertility Survey, London.

Chen, L. C., and others. ''Maternal Mortality in Rural Bangladesh.'' In *Studies in Family Planning* 5, 11:334-41, November 1974.

Coale, Ansley, and Susan Watkins, eds. 1984. *The Decline of Fertility in Europe*. Princeton, N.J.: Princeton University Press.

Cochrane, Susan H. 1983. ''Effects of Education and Urbanization on Fertility.'' In Rodolfo A. Bulatao and Ronald D. Lee, eds., *Determinants of Fertility in Developing Countries*. New York: Academic Press.

Cochrane, Susan H., Donald J. O'Hara, and Joanne Leslie. 1980. ''The Effects of Education on Health.'' World Bank Staff Working Paper no. 405. Washington, D.C.

Deevey, Edward. 1960. ''The Human Population.'' *Scientific American* 203, 3:195-204.

Demeny, Paul. 1984. ''A Perspective on Long-term Population Growth.'' Center for Policy Studies Working Paper no. 104. New York: The Population Council.

Durand, John D. 1977. ''Historical Estimates of World Population: An Evaluation.'' *Population and Development Review* 3, 3:253-96.

Easterlin, Richard, A. 1975. ''An Economic Framework for Fertility Analysis.'' *Studies in Family Planning* 6:54-63.

Easterlin, Richard, A., ed. 1980. *Population and Economic Change in Developing Countries*. Chicago, Ill.: University of Chicago Press.

Faruqee, Rashid, and Ravi Gulhati. 1983. ''Rapid Population Growth in Sub-Saharan Africa: Issues and Policies.'' World Bank Staff Working Paper no. 559. Washington, D.C.

Food and Agriculture Organization of the United Nations (FAO). 1981. *Agriculture: Toward 2000*. Economic and Social Development Series no. 23. Rome.

———. 1981. *FAO Production Yearbook* 35. Rome.

Frank, Odile. 1983. ''Infertility in Sub-Saharan Africa.'' Center for Policy Studies Working Paper no. 97. New York: The Population Council.

Freedman, Ronald. 1979. ''Theories of Fertility Decline: A Reappraisal.'' *Social Forces* 58, 1:1-17.

Gilland, Bernard. 1983. ''Considerations on World Population and Food Supply.'' *Population and Development Review* 9, 2:203-11.

Habbakuk, H., and M. Postan. 1965. *The Cambridge Economic History of Europe* 6. Cambridge: Cambridge University Press.

Henry, Alice, and Phyllis T. Piotrow. 1979. ''Age at Marriage and Fertility.'' *Population Reports*, Series M, no. 4.

Higgins, G. M., and others. 1982. *Potential Population Supporting Capacities of Lands in the Developing World*. Rome: FAO.

Ho, Teresa J. 1979. ''Time Costs of Child Rearing in the Rural Philippines.'' *Population and Development Review* 5:643-62.

Jacobsen, Judith. 1983. ''Promoting Population Stabilization: Incentives for Small Families.'' *Worldwatch Paper 54*. Washington, D.C.: Worldwatch Institute.

Johansson, E. 1977. ''The History of Literacy in Sweden in Comparison with Some Other Countries.'' *Educational Reports Umea*, 12.

Johnston, Bruce F., and William C. Clark. 1982. *Redesigning Rural Development: A Strategic Perspective*. Baltimore, Md.: Johns Hopkins University Press.

Johnston, Bruce F., and Peter Kilby. 1975. *Agriculture and Structural Transformation*. New York: Oxford University Press.

Keyfitz, N., and W. Flieger. 1968. *World Population: An Analysis of Data*. Chicago: University of Chicago Press.

Kindleberger, Charles. 1973. *World in Recession*. Berkeley: University of California Press.

King, Timothy, and others. 1974. *Population Policies and Economic Development*. Baltimore, Md.: Johns Hopkins University Press.

Lal, Deepak. 1983. *The Poverty of ''Development Economics.''* Hobart Paperback 16. London: Institute of Economic Affairs.

Lindert, Peter H. 1983. ''The Changing Economic Costs and Benefits of Having Children.'' In *Determinants of Fertility in Developing Countries*. Rodolfo A. Bulatao and Ronald D. Lee, eds. New York: Academic Press.

——. 1984. "The Malthusian Case: Preindustrial England" (unpublished bibliographical note).

Linn, Johannes. 1983. *Cities in the Developing World: Policies for Their Equitable and Efficient Growth.* New York: Oxford University Press.

McCann, Margaret F., and others. 1981. "Breastfeeding, Fertility, and Family Planning." *Population Reports*, Series J, no. 24.

Meadows, Donella H., and others. 1972. *The Limits to Growth: A Report for the Club of Rome's Project on the Predicament of Mankind.* New York: Universe Books.

Mitra, Pradeep. 1983. "Accounting for Adjustment in Selected Semi-industrial Countries." *Discussion Paper* 70. Washington D.C.: Development Research Department, World Bank.

Morris, Leo, and others. 1981. "Contraceptive Prevalence Surveys: A New Source of Family Planning Data." *Population Reports*, Series M, no. 5. Baltimore, Md.: Population Information Program, Johns Hopkins University.

Mosk, Carl. 1983. *Patriarchy and Fertility: Japan and Sweden, 1880–1960.* New York: Academic Press.

Nortman, Dorothy, and Joanne Fisher. 1982. *Population and Family Planning Programs: A Compendium of Data through 1981*, 11th ed. New York: The Population Council.

Organisation for Economic Co-operation and Development. 1983. *OECD Economic Outlook.* Paris.

Page, Hilary J., and Ron Lesthaeghe, eds. 1981. *Child-spacing in Tropical Africa.* New York: Academic Press.

Pingali, P. L., and Hans P. Binswanger. 1983. "Population Density, Farming Intensity, Patterns of Labor Use and Mechanization." *Discussion Paper 11.* Washington D.C.: Agriculture and Rural Development Department, World Bank.

Riedel, James. 1984. "Trade as the Engine of Growth in Developing Countries Revisited." *Economic Journal* 94, 373.

Rostow, W. W. 1978. *The World Economy: History and Prospect.* Austin, Tx.: University of Texas Press.

Rutstein, Shea Oscar. 1982. "Infant and Child Mortality: Levels, Trends, and Demographic Differentials." WFS Comparative Study no. 24 (London, November 1982).

Sachs, Jeffrey. 1979. "Wages, Profits, and Macroeconomic Adjustment: A Comparative Study." *Brookings Papers on Economic Activity* 2:269-320.

——. 1983. "Theoretical Issues in International Borrowing." Working Paper 1189. Cambridge, Mass.: National Bureau of Economic Research.

Schultz, T. Paul. 1981. *Economics of Population.* Reading, Mass.: Addison Wesley.

Sen, Amartya. 1967. "Isolation, Assurance, and the Social Rate of Discount." *Quarterly Journal of Economics* 81, 1.

Simon, Julian. 1982. *The Ultimate Resource.* Princeton, N.J.: Princeton University Press.

Sivard, Ruth. 1983. *World Military and Social Expenditures 1983.* Washington, D.C.: World Priorities.

Stokes, C. Shannon, and Wayne A. Schutjer. 1983. "Access to Land and Fertility in Developing Countries." Paper prepared for the Conference on Rural Development and Human Fertility, Pennsylvania State University, University Park, Pennsylvania. Mimeo.

Tien, H. Y. 1983. "China: Demographic Billionaire." *Population Bulletin* 38, 2.

Tietze, Christopher. 1983. *Induced Abortion: A World Review 1983.* 5th ed. New York: The Population Council.

UN Department of International, Economic and Social Affairs. 1966. *World Population Prospects as Assessed in 1963.* Population Studies no. 41. New York.

——. 1966 and 1980. *Demographic Yearbook.* New York.

——. 1980. *Patterns of Urban and Rural Population Growth.* Population Studies no. 68. New York.

——. Forthcoming. *World Population Trends and Policies, 1983 Monitoring Report.* New York.

UN Department of International, Economic and Social Affairs and UN Fund for Population Activities. Various years. "Population Policy Compendiums." New York.

UN Educational, Scientific and Cultural Organization. 1983. *UNESCO Statistical Yearbook.* Paris.

UN Fund for Population Activities. 1983. *Report on Population Assistance, 1981.* New York.

US Bureau of the Census. 1960. *Historical Statistics of the United States: Colonial Times to 1957.* Washington, D.C.: US Government Printing Office.

US Congress, Office of Technology Assessment. 1982. *World Population and Fertility Planning Technologies: The Next 20 Years.* Washington D.C.: Government Printing Office.

Van de Walle, E., and J. Knodel. 1980. "Europe's Fertility Transition, New Evidence and Lessons for Today's Developing World." *Population Bulletin* 34, 6:3-43. Washington, D.C.: Population Reference Bureau.

Wolf, Martin, and others. 1984. *Costs of Protecting Jobs in Textiles and Clothing.* Thames Essay no. 38. London: Trade Policy Research Centre.

World Bank. 1981. *Accelerated Development in Sub-Saharan Africa: An Agenda for Action.* Washington, D.C.

World Bank. 1982a. *IDA in Retrospect: The First Two Decades of the International Development Association.* New York: Oxford University Press.

——. 1982b. *World Development Report 1982.* New York: Oxford University Press.

World Bank. 1983. *Sub-Saharan Africa: Progress Report on Development Prospects and Programs.* Washington, D.C.

Zimmerman, L. J. 1965. *Poor Lands, Rich Lands: The Widening Gap.* New York: Random House.

Annex

World
Development
Indicators

Contents

Key

Afghanistan	29	Hong Kong	90	Paraguay	67
Albania	121	Hungary	119	Peru	60
Algeria	81	India	11	Philippines	50
Angola	68	Indonesia	43	*Poland*	125
Argentina	83	*Iran, Islamic Republic of*	93	Portugal	82
Australia	110	*Iraq*	94	Romania	120
Austria	105	Ireland	100	Rwanda	12
Bangladesh	2	Israel	89	Saudi Arabia	97
Belgium	107	Italy	102	Senegal	39
Benin	17	Ivory Coast	56	Sierra Leone	28
Bhutan	30	Jamaica	62	Singapore	91
Bolivia	42	Japan	106	Somalia	15
Brazil	79	Jordan	74	South Africa	85
Bulgaria	122	*Kampuchea, Democratic*	31	Spain	101
Burma	6	Kenya	27	Sri Lanka	23
Burundi	13	*Korea, Democratic Republic of*	70	Sudan	35
Cameroon	54	Korea, Republic of	76	Sweden	116
Canada	111	Kuwait	98	Switzerland	118
Central African Republic	18	*Lao People's Democratic Republic*	32	Syrian Arab Republic	73
Chad	1	*Lebanon*	71	Tanzania	14
Chile	78	Lesotho	41	Thailand	48
China	19	Liberia	38	Togo	24
Colombia	66	Libya	96	Trinidad and Tobago	92
Congo, People's Republic of the	58	Madagascar	22	Tunisia	65
Costa Rica	59	Malawi	8	Turkey	64
Cuba	69	Malaysia	75	Uganda	10
Czechoslovakia	123	Mali	5	*Union of Soviet Socialist Republics*	126
Denmark	114	Mauritania	36	United Arab Emirates	99
Dominican Republic	61	Mexico	80	United Kingdom	104
Ecuador	63	*Mongolia*	72	United States	115
Egypt, Arab Republic of	46	Morocco	53	Upper Volta	9
El Salvador	47	*Mozambique*	33	Uruguay	84
Ethiopia	3	Nepal	4	Venezuela	87
Finland	108	Netherlands	109	*Viet Nam*	34
France	112	New Zealand	103	Yemen Arab Republic	40
German Democratic Republic	124	Nicaragua	55	Yemen, People's Democratic Republic of	37
Germany, Federal Republic of	113	Niger	21	Yugoslavia	86
Ghana	25	Nigeria	52	Zaire	7
Greece	88	Norway	117	Zambia	44
Guatemala	57	Oman	95	Zimbabwe	51
Guinea	20	Pakistan	26		
Haiti	16	Panama	77		
Honduras	45	Papua New Guinea	49		

Introduction

The World Development Indicators, a by-product of the World Bank's statistical and analytical work, provide information on the main features of social and economic development. Most of the data collected by the World Bank are on its developing member countries. Because comparable data for industrial market economies are readily available, these are also included in the indicators. Data for nonmarket economies, a few of which are members of the World Bank, are included if available in a comparable form.

Every effort has been made to standardize concepts, definitions, coverage, timing, and other characteristics of the basic data to ensure the greatest possible degree of comparability. Nevertheless, care must be taken in how the indicators are interpreted. Although the statistics are drawn from sources generally considered the most authoritative and reliable, many of them are subject to considerable margins of error. In addition, variations in national statistical practices mean that most data are not strictly comparable. The data should thus be construed only as indicating trends and characterizing major differences among economies.

The indicators in Table 1 give a summary profile of the economies. The data in the other tables fall into the following broad areas: national accounts, agriculture, industry, energy, external trade, external debt, aid flows, other external transactions, demography, labor force, urbanization, social indicators, central government finances, and income distribution. The table on central government expenditure is an expanded version of an earlier table, and is complemented by a new table on central government current revenue.

Most of the information used in computing the indicators was drawn from the data files and publications of the World Bank, the International Monetary Fund, and the United Nations and its specialized agencies.

For ease of reference, ratios and rates of growth are shown; absolute values are reported only in a few instances. Most growth rates were calculated for two periods: 1960–70 and 1970–82, or 1970–81 if data for 1982 were not available. All growth rates are in constant prices and were computed, unless noted otherwise, by using the least-squares method. Because this method takes all observations in a period into account, the resulting growth rates are not unduly influenced by exceptional values. Table entries in italics indicate that they are for years or periods other than those specified. All dollar figures are US dollars, derived by applying the official exchange rates, with the exception of the GNP per capita figures, which are derived by applying the *World Bank Atlas* method described in the technical note to Table 1. Conversion of national currency values in this manner results in some inevitable distortions; the technical note to Table l also discusses this problem.

Some of the differences between figures shown in this year's and last year's editions reflect not only updating but also revisions to historical series.

The economies included in the World Development Indicators are classified by GNP per capita. This classification is useful in distinguishing economies at different stages of development. Many of the economies included are also classified by dominant characteristics—to distinguish oil importers from oil exporters and to distinguish industrial market from industrial nonmarket economies. The groups used in the tables are 34 low-income developing economies with a GNP per capita of less than $410 in 1982, 60 middle-income developing economies with a GNP per capita of $410 or more, 5 high-income oil exporters, 19 industrial market economies, and 8 East European nonmarket economies. Note that because of the paucity of data and differences in the method of computing national income, estimates of GNP per capita are available only for those nonmarket economies that are members of the World Bank.

The format of this edition generally follows that used in previous years. An important difference, however, is that economies for which no GNP per capita figure can be calculated are listed in italics, in alphabetical order, at the end of the appropriate income groups. All other economies are listed by group in ascending order of GNP per capita. The same order is used in all tables. The alphabetical list in the key shows the reference number of each economy; italics indicate those economies placed at the end of a group due to the unavailability of GNP per capita figures. Countries with populations of less than a million are not reported in the tables, largely for lack of comprehensive data. The technical note to Table 1 shows some basic indicators for 34 small countries that are members of the United Nations, the World Bank, or both.

Summary measures—totals, median values, or weighted averages—were calculated for the economy groups only if data were adequate and meaningful statistics could be obtained. Because China and India heavily influence the overall summary measures for the low-income economies, summary measures are separately shown for China and India and for other low-income economies. And because trade in oil affects the economic characteristics and performance of middle-income economies, summary measures are also shown for oil importers and for oil exporters. Moreover, the group of middle-income economies is divided into lower and upper categories to provide more meaningful summary measures.

The weights used in computing the summary measures are described in the technical notes. The letter w after a summary measure indicates that it is a weighted average; the letter m, that it is a median value; the letter t, that it is a total. The median is the middle value of a data set arranged in order of magnitude. Because the coverage of

Groups of economies

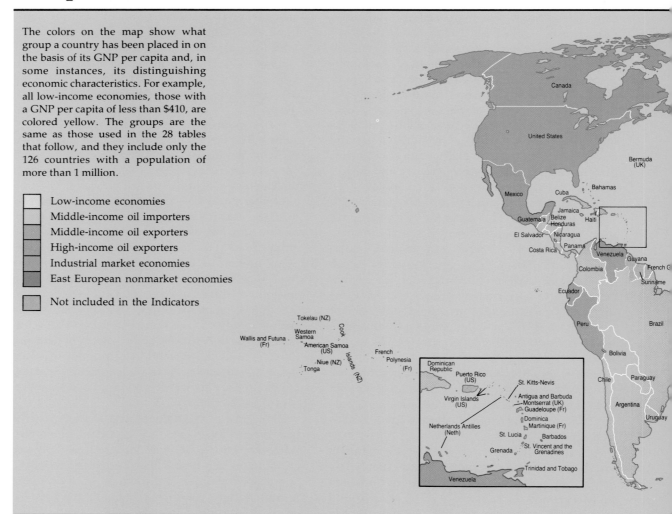

The colors on the map show what group a country has been placed in on the basis of its GNP per capita and, in some instances, its distinguishing economic characteristics. For example, all low-income economies, those with a GNP per capita of less than $410, are colored yellow. The groups are the same as those used in the 28 tables that follow, and they include only the 126 countries with a population of more than 1 million.

☐ Low-income economies
☐ Middle-income oil importers
☐ Middle-income oil exporters
☐ High-income oil exporters
☐ Industrial market economies
☐ East European nonmarket economies

☐ Not included in the Indicators

economies is not uniform for all indicators and because the variation around central tendencies can be large, readers should exercise caution in comparing the summary measures for different indicators, groups, and years or periods.

The technical notes should be referred to in any use of the data. These notes outline the methods, concepts, definitions, and data sources. The bibliography gives details of the data sources, which contain comprehensive definitions and descriptions of concepts used.

This year's edition includes four world maps. The first map shows country names and the groups in which economies have been placed. The maps on the following pages show population, life expectancy at birth, and the share of agriculture in gross domestic product (GDP). The Eckert IV projection has been used for these maps because it maintains correct areas for all countries, though at the cost of some distortions in shape, distance, and direction. The maps have been prepared exclusively for the convenience of the readers of this Report; the denominations used, and the boundaries shown, do not imply on the part of the World Bank and its affiliates any judgment on the legal status of any territory or any endorsement or acceptance of such boundaries.

The World Development Indicators are prepared under the supervision of Ramesh Chander.

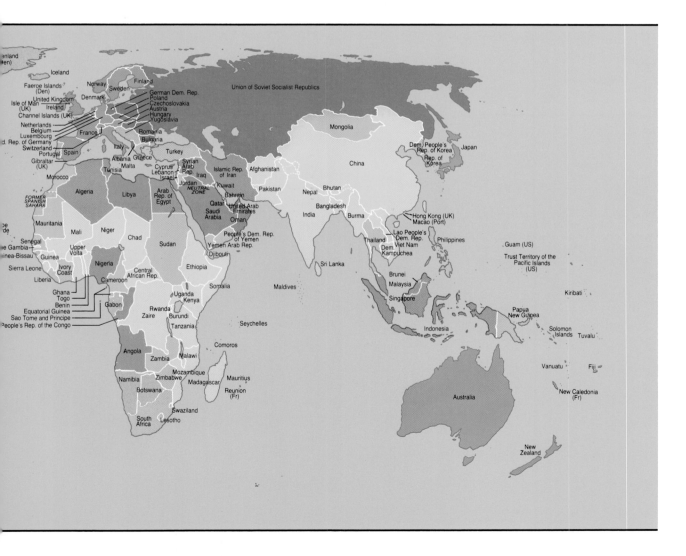

Population

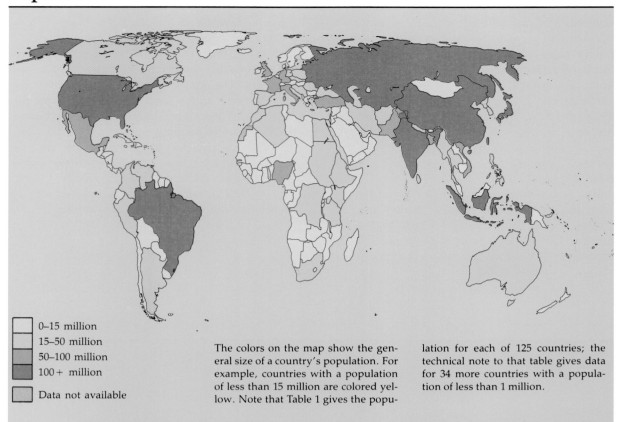

0–15 million
15–50 million
50–100 million
100 + million

Data not available

The colors on the map show the general size of a country's population. For example, countries with a population of less than 15 million are colored yellow. Note that Table 1 gives the population for each of 125 countries; the technical note to that table gives data for 34 more countries with a population of less than 1 million.

The bar chart at right shows population by country group for the years 1960 and 1982 as well as projected population for the year 2000. The country groups are those used in the map on the preceding pages and in the tables that follow.

The pie chart at right shows the proportion of total population, excluding countries with populations of less than 1 million, accounted for by each country group. "Other" refers to high-income oil producers.

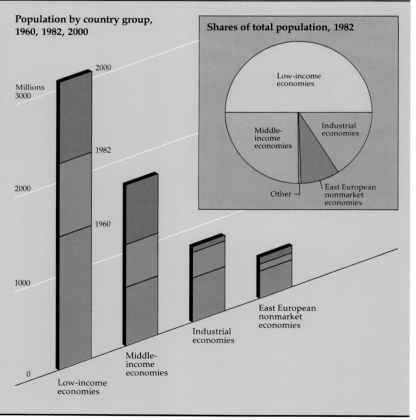

Population by country group, 1960, 1982, 2000

Shares of total population, 1982

Life expectancy

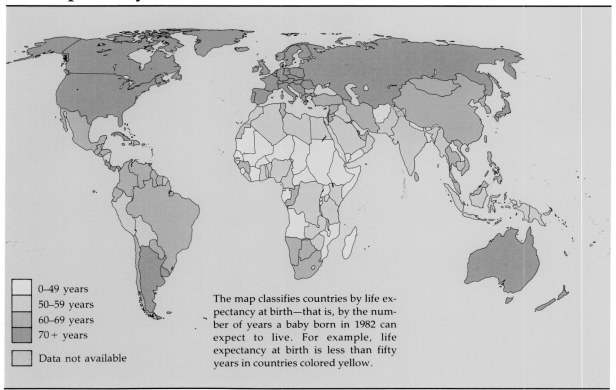

0–49 years	
50–59 years	
60–69 years	
70 + years	
Data not available	

The map classifies countries by life expectancy at birth—that is, by the number of years a baby born in 1982 can expect to live. For example, life expectancy at birth is less than fifty years in countries colored yellow.

Share of agriculture in GDP

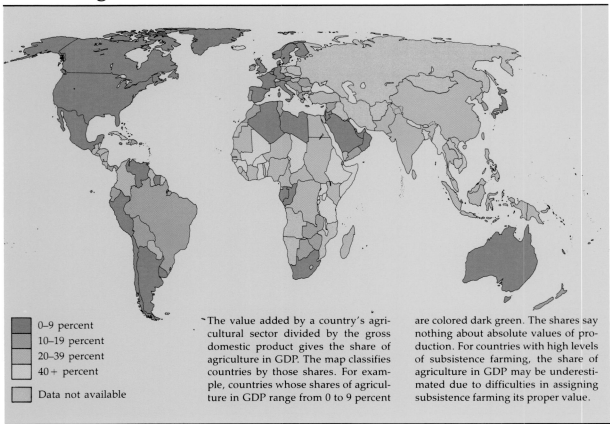

0–9 percent	
10–19 percent	
20–39 percent	
40 + percent	
Data not available	

The value added by a country's agricultural sector divided by the gross domestic product gives the share of agriculture in GDP. The map classifies countries by those shares. For example, countries whose shares of agriculture in GDP range from 0 to 9 percent are colored dark green. The shares say nothing about absolute values of production. For countries with high levels of subsistence farming, the share of agriculture in GDP may be underestimated due to difficulties in assigning subsistence farming its proper value.

Table 1. Basic indicators

	Population (millions) mid–1982	Area (thousands of square kilometers)	GNP per capita[a] Dollars 1982	GNP per capita[a] Average annual growth rate (percent) 1960–82[b]	Average annual rate of inflation[a] (percent) 1960–70[c]	Average annual rate of inflation[a] (percent) 1970–82[d]	Life expectancy at birth (years) 1982
Low-income economies	2,266.5 t	29,097 t	280 w	3.0 w	3.2 m	11.5 m	59 w
China and India	1,725.2 t	12,849 t	290 w	3.5 w	..	..	62 w
Other low-income	541.3 t	16,248 t	250 w	1.1 w	3.2 m	11.7 m	51 w
1 Chad	4.6	1,284	80	−2.8	4.6	7.8	44
2 Bangladesh	92.9	144	140	0.3	3.7	14.9	48
3 Ethiopia	32.9	1,222	140	1.4	2.1	4.0	47
4 Nepal	15.4	141	170	−0.1	7.7	8.9	46
5 Mali	7.1	1,240	180	1.6	5.0	9.8	45
6 Burma	34.9	677	190	1.3	2.7	9.7	55
7 Zaire	30.7	2,345	190	−0.3	29.9	35.3	50
8 Malawi	6.5	118	210	2.6	2.4	9.5	44
9 Upper Volta	6.5	274	210	1.1	1.3	9.7	44
10 Uganda	13.5	236	230	−1.1	3.2	47.4	47
11 India	717.0	3,288	260	1.3	7.1	8.4	55
12 Rwanda	5.5	26	260	1.7	13.1	13.4	46
13 Burundi	4.3	28	280	2.5	2.8	12.5	47
14 Tanzania	19.8	945	280	1.9	1.8	11.9	52
15 Somalia	4.5	638	290	−0.1	4.5	12.6	39
16 Haiti	5.2	28	300	0.6	4.0	9.2	54
17 Benin	3.7	113	310	0.6	1.9	9.6	48
18 Central African Rep.	2.4	623	310	0.6	4.1	12.6	48
19 China	1,008.2	9,561	310	5.0	..	..	67
20 Guinea	5.7	246	310	1.5	1.5	3.3	38
21 Niger	5.9	1,267	310	−1.5	2.1	12.1	45
22 Madagascar	9.2	587	320	−0.5	3.2	11.5	48
23 Sri Lanka	15.2	66	320	2.6	1.8	13.3	69
24 Togo	2.8	57	340	2.3	1.3	8.8	47
25 Ghana	12.2	239	360	−1.3	7.5	39.5	55
26 Pakistan	87.1	804	380	2.8	3.3	12.7	50
27 Kenya	18.1	583	390	2.8	1.6	10.1	57
28 Sierra Leone	3.2	72	390	0.9	..	12.2	38
29 Afghanistan	16.8	648	..	..	11.9	..	36
30 Bhutan	1.2	47	..	..	..	..	43
31 Kampuchea, Dem.	..	181	..	..	..	..	..
32 Lao PDR	3.6	237	..	..	..	..	43
33 Mozambique	12.9	802	..	..	..	..	51
34 Viet Nam	57.0	330	..	..	..	..	64
Middle-income economies	1,158.3 t	43,031 t	1,520 w	3.6 w	3.0 m	12.8 m	60 w
Oil exporters	519.5 t	15,036 t	1,260 w	3.6 w	3.0 m	13.9 m	57 w
Oil importers	638.8 t	27,995 t	1,710 w	3.5 w	3.0 m	12.7 m	63 w
Lower middle-income	669.6 t	20,952 t	840 w	3.2 w	2.9 m	11.7 m	56 w
35 Sudan	20.2	2,506	440	−0.4	3.9	15.2	47
36 Mauritania	1.6	1,031	470	1.4	2.1	8.7	45
37 Yemen, PDR	2.0	333	470	6.4	..	..	46
38 Liberia	2.0	111	490	0.9	1.9	8.5	54
39 Senegal	6.0	196	490	(.)	1.8	7.9	44
40 Yemen Arab Rep.	7.5	195	500	5.1	..	15.0	44
41 Lesotho	1.4	30	510	6.5	2.7	11.4	53
42 Bolivia	5.9	1,099	570	1.7	3.5	25.9	51
43 Indonesia	152.6	1,919	580	4.2	..	19.9	53
44 Zambia	6.0	753	640	−0.1	7.6	8.7	51
45 Honduras	4.0	112	660	1.0	2.9	8.7	60
46 Egypt, Arab Rep.	44.3	1,001	690	3.6	2.6	11.9	57
47 El Salvador	5.1	21	700	0.9	0.5	10.8	63
48 Thailand	48.5	514	790	4.5	1.8	9.7	63
49 Papua New Guinea	3.1	462	820	2.1	4.0	8.1	53
50 Philippines	50.7	300	820	2.8	5.8	12.8	64
51 Zimbabwe	7.5	391	850	1.5	1.1	8.4	56
52 Nigeria	90.6	924	860	3.3	4.0	14.4	50
53 Morocco	20.3	447	870	2.6	2.0	8.3	52
54 Cameroon	9.3	475	890	2.6	4.2	10.7	53
55 Nicaragua	2.9	130	920	0.2	1.8	14.3	58
56 Ivory Coast	8.9	322	950	2.1	2.8	12.4	47
57 Guatemala	7.7	109	1,130	2.4	0.3	10.1	60
58 Congo, People's Rep.	1.7	342	1,180	2.7	4.7	10.8	60
59 Costa Rica	2.3	51	1,430	2.8	1.9	18.4	74
60 Peru	17.4	1,285	1,310	1.0	10.4	37.0	58
61 Dominican Rep.	5.7	49	1,330	3.2	2.1	8.8	62
62 Jamaica	2.2	11	1,330	0.7	4.0	16.2	73
63 Ecuador	8.0	284	1,350	4.8	6.1	14.5	63
64 Turkey	46.5	781	1,370	3.4	5.6	34.4	63

Note: For data comparability and coverage see the technical notes.

		Population (millions) mid-1982	Area (thousands of square kilometers)	GNP per capita[a] Dollars 1982	GNP per capita[a] Average annual growth rate (percent) 1960-82[b]	Average annual rate of inflation[a] (percent) 1960-70[c]	Average annual rate of inflation[a] (percent) 1970-82[d]	Life expectancy at birth (years) 1982
65	Tunisia	6.7	164	1,390	4.7	3.6	8.7	61
66	Colombia	27.0	1,139	1,460	3.1	11.9	22.7	64
67	Paraguay	3.1	407	1,610	3.7	3.1	12.7	65
68	*Angola*	8.0	1,247	..	..	..	..	43
69	*Cuba*	9.8	115	..	..	..	..	75
70	*Korea, Dem. Rep.*	18.7	121	..	..	..	..	64
71	*Lebanon*	2.6	10	..	..	1.4	..	65
72	*Mongolia*	1.8	1,565	..	..	..	..	65
Upper middle-income		**488.7** *t*	**22,079** *t*	**2,490** *w*	**4.1** *w*	**3.0** *m*	**16.4** *m*	**65** *w*
73	Syrian Arab Rep.	9.5	185	1,680	4.0	2.6	*12.2*	66
74	Jordan	3.1	98	1,690	6.9	..	9.6	64
75	Malaysia	14.5	330	1,860	4.3	−0.3	7.2	67
76	Korea, Rep. of	39.3	98	1,910	6.6	17.5	19.3	67
77	Panama	1.9	77	2,120	3.4	1.5	7.5	71
78	Chile	11.5	757	2,210	0.6	33.0	144.3	70
79	Brazil	126.8	8,512	2,240	4.8	46.1	*42.1*	64
80	Mexico	73.1	1,973	2,270	3.7	3.5	20.9	65
81	Algeria	19.9	2,382	2,350	3.2	2.7	13.9	57
82	Portugal	10.1	92	2,450	4.8	3.0	17.4	71
83	Argentina	28.4	2,767	2,520	1.6	21.4	136.0	70
84	Uruguay	2.9	176	2,650	1.7	50.2	59.3	73
85	South Africa	30.4	1,221	2,670	2.1	3.0	12.8	63
86	Yugoslavia	22.6	256	2,800	4.9	12.6	20.0	71
87	Venezuela	16.7	912	4,140	1.9	1.3	12.4	68
88	Greece	9.8	132	4,290	5.2	3.2	15.4	74
89	Israel	4.0	21	5,090	3.2	6.4	52.3	74
90	Hong Kong	5.2	1	5,340	7.0	2.4	8.6	75
91	Singapore	2.5	1	5,910	7.4	1.1	5.4	72
92	Trinidad and Tobago	1.1	5	6,840	3.1	3.2	17.8	68
93	*Iran, Islamic Rep.*	41.2	1,648	..	..	−0.5	..	60
94	*Iraq*	14.2	435	..	..	1.7	..	59
High-income oil exporters		**17.0** *t*	**4,312** *t*	**14,820** *w*	**5.6** *w*	**..**	**16.0** *m*	**58** *w*
95	Oman	1.1	300	6,090	7.4	..	..	52
96	Libya	3.2	1,760	8,510	4.1	5.2	16.0	57
97	Saudi Arabia	10.0	2,150	16,000	7.5	..	22.5	56
98	Kuwait	1.6	18	19,870	−0.1	..	15.6	71
99	United Arab Emirates	1.1	84	23,770	−0.7	..	..	71
Industrial market economies		**722.9** *t*	**30,935** *t*	**11,070** *w*	**3.3** *w*	**4.3** *m*	**9.9** *m*	**75** *w*
100	Ireland	3.5	70	5,150	2.9	5.2	14.3	73
101	Spain	37.9	505	5,430	4.0	6.8	16.0	74
102	Italy	56.3	301	6,840	3.4	4.4	16.0	74
103	New Zealand	3.2	269	7,920	1.5	3.6	13.1	73
104	United Kingdom	55.8	245	9,660	2.0	4.1	14.2	74
105	Austria	7.6	84	9,880	3.9	3.7	6.1	73
106	Japan	118.4	372	10,080	6.1	5.1	6.9	77
107	Belgium	9.9	31	10,760	3.6	3.6	7.1	73
108	Finland	4.8	337	10,870	3.6	6.0	11.7	73
109	Netherlands	14.3	41	10,930	2.9	5.4	7.4	76
110	Australia	15.2	7,687	11,140	2.4	3.1	11.4	74
111	Canada	24.6	9,976	11,320	3.1	3.1	9.3	75
112	France	54.4	547	11,680	3.7	4.2	10.1	75
113	Germany, Fed. Rep.	61.6	249	12,460	3.1	3.2	4.9	73
114	Denmark	5.1	43	12,470	2.5	6.4	9.9	75
115	United States	231.5	9,363	13,160	2.2	2.9	7.3	75
116	Sweden	8.3	450	14,040	2.4	4.3	9.9	77
117	Norway	4.1	324	14,280	3.4	4.4	9.0	76
118	Switzerland	6.4	41	17,010	1.9	4.4	4.8	79
East European nonmarket economies		**383.3** *t*	**23,422** *t*	**..**	**..**	**..**	**..**	**70** *w*
119	Hungary	10.7	93	2,270	6.3	..	3.2	71
120	Romania	22.5	238	2,560	*5.1*	..	..	71
121	*Albania*	2.9	29	..	..	..	..	72
122	*Bulgaria*	8.9	111	..	..	..	..	72
123	*Czechoslovakia*	15.4	128	..	..	..	..	72
124	*German Dem. Rep.*	16.7	108	..	..	..	..	73
125	*Poland*	36.2	313	..	..	..	..	72
126	*USSR*	270.0	22,402	..	..	..	..	69

a. See the technical notes. b. Because data for the early 1960s are not always available, figures in italics are for periods other than that specified. c. Figures in italics are for 1961–70, not 1960–70. d. Figures in italics are for 1970–81, not 1970–82.

Table 2. Growth of production

	GDP 1960–70[a]	GDP 1970–82[b]	Agriculture 1960–70[a]	Agriculture 1970–82[b]	Industry 1960–70[a]	Industry 1970–82[b]	Manufacturing 1960–70[a]	Manufacturing 1970–82[b]	Services 1960–70[a]	Services 1970–82[b]
Low-income economies	4.5 w	4.5 w	2.2 m	2.3 m	6.6 m	4.2 m	5.5 m	3.4 m	4.2 m	4.5 m
China and India	4.5 w	4.9 w	1.8 m	2.3 m	8.3 m	6.3 m	..	..	5.2 m	4.9 m
Other low-income	4.5 w	3.4 w	2.7 m	2.3 m	6.6 m	4.0 m	6.3 m	3.2 m	4.2 m	4.5 m
1 Chad	0.5	−2.6	..	−1.0	..	−2.0	..	−3.2	..	−5.5
2 Bangladesh	3.7	4.1	2.7	2.3	8.0	8.7	6.6	10.4	4.2	5.5
3 Ethiopia	4.4	2.2	2.2	0.9	7.4	2.0	8.0	2.9	7.8	4.1
4 Nepal	2.5	2.7	..	..	..	..	..	..	..	..
5 Mali	3.3	4.3	..	3.8	..	2.1	..	..	..	5.4
6 Burma	2.6	5.0	4.1	5.0	2.8	5.8	3.4	4.7	1.5	5.6
7 Zaire	3.4	−0.2	..	1.5	..	−0.9	..	−2.3	..	−0.4
8 Malawi	4.9	5.1	..	4.1	..	5.4	..	5.4	..	6.0
9 Upper Volta	3.0	3.4	..	1.4	..	2.9	..	3.4	..	5.4
10 Uganda	5.6	−1.5	..	−0.6	..	−8.7	..	−8.9	..	1.3
11 India	3.4	3.6	1.9	1.8	5.4	4.3	4.7	4.5	4.6	5.5
12 Rwanda	2.7	5.3	..	..	..	..	..	..	..	..
13 Burundi	4.4	3.5	..	2.3	..	8.6	..	6.4	..	4.0
14 Tanzania	6.0	4.0	..	2.8	..	1.5	..	0.5	..	5.8
15 Somalia	1.0	3.8	−0.6	..	3.4	..	4.0	..	4.2	..
16 Haiti	0.2	3.4	−0.6	1.2	0.2	7.3	−0.1	7.5	1.1	3.3
17 Benin	2.6	3.3	..	..	..	..	..	..	..	..
18 Central African Rep.	1.9	1.4	0.8	2.3	5.4	4.0	..	−4.3	1.8	0.3
19 China	5.2	5.6	1.6	2.8	11.2	8.3	..	..	5.7	4.3
20 Guinea	3.5	3.8	..	..	..	..	..	..	..	..
21 Niger	2.9	3.4	3.3	−2.4	13.9	10.8	..	..	(.)	6.9
22 Madagascar	2.9	0.2	..	0.3	..	−0.7	..	..	..	0.4
23 Sri Lanka	4.6	4.5	3.0	3.2	6.6	4.2	6.3	2.4	4.6	5.2
24 Togo	8.8	3.0	..	1.7	..	5.5	..	−10.0	..	2.9
25 Ghana	2.2	−0.5	..	−0.2	..	−2.4	..	−1.5	..	−7.5
26 Pakistan	6.7	5.0	4.9	2.7	10.0	5.9	9.4	5.0	7.0	6.2
27 Kenya	5.9	5.5	..	4.1	..	8.1	..	9.0	..	5.6
28 Sierra Leone	4.3	2.0	..	2.5	..	−3.1	..	3.9	..	4.5
29 Afghanistan	2.0	..	..	..	..	..	..	..	..	..
30 Bhutan	..	..	..	..	..	..	..	..	..	..
31 Kampuchea, Dem.	3.1	..	..	..	..	..	..	..	..	..
32 Lao PDR	..	..	..	..	..	..	..	..	..	..
33 Mozambique	..	..	..	..	..	..	..	..	..	..
34 Viet Nam	3.8	..	..	..	..	..	..	..	..	..
Middle-income economies	6.0 w	5.4 w	3.5 m	3.0 m	7.4 m	5.8 m	7.3 m	5.5 m	5.5 m	5.5 m
Oil exporters	6.3 w	6.0 w	2.9 m	3.0 m	7.4 m	7.6 m	7.1 m	9.6 m	4.8 m	6.8 m
Oil importers	5.8 w	5.1 w	3.5 m	2.8 m	7.0 m	5.5 m	7.5 m	5.3 m	5.7 m	5.2 m
Lower middle-income	4.9 w	5.3 w	3.0 m	3.1 m	6.2 m	5.8 m	6.5 m	5.5 m	5.2 m	5.4 m
35 Sudan	0.7	6.3	..	4.1	..	5.8	..	6.0	..	8.5
36 Mauritania	6.7	2.0	1.4	3.4	14.1	−3.5	9.2	5.2	7.4	5.2
37 Yemen, PDR	..	..	..	..	..	..	..	..	..	..
38 Liberia	5.1	0.9	..	3.5	..	−0.7	..	4.5	..	1.0
39 Senegal	2.5	2.9	2.9	2.3	4.1	3.8	6.2	0.8	1.8	2.8
40 Yemen Arab Rep.	..	8.5	..	3.6	..	13.6	..	13.1	..	11.2
41 Lesotho	5.2	6.6	..	0.3	..	21.1	..	13.4	..	5.5
42 Bolivia	5.2	3.7	3.0	3.7	6.2	2.3	5.4	4.4	5.4	4.4
43 Indonesia	3.9	7.7	2.7	3.8	5.2	10.7	3.3	13.4	4.8	9.3
44 Zambia	5.0	0.9	..	1.9	..	0.4	..	1.4	..	1.3
45 Honduras	5.2	4.2	5.8	2.4	5.3	5.7	4.5	5.8	4.6	4.7
46 Egypt, Arab Rep.	4.3	8.4	2.9	3.0	5.4	8.3	4.8	9.3	4.7	11.7
47 El Salvador	5.9	2.2	3.0	2.0	8.5	2.0	8.8	1.1	6.5	2.4
48 Thailand	8.4	7.1	5.6	4.4	11.9	9.3	11.4	9.9	9.1	7.4
49 Papua New Guinea	6.7	2.0	..	2.6	..	4.9	..	5.5	..	..
50 Philippines	5.1	6.0	4.3	4.8	6.0	8.0	6.7	6.6	5.2	5.2
51 Zimbabwe	4.5	2.2	..	1.8	..	−1.9	..	−4.1	..	2.9
52 Nigeria	3.1	3.8	−0.4	−0.6	14.7	4.8	9.1	12.0	2.3	6.7
53 Morocco	4.4	5.0	4.7	0.1	4.2	5.3	4.2	4.9	4.4	6.3
54 Cameroon	3.7	7.0	..	3.4	..	12.2	..	8.4	..	7.2
55 Nicaragua	7.3	0.6	7.8	2.5	10.4	1.7	11.4	2.5	5.8	−0.9
56 Ivory Coast	8.0	5.7	4.2	4.5	11.5	8.6	11.6	5.4	9.7	5.4
57 Guatemala	5.6	5.0	4.3	3.9	7.8	6.7	8.2	5.3	5.5	5.0
58 Congo, People's Rep.	3.5	6.8	1.8	1.9	7.4	12.0	..	3.3	2.8	5.1
59 Costa Rica	6.5	4.5	5.7	2.3	9.4	6.1	10.6	6.0	5.7	4.6
60 Peru	4.9	3.0	3.7	0.7	5.0	3.3	5.7	2.5	5.3	3.4
61 Dominican Rep.	4.5	6.0	2.1	3.3	6.0	6.9	5.0	5.9	5.0	6.5
62 Jamaica	4.4	−1.1	1.4	−0.2	4.9	−3.5	5.7	−2.3	4.6	0.1
63 Ecuador	..	8.1	..	2.9	..	11.3	..	9.9	..	8.4
64 Turkey	6.0	5.1	2.5	3.2	9.6	5.6	10.9	5.2	6.9	5.9

Note: For data comparability and coverage see the technical notes.

		Average annual growth rate (percent)									
		GDP		Agriculture		Industry		Manufacturing		Services	
		1960–70[a]	1970–82[b]	1960–70[a]	1970–82[b]	1960–70[a]	1970–82[b]	1960–70[a]	1970–82[b]	1960–70[a]	1970–82[b]
65	Tunisia	4.7	7.0	2.0	3.6	10.9	8.0	7.8	11.6	2.6	7.6
66	Colombia	5.1	5.4	3.5	4.5	6.0	4.4	5.7	5.2	5.7	6.5
67	Paraguay	4.2	8.5	. .	6.7	. .	10.7	. .	7.8	. .	8.8
68	*Angola*	. .	. .	. .	. .	. .	. .	. .	. .	. .	. .
69	*Cuba*	. .	. .	. .	. .	. .	. .	. .	. .	. .	. .
70	*Korea, Dem. Rep.*	. .	. .	. .	. .	. .	. .	. .	. .	. .	. .
71	*Lebanon*	4.9	. .	6.3	. .	4.5	. .	5.0	. .	4.8	. .
72	*Mongolia*	. .	. .	. .	. .	. .	. .	. .	. .	. .	. .
Upper middle-income		**6.4** w	**5.4** w	**4.0** m	**2.6** m	**9.1** m	**5.7** m	**8.4** m	**5.8** m	**7.2** m	**6.3** m
73	Syrian Arab Rep.	4.6	8.8	. .	. .	. .	. .	. .	. .	. .	. .
74	Jordan	. .	9.3	. .	0.2	. .	13.5	. .	10.9	. .	9.4
75	Malaysia	6.5	7.7	. .	5.1	. .	9.2	. .	10.6	. .	8.4
76	Korea, Rep. of	8.6	8.6	4.4	2.9	17.2	13.6	17.6	14.5	8.9	7.8
77	Panama	7.8	4.7	5.8	2.0	9.9	4.4	10.5	2.7	7.7	5.3
78	Chile	4.4	1.9	3.1	3.1	4.4	0.6	5.5	−0.4	4.6	2.7
79	Brazil	5.4	7.6	. .	4.5	. .	8.2	. .	7.8	. .	7.7
80	Mexico	7.6	6.4	4.5	3.4	9.4	7.2	10.1	6.8	7.3	6.5
81	Algeria	4.3	6.6	0.1	3.9	11.6	7.0	7.8	10.9	−1.1	6.4
82	Portugal	6.2	4.5	1.3	−0.8	8.8	4.4	8.9	4.5	5.9	6.1
83	Argentina	4.3	1.5	1.8	2.2	5.8	1.0	5.6	−0.2	3.8	1.7
84	Uruguay	1.2	3.1	1.9	1.2	1.2	4.2	1.5	3.4	1.1	2.8
85	South Africa	6.3	3.6	. .	. .	. .	. .	. .	. .	. .	. .
86	Yugoslavia	5.8	5.5	3.3	3.1	6.2	7.2	5.7	8.2	6.9	4.5
87	Venezuela	6.0	4.1	5.8	3.0	4.6	2.4	6.4	4.8	7.3	5.3
88	Greece	6.9	4.1	3.5	1.9	9.4	3.9	10.2	4.8	7.1	4.9
89	Israel	8.1	3.1	. .	. .	. .	. .	. .	. .	. .	. .
90	Hong Kong	10.0	9.9	. .	. .	. .	. .	. .	. .	. .	. .
91	Singapore	8.8	8.5	5.0	1.6	12.5	8.9	13.0	9.3	7.7	8.6
92	Trinidad and Tobago	4.0	5.5	. .	−1.8	. .	4.0	. .	1.3	. .	6.9
93	*Iran, Islamic Rep.*	11.3	. .	4.4	. .	13.4	. .	12.0	. .	10.0	. .
94	*Iraq*	6.1	. .	5.7	. .	4.7	. .	5.9	. .	8.3	. .
High-income oil exporters		**16.7** w	**5.0** w	. .	**5.6** m	. .	**−2.8** m	. .	**9.5** m	. .	**12.4** m
95	Oman	19.5	5.8	. .	. .	. .	. .	. .	. .	. .	. .
96	Libya	24.4	2.4	. .	10.5	. .	−3.1	. .	14.7	. .	17.3
97	Saudi Arabia	. .	9.8	. .	5.6	. .	8.9	. .	6.8	. .	12.4
98	Kuwait	5.7	2.1	. .	5.5	. .	−2.8	. .	9.5	. .	9.6
99	United Arab Emirates	. .	. .	. .	. .	. .	. .	. .	. .	. .	. .
Industrial market economies		**5.1** w	**2.8** w	**1.4** m	**1.8** m	**5.9** m	**2.3** m	**5.9** m	**2.4** m	**4.5** m	**3.2** m
100	Ireland	4.2	3.8	0.9	. .	6.1	. .	. .	. .	4.3	. .
101	Spain	7.1	3.1	. .	2.0	. .	3.4	. .	4.1	. .	3.9
102	Italy	5.5	2.8	2.6	1.2	6.6	2.7	8.0	. .	5.1	3.2
103	New Zealand	3.6	1.8	. .	. .	. .	. .	. .	. .	. .	. .
104	United Kingdom	2.9	1.5	2.2	1.9	3.1	0.2	3.3	−0.8	2.8	2.4
105	Austria	4.6	3.3	1.2	1.5	5.4	3.0	5.2	3.2	4.4	3.8
106	Japan	10.4	4.6	2.1	−0.2	13.0	5.6	13.6	6.6	10.2	4.1
107	Belgium	4.7	2.7	−0.5	1.5	5.5	2.2	6.2	2.3	4.6	3.1
108	Finland	4.3	3.0	0.5	(.)	5.2	3.3	6.1	3.8	5.0	3.5
109	Netherlands	5.2	2.4	2.8	4.3	6.8	1.2	6.6	1.9	5.1	2.9
110	Australia	5.6	3.1	2.0	2.5	5.9	1.6	5.5	1.5	4.0	4.1
111	Canada	5.6	3.4	2.5	2.0	6.3	2.3	6.8	2.5	5.5	4.0
112	France	5.5	3.2	1.6	0.8	7.1	2.4	7.8	2.8	5.0	3.9
113	Germany, Fed. Rep.	4.4	2.4	1.5	2.2	4.8	2.0	5.4	2.0	4.2	3.2
114	Denmark	4.5	2.1	0.1	3.1	5.2	0.9	5.2	2.9	4.6	2.5
115	United States	4.3	2.7	0.5	1.7	4.6	1.9	5.3	2.4	4.4	3.2
116	Sweden	4.4	1.7	0.8	−0.8	6.2	0.7	5.9	0.5	3.9	2.6
117	Norway	4.3	4.3	0.7	1.9	4.8	4.8	4.8	1.1	5.0	4.1
118	Switzerland	4.3	0.7	. .	. .	. .	. .	. .	. .	. .	. .
East European nonmarket economies		. .	. .	. .	. .	. .	. .	. .	. .	. .	. .
119	Hungary[c]	5.3	4.8	3.2	3.2	6.2	5.5	6.5	5.7	6.0	4.8
120	Romania[d]	8.6	7.6	1.7	5.1	12.8	8.6	. .	. .	. .	. .
121	*Albania*	. .	. .	. .	. .	. .	. .	. .	. .	. .	. .
122	*Bulgaria*	. .	. .	. .	. .	. .	. .	. .	. .	. .	. .
123	*Czechoslovakia*	. .	. .	. .	. .	. .	. .	. .	. .	. .	. .
124	*German Dem. Rep.*	. .	. .	. .	. .	. .	. .	. .	. .	. .	. .
125	*Poland*	. .	. .	. .	. .	. .	. .	. .	. .	. .	. .
126	*USSR*	. .	. .	. .	. .	. .	. .	. .	. .	. .	. .

a. Figures in italics are for 1961–70, not 1960–70.   b. Figures in italics are for 1970–81, not 1970–82.   c. Services include the unallocated share of GDP.   d. Based on net material product.

Table 3. Structure of production

| | GDP[a] (millions of dollars) | | Distribution of gross domestic product (percent) | | | | | | | |
| | | | Agriculture | | Industry | | (Manufacturing)[b] | | Services | |
	1960[c]	1982[d]	1960[c]	1982[d]	1960[c]	1982[d]	1960[c]	1982[d]	1960[c]	1982[d]
Low-income economies			49 w	37 w	26 w	32 w	13 w	14 w	25 w	31 w
China and India			48 w	36 w	28 w	35 w	..	..	24 w	29 w
Other low-income			48 w	44 w	13 w	16 w	9 w	9 w	39 w	40 w
1 Chad	180	*400*	52	*64*	11	7	4	*4*	37	*29*
2 Bangladesh	3,170	10,940	57	47	7	14	5	7	36	39
3 Ethiopia	900	4,010	65	49	12	16	6	11	23	36
4 Nepal	410	2,510	..	..	..	..	..	..	..	..
5 Mali	270	1,030	55	43	10	10	5	5	35	47
6 Burma	1,280	5,900	33	48	12	13	8	9	55	39
7 Zaire	130	*5,380*	30	*32*	27	*24*	13	3	43	*44*
8 Malawi	160	1,320	50	..	10	..	5	..	40	..
9 Upper Volta	200	1,000	55	41	16	16	9	12	31	43
10 Uganda	540	*8,630*	52	*82*	12	*4*	9	*4*	36	*14*
11 India	29,550	150,760	50	33	20	26	14	16	30	41
12 Rwanda	120	*1,260*	80	*46*	6	*22*	1	*16*	14	*32*
13 Burundi	190	1,110	..	56	..	17	..	10	..	27
14 Tanzania	550	4,530	57	52	11	15	5	9	32	33
15 Somalia	160	..	71	..	8	..	3	..	21	..
16 Haiti	270	1,640	..	..	..	..	..	..	..	..
17 Benin	160	830	55	44	8	13	3	7	37	43
18 Central African Rep.	110	660	51	35	11	19	3	8	38	46
19 China	*42,770*	260,400	*47[e]*	37	*33[e]*	41	..	..	*20[e]*	22
20 Guinea	400	1,750	..	41	..	23	..	2	..	36
21 Niger	250	1,560	69	31	9	30	4	8	22	39
22 Madagascar	540	*2,900*	37	*41*	10	*15*	4	..	53	*44*
23 Sri Lanka	1,500	4,400	32	27	20	27	15	15	48	46
24 Togo	120	800	55	23	15	29	8	6	30	48
25 Ghana	1,220	31,220	41	51	10	8	..	5	49	41
26 Pakistan	3,500	24,660	46	31	16	25	12	17	38	44
27 Kenya	730	5,340	38	33	18	22	9	13	44	45
28 Sierra Leone	..	1,130	..	32	..	20	..	5	..	48
29 *Afghanistan*	1,190	..	..	..	..	..	..	..	..	..
30 *Bhutan*	..	..	..	..	..	..	..	..	..	..
31 *Kampuchea, Dem.*	..	..	..	..	..	..	..	..	..	..
32 *Lao PDR*	..	..	..	..	..	..	..	..	..	..
33 *Mozambique*	..	..	..	..	..	..	..	..	..	..
34 *Viet Nam*	..	..	..	..	..	..	..	..	..	..
Middle-income economies			24 w	15 w	30 w	38 w	21 w	20 w	46 w	47 w
Oil exporters			27 w	14 w	25 w	40 w	14 w	17 w	48 w	46 w
Oil importers			23 w	17 w	32 w	35 w	22 w	23 w	45 w	48 w
Lower middle-income			37 w	23 w	22 w	35 w	15 w	17 w	41 w	42 w
35 Sudan	1,160	9,290	..	36	..	14	..	7	..	50
36 Mauritania	90	640	44	29	21	25	3	8	35	46
37 Yemen, PDR	..	630	..	12	..	27	..	..	..	61
38 Liberia	220	950	..	36	..	28	..	7	..	36
39 Senegal	610	2,510	24	22	17	25	12	15	59	53
40 Yemen Arab Rep.	..	3,210	..	26	..	17	..	7	..	56
41 Lesotho	30	300	..	23	..	22	..	6	..	55
42 Bolivia	460	*7,160*	26	*17*	25	*27*	15	*14*	49	*56*
43 Indonesia	8,670	90,160	54	26	14	39	8	13	32	35
44 Zambia	680	3,830	11	14	63	36	4	19	26	50
45 Honduras	300	2,520	37	27	19	27	13	17	44	46
46 Egypt, Arab Rep.	3,880	26,400	30	20	24	34	20	27	46	46
47 El Salvador	570	3,680	32	22	19	20	15	15	49	58
48 Thailand	2,550	36,790	40	22	19	28	13	19	41	50
49 Papua New Guinea	230	*2,350*	49	..	13	..	4	..	38	..
50 Philippines	6,960	39,850	26	22	28	36	20	24	46	42
51 Zimbabwe	780	5,900	18	15	35	35	17	25	47	50
52 Nigeria	3,150	71,720	63	22	11	39	5	6	26	39
53 Morocco	2,040	14,700	23	18	26	31	16	16	51	51
54 Cameroon	550	7,370	..	27	..	31	..	11	..	42
55 Nicaragua	340	2,940	24	21	21	32	16	26	55	47
56 Ivory Coast	570	7,560	43	26	14	23	7	12	43	51
57 Guatemala	1,040	8,730	..	..	..	..	..	..	..	..
58 Congo, People's Rep.	130	2,170	23	6	17	52	10	5	60	42
59 Costa Rica	510	2,580	26	25	20	27	14	20	54	48
60 Peru	2,410	21,620	18	8	33	39	24	24	49	53
61 Dominican Rep.	720	*7,230*	27	*18*	23	*28*	17	*16*	50	*54*
62 Jamaica	700	3,180	10	7	36	32	15	16	54	61
63 Ecuador	970	12,330	26	11	20	40	16	12	54	49
64 Turkey	8,810	49,980	41	21	21	31	13	22	38	48

Note: For data comparability and coverage see the technical notes.

		GDP[a] (millions of dollars)		Distribution of gross domestic product (percent)							
				Agriculture		Industry		(Manufacturing)[b]		Services	
		1960[c]	1982[d]	1960[c]	1982[d]	1960[c]	1982[d]	1960[c]	1982[d]	1960[c]	1982[d]
65	Tunisia	770	7,090	24	15	18	36	8	13	58	49
66	Colombia	3,780	34,970	34	26	26	31	17	21	40	42
67	Paraguay	300	5,850	36	26	20	26	17	16	44	48
68	*Angola*	. .	. .	. .	. .	. .	. .	. .	. .	. .	. .
69	*Cuba*	. .	. .	. .	. .	. .	. .	. .	. .	. .	. .
70	*Korea, Dem. Rep.*	. .	. .	. .	. .	. .	. .	. .	. .	. .	. .
71	*Lebanon*	830	. .	11	. .	20	. .	13	. .	69	. .
72	*Mongolia*	. .	. .	. .	. .	. .	. .	. .	. .	. .	. .
Upper middle-income				18 *w*	11 *w*	33 *w*	41 *w*	25 *w*	22 *w*	49 *w*	48 *w*
73	Syrian Arab Rep.	890	*15,240*	. .	19	. .	31	. .	. .	. .	50
74	Jordan	. .	3,500	. .	7	. .	29	. .	14	. .	64
75	Malaysia	2,290	25,870	36	23	18	30	9	18	46	47
76	Korea, Rep. of	3,810	68,420	37	16	20	39	14	28	43	45
77	Panama	420	4,190	17	. .	18	. .	10	. .	65	. .
78	Chile	3,910	24,140	9	6	35	34	21	20	56	60
79	Brazil	14,540	248,470	16	. .	35	. .	26	. .	49	. .
80	Mexico	12,040	171,270	16	7	29	38	19	21	55	55
81	Algeria	2,740	44,930	16	6	35	55	8	10	49	39
82	Portugal	2,340	*21,290*	25	12	36	44	29	35	39	*44*
83	Argentina	12,170	64,450	16	. .	38	. .	32	. .	46	. .
84	Uruguay	1,120	9,790	19	8	28	33	21	26	53	59
85	South Africa	6,980	74,330	12	. .	40	. .	21	. .	48	. .
86	Yugoslavia	9,860	*68,000*	24	*13*	45	45	36	*32*	31	*42*
87	Venezuela	7,570	69,490	6	6	22	42	. .	16	72	52
88	Greece	3,110	33,950	23	19	26	29	16	18	51	52
89	Israel	2,030	*20,490*	11	5	32	35	23	. .	57	60
90	Hong Kong	950	24,440	4	. .	39	. .	26	. .	57	. .
91	Singapore	700	14,650	4	1	18	37	12	26	78	62
92	Trinidad and Tobago	470	6,970	8	2	45	52	24	13	47	46
93	*Iran, Islamic Rep.*	4,120	. .	29	. .	33	. .	11	. .	38	. .
94	*Iraq*	1,580	. .	17	. .	51	. .	10	. .	32	. .
High-income oil exporters				. .	1 *w*	. .	74 *w*	. .	4 *w*	. .	25 *w*
95	Oman	50	7,110	74	. .	8	. .	1	. .	18	. .
96	Libya	310	28,360	. .	2	. .	68	. .	3	. .	30
97	Saudi Arabia	. .	153,590	. .	1	. .	77	. .	4	. .	22
98	Kuwait	. .	20,060	. .	1	. .	61	. .	7	. .	38
99	United Arab Emirates	. .	29,870	. .	. .	. .	. .	. .	. .	. .	. .
Industrial market economies				6 *w*	3 *w*	40 *w*	36 *w*	30 *w*	24 *w*	54 *w*	61 *w*
100	Ireland	1,770	17,180	22	. .	26	. .	. .	. .	52	. .
101	Spain	11,430	181,250	. .	6	. .	*34*	. .	22	. .	60
102	Italy	37,190	344,580	12	6	41	41	31	29	47	53
103	New Zealand	3,940	23,820	. .	10	. .	33	. .	25	. .	57
104	United Kingdom	71,440	473,220	3	2	43	33	32	19	54	65
105	Austria	6,270	66,640	11	4	47	39	35	27	42	57
106	Japan	44,000	1,061,920	13	4	45	42	34	30	42	54
107	Belgium	11,280	85,240	6	2	41	35	30	25	53	63
108	Finland	5,010	48,930	17	8	35	35	23	24	48	57
109	Netherlands	11,580	136,520	9	4	46	33	34	24	45	63
110	Australia	16,370	164,210	12	6	40	35	28	20	48	59
111	Canada	39,930	289,570	6	4	34	29	23	16	60	67
112	France	60,060	537,260	11	4	39	34	29	25	50	62
113	Germany, Fed. Rep.	72,100	662,990	6	2	53	46	40	35	41	52
114	Denmark	5,960	57,000	11	5	31	24	21	17	58	71
115	United States	505,300	3,009,600	4	3	38	33	29	22	58	64
116	Sweden	13,950	98,770	7	3	40	31	27	21	53	66
117	Norway	4,630	56,080	9	4	33	41	21	15	58	55
118	Switzerland	8,550	96,730	. .	. .	. .	. .	. .	. .	. .	. .
East European nonmarket economies				. .	. .	. .	. .	. .	. .	. .	. .
119	Hungary[f]	. .	20,710	28	21	39	45	. .	. .	33	34
120	Romania	. .	53,020	. .	18	. .	57	. .	. .	. .	25
121	*Albania*	. .	. .	. .	. .	. .	. .	. .	. .	. .	. .
122	*Bulgaria*	. .	. .	. .	. .	. .	. .	. .	. .	. .	. .
123	*Czechoslovakia*	. .	. .	. .	. .	. .	. .	. .	. .	. .	. .
124	*German Dem. Rep.*	. .	. .	. .	. .	. .	. .	. .	. .	. .	. .
125	*Poland*	. .	. .	. .	. .	. .	. .	. .	. .	. .	. .
126	*USSR*	. .	. .	. .	. .	. .	. .	. .	. .	. .	. .

a. See the technical notes.   b. Manufacturing is a part of the industrial sector, but its share of GDP is shown separately because it typically is the most dynamic part of the industrial sector.   c. Figures in italics are for 1961, not 1960.   d. Figures in italics are for 1981, not 1982.   e. Based on net material product.   f. Based on constant price series. Services include the unallocated share of GDP.

Table 4. Growth of consumption and investment

		Average annual growth rate (percent)				
	Public consumption		Private consumption		Gross domestic investment	
	1960–70[a]	1970–82[b]	1960–70[a]	1970–82[b]	1960–70[a]	1970–82[b]
Low-income economies	4.5 *m*	5.0 *m*	3.2 *m*	3.3 *m*	4.9 *m*	3.3 *m*
China and India	..	..	3.2 *m*	3.7 *m*	7.3 *m*	5.9 *m*
Other low-income	4.6 *m*	4.2 *m*	3.2 *m*	3.3 *m*	4.6 *m*	3.2 *m*
1 Chad	4.4	−3.8	−0.7	−1.8	2.3	−5.4
2 Bangladesh	c	c	3.4	4.2	11.2	2.9
3 Ethiopia	8.1	7.7	4.3	2.7	5.7	0.7
4 Nepal	..	..	..	..		
5 Mali	6.2	6.5	2.8	4.4	4.9	3.1
6 Burma	c	c	2.8	4.5	3.6	9.4
7 Zaire	8.5	1.0	3.5	−3.3	9.6	5.7
8 Malawi	4.6	8.0	3.7	4.1	15.4	2.0
9 Upper Volta	..	8.7	..	2.8	..	3.2
10 Uganda	c	c	5.6	−4.0	7.5	−8.0
11 India	−0.2	7.3	3.9	2.2	4.8	5.3
12 Rwanda	1.1	*11.8*	4.3	3.2	3.5	*14.9*
13 Burundi	19.2	4.2	3.2	3.3	4.3	15.0
14 Tanzania	c	c	6.6	4.4	9.8	3.4
15 Somalia	3.7	..	0.4	..	4.3	..
16 Haiti	c	c	−1.0	4.7	1.7	8.0
17 Benin	1.7	2.6	4.9	3.1	4.2	12.2
18 Central African Rep.	2.2	−2.9	3.0	2.7	1.3	−7.5
19 China	c	c	2.5	5.1	9.8	6.4
20 Guinea	..	..	..	..	..	..
21 Niger	2.0	2.4	3.9	3.4	3.0	6.6
22 Madagascar	3.0	2.0	1.9	−0.5	5.4	−1.4
23 Sri Lanka	c	c	2.1	2.6	6.6	11.0
24 Togo	6.7	9.4	7.6	4.0	11.1	6.3
25 Ghana	7.2	5.7	1.7	−0.4	−3.1	−5.1
26 Pakistan	7.3	4.0	7.1	5.3	6.9	3.3
27 Kenya	10.0	8.4	2.9	5.9	10.3	2.1
28 Sierra Leone	..	−2.2	..	3.5	..	−1.1
29 *Afghanistan*	c	..	2.0	..	−1.0	..
30 *Bhutan*	..	..	..	..	..	..
31 *Kampuchea, Dem.*	2.6	..	3.2	..	0.3	..
32 *Lao PDR*	..	..	..	..	..	..
33 *Mozambique*	..	..	..	..	..	..
34 *Viet Nam*	..	..	..	..	..	..
Middle-income economies	6.2 *m*	6.3 *m*	5.2 *m*	5.2 *m*	7.6 *m*	6.6 *m*
Oil exporters	6.3 *m*	9.6 *m*	4.8 *m*	7.3 *m*	4.2 *m*	10.7 *m*
Oil importers	6.0 *m*	6.2 *m*	5.4 *m*	4.6 *m*	8.2 *m*	5.6 *m*
Lower middle-income	5.9 *m*	6.4 *m*	4.8 *m*	4.8 *m*	7.6 *m*	6.6 *m*
35 Sudan	12.1	2.3	−2.5	7.8	3.2	9.0
36 Mauritania	(.)	8.1	2.6	3.1	−2.0	6.6
37 Yemen, PDR	..	..	..	..	..	..
38 Liberia	5.6	2.5	0.7	3.1	−3.9	2.1
39 Senegal	−0.2	6.4	3.3	3.3	1.1	1.8
40 Yemen Arab Rep.	..	12.3	..	8.7	..	22.2
41 Lesotho	(.)	15.5	6.5	8.0	20.7	19.6
42 Bolivia	8.9	5.3	3.8	4.8	9.6	−1.9
43 Indonesia	0.9	11.9	4.1	9.0	4.6	13.7
44 Zambia	11.0	1.0	6.8	3.0	10.6	−10.5
45 Honduras	5.3	6.4	4.8	4.3	10.2	4.7
46 Egypt, Arab Rep.	c	c	6.7	6.6	3.1	15.5
47 El Salvador	6.4	5.0	5.7	2.4	3.5	1.4
48 Thailand	9.7	9.1	7.0	6.1	15.8	6.4
49 Papua New Guinea	6.0	−1.3	5.7	3.3	23.2	−3.2
50 Philippines	5.1	6.2	4.7	4.9	8.2	9.3
51 Zimbabwe	..	9.9	..	2.9	..	2.5
52 Nigeria	10.0	11.7	0.6	5.6	7.4	8.8
53 Morocco	4.4	..	4.1	..	8.8	..
54 Cameroon	6.1	4.7	2.7	6.1	9.3	9.4
55 Nicaragua	2.2	10.6	7.6	(.)	10.9	−2.1
56 Ivory Coast	11.8	9.8	8.0	5.3	12.7	10.1
57 Guatemala	4.7	6.5	4.7	4.6	7.9	5.6
58 Congo, People's Rep.	5.4	6.3	1.9	0.3	1.1	12.2
59 Costa Rica	8.0	5.3	6.0	3.5	7.1	2.9
60 Peru	6.3	4.8	7.1	3.1	1.0	3.4
61 Dominican Rep.	1.9	4.8	6.3	5.9	11.4	7.1
62 Jamaica	8.6	5.4	3.0	−1.5	7.8	−7.6
63 Ecuador	..	12.4	..	7.3	..	8.8
64 Turkey	6.7	5.9	5.1	3.6	8.8	5.6

Note: For data comparability and coverage see the technical notes.

		Average annual growth rate (percent)					
		Public consumption		Private consumption		Gross domestic investment	
		1960–70[a]	1970–82[b]	1960–70[a]	1970–82[b]	1960–70[a]	1970–82[b]
65	Tunisia	5.2	8.7	2.3	8.5	4.2	10.9
66	Colombia	5.5	5.7	5.5	5.3	4.5	6.7
67	Paraguay	6.9	7.1	5.3	7.6	6.8	17.2
68	*Angola*	..	..	..	..	..	..
69	*Cuba*	..	..	..	..	..	..
70	*Korea, Dem. Rep.*	..	..	..	..	..	..
71	*Lebanon*	5.9	..	4.4	..	6.2	..
72	*Mongolia*	..	..	..	..	..	..
Upper middle-income		**7.0** *m*	**6.3** *m*	**5.5** *m*	**6.1** *m*	**7.6** *m*	**7.3** *m*
73	Syrian Arab Rep.	..	..	..	..	..	..
74	Jordan	..	10.6	..	8.8	..	21.6
75	Malaysia	7.5	10.5	4.2	7.2	7.5	11.4
76	Korea, Rep. of	5.5	7.4	7.0	6.8	23.6	11.0
77	Panama	7.8	5.2	6.4	*4.6*	12.4	*1.0*
78	Chile	5.1	1.7	3.7	1.0	9.9	0.4
79	Brazil	3.7	*7.1*	5.4	*8.0*	6.1	6.5
80	Mexico	8.8	8.2	7.0	5.9	9.9	8.0
81	Algeria	1.5	10.8	2.3	9.3	−0.2	11.0
82	Portugal	7.7	8.2	5.5	3.8	7.7	2.3
83	Argentina	1.1	3.4	4.5	1.2	4.0	1.0
84	Uruguay	4.4	3.9	1.3	*1.4*	−1.8	*10.6*
85	South Africa	7.0	..	6.2	..	9.4	..
86	Yugoslavia	0.6	3.6	9.5	5.2	4.7	6.3
87	Venezuela	6.3	6.0	5.0	8.5	7.6	4.9
88	Greece	6.6	6.3	7.1	4.2	10.4	0.9
89	Israel	13.8	2.7	7.3	5.2	5.7	−0.7
90	Hong Kong	8.6	10.3	8.6	10.0	6.9	13.6
91	Singapore	12.6	6.2	5.4	6.2	20.5	8.7
92	Trinidad and Tobago	c	c	4.8	8.3	−2.3	10.5
93	*Iran Islamic Rep.*	16.0	..	10.0	..	12.2	..
94	*Iraq*	8.1	..	4.9	..	3.0	..
High-income oil exporters		..	**12.9** *m*	..	**18.7** *m*	..	**17.5** *m*
95	Oman	..	..	..	..	..	..
96	Libya	..	15.6	..	18.7	..	*10.7*
97	Saudi Arabia	..	c	..	19.6	..	35.5
98	Kuwait	..	10.1	..	13.1	..	17.5
99	United Arab Emirates	..	..	..	..	..	..
Industrial market economies		**4.2** *m*	**3.2** *m*	**4.3** *m*	**2.7** *m*	**5.8** *m*	**0.6** *m*
100	Ireland	3.9	5.4	3.8	2.5	9.0	4.2
101	Spain	3.8	5.1	7.0	3.3	11.3	0.7
102	Italy	4.1	2.6	6.1	2.7	3.7	0.6
103	New Zealand	3.6	2.9	3.3	1.5	3.2	−0.1
104	United Kingdom	2.2	2.1	2.4	1.4	5.1	0.3
105	Austria	3.3	3.7	4.3	3.3	5.9	2.0
106	Japan	6.2	4.5	9.0	4.1	14.6	3.3
107	Belgium	5.7	3.9	3.8	3.4	6.0	0.2
108	Finland	5.0	5.0	4.0	2.7	4.1	0.1
109	Netherlands	2.8	2.6	5.9	2.9	7.4	−1.3
110	Australia	7.1	5.0	5.0	2.7	6.7	1.1
111	Canada	6.2	2.3	4.9	3.9	5.8	3.3
112	France	4.0	3.1	5.3	3.8	7.7	1.3
113	Germany, Fed. Rep.	4.1	3.2	4.6	2.5	4.1	1.1
114	Denmark	5.9	4.0	4.1	1.7	5.9	−2.0
115	United States	4.2	1.0	4.4	3.4	5.0	1.3
116	Sweden	5.4	3.2	3.5	1.7	5.3	−0.8
117	Norway	6.2	4.0	3.7	4.8	5.0	−0.3
118	Switzerland	4.8	1.7	4.3	1.4	3.9	−0.6
East European nonmarket economies		..	..	..	..	..	..
119	Hungary	c	4.0	3.1	3.8	7.8	4.1
120	Romania	..	..	..	..	11.2	7.4
121	*Albania*	..	..	..	..	..	..
122	*Bulgaria*	..	..	..	..	..	..
123	*Czechoslovakia*	..	..	..	..	..	..
124	*German Dem. Rep.*	..	..	..	..	..	..
125	*Poland*	..	..	..	..	..	..
126	*USSR*	..	..	..	..	..	..

a. Figures in italics are for 1961–70, not 1960–70.　b. Figures in italics are for 1970–81, not 1970–82.　c. Separate figures are not available for public consumption, which is therefore included in private consumption.

Table 5. Structure of demand

Distribution of gross domestic product (percent)

	Public consumption		Private consumption		Gross domestic investment		Gross domestic saving		Exports of goods and nonfactor services		Resource balance	
	1960[a]	1982[b]	1960[a]	1982[b]	1960[a]	1982[b]	1960[a]	1982[b]	1960[a]	1982[b]	1960[a]	1982[b]
Low-income economies	8 w	11 w	78 w	73 w	19 w	24 w	18 w	21 w	7 w	9 w	−1 w	−3 w
China and India	..	..	77 w	69 w	21 w	27 w	20 w	27 w	4 w	8 w	−1 w	(.) w
Other low-income	10 w	11 w	82 w	86 w	13 w	13 w	10 w	5 w	17 w	11 w	−3 w	−8 w
1 Chad	13	23	82	102	11	9	5	−25	23	35	−6	−34
2 Bangladesh	6	8	86	95	7	14	8	−3	10	8	1	−17
3 Ethiopia	8	16	81	81	12	11	11	3	9	12	−1	−8
4 Nepal	..	c	..	91	..	15	..	9	..	11	..	−6
5 Mali	12	25	79	79	14	15	9	−4	12	19	−5	−19
6 Burma	c	c	89	85	12	23	11	15	20	6	−1	−8
7 Zaire	18	c	61	90	12	16	21	10	55	29	9	−6
8 Malawi	17	16	87	71	10	20	−4	13	18	21	−14	−7
9 Upper Volta	10	20	94	89	9	15	−4	−9	9	14	−13	−24
10 Uganda	9	c	75	95	11	8	16	5	26	5	5	−3
11 India	7	11	79	67	17	25	14	22	5	6	−3	−3
12 Rwanda	10	17	82	75	6	22	8	8	12	12	2	−14
13 Burundi	3	13	92	86	6	14	5	1	13	9	−1	−13
14 Tanzania	9	22	72	70	14	20	19	8	30	11	5	−12
15 Somalia	8	..	86	..	10	..	6	..	13	..	−4	..
16 Haiti	c	c	93	98	9	11	7	2	20	15	−2	−9
17 Benin	16	13	75	87	15	37	9	(.)	12	30	−6	−37
18 Central African Rep.	19	12	72	97	20	9	9	−9	23	18	−11	−18
19 China	c	c	76	70	23	28	24	30	4	10	1	2
20 Guinea	..	17	..	66	..	13	..	17	..	28	..	4
21 Niger	9	9	79	79	12	26	12	12	9	21	(.)	−14
22 Madagascar	20	15	75	81	11	14	5	4	12	13	−6	−10
23 Sri Lanka	13	8	78	80	14	31	9	12	44	27	−5	−19
24 Togo	8	17	88	78	11	26	4	5	19	28	−7	−21
25 Ghana	10	7	73	92	24	1	17	1	28	2	−7	(.)
26 Pakistan	11	10	84	85	12	17	5	5	8	10	−7	−12
27 Kenya	11	19	72	64	20	22	17	17	31	25	−3	−5
28 Sierra Leone	..	9	..	92	..	12	..	−1	..	14	..	−13
29 Afghanistan	c	..	87	..	16	..	13	..	4	..	−3	..
30 Bhutan	..	..	..	..	..	..	..	..	..	..	..	..
31 Kampuchea, Dem.	..	..	..	..	..	..	..	..	..	..	..	..
32 Lao PDR	..	..	..	..	..	..	..	..	..	..	..	..
33 Mozambique	..	..	..	..	..	..	..	..	..	..	..	..
34 Viet Nam	..	..	..	..	..	..	..	..	..	..	..	..
Middle-income economies	11 w	14 w	70 w	68 w	20 w	24 w	19 w	21 w	17 w	23 w	−1 w	−3 w
Oil exporters	11 w	13 w	70 w	64 w	18 w	25 w	19 w	24 w	21 w	24 w	1 w	−1 w
Oil importers	11 w	15 w	70 w	71 w	20 w	23 w	19 w	19 w	15 w	22 w	−1 w	−4 w
Lower middle-income	10 w	13 w	76 w	70 w	15 w	23 w	14 w	17 w	15 w	20 w	−1 w	−6 w
35 Sudan	8	13	81	89	9	16	11	−2	15	9	2	−18
36 Mauritania	25	31	71	64	38	41	4	5	15	43	−34	−36
37 Yemen, PDR	..	..	..	..	..	..	..	..	..	..	..	..
38 Liberia	7	23	58	57	28	22	35	20	39	46	7	−2
39 Senegal	17	20	68	74	16	20	15	6	40	31	−1	−14
40 Yemen Arab Rep.	..	27	..	95	..	43	..	−22	..	10	..	−64
41 Lesotho	17	31	108	146	2	29	−25	−77	12	14	−27	−106
42 Bolivia	7	13	86	73	14	14	7	14	13	14	−7	(.)
43 Indonesia	12	10	80	71	8	23	8	19	13	22	(.)	−4
44 Zambia	11	30	48	65	25	17	41	5	56	27	16	−12
45 Honduras	11	13	77	72	14	16	12	15	21	27	−2	−1
46 Egypt, Arab Rep.	17	21	71	64	13	30	12	15	20	32	−1	−15
47 El Salvador	10	15	79	80	15	11	11	5	20	22	−4	−6
48 Thailand	10	13	76	66	16	21	14	21	17	25	−2	(.)
49 Papua New Guinea	28	27	71	66	13	29	1	7	16	36	−12	−22
50 Philippines	8	9	76	70	16	29	16	21	11	16	(.)	−8
51 Zimbabwe	11	20	67	59	23	27	22	21	..	..	−1	−6
52 Nigeria	6	13	87	71	13	25	7	16	14	19	−6	−9
53 Morocco	12	22	77	70	10	23	11	8	24	20	1	−15
54 Cameroon	..	8	..	65	..	25	..	27	..	31	..	2
55 Nicaragua	9	24	79	69	15	19	12	7	24	15	−3	−12
56 Ivory Coast	10	18	73	58	15	24	17	24	37	39	2	(.)
57 Guatemala	8	8	84	82	10	14	8	10	13	15	−2	−4
58 Congo, People's Rep.	15	15	97	37	53	56	−12	48	21	55	−65	−8
59 Costa Rica	10	15	77	58	18	23	13	27	21	43	−5	4
60 Peru	9	15	63	71	25	17	28	14	20	19	3	−3
61 Dominican Rep.	13	10	68	74	12	21	19	16	24	14	7	−5
62 Jamaica	7	23	67	69	30	20	26	8	34	40	−4	−12
63 Ecuador	11	13	78	63	14	25	11	24	16	21	−3	−1
64 Turkey	11	11	76	73	16	22	13	16	3	11	−3	−6

Note: For data comparability and coverage see the technical notes.

	Distribution of gross domestic product (percent)											
	Public consumption		Private consumption		Gross domestic investment		Gross domestic saving		Exports of goods and nonfactor services		Resource balance	
	1960[a]	1982[b]	1960[a]	1982[b]	1960[a]	1982[b]	1960[a]	1982[b]	1960[a]	1982[b]	1960[a]	1982[b]
65 Tunisia	17	16	76	61	17	33	7	23	20	37	−10	−10
66 Colombia	6	9	73	69	21	26	21	22	16	11	(.)	−4
67 Paraguay	8	7	76	78	17	26	16	15	18	8	−1	−11
68 *Angola*	..	..	..	..	..	..	..	..	..	..	..	..
69 *Cuba*	..	..	..	..	..	..	..	..	..	..	..	..
70 *Korea, Dem. Rep.*	..	..	..	..	..	..	..	..	..	..	..	..
71 *Lebanon*	10	..	85	..	16	..	5	..	27	..	−11	..
72 *Mongolia*	..	..	..	..	..	..	..	..	..	..	..	..
Upper middle-income	12 *w*	15 *w*	67 *w*	67 *w*	22 *w*	24 *w*	21 *w*	23 *w*	18 *w*	24 *w*	−1 *w*	−1 *w*
73 Syrian Arab Rep.	..	25	..	86	..	..	..	..	..	..	..	..
74 Jordan	..	..	..	..	..	46	..	−11	..	49	..	−57
75 Malaysia	11	21	62	54	14	34	27	25	54	51	13	−9
76 Korea, Rep. of	15	13	84	63	11	26	1	24	3	39	−10	−2
77 Panama	11	*21*	78	56	16	29	11	23	31	*40*	−5	−6
78 Chile	9	15	79	77	14	10	12	8	14	22	−2	−2
79 Brazil	12	c	67	*81*	22	19	21	*19*	5	9	−1	(.)
80 Mexico	6	11	76	61	20	21	18	28	10	17	−2	7
81 Algeria	15	15	60	46	42	38	25	39	31	30	−17	1
82 Portugal	11	*16*	77	76	19	27	12	8	17	27	−7	−19
83 Argentina	9	18	70	60	22	19	21	22	10	13	−1	3
84 Uruguay	9	*13*	79	75	18	*15*	12	*12*	15	*15*	−6	−3
85 South Africa	9	..	64	..	22	..	27	..	30	..	5	..
86 Yugoslavia	19	16	49	51	36	34	32	33	14	23	−4	−1
87 Venezuela	14	14	53	61	21	26	33	25	32	25	12	−1
88 Greece	12	18	77	69	19	23	11	13	9	18	−8	−10
89 Israel	18	34	68	60	26	21	14	6	14	37	−12	−15
90 Hong Kong	7	8	87	67	18	29	6	25	82	100	−12	−4
91 Singapore	8	11	95	48	11	46	−3	41	163	196	−14	−5
92 Trinidad and Tobago	9	c	61	69	28	34	30	31	37	36	2	−3
93 *Iran, Islamic Rep.*	10	..	69	..	17	..	21	..	18	..	4	..
94 *Iraq*	18	..	48	..	20	..	34	..	42	..	14	..
High-income oil exporters	..	20 *w*	..	27 *w*	..	26 *w*	..	53 *w*	..	65 *w*	..	27 *w*
95 Oman	..	..	..	..	..	..	..	..	..	..	..	..
96 Libya	..	25	..	29	..	*32*	..	46	..	57	..	*14*
97 Saudi Arabia	..	19	..	24	..	25	..	56	..	68	..	31
98 Kuwait	..	20	..	50	..	23	..	30	..	59	..	7
99 United Arab Emirates	..	..	..	..	..	..	..	..	..	..	..	..
Industrial market economies	15 *w*	18 *w*	63 *w*	62 *w*	21 *w*	20 *w*	22 *w*	20 *w*	12 *w*	19 *w*	1 *w*	(.) *w*
100 Ireland	12	21	77	57	16	27	11	22	32	62	−5	−5
101 Spain	7	12	72	70	18	20	21	18	10	18	3	−2
102 Italy	13	18	63	62	25	20	24	20	14	27	−1	(.)
103 New Zealand	11	18	68	61	23	25	21	21	22	29	−2	−4
104 United Kingdom	17	22	66	58	19	18	17	20	21	27	−2	2
105 Austria	13	19	59	57	28	23	28	24	25	42	(.)	1
106 Japan	8	10	59	59	33	30	33	31	11	15	(.)	1
107 Belgium	13	19	69	67	19	17	18	13	33	69	−1	−4
108 Finland	12	20	60	55	28	24	28	25	23	32	(.)	1
109 Netherlands	13	18	59	61	27	18	28	21	48	58	1	3
110 Australia	10	18	65	62	28	22	25	20	15	15	−3	−2
111 Canada	14	21	65	56	23	19	21	23	18	27	−2	4
112 France	13	16	62	67	23	21	25	17	15	21	2	−4
113 Germany, Fed. Rep.	13	21	57	55	27	22	30	24	19	31	3	2
114 Denmark	13	28	62	55	26	17	25	17	32	36	−1	(.)
115 United States	17	19	64	66	19	16	19	15	5	9	(.)	−1
116 Sweden	16	29	60	54	25	18	24	17	23	33	−1	−1
117 Norway	13	19	59	49	30	26	28	32	41	46	−2	6
118 Switzerland	9	13	62	62	29	24	29	25	29	35	(.)	1
East European nonmarket economies	..	..	..	..	..	..	..	..	..	..	..	..
119 Hungary	c	10	74	61	28	29	26	29	..	38	..	1
120 Romania	..	..	..	..	..	29	..	..	..	23	..	4
121 *Albania*	..	..	..	..	..	..	..	..	..	..	..	..
122 *Bulgaria*	..	..	..	..	..	..	..	..	..	..	..	..
123 *Czechoslovakia*	..	..	..	..	..	..	..	..	..	..	..	..
124 *German Dem. Rep.*	..	..	..	..	..	..	..	..	..	..	..	..
125 *Poland*	..	..	..	..	..	..	..	..	..	..	..	..
126 *USSR*	..	..	..	..	..	..	..	..	..	..	..	..

a. Figures in italics are for 1961, not 1960.   b. Figures in italics are for 1981, not 1982.   c. Separate figures are not available for public consumption, which is therefore included in private consumption.

Table 6. Agriculture and food

	Value added in agriculture (millions of 1975 dollars)		Cereal imports (thousands of metric tons)		Food aid in cereals (thousands of metric tons)		Fertilizer consumption (hundreds of grams of plant nutrient per hectare of arable land)		Average index of food production per capita (1969–71=100)
	1970	1982ᵃ	1974	1982	1974/75ᵇ	1981/82ᵇ	1970ᶜ	1981	1980–82
Low-income economies			22,774 t	29,260 t	5,611 t	3,885 t	184 w	581 w	110 w
China and India			14,437 t	22,767 t	..	494 t	230 w	772 w	114 w
Other low-income			8,337 t	6,493 t	4,029 t	3,391 t	85 w	187 w	97 w
1 Chad	246	211	50	57	13	25	7	13	95
2 Bangladesh	9,475	11,027	1,719	1,375	2,130	1,076	142	436	94
3 Ethiopia	1,128	1,286	118	273	59	178	4	33	82
4 Nepal	1,012	1,183	19	23	0	10	30	94	83
5 Mali	260	369	281	143	114	67	29	64	83
6 Burma	1,479	2,671	26	14	14	5	34	165	113
7 Zaire	397	479	343	323	(.)	93	8	12	87
8 Malawi	181	311	17	88	(.)	2	52	106	99
9 Upper Volta	217	262	99	98	0	82	3	19	95
10 Uganda	1,926	1,952	37	68	16	49	13	1	86
11 India	28,962	33,565	5,261	2,402	1,582	416	114	338	101
12 Rwanda	..	394	3	21	19	13	3	3	105
13 Burundi	239	291	7	20	6	9	5	8	96
14 Tanzania	842	1,058	431	360	148	254	30	56	88
15 Somalia	357	..	42	406	110	175	31	12	60
16 Haiti	..	..	83	197	25	90	4	65	85
17 Benin	..	231	8	115	9	8	33	15	100
18 Central African Rep.	120	152	7	29	1	2	11	6	104
19 China	44,235	65,540	9,176	20,365	..	78	418	1,501	124
20 Guinea	..	647	63	110	49	41	18	18	89
21 Niger	440	327	155	120	75	71	1	10	88
22 Madagascar	691	729	114	392	7	78	56	23	94
23 Sri Lanka	841	1,178	951	481	271	195	496	769	154
24 Togo	145	183	6	61	0	5	3	24	89
25 Ghana	2,358	2,279	177	211	43	46	9	112	72
26 Pakistan	3,258	4,406	1,274	361	619	368	168	531	105
27 Kenya	706	1,247	15	194	2	115	224	344	88
28 Sierra Leone	192	236	72	124	10	29	13	19	81
29 Afghanistan	..	..	5	75	10	93	24	46	96
30 Bhutan	..	..	23	32	0	1	(.)	11	107
31 Kampuchea, Dem.	..	..	223	75	226	44	13	62	55
32 Lao PDR	..	..	53	27	13	(.)	4	45	122
33 Mozambique	..	..	62	298	34	126	27	117	68
34 Viet Nam	..	..	1,854	322	6	41	512	409	114
Middle-income economies			41,418 t	66,303 t	2,390 t	4,463 t	206 w	425 w	111 w
Oil exporters			17,941 t	30,522 t	1,074 t	2,225 t	145 w	330 w	104 w
Oil importers			23,477 t	35,781 t	1,316 t	2,238 t	238 w	470 w	116 w
Lower middle-income			16,901 t	27,423 t	1,541 t	3,924 t	167 w	375 w	108 w
35 Sudan	1,367	2,127	125	611	50	185	31	60	87
36 Mauritania	117	152	115	219	48	86	6	(.)	73
37 Yemen, PDR	..	..	149	271	38	25	(.)	88	92
38 Liberia	142	205	42	109	3	42	55	92	88
39 Senegal	491	625	341	492	28	77	20	47	93
40 Yemen Arab Rep.	221	401	158	560	0	13	1	43	93
41 Lesotho	48	46	49	111	14	34	17	151	84
42 Bolivia	348	550	207	293	22	44	13	20	100
43 Indonesia	7,896	12,593	1,919	1,912	301	107	119	744	117
44 Zambia	278	325	93	225	1	100	71	166	87
45 Honduras	312	422	52	89	31	34	160	176	79
46 Egypt, Arab Rep.	2,683	3,878	3,877	6,703	610	1,952	1,282	2,475	85
47 El Salvador	328	374	75	179	4	132	1,048	1,220	97
48 Thailand	3,591	5,837	97	133	0	5	76	177	138
49 Papua New Guinea	345	466	71	164	..	..	76	326	99
50 Philippines	3,682	6,342	817	1,287	89	54	214	324	124
51 Zimbabwe	451	685	56	3	..	(.)	466	682	87
52 Nigeria	9,061	8,563	389	2,280	7	1	3	70	92
53 Morocco	1,725	1,836	891	1,913	75	465	130	239	84
54 Cameroon	732	1,134	81	117	4	11	28	60	102
55 Nicaragua	265	367	44	70	3	103	184	480	77
56 Ivory Coast	876	1,421	172	592	4	1	71	132	107
57 Guatemala	..	..	138	105	9	11	224	537	114
58 Congo, People's Rep.	93	108	34	81	2	(.)	112	8	81
59 Costa Rica	338	436	110	164	1	45	1,086	1,514	100
60 Peru	2,232	2,417	637	1,524	37	76	297	375	87
61 Dominican Rep.	667	1,022	252	302	16	59	354	471	104
62 Jamaica	199	196	340	405	1	78	886	718	90
63 Ecuador	628	914	152	327	13	5	123	262	101
64 Turkey	7,691	11,442	1,276	546	70	(.)	166	454	115

Note: For data comparability and coverage see the technical notes.

		Value added in agriculture (millions of 1975 dollars)		Cereal imports (thousands of metric tons)		Food aid in cereals (thousands of metric tons)		Fertilizer consumption (hundreds of grams of plant nutrient per hectare of arable land)		Average index of food production per capita (1969-71=100)
		1970	1982[a]	1974	1982	1974/75[b]	1981/82[b]	1970[c]	1981	1980-82
65	Tunisia	480	816	307	946	1	96	82	180	128
66	Colombia	2,848	4,593	503	886	28	3	310	504	124
67	Paraguay	419	821	71	38	10	1	58	48	111
68	*Angola*	..	..	149	311	0	68	45	35	77
69	*Cuba*	..	..	1,622	2,241	..	..	1,539	1,872	113
70	*Korea, Dem. Rep.*	..	..	1,108	585	..	..	1,484	3,486	132
71	*Lebanon*	..	..	354	529	21	11	1,279	1,006	134
72	*Mongolia*	..	..	28	100	..	..	18	112	95
Upper middle-income				24,517 *t*	38,880 *t*	849 *t*	539 *t*	243 *w*	470 *w*	115 *w*
73	Syrian Arab Rep.	595	..	339	426	47	8	67	232	168
74	Jordan	92	132	171	668	63	73	20	53	70
75	Malaysia	2,049	3,738	1,017	1,447	1	..	436	923	150
76	Korea, Rep. of	3,995	5,812	2,679	5,538	234	429	2,466	3,513	125
77	Panama	193	248	63	110	3	3	391	521	103
78	Chile	440	565	1,737	1,425	331	18	317	202	98
79	Brazil	8,737	13,429	2,485	4,492	31	3	169	375	133
80	Mexico	8,501	12,538	2,881	2,194	..	..	246	666	104
81	Algeria	952	1,375	1,816	3,831	54	5	174	262	75
82	Portugal	2,242	2,025	1,860	3,504	0	0	411	767	73
83	Argentina	3,523	4,676	0	0	..	..	24	27	122
84	Uruguay	387	425	70	122	31	0	392	333	109
85	South Africa	..	..	127	302	..	..	425	904	193
86	Yugoslavia	3,584	5,493	992	1,267	..	..	766	1,284	126
87	Venezuela	1,362	1,861	1,270	2,575	..	..	165	388	95
88	Greece	2,851	3,711	1,341	717	..	..	858	1,335	131
89	Israel	..	..	1,176	1,599	53	(.)	1,394	1,996	107
90	Hong Kong	171	166	657	879	..	..	..	..	71
91	Singapore	100	123	682	1,819	(.)	(.)	2,667	6,714	91
92	Trinidad and Tobago	80	65	208	272	..	..	640	417	62
93	*Iran, Islamic Rep.*	3,739	..	2,076	3,183	..	..	76	423	111
94	*Iraq*	1,172	..	870	2,510	1	..	35	141	87
High-income oil exporters				1,379 *t*	7,371 *t*			58 *w*	467 *w*	42 *w*
95	Oman	..	..	52	217			(.)	395	95
96	Libya	126	388	612	849			64	375	127
97	Saudi Arabia	331	616	482	5,584			44	602	9
98	Kuwait	20	30	101	439			(.)	5,000	..
99	United Arab Emirates	..	..	132	282			(.)	2,812	..
Industrial market economies				65,494 *t*	66,103 *t*			985 *w*	1,191 *w*	114 *w*
100	Ireland	..	..	631	386			3,573	6,094	103
101	Spain	7,945	9,689	4,675	7,402			595	672	126
102	Italy	14,093	15,430	8,100	6,506			962	1,633	109
103	New Zealand	..	..	92	22			8,875	10,241	114
104	United Kingdom	5,386	7,297	7,541	3,943			2,521	3,296	126
105	Austria	1,806	2,325	165	93			2,517	2,393	129
106	Japan	24,218	25,012	19,557	24,336			3,849	3,872	91
107	Belgium[d]	1,854	2,120	4,585	6,370			5,686	4,902	107
108	Finland	3,188	3,017	222	1,030			1,931	1,938	107
109	Netherlands	3,173	5,313	7,199	4,843			7,165	7,674	120
110	Australia	4,351	5,107	2	9			246	279	98
111	Canada	6,743	8,770	1,513	904			192	419	119
112	France	17,077	20,459	654	2,482			2,424	2,984	121
113	Germany, Fed. Rep.	11,567	15,924	7,164	4,977			4,208	4,184	118
114	Denmark	1,641	2,618	462	377			2,254	2,330	125
115	United States	46,300	55,400	460	399			800	1,024	119
116	Sweden	3,133	3,219	301	112			1,639	1,639	119
117	Norway	1,409	1,676	713	726			2,471	3,033	127
118	Switzerland	..	..	1,458	1,156			3,842	4,122	127
East European nonmarket economies				18,543 *t*	50,406 *t*			635 *w*	1,098 *w*	107 *w*
119	Hungary	1,619	2,551	408	24			1,485	2,793	147
120	Romania	..	..	1,381	1,305			559	1,541	152
121	*Albania*	..	..	48	12			745	1,114	104
122	*Bulgaria*	..	..	649	397			1,446	2,506	127
123	*Czechoslovakia*	..	..	1,296	681			2,402	3,327	120
124	*German Dem. Rep.*	..	..	2,821	3,313			3,202	3,442	129
125	*Poland*	..	..	4,185	4,566		417	1,715	2,481	93
126	*USSR*	..	..	7,755	40,108			437	826	101

a. Figures in italics are for 1981, not 1982.   b. Figures are for the crop years 1974/75 and 1981/82.   c. Average for 1969–71.   d. Includes Luxembourg.

229

Table 7. Industry

		Distribution of manufacturing value added (percent; 1975 prices)					Value added in manufacturing (millions of 1975 dollars)	
		Food and agriculture 1981[a]	Textiles and clothing 1981[a]	Machinery and transport equipment 1981[a]	Chemicals 1981[a]	Other manufacturing 1981[a]	1970	1981
Low-income economies								
China and India								
Other low-income								
1	Chad	49	34	..	..	17	37	21
2	Bangladesh	30	38	4	16	12	647	1,290
3	Ethiopia	27	27	..	2	44	236	349
4	Nepal	..	..	..	..	..	..	..
5	Mali	..	..	..	..	..	44	55
6	Burma	31	14	1	4	50	287	456
7	Zaire	..	..	..	..	..	186	163
8	Malawi	54	10	..	..	36	44	81
9	Upper Volta	74	7	..	11	8	67	96
10	Uganda	54	25	..	..	21	222	87
11	India	13	18	20	14	35	10,232	16,190
12	Rwanda	58	..	..	2	40	..	106
13	Burundi	..	..	..	..	..	23	44
14	Tanzania	..	..	..	..	..	190	202
15	Somalia	..	..	..	..	..	42	..
16	Haiti	35	17	..	1	47	..	..
17	Benin	..	..	..	..	..	..	56
18	Central African Rep.	66	21	(.)	2	11	44	29
19	China	..	..	..	..	..	..	..
20	Guinea	..	..	..	..	..	..	26
21	Niger	..	..	..	..	..	54	172
22	Madagascar	27	39	2	10	22	295	272
23	Sri Lanka	46	10	..	..	44	556	714
24	Togo	50	28	..	..	22	30	14
25	Ghana	28	..	..	..	72	591	505
26	Pakistan	46	14	7	16	17	1,492	2,496
27	Kenya	24	10	33	6	27	167	531
28	Sierra Leone	..	..	..	..	..	25	37
29	Afghanistan	..	..	..	..	..	..	..
30	Bhutan	..	..	..	..	..	..	..
31	Kampuchea, Dem.	..	..	..	..	..	..	..
32	Lao PDR	..	..	..	..	..	..	..
33	Mozambique	..	..	..	..	..	..	..
34	Viet Nam	..	..	..	..	..	..	..
Middle-income economies								
Oil exporters								
Oil importers								
Lower middle-income								
35	Sudan	..	..	..	..	..	253	421
36	Mauritania	..	..	..	..	..	21	36
37	Yemen, PDR	..	..	..	..	..	..	59
38	Liberia	22	..	..	..	78	25	39
39	Senegal	43	15	..	8	34	276	298
40	Yemen Arab Rep.	..	..	..	..	..	25	102
41	Lesotho	..	..	..	..	..	3	10
42	Bolivia	..	..	..	..	..	237	390
43	Indonesia	28	8	7	12	45	1,517	5,998
44	Zambia	16	22	10	14	38	319	444
45	Honduras	47	14	1	7	31	138	254
46	Egypt, Arab Rep.	20	22	14	10	34	1,835	4,544
47	El Salvador	..	..	..	..	..	252	270
48	Thailand	31	26	15	3	25	1,675	4,636
49	Papua New Guinea	..	..	..	..	..	71	132
50	Philippines	40	11	10	7	32	2,816	5,706
51	Zimbabwe	19	19	10	11	41	564	969
52	Nigeria	33	18	12	11	26	1,191	4,020
53	Morocco	31	12	9	10	38	1,138	1,960
54	Cameroon	41	..	2	7	50	199	477
55	Nicaragua	52	15	..	..	33	262	360
56	Ivory Coast	..	..	..	..	..	398	706
57	Guatemala	..	..	..	..	..	..	..
58	Congo, People's Rep.	37	5	..	7	51	73	104
59	Costa Rica	..	..	..	..	..	261	531
60	Peru	27	14	10	11	38	2,911	4,038
61	Dominican Rep.	72	4	1	5	18	483	956
62	Jamaica	..	..	..	..	..	429	359
63	Ecuador	27	14	10	7	42	322	887
64	Turkey	24	11	15	12	38	3,678	6,532

Note: For data comparability and coverage see the technical notes.

	Distribution of manufacturing value added (percent; 1975 prices)					Value added in manufacturing (millions of 1975 dollars)	
	Food and agriculture 1981[a]	Textiles and clothing 1981[a]	Machinery and transport equipment 1981[a]	Chemicals 1981[a]	Other manufacturing 1981[a]	1970	1981
65 Tunisia	20	20	8	16	36	222	820
66 Colombia	32	15	11	12	30	1,800	3,260
67 Paraguay	34	14	10	4	38	183	430
68 *Angola*	..	..	..	..	..	..	..
69 *Cuba*	*36*	*16*	*1*	*17*	*30*	..	..
70 *Korea, Dem. Rep.*	..	..	..	..	..	..	..
71 *Lebanon*	..	..	..	..	..	..	..
72 *Mongolia*	23	29	..	5	43	..	..
Upper middle-income							
73 Syrian Arab Rep.	27	32	4	4	33	575	*1,318*
74 Jordan	..	..	..	..	..	91	286
75 Malaysia	21	8	18	6	47	941	2,918
76 Korea, Rep. of	16	23	18	11	32	2,346	10,542
77 Panama	51	12	2	6	29	204	280
78 Chile	15	5	14	12	54	1,881	2,161
79 Brazil	15	10	24	13	38	18,819	40,673
80 Mexico	19	8	20	12	41	14,592	31,115
81 Algeria	24	16	10	3	47	1,068	3,125
82 Portugal	12	18	22	14	34	3,496	6,109
83 Argentina	12	11	23	13	41	10,693	10,612
84 Uruguay	*26*	*23*	*11*	*8*	*32*	726	960
85 South Africa	14	11	18	11	46	..	..
86 Yugoslavia	15	14	20	9	42	4,832	12,605
87 Venezuela	27	6	8	8	51	3,419	5,531
88 Greece	20	26	9	9	36	2,540	4,540
89 Israel	15	12	25	8	40	..	..
90 Hong Kong	..	..	..	..	..	1,620	4,966
91 Singapore	5	3	55	4	33	827	2,556
92 Trinidad and Tobago	*14*	*4*	*9*	*7*	*66*	404	434
93 *Iran, Islamic Rep.*	14	20	10	..	56	2,601	..
94 *Iraq*	*22*	*22*	..	..	*56*	522	..
High-income oil exporters							
95 Oman	..	..	..	..	..	..	..
96 Libya	*14*	..	..	*21*	*65*	154	544
97 Saudi Arabia	4	..	..	..	96	1,726	3,568
98 Kuwait	9	..	..	17	74	368	986
99 United Arab Emirates	..	..	..	..	..	..	..
Industrial market economies							
100 Ireland	23	10	13	15	39	..	..
101 Spain	13	14	17	10	46	18,331	28,734
102 Italy	10	15	29	8	38	..	..
103 New Zealand	24	11	16	4	45	..	..
104 United Kingdom	13	8	34	10	35	58,677	52,963
105 Austria	15	9	24	7	45	9,112	13,355
106 Japan	7	5	39	8	41	118,403	252,581
107 Belgium	18	8	27	12	35	14,386	19,164
108 Finland	12	8	25	8	47	5,636	8,919
109 Netherlands	19	4	28	13	36	18,684	23,760
110 Australia	17	7	22	8	46	20,206	25,379
111 Canada	14	7	23	7	49	25,748	36,978
112 France	17	7	33	7	36	75,800	104,907
113 Germany, Fed. Rep.	10	5	37	10	38	149,113	182,717
114 Denmark	24	7	25	8	36	5,858	8,139
115 United States	11	6	33	12	38	328,200	446,700
116 Sweden	10	3	35	7	45	16,743	18,138
117 Norway	16	4	27	7	46	5,322	6,309
118 Switzerland	20	8	21	13	38	..	..
East European nonmarket economies							
119 Hungary	11	10	29	10	40	3,244	5,984
120 Romania	*12*	*15*	*33*	*12*	*28*	..	..
121 *Albania*	..	..	..	..	..	..	..
122 *Bulgaria*	25	16	16	6	37	..	..
123 *Czechoslovakia*	7	9	38	8	38	..	..
124 *German Dem. Rep.*	18	10	34	9	29	..	..
125 *Poland*	5	19	32	9	35	..	..
126 *USSR*	12	11	29	6	42	..	..

a. Figures in italics are for 1980, not 1981.

Table 8. Commercial energy

	Average annual energy growth rate (percent)				Energy consumption per capita (thousands of kilograms of oil equivalent)		Energy imports as a percentage of merchandise exports	
	Energy production		Energy consumption					
	1960–74[a]	1974–81	1960–74	1974–81	1960[b]	1981	1960	1981[c]
Low-income economies	6.2 *w*	5.7 *w*	5.8 *w*	5.5 *w*	140 *w*	253 *w*	11 *w*	61 *w*
China and India	5.9 *w*	5.7 *w*	5.9 *w*	5.7 *w*	148 *w*	307 *w*	..	..
Other low-income	14.3 *w*	6.5 *w*	4.5 *w*	3.7 *w*	52 *w*	80 *w*	10 *w*	42 *w*
1 Chad	..	..	9.8	3.8	7	20	23	..
2 Bangladesh	..	11.7	..	8.2	..	35	..	17
3 Ethiopia	14.1	5.6	14.2	6.2	7	23	11	44
4 Nepal	26.9	7.8	12.6	5.9	3	10	..	*10*
5 Mali	*41.2*	7.0	6.3	5.1	10	21	13	..
6 Burma	5.6	10.2	4.3	5.5	41	59	4	..
7 Zaire	3.0	12.2	5.0	2.0	65	76	3	..
8 Malawi	32.8	9.5	..	4.5	..	46	..	*15*
9 Upper Volta	..	..	7.8	13.1	3	22	38	71
10 Uganda	5.2	−3.2	9.2	−8.0	27	23	5	..
11 India	4.9	5.4	5.4	5.6	79	158	11	*81*
12 Rwanda	23.7	2.3	..	7.0	10	18	..	..
13 Burundi	..	30.5	..	10.6	6	15	..	..
14 Tanzania	10.6	6.7	10.8	2.4	30	50	..	*50*
15 Somalia	..	..	10.2	19.2	11	90	4	2
16 Haiti	27.1	11.0	3.7	8.3	29	55	..	..
17 Benin	..	..	10.0	−1.5	26	38	16	..
18 Central African Rep.	14.1	3.7	7.7	7.3	20	33	12	*1*
19 China	6.2	5.7	6.0	5.3	191	412	..	..
20 Guinea	*15.9*	(.)	3.4	1.3	35	54	7	..
21 Niger	..	..	15.1	10.9	3	31	6	23
22 Madagascar	7.2	−5.8	11.4	−5.4	27	41	9	13
23 Sri Lanka	10.1	7.4	4.4	1.7	122	123	8	45
24 Togo	..	24.2	13.2	16.1	15	125	10	18
25 Ghana	..	3.0	12.3	−0.1	72	161	7	..
26 Pakistan	9.2	9.1	4.8	7.8	97	179	17	52
27 Kenya	9.6	15.0	6.4	2.5	114	147	18	63
28 Sierra Leone	..	..	6.8	−0.5	74	121	11	..
29 *Afghanistan*	38.9	−4.7	10.3	2.3	16	48	12	..
30 *Bhutan*	..	..	..	..	..	..	..	..
31 *Kampuchea, Dem.*	..	..	13.5	10.1	..	59	9	..
32 *Lao PDR*	..	24.6	..	..	11	65	..	..
33 *Mozambique*	3.2	29.5	6.4	−0.5	76	85	11	..
34 *Viet Nam*	..	5.3	..	−0.2	..	103	..	..
Middle-income economies	12.4 *w*	−3.8 *w*	8.0 *w*	5.4 *w*	317 *w*	721 *w*	9 *w*	27 *w*
Oil exporters	13.5 *w*	−5.6 *w*	6.9 *w*	6.5 *w*	257 *w*	593 *w*	· 5 *w*	7 *w*
Oil importers	7.6 *w*	4.5 *w*	8.4 *w*	4.8 *w*	357 *w*	824 *w*	13 *w*	37 *w*
Lower middle-income	21.8 *w*	2.3 *w*	8.4 *w*	5.5 *w*	146 *w*	362 *w*	8 *w*	27 *w*
35 Sudan	29.7	9.6	13.1	−3.9	40	70	8	44
36 Mauritania	..	..	20.9	4.2	12	131	39	..
37 Yemen, PDR	..	..	..	8.5	..	791	..	..
38 Liberia	31.9	−0.9	19.8	1.6	66	373	3	24
39 Senegal	..	..	1.9	−2.0	381	206	8	77
40 Yemen Arab Rep.	..	..	..	17.1	..	57	..	..
41 Lesotho	..	..	..	..	..	..	..	..
42 Bolivia	17.1	−0.1	6.8	8.2	122	326	4	..
43 Indonesia	8.5	5.1	4.4	8.7	88	191	3	8
44 Zambia	..	4.5	..	0.2	..	443	..	..
45 Honduras	29.4	8.1	9.2	3.5	102	206	10	18
46 Egypt, Arab Rep.	9.3	20.4	2.6	10.8	197	448	12	10
47 El Salvador	5.1	19.8	7.3	5.9	98	210	6	27
48 Thailand	28.0	8.1	16.5	7.3	44	284	12	43
49 Papua New Guinea	12.3	14.9	17.1	4.6	37	240	7	..
50 Philippines	2.9	25.2	9.9	5.6	109	281	9	45
51 Zimbabwe	..	−2.5	..	1.4	..	578	..	..
52 Nigeria	36.6	−2.3	9.2	17.2	20	143	7	..
53 Morocco	2.0	4.7	7.9	7.4	118	283	9	50
54 Cameroon	1.1	55.4	4.7	8.5	61	122	7	13
55 Nicaragua	26.5	5.3	10.4	0.3	125	271	12	41
56 Ivory Coast	9.7	35.1	14.9	7.9	50	191	5	21
57 Guatemala	9.9	20.9	6.6	5.0	124	199	12	62
58 Congo, People's Rep.	15.8	9.3	5.9	18.5	89	139	25	7
59 Costa Rica	9.5	8.2	10.8	5.5	208	592	7	21
60 Peru	3.5	15.1	6.3	2.4	315	534	4	1
61 Dominican Rep.	1.8	−7.0	14.0	−1.2	108	349	..	40
62 Jamaica	−0.7	−0.1	9.6	0.2	449	1,182	11	51
63 Ecuador	19.1	3.8	8.5	13.6	151	571	2	*1*
64 Turkey	8.4	4.6	10.4	5.0	170	569	16	83

Note: For data comparability and coverage see the technical notes.

		Average annual energy growth rate (percent)				Energy consumption per capita (thousands of kilograms of oil equivalent)		Energy imports as a percentage of merchandise exports	
		Energy production		Energy consumption					
		1960–74[a]	1974–81	1960–74	1974–81	1960[b]	1981	1960	1981[c]
65	Tunisia	72.2	5.5	9.8	10.0	119	497	15	31
66	Colombia	3.5	2.5	6.3	4.7	355	690	3	25
67	Paraguay	..	10.4	9.0	7.8	54	172	3	..
68	*Angola*	35.5	−1.8	13.0	5.2	46	210	..	..
69	*Cuba*	21.2	5.3	4.7	4.1	624	1,051	6	..
70	*Korea, Dem. Rep.*	9.4	3.0	9.6	3.7	833	2,054	..	..
71	*Lebanon*	12.7	0.9	7.6	−1.9	512	812	68	..
72	*Mongolia*	10.4	10.9	..	11.1	364	1,161	..	..
Upper middle-income		**9.3** *w*	**−5.9** *w*	**7.8** *w*	**5.3** *w*	**540** *w*	**1,209** *w*	**10** *w*	**27** *w*
73	Syrian Arab Rep.	86.6	2.2	9.0	13.1	218	771	16	..
74	Jordan	..	..	6.8	16.1	130	706	79	101
75	Malaysia	37.5	19.6	9.5	8.3	222	689	2	18
76	Korea, Rep. of	5.9	4.2	14.7	10.4	143	1,104	70	37
77	Panama	14.7	53.6	18.5	4.6	306	2,192	..	125
78	Chile	4.0	0.8	6.2	1.1	569	754	10	20
79	Brazil	8.3	8.4	9.1	5.9	264	740	21	52
80	Mexico	5.8	17.6	7.4	9.3	540	1,340	3	..
81	Algeria	11.2	5.1	8.0	17.6	221	931	14	2
82	Portugal	4.5	0.7	7.8	4.3	363	1,145	17	58
83	Argentina	6.5	4.7	5.5	3.0	808	1,445	14	11
84	Uruguay	3.7	9.3	2.2	2.2	703	853	35	44
85	South Africa	3.6	10.0	5.2	5.0	1,512	2,392	9	(.)
86	Yugoslavia	4.2	4.0	6.7	5.0	659	1,844	8	35
87	Venezuela	1.1	−2.3	3.7	4.4	2,176	2,439	1	(.)
88	Greece	13.5	7.3	11.3	5.0	361	1,699	26	46
89	Israel	41.8	−39.4	9.3	2.1	932	1,847	17	36
90	Hong Kong	..	..	10.4	5.5	443	1,314	5	9
91	Singapore	..	..	9.4	1.6	1,448	4,492	17	44
92	Trinidad and Tobago	2.8	2.3	1.1	7.8	4,420	6,378	35	32
93	*Iran, Islamic Rep.*	14.6	−19.7	11.0	−1.7	522	808	1	..
94	*Iraq*	5.0	−2.9	5.1	11.8	411	855	(.)	..
High-income oil exporters		**17.1** *w*	**0.9** *w*	**..**	**7.1** *w*	**..**	**3,367** *w*	**..**	**1** *w*
95	Oman	44.0	−1.0	..	−2.6	..	914	..	7
96	Libya	29.1	−1.0	15.4	20.9	198	2,309	288	1
97	Saudi Arabia	14.0	4.0	14.6	7.6	874	3,326	1,271	(.)
98	Kuwait	4.5	−6.8	..	1.9	..	6,261	..	(.)
99	United Arab Emirates	37.9	−0.5	..	18.1	..	4,985	..	5
Industrial market economies		**4.0** *w*	**2.2** *w*	**5.3** *w*	**1.1** *w*	**3,141** *w*	**4,985** *w*	**12** *w*	**30** *w*
100	Ireland	−0.4	10.8	5.3	4.6	1,218	2,480	17	20
101	Spain	2.9	4.7	8.5	2.5	667	1,902	22	67
102	Italy	2.3	−0.2	8.1	0.8	1,003	2,558	18	41
103	New Zealand	4.0	5.1	5.2	2.0	2,083	3,673	7	20
104	United Kingdom	−0.9	10.8	2.2	−0.8	3,295	3,541	14	14
105	Austria	1.4	1.5	5.5	1.9	1,685	3,398	12	25
106	Japan	−1.4	5.9	11.3	1.5	880	3,087	18	48
107	Belgium	−7.2	2.8	5.1	0.3	2,790	4,636	11	23
108	Finland	3.3	20.6	9.4	5.7	1,304	5,793	11	40
109	Netherlands	16.9	−1.4	9.8	0.1	2,114	4,908	15	25
110	Australia	12.1	4.6	6.5	2.8	2,576	4,908	12	15
111	Canada	8.7	1.8	5.9	2.6	5,151	9,208	9	11
112	France	−1.4	5.3	5.7	1.7	1,964	3,619	16	33
113	Germany, Fed. Rep.	−0.6	0.8	4.4	1.4	2,645	4,342	7	23
114	Denmark	−21.6	36.1	5.9	1.0	1,914	3,616	15	26
115	United States	3.3	1.2	4.0	0.7	5,863	7,540	8	36
116	Sweden	3.6	8.5	5.2	1.9	3,122	6,138	16	25
117	Norway	6.8	19.4	6.0	3.9	3,400	8,305	15	13
118	Switzerland	4.2	5.3	6.2	1.7	1,841	3,755	10	14
East European nonmarket economies		**5.2** *w*	**3.6** *w*	**5.3** *w*	**3.5** *w*	**1,983** *w*	**4,442** *w*	**..**	**..**
119	Hungary	1.6	1.7	3.8	3.6	1,354	2,863	13	17
120	Romania	5.9	1.9	7.8	4.7	1,056	3,289	..	..
121	*Albania*	9.7	5.7	7.9	6.4	362	899	..	..
122	*Bulgaria*	3.3	4.8	9.7	4.6	935	4,164	7	19
123	*Czechoslovakia*	1.1	0.9	3.2	2.4	2,765	4,773	..	..
124	*German Dem. Rep.*	0.6	1.6	2.2	2.5	3,173	5,398	..	..
125	*Poland*	4.0	1.0	4.4	3.7	1,756	3,198	..	20
126	*USSR*	5.8	4.2	5.5	3.5	2,029	4,736	4	..

a. Figures in italics are for 1961–74, not 1960–74.   b. Figures in italics are for 1961, not 1960.   c. Figures in italics are for 1980, not 1981.

Table 9. Growth of merchandise trade

	Merchandise trade (millions of dollars)		Average annual growth rate[a] (percent)				Terms of trade (1980 = 100)	
	Exports 1982[b]	Imports 1982[b]	Exports 1960–70	Exports 1970–82[c]	Imports 1960–70	Imports 1970–82[c]	1979	1982[b]
Low-income economies	42,619 t	56,205 t	5.4 m	0.3 m	5.4 m	1.2 m	108 m	87 m
China and India	30,321 t	33,097 t	..	..	..	..	..	..
Other low-income	12,298 t	23,108 t	5.7 m	0.2 m	5.8 m	0.7 m	108 m	87 m
1 Chad	101	132	6.0	−8.6	5.1	−3.6	100	99
2 Bangladesh	769	2,300	8.1	−0.8	7.0	5.5	96	98
3 Ethiopia	404	787	3.7	1.3	6.2	0.2	139	74
4 Nepal	46	252	..	..	..	..	..	..
5 Mali	146	332	2.9	6.6	−0.4	6.6	107	102
6 Burma	380	408	−11.6	1.9	−5.6	−2.3	99	86
7 Zaire	569	480	−1.7	−5.6	5.4	−12.4	113	81
8 Malawi	262	314	11.7	5.1	7.6	1.2	111	106
9 Upper Volta	56	346	14.5	9.1	8.1	6.7	113	97
10 Uganda	371	339	6.9	−9.2	6.2	−7.9	103	74
11 India	8,446	14,088	4.7	4.7	−0.9	2.6	118	96
12 Rwanda	90	286	16.0	2.4	8.2	11.5	88	63
13 Burundi	88	214	..	..	..	..	..	..
14 Tanzania	480	1,046	3.8	−5.8	6.0	−1.5	105	86
15 Somalia	317	378	2.5	9.1	2.7	3.8	116	111
16 Haiti	380	525	..	..	..	..	..	..
17 Benin	34	889	5.2	−4.4	7.5	5.2	115	75
18 Central African Rep.	106	91	9.6	2.6	4.5	−0.2	99	90
19 China	21,875	19,009	..	..	..	..	..	..
20 Guinea	411	296	..	..	..	..	..	..
21 Niger	333	442	5.9	20.8	12.1	11.0	112	89
22 Madagascar	433	522	5.4	−3.6	4.1	−3.4	103	80
23 Sri Lanka	1,015	1,771	4.6	0.1	−0.2	1.8	126	85
24 Togo	213	526	10.5	0.3	8.6	8.6	108	112
25 Ghana	873	705	0.1	−4.7	−1.5	−4.8	136	61
26 Pakistan	2,403	5,396	9.9	4.7	5.4	3.9	119	93
27 Kenya	979	1,683	7.5	−3.3	6.5	−2.7	108	87
28 Sierra Leone	111	298	2.5	−6.6	1.9	−2.6	121	84
29 Afghanistan	373	776	2.7	7.1	0.7	8.1	99	96
30 Bhutan	..	..	..	..	..	..	..	..
31 Kampuchea, Dem.	40	62	..	..	..	..	..	..
32 Lao PDR	24	83	..	..	..	..	..	..
33 Mozambique	303	792	6.0	−13.3	7.9	−14.5	104	84
34 Viet Nam	188	637	..	..	..	..	..	..
Middle-income economies	329,558 t	380,209 t	5.4 m	2.6 m	5.9 m	3.9 m	99 m	91 m
Oil exporters	149,540 t	144,301 t	4.4 m	−1.3 m	3.6 m	8.7 m	74 m	104 m
Oil importers	180,018 t	235,908 t	6.7 m	4.0 m	7.4 m	1.5 m	102 m	85 m
Lower middle-income	97,855 t	119,668 t	5.3 m	1.6 m	6.8 m	3.3 m	98 m	89 m
35 Sudan	499	1,285	2.1	−5.1	0.5	3.5	98	85
36 Mauritania	232	273	53.8	−0.1	4.6	3.0	101	97
37 Yemen, PDR	580	1,193	..	..	..	..	..	..
38 Liberia	531	477	18.5	0.5	2.9	−2.4	121	92
39 Senegal	477	974	1.4	−1.8	2.3	1.3	110	89
40 Yemen Arab Rep.	44	1,987	..	..	..	..	..	..
41 Lesotho[d]	..	..	..	..	..	..	..	..
42 Bolivia	832	496	9.7	−3.9	8.1	3.8	77	76
43 Indonesia	22,294	16,859	3.5	4.4	1.9	12.3	73	108
44 Zambia	1,059	831	2.3	−0.5	9.7	−6.8	118	72
45 Honduras	654	712	10.9	3.4	11.7	0.8	100	81
46 Egypt, Arab Rep.	3,120	9,078	3.9	−0.3	−0.9	9.6	95	105
47 El Salvador	704	883	6.2	2.6	6.4	1.2	99	69
48 Thailand	6,945	8,548	5.2	9.1	11.3	4.3	121	78
49 Papua New Guinea	799	1,029	..	..	..	..	..	..
50 Philippines	5,010	8,229	2.3	7.9	7.2	2.1	112	83
51 Zimbabwe	663	704	..	..	..	..	81	105
52 Nigeria	19,484	20,821	6.6	−1.6	1.5	17.2	67	103
53 Morocco	2,059	4,315	2.7	−0.3	3.3	4.7	98	98
54 Cameroon	998	1,205	7.1	4.0	9.2	5.2	119	71
55 Nicaragua	406	776	9.9	1.6	10.4	−1.3	103	64
56 Ivory Coast	2,235	2,090	8.9	2.6	10.0	4.6	119	91
57 Guatemala	1,120	1,362	9.3	5.4	7.2	3.3	92	71
58 Congo, People's Rep.	923	970	6.4	1.4	−1.0	9.1	74	110
59 Costa Rica	872	887	9.6	4.5	10.1	0.1	97	88
60 Peru	3,230	3,787	2.1	4.8	3.6	1.6	99	89
61 Dominican Rep.	768	1,256	−2.1	4.0	9.9	1.3	83	82
62 Jamaica	726	1,372	4.8	−3.3	8.2	−6.1	107	85
63 Ecuador	2,341	2,189	2.8	−1.3	11.6	8.6	70	98
64 Turkey	5,685	8,812	..	4.0	..	2.0	125	89

Note: For data comparability and coverage see the technical notes.

234

	Merchandise trade (millions of dollars)		Average annual growth rate[a] (percent)				Terms of trade (1980=100)	
			Exports		Imports			
	Exports 1982[b]	Imports 1982[b]	1960–70	1970–82[c]	1960–70	1970–82[c]	1979	1982[b]
65 Tunisia	1,960	3,294	4.4	−0.1	2.3	8.7	79	99
66 Colombia	3,095	5,478	2.6	2.2	2.4	7.3	90	92
67 Paraguay	330	581	5.4	5.8	7.4	6.7	133	87
68 Angola	1,730	1,001	9.7	−15.8	11.5	0.0	74	104
69 Cuba	1,328	1,415	3.9	2.9	5.5	1.4	90	68
70 Korea, Dem. Rep.	843	899	..	..	..	..	..	..
71 Lebanon	923	3,567	15.2	1.0	5.2	3.9	96	92
72 Mongolia	37	29	..	..	..	..	..	..
Upper middle-income	**231,703** t	**260,541** t	**5.4** m	**7.1** m	**5.5** m	**7.4** m	**100** m	**96** m
73 Syrian Arab Rep.	2,026	4,015	3.5	−4.0	4.1	11.3	73	107
74 Jordan	753	3,241	10.8	17.7	3.6	13.5	102	101
75 Malaysia	11,789	12,543	6.1	3.8	2.4	7.3	97	83
76 Korea, Rep. of	21,853	24,251	34.7	20.2	19.7	9.8	127	95
77 Panama	309	1,569	10.4	−7.3	10.5	−3.9	94	84
78 Chile	3,822	3,529	0.7	9.5	4.8	1.5	120	74
79 Brazil	18,627	19,936	5.3	8.8	5.0	1.4	114	84
80 Mexico	21,006	15,042	3.4	8.6	6.4	8.7	77	106
81 Algeria	12,533	10,937	3.7	−0.3	−1.2	10.8	64	106
82 Portugal	4,111	9,313	9.6	..	14.2	..	..	..
83 Argentina	7,798	5,337	3.8	8.3	0.4	1.6	102	90
84 Uruguay	1,023	1,042	2.8	5.9	−3.0	1.9	119	80
85 South Africa[d]	17,597	18,956	5.4	..	8.2	..	101	..
86 Yugoslavia	10,265	13,346	7.7	..	8.8	..	101	..
87 Venezuela	16,443	11,670	1.1	−7.2	4.4	9.2	67	112
88 Greece	4,297	10,023	10.8	9.4	10.8	4.5	98	103
89 Israel	5,017	7,960	13.6	8.8	8.7	1.7	118	93
90 Hong Kong	20,985	23,554	12.7	9.4	9.2	11.9	100	95
91 Singapore	20,788	28,167	4.2	..	5.9	..	102	..
92 Trinidad and Tobago	3,072	3,697	4.9	−6.4	3.2	−5.3	95	97
93 Iran, Islamic Rep.	16,379	11,231	12.5	−13.8	11.5	7.5	60	98
94 Iraq	11,210	21,182	5.4	−4.8	1.7	24.1	69	118
High-income oil exporters	**133,379** t	**76,211** t	**33.5** m	**−2.9** m	**10.9** m	**19.3** m	**68** m	**114** m
95 Oman	4,421	2,682	..	..	..	..	..	..
96 Libya	16,391	15,414	66.9	−8.1	15.6	12.9	67	105
97 Saudi Arabia	79,123	40,654	10.8	2.3	11.0	32.3	67	125
98 Kuwait	16,561	8,042	5.2	−11.2	10.8	15.2	68	115
99 United Arab Emirates	16,883	9,419	56.1	2.4	5.2	23.3	73	113
Industrial market economies	**1,148,808** t	**1,212,975** t	**8.5** m	**5.6** m	**9.5** m	**4.3** m	**106** m	**99** m
100 Ireland	7,982	9,618	7.1	8.1	8.3	5.9	92	86
101 Spain	20,522	31,535	11.5	9.4	18.5	4.4	117	92
102 Italy	73,490	86,213	13.6	5.8	9.7	3.1	107	95
103 New Zealand	5,539	5,825	4.6	3.9	2.9	1.8	112	98
104 United Kingdom	97,028	99,723	4.8	6.0	5.0	3.5	102	97
105 Austria	15,685	19,557	9.6	7.0	9.6	6.1	104	99
106 Japan	138,911	131,932	17.2	8.5	13.7	3.5	125	106
107 Belgium[e]	52,381	58,037	10.9	4.6	10.3	4.5	104	94
108 Finland	13,132	13,387	6.8	4.7	7.0	2.4	112	100
109 Netherlands	66,322	62,583	9.9	4.5	9.5	3.1	102	103
110 Australia	22,022	24,187	6.5	3.8	7.2	5.2	103	100
111 Canada	68,499	55,091	10.0	4.0	9.1	4.3	99	94
112 France	92,629	115,645	8.2	6.1	11.0	6.2	107	98
113 Germany, Fed. Rep.	176,428	155,856	10.1	5.6	10.0	5.1	106	100
114 Denmark	15,527	17,162	7.1	4.8	8.2	2.1	107	99
115 United States	212,275	254,884	6.0	5.6	9.8	3.8	111	107
116 Sweden	26,817	27,591	7.7	3.2	7.2	2.3	100	99
117 Norway	17,595	15,479	9.1	6.7	9.7	4.3	86	115
118 Switzerland	26,024	28,670	8.5	3.9	9.0	4.3	109	112
East European nonmarket economies	**160,258** t	**150,004** t	**9.4** m	**6.7** m	**8.6** m	**6.0** m	**..**	**..**
119 Hungary	8,767	8,814	9.7	7.4	9.1	5.0	99	97
120 Romania	11,714	9,836	9.4	..	8.8	..	..	..
121 Albania	267	246	..	..	..	..	..	..
122 Bulgaria	1,969	2,281	14.4	11.4	12.9	7.8	..	..
123 Czechoslovakia	15,637	15,403	6.7	6.1	7.0	4.3	..	..
124 German Dem. Rep.	21,743	20,196	8.3	..	8.6	..	..	..
125 Poland	13,249	15,476	−0.3	6.7	−0.4	6.0	99	..
126 USSR	86,912	77,752	9.7	5.6	7.1	8.3	..	..

a. See the technical notes. b. Figures in italics are for 1981, not 1982. c. Figures in italics are for 1970–81, not 1970–82. d. Figures are for the South African Customs Union comprising South Africa, Namibia, Lesotho, Botswana, and Swaziland. Trade between the component territories is excluded. e. Includes Luxembourg.

Table 10. Structure of merchandise exports

	Fuels, minerals, and metals		Other primary commodities		Textiles and clothing		Machinery and transport equipment		Other manufactures	
Percentage share of merchandise exports	1960[a]	1981[b]	1960[a]	1981[b]	1960[a]	1981[b]	1960[a]	1981[b]	1960[a]	1981[b]
Low-income economies	9 w	19 w	70 w	31 w	15 w	21 w	(.) w	4 w	6 w	25 w
China and India	..	20 w	..	26 w	..	22 w	..	6 w	..	26 w
Other low-income	8 w	16 w	83 w	54 w	4 w	21 w	(.) w	1 w	5 w	8 w
1 Chad	3	..	94	..	0	..	0	..	3	..
2 Bangladesh	..	(.)	..	32	..	56	..	1	..	11
3 Ethiopia	0	8	100	91	0	(.)	0	(.)	0	1
4 Nepal	..	(.)	..	69	..	24	..	0	..	7
5 Mali	0	..	96	..	1	..	1	..	2	..
6 Burma	4	..	95	..	0	..	0	..	1	..
7 Zaire	42	..	57	..	0	..	0	..	1	..
8 Malawi	..	(.)	..	93	..	5	..	(.)	..	2
9 Upper Volta	0	(.)	100	85	0	2	0	6	(.)	7
10 Uganda	8	..	92	..	0	..	0	..	(.)	..
11 India	10	8	45	33	35	23	1	8	9	28
12 Rwanda	..	..	..	..	..	..	..	..	..	..
13 Burundi	..	..	..	..	..	..	..	..	..	..
14 Tanzania	(.)	10	87	76	0	9	0	(.)	13	5
15 Somalia	0	5	88	94	0	(.)	8	(.)	4	1
16 Haiti	0	..	100	..	0	..	0	..	0	..
17 Benin	10	..	80	..	7	..	(.)	..	3	..
18 Central African Rep.	12	(.)	86	74	(.)	(.)	1	(.)	1	26
19 China	..	24	..	23	..	21	..	5	..	27
20 Guinea	42	..	58	..	0	..	0	..	0	..
21 Niger	..	81	100	17	0	1	0	(.)	0	1
22 Madagascar	4	13	90	79	1	4	1	1	4	3
23 Sri Lanka	(.)	14	99	65	0	16	0	(.)	0	5
24 Togo	3	52	89	33	3	1	0	1	5	13
25 Ghana	7	..	83	..	0	..	0	..	10	..
26 Pakistan	0	7	73	40	23	41	1	1	3	11
27 Kenya	1	36	87	52	0	(.)	0	1	12	11
28 Sierra Leone	15	..	20	..	0	..	0	..	65	..
29 Afghanistan	(.)	..	82	..	14	..	3	..	1	..
30 Bhutan	..	..	..	..	..	..	..	..	..	..
31 Kampuchea, Dem.	0	..	100	..	0	..	0	..	0	..
32 Lao PDR	..	..	..	..	..	..	..	..	..	..
33 Mozambique	0	..	100	..	0	..	0	..	0	..
34 Viet Nam	..	..	..	..	..	..	..	..	..	..
Middle-income economies	30 w	33 w	59 w	24 w	3 w	10 w	1 w	11 w	7 w	22 w
Oil exporters	48 w	80 w	48 w	13 w	1 w	2 w	(.) w	3 w	3 w	2 w
Oil importers	15 w	13 w	68 w	28 w	5 w	14 w	2 w	14 w	10 w	31 w
Lower middle-income	20 w	43 w	76 w	39 w	1 w	6 w	(.) w	2 w	3 w	10 w
35 Sudan	0	5	100	94	0	1	0	(.)	0	(.)
36 Mauritania	4	..	69	..	1	..	20	..	6	..
37 Yemen, PDR	..	..	..	..	..	..	..	..	..	..
38 Liberia	45	67	55	31	0	(.)	0	1	0	1
39 Senegal	3	52	94	29	1	4	1	4	1	11
40 Yemen Arab Rep.	..	(.)	..	49	..	6	..	25	..	20
41 Lesotho[c]	..	..	..	..	..	..	..	..	..	..
42 Bolivia	..	..	..	..	..	..	..	..	..	..
43 Indonesia	33	83	67	13	(.)	1	(.)	1	(.)	2
44 Zambia	..	..	..	..	..	..	..	..	..	..
45 Honduras	5	6	93	83	0	2	0	(.)	2	9
46 Egypt, Arab Rep.	4	69	84	23	9	7	(.)	(.)	3	1
47 El Salvador	0	7	94	56	3	14	(.)	3	3	20
48 Thailand	7	8	91	65	(.)	10	0	5	2	12
49 Papua New Guinea	0	..	92	..	0	..	0	..	8	..
50 Philippines	10	16	86	39	1	7	0	3	3	35
51 Zimbabwe	71	..	25	..	1	..	(.)	..	3	..
52 Nigeria	8	..	89	..	0	..	0	..	3	..
53 Morocco	38	44	54	28	1	10	1	1	6	17
54 Cameroon	19	33	77	64	0	1	2	(.)	2	2
55 Nicaragua	3	2	95	88	0	1	0	(.)	2	9
56 Ivory Coast	1	8	98	82	0	3	(.)	2	1	5
57 Guatemala	2	2	95	69	1	5	0	2	2	22
58 Congo, People's Rep.	7	90	84	4	(.)	(.)	5	(.)	4	6
59 Costa Rica	0	1	95	67	0	4	0	4	5	24
60 Peru	49	64	50	19	0	8	0	2	1	7
61 Dominican Rep.	6	2	92	79	0	(.)	0	1	2	18
62 Jamaica	50	81	45	13	2	1	0	1	3	4
63 Ecuador	0	..	99	..	0	..	0	..	1	..
64 Turkey	8	7	89	56	0	19	0	4	3	14

Note: For data comparability and coverage see the technical notes.

	Percentage share of merchandise exports									
	Fuels, minerals, and metals		Other primary commodities		Textiles and clothing		Machinery and transport equipment		Other manufactures	
	1960[a]	1981[b]	1960[a]	1981[b]	1960[a]	1981[b]	1960[a]	1981[b]	1960[a]	1981[b]
65 Tunisia	24	57	66	10	1	15	1	2	8	16
66 Colombia	19	2	79	70	0	8	(.)	3	2	17
67 Paraguay	0	..	100	..	0	..	0	..	0	..
68 *Angola*	..	..	..	..	..	..	..	..	..	..
69 *Cuba*	2	5	93	*90*	1	*0*	(.)	*0*	4	5
70 *Korea, Dem. Rep.*	..	..	..	..	..	..	..	..	..	..
71 *Lebanon*	..	..	..	..	..	..	..	..	..	..
72 *Mongolia*	..	..	..	..	..	..	..	..	..	..
Upper middle-income	**38** *w*	**29** *w*	**46** *w*	**18** *w*	**4** *w*	**12** *w*	**2** *w*	**14** *w*	**10** *w*	**27** *w*
73 Syrian Arab Rep.	0	..	81	..	2	..	0	..	17	..
74 Jordan	0	33	96	24	0	6	0	2	4	35
75 Malaysia	20	36	74	44	(.)	3	(.)	12	6	5
76 Korea, Rep. of	30	2	56	8	8	30	(.)	22	6	38
77 Panama	..	24	..	67	..	3	..	(.)	..	6
78 Chile	92	65	4	25	0	(.)	0	2	4	8
79 Brazil	8	14	89	45	0	4	(.)	18	3	19
80 Mexico	24	..	64	..	4	..	1	..	7	..
81 Algeria	12	99	81	*1*	0	(.)	1	(.)	6	(.)
82 Portugal	8	9	37	20	18	27	3	13	34	31
83 Argentina	1	8	95	72	0	1	(.)	5	4	14
84 Uruguay	(.)	1	71	69	21	13	(.)	2	8	15
85 South Africa[c]	29	14	42	13	2	1	4	2	23	70
86 Yugoslavia	18	6	45	15	4	11	15	29	18	39
87 Venezuela	74	97	26	(.)	0	(.)	0	1	(.)	2
88 Greece	9	18	81	28	1	20	1	5	8	29
89 Israel	4	2	35	17	8	6	2	19	51	56
90 Hong Kong	5	1	15	2	45	42	4	18	31	37
91 Singapore	1	29	73	15	5	4	7	26	14	26
92 Trinidad and Tobago	82	90	14	2	0	(.)	0	3	4	5
93 *Iran, Islamic Rep.*	88	..	9	..	0	..	0	..	3	..
94 *Iraq*	97	..	3	..	0	..	0	..	0	..
High-income oil exporters	..	**98** *w*	..	**(.)** *w*	..	**(.)** *w*	..	**1** *w*	..	**1** *w*
95 Oman	..	94	..	1	..	(.)	..	4	..	1
96 Libya	100	100	0	(.)	0	(.)	0	(.)	0	(.)
97 Saudi Arabia	95	99	5	(.)	0	(.)	0	(.)	0	1
98 Kuwait	..	84	..	1	..	1	..	5	..	9
99 United Arab Emirates	..	..	..	..	..	..	..	..	..	..
Industrial market economies	**11** *w*	**12** *w*	**23** *w*	**15** *w*	**7** *w*	**4** *w*	**29** *w*	**37** *w*	**30** *w*	**32** *w*
100 Ireland	5	3	67	35	6	8	4	22	18	32
101 Spain	21	9	57	20	7	5	2	26	13	40
102 Italy	8	8	19	9	17	11	29	32	27	40
103 New Zealand	(.)	5	97	74	0	3	(.)	4	3	14
104 United Kingdom	7	23	9	9	8	4	44	33	32	31
105 Austria	26	5	22	11	10	10	16	27	26	47
106 Japan	11	1	10	2	28	4	23	57	28	36
107 Belgium[d]	15	14	9	12	12	7	13	22	51	45
108 Finland	3	8	50	20	1	7	13	21	33	44
109 Netherlands	15	27	34	24	8	4	18	16	25	29
110 Australia	13	33	79	42	(.)	1	3	6	5	18
111 Canada	33	26	37	22	1	1	8	28	21	23
112 France	9	8	18	19	10	5	25	34	38	34
113 Germany, Fed. Rep.	9	7	4	7	4	5	44	45	39	36
114 Denmark	2	5	63	39	3	5	19	25	13	26
115 United States	10	7	27	23	3	2	35	44	25	24
116 Sweden	10	9	29	12	1	2	31	42	29	35
117 Norway	22	60	34	9	2	1	10	13	32	17
118 Switzerland	2	3	8	4	12	7	30	34	48	52
East European nonmarket economies	**18** *w*	..	**33** *w*	..	**3** *w*	..	**34** *w*	..	**21** *w*	..
119 Hungary	6	8	28	27	7	7	38	31	21	27
120 Romania	..	..	..	..	..	..	..	..	..	..
121 *Albania*	..	..	..	..	..	..	..	..	..	..
122 *Bulgaria*	3	..	75	..	12	..	6	..	4	..
123 *Czechoslovakia*	20	5	11	8	(.)	6	45	52	25	29
124 *German Dem. Rep.*	..	..	..	..	..	..	..	..	..	..
125 *Poland*	..	17	..	8	..	7	..	47	..	21
126 *USSR*	24	..	28	..	1	..	21	..	26	..

a. Figures in italics are for 1961, not 1960.   b. Figures in italics are for 1980, not 1981.   c. Figures are for the South African Customs Union comprising South Africa, Namibia, Lesotho, Botswana, and Swaziland. Trade between the component countries is excluded.   d. Includes Luxembourg.

Table 11. Structure of merchandise imports

Percentage share of merchandise imports

	Food 1960[a]	Food 1981[b]	Fuels 1960[a]	Fuels 1981[b]	Other primary commodities 1960[a]	Other primary commodities 1981[b]	Machinery and transport equipment 1960[a]	Machinery and transport equipment 1981[b]	Other manufactures 1960[a]	Other manufactures 1981[b]
Low-income economies	22 *w*	14 *w*	7 *w*	21 *w*	18 *w*	12 *w*	26 *w*	22 *w*	27 *w*	31 *w*
China and India	..	13 *w*	..	21 *w*	..	14 *w*	..	21 *w*	..	31 *w*
Other low-income	24 *w*	16 *w*	8 *w*	21 *w*	4 *w*	6 *w*	21 *w*	26 *w*	43 *w*	31 *w*
1 Chad	19	..	12	..	4	..	19	..	46	..
2 Bangladesh	..	20	..	8	..	11	..	21	..	40
3 Ethiopia	..	9	..	23	..	4	..	35	..	29
4 Nepal	..	4	..	18	..	2	..	32	..	44
5 Mali	20	..	5	..	4	..	18	..	53	..
6 Burma	14	..	4	..	9	..	17	..	56	..
7 Zaire	..	..	..	..	..	..	..	..	..	..
8 Malawi	..	8	..	15	..	2	..	34	..	41
9 Upper Volta	21	25	4	16	1	3	24	24	50	32
10 Uganda	6	..	8	..	8	..	25	..	53	..
11 India	21	9	6	45	28	8	30	13	15	25
12 Rwanda	..	..	..	..	..	..	..	..	..	..
13 Burundi	..	..	..	..	..	..	..	..	..	..
14 Tanzania	..	13	..	21	..	3	..	35	..	28
15 Somalia	27	33	4	1	0	4	18	35	51	27
16 Haiti	..	..	..	..	..	..	..	..	..	..
17 Benin	17	..	10	..	1	..	18	..	54	..
18 Central African Rep.	15	21	9	2	2	3	26	34	48	40
19 China	..	16	..	(.)	..	20	..	27	..	37
20 Guinea	..	..	..	..	..	..	..	..	..	..
21 Niger	24	23	5	15	4	4	18	26	49	32
22 Madagascar	17	14	6	11	3	3	23	40	51	32
23 Sri Lanka	39	19	7	25	5	3	15	23	34	30
24 Togo	16	26	6	8	3	3	32	21	43	42
25 Ghana	19	..	5	..	4	..	26	..	46	..
26 Pakistan	22	14	10	28	2	8	27	23	39	27
27 Kenya	12	8	11	34	8	2	27	28	42	28
28 Sierra Leone	23	..	12	..	5	..	15	..	45	..
29 Afghanistan	14	..	7	..	4	..	14	..	61	..
30 Bhutan	..	..	..	..	..	..	..	..	..	..
31 Kampuchea, Dem.	..	..	..	..	..	..	..	..	..	..
32 Lao PDR	..	..	..	..	..	..	..	..	..	..
33 Mozambique	..	..	..	..	..	..	..	..	..	..
34 Viet Nam	..	..	..	..	..	..	..	..	..	..
Middle-income economies	15 *w*	12 *w*	9 *w*	21 *w*	13 *w*	6 *w*	28 *w*	29 *w*	35 *w*	32 *w*
Oil exporters	19 *w*	17 *w*	7 *w*	9 *w*	8 *w*	5 *w*	27 *w*	37 *w*	39 *w*	32 *w*
Oil importers	14 *w*	10 *w*	10 *w*	25 *w*	16 *w*	7 *w*	29 *w*	27 *w*	31 *w*	31 *w*
Lower middle-income	16 *w*	14 *w*	7 *w*	21 *w*	9 *w*	5 *w*	28 *w*	29 *w*	40 *w*	31 *w*
35 Sudan	17	19	8	19	3	3	14	22	58	37
36 Mauritania	5	..	3	..	3	..	39	..	50	..
37 Yemen, PDR	..	..	..	..	..	..	..	..	..	..
38 Liberia	16	22	4	27	7	2	34	25	39	24
39 Senegal	30	28	5	30	2	1	19	18	44	23
40 Yemen Arab Rep.	..	28	..	7	..	1	..	28	..	36
41 Lesotho[c]	..	..	..	..	..	..	..	..	..	..
42 Bolivia	..	..	..	..	..	..	..	..	..	..
43 Indonesia	23	11	5	13	10	6	17	36	45	34
44 Zambia	..	..	..	..	..	..	..	..	..	..
45 Honduras	13	10	9	16	3	2	24	27	51	45
46 Egypt, Arab Rep.	23	34	11	3	16	6	25	28	25	29
47 El Salvador	17	17	6	21	6	4	26	12	45	46
48 Thailand	10	4	11	30	11	8	25	26	43	32
49 Papua New Guinea	30	..	5	..	4	..	23	..	38	..
50 Philippines	15	8	10	30	5	4	36	23	34	35
51 Zimbabwe	..	..	..	..	..	..	..	..	..	..
52 Nigeria	14	..	5	..	6	..	24	..	51	..
53 Morocco	27	23	8	27	7	9	19	19	39	22
54 Cameroon	20	9	8	12	3	2	17	34	52	43
55 Nicaragua	9	18	10	20	5	1	22	21	54	40
56 Ivory Coast	18	20	6	22	2	2	27	22	47	34
57 Guatemala	12	6	10	38	7	3	26	16	45	37
58 Congo, People's Rep.	18	19	6	14	1	2	31	23	44	42
59 Costa Rica	13	9	6	16	6	4	26	22	49	49
60 Peru	16	19	5	1	5	4	37	49	37	27
61 Dominican Rep.	..	18	..	33	..	3	..	20	..	26
62 Jamaica	22	19	8	33	9	3	24	15	37	30
63 Ecuador	13	9	3	1	9	4	33	49	42	37
64 Turkey	7	3	11	44	16	6	42	22	24	25

Note: For data comparability and coverage see the technical notes.

		Percentage share of merchandise imports								
		Food		Fuels		Other primary commodities		Machinery and transport equipment		Other manufactures	
		1960[a]	1981[b]	1960[a]	1981[b]	1960[a]	1981[b]	1960[a]	1981[b]	1960[a]	1981[b]
65	Tunisia	20	14	9	21	4	8	23	27	44	30
66	Colombia	8	10	3	14	15	6	43	37	31	33
67	Paraguay	..	..	..	..	..	..	..	..	..	..
68	*Angola*	..	..	..	..	..	..	..	..	..	..
69	*Cuba*	..	..	..	..	..	..	..	..	..	..
70	*Korea, Dem. Rep.*	..	..	..	..	..	..	..	..	..	..
71	*Lebanon*	..	..	..	..	..	..	..	..	..	..
72	*Mongolia*	..	..	..	..	..	..	..	..	..	..
	Upper middle-income	**15** *w*	**11** *w*	**9** *w*	**22** *w*	**15** *w*	**7** *w*	**28** *w*	**29** *w*	**33** *w*	**31** *w*
73	Syrian Arab Rep.	24	..	8	..	5	..	15	..	48	..
74	Jordan	..	17	..	17	..	3	..	33	..	30
75	Malaysia	29	13	16	17	13	5	14	37	28	28
76	Korea, Rep. of	10	12	7	30	25	15	12	23	46	20
77	Panama	15	*10*	10	*31*	1	*1*	22	*21*	52	*37*
78	Chile	..	*15*	..	*18*	..	*4*	..	*33*	..	*30*
79	Brazil	14	9	19	51	13	4	36	18	18	18
80	Mexico	4	..	2	..	10	..	52	..	32	..
81	Algeria	26	21	4	2	2	5	14	38	54	34
82	Portugal	15	16	10	24	28	9	26	27	21	24
83	Argentina	3	5	13	11	11	6	44	43	29	35
84	Uruguay	5	7	24	32	46	5	17	32	8	24
85	South Africa[c]	6	4	7	(.)	9	4	37	42	41	50
86	Yugoslavia	11	6	5	24	25	12	37	28	22	30
87	Venezuela	18	17	1	1	10	4	36	43	35	35
88	Greece	11	11	8	22	16	7	44	28	21	32
89	Israel	20	12	7	26	18	7	28	24	27	31
90	Hong Kong	27	12	3	8	16	5	10	23	44	52
91	Singapore	21	7	15	34	38	5	7	28	19	26
92	Trinidad and Tobago	16	13	34	37	7	3	18	22	25	25
93	*Iran, Islamic Rep.*	14	..	1	..	1	..	23	..	61	..
94	*Iraq*	..	..	..	..	..	..	..	..	..	..
	High-income oil exporters	..	**14** *w*	..	**5** *w*	..	**2** *w*	..	**39** *w*	..	**40** *w*
95	Oman	..	13	..	13	..	2	..	39	..	33
96	Libya	13	18	5	1	10	2	40	38	32	41
97	Saudi Arabia	..	14	..	1	..	2	..	40	..	43
98	Kuwait	..	14	..	1	..	2	..	41	..	42
99	United Arab Emirates	..	11	..	11	..	2	..	36	..	40
	Industrial market economies	**22** *w*	**11** *w*	**11** *w*	**28** *w*	**24** *w*	**9** *w*	**16** *w*	**23** *w*	**27** *w*	**31** *w*
100	Ireland	18	13	12	15	11	4	21	27	38	41
101	Spain	16	12	22	43	25	9	22	17	15	19
102	Italy	20	12	14	35	31	11	13	20	22	22
103	New Zealand	8	6	8	20	16	5	29	32	39	37
104	United Kingdom	36	14	11	14	27	10	8	26	18	36
105	Austria	16	7	10	19	20	9	29	27	25	38
106	Japan	17	13	17	51	49	16	9	7	8	13
107	Belgium[d]	15	12	10	20	26	10	21	22	28	36
108	Finland	13	7	10	31	20	7	33	27	24	28
109	Netherlands	18	15	13	26	14	6	22	19	33	34
110	Australia	6	5	10	14	16	4	31	39	37	38
111	Canada	12	7	9	12	12	6	36	47	31	28
112	France	25	10	17	29	25	8	14	22	19	31
113	Germany, Fed. Rep.	26	12	8	24	28	9	10	20	28	35
114	Denmark	18	12	12	24	11	7	23	21	36	36
115	United States	24	8	10	31	25	7	10	26	31	28
116	Sweden	13	7	14	25	13	6	26	27	34	35
117	Norway	12	7	9	15	13	7	36	34	30	37
118	Switzerland	18	9	8	12	13	6	21	26	40	47
	East European nonmarket economies	..	**10** *w*	..	**22** *w*	..	**16** *w*	..	**29** *w*	..	**23** *w*
119	Hungary	8	9	12	17	28	11	28	28	24	35
120	Romania	..	3	..	28	..	27	..	28	..	14
121	*Albania*	..	..	..	..	..	..	..	..	..	..
122	*Bulgaria*	..	..	..	..	..	..	..	..	..	..
123	Czechoslovakia	..	10	..	23	..	14	..	35	..	18
124	*German Dem. Rep.*	..	..	..	..	..	..	..	..	..	..
125	Poland	..	18	..	20	..	10	..	31	..	21
126	USSR	12	..	4	..	18	..	30	..	36	..

a. Figures in italics are for 1961, not 1960.   b. Figures in italics are for 1980, not 1981.   c. Figures are for the South African Customs Union comprising South Africa, Namibia, Lesotho, Botswana, and Swaziland. Trade between the component territories is excluded.   d. Includes Luxembourg.

239

Table 12. Origin and destination of merchandise exports

	Destination of merchandise exports (percentage of total)							
	Industrial market economies		East European nonmarket economies		High-income oil exporters		Developing economies	
Origin	1960	1982[a]	1960	1982[a]	1960	1982[a]	1960	1982[a]
Low-income economies	51 w	52 w	21 w	5 w	1 w	4 w	27 w	39 w
China and India	39 w	48 w	36 w	6 w	(.) w	4 w	25 w	42 w
Other low-income	66 w	60 w	3 w	4 w	2 w	6 w	29 w	30 w
1 Chad	73	44	0	0	0	7	27	49
2 Bangladesh	..	38	..	10	..	1	..	51
3 Ethiopia	69	66	1	3	6	7	24	24
4 Nepal	..	50	..	0	..	(.)	..	50
5 Mali	93	62	0	1	(.)	(.)	7	37
6 Burma	23	35	3	2	(.)	3	74	60
7 Zaire	89	92	(.)	(.)	(.)	(.)	11	8
8 Malawi	..	74	..	0	..	0	..	26
9 Upper Volta	4	64	0	0	0	0	96	36
10 Uganda	62	88	0	0	0	2	38	10
11 India	66	61	7	11	2	8	25	20
12 Rwanda	..	61	..	0	..	(.)	..	39
13 Burundi	..	76	..	0	..	0	..	24
14 Tanzania	74	57	1	4	0	1	25	38
15 Somalia	85	16	..	(.)	(.)	68	15	16
16 Haiti	98	97	(.)	(.)	0	0	2	3
17 Benin	90	82	2	(.)	0	0	8	18
18 Central African Rep.	83	83	0	(.)	0	(.)	17	17
19 China	14	43	61	4	(.)	2	25	51
20 Guinea	63	87	8	(.)	(.)	(.)	19	13
21 Niger	74	76	0	0	0	0	26	24
22 Madagascar	79	57	1	6	0	(.)	20	37
23 Sri Lanka	75	46	3	4	0	4	22	46
24 Togo	74	63	0	1	0	(.)	26	36
25 Ghana	88	77	7	10	(.)	(.)	5	13
26 Pakistan	56	40	4	4	2	19	38	37
27 Kenya	77	53	0	1	(.)	4	23	42
28 Sierra Leone	99	80	0	0	0	(.)	1	20
29 Afghanistan	48	30	28	50	0	1	24	19
30 Bhutan	..	..	..	..	..	..	..	..
31 Kampuchea, Dem.	..	..	..	..	..	..	..	..
32 Lao PDR	..	15	..	0	..	(.)	..	85
33 Mozambique	29	54	(.)	0	(.)	3	71	43
34 Viet Nam	..	28	..	7	..	(.)	..	65
Middle-income economies	68 w	65 w	7 w	4 w	(.) w	3 w	25 w	28 w
Oil exporters	68 w	70 w	4 w	1 w	(.) w	2 w	28 w	27 w
Oil importers	68 w	61 w	9 w	6 w	(.) w	5 w	23 w	28 w
Lower middle-income	73 w	69 w	7 w	2 w	1 w	2 w	19 w	27 w
35 Sudan	59	38	8	7	4	22	29	33
36 Mauritania	89	95	0	0	0	(.)	11	5
37 Yemen, PDR	42	53	(.)	(.)	2	27	56	20
38 Liberia	100	64	0	1	0	(.)	(.)	35
39 Senegal	89	65	0	(.)	0	(.)	11	35
40 Yemen Arab Rep.	46	27	18	(.)	(.)	23	36	50
41 Lesotho[b]	..	..	..	..	..	..	..	..
42 Bolivia	88	34	0	4	0	0	12	62
43 Indonesia	54	75	11	(.)	(.)	(.)	42	25
44 Zambia	..	74	..	1	..	0	..	25
45 Honduras	77	87	0	0	0	(.)	23	13
46 Egypt, Arab Rep.	26	53	33	13	2	3	39	31
47 El Salvador	88	74	0	(.)	0	0	12	26
48 Thailand	47	55	2	3	3	4	48	38
49 Papua New Guinea	..	89	..	(.)	..	(.)	..	11
50 Philippines	94	73	0	2	(.)	1	6	24
51 Zimbabwe	..	49	..	1	..	1	..	49
52 Nigeria	95	89	1	2	0	(.)	4	9
53 Morocco	74	68	3	7	(.)	2	23	23
54 Cameroon	93	89	1	(.)	(.)	(.)	6	11
55 Nicaragua	91	68	(.)	6	0	(.)	9	26
56 Ivory Coast	84	71	0	3	0	(.)	16	26
57 Guatemala	94	55	0	(.)	0	3	6	42
58 Congo, People's Rep.	93	81	0	(.)	0	(.)	7	19
59 Costa Rica	93	68	(.)	2	(.)	(.)	7	30
60 Peru	84	72	(.)	2	0	(.)	16	26
61 Dominican Rep.	92	70	0	11	1	(.)	7	19
62 Jamaica	96	75	0	5	0	(.)	4	20
63 Ecuador	91	50	1	1	0	(.)	8	49
64 Turkey	71	42	12	5	(.)	12	17	41

Note: For data comparability and coverage see the technical notes.

240

	Destination of merchandise exports (percentage of total)							
	Industrial market economies		East European nonmarket economies		High-income oil exporters		Developing economies	
Origin	1960	1982[a]	1960	1982[a]	1960	1982[a]	1960	1982[a]
65 Tunisia	76	73	3	2	2	4	19	21
66 Colombia	94	73	1	4	0	(.)	5	23
67 Paraguay	61	41	0	0	0	0	39	59
68 Angola	64	67	2	(.)	0	0	34	33
69 Cuba	72	43	19	10	(.)	3	9	44
70 Korea, Dem. Rep.	..	..	..	..	..	..	..	..
71 Lebanon	21	14	8	1	32	55	39	30
72 Mongolia	..	..	..	..	..	..	..	..
Upper middle-income	**67** w	**63** w	**6** w	**4** w	**(.)** w	**4** w	**28** w	**29** w
73 Syrian Arab Rep.	39	55	19	18	11	9	31	18
74 Jordan	1	5	11	11	26	23	62	61
75 Malaysia	58	51	7	3	0	1	35	45
76 Korea, Rep. of	89	65	0	(.)	0	10	11	25
77 Panama	99	76	0	(.)	0	1	1	23
78 Chile	91	72	(.)	1	(.)	1	9	26
79 Brazil	81	60	6	6	(.)	1	13	33
80 Mexico	93	91	(.)	(.)	0	(.)	7	9
81 Algeria	93	93	0	1	(.)	(.)	7	6
82 Portugal	56	81	2	2	(.)	1	42	16
83 Argentina	75	43	5	22	(.)	(.)	20	35
84 Uruguay	82	39	7	8	0	2	11	51
85 South Africa[b]	71	82	1	(.)	(.)	0	28	18
86 Yugoslavia	48	27	31	50	1	3	20	20
87 Venezuela	62	56	0	(.)	0	(.)	38	44
88 Greece	65	60	21	8	1	11	13	21
89 Israel	76	66	1	1	0	0	23	33
90 Hong Kong	54	77	(.)	(.)	1	3	45	20
91 Singapore	38	40	4	1	1	5	57	54
92 Trinidad and Tobago	80	69	0	(.)	(.)	(.)	20	31
93 Iran, Islamic Rep.	62	55	3	(.)	1	10	34	29
94 Iraq	85	47	1	(.)	(.)	(.)	14	53
High-income oil exporters	**83** w	**56** w	**(.)** w	**1** w	**0** w	**11** w	**17** w	**35** w
95 Oman	..	11	..	0	..	70	..	19
96 Libya	67	80	7	4	0	0	26	16
97 Saudi Arabia	74	66	0	(.)	0	(.)	26	34
98 Kuwait	..	44	..	1	..	5	..	55
99 United Arab Emirates	91	12	0	(.)	0	45	9	43
Industrial market economies	**67** w	**66** w	**3** w	**3** w	**(.)** w	**4** w	**30** w	**27** w
100 Ireland	96	87	(.)	1	(.)	2	4	10
101 Spain	80	58	2	2	(.)	5	18	35
102 Italy	65	64	4	3	2	8	29	25
103 New Zealand	95	65	1	6	(.)	2	4	27
104 United Kingdom	57	70	3	2	2	5	38	23
105 Austria	69	69	13	11	(.)	3	18	17
106 Japan	45	47	2	3	2	8	51	42
107 Belgium[c]	79	83	2	2	1	2	18	13
108 Finland	69	60	19	29	(.)	1	12	10
109 Netherlands	78	83	1	2	1	2	20	13
110 Australia	75	49	3	4	1	3	21	44
111 Canada	90	84	1	3	(.)	1	9	12
112 France	53	66	3	3	(.)	4	44	27
113 Germany, Fed. Rep.	70	73	4	4	1	4	25	19
114 Denmark	83	79	4	1	(.)	3	13	17
115 United States	61	54	1	2	1	5	37	39
116 Sweden	79	79	4	3	(.)	3	17	15
117 Norway	80	88	4	1	(.)	1	16	10
118 Switzerland	72	69	3	3	1	5	24	23
East European nonmarket economies	**19** w	**..**	**59** w	**..**	**(.)** w	**..**	**22** w	**..**
119 Hungary	22	24	61	52	(.)	2	17	22
120 Romania	20	..	66	..	(.)	..	14	..
121 Albania	1	..	93	..	0	..	6	..
122 Bulgaria	13	..	80	..	(.)	..	7	..
123 Czechoslovakia	16	19	67	64	(.)	2	17	34
124 German Dem. Rep.	19	..	68	..	(.)	..	13	..
125 Poland	29	27	54	49	(.)	2	17	22
126 USSR	18	..	51	..	(.)	..	31	..

a. Figures in italics are for 1981, not 1982.   b. Figures are for the South African Customs Union comprising South Africa, Namibia, Lesotho, Botswana, and Swaziland. Trade between the component territories is excluded.   c. Includes Luxembourg.

Table 13. Origin and destination of manufactured exports

Origin	Destination of manufactured exports (percentage of total)								Value manufactured exports (millions of dollars)	
	Industrial market economies		East European nonmarket economies		High-income oil exporters		Developing economies			
	1962[a]	1981[b]	1962[a]	1981[b]	1962[a]	1981[b]	1962[a]	1981[b]	1962[a]	1981[b]
Low-income economies	57 w	50 w	..	14 w	..	8 w	..	28 w		
China and India	..	..	..	..	..	..	..	..		
Other low-income	61 w	48 w	1 w	6 w	1 w	8 w	37 w	38 w		
1 Chad	19	..	0	..	6	..	75	..	1	..
2 Bangladesh	..	36	..	8	..	1	..	55	..	448
3 Ethiopia	47	37	2	12	1	7	50	44	2	1
4 Nepal	..	73	..	0	..	(.)	..	27	..	29
5 Mali	33	..	1	..	0	..	66	..	(.)	..
6 Burma	58	..	(.)	..	0	..	42	..	3	..
7 Zaire	93	..	0	..	0	..	7	..	12	..
8 Malawi	..	33	..	(.)	..	(.)	..	67	..	18
9 Upper Volta	19	19	0	0	0	0	81	81	1	11
10 Uganda	15	..	0	..	0	..	85	..	(.)	..
11 India	56	51	5	18	2	7	37	24	630	4,424
12 Rwanda	90	..	0	..	0	..	10	..	(.)	..
13 Burundi	..	..	..	..	..	..	..	..	..	..
14 Tanzania	93	60	0	(.)	0	1	7	39	16	75
15 Somalia	61	58	0	3	4	11	35	28	(.)	1
16 Haiti	..	..	..	..	..	..	..	..	..	..
17 Benin	18	..	0	..	0	..	82	..	(.)	..
18 Central African Rep.	78	69	2	0	0	0	20	31	3	29
19 China	..	..	..	..	..	..	..	..	..	12,298
20 Guinea	..	..	..	..	..	..	..	..	..	..
21 Niger	7	30	0	(.)	0	0	93	70	1	10
22 Madagascar	87	73	0	1	0	(.)	13	26	5	25
23 Sri Lanka	63	83	2	(.)	(.)	1	35	16	6	218
24 Togo	44	9	0	1	0	0	56	90	1	32
25 Ghana	39	..	11	..	(.)	..	50	..	12	..
26 Pakistan	46	51	(.)	8	1	13	53	28	97	1,439
27 Kenya	22	12	0	(.)	2	7	76	81	11	210
28 Sierra Leone	98	..	0	..	0	..	2	..	21	..
29 Afghanistan	96	..	1	..	0	..	3	..	9	..
30 Bhutan	..	..	..	..	..	..	..	..	..	..
31 Kampuchea, Dem.	30	..	1	..	(.)	..	70	..	1	..
32 Lao PDR	35	..	0	..	0	..	65	..	(.)	..
33 Mozambique	31	..	0	..	0	..	69	..	3	..
34 Viet Nam	10	..	0	..	0	..	90	..	1	..
Middle-income economies	50 w	57 w	5 w	7 w	1 w	5 w	43 w	31 w		
Oil exporters	61 w	57 w	5 w	3 w	1 w	3 w	27 w	37 w		
Oil importers	48 w	57 w	5 w	7 w	1 w	5 w	46 w	31 w		
Lower middle-income	53 w	52 w	8 w	3 w	1 w	6 w	38 w	39 w		
35 Sudan	37	50	1	16	3	22	59	12	(.)	4
36 Mauritania	98	..	0	..	0	..	2	..	2	..
37 Yemen, PDR	..	..	..	..	..	..	..	..	..	..
38 Liberia	94	47	(.)	(.)	0	0	6	53	3	13
39 Senegal	76	24	0	1	0	(.)	24	75	5	110
40 Yemen Arab Rep.	..	59	..	0	..	7	..	34	..	12
41 Lesotho[c]	..	..	..	..	..	..	..	..	..	..
42 Bolivia	82	..	0	..	0	..	18	..	4	..
43 Indonesia	52	33	1	(.)	1	5	46	62	2	733
44 Zambia	..	..	..	..	..	..	..	..	..	..
45 Honduras	1	33	0	0	0	0	99	67	2	83
46 Egypt, Arab Rep.	23	37	35	42	3	6	39	15	69	276
47 El Salvador	1	7	0	0	0	0	99	93	11	181
48 Thailand	51	59	(.)	(.)	(.)	7	49	34	21	1,869
49 Papua New Guinea	97	..	0	..	0	..	3	..	4	..
50 Philippines	91	78	0	(.)	(.)	1	9	21	26	2,552
51 Zimbabwe	44	..	0	..	0	..	56	..	31	..
52 Nigeria	91	..	(.)	..	(.)	..	9	..	34	..
53 Morocco	52	45	2	9	(.)	9	46	37	28	655
54 Cameroon	25	77	0	0	0	0	75	23	4	50
55 Nicaragua	55	2	0	(.)	0	0	45	98	2	47
56 Ivory Coast	61	34	0	(.)	0	(.)	39	66	2	262
57 Guatemala	46	4	0	0	0	(.)	54	96	8	325
58 Congo, People's Rep.	88	88	0	0	0	0	12	12	14	64
59 Costa Rica	78	11	0	(.)	0	(.)	22	89	9	322
60 Peru	53	45	0	2	0	(.)	47	53	5	386
61 Dominican Rep.	98	80	0	0	0	0	2	20	4	186
62 Jamaica	73	74	0	8	0	1	27	17	20	611
63 Ecuador	46	..	0	..	0	..	54	..	2	..
64 Turkey	73	40	17	3	(.)	21	10	36	4	1,748

Note: For data comparability and coverage see the technical notes.

Origin	Destination of manufactured exports (percentage of total)								Value manufactured exports (millions of dollars)	
	Industrial market economies		East European nonmarket economies		High-income oil exporters		Developing economies			
	1962[a]	1981[b]	1962[a]	1981[b]	1962[a]	1981[b]	1962[a]	1981[b]	1962[a]	1981[b]
65 Tunisia	64	68	0	2	7	7	29	23	10	835
66 Colombia	57	33	0	1	0	(.)	43	66	16	838
67 Paraguay	84	..	0	..	0	..	16	..	4	..
68 *Angola*	34	..	4	..	0	..	62	..	21	..
69 *Cuba*	1	..	83	..	0	..	16	..	6	*319*
70 *Korea, Dem. Rep.*	..	..	..	..	..	..	..	..	..	..
71 *Lebanon*	22	..	4	..	14	..	60	..	11	..
72 *Mongolia*	..	..	..	..	..	..	..	..	..	..
Upper middle-income	**50** *w*	**58** *w*	**5** *w*	**8** *w*	**1** *w*	**5** *w*	**44** *w*	**31** *w*		
73 Syrian Arab Rep.	17	..	7	..	1	..	75	..	9	..
74 Jordan	12	*13*	10	*(.)*	32	*36*	46	*51*	1	*201*
75 Malaysia	11	62	0	(.)	(.)	2	89	36	58	2,359
76 Korea, Rep. of	83	62	0	0	0	10	17	28	10	19,188
77 Panama	24	*11*	0	*(.)*	0	*1*	76	*88*	1	*31*
78 Chile	45	29	0	(.)	0	2	55	69	20	737
79 Brazil	60	43	3	1	0	1	37	55	39	9,465
80 Mexico	71	..	0	..	0	..	29	..	122	..
81 *Algeria*	*50*	*58*	*0*	*36*	*0*	*(.)*	*50*	*6*	*23*	*49*
82 Portugal	56	79	(.)	2	(.)	1	44	18	205	2,961
83 Argentina	62	45	3	5	0	1	35	49	39	1,800
84 Uruguay	75	45	13	6	0	(.)	12	49	7	363
85 South Africa[c]	54	..	(.)	..	(.)	..	46	..	317	15,317
86 Yugoslavia	31	25	30	53	1	4	38	18	344	8,574
87 Venezuela	94	59	0	(.)	0	(.)	6	41	158	417
88 Greece	52	53	6	4	3	15	39	28	27	2,266
89 Israel	66	66	3	(.)	0	0	31	34	184	4,590
90 Hong Kong	63	77	0	(.)	1	3	36	20	642	20,076
91 Singapore	4	49	0	1	2	4	94	46	328	11,712
92 Trinidad and Tobago	39	72	0	(.)	0	(.)	61	28	13	315
93 *Iran, Islamic Rep.*	45	..	1	..	3	..	51	..	44	..
94 *Iraq*	26	..	(.)	..	8	..	66	..	2	..
High-income oil exporters	**13** *w*	**25** *w*	**0** *w*	**(.)** *w*	**30** *w*	**23** *w*	**57** *w*	**52** *w*		
95 Oman	..	18	..	0	..	70	..	12	..	229
96 Libya	68	68	0	(.)	0	(.)	32	32	(.)	58
97 Saudi Arabia	64	12	0	(.)	12	18	24	70	3	721
98 Kuwait	(.)	28	0	(.)	35	21	65	51	11	2,453
99 United Arab Emirates	76	..	0	..	3	..	21	..	33	..
Industrial market economies	**63** *w*	**63** *w*	**3** *w*	**3** *w*	**1** *w*	**5** *w*	**33** *w*	**29** *w*		
100 Ireland	76	91	0	(.)	(.)	1	24	8	134	4,820
101 Spain	57	53	1	2	(.)	6	42	39	205	14,320
102 Italy	65	61	5	3	2	10	28	26	3,490	62,769
103 New Zealand	90	72	0	(.)	0	1	10	27	23	1,096
104 United Kingdom	58	62	3	2	2	7	37	29	8,947	70,115
105 Austria	67	67	18	12	(.)	3	15	18	931	13,255
106 Japan	45	47	4	3	1	7	50	43	4,340	146,635
107 Belgium[d]	83	83	2	2	1	2	14	13	3,257	40,574
108 Finland	56	57	31	31	(.)	1	13	11	608	10,052
109 Netherlands	78	79	2	2	1	4	19	15	2,443	33,738
110 Australia	62	30	(.)	(.)	(.)	1	38	69	263	5,268
111 Canada	89	88	(.)	(.)	(.)	1	11	11	1,959	35,573
112 France	63	63	4	3	(.)	4	33	30	5,317	73,675
113 Germany, Fed. Rep.	74	70	4	4	1	4	21	22	11,623	151,043
114 Denmark	76	74	8	2	(.)	2	16	22	627	8,888
115 United States	48	54	(.)	(.)	1	6	51	40	13,957	157,217
116 Sweden	76	74	6	3	(.)	4	18	19	1,958	22,694
117 Norway	81	73	2	3	(.)	1	17	23	442	5,533
118 Switzerland	74	69	3	3	1	4	22	24	2,005	24,697
East European nonmarket economies	**..**	**..**	**..**	**..**	**..**	**..**	**..**	**..**	**..**	**..**
119 Hungary	..	23	..	56	..	1	..	20	..	5,591
120 Romania	..	..	..	..	..	..	..	..	..	..
121 *Albania*	..	..	..	..	..	..	..	..	..	..
122 *Bulgaria*	..	..	..	..	..	..	..	..	..	..
123 *Czechoslovakia*	..	14	..	68	..	2	..	16	..	12,971
124 *German Dem. Rep.*	..	..	..	..	..	..	..	..	..	..
125 *Poland*	..	17	..	56	..	2	..	25	..	9,983
126 *USSR*	..	..	..	..	..	..	..	..	..	..

a. Figures in italics are for 1963, not 1962.   b. Figures in italics are for 1980, not 1981.   c. Figures are for the South African Customs Union comprising South Africa, Namibia, Lesotho, Botswana, and Swaziland. Trade between the component territories is excluded.   d. Includes Luxembourg.

Table 14. Balance of payments and reserves

	Current account balance (millions of dollars)		Receipts of workers' remittances (millions of dollars)		Net direct private investment (millions of dollars)		Gross international reserves		
							Millions of dollars		In months of import coverage
	1970	1982[a]	1970	1982[a]	1970	1982[a]	1970	1982[a]	1982[a]
Low-income economies									7.3 *w*
China and India									8.1 *w*
Other low-income									3.0 *w*
1 Chad	2	19	..	..	1	(.)	2	18	2.0
2 Bangladesh	..	−632	..	329	..	..	..	207	0.9
3 Ethiopia	−32	−196	..	..	4	..	72	277	3.6
4 Nepal	..	−86	..	..	..	..	94	268	6.5
5 Mali	−2	−113	6	39	..	2	1	25	0.7
6 Burma	−63	−317	..	..	..	..	98	328	3.9
7 Zaire	−64	−375	2	..	42	..	189	312	1.8
8 Malawi	−35	−78	..	..	9	..	29	29	0.9
9 Upper Volta	9	..	18	..	(.)	..	36	67	..
10 Uganda	20	−256	..	..	4	..	57	73	0.1
11 India	−394	−2,696	113	2,293	6	..	1,023	8,109	5.4
12 Rwanda	7	−90	1	1	(.)	21	8	128	4.3
13 Burundi	..	..	..	..	..	..	15	37	..
14 Tanzania	−36	−268	..	9	..	..	65	19	0.2
15 Somalia	−6	−177	..	20	5	−1	21	15	0.3
16 Haiti	2	−93	17	95	3	13	4	12	0.3
17 Benin	−1	..	2	..	7	..	16	10	..
18 Central African Rep.	−12	−39	(.)	..	1	9	1	52	2.3
19 China	..	5,608	..	..	..	..	..	17,142	9.4
20 Guinea	..	..	..	..	..	..	..	..	..
21 Niger	(.)	..	..	..	1	..	19	35	..
22 Madagascar	10	−369	..	..	10	..	37	20	0.3
23 Sri Lanka	−59	−574	3	290	(.)	64	43	380	1.9
24 Togo	3	−152	..	..	1	..	35	173	5.6
25 Ghana	−68	83	..	1	68	21	58	318	4.0
26 Pakistan	−667	−811	..	2,580	31	65	194	1,813	3.0
27 Kenya	−49	−509	..	..	14	60	220	248	1.4
28 Sierra Leone	−16	−158	..	..	8	6	39	8	0.4
29 *Afghanistan*	..	..	..	..	..	..	49	699	..
30 *Bhutan*	..	..	..	..	..	..	..	..	..
31 *Kampuchea, Dem.*	..	..	..	..	..	..	..	..	..
32 *Lao PDR*	..	..	..	..	..	..	6	..	..
33 *Mozambique*	..	..	..	..	..	..	..	..	..
34 *Viet Nam*	..	..	..	..	..	..	243	..	..
Middle-income economies									4.7 *w*
Oil exporters									4.6 *w*
Oil importers									4.8 *w*
Lower middle-income									3.9 *w*
35 Sudan	−42	−248	..	131	..	..	22	21	0.2
36 Mauritania	−5	−252	1	2	1	15	3	144	2.7
37 Yemen, PDR	−4	−221	60	411	..	..	59	271	3.4
38 Liberia	..	−79	..	..	..	..	..	8	0.2
39 Senegal	−16	..	3	..	5	..	22	25	..
40 Yemen Arab Rep.	..	−610	..	1,118	..	24	..	558	2.9
41 Lesotho	..	−50	..	..	..	4	..	48	1.2
42 Bolivia	4	−92	(.)	1	−76	37	46	563	6.4
43 Indonesia	−310	−737	..	..	83	133	160	6,248	3.0
44 Zambia	108	−252	..	..	−297	..	515	157	1.5
45 Honduras	−64	−228	..	..	8	14	20	120	1.4
46 Egypt, Arab Rep.	−148	−2,216	29	2,074	..	650	165	1,809	1.9
47 El Salvador	9	−250	..	..	4	..	64	277	2.6
48 Thailand	−250	−1,144	..	616	43	185	912	2,674	3.0
49 Papua New Guinea	..	−487	..	..	..	84	..	374	2.9
50 Philippines	−48	−3,356	..	240	−29	253	255	2,573	2.7
51 Zimbabwe	..	−706	..	2	..	7	59	320	1.7
52 Nigeria	−368	−7,324	..	..	205	358	223	1,927	1.1
53 Morocco	−124	−1,876	63	849	20	79	141	540	1.1
54 Cameroon	−30	−525	(.)	21	16	1	81	81	0.5
55 Nicaragua	−40	..	..	..	15	..	49	171	..
56 Ivory Coast	−38	15	..	..	31	..	119	23	0.1
57 Guatemala	−8	−379	..	..	29	76	79	351	2.4
58 Congo, People's Rep.	..	−320	..	..	..	31	9	42	0.3
59 Costa Rica	−74	−200	..	..	26	33	16	250	2.3
60 Peru	202	−1,644	..	..	−70	59	339	1,987	4.0
61 Dominican Rep.	−102	−442	25	190	72	−1	32	171	1.1
62 Jamaica	−153	−403	29	75	161	−16	139	109	0.7
63 Ecuador	−113	−1,002	..	..	89	60	76	797	2.4
64 Turkey	−44	−849	273	2,187	58	150	440	2,645	3.1

Note: For data comparability and coverage see the technical notes.

	Current account balance (millions of dollars)		Receipts of workers' remittances (millions of dollars)		Net direct private investment (millions of dollars)		Gross international reserves		
							Millions of dollars		In months of import coverage
	1970	1982[a]	1970	1982[a]	1970	1982[a]	1970	1982[a]	1982[a]
65 Tunisia	−53	−657	29	372	16	339	60	692	2.1
66 Colombia	−293	−2,265	6	..	39	268	207	5,605	9.0
67 Paraguay	−16	−388	..	1	4	44	18	699	7.2
68 *Angola*	..	..	..	..	..	..	..	..	..
69 *Cuba*	..	..	..	..	..	..	..	..	..
70 *Korea, Dem. Rep.*	..	..	..	..	..	..	..	..	..
71 *Lebanon*	..	..	..	..	..	..	405	6,822	..
72 *Mongolia*	..	..	..	..	..	..	..	..	..
Upper middle-income									5.1 *w*
73 Syrian Arab Rep.	−69	−493	7	140	..	..	57	579	1.5
74 Jordan	−20	−336	..	1,084	..	56	258	1,378	3.8
75 Malaysia	8	−3,445	..	5	94	1,230	667	4,833	3.3
76 Korea, Rep. of	−623	−2,679	33	126	66	−77	610	2,946	1.1
77 Panama	−64	−454	67	13	33	37	16	101	0.2
78 Chile	−91	−2,382	..	..	−79	365	392	2,597	3.9
79 Brazil	−837	−16,332	..	6	407	2,551	1,190	3,997	1.2
80 Mexico	−1,068	−2,778	123	216	323	868	756	1,777	0.6
81 Algeria	−125	85	211	447	45	−1	352	5,915	4.6
82 Portugal	..	−3,227	..	2,607	..	136	1,565	10,540	10.7
83 Argentina	−163	−2,505	6	41	11	266	682	4,504	4.5
84 Uruguay	−45	−235	..	..	..	−14	186	1,422	8.8
85 South Africa	−1,215	−2,855	..	..	318	−573	1,057	3,944	2.0
86 Yugoslavia	−372	−465	441	4,350	..	..	143	1,625	1.0
87 Venezuela	−104	−3,456	..	(.)	−23	254	1,047	11,815	6.1
88 Greece	−402	−1,891	333	1,019	50	437	318	2,630	2.8
89 Israel	−562	−2,103	..	..	40	10	452	4,335	3.5
90 Hong Kong	..	..	21	215	..	..	..	..	..
91 Singapore	−572	−1,278	..	..	93	2,093	1,012	8,480	3.3
92 Trinidad and Tobago	−109	283	3	1	83	258	43	3,369	13.3
93 *Iran, Islamic Rep.*	−507	..	..	..	25	..	217	..	..
94 *Iraq*	105	..	..	..	24	..	472	..	..
High-income oil exporters									6.3 *w*
95 Oman	..	358	..	43	..	134	129	1,532	4.8
96 Libya	645	−2,977	..	..	139	−765	1,596	10,425	6.9
97 Saudi Arabia	71	45,125	..	(.)	20	3,376	670	34,051	5.9
98 Kuwait	..	5,786	..	(.)	..	−222	209	7,073	7.5
99 United Arab Emirates	..	..	..	..	..	..	..	2,589	..
Industrial market economies									5.6 *w*
100 Ireland	−198	−2,147	..	..	32	204	698	2,794	2.7
101 Spain	111	−4,150	469	1,124	179	1,280	1,851	14,328	4.3
102 Italy	902	−5,635	446	1,187	498	−318	5,547	44,552	5.1
103 New Zealand	−29	−1,499	..	209	22	233	258	646	0.9
104 United Kingdom	1,975	9,391	..	..	−439	−2,576	2,919	21,083	1.9
105 Austria	−75	386	13	201	104	93	1,806	14,949	6.5
106 Japan	1,980	6,977	..	189	−260	−4,085	4,877	34,404	2.4
107 Belgium	717	−2,912	154	389	140	1,652	2,947	19,544	2.8
108 Finland	−239	−943	..	..	−41	−230	455	2,098	1.5
109 Netherlands	−483	3,460	..	..	−15	−1,696	3,362	30,208	4.4
110 Australia	−837	−8,447	..	..	785	1,979	1,709	9,995	3.6
111 Canada	821	2,470	..	..	566	−1,658	4,733	12,258	1.8
112 France	50	−12,152	130	322	248	−1,248	5,199	53,928	3.9
113 Germany, Fed. Rep.	850	3,544	350	2,323	−290	−2,429	13,879	88,251	5.1
114 Denmark	−544	−2,255	..	..	75	55	488	3,010	1.5
115 United States	2,320	−11,504	..	283	−6,130	13,491	15,237	143,445	4.9
116 Sweden	−265	−3,547	..	..	−104	−718	775	6,286	2.0
117 Norway	−242	798	..	11	32	−22	813	7,414	3.4
118 Switzerland	72	3,623	23	84	..	..	5,317	53,511	18.0
East European nonmarket economies									..
119 Hungary	−25	−397	..	..	..	2	..	1,449	1.6
120 Romania	..	1,040	..	..	..	..	..	2,073	2.2
121 *Albania*	..	..	..	..	..	..	..	..	..
122 *Bulgaria*	..	..	..	..	..	..	..	..	..
123 *Czechoslovakia*	..	..	..	..	..	..	..	..	..
124 *German Dem. Rep.*	..	..	..	..	..	..	..	..	..
125 *Poland*	..	..	..	..	..	..	..	..	..
126 *USSR*	..	..	..	..	..	..	..	..	..

a. Figures in italics are for 1981, not 1982.

Table 15. Flow of public and publicly guaranteed external capital

	Public and publicly guaranteed medium- and long-term loans (millions of dollars)					
	Gross inflow		Repayment of principal		Net inflow[a]	
	1970	1982	1970	1982	1970	1982
Low-Income Economies **China and India** **Other low-income**						
1 Chad	6	(.)	2	(.)	3	(.)
2 Bangladesh	..	656	..	63	..	593
3 Ethiopia	27	122	15	33	13	89
4 Nepal	1	71	2	3	−2	68
5 Mali	21	127	(.)	3	21	124
6 Burma	16	402	18	68	−2	334
7 Zaire	31	175	28	65	3	110
8 Malawi	38	72	3	33	36	39
9 Upper Volta	2	78	2	13	(.)	65
10 Uganda	26	96	4	57	22	39
11 India	890	2,405	307	675	583	1,730
12 Rwanda	(.)	28	(.)	3	(.)	25
13 Burundi	1	52	(.)	3	1	49
14 Tanzania	50	241	10	20	40	221
15 Somalia	4	124	(.)	9	4	114
16 Haiti	4	58	4	11	1	48
17 Benin	2	92	1	19	1	73
18 Central African Rep.	2	21	2	2	−1	19
19 China	..	..	..	..	..	..
20 Guinea	90	88	10	55	79	33
21 Niger	12	116	1	66	10	50
22 Madagascar	10	278	5	70	5	208
23 Sri Lanka	61	484	27	68	34	416
24 Togo	5	50	2	11	3	39
25 Ghana	40	94	12	38	28	56
26 Pakistan	484	893	114	326	370	567
27 Kenya	30	390	16	178	15	212
28 Sierra Leone	8	57	10	8	−2	49
29 *Afghanistan*	34	..	15	..	19	..
30 *Bhutan*	..	..	..	..	..	..
31 *Kampuchea, Dem.*	..	..	..	..	..	..
32 *Lao PDR*	..	..	..	..	..	..
33 *Mozambique*	..	..	..	..	..	..
34 *Viet Nam*	..	..	..	..	..	..
Middle-income economies **Oil exporters** **Oil importers**						
Lower middle-income						
35 Sudan	60	419	22	68	39	351
36 Mauritania	4	215	3	16	1	199
37 Yemen, PDR	1	172	(.)	40	1	132
38 Liberia	7	59	12	19	−4	41
39 Senegal	15	212	5	38	10	174
40 Yemen Arab Rep.	..	261	..	45	..	216
41 Lesotho	(.)	42	(.)	4	(.)	38
42 Bolivia	54	162	17	95	37	68
43 Indonesia	441	4,250	59	1,148	382	3,102
44 Zambia	351	311	33	97	318	214
45 Honduras	29	202	3	51	26	151
46 Egypt, Arab Rep.	302	2,702	247	1,487	55	1,215
47 El Salvador	8	156	6	24	2	132
48 Thailand	51	1,420	23	306	27	1,114
49 Papua New Guinea	25	171	(.)	31	25	139
50 Philippines	128	1,880	72	494	56	1,387
51 Zimbabwe	(.)	517	5	51	−5	466
52 Nigeria	62	1,864	36	618	26	1,246
53 Morocco	163	2,178	36	779	127	1,399
54 Cameroon	28	181	4	143	24	38
55 Nicaragua	44	302	17	168	28	134
56 Ivory Coast	77	1,309	27	499	50	810
57 Guatemala	37	344	20	34	17	310
58 Congo, People's Rep.	35	523	6	181	29	342
59 Costa Rica	30	184	21	54	9	129
60 Peru	148	2,105	101	982	47	1,123
61 Dominican Rep.	38	395	7	141	31	254
62 Jamaica	15	259	6	115	9	144
63 Ecuador	42	273	16	539	26	−267
64 Turkey	328	2,196	128	886	200	1,310

Note: For data comparability and coverage see the technical notes.

	Public and publicly guaranteed medium- and long-term loans (millions of dollars)					
	Gross inflow		Repayment of principal		Net inflow[a]	
	1970	1982	1970	1982	1970	1982
65 Tunisia	87	620	45	290	42	330
66 Colombia	252	1,218	78	305	174	913
67 Paraguay	15	276	7	39	7	237
68 *Angola*	. .	. .	. .	. .	. .	. .
69 *Cuba*	. .	. .	. .	. .	. .	. .
70 *Korea, Dem. Rep.*	. .	. .	. .	. .	. .	. .
71 *Lebanon*	12	15	2	45	9	−30
72 *Mongolia*	. .	. .	. .	. .	. .	. .
Upper middle-income						
73 Syrian Arab Rep.	59	410	30	281	30	129
74 Jordan	14	374	3	132	12	242
75 Malaysia	43	2,883	45	241	−1	2,642
76 Korea, Rep. of	441	3,982	198	1,829	242	2,153
77 Panama	67	731	24	282	44	449
78 Chile	397	1,296	163	482	234	814
79 Brazil	886	7,915	255	4,007	631	3,908
80 Mexico	772	11,163	476	3,073	297	8,090
81 Algeria	292	2,238	33	2,893	259	−654
82 Portugal	18	3,112	63	798	−45	2,314
83 Argentina	487	2,422	342	1,070	146	1,353
84 Uruguay	38	574	47	71	−9	503
85 South Africa	. .	. .	. .	. .	. .	. .
86 Yugoslavia	180	826	168	380	12	445
87 Venezuela	224	1,924	42	1,593	183	331
88 Greece	164	1,695	61	596	102	1,100
89 Israel	410	2,108	25	1,118	385	990
90 Hong Kong	(.)	19	(.)	27	(.)	−7
91 Singapore	58	267	6	121	52	146
92 Trinidad and Tobago	8	39	10	37	−2	1
93 *Iran, Islamic Rep.*	940	. .	235	. .	705	. .
94 *Iraq*	63	. .	18	. .	46	. .
High-income oil exporters						
95 Oman	. .	231	. .	78	. .	153
96 Libya						
97 Saudi Arabia						
98 Kuwait						
99 United Arab Emirates						
Industrial market economies						
100 Ireland						
101 Spain						
102 Italy						
103 New Zealand						
104 United Kingdom						
105 Austria						
106 Japan						
107 Belgium						
108 Finland						
109 Netherlands						
110 Australia						
111 Canada						
112 France						
113 Germany, Fed. Rep.						
114 Denmark						
115 United States						
116 Sweden						
117 Norway						
118 Switzerland						
East European nonmarket economies						
119 Hungary	. .	1,203	. .	978	. .	225
120 Romania						
121 *Albania*						
122 *Bulgaria*						
123 *Czechoslovakia*						
124 *German Dem. Rep.*						
125 *Poland*						
126 *USSR*						

a. Gross inflow less repayment of principal may not equal net inflow because of rounding.

Table 16. External public debt and debt service ratios

	External public debt outstanding and disbursed				Interest payments on external public debt (millions of dollars)		Debt service as percentage of:			
	Millions of dollars		As percentage of GNP				GNP		Exports of goods and services	
	1970	1982	1970	1982a	1970	1982	1970	1982a	1970	1982a
Low-income economies			17.0 _w_	18.9 _w_			1.1 _w_	1.1 _w_	11.3 _w_	8.8 _w_
China and India			..	..			..	..	..	..
Other low-income			20.9 _w_	28.7 _w_			1.5 _w_	1.6 _w_	5.7 _w_	9.9 _w_
1 Chad	32	189	11.9	59.0	(.)	(.)	1.0	0.1	3.9	0.4
2 Bangladesh	..	4,353	..	38.6	..	48	..	1.0	..	8.3
3 Ethiopia	169	875	9.5	19.8	6	22	1.2	1.2	11.4	9.5
4 Nepal	3	297	0.3	11.6	(.)	3	0.3	0.2	..	2.3
5 Mali	238	822	88.1	79.4	(.)	5	0.2	0.8	1.2	3.5
6 Burma	101	1,960	4.7	33.5	3	52	0.9	2.1	15.8	_22.0_
7 Zaire	311	4,087	17.6	78.4	9	72	2.1	2.6	4.4	..
8 Malawi	122	692	43.2	48.8	3	32	2.1	4.5	7.1	22.8
9 Upper Volta	21	335	6.3	29.3	(.)	7	0.6	1.7	4.0	..
10 Uganda	138	587	10.6	8.0	4	10	0.6	0.9	2.7	_22.3_
11 India	7,940	19,487	14.9	11.4	189	476	0.9	0.7	20.9	_7.1_
12 Rwanda	2	189	0.9	_13.5_	(.)	2	0.2	0.2	1.3	3.2
13 Burundi	7	201	3.1	17.0	(.)	2	0.3	0.4	..	..
14 Tanzania	248	1,659	19.4	32.7	6	33	1.2	1.1	4.9	_5.1_
15 Somalia	77	944	24.4	78.4	(.)	10	0.3	1.6	2.1	7.2
16 Haiti	40	405	10.3	25.0	(.)	8	1.0	1.2	5.8	5.1
17 Benin	41	556	16.0	57.5	(.)	28	0.7	4.8	2.2	..
18 Central African Rep.	24	222	13.7	34.6	1	2	1.7	0.7	4.8	2.9
19 _China_	..	..	..	..	..	..	..	..	..	..
20 Guinea	314	1,230	47.4	76.8	4	24	2.2	4.9	..	..
21 Niger	32	603	8.7	40.2	1	44	0.6	7.3	3.8	..
22 Madagascar	93	1,565	10.8	56.8	2	42	0.8	4.1	3.5	..
23 Sri Lanka	317	1,969	16.1	41.8	12	68	2.0	2.9	10.3	8.3
24 Togo	40	819	16.0	104.5	1	22	0.9	4.3	2.9	..
25 Ghana	489	1,116	22.6	3.6	12	27	1.1	0.2	5.0	6.8
26 Pakistan	3,059	9,178	30.5	31.5	76	213	1.9	1.8	..	9.2
27 Kenya	316	2,359	20.5	39.2	12	147	1.8	5.4	5.4	20.3
28 Sierra Leone	59	370	14.3	29.8	2	2	2.9	0.9	9.9	20.8
29 _Afghanistan_	547	..	58.1	..	9	..	2.5	..	..	..
30 _Bhutan_	..	..	..	..	..	..	..	..	..	..
31 _Kampuchea, Dem._	..	..	..	..	..	..	..	..	..	..
32 _Lao PDR_	..	..	..	..	..	..	..	..	..	..
33 _Mozambique_	..	..	..	..	..	..	..	..	..	..
34 _Viet Nam_	..	..	..	..	..	..	..	..	..	..
Middle-income economies			12.3 _w_	24.5 _w_			1.5 _w_	4.2 _w_	10.1 _w_	16.9 _w_
Oil exporters			12.7 _w_	25.9 _w_			1.7 _w_	4.8 _w_	12.6 _w_	19.7 _w_
Oil importers			12.1 _w_	23.7 _w_			1.5 _w_	3.8 _w_	9.2 _w_	15.9 _w_
Lower middle-income			15.4 _w_	27.2 _w_			1.6 _w_	3.7 _w_	9.2 _w_	16.8 _w_
35 Sudan	319	5,093	15.8	47.7	13	11	1.7	_0.8_	10.7	7.5
36 Mauritania	27	1,001	13.9	146.5	(.)	24	1.7	5.8	3.1	11.8
37 Yemen, PDR	1	761	..	80.2	(.)	8	..	5.0	(.)	6.2
38 Liberia	158	641	49.6	68.1	6	14	5.5	3.5	..	_5.1_
39 Senegal	98	1,329	11.6	55.0	2	64	0.8	4.2	2.7	..
40 Yemen Arab Rep.	..	1,312	..	36.1	..	10	..	1.5	..	3.8
41 Lesotho	8	123	7.8	20.4	(.)	3	0.4	1.2	..	2.0
42 Bolivia	479	2,556	47.1	39.1	6	165	2.3	4.0	11.3	28.2
43 Indonesia	2,443	18,421	27.1	21.1	24	1,160	0.9	2.6	6.9	8.3
44 Zambia	623	2,381	37.0	66.3	26	88	3.5	5.1	5.9	17.4
45 Honduras	90	1,385	12.9	53.2	3	97	0.8	5.7	2.8	18.8
46 Egypt, Arab Rep.	1,644	15,468	23.8	52.8	38	391	4.1	6.4	28.7	20.2
47 El Salvador	88	801	8.6	22.2	4	27	0.9	1.4	3.6	4.6
48 Thailand	324	6,206	4.9	17.4	16	483	0.6	2.2	3.4	8.4
49 Papua New Guinea	36	748	5.8	32.8	1	63	0.1	4.1	..	10.2
50 Philippines	572	8,836	8.1	22.5	23	535	1.4	2.6	7.2	12.8
51 Zimbabwe	233	1,221	15.7	19.1	5	95	0.6	2.3	..	9.2
52 Nigeria	480	6,085	4.8	8.7	20	722	0.6	1.9	4.2	9.5
53 Morocco	711	9,030	18.0	60.8	23	615	1.5	9.4	7.7	36.8
54 Cameroon	131	1,912	12.1	26.8	4	121	0.8	3.7	3.1	15.6
55 Nicaragua	155	2,810	20.7	100.1	7	120	3.2	10.2	11.0	..
56 Ivory Coast	256	4,861	18.3	74.3	11	476	2.8	14.9	6.8	36.9
57 Guatemala	106	1,119	5.7	13.0	6	54	1.4	1.0	7.4	6.6
58 Congo, People's Rep.	135	1,370	50.4	67.5	3	92	3.3	13.4	..	22.6
59 Costa Rica	134	2,475	13.8	111.7	7	82	2.9	6.2	10.0	12.5
60 Peru	856	6,900	12.6	33.5	44	548	2.1	7.4	11.6	36.7
61 Dominican Rep.	212	1,620	14.5	21.2	4	109	0.8	3.3	4.1	18.7
62 Jamaica	154	1,511	11.5	49.9	8	128	1.1	8.0	2.5	16.8
63 Ecuador	217	3,912	13.2	34.3	7	561	1.4	9.7	9.1	_30.8_
64 Turkey	1,854	15,933	14.4	29.7	42	932	1.3	3.4	16.3	19.6

Note: For data comparability and coverage see the technical notes.

		External public debt outstanding and disbursed				Interest payments on external public debt (millions of dollars)		Debt service as percentage of:			
		Millions of dollars		As percentage of GNP				GNP		Exports of goods and services	
		1970	1982	1970	1982[a]	1970	1982	1970	1982[a]	1970	1982[a]
65	Tunisia	541	3,472	38.2	42.2	18	196	4.5	5.9	17.5	15.1
66	Colombia	1,293	6,004	18.8	15.4	44	569	1.8	2.2	11.9	17.5
67	Paraguay	112	940	19.2	16.1	4	41	1.8	1.4	11.9	10.3
68	*Angola*	..	..	..	..	..	..	..	..	..	..
69	*Cuba*	..	..	..	..	..	..	..	..	..	..
70	*Korea, Dem. Rep.*	..	..	..	..	..	..	..	..	..	..
71	Lebanon	64	213	4.2	..	1	19	0.2	..	..	..
72	*Mongolia*	..	..	..	..	..	..	..	..	..	..
Upper middle-income				10.8 *w*	23.2 *w*			1.5 *w*	4.4 *w*	10.7 *w*	16.9 *w*
73	Syrian Arab Rep.	232	2,616	12.8	15.1	6	92	2.0	2.2	10.8	14.2
74	Jordan	118	1,686	22.8	42.9	2	61	0.9	4.9	3.6	6.1
75	Malaysia	390	7,671	10.0	30.5	21	479	1.7	2.9	3.6	5.1
76	Korea, Rep. Of	1,797	20,061	20.4	28.3	70	1,887	3.0	5.2	19.4	13.1
77	Panama	194	2,820	19.5	70.6	7	332	3.1	15.4	7.7	13.8
78	Chile	2,066	5,239	25.8	23.7	78	551	3.0	4.7	18.9	18.8
79	Brazil	3,236	47,589	7.1	16.9	133	5,896	0.9	3.5	12.5	42.1
80	Mexico	3,206	50,412	9.1	31.1	216	5,892	2.0	5.5	23.6	29.5
81	Algeria	937	13,897	19.3	31.9	10	1,368	0.9	9.8	3.2	24.6
82	Portugal	485	9,598	7.8	43.9	29	904	1.5	7.8	..	20.0
83	Argentina	1,878	15,780	8.2	29.5	121	1,272	2.0	4.4	21.5	24.5
84	Uruguay	269	1,829	11.1	20.2	16	156	2.6	2.5	21.6	13.4
85	South Africa	..	..	..	..	..	..	..	..	..	..
86	Yugoslavia	1,198	5,626	8.8	9.4	72	519	1.8	1.5	8.4	4.6
87	Venezuela	728	12,122	6.6	17.8	40	1,557	0.7	4.6	2.9	15.6
88	Greece	905	6,783	8.9	17.3	41	588	1.0	3.0	7.1	13.3
89	Israel	2,274	14,900	41.3	64.6	13	1,001	0.7	9.2	2.7	20.8
90	Hong Kong	2	267	0.1	1.0	(.)	22	(.)	0.2	(.)	(.)
91	Singapore	152	1,423	7.9	10.0	6	114	0.6	1.7	0.6	0.8
92	Trinidad and Tobago	101	651	12.2	8.9	6	63	1.9	1.4	4.4	*2.9*
93	*Iran, Islamic Rep.*	2,193	..	20.8	..	85	..	3.0	..	12.2	..
94	*Iraq*	274	..	8.8	..	9	..	0.9	..	2.2	..
High-income oil exporters											
95	Oman	..	677	..	11.5	..	30	..	1.8	..	2.2
96	Libya										
97	Saudi Arabia										
98	Kuwait										
99	United Arab Emirates										
Industrial market economies											
100	Ireland										
101	Spain										
102	Italy										
103	New Zealand										
104	United Kingdom										
105	Austria										
106	Japan										
107	Belgium										
108	Finland										
109	Netherlands										
110	Australia										
111	Canada										
112	France										
113	Germany, Fed. Rep.										
114	Denmark										
115	United States										
116	Sweden										
117	Norway										
118	Switzerland										
East European nonmarket economies											
119	Hungary	..	6,739	..	30.0	..	808	..	8.0	..	17.0
120	Romania										
121	*Albania*										
122	*Bulgaria*										
123	*Czechoslovakia*										
124	*German Dem. Rep.*										
125	*Poland*										
126	*USSR*										

a. Figures in italics are for 1981, not 1982.

Table 17. Terms of public borrowing

	Commitments (millions of dollars)		Average interest rate (percent)		Average maturity (years)		Average grace period (years)	
	1970	1982[a]	1970	1982[a]	1970	1982[a]	1970	1982[a]
Low-income economies	3,008 t	10,046 t	2.8 w	4.9 w	31 w	30 w	9 w	7 w
China and India	..	..	..	..	..	..	..	..
Other low-income	2,074 t	6,362 t	3.0 w	3.7 w	29 w	32 w	9 w	8 w
1 Chad	4	21	4.8	0.8	7	49	2	9
2 Bangladesh	..	1,036		1.5	..	39	..	9
3 Ethiopia	21	107	4.3	3.8	32	26	7	5
4 Nepal	17	107	2.8	1.4	27	40	6	10
5 Mali	30	234	0.3	2.0	27	40	11	9
6 Burma	57	662	4.3	3.3	16	30	4	8
7 Zaire	257	268	6.5	2.3	13	39	4	8
8 Malawi	13	51	3.8	3.5	30	34	6	7
9 Upper Volta	9	168	2.3	1.8	37	36	8	8
10 Uganda	12	251	3.7	3.6	28	33	7	7
11 India	933	3,684	2.4	7.0	35	27	8	7
12 Rwanda	9	80	0.8	1.2	50	45	11	9
13 Burundi	1	90	2.9	5.4	5	23	2	6
14 Tanzania	283	234	1.2	2.5	40	32	11	8
15 Somalia	2	84	(.)	1.7	4	22	4	5
16 Haiti	5	64	6.7	2.4	9	43	1	9
17 Benin	7	140	1.8	7.2	32	21	7	4
18 Central African Rep.	7	75	2.0	3.5	36	32	8	7
19 China	..	..	..	..	..	..	..	..
20 Guinea	158	86	2.6	3.4	15	27	6	7
21 Niger	18	164	1.2	5.9	40	22	8	5
22 Madagascar	23	218	2.3	5.0	39	23	9	6
23 Sri Lanka	79	642	3.0	7.0	27	26	5	6
24 Togo	3	12	4.6	4.7	17	30	4	8
25 Ghana	41	48	2.4	3.2	39	29	10	8
26 Pakistan	935	965	2.8	4.2	32	33	12	8
27 Kenya	41	524	3.0	5.9	36	30	8	7
28 Sierra Leone	24	50	3.5	2.4	27	25	6	5
29 *Afghanistan*	19	..	1.7	..	33	..	8	..
30 *Bhutan*	..	..	..	..	..	..	..	..
31 *Kampuchea, Dem.*	..	..	..	..	..	..	..	..
32 *Lao PDR*	..	..	..	..	..	..	..	..
33 *Mozambique*	..	..	..	..	..	..	..	..
34 *Vietnam*	..	..	..	..	..	..	..	..
Middle-income economies	10,585 t	76,755 t	6.0 w	11.7 w	17 w	12 w	4 w	4 w
Oil exporters	4,013 t	34,197 t	6.0 w	12.3 w	16 w	11 w	4 w	4 w
Oil importers	6,572 t	42,558 t	6.0 w	11.2 w	15 w	14 w	4 w	4 w
Lower middle-income	3,710 t	32,887 t	4.5 w	9.8 w	22 w	16 w	6 w	4 w
35 Sudan	118	701	1.9	3.6	16	21	7	6
36 Mauritania	7	204	6.5	2.6	11	20	3	4
37 Yemen, PDR	62	100	(.)	1.8	21	28	11	6
38 Liberia	11	126	5.4	4.4	19	32	5	7
39 Senegal	8	441	4.4	4.3	28	32	8	8
40 Yemen Arab Rep.	9	313	5.2	3.4	5	18	3	4
41 Lesotho	(.)	10	5.1	8.3	25	23	2	5
42 Bolivia	13	145	3.7	8.9	26	18	6	7
43 Indonesia	518	5,777	2.7	9.4	34	15	9	5
44 Zambia	555	420	4.2	6.8	23	21	6	6
45 Honduras	23	147	4.1	6.4	30	29	7	7
46 Egypt, Arab Rep.	246	2,869	5.6	8.1	14	24	3	3
47 El Salvador	12	325	4.7	5.3	23	19	6	5
48 Thailand	106	2,094	6.8	9.4	19	19	4	6
49 Papua New Guinea	58	166	6.0	13.5	24	14	8	6
50 Philippines	158	2,118	7.4	11.3	11	16	2	5
51 Zimbabwe	..	715		8.9	..	16	..	5
52 Nigeria	79	2,753	5.8	13.9	17	9	6	4
53 Morocco	182	1,794	4.6	10.2	20	11	4	3
54 Cameroon	41	347	4.7	9.2	29	18	8	5
55 Nicaragua	23	334	7.1	5.9	18	14	4	3
56 Ivory Coast	71	1,253	5.8	12.7	19	12	5	4
57 Guatemala	50	194	5.2	6.4	26	13	6	4
58 Congo, People's Rep.	43	497	3.0	10.4	17	8	6	2
59 Costa Rica	58	265	5.6	4.9	28	20	6	7
60 Peru	125	2,746	7.4	11.9	13	10	4	3
61 Dominican Rep.	20	406	2.5	5.5	28	17	5	4
62 Jamaica	24	317	6.0	8.8	16	17	3	5
63 Ecuador	78	407	6.1	8.8	20	18	4	7
64 Turkey	487	1,577	3.6	11.3	19	13	5	4

Note: For data comparability and coverage see the technical notes.

	Commitments (millions of dollars)		Average interest rate (percent)		Average maturity (years)		Average grace period (years)	
	1970	1982ᵃ	1970	1982ᵃ	1970	1982ᵃ	1970	1982ᵃ
65 Tunisia	141	566	3.4	7.7	27	18	6	4
66 Colombia	362	2,371	5.9	10.7	21	14	5	5
67 Paraguay	14	383	5.6	9.1	25	16	6	4
68 *Angola*	..	..	..	..	..	..	..	..
69 *Cuba*	..	..	..	..	..	..	..	..
70 *Korea, Dem. Rep.*	..	..	..	..	..	..	..	..
71 Lebanon	7	*13*	2.7	*11.1*	21	*13*	1	*4*
72 *Mongolia*	..	..	..	..	..	..	..	..
Upper middle-income	6,875 *t*	43,868 *t*	6.9 *w*	13.2 *w*	13 *w*	10 *w*	4 *w*	4 *w*
73 Syrian Arab Rep.	14	218	4.4	6.4	9	17	2	4
74 Jordan	33	245	3.9	6.0	12	20	5	5
75 Malaysia	83	2,863	6.1	11.9	19	12	5	6
76 Korea, Rep. of	677	3,759	6.0	11.5	19	13	5	4
77 Panama	111	552	6.9	13.1	15	11	4	4
78 Chile	343	1,432	6.9	14.4	12	8	3	4
79 Brazil	1,362	10,712	7.1	13.0	14	11	3	3
80 Mexico	826	10,799	8.0	14.8	12	6	3	3
81 Algeria	288	1,964	6.5	8.9	10	8	2	2
82 Portugal	59	2,446	4.3	11.3	17	8	4	3
83 Argentina	488	1,010	7.4	11.9	12	11	3	3
84 Uruguay	72	450	7.9	14.1	12	8	3	2
85 South Africa	..	..	..	..	..	..	..	..
86 Yugoslavia	198	490	7.1	14.5	17	10	6	4
87 Venezuela	198	2,591	8.2	17.6	8	8	2	2
88 Greece	242	1,442	7.2	12.6	9	10	4	4
89 Israel	439	2,316	7.3	13.6	13	20	5	5
90 Hong Kong	(.)	1	(.)	7.9	(.)	12	(.)	4
91 Singapore	69	432	6.8	10.9	17	11	4	3
92 Trinidad and Tobago	3	148	7.5	13.1	10	9	1	6
93 *Iran, Islamic Rep.*	1,342	..	6.2	..	12	..	3	..
94 *Iraq*	28	..	3.3	..	11	..	2	..
High-income oil exporters								
95 Oman								
96 Libya								
97 Saudi Arabia								
98 Kuwait								
99 United Arab Emirates								
Industrial market economies								
100 Ireland								
101 Spain								
102 Italy								
103 New Zealand								
104 United Kingdom								
105 Austria								
106 Japan								
107 Belgium								
108 Finland								
109 Netherlands								
110 Australia								
111 Canada								
112 France								
113 Germany, Fed. Rep.								
114 Denmark								
115 United States								
116 Sweden								
117 Norway								
118 Switzerland								
East European nonmarket economies								
119 Hungaryᵇ	..	1,117	..	11.7	..	4.1	..	1.8
120 Romania								
121 *Albania*								
122 *Bulgaria*								
123 *Czechoslovakia*								
124 *German Dem. Rep.*								
125 *Poland*								
126 *USSR*								

a. Figures in italics are for 1981, not 1982.   b. Includes only debt in convertible currencies.

Table 18. Official development assistance from OECD & OPEC members

				Amount						
	1960	1965	1970	1975	1978	1979	1980	1981	1982	1983[a]
OECD					**Millions of US dollars**					
102 Italy	77	60	147	182	376	273	683	666	814	827
103 New Zealand	..	..	14	66	55	68	72	68	65	61
104 United Kingdom	407	472	500	904	1,465	2,156	1,852	2,191	1,792	1,601
105 Austria	..	10	11	79	154	131	178	314	354	157
106 Japan	105	244	458	1,148	2,215	2,685	3,353	3,171	3,023	3,761
107 Belgium	101	102	120	378	536	643	595	575	501	477
108 Finland	..	2	7	48	55	90	111	135	144	153
109 Netherlands	35	70	196	608	1,074	1,472	1,630	1,510	1,474	1,195
110 Australia	59	119	212	552	588	629	667	650	882	754
111 Canada	75	96	337	880	1,060	1,056	1,075	1,189	1,197	1,424
112 France	823	752	971	2,093	2,705	3,449	4,162	4,177	4,028	3,915
113 Germany, Fed. Rep.	223	456	599	1,689	2,347	3,393	3,567	3,181	3,163	3,181
114 Denmark	5	13	59	205	388	461	481	403	415	394
115 United States	2,702	4,023	3,153	4,161	5,663	4,684	7,138	5,782	8,202	7,950
116 Sweden	7	38	117	566	783	988	962	919	980	779
117 Norway	5	11	37	184	355	429	486	467	559	584
118 Switzerland	4	12	30	104	173	213	253	237	252	318
Total	4,628	6,480	6,968	13,847	19,992	22,820	27,265	25,635	27,845	27,531
OECD					**As percentage of donor GNP**					
102 Italy	.22	.10	.16	.11	.14	.08	.17	.19	.24	.24
103 New Zealand	..	..	.23	.52	.34	.33	.33	.29	.28	.28
104 United Kingdom	.56	.47	.41	.39	.46	.52	.35	.43	.37	.36
105 Austria	..	.11	.07	.21	.27	.19	.23	.48	.53	.23
106 Japan	.24	.27	.23	.23	.23	.27	.32	.28	.29	.33
107 Belgium	.88	.60	.46	.59	.55	.57	.50	.59	.60	.59
108 Finland	..	.02	.06	.18	.16	.22	.22	.28	.30	.33
109 Netherlands	.31	.36	.61	.75	.82	.98	1.03	1.08	1.08	.91
110 Australia	.37	.53	.59	.65	.55	.53	.48	.41	.57	.49
111 Canada	.19	.19	.41	.54	.52	.48	.43	.43	.42	.47
112 France	1.35	.76	.66	.62	.57	.60	.64	.73	.75	.76
113 Germany, Fed. Rep.	.31	.40	.32	.40	.37	.45	.44	.47	.48	.48
114 Denmark	.09	.13	.38	.58	.75	.77	.74	.73	.77	.73
115 United States	.53	.58	.32	.27	.27	.20	.27	.20	.27	.24
116 Sweden	.05	.19	.38	.82	.90	.97	.79	.83	1.02	.88
117 Norway	.11	.16	.32	.66	.90	.93	.85	.82	.99	1.10
118 Switzerland	.04	.09	.15	.19	.20	.21	.24	.24	.25	.31
OECD					**National currencies**					
101 Italy (billions of lire)	48	38	92	119	319	227	585	757	1,101	1,255
103 New Zealand (millions of dollars)	..	..	13	54	53	66	74	78	86	92
104 United Kingdom (millions of pounds)	145	169	208	407	763	1,016	796	1,080	1,024	1,055
105 Austria (millions of schillings)	..	260	286	1,376	2,236	1,751	2,303	5,001	6,039	2,813
106 Japan (billions of yen)	38	88	165	341	466	588	760	699	753	893
107 Belgium (millions of francs)	5,050	5,100	6,000	13,902	16,880	18,852	17,400	21,350	22,891	24,364
108 Finland (millions of markkaa)	..	6	29	177	226	351	414	583	694	854
109 Netherlands (millions of guilders)	133	253	710	1,538	2,324	2,953	3,241	3,768	3,936	3,412
110 Australia (millions of dollars)	53	106	189	421	514	563	585	566	867	844
111 Canada (millions of dollars)	73	104	353	895	1,209	1,237	1,257	1,425	1,477	1,755
112 France (millions of francs)	4,063	3,713	5,393	8,971	12,207	14,674	17,589	22,700	26,474	29,837
113 Germany, Fed. Rep. (millions of deutsche marks)	937	1,824	2,192	4,155	4,714	6,219	6,484	7,189	7,675	8,123
114 Denmark (millions of kroner)	35	90	443	1,178	2,140	2,425	2,711	2,871	3,458	3,599
115 United States (millions of dollars)	2,702	4,023	3,153	4,161	5,663	4,684	7,138	5,782	8,202	7,950
116 Sweden (millions of kronor)	36	197	605	2,350	3,538	4,236	4,069	4,653	6,201	5,975
117 Norway (millions of kroner)	36	79	264	962	1,861	2,172	2,400	2,680	3,608	4,258
118 Switzerland (millions of francs)	17	52	131	268	309	354	424	466	512	667
OECD					**Summary**					
ODA (billions of US dollars, nominal prices)	4.63	6.48	6.97	13.85	19.99	22.82	27.27	25.64	27.85	27.53
ODA as percentage of GNP	.51	.49	.34	.36	.35	.35	.38	.35	.38	.37
ODA (billions of US dollars, constant 1980 prices)	16.41	20.19	18.15	21.60	24.09	24.89	27.27	25.82	28.31	27.37
GNP (trillions of US dollars, nominal prices)	.90	1.30	2.00	3.90	5.70	6.50	7.20	7.30	7.24	7.52
GDP deflator[b]	.28	.32	.38	.64	.83	.92	1.00	.99	.98	1.01

Note: For data comparability and coverage see the technical notes.

	Amount							
	1975	1976	1977	1978	1979	1980	1981	1982[c]
OPEC	**Millions of US dollars**							
54 Nigeria	14	83	50	26	29	33	141	58
81 Algeria	41	54	42	41	281	103	97	128
87 Venezuela	31	108	24	87	107	125	67	216
93 Iran, Islamic Rep.	593	753	169	240	−19	−90	−157	−178
94 Iraq	215	231	62	172	847	876	148	. .
96 Libya	259	94	101	139	105	382	293	43
97 Saudi Arabia	2,756	3,028	3,086	5,464	4,238	5,943	5,664	4,428
98 Kuwait	946	531	1,292	978	971	1,140	1,154	1,295
99 United Arab Emirates	1,046	1,021	1,052	885	970	909	811	563
Qatar	338	195	189	98	287	269	248	251
Total OAPEC[d]	5,601	5,154	5,824	7,777	7,699	9,622	8,415	6,708
Total OPEC	6,239	6,098	6,067	8,130	7,816	9,690	8,466	6,804
OPEC	**As percentage of donor GNP**							
54 Nigeria	.04	.19	.10	.05	.04	.04	.20	.08
81 Algeria	.28	.33	.21	.16	.92	.26	.24	.29
87 Venezuela	.11	.34	.07	.22	.22	.21	.10	.32
93 Iran, Islamic Rep.	1.12	1.16	.22	.33	. .	. .	. .	. .
94 Iraq	1.62	1.44	.33	.76	2.53	2.39	.40	. .
96 Libya	2.29	.63	.57	.79	.43	1.18	1.11	.18
97 Saudi Arabia	7.76	6.46	5.24	8.39	5.55	5.09	3.58	2.82
98 Kuwait	7.40	3.63	8.10	5.46	3.50	3.40	3.55	4.86
99 United Arab Emirates	11.68	8.88	7.23	6.35	5.09	3.30	2.88	2.06
Qatar	15.58	7.95	7.56	3.38	6.18	4.03	3.75	3.80
Total OAPEC[d]	5.73	4.23	3.95	4.69	3.54	3.44	2.87	2.42
Total OPEC	2.92	2.32	1.96	2.47	1.86	2.21	1.93	1.65

	Net Bilateral flow to low-income countries								
	1960	1965	1970	1975	1978	1979	1980	1981	1982
OECD	**Percentage of donor GNP**								
101 Italy	.03	.04	.06	.01	.01	.01	.01	.02	.04
102 New Zealand	. .	. .	. .	.14	.03	.01	.01	.01	.00
104 United Kingdom	.22	.23	.15	.11	.15	.15	.12	.13	.07
105 Austria	. .	.06	.05	.02	.01	.02	.03	.03	.01
106 Japan	.12	.13	.11	.08	.07	.08	.07	.06	.11
107 Belgium	.27	.56	.30	.31	.23	.27	.24	.25	.21
108 Finland	. .	. .	. .	.06	.04	.06	.08	.09	.08
109 Netherlands	.19	.08	.24	.24	.34	.26	.32	.37	.29
110 Australia	. .	.08	.09	.10	.08	.06	.04	.06	.08
111 Canada	.11	.10	.22	.24	.17	.13	.11	.12	.13
112 France	.01	.12	.09	.10	.08	.07	.08	.11	.10
113 Germany, Fed. Rep.	.13	.14	.10	.12	.07	.09	.09	.11	.13
114 Denmark	. .	.02	.10	.20	.21	.28	.28	.20	.22
115 United States	.22	.26	.14	.08	.04	.03	.03	.03	.03
116 Sweden	.01	.07	.12	.41	.37	.41	.34	.31	.36
117 Norway	.02	.04	.12	.25	.39	.33	.28	.25	.33
118 Switzerland	. .	.02	.05	.10	.08	.06	.08	.07	.09
Total	.18	.20	.13	.11	.09	.08	.07	.08	.08

a. Preliminary estimates. b. See the technical notes. c. Provisional. d. Organization of Arab Petroleum Exporting Countries.

Table 19. Population growth and projections

	Average annual growth of population (percent)			Population (millions)			Hypothetical size of stationary population (millions)	Assumed year of reaching net reproduction rate of 1	Population momentum 1980
	1960–70	1970–82	1980–2000	1982	1990ᵃ	2000ᵃ			
Low-income economies	2.3 w	1.9 w	1.7 w	2,269 t	2,621 t	3,097 t			
China and India	2.3 w	1.7 w	1.3 w	1,725 t	1,938 t	2,190 t			
Other low-income	2.5 w	2.6 w	2.9 w	544 t	683 t	907 t			
1 Chad	1.9	2.0	2.5	5	6	7	22	2040	1.8
2 Bangladesh	2.5	2.6	2.9	93	119	157	454	2035	1.9
3 Ethiopia	2.4	2.0	3.1	33	42	57	231	2045	1.9
4 Nepal	1.9	2.6	2.6	15	19	24	71	2040	1.9
5 Mali	2.5	2.7	2.8	7	9	12	42	2040	1.8
6 Burma	2.2	2.2	2.4	35	43	53	115	2025	1.8
7 Zaire	2.0	3.0	3.3	31	40	55	172	2030	1.9
8 Malawi	2.8	3.0	3.4	7	8	12	48	2040	1.9
9 Upper Volta	2.0	2.0	2.4	7	8	10	35	2040	1.7
10 Uganda	3.0	2.7	3.4	14	17	25	89	2035	2.0
11 India	2.3	2.3	1.9	717	844	994	1,707	2010	1.7
12 Rwanda	2.6	3.4	3.6	6	7	11	47	2040	1.9
13 Burundi	1.4	2.2	3.0	4	5	7	27	2040	1.9
14 Tanzania	2.7	3.4	3.5	20	26	36	117	2030	2.0
15 Somalia	2.8	2.8	2.4	5	5	.7	23	2045	1.8
16 Haiti	1.6	1.7	1.8	5	6	7	14	2025	1.8
17 Benin	2.6	2.7	3.3	4	5	7	23	2035	2.0
18 Central African Rep.	1.6	2.1	2.8	2	3	4	13	2040	1.9
19 China	2.3	1.4	1.0	1,008	1,094	1,196	1,461	2000	1.7
20 Guinea	1.5	2.0	2.4	6	7	9	28	2045	1.8
21 Niger	3.4	3.3	3.3	6	8	11	40	2040	1.9
22 Madagascar	2.2	2.6	3.2	9	12	16	54	2035	1.9
23 Sri Lanka	2.4	1.7	1.8	15	18	21	32	2005	1.8
24 Togo	3.0	2.6	3.3	3	4	5	17	2035	2.0
25 Ghana	2.3	3.0	3.9	12	17	24	83	2030	2.0
26 Pakistan	2.8	3.0	2.7	87	107	140	377	2035	1.9
27 Kenya	3.2	4.0	4.4	18	26	40	153	2030	2.1
28 Sierra Leone	1.7	2.0	2.4	3	4	5	16	2045	1.9
29 Afghanistan	2.2	2.5	2.3	17	20	25	76	2045	1.9
30 Bhutan	1.3	2.0	2.2	1	1	2	4	2035	1.8
31 Kampuchea, Dem.	2.5	. .	. .	. .	. .	. .			. .
32 Lao PDR	1.9	2.0	2.6	4	4	6	19	2040	1.8
33 Mozambique	2.1	4.3	3.4	13	17	24	82	2035	2.0
34 Viet Nam	3.1	2.8	2.5	57	70	88	171	2015	1.9
Middle-income economies	2.6 w	2.4 w	2.2 w	1,163 t	1,404 t	1,741 t			
Oil exporters	2.6 w	2.7 w	2.5 w	521 t	641 t	819 t			
Oil importers	2.5 w	2.3 w	2.0 w	642 t	763 t	922 t			
Lower middle-income	2.5 w	2.5 w	2.4 w	673 t	816 t	1,023 t			
35 Sudan	2.2	3.2	2.9	20	25	34	112	2035	1.8
36 Mauritania	2.3	2.3	2.6	2	2	3	8	2035	1.8
37 Yemen, PDR	2.2	2.2	3.1	2	2	3	12	2040	1.9
38 Liberia	3.2	3.5	3.5	2	3	4	12	2030	1.8
39 Senegal	2.3	2.7	3.1	6	8	10	36	2040	1.9
40 Yemen Arab Rep.	2.3	3.0	2.9	8	9	12	43	2040	1.9
41 Lesotho	2.0	2.4	2.8	1	2	2	7	2030	1.8
42 Bolivia	2.4	2.6	2.4	6	7	9	22	2030	1.8
43 Indonesia	2.1	2.3	1.9	153	179	212	370	2010	1.9
44 Zambia	2.6	3.1	3.6	6	8	11	37	2030	2.0
45 Honduras	3.1	3.4	3.1	4	5	7	17	2025	2.0
46 Egypt, Arab Rep.	2.5	2.5	2.0	44	52	63	114	2015	1.8
47 El Salvador	3.4	3.0	2.6	5	6	8	17	2015	1.9
48 Thailand	3.1	2.4	1.9	49	57	68	111	2010	1.8
49 Papua New Guinea	2.2	2.1	2.2	3	4	5	10	2030	1.8
50 Philippines	3.0	2.7	2.1	51	61	73	127	2010	1.8
51 Zimbabwe	3.6	3.2	4.4	8	11	16	62	2030	2.1
52 Nigeria	2.5	2.6	3.5	91	119	169	618	2035	2.0
53 Morocco	2.6	2.6	2.5	20	25	31	70	2025	1.9
54 Cameroon	2.0	3.0	3.5	9	12	17	65	2035	1.9
55 Nicaragua	2.6	3.9	3.0	3	4	5	12	2025	2.0
56 Ivory Coast	3.7	4.9	3.7	9	12	17	58	2035	2.0
57 Guatemala	3.0	3.1	2.6	8	10	12	25	2020	1.9
58 Congo, People's Rep.	2.4	3.0	3.8	2	2	3	10	2025	1.9
59 Costa Rica	3.3	2.5	2.2	2	3	3	5	2005	1.9
60 Peru	2.9	2.8	2.2	17	21	26	49	2020	1.9
61 Dominican Rep.	2.9	3.0	2.2	6	7	8	15	2010	1.9
62 Jamaica	1.4	1.5	1.4	2	3	3	4	2005	1.6
63 Ecuador	2.9	2.6	2.6	8	10	13	27	2020	1.9
64 Turkey	2.5	2.3	2.0	47	55	65	111	2010	1.8

Note: For data comparability and coverage see the technical notes.

		Average annual growth of population (percent)			Population (millions)			Hypothetical size of stationary population (millions)	Assumed year of reaching net reproduction rate of 1	Population momentum 1980
		1960–70	1970–82	1980–2000	1982	1990[a]	2000[a]			
65	Tunisia	2.0	2.3	2.3	7	8	10	19	2015	1.8
66	Colombia	3.0	1.9	1.9	27	32	38	62	2010	1.8
67	Paraguay	2.6	2.6	2.3	3	4	5	8	2010	1.9
68	*Angola*	2.1	2.5	2.8	8	10	13	44	2040	1.9
69	*Cuba*	2.1	1.1	1.0	10	11	12	15	2010	1.6
70	*Korea, Dem. Rep.*	2.8	2.5	2.1	19	22	27	46	2010	1.8
71	*Lebanon*	2.9	0.5	1.3	3	3	3	6	2005	1.6
72	*Mongolia*	3.0	2.9	2.4	2	2	3	5	2015	1.9
	Upper middle-income	**2.6** w	**2.3** w	**2.1** w	**490** t	**588** t	**718** t			
73	Syrian Arab Rep.	3.2	3.5	3.5	10	13	17	42	2020	2.0
74	Jordan	3.1	2.5	3.9	3	4	6	16	2020	2.0
75	Malaysia	2.8	2.5	2.0	15	17	21	33	2005	1.8
76	Korea, Rep. of	2.6	1.7	1.4	39	45	51	70	2000	1.7
77	Panama	2.9	2.3	1.9	2	2	3	4	2005	1.8
78	Chile	2.1	1.7	1.4	12	13	15	21	2005	1.7
79	Brazil	2.8	2.4	2.0	127	152	181	304	2010	1.8
80	Mexico	3.3	3.0	2.3	73	89	109	199	2010	1.9
81	Algeria	2.4	3.1	3.7	20	27	39	119	2025	1.9
82	Portugal	0.3	0.8	0.6	10	10	11	14	2000	1.4
83	Argentina	1.5	1.4	1.3	28	32	36	54	2010	1.5
84	Uruguay	1.0	0.4	0.7	3	3	3	4	2005	1.3
85	South Africa	2.4	2.8	3.1	30	39	52	123	2020	1.8
86	Yugoslavia	1.0	0.9	0.6	23	24	25	29	2010	1.4
87	Venezuela	3.8	3.6	2.6	17	21	26	46	2010	2.0
88	Greece	0.6	1.0	0.4	10	10	11	12	2000	1.3
89	Israel	3.5	2.5	1.6	4	5	5	8	2005	1.7
90	Hong Kong	2.5	2.4	1.4	5	6	7	8	2000	1.6
91	Singapore	2.3	1.5	1.0	3	3	3	3	2000	1.6
92	Trinidad and Tobago	2.1	0.5	1.7	1	1	2	2	2010	1.7
93	*Iran, Islamic Rep.*	3.4	3.1	3.1	41	53	70	159	2020	1.9
94	*Iraq*	3.2	3.5	3.4	14	19	26	68	2025	2.0
	High-income oil exporters	**4.2** w	**5.0** w	**3.8** w	**17** t	**24** t	**33** t			
95	Oman	2.6	4.3	2.9	1	1	2	4	2020	1.9
96	Libya	3.9	4.1	4.3	3	5	7	21	2025	2.1
97	Saudi Arabia	3.5	4.8	3.7	10	14	19	62	2030	1.9
98	Kuwait	9.9	6.3	3.5	2	2	3	5	2010	2.1
99	United Arab Emirates	9.3	15.5	3.7	1	2	2	4	2015	1.6
	Industrial market economies	**1.1** w	**0.7** w	**0.4** w	**723** t	**749** t	**780** t			
100	Ireland	0.4	1.5	1.1	4	4	4	6	2000	1.5
101	Spain	1.0	1.0	0.7	38	40	43	51	2000	1.3
102	Italy	0.7	0.4	0.1	56	57	58	57	2010	1.2
103	New Zealand	1.8	1.0	0.6	3	3	4	4	2010	1.4
104	United Kingdom	0.6	0.1	0.1	56	56	57	59	2010	1.2
105	Austria	0.5	0.1	0.1	8	8	8	8	2010	1.2
106	Japan	1.0	1.1	0.4	118	123	128	128	2010	1.2
107	Belgium	0.6	0.2	0.1	10	10	10	10	2010	1.2
108	Finland	0.4	0.4	0.1	5	5	5	5	2010	1.3
109	Netherlands	1.3	0.7	0.4	14	15	15	15	2010	1.3
110	Australia	2.0	1.5	1.0	15	16	18	21	2010	1.5
111	Canada	1.8	1.2	1.0	25	27	29	33	2010	1.5
112	France	1.1	0.5	0.4	54	56	58	62	2010	1.3
113	Germany, Fed. Rep.	0.9	0.1	−0.1	62	61	60	54	2010	1.1
114	Denmark	0.8	0.3	0.1	5	5	5	5	2010	1.2
115	United States	1.3	1.0	0.7	232	245	259	292	2010	1.4
116	Sweden	0.7	0.3	0.1	8	8	9	8	2010	1.1
117	Norway	0.8	0.5	0.2	4	4	4	4	2010	1.2
118	Switzerland	1.5	0.1	0.1	6	6	6	6	2010	1.0
	East European nonmarket economies	**1.1** w	**0.8** w	**0.6** w	**384** t	**407** t	**431** t			
119	Hungary	0.3	0.3	0.1	11	11	11	12	2010	1.2
120	Romania	0.9	0.9	0.7	23	24	25	31	2000	1.3
121	*Albania*	2.8	2.5	1.8	3	3	4	6	2000	1.8
122	*Bulgaria*	0.8	0.4	0.3	9	9	10	10	2010	1.2
123	*Czechoslovakia*	0.5	0.6	0.4	15	16	17	20	2000	1.3
124	*German Dem. Rep.*	−0.1	−0.2	0.2	17	17	17	18	2010	1.2
125	*Poland*	1.0	0.9	0.7	36	39	41	49	2000	1.4
126	*USSR*	1.2	0.9	0.7	270	288	306	377	2000	1.4
	Total[b]				4,556	5,205	6,082			

a. For the assumptions used in the projections see the technical notes.   b. Excludes countries with populations of less than 1 million.

Table 20. Demographic and fertility-related indicators

	Crude birth rate per thousand population		Crude death rate per thousand population		Percentage change in:		Total fertility rate		Percentage of married women of childbearing age using contraception[a]	
					Crude birth rate	Crude death rate				
	1960	1982	1960	1982	1960–82	1960–82	1982	2000	1970	1981
Low-income economies	44 *w*	30 *w*	24 *w*	11 *w*	−34.2 *w*	−54.7 *w*	4.1 *w*	3.2 *w*	..	..
China and India	43 *w*	25 *w*	24 *w*	9 *w*	−42.6 *w*	−61.5 *w*	3.4 *w*	2.4 *w*	..	..
Other low-income	47 *w*	44 *w*	24 *w*	16 *w*	−7.2 *w*	−32.8 *w*	6.1 *w*	5.2 *w*	..	..
1 Chad	45	42	29	21	−6.6	−27.7	5.5	5.6	..	..
2 Bangladesh	47	47	22	17	0.2	−24.7	6.3	5.1	..	19
3 Ethiopia	51	47	28	18	−7.0	−35.9	6.5	6.1	..	..
4 Nepal	46	43	26	19	−6.5	−27.3	6.3	5.3	..	7
5 Mali	50	48	27	21	−3.2	−23.0	6.5	6.0	..	..
6 Burma	43	38	21	13	−11.3	−37.9	5.3	3.6	..	..
7 Zaire	48	46	24	16	−4.1	−34.2	6.3	5.8	..	..
8 Malawi	56	56	27	23	0.2	−15.7	7.8	7.1	..	..
9 Upper Volta	49	48	27	21	−1.5	−20.1	6.5	6.0	..	..
10 Uganda	49	50	21	19	1.4	−11.6	7.0	6.4	..	..
11 India	48	34	24	13	−28.3	−46.8	4.8	2.9	12	28
12 Rwanda	53	54	27	20	0.9	−27.4	8.3	7.6	..	..
13 Burundi	45	47	25	19	2.9	−23.7	6.5	6.0	..	..
14 Tanzania	47	47	22	15	0.8	−33.4	6.5	5.8	..	..
15 Somalia	48	48	29	25	0.2	−12.3	6.5	6.1	..	..
16 Haiti	39	32	19	13	−17.4	−35.7	4.6	3.7	..	19
17 Benin	51	49	27	18	−2.5	−32.2	6.5	5.9	..	17
18 Central African Rep.	43	41	26	17	−3.9	−35.4	5.5	5.6	..	..
19 China	39	19	24	7	−52.8	−71.9	2.3	2.0	..	69
20 Guinea	48	49	35	27	1.8	−22.6	6.5	6.1	..	..
21 Niger	52	52	27	20	0.7	−24.5	7.0	6.4	..	..
22 Madagascar	47	47	27	18	−0.1	−33.0	6.5	5.9	..	..
23 Sri Lanka	36	27	9	6	−25.7	−34.8	3.4	2.3	..	55
24 Togo	51	49	23	19	−2.7	−17.6	6.5	5.9	..	..
25 Ghana	50	49	20	13	−1.8	−35.7	7.0	6.3	..	10
26 Pakistan	49	42	23	15	−13.6	−34.3	5.8	4.8	6	..
27 Kenya	55	55	24	12	0.2	−47.9	8.0	7.1	6	7
28 Sierra Leone	49	49	34	27	−0.2	−20.6	6.5	6.1	..	..
29 *Afghanistan*	50	54	31	29	7.4	−6.5	8.0	5.6	2	..
30 *Bhutan*	43	43	25	21	−0.2	−15.3	6.2	5.1	..	..
31 *Kampuchea, Dem.*	45	..	21	..	..	..	..	..	..	..
32 *Lao PDR*	44	42	23	20	−4.7	−12.0	6.4	5.9	..	..
33 *Mozambique*	..	49	..	16	..	..	6.5	5.9	..	..
34 *Viet Nam*	47	35	21	8	−24.9	−62.3	5.0	3.1	..	..
Middle-income economies	43 *w*	35 *w*	17 *w*	10 *w*	−22.0 *w*	−39.6 *w*	4.7 *w*	3.6 *w*	..	..
Oil exporters	47 *w*	38 *w*	21 *w*	12 *w*	−19.1 *w*	−42.9 *w*	5.3 *w*	4.0 *w*	..	..
Oil importers	40 *w*	31 *w*	15 *w*	9 *w*	−24.5 *w*	−37.0 *w*	4.2 *w*	3.3 *w*	..	..
Lower middle-income	46 *w*	37 *w*	20 *w*	12 *w*	−21.2 *w*	−42.0 *w*	5.0 *w*	3.9 *w*	..	..
35 Sudan	47	45	25	18	−3.4	−29.9	6.6	6.0	..	5
36 Mauritania	51	43	27	19	−14.3	−28.3	6.0	5.9	..	1
37 Yemen, PDR	50	48	29	19	−5.6	−33.9	6.9	6.3	..	..
38 Liberia	50	50	21	14	−0.3	−30.6	6.9	6.2	..	..
39 Senegal	48	48	26	21	(.)	−22.5	6.5	6.0	..	4
40 Yemen Arab Rep.	50	48	29	22	−2.8	−25.1	6.8	6.2	..	1
41 Lesotho	42	42	23	15	(.)	−35.8	5.8	5.2	..	5
42 Bolivia	46	43	22	16	−7.2	−28.7	6.3	4.2	..	..
43 Indonesia	44	34	23	13	−23.9	−43.2	4.3	2.8	..	53
44 Zambia	51	50	24	16	−2.2	−36.5	6.8	6.1	..	..
45 Honduras	51	44	19	10	−14.2	−45.1	6.5	4.1	..	27
46 Egypt, Arab Rep.	44	35	20	11	−22.1	−44.6	4.6	3.0	..	24
47 El Salvador	48	40	17	8	−17.4	−52.1	5.6	3.3	..	34
48 Thailand	44	28	15	8	−36.2	−48.1	3.6	2.6	15	59
49 Papua New Guinea	44	34	23	13	−22.3	−43.1	5.0	3.6	..	..
50 Philippines	47	31	15	7	−34.0	−53.4	4.2	2.7	15	36
51 Zimbabwe	55	54	17	12	−1.8	−25.0	8.0	7.1	..	15
52 Nigeria	52	50	25	16	−4.7	−35.6	6.9	6.3	..	6
53 Morocco	50	40	21	15	−19.8	−30.7	5.8	3.8	..	19
54 Cameroon	38	46	21	15	21.2	−30.7	6.5	6.4	..	2
55 Nicaragua	51	45	18	11	−11.3	−39.8	6.3	4.0	..	..
56 Ivory Coast	49	48	24	17	−2.7	−28.2	7.0	6.4	..	3
57 Guatemala	48	38	18	9	−21.0	−49.1	5.2	3.4	..	18
58 Congo, People's Rep.	40	43	18	10	6.8	−46.0	6.0	5.7	..	..
59 Costa Rica	48	30	8	4	−36.8	−51.3	3.5	2.3	..	65
60 Peru	47	34	19	11	−27.4	−42.1	4.5	3.2	..	41
61 Dominican Rep.	49	34	17	8	−31.1	−54.0	4.2	2.7	..	42
62 Jamaica	42	27	9	6	−35.0	−36.4	3.4	2.3	..	55
63 Ecuador	47	37	17	8	−20.5	−49.3	5.4	3.5	..	34
64 Turkey	43	31	16	9	−28.0	−43.4	4.1	2.7	32	38

Note: For data comparability and coverage see the technical notes.

		Crude birth rate per thousand population		Crude death rate per thousand population		Percentage change in:		Total fertility rate		Percentage of married women of childbearing age using contraception[a]	
						Crude birth rate	Crude death rate				
		1960	1982	1960	1982	1960–82	1960–82	1982	2000	1970	1981
65	Tunisia	47	34	19	9	−27.0	−51.9	4.9	3.1	..	41
66	Colombia	47	29	17	7	−38.8	−57.5	3.6	2.6	..	49
67	Paraguay	43	31	13	7	−27.2	−44.6	4.2	2.7	..	36
68	*Angola*	50	49	31	22	−1.8	−28.6	6.5	6.0	..	..
69	*Cuba*	31	16	9	6	−46.7	−36.7	2.0	2.0	..	..
70	*Korea, Dem. Rep.*	41	30	13	7	−25.9	−42.0	4.0	2.6	..	..
71	*Lebanon*	43	29	14	9	−33.2	−40.2	3.8	2.4	53	..
72	*Mongolia*	41	34	15	7	−17.0	−52.7	4.8	3.1	..	..
	Upper middle-income	**40** *w*	**31** *w*	**13** *w*	**8** *w*	**−23.2** *w*	**−36.4** *w*	**4.2** *w*	**3.1** *w*	**..**	**..**
73	Syrian Arab Rep.	47	46	18	7	−1.5	−62.1	7.2	4.0	22	20
74	Jordan	47	45	20	8	−5.5	−59.3	7.4	5.2	22	25
75	Malaysia	44	29	15	6	−34.1	−57.0	3.7	2.4	33	..
76	Korea, Rep. of	43	23	14	6	−46.7	−53.3	2.7	2.1	25	54
77	Panama	41	28	10	5	−31.9	−47.6	3.5	2.3	..	61
78	Chile	34	23	13	7	−32.8	−46.8	2.7	2.2	..	..
79	Brazil	43	31	13	8	−26.9	−37.4	3.9	2.6	..	..
80	Mexico	45	34	12	7	−25.3	−41.5	4.6	2.8	..	39
81	Algeria	51	47	20	13	−7.8	−36.7	7.0	6.1	..	..
82	Portugal	24	18	11	10	−26.4	−8.3	2.3	2.1	..	66
83	Argentina	23	25	9	9	6.5	3.4	3.4	2.5	..	..
84	Uruguay	22	18	10	9	−17.4	−5.2	2.6	2.2	..	..
85	South Africa	39	40	15	9	1.3	−43.2	5.1	4.4	..	..
86	Yugoslavia	24	15	10	9	−36.6	−10.1	2.0	2.1	59	55
87	Venezuela	46	35	11	6	−24.4	−50.9	4.3	2.7	..	49
88	Greece	19	14	7	9	−24.3	19.2	2.3	2.1	..	..
89	Israel	27	24	6	7	−12.3	19.3	3.1	2.3	..	..
90	Hong Kong	35	18	7	5	−47.2	−20.9	2.1	2.1	42	72
91	Singapore	39	17	6	5	−55.3	−16.1	1.7	2.1	60	71
92	Trinidad and Tobago	38	29	8	7	−22.1	−17.2	3.3	2.4	44	52
93	*Iran, Islamic Rep.*	53	41	19	10	−23.8	−48.7	5.6	4.2	..	..
94	*Iraq*	49	45	20	11	−9.2	−46.2	6.7	4.9	14	..
	High-income oil exporters	**49** *w*	**42** *w*	**22** *w*	**11** *w*	**−12.9** *w*	**−49.8** *w*	**6.9** *w*	**5.8** *w*	**..**	**..**
95	Oman	51	47	28	15	−7.0	−47.1	7.1	4.0	..	..
96	Libya	49	45	19	11	−7.1	−42.9	7.2	6.3	..	..
97	Saudi Arabia	49	43	23	12	−11.2	−45.8	7.1	6.3	..	..
98	Kuwait	44	35	10	3	−21.4	−65.2	5.7	3.0	..	..
99	United Arab Emirates	46	28	19	3	−39.1	−82.1	6.0	4.8	..	..
	Industrial market economies	**20** *w*	**14** *w*	**10** *w*	**9** *w*	**−31.4** *w*	**−5.4** *w*	**1.7** *w*	**2.0** *w*	**..**	**..**
100	Ireland	21	20	12	9	−5.1	−18.3	3.2	2.1	..	..
101	Spain	22	15	9	9	−29.5	1.1	2.2	2.1	..	51
102	Italy	18	11	10	11	−37.0	9.4	1.6	1.9	..	78
103	New Zealand	27	16	9	8	−40.4	−8.0	1.9	2.0	..	..
104	United Kingdom	18	13	12	12	−27.4	3.5	1.8	2.0	69	77
105	Austria	18	13	13	12	−30.2	−5.5	1.6	1.9	..	..
106	Japan	17	13	8	7	−25.4	−13.2	1.7	1.9	56	..
107	Belgium	17	12	12	12	−28.4	−4.8	1.6	1.9	..	..
108	Finland	19	14	9	9	−25.9	..	1.6	1.9	77	80
109	Netherlands	21	12	8	8	−42.3	6.5	1.4	1.8	..	..
110	Australia	22	16	9	8	−28.1	−9.3	2.0	2.0	..	..
111	Canada	27	15	8	7	−43.4	−11.5	1.8	2.0	..	..
112	France	18	14	11	11	−23.5	−3.5	1.8	2.0	64	79
113	Germany, Fed. Rep.	18	10	12	12	−42.3	(.)	1.4	1.8	..	..
114	Denmark	17	10	10	11	−38.0	13.7	1.5	1.9	67	..
115	United States	24	16	10	9	−32.5	−9.5	1.8	2.0	65	68
116	Sweden	14	11	10	11	−19.0	9.0	1.7	1.9	..	..
117	Norway	17	12	9	10	−28.3	9.9	1.7	1.9	..	71
118	Switzerland	18	11	10	9	−35.2	−3.1	1.9	2.0	..	..
	East European nonmarket economies	**23** *w*	**18** *w*	**8** *w*	**10** *w*	**−20.5** *w*	**34.4** *w*	**2.3** *w*	**2.1** *w*	**..**	**..**
119	Hungary	15	13	10	14	−15.0	32.4	2.0	2.0	67	74
120	Romania	19	17	9	10	−9.4	11.5	2.4	2.1	..	58
121	*Albania*	43	28	10	6	−35.9	−47.1	3.6	2.2	..	..
122	*Bulgaria*	18	15	8	10	−18.0	28.4	2.1	2.1	..	76
123	*Czechoslovakia*	16	15	9	12	−4.4	27.2	2.2	2.1	..	..
124	*German Dem. Rep.*	17	15	14	13	−14.7	−6.6	1.9	2.0	..	..
125	*Poland*	23	19	8	9	−14.2	21.1	2.3	2.1	60	75
126	*USSR*	25	19	7	10	−23.7	42.3	2.4	2.1	..	..

a. Figures include women whose husbands practice contraception. Figures in italics are for years other than those specified. See the technical notes.

Table 21. Labor force

	Percentage of population of working age (15–64 years)		Percentage of labor force in:						Average annual growth of labor force (percent)		
			Agriculture		Industry		Services				
	1960	1982	1960	1980	1960	1980	1960	1980	1960–70	1970–82	1980–2000
Low-income economies	55 w	59 w	77 w	72 w	9 w	13 w	14 w	15 w	1.7 w	2.0 w	2.0 w
China and India	56 w	61 w	. .	69 w	. .	17 w	. .	14 w	1.7 w	1.9 w	1.8 w
Other low-income	54 w	53 w	82 w	73 w	7 w	11 w	11 w	16 w	1.8 w	2.3 w	3.0 w
1 Chad	57	54	95	85	2	7	3	8	1.5	1.8	2.6
2 Bangladesh	53	55	87	74	3	11	10	15	2.1	2.9	3.0
3 Ethiopia	53	52	88	80	5	7	7	13	2.0	1.7	3.0
4 Nepal	57	55	95	93	2	2	3	5	1.3	2.4	2.7
5 Mali	54	51	94	73	3	12	3	15	2.1	2.1	2.9
6 Burma	59	55	. .	67	. .	10	. .	23	1.1	1.5	2.3
7 Zaire	53	52	83	75	9	13	8	12	1.4	2.3	3.2
8 Malawi	52	50	92	86	3	5	5	9	2.4	2.5	3.2
9 Upper Volta	54	52	92	82	5	13	3	5	1.6	1.6	2.5
10 Uganda	54	52	89	83	4	6	7	11	2.6	2.1	3.5
11 India	54	57	74	71	11	13	15	16	1.7	2.1	2.1
12 Rwanda	53	52	95	91	1	2	4	7	2.2	3.2	3.5
13 Burundi	55	53	90	84	3	5	7	11	0.9	1.6	2.8
14 Tanzania	54	51	89	83	4	6	7	11	2.1	2.6	3.4
15 Somalia	54	54	88	82	4	8	8	10	2.1	2.9	2.0
16 Haiti	55	53	80	74	6	7	14	19	0.6	1.3	2.0
17 Benin	53	51	54	46	9	16	37	38	2.1	2.1	2.8
18 Central African Rep.	58	55	94	88	2	4	4	8	1.1	1.5	2.4
19 China	56	63	. .	69	. .	19	. .	12	1.7	1.8	1.6
20 Guinea	55	53	88	82	6	11	6	7	1.1	1.3	2.3
21 Niger	53	51	95	91	1	3	4	6	3.0	3.0	3.4
22 Madagascar	55	53	93	87	2	4	5	9	1.7	2.1	3.0
23 Sri Lanka	54	60	56	54	14	14	30	32	2.1	2.1	2.1
24 Togo	53	51	80	67	8	15	12	18	2.5	1.8	3.2
25 Ghana	53	51	64	53	14	20	22	27	1.6	2.3	3.9
26 Pakistan	52	51	61	57	18	20	21	23	1.9	2.7	3.1
27 Kenya	50	47	86	78	5	10	9	12	2.7	3.3	4.2
28 Sierra Leone	55	53	78	65	12	19	10	16	1.0	1.6	2.4
29 Afghanistan	55	52	85	79	6	8	9	13	1.9	2.1	2.6
30 Bhutan	56	56	95	93	2	2	3	5	0.3	2.1	2.3
31 Kampuchea, Dem.	53	. .	82	. .	4	. .	14	. .	2.0	. .	. .
32 Lao PDR	56	51	83	75	4	6	13	19	1.1	0.8	2.7
33 Mozambique	56	53	81	66	8	18	11	16	1.8	3.4	3.1
34 Viet Nam	. .	54	81	71	5	10	14	19	. .	. .	2.7
Middle-income economies	55 w	56 w	62 w	46 w	15 w	21 w	23 w	34 w	2.1 w	2.4 w	2.6 w
Oil exporters	54 w	54 w	66 w	48 w	13 w	20 w	22 w	32 w	2.1 w	2.6 w	2.9 w
Oil importers	55 w	57 w	60 w	44 w	16 w	21 w	24 w	35 w	2.1 w	2.3 w	2.4 w
Lower middle-income	54 w	55 w	71 w	56 w	11 w	16 w	18 w	28 w	1.9 w	2.4 w	2.6 w
35 Sudan	53	53	86	78	6	10	8	12	2.1	2.8	3.0
36 Mauritania	53	51	91	69	3	8	6	23	1.9	2.0	2.4
37 Yemen, PDR	52	52	70	45	15	15	15	40	1.7	1.7	3.6
38 Liberia	52	51	80	70	10	14	10	16	2.4	3.0	3.5
39 Senegal	54	52	84	77	5	10	11	13	1.7	2.0	2.7
40 Yemen Arab Rep.	54	52	83	75	7	11	10	14	1.6	2.0	3.4
41 Lesotho	57	55	93	87	2	4	5	9	1.6	1.9	2.7
42 Bolivia	55	53	61	50	18	24	21	26	1.7	2.3	2.9
43 Indonesia	56	57	75	58	8	12	17	30	1.7	2.5	1.9
44 Zambia	53	50	79	67	7	11	14	22	2.1	2.3	3.2
45 Honduras	52	50	70	63	11	20	19	17	2.5	3.2	3.5
46 Egypt, Arab Rep.	55	57	58	50	12	30	30	20	2.2	2.5	2.4
47 El Salvador	52	52	62	50	17	22	21	28	3.0	2.8	3.5
48 Thailand	53	56	84	76	4	9	12	15	2.1	2.8	2.2
49 Papua New Guinea	57	55	89	82	4	8	7	10	1.7	1.7	2.0
50 Philippines	52	53	61	46	15	17	24	37	2.1	2.5	2.7
51 Zimbabwe	52	50	69	60	11	15	20	25	3.1	2.3	4.5
52 Nigeria	52	50	71	54	10	19	19	27	1.8	1.8	3.5
53 Morocco	53	51	62	52	14	21	24	27	1.5	2.8	3.5
54 Cameroon	57	54	87	83	5	7	8	10	1.5	2.2	3.2
55 Nicaragua	50	50	62	39	16	14	22	47	2.3	3.8	3.9
56 Ivory Coast	54	53	89	79	2	4	9	17	3.6	4.1	3.3
57 Guatemala	51	54	67	55	14	21	19	24	2.8	3.2	2.9
58 Congo, People's Rep.	56	52	52	34	17	26	31	40	1.8	2.2	3.9
59 Costa Rica	50	59	51	29	19	23	30	48	3.3	3.8	2.8
60 Peru	52	54	53	40	20	19	27	41	2.1	2.8	2.9
61 Dominican Rep.	49	53	67	49	12	18	21	33	2.2	3.6	3.0
62 Jamaica	54	54	39	35	25	18	36	47	0.4	2.3	2.8
63 Ecuador	52	52	57	52	19	17	24	31	2.7	2.8	3.4
64 Turkey	55	59	79	54	11	13	10	33	1.4	2.0	2.3

Note: For data comparability and coverage see the technical notes.

		Percentage of population of working age (15–64 years)		Percentage of labor force in:						Average annual growth of labor force (percent)		
				Agriculture		Industry		Services				
		1960	1982	1960	1980	1960	1980	1960	1980	1960–70	1970–82	1980–2000
65	Tunisia	52	56	56	35	18	32	26	33	0.7	3.1	3.1
66	Colombia	50	60	51	26	19	21	30	53	3.0	3.3	2.4
67	Paraguay	51	53	56	49	19	19	25	32	2.3	2.9	3.0
68	*Angola*	55	53	69	59	12	16	19	25	1.6	2.0	2.9
69	*Cuba*	61	61	39	23	22	31	39	46	0.8	1.8	1.8
70	*Korea, Dem. Rep.*	53	56	62	49	23	33	15	18	2.3	2.9	2.8
71	*Lebanon*	53	56	38	11	23	27	39	62	2.1	1.1	2.2
72	*Mongolia*	54	54	70	55	13	22	17	23	2.1	2.5	3.1
Upper middle-income		**55** *w*	**57** *w*	**49** *w*	**30** *w*	**20** *w*	**28** *w*	**31** *w*	**42** *w*	**2.3** *w*	**2.3** *w*	**2.5** *w*
73	Syrian Arab Rep.	52	49	54	33	19	31	27	36	2.1	3.3	4.4
74	Jordan	52	51	44	20	26	20	30	60	2.8	2.5	4.4
75	Malaysia	51	56	63	50	12	16	25	34	2.7	2.9	3.0
76	Korea, Rep. of	54	62	66	34	9	29	25	37	3.1	2.6	2.1
77	Panama	52	56	51	33	14	18	35	49	3.4	2.4	2.5
78	Chile	57	62	30	19	20	19	50	62	1.4	2.1	2.1
79	Brazil	54	55	52	30	15	24	33	46	2.7	2.3	2.6
80	Mexico	51	52	55	36	20	26	25	38	2.8	3.2	3.3
81	Algeria	52	49	67	25	12	25	21	50	0.5	3.5	4.8
82	Portugal	63	63	44	28	29	35	27	37	0.4	0.6	0.8
83	Argentina	64	63	20	13	36	28	44	59	1.3	1.3	1.3
84	Uruguay	64	63	21	11	30	32	49	57	0.8	0.3	0.9
85	South Africa	55	55	32	30	30	29	38	41	3.0	2.9	3.3
86	Yugoslavia	63	67	63	29	18	35	19	36	0.6	0.6	0.6
87	Venezuela	51	55	35	18	22	27	43	55	3.1	4.1	3.3
88	Greece	65	64	56	37	20	28	24	35	0.0	0.8	0.5
89	Israel	59	58	14	7	35	36	51	57	3.6	2.4	2.1
90	Hong Kong	56	66	8	3	52	57	40	40	3.3	3.5	1.4
91	Singapore	55	66	8	2	23	39	69	59	2.7	2.6	1.2
92	Trinidad and Tobago	53	63	22	10	34	39	44	52	2.5	1.8	2.2
93	*Iran, Islamic Rep.*	51	52	54	39	23	34	23	27	3.1	2.9	3.8
94	*Iraq*	51	51	53	42	18	26	29	32	2.9	3.1	3.9
High-income oil exporters		**54** *w*	**52** *w*	**62** *w*	**46** *w*	**13** *w*	**19** *w*	**25** *w*	**35** *w*	**3.8** *w*	**4.5** *w*	**3.8** *w*
95	Oman	54	52	..	..	..	..	..	..	..	..	..
96	Libya	53	51	53	19	17	28	30	53	3.6	3.6	4.4
97	Saudi Arabia	54	52	71	61	10	14	19	25	3.3	4.7	3.7
98	Kuwait	63	52	1	2	34	34	65	64	7.0	4.8	3.4
99	United Arab Emirates	..	..	..	..	..	..	..	..	..	..	..
Industrial market economies		**63** *w*	**66** *w*	**18** *w*	**6** *w*	**38** *w*	**38** *w*	**44** *w*	**56** *w*	**1.2** *w*	**1.2** *w*	**0.6** *w*
100	Ireland	58	59	36	18	25	37	39	45	0.0	1.3	1.5
101	Spain	64	63	42	14	31	40	27	46	0.2	1.2	0.8
102	Italy	66	65	31	11	40	45	29	44	-0.1	0.6	0.3
103	New Zealand	58	64	15	10	37	35	48	55	2.2	1.7	1.0
104	United Kingdom	65	64	4	2	48	42	48	56	0.6	0.4	0.2
105	Austria	66	65	24	9	46	37	30	54	-0.7	0.9	0.3
106	Japan	64	68	33	12	30	39	37	49	1.9	1.3	0.7
107	Belgium	65	66	8	3	48	41	44	56	0.3	0.7	0.2
108	Finland	62	68	36	11	31	35	33	54	0.4	0.9	0.3
109	Netherlands	61	67	11	6	43	45	46	49	1.6	1.3	0.5
110	Australia	61	65	11	6	40	33	49	61	2.6	1.8	1.1
111	Canada	59	67	13	5	34	29	52	66	2.5	2.0	1.1
112	France	62	64	22	8	39	39	39	53	0.7	1.0	0.6
113	Germany, Fed. Rep.	68	67	14	4	48	46	38	50	0.2	0.8	(.)
114	Denmark	64	65	18	7	37	35	45	58	1.1	0.6	0.4
115	United States	60	66	7	2	36	32	57	66	1.8	1.7	0.9
116	Sweden	66	64	14	5	45	34	41	61	1.0	0.3	0.4
117	Norway	63	63	20	7	37	37	44	56	0.5	0.7	0.6
118	Switzerland	66	67	11	5	50	46	38	49	2.0	0.4	0.2
East European nonmarket economies		**63** *w*	**66** *w*	**42** *w*	**18** *w*	**30** *w*	**44** *w*	**28** *w*	**39** *w*	**0.8** *w*	**1.1** *w*	**0.6** *w*
119	Hungary	66	65	39	21	34	43	27	36	0.5	0.3	0.1
120	Romania	64	64	65	29	15	36	20	35	0.9	0.6	0.7
121	*Albania*	54	58	71	61	18	25	11	14	2.3	2.7	2.4
122	Bulgaria	66	66	57	37	25	39	18	24	0.7	0.2	0.2
123	Czechoslovakia	64	64	26	11	46	48	28	41	0.8	0.7	0.6
124	*German Dem. Rep.*	65	64	18	10	48	50	34	40	-0.2	0.5	0.3
125	*Poland*	61	66	48	31	29	39	23	30	1.7	1.4	0.8
126	*USSR*	63	66	42	14	29	45	29	41	0.7	1.2	0.6

Table 22. Urbanization

	Urban population				Percentage of urban population				Number of cities of over 500,000 persons	
	As percentage of total population		Average annual growth rate (percent)		In largest city		In cities of over 500,000 persons			
	1960[a]	1982[a]	1960–70	1970–82	1960	1980	1960	1980	1960	1980
Low-income economies	17 *w*	21 *w*	4.1 *w*	4.4 *w*	10 *w*	16 *w*	31 *w*	55 *w*	55 *t*	145 *t*
China and India	18 *w*	22 *w*	..	..	7 *w*	6 *w*	33 *w*	59 *w*	49 *t*	114 *t*
Other low-income	12 *w*	20 *w*	5.2 *w*	5.2 *w*	25 *w*	28 *w*	19 *w*	40 *w*	6 *t*	31 *t*
1 Chad	7	19	6.8	6.4	..	39	0	0	0	0
2 Bangladesh	5	12	6.2	6.0	20	30	20	51	1	3
3 Ethiopia	6	15	6.5	5.6	30	37	0	37	0	1
4 Nepal	3	6	4.2	6.7	41	27	0	0	0	0
5 Mali	11	19	5.4	4.7	32	24	0	0	0	0
6 Burma	19	28	3.9	3.9	23	23	23	23	1	2
7 Zaire	16	38	5.2	7.6	14	28	14	38	1	2
8 Malawi	4	10	6.6	6.4	..	19	0	0	0	0
9 Upper Volta	5	11	5.7	6.0	..	41	0	0	0	0
10 Uganda	5	9	7.1	3.4	38	52	0	52	0	1
11 India	18	24	3.3	3.9	7	6	26	39	11	36
12 Rwanda	2	5	5.4	6.4	..	0	0	0	0	0
13 Burundi	2	2	1.3	2.5	..	..	0	0	0	0
14 Tanzania	5	13	6.3	8.5	34	50	0	50	0	1
15 Somalia	17	32	5.7	5.4	..	34	0	0	0	0
16 Haiti	16	26	3.9	4.0	42	56	0	56	0	1
17 Benin	10	15	5.4	4.4	..	63	0	63	0	1
18 Central African Rep.	23	37	4.7	3.5	40	36	0	0	0	0
19 China	18	21	..	..	6	6	42	45	38	78
20 Guinea	10	20	4.9	5.2	37	80	0	80	0	1
21 Niger	6	14	7.0	7.2	..	31	0	0	0	0
22 Madagascar	11	20	5.0	5.2	44	36	0	36	0	1
23 Sri Lanka	18	24	4.3	2.5	28	16	0	16	0	1
24 Togo	10	21	5.8	6.6	..	60	0	0	0	0
25 Ghana	23	37	4.6	5.0	25	35	0	48	0	2
26 Pakistan	22	29	4.0	4.3	20	21	33	51	2	7
27 Kenya	7	15	6.4	7.3	40	57	0	57	0	1
28 Sierra Leone	13	23	4.9	3.9	37	47	0	0	0	0
29 *Afghanistan*	8	17	5.4	5.8	33	17	0	17	0	1
30 *Bhutan*	3	4	3.3	3.6	0	0	0	0	0	0
31 *Kampuchea, Dem.*	10	..	3.7	..	..	..	..	..	..	..
32 *Lao PDR*	8	14	3.8	4.7	69	48	0	0	0	0
33 *Mozambique*	4	9	6.5	8.1	75	83	0	83	0	1
34 *Viet Nam*	15	19	5.3	3.2	32	21	32	50	1	4
Middle-income	33 *w*	46 *w*	4.4 *w*	4.2 *w*	28 *w*	29 *w*	35 *w*	48 *w*	54 *t*	128 *t*
Oil exporters	27 *w*	40 *w*	4.2 *w*	4.4 *w*	27 *w*	30 *w*	32 *w*	48 *w*	15 *t*	42 *t*
Oil importers	37 *w*	52 *w*	4.5 *w*	4.1 *w*	28 *w*	28 *w*	36 *w*	48 *w*	39 *t*	86 *t*
Lower middle-income	24 *w*	34 *w*	4.4 *w*	4.4 *w*	27 *w*	32 *w*	28 *w*	47 *w*	22 *t*	58 *t*
35 Sudan	10	23	6.8	5.8	30	31	0	31	0	1
36 Mauritania	3	26	15.5	8.1	..	39	0	0	0	0
37 Yemen, PDR	28	38	3.5	3.7	61	49	0	0	0	0
38 Liberia	21	34	5.6	5.7	..	..	0	0	0	0
39 Senegal	23	34	4.9	3.7	53	65	0	65	0	1
40 Yemen Arab Rep.	3	14	10.2	8.3	..	25	0	0	0	0
41 Lesotho	2	13	7.5	15.4	..	..	0	0	0	0
42 Bolivia	34	45	4.1	3.3	47	44	0	44	0	1
43 Indonesia	15	22	3.6	4.5	20	23	34	50	3	9
44 Zambia	23	45	5.2	6.5	..	35	0	35	0	1
45 Honduras	23	37	5.5	5.5	31	33	0	0	0	0
46 Egypt, Arab Rep.	38	45	3.5	2.9	38	39	53	53	2	2
47 El Salvador	38	42	3.6	3.4	26	22	0	0	0	0
48 Thailand	13	17	3.6	4.3	65	69	65	69	1	1
49 Papua New Guinea	3	17	15.2	6.6	..	25	0	0	0	0
50 Philippines	30	38	3.8	3.8	27	30	27	34	1	2
51 Zimbabwe	13	24	6.7	6.0	40	50	0	50	0	1
52 Nigeria	13	21	4.7	4.9	13	17	22	58	2	9
53 Morocco	29	42	4.2	4.1	16	26	16	50	1	4
54 Cameroon	14	37	5.8	8.0	26	21	0	21	0	1
55 Nicaragua	41	55	4.0	5.0	41	47	0	47	0	1
56 Ivory Coast	19	42	7.3	8.2	27	34	0	34	0	1
57 Guatemala	33	40	3.8	4.0	41	36	41	36	1	1
58 Congo, People's Rep.	30	46	5.0	4.4	77	56	0	0	0	0
59 Costa Rica	37	43	4.0	3.2	67	64	0	64	0	1
60 Peru	46	66	5.0	3.7	38	39	38	44	1	2
61 Dominican Rep.	30	53	5.6	5.3	50	54	0	54	0	1
62 Jamaica	34	48	3.5	2.6	77	66	0	66	0	1
63 Ecuador	34	46	4.2	3.8	31	29	0	51	0	2
64 Turkey	30	44	3.5	4.7	18	24	32	42	3	4

Note: For data comparability and coverage see the technical notes.

	Urban population				Percentage of urban population				Number of cities of over 500,000 persons	
	As percentage of total population		Average annual growth rate (percent)		In largest city		In cities of over 500,000 persons			
	1960ᵃ	1982ᵃ	1960–70	1970–82	1960	1980	1960	1980	1960	1980
65 Tunisia	36	54	3.8	4.0	40	30	40	30	1	1
66 Colombia	48	65	5.2	2.7	17	26	28	51	3	4
67 Paraguay	36	40	2.9	3.3	44	44	0	44	0	1
68 *Angola*	10	22	5.7	5.8	44	64	0	64	0	1
69 *Cuba*	55	68	2.9	2.1	32.	38	32	38	1	1
70 *Korea, Dem. Rep.*	40	63	5.0	4.2	15	12	15	19	1	2
71 *Lebanon*	40	77	6.9	2.8	64	79	64	79	1	1
72 *Mongolia*	36	53	5.3	4.2	53	52	0	0	0	0
Upper middle-income	**45** *w*	**63** *w*	**4.4** *w*	**3.9** *w*	**28** *w*	**29** *w*	**38** *w*	**51** *w*	**32** *t*	**70** *t*
73 Syrian Arab Rep.	37	49	4.8	4.4	35	33	35	55	1	2
74 Jordan	43	60	4.7	4.0	31	37	0	37	0	1
75 Malaysia	25	30	3.5	3.4	19	27	0	27	0	1
76 Korea, Rep. of	28	61	6.5	5.0	35	41	61	77	3	7
77 Panama	21	53	11.1	3.2	61	66	0	66	0	1
78 Chile	68	82	3.1	2.4	38	44	38	44	1	1
79 Brazil	45	69	5.0	4.1	14	15	35	52	6	14
80 Mexico	51	68	4.7	4.2	28	32	36	48	3	7
81 Algeria	30	45	3.5	5.4	27	12	27	12	1	1
82 Portugal	23	32	1.8	2.5	47	44	47	44	1	1
83 Argentina	74	83	2.1	1.9	46	45	54	60	3	5
84 Uruguay	80	84	1.3	0.6	56	52	56	52	1	1
85 South Africa	47	50	2.6	3.2	16	13	44	53	4	7
86 Yugoslavia	28	44	3.2	2.8	11	10	11	23	1	3
87 Venezuela	67	84	5.1	4.3	26	26	26	44	1	4
88 Greece	43	64	2.6	2.5	51	57	51	70	1	2
89 Israel	77	90	4.3	3.1	46	35	46	35	1	1
90 Hong Kong	89	91	2.6	2.4	100	100	100	100	1	1
91 Singapore	100	100	2.3	1.5	100	100	100	100	1	1
92 Trinidad and Tobago	22	22	1.8	0.7	. .	. .	0	0	0	0
93 *Iran, Islamic Rep.*	34	52	5.3	5.1	26	28	26	47	1	6
94 *Iraq*	43	70	5.8	5.3	35	55	35	70	1	3
High-income oil exporters	**28** *w*	**67** *w*	**8.5** *w*	**8.6** *w*	**29** *w*	**28** *w*	**0** *w*	**34** *w*	**0** *t*	**3** *t*
95 Oman	4	20	6.3	15.6	. .	. .	. .	. .	. .	. .
96 Libya	23	58	8.4	8.0	57	64	0	64	0	1
97 Saudi Arabia	30	69	8.4	7.6	15	18	0	33	0	2
98 Kuwait	72	91	10.1	7.4	75	30	0	0	0	0
99 United Arab Emirates	40	79	14.9	14.4	. .	. .	. .	. .	. .	. .
Industrial market economies	**68** *w*	**78** *w*	**1.9** *w*	**1.3** *w*	**18** *w*	**18** *w*	**48** *w*	**55** *w*	**104** *t*	**152** *t*
100 Ireland	46	59	1.6	2.5	51	48	51	48	1	1
101 Spain	57	76	2.6	2.1	13	17	37	44	5	6
102 Italy	59	70	1.5	1.1	13	17	46	52	7	9
103 New Zealand	76	85	2.3	1.5	25	30	0	30	0	1
104 United Kingdom	86	91	0.9	0.3	24	20	61	55	15	17
105 Austria	50	55	0.9	0.7	51	39	51	39	1	1
106 Japan	63	78	2.4	1.8	18	22	35	42	5	9
107 Belgium	66	73	1.2	0.4	17	14	28	24	2	2
108 Finland	38	64	3.2	2.4	28	27	0	27	0	1
109 Netherlands	80	76	1.0	0.6	9	9	27	24	3	3
110 Australia	81	89	2.5	2.0	26	24	62	68	4	5
111 Canada	69	76	2.7	1.2	14	18	31	62	2	9
112 France	62	79	2.4	1.4	25	23	34	34	4	6
113 Germany, Fed. Rep.	77	85	1.4	0.5	20	18	48	45	11	11
114 Denmark	74	85	1.6	0.8	40	32	40	32	1	1
115 United States	70	78	1.8	1.5	13	12	61	77	40	65
116 Sweden	73	88	1.8	1.0	15	15	15	35	1	3
117 Norway	32	54	3.5	2.6	50	32	50	32	1	1
118 Switzerland	51	59	2.2	0.8	19	22	19	22	1	1
East European nonmarket economies	**48** *w*	**62** *w*	**2.6** *w*	**1.8** *w*	**9** *w*	**7** *w*	**23** *w*	**32** *w*	**36** *t*	**65** *t*
119 Hungary	40	55	2.1	1.4	45	37	45	37	1	1
120 Romania	32	51	3.4	2.7	22	17	22	17	1	1
121 *Albania*	31	38	3.8	3.4	27	25	0	0	0	0
122 *Bulgaria*	39	66	3.8	2.3	23	18	23	18	1	1
123 *Czechoslovakia*	47	64	2.1	1.8	17	12	17	12	1	1
124 *German Dem. Rep.*	72	77	0.1	0.2	9	9	14	17	2	3
125 *Poland*	48	58	1.8	1.7	17	15	41	47	5	8
126 *USSR*	49	63	2.7	1.8	6	4	21	33	25	50

a. Figures in italics are for years other than those specified.

Table 23. Indicators related to life expectancy

	Life expectancy at birth (years) Male 1960	Male 1982	Female 1960	Female 1982	Infant mortality rate (aged under 1) 1960	1982	Child death rate (aged 1–4) 1960	1982
Low-income economies	42 *w*	58 *w*	41 *w*	60 *w*	165 *w*	87 *w*	27 *w*	11 *w*
China and India	42 *w*	61 *w*	41 *w*	62 *w*	165 *w*	78 *w*	26 *w*	9 *w*
Other low-income	42 *w*	50 *w*	43 *w*	52 *w*	163 *w*	114 *w*	31 *w*	19 *w*
1 Chad	33	42	36	45	210	161	60	37
2 Bangladesh	45	48	42	49	159	133	25	19
3 Ethiopia	35	45	38	49	172	122	42	25
4 Nepal	39	46	38	45	195	145	33	22
5 Mali	36	43	39	47	179	132	45	27
6 Burma	42	53	45	56	158	96	25	12
7 Zaire	38	49	42	52	150	106	32	20
8 Malawi	36	43	37	46	206	137	58	29
9 Upper Volta	36	43	39	46	234	157	71	36
10 Uganda	41	46	45	48	139	120	28	22
11 India	43	55	42	54	165	94	26	11
12 Rwanda	38	45	41	48	167	126	40	25
13 Burundi	37	45	40	48	143	123	31	24
14 Tanzania	40	51	43	54	144	98	31	18
15 Somalia	32	38	36	40	213	184	61	47
16 Haiti	44	53	45	56	182	110	47	17
17 Benin	38	46	41	50	173	117	42	23
18 Central African Rep.	37	46	40	49	170	119	41	23
19 China	41	65	41	69	165	67	26	7
20 Guinea	31	37	34	38	222	190	65	50
21 Niger	36	43	39	47	178	132	45	27
22 Madagascar	36	46	39	50	177	116	45	23
23 Sri Lanka	62	67	62	71	71	32	7	3
24 Togo	41	45	41	49	201	122	55	25
25 Ghana	43	53	46	57	132	86	27	15
26 Pakistan	44	51	42	49	162	121	25	17
27 Kenya	45	55	48	59	112	77	21	13
28 Sierra Leone	29	37	32	38	235	190	72	50
29 *Afghanistan*	33	35	34	37	233	205	41	35
30 *Bhutan*	33	43	31	42	243	163	43	26
31 *Kampuchea, Dem.*	41	42	44	45	146	. .	22	. .
32 *Lao PDR*	39	42	42	45	180	159	29	25
33 *Mozambique*	40	49	43	52	154	105	34	20
34 *Viet Nam*	42	62	45	66	163	53	26	4
Middle-income economies	49 *w*	58 *w*	52 *w*	62 *w*	126 *w*	76 *w*	23 *w*	10 *w*
Oil exporters	45 *w*	55 *w*	47 *w*	59 *w*	146 *w*	90 *w*	28 *w*	12 *w*
Oil importers	52 *w*	61 *w*	56 *w*	65 *w*	110 *w*	64 *w*	19 *w*	8 *w*
Lower middle-income	44 *w*	55 *w*	47 *w*	58 *w*	144 *w*	89 *w*	29 *w*	13 *w*
35 Sudan	38	46	40	49	168	119	40	23
36 Mauritania	36	43	39	47	178	132	45	27
37 Yemen, PDR	35	45	37	48	210	140	59	28
38 Liberia	43	52	45	56	173	91	42	16
39 Senegal	36	44	39	46	178	155	45	34
40 Yemen Arab Rep.	35	43	36	45	212	163	60	38
41 Lesotho	41	51	44	55	137	94	29	17
42 Bolivia	41	49	45	53	167	126	40	22
43 Indonesia	40	52	42	55	150	102	23	13
44 Zambia	38	49	41	52	164	105	38	20
45 Honduras	45	58	48	62	145	83	30	8
46 Egypt, Arab Rep.	46	56	47	59	128	104	23	14
47 El Salvador	49	62	52	66	136	72	26	7
48 Thailand	50	61	55	65	103	51	13	4
49 Papua New Guinea	41	53	40	53	165	99	26	13
50 Philippines	51	62	54	66	106	51	14	4
51 Zimbabwe	47	54	51	58	100	83	19	14
52 Nigeria	37	48	40	52	190	109	50	20
53 Morocco	46	51	48	54	161	125	37	22
54 Cameroon	41	52	45	55	134	92	28	16
55 Nicaragua	46	56	48	60	144	86	30	9
56 Ivory Coast	37	46	40	49	167	119	40	23
57 Guatemala	46	58	48	62	92	66	10	5
58 Congo, People's Rep.	47	59	49	62	118	68	23	10
59 Costa Rica	60	72	63	76	74	18	8	1
60 Peru	47	57	49	60	163	83	38	8
61 Dominican Rep.	49	61	53	65	120	65	20	5
62 Jamaica	61	71	65	75	52	10	4	(.)
63 Ecuador	49	61	52	65	140	78	28	7
64 Turkey	49	61	52	66	184	83	47	9

Note: For data comparability and coverage see the technical notes.

		Life expectancy at birth (years)				Infant mortality rate (aged under 1)		Child death rate (aged 1–4)	
		Male		Female					
		1960	1982	1960	1982	1960	1982	1960	1982
65	Tunisia	48	60	49	63	159	65	36	6
66	Colombia	49	62	57	66	93	54	11	4
67	Paraguay	54	63	58	67	86	45	9	3
68	*Angola*	32	42	35	44	216	165	63	39
69	*Cuba*	62	73	65	77	35	17	2	1
70	*Korea, Dem. Rep.*	52	63	56	67	78	32	9	2
71	*Lebanon*	58	63	62	67	68	39	6	3
72	*Mongolia*	51	63	54	67	109	51	14	4
Upper middle-income		**55** *w*	**63** *w*	**58** *w*	**67** *w*	**101** *w*	**58** *w*	**15** *w*	**6** *w*
73	Syrian Arab Rep.	49	65	51	69	132	58	25	5
74	Jordan	46	62	48	65	136	65	26	6
75	Malaysia	52	65	56	69	72	29	8	2
76	Korea, Rep. of	52	64	56	71	78	32	9	2
77	Panama	61	69	63	73	68	33	6	2
78	Chile	54	68	59	72	119	27	20	2
79	Brazil	53	62	57	66	118	73	19	8
80	Mexico	55	64	59	68	91	53	10	4
81	Algeria	46	55	48	59	165	111	39	17
82	Portugal	61	68	66	74	78	26	9	1
83	Argentina	62	66	68	73	61	44	5	2
84	Uruguay	65	71	71	75	51	34	4	2
85	South Africa	51	60	55	65	92	55	16	5
86	Yugoslavia	61	69	64	74	88	34	10	2
87	Venezuela	55	65	60	71	85	39	9	2
88	Greece	67	72	70	76	40	14	3	1
89	Israel	70	72	73	76	31	16	2	1
90	Hong Kong	61	74	69	78	37	10	2	(.)
91	Singapore	62	70	66	75	35	11	2	(.)
92	Trinidad and Tobago	62	66	66	70	45	26	3	1
93	*Iran, Islamic Rep.*	50	60	50	60	163	102	26	13
94	*Iraq*	47	57	50	61	139	73	28	8
High-income oil exporters		**43** *w*	**56** *w*	**45** *w*	**60** *w*	**175** *w*	**96** *w*	**44** *w*	**13** *w*
95	Oman	38	51	39	54	193	123	52	21
96	Libya	46	56	48	59	158	95	36	11
97	Saudi Arabia	42	54	45	58	185	108	48	16
98	Kuwait	58	69	61	74	89	32	10	1
99	United Arab Emirates	51	69	54	73	135	50	26	3
Industrial market economies		**68** *w*	**71** *w*	**73** *w*	**78** *w*	**29** *w*	**10** *w*	**2** *w*	**(.)** *w*
100	Ireland	68	70	71	76	29	11	2	(.)
101	Spain	67	71	71	78	44	10	3	(.)
102	Italy	67	71	72	78	44	14	3	1
103	New Zealand	68	70	74	77	23	12	1	(.)
104	United Kingdom	68	71	74	77	23	11	1	(.)
105	Austria	66	69	72	77	38	13	3	1
106	Japan	65	74	70	79	30	7	2	(.)
107	Belgium	67	70	73	77	31	12	2	(.)
108	Finland	65	69	72	78	22	7	1	(.)
109	Netherlands	71	73	75	79	18	8	1	(.)
110	Australia	68	71	74	78	20	10	1	(.)
111	Canada	68	71	74	79	27	10	2	(.)
112	France	67	71	74	79	27	10	2	(.)
113	Germany, Fed. Rep.	67	70	72	77	34	12	2	(.)
114	Denmark	70	72	74	78	22	8	1	(.)
115	United States	67	71	73	78	26	11	1	(.)
116	Sweden	71	75	75	80	17	7	1	(.)
117	Norway	71	73	76	79	19	8	1	(.)
118	Switzerland	69	77	74	81	21	8	1	(.)
East European nonmarket economies		**65** *w*	**66** *w*	**72** *w*	**74** *w*	**38** *w*	**21** *w*	**3** *w*	**1** *w*
119	Hungary	66	68	70	75	48	20	4	1
120	Romania	64	68	67	74	76	29	8	2
121	*Albania*	61	69	63	73	83	44	9	3
122	*Bulgaria*	67	70	70	75	45	20	3	1
123	*Czechoslovakia*	67	68	73	75	24	16	1	1
124	*German Dem. Rep.*	67	70	72	76	39	12	3	(.)
125	*Poland*	65	68	70	76	56	20	5	1
126	*USSR*	65	65	72	74	33	. .	2	. .

Table 24. Health-related indicators

| | | Population per: | | | Daily calorie supply per capita | |
| | Physician | | Nursing person | | Total | As percentage of requirement |
	1960[a]	1980[a]	1960[a]	1980[a]	1981[a]	1981[a]
Low-income economies	12,088 *w*	5,772 *w*	7,226 *w*	4,841 *w*	2,219 *w*	97 *w*
China and India	7,019 *w*	2,591 *w*	6,734 *w*	3,315 *w*	2,262 *w*	98 *w*
Other low-income	37,092 *w*	15,931 *w*	9,759 *w*	9,716 *w*	2,082 *w*	91 *w*
1 Chad	72,190	47,530	5,780	3,850	1,818	76
2 Bangladesh	. .	10,940	. .	24,450	1,952	84
3 Ethiopia	100,470	58,490	14,920	5,440	1,758	76
4 Nepal	73,470	30,060	. .	33,420	1,929	86
5 Mali	64,130	22,130	4,710	2,380	1,621	72
6 Burma	15,560	4,660	8,520	4,750	2,303	113
7 Zaire	79,620	14,780	3,510	1,920	2,135	94
8 Malawi	35,250	40,950	12,940	3,830	2,138	94
9 Upper Volta	81,650	48,510	3,980	4,950	2,008	95
10 Uganda	15,050	26,810	10,030	4,180	1,778	80
11 India	4,850	3,690	10,980	5,460	1,906	86
12 Rwanda	143,290	31,510	11,620	9,840	2,194	88
13 Burundi	98,900	45,020	4,640	6,180	2,152	95
14 Tanzania	18,220	17,560	11,890	2,980	1,985	83
15 Somalia	36,570	14,290	4,810	2,330	2,119	100
16 Haiti	9,230	8,200	4,020	2,490	1,879	96
17 Benin	23,030	16,980	2,700	1,660	2,284	101
18 Central African Rep.	51,170	26,430	3,410	1,720	2,164	96
19 China	8,390	1,810	4,050	1,790	2,526	107
20 Guinea	33,770	17,110	4,040	2,570	1,877	75
21 Niger	82,170	38,790	8,460	4,650	2,489	102
22 Madagascar	8,900	10,170	3,110	3,660	2,474	109
23 Sri Lanka	4,490	7,170	4,170	1,340	2,250	102
24 Togo	47,060	18,100	5,340	1,430	1,889	83
25 Ghana	21,600	7,630	5,430	780	1,995	88
26 Pakistan	5,400	3,480	16,960	5,820	2,313	106
27 Kenya	10,690	7,890	2,270	550	2,056	88
28 Sierra Leone	20,070	16,220	2,880	1,890	2,053	101
29 Afghanistan	28,700	16,730	19,590	26,000	1,758	72
30 Bhutan	. .	18,160	. .	7,960	. .	103
31 Kampuchea, Dem.	35,280	. .	3,980	. .	1,998	95
32 Lao PDR	53,520	20,060	4,950	3,040	1,986	97
33 Mozambique	20,390	39,110	4,720	5,600	1,881	70
34 Viet Nam	. .	4,190	. .	2,930	1,961	90
Middle-income economies	17,257 *w*	5,414 *w*	3,838 *w*	1,886 *w*	2,607 *w*	111 *w*
Oil exporters	30,075 *w*	6,997 *w*	4,188 *w*	1,966 *w*	2,508 *w*	108 *w*
Oil importers	7,161 *w*	4,083 *w*	3,560 *w*	1,812 *w*	2,686 *w*	113 *w*
Lower middle-income	28,478 *w*	7,765 *w*	4,697 *w*	2,462 *w*	2,454 *w*	107 *w*
35 Sudan	33,230	8,930	3,010	1,430	2,406	99
36 Mauritania	40,420	14,350	5,430	2,080	2,082	97
37 Yemen, PDR	13,270	7,200	. .	830	2,067	86
38 Liberia	12,600	9,610	1,410	1,420	2,510	114
39 Senegal	24,990	13,800	3,150	1,400	2,434	101
40 Yemen Arab Rep.	130,090	11,670	. .	4,580	2,239	76
41 Lesotho	23,490	18,640	6,540	4,330	2,535	111
42 Bolivia	3,830	. .	4,170	. .	2,179	91
43 Indonesia	46,780	11,530	4,510	2,300	2,342	110
44 Zambia	9,540	7,670	9,920	1,730	2,094	93
45 Honduras	12,620	3,120	3,110	700	2,171	96
46 Egypt, Arab Rep.	2,550	970	1,930	1,500	2,941	116
47 El Salvador	5,330	3,220	. .	910	2,146	94
48 Thailand	7,900	7,100	4,830	2,400	2,303	105
49 Papua New Guinea	19,320	13,590	. .	960	2,323	92
50 Philippines	6,940	7,970	1,440	6,000	2,318	116
51 Zimbabwe	4,790	6,580	1,000	1,190	2,025	90
52 Nigeria	73,710	12,550	4,040	3,010	2,361	91
53 Morocco	9,410	10,750	. .	1,830	2,643	115
54 Cameroon	45,230	13,990	3,080	1,950	2,439	102
55 Nicaragua	2,690	1,800	1,250	550	2,184	99
56 Ivory Coast	29,190	21,040	2,920	1,590	2,670	112
57 Guatemala	4,640	8,610	9,040	1,620	2,045	93
58 Congo, People's Rep.	16,100	5,510	1,300	790	2,199	94
59 Costa Rica	2,740	1,460	720	450	2,686	118
60 Peru	1,910	1,390	3,530	970	2,183	98
61 Dominican Rep.	8,220	2,320	. .	2,150	2,192	106
62 Jamaica	2,590	2,830	420	630	2,643	119
63 Ecuador	2,670	760	2,360	570	2,100	97
64 Turkey	2,800	1,630	16,300	1,130	3,019	122

Note: For data comparability and coverage see the technical notes.

		Population per:				Daily calorie supply per capita	
		Physician		Nursing person		Total	As percentage of requirement
		1960[a]	1980[a]	1960[a]	1980[a]	1981[a]	1981[a]
65	Tunisia	10,030	3,690	. .	890	2,782	116
66	Colombia	2,640	1,710	4,220	800	2,521	108
67	Paraguay	1,810	1,710	1,380	1,100	3,005	139
68	Angola	14,910	. .	6,650	. .	2,096	83
69	Cuba	1,060	710	950	360	2,766	121
70	Korea, Dem. Rep.	. .	430	. .	. .	3,009	129
71	Lebanon	1,210	540	2,080	730	2,476	99
72	Mongolia	1,070	450	300	240	2,691	111
Upper middle-income		**2,532** w	**2,021** w	**2,752** w	**1,024** w	**2,816** w	**117** w
73	Syrian Arab Rep.	4,630	2,270	10,850	1,410	2,908	120
74	Jordan	5,800	1,700	1,930	1,180	2,260	102
75	Malaysia	7,060	7,910	1,800	940	2,662	121
76	Korea, Rep. of	3,540	1,440	3,240	350	2,931	126
77	Panama	2,730	980	760	420	2,271	103
78	Chile	1,780	1,930	640	450	2,790	114
79	Brazil	2,210	. .	2,810	. .	2,529	107
80	Mexico	1,830	. .	3,650	. .	2,805	121
81	Algeria	5,530	2,630	. .	740	2,433	89
82	Portugal	1,250	540	1,420	650	2,675	110
83	Argentina	740	430	760	. .	3,405	125
84	Uruguay	960	540	800	190	2,912	110
85	South Africa	2,180	. .	480	. .	2,825	118
86	Yugoslavia	1,620	550	630	280	3,662	144
87	Venezuela	1,500	990	2,830	380	2,642	107
88	Greece	800	420	800	600	3,748	150
89	Israel	400	370	360	130	2,946	115
90	Hong Kong	3,060	1,210	2,910	790	2,920	129
91	Singapore	2,380	1,150	650	320	3,078	133
92	Trinidad and Tobago	2,370	1,360	670	380	2,694	121
93	Iran, Islamic Rep.	3,860	6,090	7,690	2,520	2,795	114
94	Iraq	5,280	1,800	3,040	2,160	3,086	127
High-income oil exporters		**14,738** w	**1,355** w	**4,996** w	**836** w	**2,969** w	**124** w
95	Oman	31,180	1,900	. .	500	. .	. .
96	Libya	6,580	730	1320	400	3,459	147
97	Saudi Arabia	16,370	1,670	5,850	1,170	2,895	116
98	Kuwait	1,210	570	270	180	. .	. .
99	United Arab Emirates	. .	900	. .	340	. .	. .
Industrial market economies		**816** w	**554** w	**470** w	**180** w	**3,396** w	**132** w
100	Ireland	950	780	190	120	3,495	135
101	Spain	850	460	1,300	330	3,142	127
102	Italy	640	340	1,330	. .	3,716	150
103	New Zealand	850	650	. .	120	3,480	129
104	United Kingdom	940	650	210	140	3,322	132
105	Austria	550	400	440	230	3,539	134
106	Japan	930	780	310	240	2,740	117
107	Belgium	780	400	520	120	3,916	160
108	Finland	1,570	530	170	100	2,799	103
109	Netherlands	900	540	. .	130	3,588	133
110	Australia	750	560	. .	120	3,210	119
111	Canada	910	550	170	90	3,321	126
112	France	930	580	530	120	3,360	133
113	Germany, Fed. Rep.	670	450	370	170	3,538	133
114	Denmark	810	480	220	210	3,567	133
115	United States	750	520	340	140	3,647	138
116	Sweden	1,050	490	100	60	3,196	119
117	Norway	900	520	330	90	3,173	118
118	Switzerland	740	410	350	160	3,561	133
East European nonmarket economies		**683** w	**349** w	**358** w	**131** w	**3,351** w	**131** w
119	Hungary	720	400	330	150	3,509	134
120	Romania	790	680	420	270	3,337	126
121	Albania	3,620	960	530	310	2,701	112
122	Bulgaria	710	410	550	190	3,644	146
123	Czechoslovakia	620	360	230	130	3,472	141
124	German Dem. Rep.	1,180	520	. .	. .	3,780	144
125	Poland	1,070	570	460	240	3,210	123
126	USSR	560	270	340	100	3,328	130

a. Figures in italics are for years other than those specified. See the technical notes.

Table 25. Education

	Number enrolled in primary school as percentage of age group						Number enrolled in secondary school as percentage of age group		Number enrolled in higher education as percentage of population aged 20–24	
	Total		Male		Female					
	1960	1981[a]	1960	1981[a]	1960	1981[a]	1960	1981[a]	1960	1981[a]
Low-income economies	80 *w*	94 *w*	69 *w*	107 *w*	34 *w*	81 *w*	18 *w*	34 *w*	2 *w*	4 *w*
China and India	90 *w*	102 *w*		115 *w*	40 *w*	89 *w*	21 *w*	38 *w*		4 *w*
Other low-income	38 *w*	72 *w*	51 *w*	84 *w*	25 *w*	58 *w*	7 *w*	19 *w*	1 *w*	2 *w*
1 Chad	17	35	29	51	4	19	..	3	..	(.)
2 Bangladesh	47	62	66	76	26	47	8	15	1	3
3 Ethiopia	7	46	11	60	3	33	..	12	(.)	1
4 Nepal	10	91	19	126	1	53	6	21	1	3
5 Mali	10	27	14	35	6	20	1	9	..	1
6 Burma	56	84	61	87	52	81	10	20	1	4
7 Zaire	60	90	88	104	32	75	3	23	(.)	1
8 Malawi	..	62	..	73	..	51	1	4	..	(.)
9 Upper Volta	8	20	12	26	5	15	1	3	..	(.)
10 Uganda	49	54	65	62	32	46	3	5	(.)	1
11 India	61	79	80	93	40	64	20	30	3	8
12 Rwanda	49	72	68	75	30	69	2	2	..	(.)
13 Burundi	18	32	27	40	9	25	1	3	(.)	1
14 Tanzania	25	102	33	107	18	98	2	3	..	(.)
15 Somalia	9	30	13	38	5	21	1	11	(.)	1
16 Haiti	46	69	50	74	42	64	4	13	(.)	1
17 Benin	27	65	38	88	15	42	2	18	..	1
18 Central African Rep.	32	68	53	89	12	49	1	13	..	1
19 China	109	118	..	130	..	106	21	44	..	1
20 Guinea	30	33	44	44	16	22	2	16	..	5
21 Niger	5	23	7	29	3	17	..	6	..	(.)
22 Madagascar	52	100	58	..	45	..	4	14	(.)	3
23 Sri Lanka	95	103	100	106	90	100	27	51	1	3
24 Togo	44	111	63	135	24	87	2	31	..	2
25 Ghana	38	69	52	77	25	60	5	36	(.)	1
26 Pakistan	30	56	46	78	13	31	11	17	1	2
27 Kenya	47	109	64	114	30	101	2	19	(.)	1
28 Sierra Leone	23	39	30	45	15	30	2	12	(.)	1
29 *Afghanistan*	9	34	15	54	2	13	1	11	(.)	2
30 *Bhutan*	3	21	..	25	..	17	3	3	..	(.)
31 *Kampuchea, Dem.*	64	..	82	..	46	..	3	..	(.)	..
32 *Lao PDR*	25	97	34	105	16	89	1	18	(.)	(.)
33 *Mozambique*	48	90	60	102	36	78	2	6	..	(.)
34 *Viet Nam*	..	113	..	120	..	105	..	48	..	3
Middle-income economies	75 *w*	102 *w*	83 *w*	106 *w*	68 *w*	95 *w*	14 *w*	41 *w*	3 *w*	11 *w*
Oil exporters	64 *w*	106 *w*	75 *w*	111 *w*	52 *w*	95 *w*	9 *w*	37 *w*	2 *w*	8 *w*
Oil importers	84 *w*	99 *w*	90 *w*	102 *w*	80 *w*	95 *w*	18 *w*	44 *w*	4 *w*	13 *w*
Lower middle-income	66 *w*	101 *w*	76 *w*	106 *w*	56 *w*	91 *w*	10 *w*	34 *w*	3 *w*	9 *w*
35 Sudan	25	52	35	61	14	43	3	18	(.)	2
36 Mauritania	8	33	13	43	3	23	..	10	..	..
37 Yemen, PDR	13	64	20	94	5	34	5	18	..	2
38 Liberia	31	66	45	82	18	50	2	20	(.)	2
39 Senegal	27	48	36	58	17	38	3	12	1	3
40 Yemen Arab Rep.	8	47	14	82	..	12	..	5	..	1
41 Lesotho	83	104	63	84	102	123	3	17	(.)	2
42 Bolivia	64	86	78	93	50	78	12	34	4	12
43 Indonesia	71	100	86	106	58	94	6	30	1	3
44 Zambia	42	96	51	102	34	90	2	16	..	2
45 Honduras	67	95	68	96	67	95	8	30	1	8
46 Egypt, Arab Rep.	66	76	80	89	52	63	16	52	5	15
47 El Salvador	80	61	82	61	77	61	13	20	1	4
48 Thailand	83	96	88	95	79	93	13	29	2	20
49 Papua New Guinea	32	65	59	73	7	58	1	13	..	2
50 Philippines	95	110	98	111	93	108	26	63	13	26
51 Zimbabwe	96	126	107	130	86	121	6	15	(.)	(.)
52 Nigeria	36	98	46	94	27	70	4	16	(.)	3
53 Morocco	47	78	67	97	27	60	5	26	1	6
54 Cameroon	65	107	87	117	43	97	2	19	..	2
55 Nicaragua	66	104	65	101	66	107	7	41	1	12
56 Ivory Coast	46	76	68	92	24	60	2	17	(.)	3
57 Guatemala	45	69	50	74	39	63	7	16	2	7
58 Congo, People's Rep.	78	156	103	163	53	148	4	69	1	6
59 Costa Rica	96	108	97	109	95	107	21	48	5	26
60 Peru	83	112	95	116	71	108	15	57	4	19
61 Dominican Rep.	98	109	99	..	98	..	7	41	1	10
62 Jamaica	92	99	92	99	93	100	45	58	2	6
63 Ecuador	83	107	87	109	79	105	12	40	3	35
64 Turkey	75	102	90	110	58	95	14	42	3	5

Note: For data comparability and coverage see the technical notes.

		Number enrolled in primary school as percentage of age group						Number enrolled in secondary school as percentage of age group		Number enrolled in higher education as percentage of population aged 20–24	
		Total		Male		Female					
		1960	1981[a]	1960	1981[a]	1960	1981[a]	1960	1981[a]	1960	1981[a]
65	Tunisia	66	106	88	119	43	92	12	30	1	5
66	Colombia	77	130	77	129	77	132	12	48	2	12
67	Paraguay	98	102	105	106	90	98	11	26	2	7
68	*Angola*	21	..	28	..	13	..	2	..	(.)	(.)
69	*Cuba*	109	107	109	110	109	104	14	75	3	20
70	*Korea, Dem. Rep.*	..	116	..	118	..	114	..	..	..	..
71	*Lebanon*	102	118	105	123	99	114	19	58	6	28
72	*Mongolia*	79	105	79	107	78	102	51	89	8	9
Upper middle-income		**88** *w*	**104** *w*	**93** *w*	**107** *w*	**83** *w*	**101** *w*	**20** *w*	**51** *w*	**4** *w*	**14** *w*
73	Syrian Arab Rep.	65	101	89	112	39	89	16	48	4	18
74	Jordan	77	103	94	105	59	100	25	77	1	27
75	Malaysia	96	92	108	94	83	91	19	53	1	5
76	Korea, Rep. of	94	107	99	108	89	105	27	85	5	18
77	Panama	96	111	98	113	94	108	29	65	5	27
78	Chile	109	115	111	115	107	114	24	57	4	13
79	Brazil	95	93	97	93	93	93	11	32	2	12
80	Mexico	80	121	82	122	77	120	11	51	3	15
81	Algeria	46	94	55	106	37	81	8	36	(.)	5
82	Portugal	..	103	..	..	..	..	..	56	4	11
83	Argentina	98	119	98	120	99	119	23	59	11	25
84	Uruguay	111	122	111	124	111	120	37	70	8	20
85	South Africa	89	..	94	..	85	..	15	..	3	..
86	Yugoslavia	111	99	113	100	108	98	58	83	9	22
87	Venezuela	100	105	100	105	100	104	21	40	4	20
88	Greece	102	103	104	103	101	102	37	81	4	17
89	Israel	98	95	99	94	97	96	48	74	10	26
90	Hong Kong	87	106	93	108	79	104	20	65	4	10
91	Singapore	111	104	121	106	101	103	32	65	6	8
92	Trinidad and Tobago	88	94	89	93	87	95	24	61	1	5
93	*Iran, Islamic Rep.*	41	95	56	111	27	78	12	45	1	5
94	*Iraq*	65	113	94	117	36	109	19	59	2	9
High-income oil exporters		**29** *w*	**83** *w*	**44** *w*	**93** *w*	**12** *w*	**73** *w*	**5** *w*	**43** *w*	**1** *w*	**8** *w*
95	Oman	..	74	..	90	..	57	..	22	..	..
96	Libya	59	123	92	128	24	119	9	67	1	6
97	Saudi Arabia	12	64	22	77	2	51	2	30	(.)	8
98	Kuwait	117	94	131	96	102	93	37	76	..	14
99	United Arab Emirates	..	127	..	127	..	127	..	61	(.)	4
Industrial market economies		**114** *w*	**101** *w*	**107** *w*	**103** *w*	**112** *w*	**103** *w*	**64** *w*	**90** *w*	**16** *w*	**37** *w*
100	Ireland	110	102	107	101	112	102	35	93	9	21
101	Spain	110	110	106	110	116	109	23	88	4	23
102	Italy	111	101	112	102	109	102	34	73	7	27
103	New Zealand	108	102	110	103	106	101	73	81	13	26
104	United Kingdom	92	103	92	103	92	103	66	83	9	20
105	Austria	105	99	106	99	104	98	50	73	8	24
106	Japan	103	100	103	100	102	100	74	92	10	30
107	Belgium	109	100	111	100	108	101	69	90	9	26
108	Finland	97	96	100	96	95	96	74	98	7	31
109	Netherlands	105	100	105	99	104	101	58	95	13	31
110	Australia	103	110	103	110	103	110	51	86	13	26
111	Canada	107	106	108	106	105	104	46	93	16	37
112	France	144	110	98	112	143	111	46	86	10	26
113	Germany, Fed. Rep.	133	100	132	100	134	100	53	94	6	28
114	Denmark	103	97	103	97	103	98	65	105	10	29
115	United States	118	100	..	100	..	100	86	97	32	58
116	Sweden	96	98	95	98	96	98	55	85	9	37
117	Norway	100	100	100	100	100	100	57	97	7	26
118	Switzerland	118	..	118	..	118	..	26	..	7	18
East European nonmarket economies		**101** *w*	**105** *w*	**101** *w*	**99** *w*	**101** *w*	**99** *w*	**45** *w*	**88** *w*	**11** *w*	**20** *w*
119	Hungary	101	99	103	99	100	99	23	42	7	14
120	Romania	98	103	101	104	95	103	24	68	5	11
121	*Albania*	94	106	102	109	86	103	20	65	5	5
122	*Bulgaria*	93	99	94	100	92	99	55	83	11	15
123	*Czechoslovakia*	93	90	93	90	93	91	25	46	11	18
124	*German Dem. Rep.*	112	95	111	95	113	97	39	89	16	30
125	*Poland*	109	100	110	100	107	99	50	77	9	17
126	*USSR*	100	107	100	..	100	..	49	96	11	21

a. Figures in italics are for years other than those specified. See the technical notes.

Table 26. Central government expenditure

	Percentage of total expenditure												Total expenditure (percent of GNP)		Overall surplus/ deficit (percent of GNP)	
	Defense		Education		Health		Housing and community amenities; social security and welfare		Economic services		Other[a]					
	1972	1981[b]	1972	1981[b]	1972	1981[b]	1972	1981[b]	1972	1981[b]	1972	1981[b]	1972	1981[b]	1972	1981[b]
Low-income economies	11.4 w	18.3 w	16.4 w	5.9 w	6.2 w	2.9 w	4.7 w	5.0 w	26.8 w	25.7 w	34.5 w	42.2 w	21.0 w	15.4 w	−4.4 w	−5.6 w
China and India	..	..	..	..	..	..	..	..	..	..	..	..	..	..	..	..
Other low-income	11.4 w	15.4 w	16.4 w	11.5 w	6.2 w	4.4 w	4.7 w	6.1 w	26.8 w	29.0 w	34.5 w	33.6 w	21.0 w	17.6 w	−4.4 w	−5.0 w
1 Chad	24.6	..	14.8	..	4.4	..	1.7	..	21.8	..	32.7	..	18.1	..	−3.2	..
2 Bangladesh	..	..	..	..	..	..	..	..	..	..	..	..	..	..	..	..
3 Ethiopia	14.3	..	14.4	..	5.7	..	4.4	..	22.9	..	38.3	..	13.8	..	−1.4	..
4 Nepal	7.2	6.5	7.2	9.7	4.7	4.1	0.7	1.5	57.2	57.1	23.0	21.0	8.5	13.4	−1.2	−2.5
5 Mali	..	11.1	..	15.7	..	3.1	..	3.0	..	11.4	..	55.6	..	25.9	..	−5.6
6 Burma	..	21.7	..	10.1	..	6.1	..	9.2	..	35.5	..	17.3	..	16.5	..	1.7
7 Zaire	..	..	..	..	..	..	..	..	..	..	..	..	38.6	33.8	−7.5	−5.9
8 Malawi	3.1	8.4	15.8	11.1	5.5	5.2	5.8	2.9	33.1	38.2	36.8	34.3	22.1	35.3	−6.2	−12.0
9 Upper Volta	..	..	..	..	..	..	..	..	..	..	..	..	..	14.6	..	..
10 Uganda	23.1	34.5	15.3	10.9	5.3	4.0	7.3	2.8	12.4	13.7	36.6	34.1	21.8	3.2	−8.1	−2.5
11 India	..	20.4	..	1.9	..	1.8	..	4.2	..	23.3	..	48.4	..	14.0	..	−6.0
12 Rwanda	..	13.1	..	18.8	..	4.5	..	4.1	..	41.4	..	18.0	..	14.4	..	−1.8
13 Burundi	..	..	..	..	..	..	..	..	..	..	..	..	..	21.2	..	−5.0
14 Tanzania	11.9	11.2	17.3	12.1	7.2	5.5	2.1	2.4	39.0	37.4	22.6	31.5	19.7	33.3	−5.0	..
15 Somalia	23.3	..	5.5	..	7.2	..	1.9	..	21.6	..	40.5	..	13.5	..	0.6	..
16 Haiti	..	..	..	..	..	..	..	..	..	..	..	..	14.5	19.4	..	−5.0
17 Benin	..	..	..	..	..	..	..	..	..	..	..	..	..	..	..	..
18 Central African Rep.	..	9.3	..	16.9	..	4.9	..	6.1	..	18.8	..	43.9	..	23.5	..	−4.5
19 China	..	..	..	..	..	..	..	..	..	..	..	..	..	..	..	..
20 Guinea	..	..	..	..	..	..	..	..	..	..	..	..	..	..	..	..
21 Niger	..	3.8	..	18.0	..	4.1	..	3.8	..	32.4	..	38.0	..	25.9	..	−6.6
22 Madagascar	3.6	..	9.1	..	4.2	..	9.9	..	40.5	..	32.7	..	20.8	..	−2.5	..
23 Sri Lanka	..	1.7	..	7.2	..	3.5	..	13.7	..	13.6	..	60.3	..	33.9	..	−12.8
24 Togo	..	..	..	..	..	..	..	..	..	..	..	..	..	35.3	..	−2.2
25 Ghana	8.0	3.7	20.1	22.0	6.2	7.0	4.1	6.8	15.0	20.7	46.6	39.8	19.5	10.1	−5.8	−6.2
26 Pakistan	..	28.5	..	3.1	..	1.6	..	7.2	..	32.4	..	27.2	..	17.7	..	−5.4
27 Kenya	6.0	10.7	21.9	20.6	7.9	7.8	3.9	0.8	30.1	30.0	30.2	30.0	21.0	28.4	−3.9	−6.8
28 Sierra Leone	..	..	..	..	..	..	..	..	..	..	..	..	..	27.2	..	−9.2
29 Afghanistan	..	..	..	..	..	..	..	..	..	..	..	..	..	..	..	..
30 Bhutan	..	..	..	..	..	..	..	..	..	..	..	..	..	..	..	..
31 Kampuchea, Dem.	..	..	..	..	..	..	..	..	..	..	..	..	..	..	..	..
32 Lao PDR	..	..	..	..	..	..	..	..	..	..	..	..	..	..	..	..
33 Mozambique	..	..	..	..	..	..	..	..	..	..	..	..	..	..	..	..
34 Viet Nam	..	..	..	..	..	..	..	..	..	..	..	..	..	..	..	..
Middle-income economies	15.2 w	9.6 w	12.4 w	14.3 w	6.6 w	5.3 w	20.3 w	13.8 w	24.5 w	27.0 w	21.0 w	30.0 w	19.6 w	24.5 w	−3.0 w	−3.8 w
Oil exporters	16.3 w	6.2 w	15.4 w	16.6 w	5.7 w	5.6 w	11.1 w	8.7 w	29.0 w	30.7 w	22.5 w	32.2 w	17.2 w	27.8 w	−2.8 w	−3.9 w
Oil importers	14.7 w	15.8 w	11.0 w	10.0 w	6.9 w	4.6 w	24.5 w	23.2 w	22.4 w	20.2 w	22.0 w	27.0 w	20.7 w	21.8 w	−3.1 w	−3.8 w
Lower middle-income	17.4 w	14.1 w	18.8 w	14.2 w	4.8 w	4.2 w	5.1 w	4.9 w	30.2 w	26.3 w	23.7 w	36.3 w	16.6 w	20.8 w	−2.3 w	−3.6 w
35 Sudan	24.1	13.2	9.3	9.8	5.4	1.4	1.4	0.9	15.8	19.8	44.1	54.9	19.2	19.1	−0.8	−3.2
36 Mauritania	..	..	..	..	..	..	..	..	..	..	..	..	..	..	..	..
37 Yemen, PDR	..	..	..	..	..	..	..	..	..	..	..	..	..	..	..	..
38 Liberia	..	11.3	..	16.0	..	7.6	..	3.3	..	33.0	..	28.8	..	33.7	..	−11.5
39 Senegal	..	15.6	..	21.3	..	4.3	..	9.9	..	20.6	..	28.1	17.4	29.3	−0.8	−3.3
40 Yemen Arab Rep.	..	32.6	..	14.0	..	3.6	..	..	..	13.6	..	36.2	..	41.8	..	−19.7
41 Lesotho	..	..	19.5	..	8.0	..	6.5	..	24.5	..	41.5	..	16.6	..	−0.9	..
42 Bolivia	16.2	22.7	30.6	24.4	8.6	7.2	2.9	2.7	12.4	17.2	29.3	25.8	9.2	12.7	−1.4	−4.1
43 Indonesia	..	12.7	..	7.9	..	2.5	..	1.2	..	29.4	..	46.2	16.2	27.3	−2.6	−2.2
44 Zambia	..	..	19.0	11.9	7.4	6.1	1.3	0.6	26.7	21.9	45.7	59.6	35.4	39.8	−14.4	−14.0
45 Honduras	12.4	..	22.3	..	10.2	..	8.7	..	28.3	..	18.1	..	15.4	..	−2.7	..
46 Egypt, Arab Rep.	..	..	..	..	..	..	..	..	..	..	..	..	..	..	..	..
47 El Salvador	6.6	16.8	21.4	17.9	10.9	8.4	7.6	5.4	14.4	24.7	39.0	26.9	12.8	18.5	−1.0	−7.4
48 Thailand	20.2	20.6	19.9	19.3	3.7	4.3	7.0	5.6	25.7	23.3	23.5	27.0	17.2	18.5	−4.3	−3.5
49 Papua New Guinea	..	4.0	..	17.7	..	9.1	..	3.2	..	19.6	..	46.5	..	39.8	..	−5.5
50 Philippines	10.9	14.2	16.3	14.2	3.2	5.0	4.3	5.8	17.6	55.3	47.7	5.5	13.5	12.8	−2.0	−4.0
51 Zimbabwe	..	19.9	..	19.5	..	6.9	..	7.5	..	19.5	..	26.6	..	31.3	..	−7.3
52 Nigeria	40.2	..	4.5	..	3.6	..	0.8	..	19.6	..	31.4	..	9.9	..	−0.9	..
53 Morocco	12.3	16.2	19.2	16.5	4.8	3.0	8.4	5.6	25.6	28.0	29.7	30.7	22.4	39.8	−3.8	−13.6
54 Cameroon	..	5.1	..	7.5	..	2.7	..	5.1	..	10.0	..	69.6	..	21.6	..	−3.4
55 Nicaragua	12.3	11.0	16.6	11.6	4.0	14.6	16.4	7.4	27.1	20.6	23.6	34.9	15.5	30.2	−4.0	−6.8
56 Ivory Coast	..	3.9	..	16.3	..	3.9	..	4.3	..	13.4	..	58.1	..	32.2	..	−11.0
57 Guatemala	11.0	..	19.4	..	9.5	..	10.4	..	23.8	..	25.8	..	9.9	16.2	−2.2	−6.2
58 Congo, People's Rep.	..	..	..	..	..	..	..	..	..	..	..	..	..	54.6	..	−5.8
59 Costa Rica	2.8	2.6	28.3	23.7	3.8	29.7	26.7	12.6	21.8	15.2	16.7	16.2	18.9	23.7	−4.5	−3.2
60 Peru	14.8	13.8	22.7	11.3	6.2	5.3	2.9	1.1	30.3	..	23.1	68.5	17.1	20.2	−1.1	−3.5
61 Dominican Rep.	..	8.9	..	13.9	..	9.7	..	13.5	..	37.3	..	16.8	18.5	17.0	−0.2	−2.7
62 Jamaica	..	..	..	..	..	..	..	..	..	..	..	..	..	44.9	..	−16.6
63 Ecuador	..	11.8	..	30.1	..	7.9	..	1.3	..	19.4	..	29.5	..	17.1	..	−5.1
64 Turkey	15.4	15.2	18.2	16.8	3.3	2.1	3.3	8.9	41.9	25.7	17.9	31.3	21.8	23.3	−2.1	−1.8

Note: For data comparability and coverage see the technical notes.

	Percentage of total expenditure												Total expenditure (percent of GNP)		Overall surplus/ deficit (percent of GNP)	
	Defense		Education		Health		Housing and community amenities; social security and welfare		Economic services		Other[a]					
	1972	1981[b]	1972	1981[b]	1972	1981[b]	1972	1981[b]	1972	1981[b]	1972	1981[b]	1972	1981[b]	1972	1981[b]
65 Tunisia	4.9	8.3	30.5	15.3	7.4	7.7	8.8	13.6	23.3	34.0	25.1	21.1	22.5	32.4	−0.9	−2.5
66 Colombia	..	..	..	..	..	..	..	..	..	..	..	..	13.3	..	−2.6	..
67 Paraguay	13.8	13.2	12.1	11.8	3.5	4.5	18.3	22.8	19.6	19.0	32.7	28.8	13.1	10.7	−1.7	−1.5
68 *Angola*	..	..	..	..	..	..	..	..	..	..	..	..	..	..	..	..
69 *Cuba*	..	..	..	..	..	..	..	..	..	..	..	..	..	..	..	..
70 *Korea, Dem. Rep.*	..	..	..	..	..	..	..	..	..	..	..	..	..	..	..	..
71 *Lebanon*	..	..	..	..	..	..	..	..	..	..	..	..	..	..	..	..
72 *Mongolia*	..	..	..	..	..	..	..	..	..	..	..	..	..	..	..	..
Upper middle-income	14.6*w*	8.8*w*	10.8*w*	14.3*w*	7.0*w*	5.5*w*	24.2*w*	15.4*w*	23.0*w*	27.1*w*	20.4*w*	28.9*w*	15.0*w*	20.6*w*	−2.4*w*	−3.1*w*
73 Syrian Arab Rep.	37.2	37.7	11.3	7.1	1.4	1.1	3.6	11.4	39.9	30.9	6.7	11.8	28.1	41.3	−3.4	−6.8
74 Jordan	..	25.3	..	7.6	..	3.8	..	14.5	..	28.3	..	20.6	..	35.8	..	−7.6
75 Malaysia	18.5	15.1	23.4	15.9	6.8	4.4	4.4	10.5	14.2	29.0	32.7	25.2	27.7	40.8	−9.8	−15.8
76 Korea, Rep. of	25.8	35.2	15.9	17.9	1.2	1.3	5.8	6.7	25.6	14.4	25.7	24.5	18.6	19.0	−4.0	−3.7
77 Panama	..	..	..	12.8	..	13.2	..	12.8	..	18.4	..	42.8	..	36.1	..	−9.1
78 Chile	6.1	12.0	14.3	14.4	8.2	6.4	39.8	42.6	15.3	11.4	16.3	13.3	42.3	31.0	−13.0	2.7
79 Brazil	8.3	3.4	6.8	3.8	6.4	7.4	36.0	34.8	24.6	24.1	17.9	26.5	16.6	19.5	−0.4	−2.4
80 Mexico	4.2	2.5	16.6	18.2	5.1	1.9	24.9	18.8	34.3	36.4	15.0	22.3	12.1	20.8	−3.1	−6.9
81 *Algeria*	..	..	..	..	..	..	..	..	..	..	..	..	..	..	..	..
82 *Portugal*	..	..	..	..	..	..	..	..	..	..	..	..	..	..	..	..
83 Argentina	8.8	11.4	8.8	7.3	2.9	1.4	23.5	34.2	14.7	17.9	41.2	27.8	16.5	23.6	−3.4	−8.5
84 Uruguay	5.6	12.9	9.5	7.7	1.6	3.8	52.3	51.7	9.8	13.3	21.2	10.7	25.0	24.4	−2.5	−1.5
85 South Africa	..	..	..	..	..	..	..	..	..	..	..	..	21.9	22.7	−4.2	−2.4
86 Yugoslavia	20.5	50.4	..	..	24.8	..	35.6	7.2	12.0	16.6	7.0	25.8	21.1	8.5	−0.4	−0.1
87 Venezuela	10.3	3.9	18.3	18.3	11.7	7.3	8.2	6.8	25.8	32.8	25.7	30.9	21.3	28.9	−1.0	−2.6
88 Greece	14.9	..	9.0	..	7.3	..	30.7	..	27.9	..	10.3	..	27.5	34.4	−1.7	−4.8
89 Israel	39.8	39.8	9.0	9.4	3.5	3.5	7.8	19.2	16.3	3.9	23.5	24.1	44.1	78.4	−16.3	−18.6
90 Hong Kong	..	..	..	..	..	..	..	..	..	..	..	..	..	..	..	..
91 Singapore	35.3	21.7	15.7	19.1	7.8	7.2	3.9	8.4	9.9	15.2	27.3	28.5	16.8	25.2	1.3	0.1
92 Trinidad and Tobago	..	2.0	..	11.2	..	5.9	..	17.3	..	31.1	..	32.4	..	31.0	..	3.3
93 *Iran, Islamic Rep.*	24.1	11.7	10.4	15.9	3.6	5.4	6.1	11.5	30.6	22.9	25.2	32.6	30.8	..	−4.6	..
94 *Iraq*	..	..	..	..	..	..	..	..	..	..	..	..	..	..	..	..
High-income oil exporters	12.9*w*	28.0*w*	13.5*w*	9.2*w*	5.5*w*	5.5*w*	12.5*w*	9.5*w*	17.7*w*	16.2*w*	37.9*w*	31.6*w*	36.6*w*	26.3*w*	14.7*w*	17.7*w*
95 Oman	39.3	50.8	3.7	5.3	5.9	3.0	3.0	1.6	24.4	23.8	23.6	15.4	62.1	51.9	−15.3	2.4
96 *Libya*	..	..	..	..	..	..	..	..	..	..	..	..	..	..	..	..
97 *Saudi Arabia*	..	..	..	..	..	..	..	..	..	..	..	..	..	..	..	..
98 Kuwait	8.4	9.8	15.0	9.0	5.5	4.9	14.2	15.2	16.6	19.3	40.1	41.9	34.4	28.9	17.4	34.0
99 United Arab Emirates	24.5	47.5	16.2	11.7	4.5	7.9	6.4	3.9	18.2	6.1	30.2	22.9	..	18.1	..	2.3
Industrial market economies	23.4*w*	13.6*w*	4.3*w*	5.1*w*	9.9*w*	11.4*w*	36.4*w*	41.7*w*	11.6*w*	9.9*w*	14.4*w*	18.2*w*	21.7*w*	28.3*w*	−0.9*w*	−2.7*w*
100 Ireland	..	..	..	..	..	..	..	..	..	..	..	..	33.0	51.7	−5.5	−14.5
101 Spain	6.5	4.4	8.3	7.9	0.9	0.7	49.8	58.5	17.5	13.7	17.0	14.9	19.8	27.3	−0.5	−4.3
102 Italy	..	3.4	..	9.2	..	11.0	..	32.0	..	7.5	..	36.9	..	47.3	..	−12.9
103 New Zealand	5.8	5.4	16.9	13.5	14.9	14.4	25.5	28.9	16.4	15.7	20.4	22.2	28.5	39.6	−3.8	−7.6
104 United Kingdom	16.7	..	2.6	..	12.2	..	26.5	..	11.1	..	30.8	..	32.7	40.8	−2.7	−4.7
105 Austria	..	2.9	..	9.5	..	12.9	..	48.4	..	12.7	..	13.6	..	39.4	..	−2.9
106 Japan	..	..	..	..	..	..	..	..	..	..	..	..	12.7	19.0	..	..
107 Belgium	6.7	5.5	15.5	14.8	1.5	1.7	41.0	45.0	18.9	18.4	16.4	14.6	39.2	55.8	−4.3	−11.7
108 Finland	6.1	5.1	15.3	14.5	10.6	11.2	28.4	28.8	27.9	26.9	11.6	13.5	24.8	29.9	1.3	−1.0
109 Netherlands	..	5.6	..	12.6	..	11.8	..	40.2	..	11.2	..	18.6	..	55.5	..	−6.6
110 Australia	14.1	9.6	4.4	8.2	8.2	10.1	21.0	29.4	13.1	8.1	39.2	34.6	19.5	24.6	−0.3	−0.7
111 Canada	..	7.8	..	3.5	..	6.2	..	34.1	..	18.4	..	29.9	..	23.3	..	−2.6
112 France	..	7.5	..	8.7	..	15.0	..	47.5	..	6.9	..	14.3	32.5	42.1	0.7	−2.7
113 Germany, Fed. Rep.	12.4	9.2	1.5	0.8	17.5	18.5	46.9	51.8	11.3	6.6	10.4	13.1	24.2	31.0	0.7	−2.3
114 Denmark	7.2	..	15.9	..	10.0	..	41.3	..	11.8	..	13.8	..	32.9	43.8	2.7	−6.3
115 United States	32.2	21.8	3.2	2.5	8.6	10.7	35.3	36.9	10.6	9.8	10.1	18.3	19.4	23.4	−1.6	−2.7
116 Sweden	12.5	7.3	14.8	10.5	3.6	2.0	44.3	49.6	10.6	10.5	14.3	20.2	28.0	43.7	−1.2	−9.2
117 Norway	9.7	..	9.9	..	12.3	..	39.9	..	20.2	..	8.0	..	35.0	38.9	−1.5	2.1
118 Switzerland	15.1	10.6	4.2	3.3	10.0	12.7	39.5	49.0	18.4	13.3	12.8	11.1	13.3	18.3	0.9	(.)
East European nonmarket economies	..	..	..	..	..	..	..	..	..	..	..	..	..	..	..	..
119 *Hungary*	..	..	..	..	..	..	..	..	..	..	..	..	..	..	..	..
120 *Romania*	..	..	..	..	..	..	..	..	..	..	..	..	..	..	..	..
121 *Albania*	..	..	..	..	..	..	..	..	..	..	..	..	..	..	..	..
122 *Bulgaria*	..	..	..	..	..	..	..	..	..	..	..	..	..	..	..	..
123 *Czechoslovakia*	..	..	..	..	..	..	..	..	..	..	..	..	..	..	..	..
124 *German Dem. Rep.*	..	..	..	..	..	..	..	..	..	..	..	..	..	..	..	..
125 *Poland*	..	..	..	..	..	..	..	..	..	..	..	..	..	..	..	..
126 *USSR*	..	..	..	..	..	..	..	..	..	..	..	..	..	..	..	..

a. See the technical notes.   b. Figures in italics are for 1980, not 1981.

Table 27. Central government current revenue

	Taxes on income, profit, and capital gain		Social security contributions		Domestic taxes on goods and services		Taxes on international trade and transactions		Other taxes[a]		Current nontax revenue		Total current revenue (percent of GNP)	
	1972	1981[b]	1972	1981[b]	1972	1981[b]	1972	1981[b]	1972	1981[b]	1972	1981[b]	1972	1981[b]
Low-income economies	21.6 w	19.8 w	..	..	24.1 w	38.6 w	35.2 w	25.3 w	7.4 w	0.9 w	11.7 w	15.4 w	18.4 w	14.3 w
China and India	..	..	..	..	..	..	..	..	..	..	..	..	..	..
Other low-income	21.6 w	20.4 w	..	..	24.1 w	34.8 w	35.2 w	30.3 w	7.4 w	1.4 w	11.7 w	13.1 w	18.4 w	16.7 w
1 Chad	16.7	..	..	..	12.3	..	45.2	..	20.5	..	5.3	..	13.1	..
2 Bangladesh	..	..	..	..	..	..	..	..	..	..	..	..	..	..
3 Ethiopia	23.0	..	..	..	27.8	..	32.5	..	5.6	..	11.1	..	10.5	..
4 Nepal	4.1	6.1	..	..	26.5	36.8	36.7	34.4	19.0	8.7	13.7	14.0	5.2	8.1
5 Mali	..	18.8	..	..	..	39.7	..	20.7	..	13.2	..	7.6	..	14.4
6 Burma	..	2.7	..	..	..	39.0	..	16.7	..	..	..	41.7	..	17.1
7 Zaire	22.2	34.9	2.2	1.0	12.7	15.3	57.9	30.1	1.4	3.7	3.7	15.0	27.9	21.5
8 Malawi	31.4	28.5	..	..	24.2	30.3	20.0	23.1	0.5	0.4	23.8	17.8	16.0	19.5
9 Upper Volta	..	..	..	..	..	..	..	..	..	..	..	..	..	..
10 Uganda	22.1	19.7	..	..	32.9	36.6	36.2	37.8	0.3	0.3	8.5	5.7	13.7	0.7
11 India	..	19.4	..	..	..	41.0	..	22.1	..	0.6	..	16.9	..	12.8
12 Rwanda	..	17.8	..	4.1	..	19.3	..	42.4	..	2.4	..	14.0	..	12.9
13 Burundi	..	22.4	..	2.9	..	28.7	..	24.0	..	11.2	..	10.8	..	11.9
14 Tanzania	29.9	31.1	..	..	29.1	50.6	21.7	10.2	0.5	0.9	18.8	7.2	15.8	19.6
15 Somalia	10.7	..	..	..	24.7	..	45.3	..	5.2	..	14.0	..	13.7	..
16 Haiti	..	13.9	..	..	..	15.5	..	48.4	..	9.6	..	12.6	..	11.3
17 Benin	..	..	..	..	..	..	..	..	..	..	..	..	..	..
18 Central African Rep.	..	16.1	..	6.4	..	20.8	..	39.8	..	7.8	..	9.1	..	16.9
19 China	..	..	..	..	..	..	..	..	..	..	..	..	..	..
20 Guinea	..	..	..	..	..	..	..	..	..	..	..	..	..	..
21 Niger	..	23.8	..	4.0	..	18.0	..	36.4	..	2.6	..	15.3	..	20.3
22 Madagascar	13.0	..	7.2	..	29.8	..	33.6	..	5.4	..	10.9	..	18.4	..
23 Sri Lanka	..	13.3	..	..	..	32.5	..	47.0	..	1.8	..	5.3	..	18.3
24 Togo	..	34.4	..	5.8	..	15.3	..	31.8	..	−1.7	..	14.4	..	34.8
25 Ghana	18.2	24.8	..	..	29.1	39.1	40.8	27.9	0.4	0.1	11.4	8.2	15.1	4.2
26 Pakistan	..	15.6	..	..	..	33.2	..	34.0	..	0.3	..	17.0	..	15.1
27 Kenya	35.6	29.1	..	..	19.9	38.2	24.3	22.0	1.4	0.6	18.8	10.0	18.0	23.1
28 Sierra Leone	..	23.9	..	..	..	20.4	..	44.4	..	1.5	..	9.8	..	16.8
29 Afghanistan	..	..	..	..	..	..	..	..	..	..	..	..	..	..
30 Bhutan	..	..	..	..	..	..	..	..	..	..	..	..	..	..
31 Kampuchea, Dem.	..	..	..	..	..	..	..	..	..	..	..	..	..	..
32 Lao PDR	..	..	..	..	..	..	..	..	..	..	..	..	..	..
33 Mozambique	..	..	..	..	..	..	..	..	..	..	..	..	..	..
34 Viet Nam	..	..	..	..	..	..	..	..	..	..	..	..	..	..
Middle-income economies	24.9 w	43.4 w	14.5 w	8.2 w	27.6 w	21.8 w	14.0 w	11.9 w	3.3 w	0.5 w	15.7 w	14.2 w	19.6 w	26.3 w
Oil exporters	33.2 w	62.9 w	8.5 w	5.2 w	23.4 w	10.9 w	14.5 w	12.2 w	−0.4 w	−3.1 w	20.8 w	11.7 w	18.1 w	27.7 w
Oil importers	20.6 w	20.6 w	17.5 w	11.5 w	29.7 w	34.5 w	13.8 w	11.5 w	5.3 w	4.7 w	13.1 w	17.2 w	20.2 w	23.8 w
Lower middle-income	27.5 w	38.4 w	..	..	29.3 w	25.3 w	20.5 w	17.5 w	10.5 w	5.6 w	12.2 w	13.2 w	15.9 w	21.8 w
35 Sudan	11.8	14.4	..	..	30.4	26.0	40.5	42.6	1.5	0.7	15.7	16.3	18.0	13.4
36 Mauritania	..	..	..	..	..	..	..	..	..	..	..	..	..	..
37 Yemen, PDR	..	..	..	..	..	..	..	..	..	..	..	..	..	..
38 Liberia	..	32.4	..	..	..	24.2	..	36.3	..	3.3	..	3.8	..	22.7
39 Senegal	17.6	17.4	..	3.9	24.5	18.8	30.9	18.9	23.8	24.4	3.2	16.6	16.8	25.9
40 Yemen Arab Rep.	..	8.8	..	..	..	10.0	..	49.2	..	12.5	..	19.5	..	22.0
41 Lesotho	14.3	..	..	..	2.0	..	62.9	..	9.5	..	11.3	..	11.7	..
42 Bolivia	14.5	15.2	..	..	28.4	37.8	46.0	29.4	5.3	3.7	5.7	13.9	7.8	8.5
43 Indonesia	45.5	72.5	..	..	22.7	7.8	17.5	4.8	3.6	1.0	10.6	13.9	14.4	26.4
44 Zambia	49.7	35.2	..	..	20.2	46.8	14.3	7.7	0.1	3.3	15.6	6.9	24.2	25.1
45 Honduras	19.2	24.2	3.0	..	33.8	25.9	28.2	42.4	2.3	1.9	13.5	5.7	12.6	14.8
46 Egypt, Arab Rep.	..	..	..	..	..	..	..	..	..	..	..	..	..	..
47 El Salvador	15.2	20.9	..	..	25.6	35.2	36.1	29.8	17.2	4.9	6.0	9.2	11.6	12.4
48 Thailand	12.1	19.6	..	..	46.3	45.5	28.7	22.8	1.8	1.8	11.2	10.2	12.9	14.4
49 Papua New Guinea	..	58.0	..	..	..	12.3	..	18.1	..	1.0	..	10.6	..	23.5
50 Philippines	13.8	21.7	..	..	24.3	41.9	23.0	22.3	29.7	2.8	9.3	11.4	12.5	11.7
51 Zimbabwe	..	47.7	..	..	..	30.5	..	9.1	..	1.2	..	11.5	..	26.3
52 Nigeria	43.0	..	..	..	26.3	..	17.5	..	0.2	..	13.0	..	11.3	..
53 Morocco	16.4	18.5	5.9	5.4	45.7	31.6	13.2	20.9	6.1	7.0	12.6	16.6	18.1	25.8
54 Cameroon	..	28.2	..	6.2	..	16.0	..	34.1	..	4.4	..	11.2	..	18.3
55 Nicaragua	9.6	7.8	14.0	8.9	37.4	37.3	24.3	25.2	8.9	10.7	5.8	10.1	12.6	23.1
56 Ivory Coast	..	12.9	..	5.7	..	25.0	..	42.8	..	6.0	..	7.5	..	23.4
57 Guatemala	12.7	12.0	..	11.2	36.1	29.5	26.2	19.9	15.6	14.9	9.4	12.5	8.9	10.4
58 Congo, People's Rep.	19.3	48.7	..	4.4	40.3	7.6	26.5	13.0	6.4	2.7	7.4	23.5	18.4	39.0
59 Costa Rica	17.7	14.6	13.4	25.2	38.1	25.7	18.0	27.3	1.6	1.8	11.1	5.3	15.8	20.1
60 Peru	17.5	15.8	..	..	32.2	41.8	15.7	29.2	22.1	5.2	12.4	8.1	16.0	16.6
61 Dominican Rep.	17.9	19.0	3.9	3.7	19.0	25.6	40.3	28.6	1.8	1.7	17.0	21.5	17.9	14.1
62 Jamaica	..	..	..	..	..	..	..	..	..	..	..	..	..	..
63 Ecuador	..	43.7	..	..	..	19.3	..	26.8	..	1.4	..	8.9	..	12.0
64 Turkey	30.8	51.7	..	..	31.1	19.9	14.5	5.3	6.1	6.7	17.6	16.4	19.7	22.0

Note: For data comparability and coverage see the technical notes.

	Percentage of total current revenue												
	Tax revenue												Total current revenue (percent of GNP)	
	Taxes on income, profit, and capital gain		Social security contributions		Domestic taxes on goods and services		Taxes on international trade and transactions		Other taxes[a]		Current nontax revenue			
	1972	1981[b]	1972	1981[b]	1972	1981[b]	1972	1981[b]	1972	1981[b]	1972	1981[b]	1972	1981[b]
65 Tunisia	15.9	15.3	7.1	8.8	31.6	23.4	21.8	25.5	7.8	3.2	15.7	23.9	23.0	31.8
66 Colombia	37.2	..	13.9	..	16.0	..	20.3	..	7.2	..	5.5	..	10.8	..
67 Paraguay	8.8	16.2	10.4	14.6	26.2	16.5	24.8	21.0	17.0	22.5	12.8	9.2	11.5	10.3
68 *Angola*	..	..	..	..	..	..	..	..	..	..	..	..	..	..
69 *Cuba*	..	..	..	..	..	..	..	..	..	..	..	..	..	..
70 *Korea, Dem. Rep.*	..	..	..	..	..	..	..	..	..	..	..	..	..	..
71 *Lebanon*	..	..	..	..	..	..	..	..	..	..	..	..	..	..
72 *Mongolia*	..	..	..	..	..	..	..	..	..	..	..	..	..	..
Upper middle-income	**23.8***w*	**46.4***w*	**20.4***w*	**10.3***w*	**26.9***w*	**21.0***w*	**11.5***w*	**10.6***w*	**0.3***w*	**−2.8***w*	**17.1***w*	**14.5***w*	**20.7***w*	**27.0***w*
73 Syrian Arab Rep.	6.8	12.5	..	..	10.4	6.2	17.3	14.6	12.1	6.1	53.4	60.7	24.5	24.2
74 Jordan	..	13.7	..	..	..	7.5	..	42.2	..	9.9	..	26.7	..	19.2
75 Malaysia	25.2	36.9	0.1	0.5	24.2	15.4	27.9	28.3	1.4	1.8	21.2	17.0	21.2	29.1
76 Korea, Rep. of	29.2	23.0	0.8	1.0	41.7	44.7	10.7	13.9	5.2	3.7	12.3	13.7	13.6	20.1
77 Panama	..	24.9	..	18.9	..	16.7	..	10.7	..	9.2	..	19.7	..	28.1
78 Chile	12.9	16.9	27.1	15.3	28.6	40.9	10.0	5.5	4.3	4.7	17.1	16.8	30.2	31.8
79 Brazil	18.3	13.2	27.4	25.7	37.6	27.5	7.0	3.0	3.7	4.8	6.0	25.8	17.7	23.5
80 Mexico	36.5	37.1	19.4	14.4	32.4	31.8	13.1	29.1	−9.9	−18.6	8.4	6.2	10.4	15.7
81 *Algeria*	..	..	..	..	..	..	..	..	..	..	..	..	..	..
82 *Portugal*	..	..	..	..	..	..	..	..	..	..	..	..	..	..
83 Argentina	7.4	5.4	25.9	15.8	14.8	44.0	18.5	10.7	−3.7	5.3	37.0	18.9	13.1	17.7
84 Uruguay	4.7	7.3	30.0	24.6	24.5	43.9	6.1	11.7	22.0	5.7	12.6	6.7	22.7	23.2
85 South Africa	54.8	55.8	1.2	*1.1*	21.5	23.8	4.6	3.3	5.0	3.2	12.9	12.8	21.3	24.1
86 Yugoslavia	..	..	52.3	..	24.5	68.2	19.5	30.1	..	..	3.7	1.7	20.7	8.4
87 Venezuela	53.8	75.0	5.9	3.6	6.7	2.9	6.1	5.7	1.1	0.8	26.4	12.0	21.9	33.3
88 Greece	12.0	..	23.5	..	34.9	..	6.7	..	11.9	..	11.0	..	26.9	..
89 Israel	36.2	*41.4*	..	10.3	23.0	25.0	21.6	3.6	6.8	7.3	12.4	12.3	32.0	*55.1*
90 *Hong Kong*	..	..	..	..	..	..	..	..	..	..	..	..	..	..
91 Singapore	24.4	35.6	..	..	17.6	14.1	11.1	5.6	15.5	15.5	31.4	29.2	21.6	28.0
92 Trinidad and Tobago	..	70.0	..	2.0	..	4.1	..	6.5	..	0.6	..	16.8	..	44.1
93 *Iran, Islamic Rep.*	7.9	11.7	2.7	7.3	6.4	3.0	14.6	8.2	4.9	3.9	63.6	65.9	26.2	..
94 *Iraq*	..	..	..	..	..	..	..	..	..	..	..	..	..	..
High-income oil exporters	..	..	..	..	..	..	..	..	..	..	..	..	..	..
95 Oman	71.1	28.9	..	..	..	0.3	3.0	1.1	2.3	0.2	23.6	69.4	47.4	54.2
96 *Libya*	..	..	..	..	..	..	..	..	..	..	..	..	..	..
97 *Saudi Arabia*	..	..	..	..	..	..	..	..	..	..	..	..	..	..
98 Kuwait	68.8	2.4	..	..	19.7	0.5	1.5	1.1	0.2	0.1	9.9	95.9	55.2	71.1
99 *United Arab Emirates*	..	..	..	..	..	..	..	..	..	..	..	..	..	0.2
Industrial market economies	**45.2***w*	**41.2***w*	**26.8***w*	**30.8***w*	**17.1***w*	**15.8***w*	**2.0***w*	**1.5***w*	**2.6***w*	**2.0***w*	**6.3***w*	**8.7***w*	**24.6***w*	**30.1***w*
100 Ireland	28.1	*34.7*	8.9	*13.6*	32.6	*25.1*	16.6	*13.5*	3.2	*2.1*	10.5	*11.1*	30.6	39.8
101 Spain	15.9	23.9	38.9	47.1	23.4	16.8	10.0	6.0	0.7	−0.8	11.1	7.0	20.0	*24.8*
102 Italy	..	34.2	..	32.9	..	23.2	..	0.2	..	2.7	..	6.9	..	35.3
103 New Zealand	61.4	66.8	..	..	20.0	18.4	4.1	3.6	4.5	1.4	10.0	9.7	27.3	34.9
104 United Kingdom	39.4	39.7	15.1	15.6	27.1	26.4	1.7	(.)	5.6	5.9	11.2	12.4	33.5	36.3
105 Austria	..	20.6	..	35.3	..	25.1	..	1.4	..	8.7	..	8.9	..	36.8
106 *Japan*	..	..	..	..	..	..	..	..	..	..	..	..	..	..
107 Belgium	31.3	37.4	32.4	30.6	28.9	25.0	1.0	(.)	3.3	2.2	3.1	4.9	35.0	44.8
108 Finland	30.0	30.5	10.7	9.7	47.7	48.0	3.1	1.5	2.9	2.9	5.5	7.3	27.1	29.7
109 Netherlands	..	28.3	..	37.4	..	19.1	..	(.)	..	2.3	..	12.8	..	50.8
110 Australia	58.3	62.4	..	..	21.9	23.1	5.2	5.2	2.1	0.2	12.5	9.0	21.4	24.4
111 Canada	..	47.5	..	11.1	..	12.0	..	6.1	..	10.0	..	13.4	..	22.1
112 France	16.9	18.0	37.1	42.5	37.9	30.1	0.3	(.)	2.9	3.5	4.9	5.9	33.6	40.5
113 Germany, Fed. Rep.	19.7	17.6	46.6	55.2	28.1	22.7	0.8	(.)	0.8	0.1	4.0	4.4	25.2	29.0
114 Denmark	40.0	35.5	5.1	2.7	42.0	46.6	3.1	0.8	3.0	2.7	6.8	11.8	35.5	36.2
115 United States	59.4	54.2	23.6	28.0	7.1	6.4	1.6	1.3	2.5	1.1	5.7	9.1	18.0	21.7
116 Sweden	27.0	16.0	21.6	38.7	34.0	29.7	1.5	1.2	4.6	1.2	11.3	13.2	32.5	37.9
117 Norway	22.5	28.7	20.5	22.0	47.9	38.2	1.6	0.7	1.0	1.1	6.6	9.3	37.0	44.1
118 Switzerland	13.9	14.3	37.3	48.2	21.5	19.4	16.7	9.1	2.6	2.3	8.0	6.7	14.5	18.4
East European nonmarket economies	..	..	..	..	..	..	..	..	..	..	..	..	..	..
119 *Hungary*	..	..	..	..	..	..	..	..	..	..	..	..	..	..
120 *Romania*	..	..	..	..	..	..	..	..	..	..	..	..	..	..
121 *Albania*	..	..	..	..	..	..	..	..	..	..	..	..	..	..
122 *Bulgaria*	..	..	..	..	..	..	..	..	..	..	..	..	..	..
123 *Czechoslovakia*	..	..	..	..	..	..	..	..	..	..	..	..	..	..
124 *German Dem. Rep.*	..	..	..	..	..	..	..	..	..	..	..	..	..	..
125 *Poland*	..	..	..	..	..	..	..	..	..	..	..	..	..	..
126 *USSR*	..	..	..	..	..	..	..	..	..	..	..	..	..	..

a. See the technical notes.   b. Figures in italics are for 1980, not 1981.

Table 28. Income distribution

	Year	Percentage share of household income, by percentile groups of households[a]					
		Lowest 20 percent	Second quintile	Third quintile	Fourth quintile	Highest 20 percent	Highest 10 percent
Low-income economies							
China and India							
Other low-income							
1 Chad		..	..	..	..	..	..
2 Bangladesh	1973–74	6.9	11.3	16.1	23.5	42.2	27.4
3 Ethiopia		..	..	..	..	..	..
4 Nepal	1976–77	4.6	8.0	11.7	16.5	59.2	46.5
5 Mali		..	..	..	..	..	..
6 Burma		..	..	..	..	..	..
7 Zaire		..	..	..	..	..	..
8 Malawi	1967–68	10.4	11.1	13.1	14.8	50.6	40.1
9 Upper Volta		..	..	..	..	..	..
10 Uganda		..	..	..	..	..	..
11 India	1975–76	7.0	9.2	13.9	20.5	49.4	33.6
12 Rwanda		..	..	..	..	..	..
13 Burundi		..	..	..	..	..	..
14 Tanzania	1969	5.8	10.2	13.9	19.7	50.4	35.6
15 Somalia		..	..	..	..	..	..
16 Haiti		..	..	..	..	..	..
17 Benin		..	..	..	..	..	..
18 Central African Rep.		..	..	..	..	..	..
19 China		..	..	..	..	..	..
20 Guinea		..	..	..	..	..	..
21 Niger		..	..	..	..	..	..
22 Madagascar		..	..	..	..	..	..
23 Sri Lanka	1969–70	7.5	11.7	15.7	21.7	43.4	28.2
24 Togo		..	..	..	..	..	..
25 Ghana		..	..	..	..	..	..
26 Pakistan		..	..	..	..	..	..
27 Kenya	1976	2.6	6.3	11.5	19.2	60.4	45.8
28 Sierra Leone	1967–69	5.6	9.5	12.8	19.6	52.5	37.8
29 Afghanistan		..	..	..	..	..	..
30 Bhutan		..	..	..	..	..	..
31 Kampuchea, Dem.		..	..	..	..	..	..
32 Lao PDR		..	..	..	..	..	..
33 Mozambique		..	..	..	..	..	..
34 Viet Nam		..	..	..	..	..	..
Middle-income economies							
Oil exporters							
Oil importers							
Lower middle-income							
35 Sudan	1967–68	4.0	8.9	16.6	20.7	49.8	34.6
36 Mauritania		..	..	..	..	..	..
37 Yemen, PDR		..	..	..	..	..	..
38 Liberia		..	..	..	..	..	..
39 Senegal		..	..	..	..	..	..
40 Yemen Arab Rep.		..	..	..	..	..	..
41 Lesotho		..	..	..	..	..	..
42 Bolivia		..	..	..	..	..	..
43 Indonesia	1976	6.6	7.8	12.6	23.6	49.4	34.0
44 Zambia		..	..	..	..	..	..
45 Honduras		..	..	..	..	..	..
46 Egypt, Arab Rep.		..	..	..	..	..	..
47 El Salvador		..	..	..	..	..	..
48 Thailand	1975–76	5.6	9.6	13.9	21.1	49.8	34.1
49 Papua New Guinea		..	..	..	..	..	..
50 Philippines	1970–71	5.2	9.0	12.8	19.0	54.0	38.5
51 Zimbabwe		..	..	..	..	..	..
52 Nigeria		..	..	..	..	..	..
53 Morocco		..	..	..	..	..	..
54 Cameroon		..	..	..	..	..	..
55 Nicaragua		..	..	..	..	..	..
56 Ivory Coast		..	..	..	..	..	..
57 Guatemala		..	..	..	..	..	..
58 Congo, People's Rep.		..	..	..	..	..	..
59 Costa Rica	1971	3.3	8.7	13.3	19.9	54.8	39.5
60 Peru	1972	1.9	5.1	11.0	21.0	61.0	42.9
61 Dominican Rep.		..	..	..	..	..	..
62 Jamaica		..	..	..	..	..	..
63 Ecuador		..	..	..	..	..	..
64 Turkey	1973	3.5	8.0	12.5	19.5	56.5	40.7

Note: For data comparability and coverage see the technical notes.

	Year	Percentage share of household income, by percentile groups of households[a]					
		Lowest 20 percent	Second quintile	Third quintile	Fourth quintile	Highest 20 percent	Highest 10 percent
65 Tunisia		..	..	..	..	..	..
66 Colombia		..	..	..	..	..	..
67 Paraguay		..	..	..	..	..	..
68 *Angola*		..	..	..	..	..	..
69 *Cuba*		..	..	..	..	..	..
70 *Korea, Dem. Rep.*		..	..	..	..	..	..
71 *Lebanon*		..	..	..	..	..	..
72 *Mongolia*		..	..	..	..	..	..

Upper middle-income

	Year	Lowest 20 percent	Second quintile	Third quintile	Fourth quintile	Highest 20 percent	Highest 10 percent
73 Syrian Arab Rep.		..	..	..	..	..	..
74 Jordan		..	..	..	..	..	..
75 Malaysia	1973	3.5	7.7	12.4	20.3	56.1	39.8
76 Korea, Rep. of	1976	5.7	11.2	15.4	22.4	45.3	27.5
77 Panama	1970	2.0	5.2	11.0	20.0	61.8	44.2
78 Chile	1968	4.4	9.0	13.8	21.4	51.4	34.8
79 Brazil	1972	2.0	5.0	9.4	17.0	66.6	50.6
80 Mexico	1977	2.9	7.0	12.0	20.4	57.7	40.6
81 Algeria		..	..	..	..	..	..
82 Portugal		..	..	..	..	..	..
83 Argentina	1970	4.4	9.7	14.1	21.5	50.3	35.2
84 Uruguay		..	..	..	..	..	..
85 South Africa		..	..	..	..	..	..
86 Yugoslavia	1978	6.6	12.1	18.7	23.9	38.7	22.9
87 Venezuela	1970	3.0	7.3	12.9	22.8	54.0	35.7
88 Greece		..	..	..	..	..	..
89 Israel	1979–80	6.0	12.0	17.7	24.4	39.9	22.6
90 Hong Kong	1980	5.4	10.8	15.2	21.6	47.0	31.3
91 Singapore		..	..	..	..	..	..
92 Trinidad and Tobago	1975–76	4.2	9.1	13.9	22.8	50.0	31.8
93 *Iran, Islamic Rep.*		..	..	..	..	..	..
94 *Iraq*		..	..	..	..	..	..

High-income oil exporters

	Year	Lowest 20 percent	Second quintile	Third quintile	Fourth quintile	Highest 20 percent	Highest 10 percent
95 Oman		..	..	..	..	..	..
96 Libya		..	..	..	..	..	..
97 Saudi Arabia		..	..	..	..	..	..
98 Kuwait		..	..	..	..	..	..
99 United Arab Emirates		..	..	..	..	..	..

Industrial market economies

	Year	Lowest 20 percent	Second quintile	Third quintile	Fourth quintile	Highest 20 percent	Highest 10 percent
100 Ireland	1973	7.2	13.1	16.6	23.7	39.4	25.1
101 Spain	1974	6.0	11.8	16.9	23.1	42.2	26.7
102 Italy	1977	6.2	11.3	15.9	22.7	43.9	28.1
103 New Zealand		..	..	..	..	..	..
104 United Kingdom	1979	7.0	11.5	17.0	24.8	39.7	23.4
105 Austria		..	..	..	..	..	..
106 Japan	1979	8.7	13.2	17.5	23.1	36.8	21.2
107 Belgium	1974–75	7.7	12.4	17.0	23.1	39.8	24.3
108 Finland	1977	6.8	12.8	18.7	24.9	36.8	21.2
109 Netherlands	1977	8.1	13.7	17.9	23.3	37.0	22.1
110 Australia	1975–76	5.4	10.0	15.0	22.5	47.1	30.5
111 Canada	1977	3.8	10.7	17.9	25.6	42.0	26.9
112 France	1975	5.3	11.1	16.0	21.8	45.8	30.5
113 Germany, Fed. Rep.	1978	7.9	12.5	17.0	23.1	39.5	24.0
114 Denmark	1976	7.4	12.6	18.3	24.2	37.5	22.4
115 United States	1978	4.6	8.9	14.1	22.1	50.3	33.4
116 Sweden	1979	7.2	12.8	17.4	25.4	37.2	21.2
117 Norway	1970	6.3	12.9	18.8	24.7	37.3	22.2
118 Switzerland		..	..	..	..	..	..

East European nonmarket economies

	Year	Lowest 20 percent	Second quintile	Third quintile	Fourth quintile	Highest 20 percent	Highest 10 percent
119 Hungary		..	..	..	..	..	..
120 Romania		..	..	..	..	..	..
121 *Albania*		..	..	..	..	..	..
122 *Bulgaria*		..	..	..	..	..	..
123 *Czechoslovakia*		..	..	..	..	..	..
124 *German Dem. Rep.*		..	..	..	..	..	..
125 *Poland*		..	..	..	..	..	..
126 *USSR*		..	..	..	..	..	..

a. These estimates should be treated with caution. See the technical notes.

Technical notes

This edition of the World Development Indicators provides economic indicators for periods of years and social indicators for selected years in a form suitable for comparing economies and groups of economies. The statistics and measures have been carefully chosen to give a comprehensive picture of development. Considerable effort has been made to standardize the data; nevertheless, statistical methods, coverage, practices, and definitions differ widely. In addition, the statistical systems in many developing economies still are weak, and this affects the availability and reliability of the data. Readers are urged to take these limitations into account in interpreting the indicators, particularly when making comparisons across economies.

All growth rates shown are in constant prices and, unless otherwise noted, have been computed by using the least-squares method. The least-squares growth rate, r, is estimated by fitting a least-squares linear trend line to the logarithmic annual values of the variable in the relevant period using the logarithmic form: Log $X_t = a + bt + e_t$, where X_t is the variable, a is the intercept, b is the slope coefficient, t is time, and e_t is the error term. Then r is equal to [antilog b] − 1, the least-squares estimate of the growth rate.

Table 1. Basic indicators

The estimates of *population* for mid-1982 are primarily based on data from the UN Population Division. In many cases the data take into account the results of recent population censuses. The data on *area* are from the computer tape for the FAO *Production Yearbook 1982*.

Gross national product (GNP) measures the total domestic and foreign output claimed by residents. It comprises gross domestic product (see the note for Table 2) and factor incomes (such as investment income, labor income, and workers' remittances) accruing to residents from abroad, less the income earned in the domestic economy accruing to persons abroad. It is calculated without making deductions for depreciation.

The *GNP per capita* figures were calculated according to the *World Bank Atlas* method, under which the conversion of GNP proceeds in the following manner. The first step is to convert the GNP series in constant market prices and national currency units to one measured in constant average 1980–82 prices. This is done by multiplying the original constant price series by the weighted-average domestic GNP deflator for the base period (that is, by the ratio of total GNP in current prices to total GNP in constant prices for the 1980–82 period). The second step is to convert the series measured in constant average 1980–82 prices in national currency to one in US dollars by dividing that series by the weighted-average exchange rate for the base period. The weighted-average exchange rate is the ratio of the sum of GNP in current prices to the sum of the GNP divided by the annual average exchange rate in national currency per US dollar for 1980, 1981, and 1982. The third step is to convert the series measured in constant average 1980–82 US dollars to one measured in current US dollars by multiplying that series by the implicit US GNP deflator for 1980–82. This procedure was followed for most economies.

The *GNP per capita* figures were obtained by dividing GNP at market prices in US dollars by the population in mid-1982. The use of the three-year base period is intended to smooth the impact of fluctuations in prices and exchange rates. As the base period is changed every year, the per capita estimates presented in the various editions of the World Development Indicators are not comparable.

Because of problems associated with the availability of data and the determination of exchange rates, information on GNP per capita is shown only for East European nonmarket economies that are members of the World Bank. The World Bank has a research project under way to estimate GNP per capita for nonmarket economies that are not members. But until a broadly acceptable method is prepared, figures will not be shown for the GNP per capita of such economies.

For Romania the GNP per capita figure has been derived, following the *World Bank Atlas* method, by using adjusted official Romanian national accounts data and converting them into US dollars at the effective exchange rate for foreign trade transactions in convertible currencies.

The World Bank, for its own operational purposes, attempts to estimate internationally comparable and consistent GNP per capita figures. This task is made difficult, however, by conceptual and coverage as well as quality differences in the basic data and by the fact that prevailing exchange rates do not fully reflect the rate at which transactions take place. Recognizing that these shortcomings affect the comparability of the GNP per capita estimates, the World Bank recently initiated a process aimed at revision of the *World Bank Atlas* methodology described above. It is systematically evaluating the GNP estimates of its member countries, focusing on the coverage and concepts employed, and where appropriate will make adjustments to increase comparability. This evaluation of national accounts data will be based on documentation on the sources and methods underlying the compilations, obtained either directly from national governments or from other international agencies such as the UN Statistical Office, OECD, and the Statistical Office of the European Communities.

The World Bank is also undertaking a systematic review to improve the conversion factors. For 1983 on, GNP per capita for a specified year in US dollars will be estimated by converting GNP in national currencies using a mean of the official exchange rate for that year and the two preceding years, adjusted for relative price changes between the economy in question and the United States. An alternative conversion factor will be used when the official exchange rate is judged to be egregiously different from the rate effectively applied to foreign transactions.

GNP per capita estimates calculated using the new methodology will be published in the next editions of the *World Bank Atlas* and the World Development Indicators, together with detailed technical notes.

Given the data and conversion factor considerations discussed above, this year's GNP per capita figures must be interpreted with great caution.

The *average annual rate of inflation* is the least-squares growth rate of the implicit gross domestic product (GDP) deflator for each of the periods shown. The GDP deflator is first calculated by dividing, for each year of the period, the value of GDP in current market prices by the value of GDP in constant market prices, both in national currency. The least-squares method is then used to calculate the growth rate of the GDP deflator for the period. This measure of inflation has limita-

tions, in particular for the oil-producing countries during the period of sharp increases in oil prices. It is used as an indicator of inflation because it is the most broadly based deflator, showing annual price movements for all goods and services produced in an economy.

Life expectancy at birth indicates the number of years newborn children would live if subject to the mortality risks prevailing for the cross-section of population at the time of their birth. Data are from the UN Population Division, supplemented by World Bank estimates.

The table on this page shows basic indicators for 34 countries that have a population of less than a million and are members of the United Nations, the World Bank, or both. For most of these countries, comprehensive data are not available.

The averages in this table are weighted by population.

Tables 2 and 3. Growth and structure of production

Most of the definitions used are those of the UN *System of National Accounts*.

Gross domestic product (GDP) measures the total final output of goods and services produced by an economy—that is, by residents and nonresidents, regardless of the allocation to domestic and foreign claims. It is calculated without making deductions for depreciation. For many countries, GDP by industrial origin is measured at factor cost; for other countries without complete national accounts series at factor cost, market price series were used. GDP at factor cost is equal to GDP at market prices, less indirect taxes net of subsidies. The figures for GDP are dollar values converted from domestic currency by using the average annual official exchange rate for the year in question: that is, they were not calculated by using the *World Bank Atlas* method described in the note for Table 1. Because of these differences in concept and in method of conversion, the figures in these tables are not comparable with the GNP-based numbers in Table 1.

As in Table 1, data are shown only for East European nonmarket economies that are members of the World Bank.

The *agricultural sector* comprises agriculture, forestry, hunting, and fishing. In developing countries with high levels of subsistence farming, much of the agricultural production is either not exchanged or not exchanged for money. Due to difficulties in assigning subsistence farming its proper value, the share of agriculture in GDP may be underestimated. The *industrial sector* comprises mining, *manufacturing*, construction, and electricity, water, and gas. All other branches of economic activity are categorized as *services*.

National accounts series in domestic currency units were used to compute the indicators in these tables. The growth rates in Table 2 were calculated from constant price series; the sectoral shares of GDP in Table 3, from current price series.

The average growth rates for the summary measures in Table 2 are weighted by country GDP in 1970 dollars. The average sectoral shares in Table 3 are weighted by GDP in current dollars for the years in question.

Tables 4 and 5. Growth of consumption and investment; Structure of demand

GDP is defined in the note for Table 2.

Public consumption (or general government consumption) includes all current expenditure for purchases of goods and services by all levels of government. Capital expenditure on national

Basic indicators for UN/World Bank members with a population of less than 1 million

| | | | GNP per capita | | | | |
| | Population (millions) mid-1982 | Area (thousands of square kilometers) | Dollars 1982 | Average annual growth rate (percent) 1960–82 [a] | Average annual rate of inflation (percent) | | Life expectancy at birth (years) 1982 [c] |
UN/World Bank member					1960–70	1970–82 [b]	
Guinea-Bissau	0.8	36	170	−1.7	. .	7.1	38
Comoros	0.4	2	340	0.9	3.4	11.7	48
Cape Verde	0.3	4	350	. .	. .	11.9	61
Gambia, The	0.7	11	360	2.5	2.2	9.7	36
Sao Tome and Principe	0.1	1	370	1.2	. .	7.5	62
St. Vincent and the Grenadines	0.1	(.)	620	0.6	4.0	12.9	. .
Solomon Islands	0.2	28	660	1.3	3.0	8.3	. .
Guyana	0.8	215	670	1.7	2.4	9.9	68
Dominica	0.1	1	710	−0.8	3.8	16.5	58
St. Lucia	0.1	1	720	3.4	3.6	11.0	. .
St. Kitts-Nevis	0.1	(.)	750	1.1	5.5	9.8	. .
Grenada	0.1	(.)	760	1.6	3.4	15.0	69
Botswana	0.9	600	900	6.8	2.4	11.5	60
Swaziland	0.7	17	940	4.2	2.4	12.8	54
Belize	0.2	23	1,080	3.4	3.4	9.5	. .
Mauritius	0.9	2	1,240	2.1	2.2	15.0	66
Antigua and Barbuda	0.1	(.)	1,740	−0.2	3.1	14.0	. .
Fiji	0.7	18	1,950	3.2	2.5	11.7	68
Barbados	0.3	(.)	2,900	4.5	2.3	13.8	72
Malta	0.4	(.)	3,800	8.0	1.5	4.9	72
Bahamas	0.2	14	3,830	−0.4	3.4	7.4	69
Cyprus	0.6	9	3,840	5.9	1.3	7.3	74
Gabon	0.7	268	4,000	4.4	5.4	19.5	49
Bahrain	0.4	1	9,280	. .	. .	. .	68
Iceland	0.2	103	12,150	3.2	12.2	38.2	77
Luxembourg	0.4	3	14,340	4.0	3.7	6.8	73
Qatar	0.3	11	21,880	. .	2.6	29.4	71
Djibouti	0.4	22	. .	. .	. .	. .	50
Equatorial Guinea	0.4	28	. .	. .	3.4	. .	43
Maldives	0.2	(.)	. .	. .	1.0	. .	47
Seychelles	0.1	(.)	. .	. .	. .	. .	66
Suriname	0.4	163	. .	. .	. .	. .	65
Vanuatu	0.1	15	. .	. .	. .	. .	. .
Western Samoa	0.2	3	. .	. .	. .	. .	65

a. Because data for the early 1960s are not available, figures in italics are for periods other than that specified. b. Figures in italics are for 1970–81, not 1970–82. c. Figures in italics are for years other than 1982. See the technical notes.

defense and security is regarded as consumption expenditure.

Private consumption is the market value of all goods and services purchased or received as income in kind by households and nonprofit institutions. It includes imputed rent for owner-occupied dwellings.

Gross domestic investment consists of the outlays for additions to the fixed assets of the economy, plus changes in the net value of inventories.

Gross domestic saving shows the amount of gross domestic investment financed from domestic output. Comprising public and private saving, it is gross domestic investment plus the net exports of goods and nonfactor services.

Exports of goods and nonfactor services represent the value of all goods and nonfactor services sold to the rest of the world; they include merchandise, freight, insurance, travel, and other nonfactor services. The value of factor services, such as investment income, labor income, and workers' remittances from abroad, is excluded.

The *resource balance* is the difference between exports and imports of goods and nonfactor services.

National accounts series in domestic currency units were used to compute the indicators in these tables. The growth rates in Table 4 were calculated from constant price series; the shares of GDP in Table 5, from current price series.

The summary measures in Table 4 are weighted by country GDP in 1970 dollars; those in Table 5, by GDP in current dollars for the years in question.

Table 6. Agriculture and food

The basic data for *value added in agriculture* are from the World Bank's national accounts series in national currencies. The 1975 value added in current prices in national currencies is converted to US dollars by applying the official exchange rate for 1975. The growth rates of the constant price series in national currencies are applied to the 1975 value added in US dollars to derive the values, in 1975 US dollars, for 1970 and 1982.

Cereal imports and *food aid in cereals* are measured in grain equivalents and defined as comprising all cereals under the Revised Standard International Trade Classification (SITC) Groups 041–046. The figures are not directly comparable since cereal imports are based on calendar-year and recipient-country data, whereas food aid in cereals is based on crop-year and donor-country data.

Fertilizer consumption is measured in relation to

arable land, defined as comprising arable land and land under permanent crops. This includes land under temporary crops (double-cropped areas are counted once), temporary meadows for mowing or pastures, land under market and kitchen gardens, land temporarily fallow or lying idle, as well as land under permanent crops.

The figures on food and fertilizer are from the Food and Agriculture Organization (FAO): from computer tapes for *Production Yearbook 1982, Trade Yearbook 1982,* and *Fertilizer Yearbook 1982;* and from *Food Aid Bulletin,* October 1980 and July 1983. In some instances data are for 1974 because they provide the earliest available information.

The *index of food production per capita* shows the average annual quantity of food produced per capita in 1980–82 in relation to that in 1969–71. The estimates were derived from those of the FAO, which are calculated by dividing indices of the quantity of food production by indices of total population. For this index, food is defined as comprising cereals, starchy roots, sugar cane, sugar beet, pulses, edible oils, nuts, fruits, vegetables, livestock, and livestock products. Quantities of food production are measured net of animal feed, seeds for use in agriculture, and food lost in processsing and distribution. Given the weaknesses in agricultural production statistics, caution should be exercised in interpreting them.

Table 7. Industry

The percentage *distribution of value added* among manufacturing industries was calculated from data obtained from the UN Industrial Development Organization (UNIDO), with the base values expressed in 1975 dollars.

The classification of manufacturing industries is in accord with the UN International Standard Industrial Classification of All Economic Activities (ISIC). *Food and agriculture* comprise ISIC Major Groups 311, 313, and 314; *textiles and clothing* 321–24; *machinery and transport equipment* 382–84; and *chemicals* 351 and 352. *Other manufacturing* generally comprises ISIC Major Division 3, less all of the above; however, for some economies for which complete data are not available, other categories are included as well.

The basic data for *value added in manufacturing* are from the World Bank's national accounts series in national currencies. The 1975 value added in current prices in national currencies is converted to US dollars by applying the official exchange rate for 1975. The growth rates of the constant price series in national currencies are applied to the 1975 value added in US dollars to derive the values, in 1975 US dollars, for 1970 and 1981.

Table 8. Commercial energy

The data on energy generally are from UN sources. They refer to commercial forms of primary energy: petroleum and natural gas liquids, natural gas, solid fuels (coal, lignite, and so on), and primary electricity (nuclear, geothermal, and hydroelectric power)—all converted into oil equivalents. Figures on liquid fuel consumption include petroleum derivatives that have been consumed in non-energy uses. For converting primary electricity into oil equivalents, a notional thermal efficiency of 34 percent has been assumed. The use of firewood and other traditional fuels, though substantial in some developing countries, is not taken into account because reliable and comprehensive data are not available.

The summary measures of growth rates of *energy production* are weighted by volumes of production in 1974; those of growth rates of *energy consumption,* by volumes of consumption in 1974; those of *energy consumption per capita,* by population in 1974.

Energy imports refer to the dollar value of energy imports—Section 3 in the Revised Standard International Trade Classification (SITC)—and are expressed as a percentage of earnings from merchandise exports. The summary measures are weighted by merchandise exports in current dollars.

Because data on energy imports do not permit a distinction between petroleum imports for fuel and for use in the petrochemicals industry, these percentages may overestimate the dependence on imported energy.

Table 9. Growth of merchandise trade

The statistics on merchandise trade are from UN publications and the UN trade data system, supplemented by statistics from the UN Conference on Trade and Development (UNCTAD), the International Monetary Fund (IMF), and in a few cases World Bank country documentation.

Merchandise exports and imports cover, with some exceptions, all international changes in ownership of goods passing across customs borders. Exports are valued f.o.b. (free on board), imports c.i.f. (cost, insurance, and freight), unless otherwise specified in the foregoing sources. These values

are in dollars at prevailing exchange rates. Note that they do not include trade in services.

The *growth rates of merchandise exports and imports* are in real terms and are calculated from quantum (volume) indices of exports and imports. Quantum indices are the ratios of the export or import value index to the corresponding unit value index. For most developing economies these indices are from the UNCTAD *Handbook of International Trade and Development Statistics* and supplementary data. For industrial economies the indices are from the UN *Yearbook of International Trade Statistics* and *Monthly Bulletin of Statistics.* The summary measures are median values. Note again that these values do not include trade in services.

The *terms of trade,* or net barter terms of trade, measure the relative level of export prices compared to import prices. Calculated as the ratio of a country's export unit value index to the import unit value index, this indicator shows changes over time in the level of export prices as a percentage of import prices. The terms-of-trade index numbers are shown for 1979 and 1982, with 1980 = 100. The unit value indices are from the same sources cited above for the growth rates of exports and imports.

Tables 10 and 11. Structure of merchandise trade

The shares in these tables are derived from trade values in current dollars reported in UN trade tapes and the UN *Yearbook of International Trade Statistics,* supplemented by other regular statistical publications of the UN and the IMF.

Merchandise exports and imports are defined in the note for Table 9. The categorization of exports and imports follows the Revised Standard International Trade Classification (SITC).

In Table 10, *fuels, minerals, and metals* are the commodities in SITC Section 3, Divisions 27 and 28 (minerals, crude fertilizers, and metalliferous ores), and Division 68 (nonferrous metals). *Other primary commodities* comprise SITC Sections 0, 1, 2, and 4 (food and live animals, beverages and tobacco, inedible crude materials, oils, fats, and waxes) less Divisions 27 and 28. *Textiles and clothing* represent SITC Divisions 65 and 84 (textiles, yarns, fabrics, and clothing). *Machinery and transport equipment* are the commodities in SITC Section 7. *Other manufactures,* calculated as the residual from the total value of manufactured exports, represent SITC Sections 5 through 9 less Section 7 and Divisions 65, 68, and 84.

In Table 11, *food* commodities are those in SITC Sections 0, 1, and 4 and in Division 22 (food and live animals, beverages and tobacco, and oils and fats). *Fuels* are the commodities in SITC Section 3 (mineral fuels, lubricants, and related materials). *Other primary commodities* comprise SITC Section 2 (crude materials excluding fuels) less Division 22 (oilseeds and nuts) plus Division 68 (nonferrous metals). *Machinery and transport equipment* are the commodities in SITC Section 7. *Other manufactures,* calculated as the residual from the total value of manufactured imports, represent SITC Sections 5 through 9 less Section 7 and Division 68.

The summary measures in Table 10 are weighted by merchandise exports in current dollars; those in Table 11, by merchandise imports in current dollars.

Table 12. Origin and destination of merchandise exports

Merchandise exports are defined in the note for Table 9. Trade shares in this table are based on statistics on the value of trade in current dollars from the UN and the IMF. Unallocated exports are distributed among the economy groups in proportion to their respective shares of allocable trade. *Industrial market economies* also include Gibraltar, Iceland, and Luxembourg; *high-income oil exporters* also include Bahrain, Brunei Darussalam, and Qatar. The summary measures are weighted by merchandise exports in current dollars.

Table 13. Origin and destination of manufactured exports

The data in this table are from the UN and are among those used to compute special Table B in the UN *Yearbook of International Trade Statistics.* *Manufactured goods* are the commodities in SITC (Revised) Sections 5 through 9 (chemicals and related products, manufactured articles, and machinery and transport equipment) excluding Division 68 (nonferrous metals).

The economy groups are the same as those in Table 12. The summary measures are weighted by manufactured exports in current dollars.

Table 14. Balance of payments and reserves

The *current account balance* is the difference between (1) exports of goods and services plus inflows of unrequited official and private transfers and (2) imports of goods and services plus unre-quited transfers to the rest of the world. The current account estimates are primarily from IMF data files.

Workers' remittances cover remittances of income by migrants who are employed or expected to be employed for a year or more in their new economy, where they are considered residents.

Net direct private investment is the net amount invested or reinvested by nonresidents in enterprises in which they or other nonresidents exercise significant managerial control. Including equity capital, reinvested earnings, and other capital, these net figures also take into account the value of direct investment abroad by residents of the reporting country. These estimates were compiled primarily from IMF data files.

Gross international reserves comprise holdings of gold, special drawing rights (SDRs), the reserve position of IMF members in the Fund, and holdings of foreign exchange under the control of monetary authorities. The data on holdings of international reserves are from IMF data files. The gold component of these reserves is valued throughout at year-end London prices: that is, $37.37 an ounce in 1970 and $456.90 an ounce in 1982. The reserve levels for 1970 and 1982 refer to the end of the year indicated and are in current dollars at prevailing exchange rates. Due to differences in the definition of international reserves, in the valuation of gold, and in reserve management practices, the levels of reserve holdings published in national sources do not have strictly comparable significance. Reserve holdings at the end of 1982 are also expressed in terms of the number of months of imports of goods and services they could pay for, with imports at the average level for 1981 or 1982. The summary measures are weighted by imports of goods and services in current dollars.

Table 15. Flow of public and publicly guaranteed external capital

The data on debt in this and successive tables are from the World Bank Debtor Reporting System. That system is concerned solely with developing economies and does not collect data on external debt for other groups of borrowers. Nor are comprehensive comparable data available from other sources.

Data on the *gross inflow* and *repayment of principal* (amortization) are for public and publicly guaranteed medium- and long-term loans. The *net inflow* is the gross inflow less the repayment of principal.

Public loans are external obligations of public debtors, including the national government, its agencies, and autonomous public bodies. Publicly guaranteed loans are external obligations of private debtors that are guaranteed for repayment by a public entity.

The data in this table and in successive tables on debt do not cover nonguaranteed private debt because comprehensive data are not available; for some borrowers such debt is substantial. The debt contracted for purchases of military equipment is also excluded because it usually is not reported.

Table 16. External public debt and debt service ratio

External public debt outstanding and disbursed represents the amount of public and publicly guaranteed loans that has been disbursed, net of repayments of principal and write-offs at year-end. In estimating external public debt as a percentage of GNP, GNP was converted from national currencies to dollars at the average official exchange rate for the year in question. The summary measures are weighted by GNP in current dollars.

Interest payments are those on the disbursed and outstanding public and publicly guaranteed debt in foreign currencies, goods, or services; they include commitment charges on undisbursed debt if information on those charges was available.

Debt service is the sum of interest payments and repayments of principal on external public and publicly guaranteed debt. The ratio of debt service to exports of goods and services is one of several rules of thumb commonly used to assess the ability to service debt. The average ratios of debt service to GNP for the economy groups are weighted by GNP in current dollars. The average ratios of debt service to exports of goods and services are weighted by exports of goods and services in current dollars.

Table 17. Terms of public borrowing

Commitments refer to the public and publicly guaranteed loans for which contracts were signed in the year specified.

Interest rates, maturities, and *grace periods* are averages weighted by the amounts of loans. Interest is the major charge levied on a loan and is usually computed on the amount of principal drawn and outstanding. The maturity of a loan is the interval between the agreement date, when a loan agreement is signed or bonds are issued, and the date of

final repayment of principal. The grace period is the interval between the agreement date and the date of the first repayment of principal.

The summary measures in this table are weighted by the amounts of loans.

Table 18. Official development assistance from OECD and OPEC members

Official development assistance (ODA) consists of net disbursements of loans and grants made at concessional financial terms by official agencies of the members of the Development Assistance Committee (DAC) of the Organisation for Economic Cooperation and Development (OECD) and of the members of the Organization of Petroleum Exporting Countries (OPEC) with the objective of promoting economic development and welfare. It includes the value of technical cooperation and assistance. All data shown were supplied by the OECD.

Amounts shown are net disbursements to developing countries and multilateral institutions. The disbursements to multilateral institutions are now reported for all DAC members on the basis of the date of issue of notes; some DAC members previously reported on the basis of the date of encashment. *Net bilateral flows to low-income countries* exclude unallocated bilateral flows and all disbursements to multilateral institutions.

The nominal values shown in the summary for ODA from OECD countries were converted into 1980 prices using the dollar GNP deflator. This deflator is based on price increases in OECD countries (excluding Greece, Portugal, and Turkey) measured in dollars. It takes into account the parity changes between the dollar and national currencies. For example, when the dollar depreciates, price increases measured in national currencies have to be adjusted upward by the amount of the depreciation to obtain price increases in dollars.

The table, in addition to showing totals for OPEC, shows totals for the Organization of Arab Petroleum Exporting Countries (OAPEC). The donor members of OAPEC are Algeria, Iraq, Kuwait, Libya, Qatar, Saudi Arabia, and United Arab Emirates. ODA data for OPEC and OAPEC were also obtained from the OECD.

Table 19. Population growth and projections

The *growth rates of population* are period averages calculated from midyear populations. The summary measures are weighted by population in 1970.

The estimates of *population* for mid-1982 are primarily based on data from the UN Population Division. In many cases the data take into account the results of recent population censuses.

The *projections of population* for 1990 and 2000, and to the year in which it will eventually become stationary, were made for each economy separately. Starting with information on total population by age and sex, fertility rates, mortality rates, and international migration rates in the base year 1980, these parameters were projected at five-year intervals on the basis of generalized assumptions until the population became stationary. The base-year estimates are from updated computer print-outs of the UN *World Population Prospects as Assessed in 1982,* from the most recent issues of the UN *Population and Vital Statistics Report* and *International Migration: Levels and Trends,* and from the World Bank, the Population Council, the US Bureau of the Census, and recent national censuses.

The *net reproduction rate* (NRR) indicates the number of daughters that a newborn girl will bear during her lifetime, assuming fixed age-specific fertility rates and a fixed set of mortality rates. The NRR thus measures the extent to which a cohort of newborn girls will reproduce themselves under given schedules of fertility and mortality. An NRR of 1 indicates that fertility is at replacement level: at this rate childbearing women, on the average, bear only enough daughters to replace themselves in the population.

A *stationary population* is one in which age- and sex-specific mortality rates have not changed over a long period, while age-specific fertility rates have simultaneously remained at replacement level (NRR=1). In such a population, the birth rate is constant and equal to the death rate, the age structure also is constant, and the growth rate is zero.

Population momentum is the tendency for population growth to continue beyond the time that replacement-level fertility has been achieved; that is, even after NRR has reached unity. The momentum of a population in the year *t* is measured as a ratio of the ultimate stationary population to the population in the year *t,* given the assumption that fertility remains at replacement level from the year *t* onward. In India, for example, in 1980 the population was 687 million, the ultimate stationary population assuming that NRR = 1 from 1980 onward was 1,195 million, and the population momentum was 1.74.

A population tends to grow even after fertility has declined to replacement level because past high growth rates will have produced an age distribution with a relatively high proportion of women in, or still to enter, the reproductive ages. Consequently, the birth rate will remain higher than the death rate and the growth rate will remain positive for several decades. A population takes 50–75 years, depending on the initial conditions, before its age distribution fully adjusts to the changed fertility rates.

To make the projections, assumptions about future mortality rates were made in terms of female life expectancy at birth (that is, the number of years a newborn girl would live if subject to the mortality risks prevailing for the cross-section of population at the time of her birth). Economies were first divided according to whether their primary-school enrollment ratio for females was above or below 70 percent. In each group a set of annual increments in female life expectancy was assumed, depending on the female life expectancy in 1980–85. For a given life expectancy at birth, the annual increments during the projection period are larger in economies having a higher primary-school enrollment ratio and a life expectancy of up to 62.5 years. At higher life expectancies, the increments are the same.

To project the fertility rates, the first step was to estimate the year in which fertility would reach replacement level. These estimates are speculative and are based on information on trends in crude birth rates (defined in the note for Table 20), total fertility rates (also defined in the note for Table 20), female life expectancy at birth, and the performance of family planning programs. For most economies it was assumed that the total fertility rate would decline between 1980 and the year of reaching a net reproduction rate of 1, after which fertility would remain at replacement level. For most countries in sub-Saharan Africa, however, total fertility rates were assumed to remain constant until 1990–95 and then to decline until replacement level was reached; for a few they were assumed to increase until 1990–95 and then to decline. Also for a few countries in Asia and the Middle East, the rates were assumed to remain constant for some years before beginning to decline. In several industrial economies, fertility is already below replacement level. Because a population will not remain stationary if its net reproduction rate is other than 1, it was assumed that fertility rates in these economies would regain replacement levels in order to make estimates of the stationary population for them. For the sake of consistency with the other estimates, the total fertility rates in the industrial economies were assumed to remain constant until 1985–90 and then to increase to replacement level by 2010.

International migration rates are based on past and present trends in migration flow. The estimates of future net migration are speculative. For most economies the net migration rates were assumed to be zero by 2000, but for a few they were assumed to be zero by 2025.

The estimates of the hypothetical size of the stationary population and the assumed year of reaching replacement-level fertility are speculative. *They should not be regarded as predictions.* They are included to provide a summary indication of the long-run implications of recent fertility and mortality trends on the basis of highly stylized assumptions. A fuller description of the methods and assumptions used to calculate the estimates is available from the Population, Health, and Nutrition Department of the World Bank.

Table 20. Demographic and fertility-related indicators

The *crude birth and death rates* indicate the number of live births and deaths per thousand population in a year. They are from the same sources mentioned in the note for Table 19. Percentage changes are computed from unrounded data.

The *total fertility rate* represents the number of children that would be born per woman, if she were to live to the end of her childbearing years and bear children at each age in accord with prevailing age-specific fertility rates. The rates given are from the same sources mentioned in the note for Table 19.

The *percentage of married women of childbearing age using contraception* refers to women who are practicing, or whose husbands are practicing, any form of contraception. These generally comprise male and female sterilization, intrauterine device (IUD), condom, injectable contraceptives, spermicides, diaphragm, rhythm, withdrawal, and abstinence. The figures for Bulgaria, Denmark, Poland, and Romania, however, as well as the 1970 figures for the United Kingdom, exclude sterilization. Women of childbearing age are generally women aged 15–49, although for some countries contraceptive usage is measured for other age groups.

Data are mainly derived from the UN *Monitoring Report* and publications of the World Fertility Survey and the Contraceptive Prevalence Survey. For a few countries for which no survey data are available, program statistics are used; these include India, Indonesia, and Zimbabwe. Program statistics may understate contraceptive prevalence because they do not measure use of methods such as rhythm, withdrawal, or abstinence, or of contraceptives not obtained through the official family planning program. The data refer to a variety of years, generally not more than two years distant from those specified.

All summary measures are weighted by population.

Table 21. Labor force

The *population of working age* refers to the population aged 15–64. The estimates are based on the population estimates of the World Bank for 1981 and previous years. The summary measures are weighted by population.

The *labor force* comprises economically active persons aged 10 years and over, including the armed forces and the unemployed, but excluding housewives, students, and other economically inactive groups. *Agriculture, industry, and services* are defined in the same manner as in Table 2. The estimates of the sectoral distribution of the labor force are from International Labour Office (ILO), *Labour Force Estimates and Projections, 1950–2000,* and from the World Bank. The summary measures are weighted by labor force.

The *labor force growth rates* were derived from the Bank's population projections and from ILO data on age-specific activity rates in the source cited above. The summary measures for 1960–70 and 1970–82 are weighted by labor force in 1970; those for 1980–2000, by estimates of labor force in 1980.

The application of ILO activity rates to the Bank's latest population estimates may be inappropriate for some economies in which there have been important changes in unemployment and underemployment, in international and internal migration, or in both. The labor force projections for 1980–2000 should thus be treated with caution.

Table 22. Urbanization

The data on *urban population as a percentage of total population* are from the UN *Patterns of Urban and Rural Population Growth,* 1980, supplemented by data from the World Bank and from various issues of the UN *Demographic Yearbook.*

The *growth rates of urban population* were calculated from the World Bank's population estimates; the estimates of urban population shares were calculated from the sources cited above. Data on urban agglomeration are also from the United Nations.

Because the estimates in this table are based on different national definitions of what is "urban," cross-country comparisons should be interpreted with caution.

The summary measures for urban population as a percentage of total population are weighted by population; the other summary measures in this table are weighted by urban population.

Table 23. Indicators related to life expectancy

Life expectancy at birth is defined in the note for Table 1.

The infant mortality rate is the number of infants who die before reaching one year of age, per thousand live births in a given year. The data are from a variety of sources—including issues of the UN Demographic Yearbook and Population and Vital Statistics Report; and UN, "Infant Mortality: World Estimates and Projections, 1950-2025," Population Bulletin of the United Nations, 1982—and from the World Bank.

The child death rate is the number of deaths of children aged 1–4 per thousand children in the same age group in a given year. Estimates were based on the data on infant mortality and on the relation between the infant mortality rate and the child death rate implicit in the appropriate Coale-Demeny Model life tables; see Ansley J. Coale and Paul Demeny, Regional Model Life Tables and Stable Populations (Princeton, N.J.: Princeton University Press, 1966).

The summary measures in this table are weighted by population.

Table 24. Health-related indicators

The estimates of population per physician and nursing person were derived from World Health Organization (WHO) data, some of which have been revised to reflect new information. They also take into account revised estimates of population. Nursing persons include graduate, practical, assistant, and auxiliary nurses; the inclusion of auxiliary nurses enables a better estimation of the availability of nursing care. Because definitions of nursing personnel vary—and because the data shown are for a variety of years, generally not more than two years distant from those specified— the data for these two indicators are not strictly comparable across countries.

The daily calorie supply per capita was calculated by dividing the calorie equivalent of the food supplies in an economy by the population. Food supplies comprise domestic production, imports less exports, and changes in stocks; they exclude animal feed, seeds for use in agriculture, and food lost in processing and distribution. The daily calorie requirement per capita refers to the calories needed to sustain a person at normal levels of activity and health, taking into account age and sex distributions, average body weights, and environmental temperatures. Both sets of estimates are from the Food and Agriculture Organization (FAO).

The summary measures in this table are weighted by population.

Table 25. Education

The data in this table refer to a variety of years, generally not more than two years distant from those specified, and are mostly from UNESCO.

The data on number enrolled in primary school refer to estimates of total, male, and female enrollment of students of all ages in primary school; they are expressed as percentages of the total, male, or female populations of primary-school age to give gross primary enrollment ratios. Although primary-school age is generally considered to be 6–11 years, the differences in country practices in the ages and duration of schooling are reflected in the ratios given. For countries with universal primary education, the gross enrollment ratios may exceed 100 percent because some pupils are below or above the official primary-school age.

The data on number enrolled in secondary school were calculated in the same manner, with secondary-school age generally considered to be 12–17 years.

The data on number enrolled in higher education are from UNESCO.

The summary measures in this table are weighted by population.

Table 26. Central government expenditure

The data on central government finance in Tables 26 and 27 are from the IMF Government Finance Statistics Yearbook, IMF data files, and World Bank country documentation. The accounts of each country are reported using the system of common definitions and classifications found in the IMF Draft Manual on Government Finance Statistics. Due to differences in coverage of available data, the individual components of central government expenditure and current revenue shown in these tables may not be strictly comparable across all economies. The shares of total expenditure and revenue by category are calculated from national currencies.

The inadequate statistical coverage of state, provincial, and local governments has dictated the use of central government data only. This may seriously understate or distort the statistical portrayal of the allocation of resources for various purposes, especially in large countries where lower levels of government have considerable autonomy and are responsible for many social services.

It must be emphasized that the data presented, especially those for education and health, are not comparable for a number of reasons. In many economies private health and education services are substantial; in others public services represent the major component of total expenditure but may be financed by lower levels of government. Great caution should therefore be exercised in using the data for cross-economy comparisons.

Central government expenditure comprises the expenditure by all government offices, departments, establishments, and other bodies that are agencies or instruments of the central authority of a country. It includes both current and capital (development) expenditure.

Defense comprises all expenditure, whether by defense or other departments, for the maintenance of military forces, including the purchase of military supplies and equipment, construction, recruiting, and training. Also falling under this category is expenditure for strengthening the public services to meet wartime emergencies, for training civil defense personnel, and for foreign military aid and contributions to military organizations and alliances.

Education comprises public expenditure for the provision, management, inspection, and support of preprimary, primary, and secondary schools; of universities and colleges; and of vocational, technical, and other training institutions by central governments. Also included is expenditure on the general administration and regulation of the education system; on research into its objectives, organization, administration, and methods; and on such subsidiary services as transport, school meals, and medical and dental services in schools.

Health covers public expenditure on hospitals, medical and dental centers, and clinics with a major medical component; on national health and medical insurance schemes; and on family planning and preventive care. Also included is expend-

iture on the general administration and regulation of relevant government departments, hospitals and clinics, health and sanitation, and national health and medical insurance schemes.

Housing and community amenities, and social security and welfare cover (1) public expenditure on housing, such as income-related schemes; on provision and support of housing and slum clearance activities; on community development; and on sanitary services; and (2) public expenditure for compensation to the sick and temporarily disabled for loss of income; for payments to the elderly, the permanently disabled, and the unemployed; and for family, maternity, and child allowances. The second category also includes the cost of welfare services such as care of the aged, the disabled, and children, as well as the cost of general administration, regulation, and research associated with social security and welfare services.

Economic services comprise public expenditure associated with the regulation, support, and more efficient operation of business, economic development, redress of regional imbalances, and creation of employment opportunities. Research, trade promotion, geological surveys, and inspection and regulation of particular industry groups are among the activities included. The five major categories of economic services are fuel and energy, agriculture, industry, transportation and communication, and other economic affairs and services.

Other covers expenditure for the general administration of government not included elsewhere; for a few economies it also includes amounts that could not be allocated to other components.

Overall surplus/deficit is defined as current and capital revenue and grants received less total expenditure less lending minus repayments.

The summary measures for the components of central government expenditure are weighted by central government expenditure in current dollars; those for total expenditure as a percentage of GNP and for overall surplus/deficit as a percentage of GNP are weighted by GNP in current dollars.

Table 27. Central government current revenue

Information on data sources and comparability is given in the note for Table 26. Current revenue by source is expressed as a percentage of total current revenue, which is the sum of tax revenue and current nontax revenue, and is calculated from national currencies.

Tax revenue is defined as all government revenue from compulsory, unrequited, nonrepayable receipts for public purposes, including interest collected on tax arrears and penalties collected on nonpayment or late payment of taxes. Tax revenue is shown net of refunds and other corrective transactions. *Taxes on income, profit, and capital gain* are taxes levied on the actual or presumptive net income of individuals, on the profits of enterprises, and on capital gains, whether realized on land sales, securities, or other assets. *Social Security contributions* include employers' and employees' social security contributions as well as those of self-employed and unemployed persons. *Domestic taxes on goods and services* include general sales, turnover, or value added taxes, selective excises on goods, selective taxes on services, taxes on the use of goods or property, and profits of fiscal monopolies. *Taxes on international trade and transactions* include import duties, export duties, profits of export or import marketing boards, transfers to government, exchange profits, and exchange taxes. *Other taxes* include employers' payroll or manpower taxes, taxes on property, and other taxes not allocable to other categories.

Current nontax revenue comprises all current government revenue that is not a compulsory nonrepayable payment for public purposes. Proceeds of grants and borrowing, funds arising from the repayment of previous lending by governments, incurrence of liabilities, and proceeds from the sale of capital assets are not included.

The summary measures for the components of current revenue are weighted by total current revenue in current dollars; those for current revenue as a percentage of GNP are weighted by GNP in current dollars.

Table 28. Income distribution

The data in this table refer to the distribution of total disposable household income accruing to percentile groups of households ranked by total household income. The distributions cover rural and urban areas and refer to different years between 1966 and 1981.

The estimates for developing economies in Asia and Africa are from the results of a joint project of the World Bank and the International Labour Organisation (ILO). Those for Turkey, Hong Kong, Malaysia, Israel, and the Republic of Korea are from data gathered by the World Bank from national sources but not adjusted. The estimates for Sri Lanka are from the results of a joint project of the World Bank and the Economic and Social Commission for Asia and the Pacific. The estimates for Latin American countries other than Mexico come from the results of two joint projects of the World Bank, one with the ILO, the other with the Economic Commission for Latin America. Those for Mexico are the results from the 1977 Household Budget Survey.

Data for Australia, Belgium, the Federal Republic of Germany, Ireland, Japan, the Netherlands, the United Kingdom, and the United States are from national sources. Data for industrial market economies other than those listed are from Sawyer 1976; the joint project of the ILO and the World Bank; and the UN *Survey of National Sources of Income Distribution Statistics,* 1981.

Because the collection of data on income distribution has not been systematically organized and integrated with the official statistical system in many countries, estimates were typically derived from surveys designed for other purposes, most often consumer expenditure surveys, which also collect some information on income. These surveys use a variety of income concepts and sample designs. Furthermore, the coverage of many of these surveys is too limited to provide reliable nationwide estimates of income distribution. Thus, although the estimates shown are considered the best available, they do not avoid all these problems and should be interpreted with extreme caution.

The scope of the indicator is similarly limited. Because households vary in size, a distribution in which households are ranked according to per capita household income rather than according to total household income is superior for many purposes. The distinction is important because households with low per capita incomes frequently are large households whose total income may be relatively high. Information on the distribution of per capita household income exists, however, for only a few countries. The World Bank Living Standards Measurement Study is developing procedures and applications that can assist countries in improving their collection and analysis of data on income distribution.

Bibliography of data sources

National accounts and economic indicators	International Monetary Fund. 1974. *Draft Manual on Government Finance Statistics.* Washington, D.C.
	———. 1983. *Government Finance Statistics Yearbook.* Vol. VII. Washington, D.C.
	Sawyer, Malcolm. 1976. *Income Distribution in OECD Countries.* OECD Occasional Studies. Paris.
	UN Department of International Economic and Social Affairs. Various years. *Statistical Yearbook.* New York.
	———. 1968. *A System of National Accounts.* New York.
	———. 1981. *A Survey of National Sources of Income Distribution Statistics.* Statistical Papers, Series M, no. 72. New York.
	FAO, IMF, and UNIDO data files.
	National sources. World Bank country documentation. World Bank data files.
Energy	UN Department of International Economic and Social Affairs. Various years. *World Energy Supplies.* Statistical Papers, Series J. New York.
	World Bank data files.
Trade	International Monetary Fund. Various years. *Direction of Trade.* Washington, D.C.
	———. Various years. *International Financial Statistics.* Washington, D.C.
	UN Conference on Trade and Development. Various years. *Handbook of International Trade and Development Statistics.* New York.
	UN Department of International Economic and Social Affairs. Various years. *Monthly Bulletin of Statistics.* New York.
	———. Various years. *Yearbook of International Trade Statistics.* New York.
	United Nations trade tapes. World Bank country documentation.
Balance of payments, capital flows, and debt	International Monetary Fund. 1977. *Balance of Payments Manual,* 4th ed. Washington, D.C.
	The Organisation for Economic Co-operation and Development. Various years. *Development Co-operation.* Paris.
	IMF balance of payments data files. World Bank Debtor Reporting System.
Labor force	International Labour Office. 1977. *Labour Force Estimates and Projections, 1950–2000,* 2nd ed. Geneva.
	International Labour Organisation tapes. World Bank data files.
Population	UN Department of International Economic and Social Affairs. Various years. *Demographic Yearbook.* New York.
	———. Various years. *Population and Vital Statistics Report.* New York.
	———. 1980. *Patterns of Urban and Rural Population Growth.* New York.
	———. 1982. "Infant Mortality: World Estimates and Projections, 1950–2025." *Population Bulletin of the United Nations,* no. 14. New York.
	———. Updated printout. *World Population Prospects as Assessed in 1982.* New York.
	———. Forthcoming. *World Population Trends and Policies: 1983 Monitoring Report.* New York.
	US Bureau of the Census. 1983. *World Population: 1983.* Washington, D.C.
	World Bank data files.
Social indicators	Food and Agriculture Organization. October 1980; July 1983. *Food Aid Bulletin.* Rome.
	———. 1982. *Production Yearbook 1982.* Rome.
	UN Department of International Economic and Social Affairs. Various years. *Demographic Yearbook.* New York.
	———. Various years. *Statistical Yearbook.* New York.
	UNESCO. Various years. *Statistical Yearbook.* Paris.
	World Health Organization. Various years. *World Health Statistics Annual.* Geneva.
	———. 1976. *World Health Statistics Report,* vol. 29, no. 10. Geneva.
	World Bank data files.